OCLC
19.95
#36318723

Cult TV

D1254688

The essential critical guide   Jon E. Lewis   Penny Stempel

791.457
L674.5c

PAVILION

East Baton Rouge Parish Library
Baton Rouge, Louisiana

This edition published in Great Britain in 1996 by
PAVILION BOOKS LIMITED
26 Upper Ground, London SE 1 9PD

First published in 1993

Text copyright © Jon E. Lewis and Penny Stempel 1993, 1996
Foreword copyright © Patrick McGoohan 1993
Inside photographs copyright © Scope Features; with the exception
of pages 68, 100, 105, 174, 181, 209 © PolyGram International
Television/Pictorial Press and pages 13, 25, 42, 66, 95,
194 © The Kobal Collection

Cover illustrations front cover: main picture © Zefa Pictures;
others © The Kobal Collection; *The Prisoner* © PolyGram
International Television/Pictorial Press
back cover: *Dr. Who* and *Absolutely Fabulous* © BBC;
Star Trek: Voyager, *Columbo* and *I Love Lucy*
© The Kobal Collection

Designed by Roy Cole
Cover design by M2/Planet X

The moral right of the authors has been asserted

All rights reserved. No part of this publication may be
reproduced, stored in a retrieval system, or transmitted,
in any form or by any means, electronic, mechanical,
photocopying, recording or otherwise, without the prior
permission of the copyright holder

A CIP catalogue record for this book is available from the
British Library

ISBN 1 85793 926 3

Printed and bound in Spain by Bookprint

2 4 6 8 10 9 7 5 3 1

This book may be ordered by post direct from the publisher
Please contact the Marketing Department
But try your bookshop first

Contents

Foreword

The Prisoner is described in this book as 'probably the cultiest of cult TV'. But on its first broadcast, September 1967 in England, *The Prisoner* was far from an immediate success. It was watched mostly by people who had followed the recently completed *Danger Man*. People expected the same straightforward plots and the same identifiable hero and villain. They were disappointed. What was this new series all about? A man held in a strange village no one knows where. A village populated by enigmatic characters called by numbers instead of names. Each of the episodes compounded the mystery instead of solving it. Who was The Prisoner? What did the name 'Number Six' mean? Who was Number One?

In the last episode I revealed the identity of Number One, the ultimate villain, as the alter ego of Number Six. This did little to pacify frustrated viewers. Outraged, they jammed the switchboard at ITV: they had been led on, swindled, double-crossed.

More than twenty-five years later it is suggested that on any day *The Prisoner* is being shown on some channel, in some country, in some part of the world. There are appreciation societies, magazines published, books written, memorabilia sales, symposia on the meaning and message of the series. People travel across oceans to visit Portmeirion where the series was filmed.

What happened? *The Prisoner* became a cult. Let us look at what makes a cult TV series. Should it be enigmatic? Then what of *Bonanza*, *Thunderbirds*, or *Danger Man*? Should it be old? Perhaps; but what of *Red Dwarf*, *Black Adder*, *Absolutely Fabulous*? Should it be disliked by the establishment on first showing? What of *The Six Million Dollar Man*, *Lost in Space*, *The Time Tunnel*? Controversy? Then what about *Space 1999*, *UFO*, *The Addams Family*? There are some (*Star Trek* is the obvious example) which make it early into the mainstream and still command cult status.

All the programmes herein are described as cult TV. They attract a fanatical following. They have something that fascinates their acolytes who view favourite shows time after time without diminution of enjoyment. Why? Perhaps the answer is that these programmes were made by enthusiasts who believed passionately in their work, and the energy of their belief is transmitted to a select audience sympathetic to the theme and hungry themselves for an enthusiasm.

The authors of this comprehensive work should be complimented on researching their subject with the attention demanded when addressing a discriminating audience, demonstrated by a note on *The Prisoner*: 'McGoohan intended it to be an allegorical conundrum (his production company was called Everyman, in direct reference to the morality plays of the Middle Ages)'. Thank you!

We who are fortunate to be included in this book should be grateful to those who have warmly supported us over the years and given longer life and a broader audience to our work.

Patrick McGoohan

Introduction

'If you let a TV through your door, life will never be the same.' So warned the *Daily Mirror* in 1950. A lot of people did, though, and life never was. By the end of the 1950s watching Logie Baird's flickering box in the corner of the sitting room had become the new family entertainment, especially after ITV raised its transmitter to the TV heavens in 1955. Virtually everybody born since 1940 is part of the TV generation, their childhood and life shaped by TV. Of the thousands of programmes which have since come from the tube of delight some have been good, some bad . . . and some, well, some have become cults.

This is a book about those special cult programmes, over 300 of them, from the *Addams Family* to *Zorro*. But what exactly, you might wonder, is cult TV? It sounds good, but what does it mean? By dictionary definition 'cult' is set apart from the mainstream, and the big divide we felt was fervour – its depth and nature. Cult programmes are objects of special devotion. In selecting the programmes to be included we started off with a list of over 600 possibles, and chipped it down by asking TV fans and experts which programmes they viewed with passion: If it was an old programme, could they remember in loving detail its stars, its theme tune (and the words to it), its catch phrases? If it was a new programme, would they cancel engagements to rush home to see it, collect the whole series on video? Would they seek out like-minded TV addicts the next day to recreate the shots and retell the jokes (in appropriate funny voices)? Better still did the series give birth to merchandising, a fan club, a fanzine, conventions or a secret language?

If the answer to these questions was 'yes' then we had a cult programme on our hands. Such indisputable qualifiers include *The Prisoner* (fan club, Six of One, fanzines and merchandising unabated), *Star Trek* (which spawned that new species of earthling, the Trekkie), *Crossroads* (whose fans still magnificently and stubbornly gather to progress its storylines), and the Australian lesbian melodrama *Prisoner: Cell Block H*.

These were the easy cases. More difficult was to disentangle the cult from the merely popular. A series that is still ardently viewed five – or even forty – years after its end (and with syndication in the States and satellite in Britain, reruns mean some series have been playing somewhere ever since they were made) clearly has a devoted following. But is every much-loved and much-repeated programme cult? No. We sought something a little extra from a series to allow it into the hallowed precincts of the cult collection – something unusual, or adventurous, and preferably kitsch. Indeed, cult TV is often distinguished by its high style (witness the wilfully contemporary sideburns and flares of Jason King in *Department S*), its innovative subject matter (such as new roles for blacks, see *I Spy* and *Julia*, and improved ones for women, see *Cagney and Lacey* and *Golden Girls*), its sexual outrageousness (*Soap*), or its uncompromising political stance (*Combat*). All this means that cult TV often succeeds only after a troubled start. First the TV executives, then the audiences are slow to catch on. A number of cult programmes only survived because of campaigns by devotees.

And yet, even after all these selection rules were applied there were still too many programmes to be included so we decided to restrict our list to drama series and serials – fiction shows with continuing characters and storylines. These we felt offered more scope for critical endeavour. Thus out went game shows, sketch shows and anthology series. A brief roll call of honour of the programmes that got away includes *Opportunity Knocks* ('I mean that most sincerely folks'), *The Golden Shot* ('Bernie, the bolt'), *Take Your Pick* with Michael Miles ('Take the money! Open the box!'), the kids' shows *Tiswas* and the seminal *Sesame Street*, the comedic *Morecambe and Wise*, *Monty Python's Flying Circus*, *Vic Reeves' Big Night Out*, and the light entertainments of *Blind Date*, *Candid Camera*, and *The Eurovision Song Contest* ('Norway, nil points').

Which leads us to the programmes included in *Cult TV*. These span the fifties to the present day and cross six genres: Science Fiction, Crime and Mystery, Westerns, Children, Melodrama and Adventure, and Comedy. Although many classic cult TV shows are here from such Golden Ages of TV as the late 1950s, when the Western rode tall and proud across the small screen, this is not simply a book of nostalgia, for many current shows are examined here, so too shows enjoying a repeat. We have also disinterred from the vault of obscurity series which have been unjustly neglected by programmers, or not even shown in the UK. These 'forgotten cults' include the hyper-realistic war series *Combat*, sci-fi comedy *Quark*, and the Western shows *The Westerner* and *Maverick*. The entry on each programme – see the User's Guide – gives full credits and transmission and production history, plus a critical review of the show. Whether your interest is trivia, anecdotes, budgets, stars or directors, you will find it here. Emmy Awards – the Oscars for TV – are also noted.

Those with an interest in TV's movers and shakers, meanwhile, can use the index to follow individual careers. Look up top producer/creator Aaron Spelling, latterly of *Dynasty* and *Beverly Hills 90210*, and you will find his beginnings as a humble scribe on such horse operas as *Wagon Train*. In the critical review we have tried to provide some insight into the programme, its historical context and its meaning. (It's a curiosity, but TV is not usually treated seriously as a cultural form. Usually it is seen as the poor cousin of film; in fact, as a flip through the index of this book proves, many great film directors – the likes of Sam Peckinpah, Robert Altman, Ridley Scott and Michael Mann – came up through TV, as did such glittering stars as Julie Christie, Steve McQueen, Michael Douglas, and Clint Eastwood. And the 1990s have even seen a glut of cinema features

based on TV series, among them *The Addams Family*, *The Fugitive*, and *The Flintstones*.)

In recognition of the crucial role music plays in the making of a cult TV show – try thinking of *Miami Vice* without Jan Hammer's soundtrack, or *Dragnet* without Walter Schumann's dum-de-dum-dum overture, or *Mission: Impossible* without the great Lalo Schifrin's theme – we have included a music credit. There is also plenty of gossip and bizarre TV trivia including first-time appearances by the yet-to-be famous, show catchphrases and in-joke language such as the 'Kookie speak' of *77 Sunset Strip*. Some of our favourite bits of trivia are that the man who trained the dolphin who took the part of Flipper previously played the title role in *The Creature from the Black Lagoon*; that Diana Ross and The Supremes guested as nuns in *Tarzan*; and that *Dallas* was originally conceived as a 'Linda Evans vehicle', but she considered soap beneath her talents and dignity (until *Dynasty*, that is).

Not the least important part of each entry is a cast list, to help settle those perennial couch potato arguments, such as the actress who played the third *Avengers* girl and the names of all the *Wombles*. Indeed, this book was born out of such an argument (which *Bilko* actor voiced Benny the Ball in *Top Cat*) and the lack of a good reference book to settle it. Eventually, we decided to write it ourselves.

We would like to suggest that you keep this book on top of your set, so when a cult show comes on your terrestrial or satellite channel, you take a moment to read it up. We think this will add to your enjoyment and appreciation of the show the next time you press the ON switch on the magic box. In the meantime, good viewing. Be seeing you.

Jon E. Lewis   Penny Stempel

User's Guide

Entries are divided into six main genres: Science Fiction, Crime and Mystery, Westerns, Children's, Melodrama and Adventure, and Comedy. Within each genre, programmes are listed alphabetically.

Key to entry credits

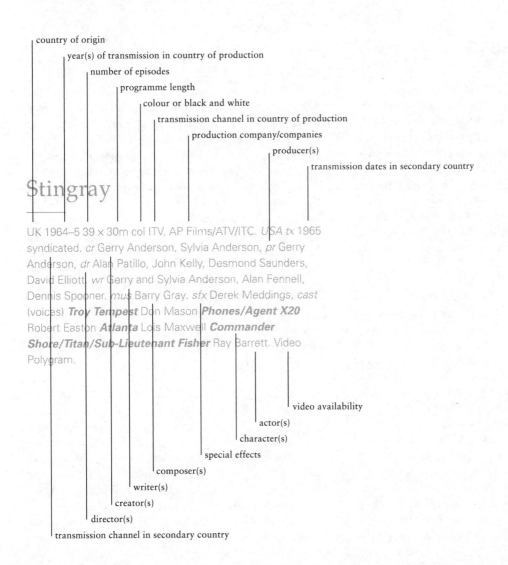

country of origin

year(s) of transmission in country of production

number of episodes

programme length

colour or black and white

transmission channel in country of production

production company/companies

producer(s)

transmission dates in secondary country

Stingray

UK 1964–5 39 × 30m col ITV. AP Films/ATV/ITC. *USA tx* 1965 syndicated. *cr* Gerry Anderson, Sylvia Anderson, *pr* Gerry Anderson, *dr* Alan Patillo, John Kelly, Desmond Saunders, David Elliott. *wr* Gerry and Sylvia Anderson, Alan Fennell, Dennis Spooner. *mus* Barry Gray. *sfx* Derek Meddings, *cast (voices)* **Troy Tempest** Don Mason **Phones/Agent X20** Robert Easton **Atlanta** Lois Maxwell **Commander Shore/Titan/Sub-Lieutenant Fisher** Ray Barrett. Video Polygram.

video availability

actor(s)

character(s)

special effects

composer(s)

writer(s)

creator(s)

director(s)

transmission channel in secondary country

Science Fiction

A for Andromeda

UK 1961 7 × 45 m bw BBC. BBC. *pr* Michael Hayes, Norman James. *wr* Fred Hoyle, John Elliot. *cast* **John Fleming** Peter Halliday **Prof Reinhart** Esmond Knight **Madeleine Dawnay** Mary Morris **Dr Geers** Geoffrey Lewis **Christine/Andromeda** Julie Christie **Dennis Bridger** Frank Windsor **Harvey** John Murray-Scott **Dr Hunter** Peter Ducrow **Judy Adamson** Patricia Kneale **Maj Quadring** Jack May **Harries** John Nettleton **J M Osborne** Noel Johnson **Gen Vandenberg** Donald Stewart **Minister of Science** Ernest Hare **Prime Minister** Maurice Hedley **Defence Minister** David King **Kaufman** John Hollis **Egon** Peter Henchie.

An early classic of British sci-fi and the first series to attempt adult fantasy since the >*Quatermass* cycle of the fifties. The year is 1970. While conducting routine checks at a new radio-telescope in the Yorkshire Dales, Prof Reinhart's staff pick up unexpected signals from a source a thousand million million miles away – constellation Andromeda. These are taped and decoded by brilliant young scientist John Fleming who reveals them to be instructions for building a computer so advanced that it is capable of generating human life. After initial suspicion, Whitehall gives the go-ahead and the machine is built in a top secret location off the Scottish coast.

News of Project Andromeda soon leaks out however and foreign governments, scientists, the military and evil international business agency, Intel, all try to gain control of the experiment. Worse, the computer itself runs out of control and sets about its true aim of mastering the world. The hero of the series – idealistic Dr John Fleming, a man with a conscience in the grand *Quatermass* tradition – sets about doing battle with the above villainry, as well as ambitious, amoral biologist Dr Madeleine Dawnay who refuses to halt the experiment.

But the series is probably best remembered for rocketing then unknown actress Julie Christie to stardom. Christie, plucked from drama school for the part, plays (brunette) lab assistant Christine who is killed by the machine only to be reborn as a beautiful, blonde replica of her former self. It is over her favours that science and man must fight. The exquisite android, christened Andromeda, has an intuitive bond with the machine that created her but Fleming, who is harbouring interests of a warmer and altogether more human nature, convinces her to break free. Together they wreck the machine, and escape into the night . . .

Based on an original storyline by renowned astronomer and novelist Fred Hoyle, Professor of Astronomy and Experimental Philosophy at Cambridge, *A for Andromeda* was scripted by BBC producer John Elliot. Elliot had an enduring interest in the machinations of governments and big business (he later produced *The Troubleshooters*), while Hoyle's novels *Black Cloud* and *Ossian's Ride* had expounded the thesis that contact from aliens would come through radio-astronomy.

A for Andromeda was a huge success, with the audience growing to an unprecedented one million viewers each week. A sequel lacking Julie Christie, *The Andromeda Breakthrough* (also BBC, 1962, six 45 mins episodes), in which Andromeda's relationship with Fleming blossoms and the two unite with Dawnay to fight the legacy of the destroyed machine, failed to make a similar impact. The part of Andromeda was taken by Susan Hampshire (>*Forsyte Saga*). Also missing from the new series was Frank Windsor (*Softly Softly, Z Cars*) who appeared in series one as Fleming's self-seeking colleague Dennis Bridger.

Eric Pierpoint donned a mottled cranium to star as Tenctonese-born Los Angeles detective George Francisco in *Alien Nation*. He later gave birth to a baby daughter.

Alien Nation

USA 1989–90 1 × 120m/21 × 60m col FBC. Kenneth Johnson Productions/20th Century Fox. *UK tx* British Sky Broadcasting 1990–1. *cr* Kenneth Johnson, Rockne O'Bannon. *exec pr* Kenneth Johnson. *pr* Andrew Schneider, Arthur Seidel, Tom Chehak. *dr* Various, including Kenneth Johnson, Gwen Arner, John McPherson, Kevin Hooks, Rob Bowman, Steve Dubin. *wr* Various, including Kenneth Johnson, Steven Long Mitchell, Craig W Van Sickel, Diane Frolov, Tom Chehak, Andrew Schneider. *mus* Steve Dorff, Larry Herbstritt, Kenneth Johnson and David Kurtz (theme). *sfx* Burt Dalton, Rick Stratton. *cast* **Detective Matthew Sikes** Gary Graham **Detective George Francisco** Eric Pierpoint **Susan Francisco** Michelle Scarabelli **Emily Francisco** Lauren Woodland **Buck Francisco** Sean Six **Cathi Frankel** Terri Treas **Albert Einstein** Jeff Marcus.

Set in Los Angeles in 1995, this Kenneth Johnson (>*V*, >*The Incredible Hulk*) series featured Matthew Sikes and George Francisco, LAPD detectives doing the usual tough job on Chandleresque streets. What made the duo unusual was that Francisco was an alien, one of 250,000 from the planet Tencton whose slave transporter spaceship had crashed in the Mojave Desert. Humanoid in appearance, except for their vestigial ears and bald, mottled craniums (an inexpensive but effective make-up), the Tenctonese were physically and intellectually superior to Earthlings, qualities which failed to endear them to the more reactionary of Angelenos.

Although spun-off from the 1989 movie of the same title (starring James Caan and Mandy Patinkin), the TV series was notably different in style and concerns. In particular, the TV version gave considerable time to the Tenctonese's rituals, homelife, and their problems of biology (salt and water could kill them), racial integration, all of which were seen through the eyes of George Francisco's family, wife Susan (Michelle Scarabelli, formerly Connie Hall in >Dallas), daughter Emily and son with attitude, the appropriately named Buck. George's salary as the first and only Tenctonese – or pejoratively, 'Slag' – detective in the LAPD meant that the family moved out of the Newcomer ghetto to an all-human neighbourhood. One of the most moving episodes related Emily's first day at the local school, where she was greeted by an anti-alien protest.

As a commentary on racism, the series was cleverly done: to the point without being soap-boxy. The alien culture developed by Johnson was fascinating and even included an invented language, subtitled on screen. The alien's method of reproduction was novel, too: Susan Francisco was first 'serviced' by a 'Binnom' (a sort of religious proxy husband), then by George, and only carried the foetus for the initial stage of pregnancy; thereafter it was carried by her husband, who actually gave birth to the baby, later ceremonially named Vesta.

The cop element of the show, however, was orthodox stuff. George was introspective, intellectual and pacific, Sikes was impulsive, unkempt and divorced. They might have been chalk and cheese but, of course, they male-bonded like glue.

In Britain, the series was first aired on British Sky Broadcasting, 1990–91.

Although the show was cancelled after a single season, the adventures and woes of the Tenctonese in LA continued in a 1994 TV movie, *Alien Nation: Dark Horizon*, which saw their former slave masters, the Overseers (many of which had escaped the crash in the desert), attempt a new subjugation. Another two *Alien Nation* made-for-TV features followed, *Body and Soul* and *The Change*.

Babylon 5

USA 1993– 1 × 90m/64+ × 60m col Syndicated. Babylonian Productions Inc. (pilot: Rattlesnake Productions Inc.). *UK tx* 1994– C4. *cr* J Michael Straczynski. *exec pr* J Michael Straczynski. *pr* Robert Latham Brown, John Copeland, Richard Compton. *dr* Various, including Richard Compton, Jim Johnston, Bruce Seth Green, Janet Greek, Lorraine Senna Ferrara, John C Flinn III. *wr* Various, including J Michael Straczynski, Scott Frost, D C Fontana, Lawrence G Ditillo, David Gerrold, Mark Scott Zicree, Kathryn M Drennan, Christy Marx. *mus* Stewart Copeland (pilot), Christopher Franke. *sfx* Ron Thornton (visual effects designer). *cast* **Cmdr Jeffrey Sinclair** Michael O'Hare **Capt John Sheridan** Bruce Boxleitner **Ambassador Delenn** Mira Furlan **Ambassador Londo Mollari** Peter Jurasik **Security Chief Garibaldi** Jerry Doyle **Ambassador G'Kar** Andreas Katsulas **Lt Cmdr Susan Ivanova** Claudia Christian **Talia Winters** Andrea Thompson **Dr Stephen Franklin** Richard Biggs **Carn Mollari** Peter Trencher **Lyta Alexander** Patricia Tallman **Marcus Cole** Jason Carter **Lennier** Bill Mumu **Na'Toth** Caitlin Brown **Vir Cotto** Stephen Furst. *Video* Warner Bros.

Epic galactic drama. In 2258 AD, years of interplanetary conflict between the five major solar systems – the Earth Alliance, Minbari Federation, Narn Regime, Vorlon Empire and Centauri Republic – end in a fragile peace, overseen by a council of humans and aliens which sits aboard lone space-station *Babylon 5*. This spinning 2,500,000 tons of metal is commanded by Jeffrey Sinclair (later replaced by Captain John Sheridan), who is also Earth Alliance representative on the council, the other chief members of which are: Ambassador G'Kar of the hegemonic Narn; wily, fan-haired Ambassador Londo Mollari of the once-great Centauri ('we have become a tourist attraction'); mysterious Ambassador Kosh Naranek of the Vorlon Empire, who moves around in a veiling protective encounter suit; and Ambassador Delenn of the Minbari, whose federation inexplicably declared peace on Earth just as they seemed poised to crush it. (The mystery was answered in an episode which revealed that Sinclair, captured during the 'Battle of the Line' was found to have a Minbari soul.) Over the seasons, the bald Delenn was increasingly beautified to become a Human-Minbari hybrid, forming romantic attachments with both Sinclair (whom she may have married in a Minbari ceremony) and Sheridan.

The brain-child of J(oseph) Michael Straczynski, *B5* has been judged to be a reworking of everything from

Ambassador G'Kar (Andreas Katsulas) of the Narn Republic, one of the council of aliens and humans aboard lone TV spaceship *Babylon 5*, the last hope for inter-galactic peace.

J R R Tolkien's novel *Lord of the Rings* to *Dune*. Certainly, it has similarities with >*Star Trek: The Next Generation*, not least for its sympathetic, 'intuitive' women characters (namely resident telepaths Lyta Alexander and Talia Winters). It also owes something to real history; Straczynski has consciously used the Yugoslavian background of actress Mira Furlan to inform both the character of Delenn and the series overall. The distinctive hallmark of the show is its remarkable computer graphic effects, overseen by Ron Thornton (also the >*Thunderbirds*-anime melding *Hypernauts*), plus its complex story, which is almost novel-like in its structure, having a beginning, middle and definite end. Intended by Straczynski to be precisely five TV seasons in length, *B5*'s first two seasons were introductions ('foreplay', in Straczynski's own phrase), which culminated in a shoot-'em-up star war between the Centauri Republic and the Nairn Regime, the latter being utterly destroyed by 2259. To ensure victory, the Centauri allied themselves with the forces of evil, the Shadows, a species amassing predatorily at the edge of the Universe. With the ending of peace, the role of *Babylon 5* altered; no longer was it the 'last, best hope for peace', but was 'our last, best hope for victory' in the fight to save the Universe from the Shadows.

Among the best episodes are: 'The Fall of Night' (in which Kosh is revealed to be an angel-like being of awesome power), 'Divided Loyalties', 'The Long, Twilight Struggle', 'In the Shadows of Z'ha'dum', and 'Babylon Squared'.

Passing through the portals of *B5* have been such sci-fi notables as David 'Sapphire and Steel' McCallum in the segment 'Infection', Walter 'Star Trek' Koenig in 'Mind War', and Billy Mumy, once upon a sixties time-warp Will Robinson of >*Lost in Space*, who appears as the semi-regular Minbari attaché Lennier. As if to prove the *B5*'s stellar pedigree the episode 'The Quality of Mercy' featured actress June Lockhart, who had been Mumy's *Lost in Space* mother.

Battlestar Galactica

USA 1978–9 1 × 180m/1 × 120m/19 × 60m col ABC. Glen A Larson Production/Universal Television. *UK tx* 1980–1 ITV. *cr*

Glen A Larson. *exec pr* Glen A Larson. *pr* Don Bellisario, John Dykstra, Paul Playdon, David O'Connell, Leslie Stevens. *dr* Richard Colla, Christian Nyby, Alan Levi, Don Bellisario, Rod Holcomb, Dan Haller, Vince Edwards, Rick Kolbe. *wr* Glen A Larson, Richard Colla, Don Bellisario, Leslie Stevens, Jim Carlson, Terrence McDonnell, Frank Lupo, Paul Playdon. *mus* Stu Philips, Glen A Larson. *sfx* John Dykstra. *cast* **Commander Adama** Lorne Greene **Lieutenant Starbuck** Dirk Benedict **Captain Apollo** Richard Hatch **Athena** Maren Jensen **Boxey** Noah Hathaway **Cassiopea** Laurette Spang. *Video* CIC.

According to its creator, this grandiose space opera was an intergalactic version of Moses' leading of the Israelites to the Promised Land. More prosaically, the series owed much to TV's >*Wagon Train*.

In the seventh millennium AD – so the premise went – twelve tribes of space humans were ambushed and virtually extinguished by a robot race called Cylons. One human battlestar, the *Galactica*, remained and this led a caravan of 220 battered vessels in search of a 'lost' 13th human colony known as Earth. Inevitably, the Cylons gave chase across the heavens.

In charge of the *Galactica* was the robed Moses/Major Adams-like Commander Adama (Lorne Greene), whose top crew members were Starfighter pilots Lieutenant Starbuck (Dirk Benedict, later 'The Faceman' in >*The A-Team*) and Captain Apollo. Other characters were Adama's daughter, the navigator Athena, and orphan boy Boxey, and traitor Count Baltar (John Colicos).

On its US première, the much-hyped and hyper-expensive show achieved stratospheric ratings. The space battles staged by John Dykstra, who won an Oscar for his work on *Star Wars*, were the most spectacular ever to flash across the small screen. But the scripts soon began to lose imagination, Larson's biblical references became ever more overblown (there were even representations of Lucifer and Mary Magdalene), and the characters were revealed as handsome but bland. Another problem was that most viewers still thought of Lorne Greene as >*Bonanza* paterfamilias Ben Cartwright. Moreover, the producers of *Star Wars* issued writs against the show claiming plagiarism. As a result, the series was cancelled at the end of its debut season, having cost over $40 million. A revival for kids *Galactica 1980*, was tried but

similarly flopped. To maximise profits in Britain, Universal released an edited-from-TV feature film version of *Battlestar Galactica* before the small screen transmission. The episodes were: Saga of a Star World (GC Jane Seymour, Lew Ayres, Wilfred Hyde White)/Lost Planet of the Gods, parts I and II/The Lost Warrior/The Long Patrol/The Gun on Ice Planet Zero, parts I and II (GC Roy Thinnes and Britt Ekland)/The Magnificent Warriors/The Young Lords/Mission Galactica, parts I and II/Fire in Space, Wars of the Gods, parts I and II (GC Patrick Macnee as The Imperious Leader)/The Man with Nine Lives (GC Fred Astaire)/Murder on the Rising Star/Greetings from Earth/Baltar's Escape/Experiment in Terra/Take the Celestra/The Hand of God.

Blake's 7

UK 1978–81 52 × 50m col BBC. BBC. *cr* Terry Nation. *pr* David Maloney, Vere Lorrimer. *dr* Various, including Michael Briant, Pennant Roberts, Vere Lorrimer, Douglas Camfield, Jonathan Wright Miller, George Spenton Foster, Derek Martinus, David Maloney, Desmond McCarthy, Fiona Cumming, Mary Ridge, David Sullivan Proudfoot, Vivienne Cozens, Viktors Ritelis. *wr* Various, including Terry Nation, Chris Boucher (script editor), Allan Prior, Robert Holmes, Roger Parkes, James Follett, Ben Steed, Tanith Lee, Trevor Hoyle, Rod Beacham, Bill Lyons, Colin Davis, Simon Masters. *mus* Dudley Simpson. *cast* **Blake** Gareth Thomas **Avon** Paul Darrow **Jenna** Sally Knyvette **Vila** Michael Keating **Gan** David Jackson **Cally** Jan Chappell **Zen** Peter Tuddenham (voice) **Orac** Peter Tuddenham (voice) **Servalan** Jacqueline Pearce **Travis** Stephen Greif/Bryan Groucher **Dayna** Josette Simon **Tarrant** Steven Pacey **Soolin** Glynis Barber. *Video* BBC.

Terry Nation's great gift to the sci-fi genre, the story of a motley group of outlaw revolutionaries led by a patriot-hero who fight the fascistic Federation (motto: 'Strength from Unity') in the second century of the third calendar.

The serial was born out of a moment of desperation at a BBC interview where Nation (inventor of the Daleks, creator of >*Survivors*, prolific writer for >*The Avengers* and >*The Saint*), having failed to sell other wares, suddenly started on the premise above. 'Have you got a title?' someone asked. 'Blake's 7,' replied Nation without hesitation. And so the cultiest of British cult sci-fi serials of the 1970s was born, one watched by 10 million viewers at its peak, an enormous number for a space opera.

Although *Blake's 7* bears the heavy imprint of Nation's own pessimistic ideas ('I can only see terror in space,' he once remarked), the show also borrowed from sources as diverse as >*Star Trek* and the legend of Robin Hood. And other *Blake's 7* contributors, on screen and off, added much to the serial's appeal, particularly script editor Chris Boucher (later creator of >*Star Cops*) and veteran BBC director/producer Vere Lorrimer. It was Boucher and Lorrimer, for instance, who gave the serial its emphasis on character. Not only were Blake's merry men and women highly individual and realistically complex personalities (the seven fought each other almost as much as they did the Federation), but the show came to be something of a character study of a revolutionary leader fighting long and near impossible odds.

The members of Blake's band who fought – and tried to evade – the Terran Federation in the near galaxy were: Roj Blake, the leader, a resistance hero who escaped from a convict ship on the way to exile on planet Cygnus Alpha; Jenna Stannis, smuggler and ace space-pilot; Kerr Avon, a *louche*, supercilious computer expert, caught by the Federation attempting to embezzle 500 million credits; Vila Restal, cowardly, sardonic lock-picker (he and Avon developed a wonderfully sniping relationship); Olag Gan, a gentle-giant muscle man; Cally, an alien from Auron; Zen, the computer on the *Liberator*, the band's first spaceship.

The membership of the band changed, however, because *Blake's 7* overturned accepted drama practice and killed off a number of its lead characters. Gan died on Earth during an attempt to destroy Control, the Federation's communications centre in 'Pressure Point' (season two); the master computer Zen was destroyed, along with the *Liberator*, by fluid particles in 'Terminal' (season four); and shortly afterwards, Cally was killed in 'Rescue' (season four). But most unusually of all, Blake himself disappeared MIA in 'Star One' (season two).

With the disappearance of Blake, the increasingly paranoid Avon (Paul Darrow) took over leadership of the group, while the loss of personnel was made up by the gradual recruitment of: Captain Del Tarrant, bully and mercenary; Dayna Mellanby, trigger-happy black gunwoman; Soolin, a native of Gauda Prime, who fought to avenge her parents' death (played by Glynis Barber, later *Dempsey and Makepeace*); Orac, the mother of all computers; and *Scorpio*, a souped-up, Wanderer-class planet-hopper Mark II spaceship.

It was not only in its proclivity for dispensing with major characters that *Blake's 7* played with conventions. It also eschewed moral blacks and whites and, in one episode, 'Star One', had Blake's 7 allied with the enemy Federation to fight off an invasion by Andromedans. Indeed, the enemy were as multi-dimensionally presented as the heroes, notably the Federation Supreme Commander Servalan (a woman) and Space Commander Travis, a man who hated Blake so much he was prepared to pursue him to the ends of the galaxy. The final episode – where Avon killed the re-appeared Blake, his former leader, then turned to face the approaching Federation troopers with a smile on his lips – was the most enigmatic conclusion to a serial since McGoohan's >*The Prisoner*.

Quality was an almost constant in *Blake's 7*. As long as you closed your eyes to sets literally held together by Sellotape.

A selection of the best episodes is: The Way Back/Rumours of Death/Sarcophagus/Terminal/Rescue/ Gold/Orbit/Blake.

The Champions

UK 1968–9 30 × 60m col ITV. ATV Midlands. *USA* 1968–9 NBC. *cr* Monty Berman and Dennis Spooner. *pr* Monty Berman. *dr* Cyril Frankel, Sam Wanamaker, Paul Dickson, John Moxey, John Gilling, Leslie Norman, Freddie Francis, Robert Asher, Don Sharp, Roy Ward Baker. *wr* Dennis Spooner, Donald James, Philip Broadley, Ralph Smart, Tony Williamson, Terry Nation, Brian Clemens, Gerald Kelsey, Ian Stuart Black. *mus* Edwin Astley, Tony Hatch (theme). *cast* **Craig Stirling** Stuart Damon **Richard Barrett** William Gaunt **Sharron Macready** Alexandra Bastedo **Tremayne** Anthony Nicholls. *Video* ITC.

'Craig Stirling, Sharron Macready and Richard Barrett . . . The Champions. Endowed with the qualities and skill of superhumans . . . qualities and skills, both physical and mental, to the peak of human performance. Gifts given to them by the unknown race of people from a lost city in Tibet. Gifts that are a secret to be closely guarded . . . a secret that enables them to use their powers to their best advantage . . . as the Champions of Law, Order and Justice. Operators of the International Agency of Nemesis!'

So opened each episode of *The Champions*, a superior, if earnest, sixties sci-fi thriller series, usually remembered as American but in fact from British ITV company, ATV Midlands. *The Champions* were improved human beings whose extraordinary skills were given after a 'fatal' plane crash in episode one, 'The Beginning'. As a result of their endowment by a lost Tibetan tribe, Craig Stirling, Richard Barrett and Sharron Macready had amazing intuition, computer-like intelligence and Olympian levels of strength and endurance. They could also communicate by telepathy.

Luckily for humanity, *The Champions* worked for Geneva-based Nemesis, a mini United Nations-style agency dedicated to preserving the world balance of power (a similar premise to that of >*Man from UNCLE*, aired in Britain a few years earlier; international cooperation was clearly an idea whose time had come in the late sixties). On the organisation's behalf the super-agents were despatched to any situation judged capable of causing a serious threat to world stability. In 'The Experiment' the Nemesis agents combat a power-mad scientist who plans to create a race of super-humans, while several episodes, including 'Happening' and 'The Dark Island', concern plans by rogue organisations to launch atomic wars from which they will emerge the omnipotent survivors.

What helped lift *The Champions* above the ordinary was undoubtedly the screen presence of its leading players, American heart-throb Stuart Damon, cast again by producer Monty Berman in spy series *The Adventurer* (1972), William Gaunt (later in the British sit-com *No Place Like Home*), and blonde bombshell-with-brains Alexandra Bastedo (whose real-life talents include fluency in French, German and Italian), more recently seen as a guest star in the award-winning comedy series

>*Absolutely Fabulous*. Not to mention Anthony Nicholls as the trio's imperturbable boss at Nemesis, Tremayne. Guest stars included Peter Wyngarde for 'The Invisible Man' and Patrick Macnee for 'The Ghost Plane' while the American actor Sam Wanamaker moved behind the camera to direct 'To Trap a Rat'.

The creative talents behind the scenes of *The Champions* – which was still being repeated in the 1990s – were producer Monty Berman, whose previous credits included >*The Baron*, >*The Saint* and >*The Persuaders*, and Dennis Spooner, co-creator of sixties crime series >*Man in a Suitcase* and scriptwriter on >*Dr Who*, Gerry Anderson's >*Fireball XL5*, >*Thunderbirds* and >*Stingray*. High-calibre writers on *The Champions* included Brian Clemens and Terry Nation, the man who not only invented the Daleks in *Dr Who* but also went on to create the ultimate British cult sci-fi series of the seventies, >*Blake's 7*.

Doctor Who

UK 1963– 679 × 30m/15 × 50m/1 × 90m bw/col BBC. BBC. *cr* Sydney Newman. *pr* Various, including Verity Lambert, Innes Lloyd, Peter Bryant, Derrick Sherwin, Barry Letts, Philip Hinchcliffe, Graham Williams, John Nathan-Turner. *dr* Various, including Waris Hussein, Douglas Camfield, Mervyn Pinfield, Derek Martinus, Christopher Barry, Raymond Cusik, Richard Martin, Julia Smith, George Spenton Foster, Michael E Briant, Paddy Russell, Pennant Roberts, Peter Grimwade, David Maloney, Morris Barry, Peter Moffat, Timothy Combe, Graeme Harper. *wr* Various, including Anthony Coburn, C E Weber, Terry Nation, Dennis Spooner, David Whitaker, John Lucarotti, Kit Pedler, Gerry Davis, Brian Hayles, Terrance Dicks, Robert Holmes, Malcolm Hulke, Robert Banks Stewart, Louis Marks, Chris Boucher, Douglas Adams, Eric Saward, Christopher H Bidemead, Terence Dudley, Guy Leopold (aka Robert Sloman), Barry Letts, Peter Grimwade, Don Houghton. *mus* Ron Grainer (theme), BBC Radiophonic Workshop. *cast* **Dr Who I (1963–6)** William Hartnell **Susan Foreman** Carole Ann Ford **Ian Chesterton** William Russell **Barbara Wright** Jacqueline Hill **Vicki** Maureen O'Brien **Steven Taylor** Peter Purves/**Dr Who II (1966–9)** Patrick Troughton **Polly** Anneke

Wills **Ben** Michael Craze **Jamie** Frazer Hines **Zoe** Wendy Padbury/**Dr Who III (1969–74)** John Pertwee **Liz Shaw** Caroline John **Brigadier Lethbridge-Stewart** Nicholas Courtney/**Dr Who IV (1974–81)** Tom Baker **Sarah Jane Smith** Elizabeth Sladen **Harry Sullivan** Ian Marter **Leela** Louise Jameson **Romana** Mary Tamm/Lalla Ward **K9** John Leeson (voice)/**Dr Who V (1982–4)** Peter Davison **Tegan** Janet Fielding **Nyssa** Sarah Sutton **Adric** Matthew Waterhouse **Turlough** Mark Strickson/**Dr Who VI (1984–6)** Colin Baker **Perpugilliam 'Peri' Brown** Nicola Bryant **Melanie Bush** Bonnie Langford/**Dr Who VII (1987–92)** Sylvester McCoy **Ace** Sophie Aldred. *Video* BBC. *The various assistants to Dr Who are grouped with the main incarnation of The Doctor they served.*

The longest-running sci-fi serial in TV history actually began as a children's education programme. It was the creation of then head of BBC drama Sydney Newman, who intended the time-space travels of Dr Who to be a means of explaining past ages and the physical sciences. 'No cheap-jack bug-eyed monsters' he instructed the programme's first producer, Verity Lambert. Thankfully for telefantasy, Lambert ignored the caution and introduced the Daleks in *Dr Who's* second story, 'The Dead Planet', December 1963. Devised by Terry Nation and designed by Ray Cusik, the Daleks became a phenomenon amongst children and their menacing catchline, 'Ex-ter-minate! Ex-ter-minate!' much imitated by tots with saucepans on their heads. *Dr Who* shot up the ratings and, despite variations in quality and frequency over the subsequent thirty years, has remained a particular object of public and TV sci-fi fandom affection.

The eponymous Time Lord of the serial was a 720-year-old with two hearts from the planet of Gallifrey who stole a faulty time travel-machine, or TARDIS (acronym for Time and Relative Dimension in Space), and set out to wander the cosmos. Eventually, he moved from objective observer of events to a fighter against evil. As the TARDIS had defective navigation, it could land anywhere in time or space.

To date there have been seven television-series incarnations of Doctor Who, all different in character, due to the need for Time Lords to 'regenerate'. The first, played by *Army Game* regular William Hartnell, was

'Exterminate! Exterminate!' The Daleks were amongst the most feared adversaries of time-travelling 720-year-old Dr Who. Originally intended as a children's educational programme, *Dr Who* became the longest-running sci-fi serial in TV history.

grandfatherly Edwardian, but was replaced by a Chaplinesque hobo version (Patrick Troughton), who in turn was succeeded by the dandyish, gadget-crazy, car-driving interpretation of Jon Pertwee (later *Worzel Gummidge*). Tom Baker then played The Doctor for seven years as scarf-trailing wit (many consider Baker's version definitive), before the character was re-invented as a sensitive clean-cut preppy (Peter Davison, also *All Creatures Great and Small*). Colin Baker's tenure saw an abrasive Doctor, while the seventh Doctor, Sylvester McCoy, was clownishly extrovert. The last three incumbents were less successful than their predecessors and, as a result, the show lost impact and ratings, which declined from a peak of 14.5 million for the fourth part of the 1979 'City of Death' story, to 4.5 million by the later 1980s.

As well as The Doctor himself, a series trademark was a succession of 'companions'. The first of these were granddaughter Susan and two of her teachers, history mistress Barbara Wright and science master Ian Chesterton (their respective disciplines being those beloved by Newman). Many of The Doctor's assistants were stereotypical helpless women, with some, like Jo Grant, seemingly only aboard the time-machine to sex things up. More advanced female characters appeared on occasion – the Liberationist Sarah Jane, and warrior-like Leela, for example – but these invariably slipped back to the norm. Some of The Doctor's male acquaintances, however, were fairly stereotyped too, including the crusty Brigadier Lethbridge-Stewart, head of the UNIT, to whom fell the serial's classic line: 'That chap with the wings, five rounds quick fire, sergeant!' ('The Daemons').

Although produced on a shoestring budget and shot on video (many episodes were wiped or lost), hardware and special effects were essential to *Dr Who's* appeal. Sheer inventiveness produced the Daleks at a pittance (their flashing lights came from the indicators of a Morris Eight car, and they were propelled by a stuntman who sat inside on a stool with castors and pushed), while the TARDIS was a police box which was simply claimed to be bigger inside than outside. It is estimated that some 140 different types of alien appeared on the show (mostly humanoid so that actors could just be dressed to play them), including the Yeti, the Cyberman, the Ice Warriors, the Sea Devils and The Tractators. The Doctor's nemesis was the evil The Master (most memorably played by Roger Delgado).

However, the low, low budget meant that on occasion the monsters were unintentionally amusing.

As not only the backbone of British sci-fi TV but a long-running drama serial, *Dr Who* has launched many in-front and behind-camera careers. The serial's first producer, Verity Lambert, is now one of the industry's most important (*GBH*, *Eldorado*), while its writers included Douglas Adams (later creator of *Hitchhiker's Guide to the Galaxy*) and Chris Boucher (*Star Cops*). Doctor's assistants actors Peter Purves and Frazer Hines went on to *Blue Peter* and *Emmerdale Farm*. A few of the more intriguing bit-appearances were Gareth 'New Avengers' Hunt ('Planet of the Spiders', 1974), John Cleese ('City of Death', 1979) and comedian Alexei Sayle ('Revelation of the Daleks', 1985).

Presently the serial awaits its future with the BBC, although in 1996 the Corporation (with Universal TR of America) produced a full-length TV movie starring Paul McGann to join the previous *Who* features, the 1965 *Doctor Who and the Daleks* and the 1966 *Daleks-Invasion Earth*, both featuring Peter Cushing as the time traveller.

Among the serial's classic stories were: The Dead Planet (wr Terry Nation)/Terror of the Autons/The Daemons/The Sea Devils/The Ark in Space/Genesis of the Daleks (wr Terry Nation)/Pyramids of Mars/ Earthshock/Mawdryn Undead/The Five Doctors (a twentieth-anniversary special in which Richard Hurdnell replaced the late William Hartnell)/The Caves of Androzani.

Doomwatch

UK 1970–2 38 × 50m col BBC 1. BBC. *cr* Gerry Davis and Kit Pedler. *pr* Terence Dudley. *dr* Various, including Paul Ciappessoni, Jonathan Alwyn, Terence Dudley, Vere Lorrimer, David Proudfoot, Pennant Roberts. *wr* Various, including Kit Pedler, Gerry Davis, Dennis Spooner, Terence Dudley, Roger Parkes, Robert Holmes, Eric Hills, Ian Curteis, Stuart Douglass. *mus* Max Harris. *cast* **Dr Spencer Quist** John Paul **Dr John Ridge** Simon Oates **Tobias Wren** Robert Powell **Colin Bradley** Joby Blanshard **Pat Hunnisett** Wendy Hall. *Video* BBC.

Doomwatch – or the Department of Measurement of Science Work – was a fictional environmental agency headed by Dr Spencer Quist ('We must have more data!'), a brusque but brilliant scientist dedicated to keeping Earth alive. Each episode related the efforts of Quist and his team – notably, charmer Dr John Ridge and young Tobias 'Toby' Wren – to counter particular out-of-control environmental problems, from toxic waste ('Burial at Sea') to genetic engineering (the veritable video nasty 'Tomorrow, The Rat').

Stagey but prescient, this green-drama series, devised by *Dr Who* writers Kit 'Cyberman' Pedler and Gerry Davis, caught the incipient eco mood of the times. It became a viewer phenomenon and its title even entered the English lexicon. Among its players was a débuting Robert Powell, whose character, Tobias Wren, was killed defusing a bomb at the beginning of season two. Powell himself, of course, had a second coming in the 1977 TV movie, *Jesus of Nazareth*.

Earth 2

USA 1996 1 × 120/12 × 60m col NBC. Amblin Television and Universal Television. *UK tx* 1996 Sky 1. *cr* Michael Duggan, Carol Flint, Mark Levin. *exec pr* Michael Duggan, Carol Flint, Marl Levin. *pr* P K Simmonds, Tony To, Cleve Landsberg, John Melfi. *dr* Various, including Scott Winant. *wr* Various, including Michael Duggan, Carol Flint, Mark Levin. *mus* David Bergeaud. *sfx* Greg Cannon (creature design). *cast* **Devon Adair** Debrah Farentino **Alonzo Solace** Antonio Sabato Jr **John Danziger** Clancy Brown **Yale** Sullivan Walker **Julia Heller MD** Jessica Steen **Commander Broderick O'Neill** Richard Bradford **Morgan Martin** John Gegenhuber **Bess Martin** Rebecca Gayheart **Zero** Tierre Turner **Ulysses Adair** Joey Zimmerman **True Danziger** J Madison Wright **Dison Blalock** David Clennon **Navigator** Marsha Firesten.

Made by Steven Spielberg's Amblin Production Company, *Earth 2* was a latterday mix of >*Lost in Space* and venerable oater >*Wagon Train*. Filmed in the majestic New Mexico desert (and at nearby Garson Studios) it concerned a group of diverse twenty-first-century pioneers, led by visionary Devon Adair, who flee their space-station after it is ravaged by a mysterious syndrome which physically impairs human young (including Adair's own son, Ulysses). The expeditionists head for pristine planet G889, the so-called Earth 2, only to crash-land on the wrong, barren side, 3,400 miles from the verdant New Pacifica region, the only place capable of supporting civilisation. Under-equipped and riven by mutual hostilities, the colonists of Eden Advance are obliged to trek epically to the promised land, encountering *en route* mystical occurrences and such aliens as animal-like Kobas, Terrians (underground humanoids) and Grendlers (reptilian scavengers). Creature design was by Greg Cannon, Academy Award winner for *Dracula* and *Mrs Doubtfire*.

Aside from Adair and son, those struggling to survive Earth 2 included hired gun John Danziger (Clancy Brown, *Highlander*, *The Adventures of Buckaroo Banzai*, and son of a former US Representative for Ohio), crippled pilot Alonzo Solace, government official Morgan Martin, tyro medic Julia Heller, and teacher Yale. Their basic incompatibility was exacerbated wonderfully by baddie Gaal (Tim Curry, *The Rocky Horror Picture Show*, *The Shadow*, in a virtuoso performance), who claimed to be a fellow crashed survivor.

Despite solid acting, awe-inspiring settings and a passable concept, *Earth 2* was unable to beat off slow plotting and bouts of melodrama. The show lasted a mere season before being 'suspended' by NBC, with the characters still many miles from their Elysian goal.

Hitchhiker's Guide To The Galaxy

UK 1981 6 × 35m BBC2. BBC. *US tx* 1982 NBC. *cr* Douglas Adams. *pr* Alan J W Bell. *wr* Douglas Adams. *mus* Paddy Kingsland. *cast* **Arthur Dent** Simon Jones **Ford Prefect** David Dixon **Voice of the Book** Peter Jones **Zaphod Beeblebrox** Mark Wing-Davey **Trillian** Sandra Dickinson **Marvin** David Learner **Voice of Marvin** Stephen Moore. *Video* BBC.

Seconds before the Earth is destroyed by a Vogon Constructor Fleet (to make way for a hyperspace bypass), Ford Prefect, an alien from planet Betelgeuse and researcher for the bestselling intergalactic reference book *The Hitchhiker's Guide* rescues typical Englishman Arthur Dent from the impending doom. Arthur, surprised to hear that Ford Prefect is not, in fact, from Guildford, soon finds himself marooned in space with his alien friend. Together the two discover what a groovy place the Universe can be and seek the answers to many burning questions: Why are people born? Why do they die? Why do they spend so much of the intervening time wearing digital watches? and so on.

Their adventures take them on a trip through the galaxy that is a satire on modern times – part fantasy, part wordplay, always very droll. They start out on spaceship *Heart of Gold* where they meet part-time galactic President Zaphod Beeblebrox, his girlfriend Trillian and Marvin the paranoid android. They bump into the ugly green Vogons who write the worst poetry in the universe, the Golgafrinchians – ad execs and telephone sanitisers who were thrown off the planet for being useless – and a pair of pan-dimensional beings who are searching for the Ultimate Question to Life, the Universe and Everything (they already have the answer – it's forty-two). They finish in The Restaurant at the End of the Universe, with a prime view over the exploding galaxy.

The Hitchhiker's Guide (first a BBC Radio show, then a bestselling novel) was as inventive on the small screen as in its previous incarnations. Sophisticated computer animation converted the viewer's screen into the Guide when necessary and any space wars were represented by video games (the high cost of the special effects nearly led to the show being cancelled after the first episode).

As befits a series of this type, guest stars were all part of the in-joke. Creator Douglas Adams was seen disrobing and walking naked into the sea in the second episode; Peter Davison, the fifth Doctor Who, made a guest appearance as talking dinner Dish of the Day (Davison's wife played Trillian in the series) and David Prowse, who played Darth Vader, was bodyguard for Plutonium rock 'n' roller Hotblack Desiado. Shootie and Bang-Bang, the two enlightened liberal galactic cops who shoot people and then agonise about it with their girlfriends afterwards, were take-offs of *Starsky and Hutch*.

The Incredible Hulk

USA 1978–82 80 × 60m/2 × 120m col CBS. An MCA Television Production. *UK tx* 1978–82. *cr* Stan Lee. *exec pr* Kenneth Johnson. *pr* Chuck Bowman, Jim Parriott, Nicholas Corea, James G Hirsch, Bob Steinhauer, Karen Harris, Jill Sherman. *dr* Various, including Reza S Badiyi, Bill Bixby, Chuck Bowman, Nick Corea, Ray Danton, Jeffrey Hayden, Alan J Levi, Frank Orsatti, Joseph Pevney, Kenneth Johnson, Sig Neufeld. *wr* Various, including Kenneth Johnson, Richard Matheson, Nick Corea, Jill Sherman, Karen Harris, Chuck Bowman, Jim Hirsch. *mus* Joseph Harnell. *cast* **David Bruce Banner** Bill Bixby **The Incredible Hulk** Lou Ferrigno **Jack McGee** Jack Colvin.

Mild, compassionate scientist Dr David Banner has been accidentally injected with an overdose of gamma rays during an experiment. Now he is in the grip of a Jekyll-and-Hyde split over which he has no control – at moments of stress he becomes *The Incredible Hulk*, a raging, green-skinned man-beast of superhuman strength. The world thinks Banner is dead but in reality he is a man on the run from society and his other self, searching for answers and the antidote.

Travelling from town to town and taking odd jobs to support himself, Banner 'hulks out' whenever annoyed by wrongdoers. Adding to his troubles is Jack McGee, the headline-hunting *National Register* reporter who suspects Banner's identity and mistakenly believes The Hulk to be a killer. Each time Banner moves on he is only moments ahead of his pursuer.

The role of the Incredible Hulk required two actors – one Bill Bixby (star of *The Magician*, 1973) to portray normal human doctor David Banner; the other weight-lifter Lou Ferrigno to play the noble, wordless Hulk into which he was transformed. It took two hours to transform former Mr Universe Ferrigno, 6 feet 5 inches tall and 19½ stone in weight (co-star of Arnold Schwarzenegger's début film *Pumping Iron*, 1976), into the Hulk. He had to be fitted with a rubber nose and forehead, white contact lenses and a green wig, and have his body sprayed with green paint. The metamorphosis sequences – as well as the famous splitting shirt – required specially graded contact lenses to effect the colour change of Banner's eyes.

But if no expense was spared on special effects, money was also saved where possible. Keen-eyed fans watching the episode in which Banner was pursued on a highway by a malevolent lorry would have spotted that the scene came from Steven Spielberg's 1971 movie *Duel*. Stock film from *Airport* was also featured later in the series.

MCA TV press handouts claimed that The Hulk wrestled with the philosophical question: 'how can man learn to control the demon within him?' This was perhaps stretching a point (after all The Hulk was a hero not a villain), but the show did take on controversial subjects such as child-beating, teenage alcoholism and psycho-surgery. As a result it was popular with adults – Ferrigno received fan mail from scores of women wanting to marry him – as well as children, who perceived him as a jolly green giant.

Hulk – the live-action version of the *Marvel* comic book superhero created by Stan Lee – was produced by Ken Johnson, already responsible for sci-fi series *The Bionic Woman* and who went on to create fantasy hits >*V* and >*Alien Nation*.

A cartoon version of *The Incredible Hulk*, featuring Banner's cousin She-Hulk, was also produced and aired by NBC in the States and by ITV in Britain.

The Invaders

USA 1967–8 43 × 60m col ABC. A Quinn Martin Production. *UK tx* 1967–8 ITV. *cr* Larry Cohen. *exec pr* Quinn Martin. *pr* Alan Armer. *dr* Various, including Paul Wendkos, Joseph Sargent, Don Medford, William Hale, Sutton Roley, Robert Butler, Richard Benedict, John Meredyth Lucas. *wr* Various, including Don Brinkley, George Eckstein, John W Bloch, Clyde Ware, Anthony Wilson, Jerry Sohl, Dan Ullman, Earl Hamner Jr., Robert Collins. *mus* Dominic Frontiere. *cast* **David Vincent** Roy Thinnes **Edgar Scoville** Kent Smith.

'How does a nightmare begin?' For architect David Vincent (Roy Thinnes) it begins when, alone at night on a remote country road, he witnesses the landing of a UFO. Later, when he returns to the scene with the police he finds nothing there except for a honeymooning couple. Vincent notices, however, that the couple's little fingers are

After a radiation experiment which went disastrously wrong, Dr David Banner transformed into the Incredible Hulk whenever he became angry. The Hulk, played by muscleman Lou Ferrigno, received 2,000 fan letters a week and was dubbed 'the Clark Gable of the eighties'.

Architect David Vincent (played by Roy Thinnes) witnesses the aliens landing in the paranoid sixties series *The Invaders.*

crooked . . . He has stumbled on to an awesome secret: aliens from a doomed planet, disguised as humans, are infiltrating Earth. He tries to tell the sceptical world but no one believes him. After all, the aliens look human; only the stiff pinkies, a lack of heartbeat and a tendency to glow when regenerating to maintain their human form gives them away. As if to complete Vincent's misery, he becomes Human Enemy Number One for the aliens.

The Invaders was the TV series most closely modelled on the Hollywood Red Scare films of the 1950s such as *Invasion of the Body Snatchers*, but sought to drop their overt anti-Commie content whilst retaining their sense of paranoia: 'They're among us now . . . in your city . . . maybe on your block', as the TV trailer put it. Another clear influence was the Cassandra myth, whilst Vincent's ceaseless criss-crossing of America was more than reminiscent of executive producer Quinn Martin's earlier series >*The Fugitive*.

There are people who like *The Invaders* but most found it repetitive and depressing. No matter how many aliens Vincent vapourised, more came along. In season two the scriptwriters, no doubt feeling sorry for the lonely hero (who actually succeeded in being less animated than the emotionless aliens), gave him seven supportive friends. These were The Believers, led by businessman Edgar Scoville. More useful would have been some good storylines. The show ended suddenly in mid run after forty-three episodes.

A few of the many guest cast were Gene Hackman, Jack Lord (>*Stoney Burke*, >*Hawaii Five-O*), Roddy McDowall (>*Planet of the Apes*) and Karen Black. Thinnes' subsequent and uneven career has included a reuniting with Quinn Martin in the US version of Tales of the Unexpected, *Twist in the Tail* (1978).

The series was the invention of Larry Cohen, who was the creator of >*Branded*.

The Invisible Man

UK 1958–9 26 × 25m bw ITV. Official Films/ITP Ralph Smart. *USA tx* 1958–60 CBS. *cr* Ralph Smart. *pr* Ralph Smart. *dr* Pennington Richards, Peter Maxwell, Ralph Smart, Quentin Lawrence. *wr* Various, including Michael Connor, Ralph

Smart, Stanley Mann, Leslie Arliss, Ian Stuart Black, Doreen Montgomery, Michael Cramoy, Tony O'Grady (alias Brian Clemens). *mus* Sidney John Key. *sfx* Jack Whitehead. *cast* **The Invisible Man** Tim Turner (voice)/Johnny Scripps (body). **Diane** Lisa Daniely **Sally** Deborah Watling **Tania** Zena Marshall **Sir Charles** Ernest Clark.

The first and best of the four TV series based on H G Wells' classic novel, particularly notable for its excellent-for-the-time special effects.

While testing his theory of optical density in the 1950s brilliant young scientist Dr Peter Grady accidentally renders himself invisible and is unable to reverse the process. Grady is *The Invisible Man*. At first HM Government sees him as a security risk, but then employs him for espionage work, not infrequently against Communist adversaries ('The Locked Room', 'Shadow on the Screen' and 'Point of Destruction').

Making the best of his invisibility, Grady also freelances as a sleuth, investigating cases of blackmail, drug-smuggling, and power-crazy dictators. A running storyline through the series was the Invisible Man's unsuccessful quest for an antidote to his transparent nature.

The most the viewer saw of the Invisible Man – who, incidentally, lacked the dark madness of H G Wells' original – was a suit of clothes, a head swathed in bandages and sunglasses. His naked presence, however, was indicated by deft special effects work by Jack Whitehead. Using wires, Whitehead raised wineglasses to invisible lips, pulled down springs on chairs to reproduce sitting and got a cigarette to puff in mid air.

To maintain the mystique of the Invisible Man, producer Ralph Smart (>*The Adventures of William Tell*, >*Danger Man*) steadfastly refused to reveal the identity of the actor who played the part. It is now known, however, that his voice was dubbed by actor Tim Turner and stuntman Johnny Scripps played by the body. Guest stars included Rupert Davies (*Maigret*), Joan Hickson (*Miss Marple*), Honor Blackman (>*The Avengers*), and Ian Hendry (*Police Surgeon*).

The other *The Invisible Man* series were an American version by Harve Bennett in 1975 (with ex-Man from UNCLE, David McCallum, in the title role), the 1976 US *Gemini Man* and a BBC six-parter in 1984.

Knight Rider

USA 1982–7 90 × 60m col NBC. Universal TV/Glen A Larson. *UK tx* 1983–7 ITV. *cr* Glen A Larson. *exec pr* Glen A Larson, Robert Cinader, Rober Foster. *pr* Various. *dr* Various, including Virgil Vogel, Rick Kolbe, Dan Haller, Sidney Hayers, Bernie Kowalski, Peter Crane, Bruce Kessler, Chris Nyby, Jeff Hayden. *wr* Various, including Glen A Larson, R A Cinader, Karen Harris, Deborah Davis, Stephen B Katz, Hannah Shearer, Richard Matheson. *mus* Stu Phillips. *cast* **Michael Knight** David Hasselhoff **Devon Miles** Edward Mulhare **Bonnie Barstow** Patricia McPherson **Voice of KITT** William Daniels **April Curtis** Rebecca Holden **Reginald Cornelius III** ('RC3') Peter Parros **Wilton Knight** Richard Basehart. *Video* CIC.

The adventures of a rebuilt ex-cop and his incredible talking car. Allegedly tailor-created for handsome but hardly loquacious actor David 'The Young and the Restless' Hasselhoff, the series was a big hit with kids, heterosexual woman and those men who understood that it was not intended to be wholly serious. In episode one Hasselhoff's character was rescued from death and disfigurement by terminally ill industrialist Wilton Knight, who bequeathed the cop his surname, a plastic visage, tight jeans, a mission to fight for justice, and, best of all, a supercar – the Knight Industries Two Thousand (KITT). This was a black Pontiac Trans Am with such optional extras as a cruising speed of 300mph, more armaments than most Third World nations and the ability to jump fifty feet into the air. More, the car could converse, and even had its own – somewhat truculent – personality. Difficult though KITT could be, it was fiercely protective of its owner and would drive through anything to save him.

Fortuitously, the industrialist (played by >*Voyage to the Bottom of the Sea* commander Richard Basehart) also left Michael Knight a fortune to finance the Foundation for Law and Government mission, plus a mansion HQ and a valued underling, Devon. Car maintenance was provided by, in order, Bonnie Barstow, April Curtis, and black homeboy Reginald Cornelius III. After *Knight Rider*, David Hasselhoff flexed his pecs as Lt Mitch Bucannon in >*Baywatch*.

You got it.

Kolchak: The Night Stalker

USA 1974–5 20 × 60m ABC. Francy Productions for Universal TV. *UK tx* 1983–5 Central. *cr* Jeff Rice. *exec pr* Darren McGavin. *pr* Paul Playdon, Cy Chermak. *dr* Allen Baron, Alex Grasshoff, Don Weiss, Michael T Caffey, Gene Levitt, Robert Scherer, Bruce Kessler, Michael Kozoll, Don McDougall, Vincent McEveety. *wr* Rudolph Borchert, Zekial Markal, David Chase, Paul Playdon, Bill Ballinger, Don Mullally, L Ford Neale, Al Friedman, Arthur Rowe, Jimmy Sangster, Steve Fisher, Stephen Lord, Michael Kozoll. *mus* Gil Melle. *cast* **Carl Kolchak** Darren McGavin **Tony Vincenzo** Simon Oakland **Ron Updyke** Jack Grinnage **Edith Cowles** Ruth McDevitt.

Even in twentieth-century America, ancient, fabled monsters stalk the dark corners of cities, streets and alleyways. And Carl Kolchak, the down-at-heel newsman with a nose for a scoop, knows it all too well. Diligent and relentless, he stalks these beasts till they have no hiding place; he finds vampires in Los Angeles, alchemists in Seattle and Jack the Ripper prowling Chicago. But the authorities want it hushed up, ulcer-ridden editor Tony Vincenzo will never print and Kolchak is left holding the evidence with no front page in sight.

Hapless reporter Kolchak, a pastiche of old newspaper-hack clichés, first took to the night-time city streets in Jeff Rice's novel *The Kolchak Papers* (1970). Darren McGavin starred as the eponymous hero in two TV movies (*The Night Stalker* and *The Night Strangler*) which were adapted from the book, and loved the character so much he decided to co-produce his own series. It was an ambitious project combining documentary-style photography, shadowy man-killing creatures and wisecracking humour. Episodes such as Jimmy Sangster's 'Horror in the Heights' (guest-cameo Phil Silvers) where the monster took the shape of its victims' loved ones showed the series at its chilling best.

But perhaps the series' blend was a bit too odd. Either way its twenty episodes went almost unnoticed, the network was sued by author Jeff Rice for producing a weekly spin-off without permission and a new programming boss, Fred Silverman, took over at ABC. *Kolchak's* demise was inevitable.

Darren McGavin had come to the role of Kolchak with a string of TV crime credits to his name – *The Old Nickerbocker Music Hall* (1948), *Crime Photographer* (1951), *Mickey Spillane's Mike Hammer* (1958), *The Outsider* (1968–9), *Rookies* (1972) – but his enterprise and eye for the unusual were not rewarded. After *Kolchak* he starred in a couple of unsuccessful comedy pilots and one short-lived series, *Small and Frye* (1983).

Episode titles for *Kolchak: The Night Stalker* were as follows: The Ripper/The Zombie/UFO (aka They Have Been, They Are, They Will Be . . .)/The Vampire/The Werewolf/Firefall (aka The Doppelganger)/The Devil's Platform/Bad Medicine/The Spanish Moss Murders/The Energy Eater (aka Matchemonedo)/The Primal Scream (aka The Humanoids)/The Trevi Collection/Chopper/Demon in Lace/Legacy of Terror/The Knightly Murders/The Youth Killers/The Sentry.

Land of the Giants

USA 1968–70 51 × 60m col ABC. An Irwin Allen Production for 20th Century Fox TV. *UK tx* 1968–72 ITV. *cr* Irwin Allen. *exec pr* Irwin Allen. *pr* Irwin Allen, Bruce Fowler. *dr* Irwin Allen, Harry Harris, Sobey Martin, Nathan Juran, Harmon Jones. *wr* Various, including Anthony Wilson, Dan Ullman, Bob and Esther Mitchell, Arthur Weiss, William Welch, Richard Shapiro, William Stuart, Sheldon Stark, Jack Turley. *mus* Johnny Williams. *sfx* LB Abbott, Art Cruickshank, Emil Kosa Jr. *cast* **Steve Burton** Gary Conway **Dan Erickson** Don Marshall **Betty Hamilton** Heather Young **Alexander Fitzhugh** Kurt Kasznar **Mark Wilson** Don Matheson **Valerie Scott** Deanna Lund **Barry Lockridge** Stefan Arngrim **Insp Kobick** Kevin Hagen.

The last of Irwin Allen's sixties telefantasy quartet (>*Voyage to the Bottom of the Sea*, >*Time Tunnel*, >*Lost in Space*) was a space-age version of *Gulliver's Travels* with US commercial rocketship *Spindrift* entering a 'spacewarp' *en route* to London in 1983 and coming out in a land where everything mirrored Earth – but was twelve times normal size. The crew and passengers trapped in this land of giants were captain Steve Burton, co-pilot Dan Erickson, engineer-tycoon Mark Wilson, stewardess Betty Hamilton, heiress Valerie Scott, mystery passenger Fitzhugh and orphaned boy Barry Lockridge (plus his dog Chipper which, in the first episode, dug up a tape-recorder with a message from previous crashed earthlings). Menaced by gigantic cats, insects, scientists who tried to experiment on them, imprisoned in dolls' houses and hunted by hulking Inspector Kobick, the castaways tried to repair their ship and escape from the Brobdingnagian planet.

One of the most giant things about the series was the budget which, at $250, 000 per episode, made *Land of the Giants* the most expensive TV series to date. Much of the money went on extensive special effects and props (all of which had to be constructed on enormous scale, like slices of 'bread' made from four-foot slabs of foam rubber). The guest cast included boxer Sugar Ray Robinson in 'Giants and All That Jazz', Jonathan Harris (>*Lost in Space*) as the piper in 'Pay the Piper', and Bruce Dern in the concluding 'Wild Journey' episode.

Lois & Clark: The New Adventures of Superman

USA 1993– 1 × 120/40+ × 45m col. Roundelay/December 3rd Production/Warner Bros. *cr* Jerry Siegel & Joe Shuster; developed for television by Deborah Joy LeVine. *exec pr* Deborah Joy LeVine, David Jacobs, Robert Butler, Robert Singer. *dr* Various, including Robert Butler, Randall Zisk, Gene Reynolds, Les Landau, Bill D'Elia, James A Contner, Felix Enrique Alcala, Mark Sobel, Robert Singer, Alan J Levi, Michael Watkins, Mel Damski, Philip J Sgriccia, James R Bagdonas. *wr* Various, including Deborah Joy LeVine, Bryce Zabel, Dan Levine, Robert Killebrew, Thania St John, Paris Qualles, Bradley Moore, Tony Blake, Paul Jackson, H B Cobb, Chris Ruppenthal, Grant Rosenberg, Eugenie Ross-Leming, Brad Buckner. *mus* Jay Gruska. *sfx* John Sheele. *cast* **Clark Kent/Superman** Dean Cain **Lois** Teri Hatcher **Perry White** Lane Smith **Lex Luthor** John Shea **Jimmy Olsen** Michael Landes/Justin Whalen (from season two) **Catherine 'Cat' Grant** Tracy Scoggins **Martha Kent** K Callan **Jonathan Kent** Eddie Jones.

Dean Cain played the superhero with his underwear outside his tights in Deborah Joy LeVine's *Moonlighting*-ish makeover of *Superman, Lois and Clark*.

Clever makeover of the Man of Steel saga, which reduced the spandexed acrobatics and upped the romance between Clark Kent (Superman's human alter ego) and *The Daily Planet* newshound Lois Lane. The question of 'will-they-won't-they?' (shades of >*Moonlighting*) teetered and titillated through the seasons, with the path of true love made rockier by villainous billionaire Lex Luthor's courtship of Lois (which ends when Luthor's misdeeds are exposed on their wedding day), the pursuit of Clark by *Planet* maneater Cat Grant, and Clark's flirtation with district attorney Mayson Drake. The writing was witty and deftly comic, with the Kryptonite-powered hero given a pleasingly downhome persona; in the pilot his red, blue and yellow Superman outfit was run up by his adopted mother on a sewing machine; in the episode 'Individual Responsibility' Superman, concerned about his erratic behaviour, visited a psychotherapist.

Although it remoulded the story of Superman into a romantic comedy (with the title twosome eventually tying the knot), the caped hero of *Lois & Clark* was still able to fly through the air with the greatest of ease, whizz around the world in seconds, and perform feats of herculean strength – all to save Metropolis from evil. Orthodox crime fighting concentrated initially on Luthor, then a varied line up of villains, among them Intergang. Despite many of the special effects being computer generated, actor Dean Cain (previously Brenda Walsh's boyfriend in >*Beverly Hills 90210*) was still required to take to a wire harness for the flying sequences.

As if to leave nothing to chance, the producers imported a distinguished guest star for almost every episode. Those performing cameos numbered amongst them Elliot Gould, Robert Culp, Raquel Welch, Denise Crosby, Larry Linville (>*M*A*S*H*), Sonny Bono and Morgan Fairchild.

In Britain the series was broadcast as *The New Adventures of Superman*, achieving regular ratings of circa 8 million.

Lost in Space

USA 1965–8 83 × 60m bw (season one) col (season two). CBS/Irwin Allen production in assoc w Jodi Production Inc, Van Bernard Productions for 20th Century Fox Television. *UK tx* 1965–70 ITV (regions). *cr* Irwin Allen. *exec pr* Irwin Allen. *dr* Tony Leader, Alex Singer, Leo Penn, Sobey Martin, Alvin Ganzer, Paul Stanley, Leonard Horn, Sutton Roley, J Addiss, Jerry Juran, Nathan Juran, Donald Richardson, Harry Harris, Robert Douglas, Ezra Stone, S Robbie, J Richardson, I Moore. *wr* Shimon Wincelberg, Peter Packer, Norman Lessing, William Welch, Jackson Gillis, Barney Slater, Herman Groves, William Read Woodfield and Allan Balter, Carey Wilbur, Bob and Wanda Duncan, Margaret Brookman Hill, Michael Fessier, Robert Hamner, Jack Turley. *mus* Johnny Williams. *sfx* L B Abbott, Hal Lydecker. *cast* **Prof John Robinson** Guy Williams **Maureen Robinson** June Lockhart **Judy** Marta Kristen **Penny** Angela Cartwright **Will** Billy Mumy **Don West** Mark Goddard **Dr Zachary Smith** Jonathan Harris **Robot** Bob May **Robot's voice** Dick Tufeld. *Video* Fox.

After his success with >*Voyage to the Bottom of the Sea*, sci-fi supremo Irwin Allen looked heavenward for his next project, the American Family Robinson *Lost in Space*.

The year was 1997 and overpopulation was strangling the Earth. The Robinsons had been chosen from millions of volunteers to be space pioneers and, once aboard spaceship *Jupiter 2*, they were to rest in suspended animation for ninety-eight years until reaching their destination, Alpha Centauri. But foreign agent Dr Zachary Smith crept on board, intending to sabotage the project. Instead the villain trapped himself in the spaceship and put it on course for a crash landing. The crew woke up to find themselves on an unknown planet, out of communication with the rest of the universe.

Lost in space aboard the *Jupiter 2* were forty-year-old astrophysicist John Robinson, his biochemist wife Maureen, beautiful eldest daughter Judy, eleven-year-old geology student Penny and precocious nine-year-old electronics wizard Will. Pilot Major Donald West, expert in celestial geology and Judy's boyfriend and the Robot completed the crew.

This unhappy combination of characters wandered from planet to planet for three years trying to find their way home, a journey fraught with perils from giant cyclamen plants, space dogs, carrot monsters and galactic showmen, as well as from the weaselly and unprincipled Dr Smith, whose conniving with extraterrestrials to try to save his own skin was guaranteed to create problems every week. Arch villain Zachary, only added to plans at the last minute to create plot possibilities, swiftly became the show's star.

The Robot, whose skills ranged from setting Mrs Robinson's hair to writing poetry, also stole the show. Created by Bob Kinoshita, who designed Robby the Robot for classic sci-fi film *Forbidden Planet*, the Robot was no hi-tech wonder; actor Bob May hit keys to work the lights on his chest and was pulled along on wheeled blocks by hidden wires.

In fact, although the show was famously cheap – Irwin Allen, when informed that an alien's spaceship was budgeted at $10,000 is said to have screamed 'Let him walk!' – the first soap opera of the space age was a good-fun show in its first season. But it soon fell victim to ratings wars. In January 1966 ABC stuck *Batman* into the slot opposite the show and triumphed in the ratings. When Irwin Allen tried to emulate Batman's camp humour *Lost in Space* rapidly became unwatchable.

Guest stars in the series included Kurt Russell, >*Hill Street Blues* star Daniel J Travanti and mechanical villain Robby the Robot.

Man From Atlantis

USA 1977–8 3 × 100 m/1 × 75m/13 × 60m col NBC. A Solow Production for NBC. *UK tx* 1977–8. *exec pr* Herbert F Solow. *pr* Herbert F Solow, Herman Miller, Robert Justman. *dr* Lee H Katzin, Marc Daniels, Reza Badiyi, Charles Dubin, Virgil Vogel, Harry Harris, Richard Benedict, Michael O'Herlihy, Barry Crane, David Moessinger, Robert Douglas, Ed Abroms, Dann Cahn, Dennis Donnelly, Paul Krasny. *wr* Mayo Simon, Robert Lewin, John D F Black, Jerry Sohl, Luther Murdoch, Tom Greene, Alan Caillou, David Balkan, Michael Wagner, Larry Alexander, Stephen Kandel, Shimon Wincelberg, Peter Allan Fields. *mus* Fred Karlin. *cast* **Mark Harris** Patrick Duffy **Dr Elizabeth Merrill** Belinda Montgomery **C W Crawford** Alan Fudge **Mr Schubert** Victor Buono **Brent** Robert Lussier **Jomo** Richard Williams **Chuey** J Victor Lopez **Jane** Jean Marie Hon **Allen** Anson Downes.

After a heavy storm a handsome young man is washed up on a Californian beach where he is discovered by beautiful Dr Elizabeth Merrill. The Doctor rushes him to a naval hospital and soon realises that this is no ordinary human. He is in fact The Man From Atlantis, last survivor of the lost continent, and he has piercing green eyes, gills instead of lungs and webbed hands and feet. He also has abilities that make him useful to the Doctor – he can swim faster than a dolphin and has superhuman strength and senses. When his health returns she christens him Mark Harris and recruits him to join her and her colleagues at the Foundation for Oceanic Research.

Together Dr Merrill (played by Belinda Montgomery, later in >*Dynasty* and >*Miami Vice*) and the Atlantean take to the deep in supersub *Cetacean* to do battle against extraterrestrial life, evil scientists and threats of any kind to the US government. Chief villain of the piece is mad scientist Mr Schubert who hatches evil plots in a habitat several miles below the sea.

Unfortunately, hero Mark Harris was just too good and the plots too bad to be true. Three 100–minute pilots attempted some exploration of the hero's origins but the series proper featured a relentless diet of implausible villains and sea monsters: another mad scientist, Dr Mary Harris, made an appearance; time travel took our hero back to the Old West and Romeo and Juliet's Italy; a mudworm developed human characteristics; and the wicked Mr Schubert melted the polar ice caps.

Today the unfortunate *Man From Atlantis* is remembered only, if at all, for the actor who played him (Patrick Duffy aka Bobby Ewing of >*Dallas*) and for his remarkable yellow swimming trunks. He may, however, take some solace from the fact that he is a major star in mainland China. The *Man From Atlantis* was the first American entertainment TV programme ever shown there.

Manimal

USA 1983–4 1 × 120m/7 × 50m col NBC. A Glen A Larson Production/20th Century Fox Television. *UK tx* 1984 BBC1. *cr* Glen A Larson. *exec pr* Glen A Larson, Paul Mason. *pr* Donald R Boyle, Paul Radin, Michael Berk, Douglas

Schwantz, Harker Wade, Randall Torno. *dr* Russ Mayberry, Sidney Hayers, Dan Haller, Chuck Bail, Les Martinson, George J Fenady. *wr* Glen A Larson, Donald R Boule, Michael Berk, Douglas Schwantz, Sam Egan, Paul Mason, Joseph Gunn. *sfx* Stan Winston (make up), Al Wright. *cast* **Jonathan Chase** Simon MacCorkindale **Brooke McKenzie** Melody Anderson **Tyrone 'Ty' Earl** Michael D Roberts **Lt Rivera** Reni Santoni.

Fantasy series featuring criminology professor Jonathan Chase who has the ability, inherited from his explorer father, to transform himself at will into any animal. (Thus the title 'Manimal' – man to animal). With the help of his Vietnam war buddy and confidant (read servant) Tyrone 'Ty' Earl, Chase used his unusual powers to aide NYPD woman police detective Brooke McKenzie in the solving of major crimes – often where the guilty party seemed untouchable by the standard due processes of the law. In the pilot episode, a traitorous army colonel, Hunt, receives justice in the shape of a great white shark (ie Chase) in his swimming pool; in 'Night of the Beast' a syndicate of gangsters, who enjoy protection in the form of the local corrupt sheriff, is bested when Chase assumes the form of a golden bear, surprising the mobsters and allowing gun-totting McKenzie to capture them; in 'Illusion' a Bulgarian fur smuggler who has immunity from prosecution thanks to his diplomatic status is persuaded to surrender his privilege when Chase, duly transformed into a black panther (a favourite guise), corners him in a warehouse.

Manimal died an early death, cancelled after a mere seven episodes, plus pilot. If intriguing, it was also flawed. Jonathan Chase (played by amiable British leading man Simon MacCorkindale, also *Jaws 3D*, Zeferrelli's *Jesus of Nazareth*, *The Manions of America*) charmed, but Ty Earl (Michael D Roberts, Rooster in >*Baretta*) was one of several embarrassing camp, streetwise blacks to appear on TV in the late seventies/early eighties (see Huggy Bear in >*Starsky and Hutch*). The glossy, blonde-haired Brooke McKenzie (Melody Anderson, Dale Arden in DeLaurentis' *Flash Gordon*) might have walked off the set of *Charlie's Angels*.

The crime-caper storylines were standard models, but the show's real weakness was Chase's 'manimal' transformations: they took so long to effect that even the most decrepit villain could hardly have helped but escape. Moreover, Chase implausibly always returned back to human form fully dressed.

Manimal was produced by Glen A 'Mr Prime Time' Larson, and was a rare flop in a run of shows which included *Magnum P.I.* and >*Knight Rider*.

The episodes were: Manimal/High Stakes/Night of the Beast/Female of the Species/Illusion/Scrimshaw/Night of the Scorpion/Breath of the Dragon.

Mork & Mindy

USA 1978–82 95 × 30m col. ABC Miller-Milkis Productions/Henderson Production Company/Paramount TV. *UK tx* 1979–83 ITV. *cr* Garry K Marshall, Tony Marshall, Dale McRaven, Joe Gauberg. *exec pr* Garry K Marshall, Tony Marshall. *pr* Bruce Johnson, Dale McRaven. *dr* Various, including Bob Claver, Jeff Chambers, Howard Storm. *wr* Various, including Robin Williams, April Kelly, Tom Tenowich, Bruce Johnson, Dale McRaven, Deborah Raznicka, Ed Scharlach. *cast* **Mork** Robin Williams **Mindy McConnell** Pam Dawber **Frederick McConnell** Conrad Janis **Cora Hudson** Elizabeth Kerr **Orson** Ralph James **Exidor** Robert Donner **Mearth** Jonathan Winters.

A spin-off from a 1978 episode of >*Happy Days* in which Mork from Ork (Robin Williams) landed on Earth and tried to kidnap Ritchie Cunningham. Audience reaction to the episode was so favourable that it was decided to give the alien a show of his own.

For his second earthly visit Mork landed at Boulder, Colorado, in a giant egg and with a mission to study earthlings, and reported back his findings to His Immenseness, Orkan leader Orson. In Boulder, Mork was befriended by Mindy McConnell, daughter of music store owner Fred. To the latter's oft-expressed disapproval, Mork moved into Mindy's apartment. Initially their relationship was, in fact, platonic but eventually they married, honeymooning on Ork – where Mork discovered he was pregnant and laid an egg. From this emerged their son, Mearth, played by middle-aged 225–pound US comedian Jonathan Winters. On Ork beings grew younger, not older.

Mork & Mindy was a pleasant twist to a sci-fi perennial, for invading alien Mork was no BEM but a zany and endearing child-man, an innocent abroad in the universe (although both Gore Vidal's play *Visit to a Small Planet* and the 1963 TV show *My Favourite Martian* have strong similarities). Mork's habits were strange – he slept upside down in a cupboard, he drank through his finger and said 'Shazbat!' a lot – but he was likeable. And funny.

The role of Mork, initially offered to Dom DeLuise, was perfectly suited to the wacky, stream-of-consciousness style of Williams, a former stand-up comic at Los Angeles' Comedy Store. Understanding this, the producers allowed Williams to do his own stuff, marking scripts: 'Mork can go off here'. The show made Williams a star, and he has followed it with a string of major films, including *Good Morning Vietnam* (1987), *The Fisher King* (1989) and *Toys* (1992).

Williams' comic skill aside, the series had an almost catastrophic tumble in quality in season two, when the producers jettisoned the show's zappy sci-fi sitcom format in favour of would-be clever surrealism. Two principal cast members were sacked, Conrad Janis (an accomplished jazz player, who has cut records with Coleman Hawkins) and Elizabeth Kerr, who played Cora Hudson, Mindy's with-it grandma. The audience ratings plummeted, and the producers restored the old format – plus Janis and Kerr – for season three. Among the other characters which appeared regularly were Exidor, a UFO prophet who thought Mork was crazy and neighbour Mr Bickley (Tom Poston). Jim Stahl played Mindy's yuppie cousin, Nelson.

If *Mork & Mindy* was something unusual in sci-fi, it also used some classic genre techniques, juxtaposing the Alien to the Human as a means of commentary on the latter. In case the audience missed the point, Mork's end-of-episode reports to Orson were explicit comments on the state of humanity. Unfortunately, these tended to be cute (people should be nice to each other), rather than meaningful.

Na nu, na nu.

The Planet Of The Apes

USA 1974 14 × 50m col CBS. A 20th Century Fox TV Production. *UK tx* 1974–5 ITV. *cr* Pierre Boulle. *exec pr* Herbert Hirschman. *pr* Stan Hough. *dr* Don Weiss, Don McDougall, Arnold Laven, Bernard McEveety, Jack Starrett, Alf Kjellin, Ralph Senensky, John Meredyth Lucas. *wr* Art Wallace, Edward J Lasko, Robert W Lenski, Robert Hamner, Barry Oringer, Anthony Lawrence, David P Lewis, Booker Bradshaw, Richard Collins, Walter Black, Howard Dimsdale, S Bar David, Arthur Browne Jr. *mus* Lalo Schifrin. *cast* **Galen** Roddy McDowall **Virdon** Ron Harper **Burke** James Naughton **Urko** Mark Lennard **Zauis** Booth Colman.

Developed from the 1967 movie of the same title directed by Franklin J Schaffer, itself based on the novel by Pierre Boulle. Spacemen Virdon and Burke pass through a timewarp and land back on Earth in the year 3085 AD – to find a topsy-turvy world where the apes rule and human beings are just the unpaid help. In the new ape society orang-utans like wily Zauis are the ruling class, chimpanzees the intellectuals, and gorillas the military class. An inquisitive young chimp called Galen – Roddy McDowall, reprising his film role – helps Virdon and Burke avoid the gorillas, led by Urko, who ruthlessly hunt the astronauts for fear that they will destabilise ape society.

The plight of Virdon and Burke was never resolved because low ratings caused the American network CBS to cancel the show after fourteen of the planned twenty-four episodes. British audiences appreciated it more, and it drew audiences of 12 million on its UK transmission. The series retained much of the splendid outlandish look of the film, together with most of the metaphorical nature of Boulle's book. Actress Sandra Locke (ex-partner of Clint Eastwood) guest-starred in episode 12 'The Cure'.

A thirty-cartoon series *Return to the Planet of the Apes* was made in 1975 by David de Patrie and Fritz Freleng for NBC.

Quantum Leap

USA 1989–93 2 × 90m/94 × 50m col NBC. Bellisarius Productions. *UK tx* 1990–4 BBC2. *cr* Donald P Bellisario. *pr* Donald P Bellisario, Deborah Pratt, Chris Ruppenthal, Tommy Thompson, John Hill, Harker Wade, Michael

Zinberg, Charles Johnson. *dr* Various, including David Hemmings, Mark Sobel, Scott Bakula, Gil Shilton, James Whitmore, Gil Dixon, Aaron Lipstadt, Alan J Levi. *wr* Various, including Donald P Bellisario, Deborah Pratt, John Hill, Deborah Arakelian, Aaron Lipstadt, Chris Ruppenthal, Tommy Thompson, Richard C Okie, Robin Jill Bernhein. *mus* Velton Ray Brunch. *cast* **Dr Sam Beckett** Scott Bakula **Al Calavicci ('The Observer')** Dean Stockwell **Gushie** Dennis Wolfberg.

A feel good sci-fi series for the nostalgic nineties from Donald P Bellisario, the man behind *Magnum*.

Adding his name to a long list of eminent sci-fi heroes, Dr Sam Beckett (Scott Bakula) is a brilliant physicist, doomed to travel in time because of a flawed experiment (albeit his own). But, unlike other time-travel series, notably >*The Time Tunnel*, Beckett can only travel within the dates of his own lifespan, from the mid fifties to the mid nineties. (This allows the viewer to tour the more optimistic decades of recent memory; Beckett's journeys have included cameos by such fifties and sixties sound-makers as Chubby Checker and Peter Noone of Herman's Hermits.) There are other rules which govern Beckett's trips in time and space: his leaps into other decades take him straight into the bodies of total strangers – they, incidentally, have no choice in the matter – and the people who 'lend' him their bodies can be anything from a secretary subjected to sexual harassment to an elderly black man in the pre-civil rights South, or a Vietnam veteran, even Elvis Presley. (Censorship problems followed an episode in which Sam leapt into a gay man.) But unlike the *Tunnel* time-travellers and >*Dr Who*, Beckett is permitted to change the past, even if only to improve his host's life.

Knowing nothing about these people until he 'arrives', Beckett often has to improvise. This can be hair-raising, as when Beckett, who has no idea how to fly a plane, finds himself in the body of a test pilot in the feature-length opening episode. No matter in whose body he lands, for the viewer Beckett appears as himself, and it is only when he looks in the mirror that we (and he) see the new him, whether rabbi, mafia hitman or Lee Harvey Oswald.

Accompanying Beckett on his leaps is rumpled, crumpled Al Calavicci – played by Dean Stockwell, whose cult status has already been assured by appearances in the films *Paris Texas* and *Blue Velvet* – a holographic observer and guardian angel invisible to everyone but Sam, children, small animals and blondes. Al carries with him a small device linked to the lab computer Ziggy which provides the facts needed to help Beckett out in his current tricky situation.

Quantum Leap (like close relative *Highway to Heaven*, starring Michael Landon as an angel) has obvious quasi-religious overtones, and religious references are nothing new for creator Bellisario. Another of his series, *Airwolf*, was full of born-again symbolism and *Magnum* ended with an invisible Tom Selleck acting as guardian angel to his wife.

On its initial American transmission, the exploits of Beckett – for all the world, with his skin-tight white suit, a latter-day Lone Ranger – languished at number eighty-eight in the ratings, but in more recent times NBC ran daily repeats which pulled in audiences of around 60 million.

The show ended with a confusing last episode in which Sam materialised on the day of his birth and pontificated on his destiny with a bartender whom he believed to be God. He never made it home.

Quark

USA 1978 1 × 60m/7 × 30m col NBC/Columbia. *cr* Buck Henry. *pr* Buck Henry (pilot), David Gerber, Mace Neufeld, Bruce Johnson. *wr* Buck Henry, Steve Zacharias. *dr* Peter H Hunt, Hy Averback. *mus* Perry Botkin Jr. *cast* **Adam Quark** Richard Benjamin **Gene/Jean** Tim Thomerson **Ficus Panderato** Richard Kelton **Betty I** Tricia Barnstable **Betty II** Cyb Barnstable **Andy the Robot** Bobby Porter **Otto Palindrome** Conrad Janis **The Head** Alan Caillou.

It is 2222 AD and Commander Adam Quark is head of an interplanetary garbage crew whose mission on behalf of the United Galaxy Sanitation Patrol is to clean up the Milky Way. In order to receive his assignments he returns his patrol ship to giant space station Perma One, operation headquarters, where disembodied Secretary General The Head rules the universe from a TV screen. Orders also come from Superintendent Otto Palindrome,

Perma One's woolly brained chief architect with four arms and golden braids.

Quark gave orders to First Officer Gene/Jean, a transmute with male and female chromosomes who was sometimes tough and sometimes delicate, Science Officer Ficus, a humanoid vegetable, glamorous ex-cheerleader Co-pilots Betty I and her clone Betty II, so similar that no one could tell them apart, Andy the Robot, a walking junkpile, and Ergo, the ship's mascot, a temperamental blob of protoplasm with one angry eye.

Whilst ridding the galaxy of superfluous litter this motley crew met adventures with such colourful space inhabitants as the evil High Gorgon, Zoltar the Magnificent and Zorgon the Malevolent. But the series was intended first and foremost as a spoof on space adventure epics: *Star Wars* was its first target (the hit feature film came out a year earlier in 1977), others included *2001: A Space Odyssey* and *Flash Gordon*.

Quark first appeared as a pilot in 1977 and débuted as a TV series in February 1978 with a one-hour special. Its slick blend of in-jokes, innuendo and slapstick gained a cult following but not a mass audience and it was soon cancelled. Mastermind of the series was Buck Henry who earlier had more success with spoof show, >*Get Smart*.

Quatermass

UK 1953–9 6 × 30m/6 × 35m bw BBC. BBC. *cr* Nigel Kneale. *pr* Rudolph Cartier. *dr* Rudolph Cartier. *wr* Nigel Kneale. *mus* Trevor Duncan. *sfx* Rudolf Cartier, Nigel Kneale, Bernard Wilkie, Jack Kine. *cast* **Professor Bernard Quatermass** Reginald Tate (1953)/John Robinson (1955)/André Morell (1958–9). *Video* BBC (*Quatermass and the Pit*).

The foundation of British sci-fi TV. In 1953, the BBC spent its entire adult drama budget (£250) on commissioning a script from Nigel Kneale, winner of the 1950 Somerset Maugham Prize for Literature. Their return was *Quatermass*, an eerie and sensational story about a professorial scientist of that surname whose experimental spaceship returns to Earth with its sole surviving occupant (Victor Caroon, played by Duncan Lamont) contaminated by an alien virus which subsequently transmuted him into a 100-foot vegetable. The serial, which played cleverly on contemporary fears about space travel, held the new TV nation agog.

But the success of *Quatermass* was due to more than Kneale's script; its production and direction – it went out live – by Rudolph Cartier was pioneeringly brilliant, rejecting the stagey theatricality of existing TV drama. In one of the first examples of special effects on TV, Caroon's alien look was achieved by covering a leather glove with bits of foliage and using a blown-up still of Westminster Abbey as background. It worked.

In *Quatermass II* (1955) Kneale and Cartier collaborated on a story in which Bernard Quatermass (now played by John Robinson), accidentally discovered a Martian plan to take over the world by infiltrating human minds. Eventually, Quatermass is able to prevent the invasion, although the upper classes proved particularly susceptible to the Martians' manoeuvres (a veiled political criticism by Kneale of the British establishment's past flirtations with fascism). The special effects were superior, thanks to the recent creation of a BBC Visual Effects Department, headed by Bernard Wilkie and John Kine.

Kneale and Cartier's *Quatermass and the Pit* (1958–9) was a dark, cabalistic tale of the excavation of an ancient alien-insect capsule in Knightsbridge, London, with the thoroughly human Quatermass (André Morell) battling to prevent the reawakened influence of the Martians on the human race. (Part of the scariness of the monsters in the *Quatermass* cycle was that they were intelligent, even advanced life forms.) The tense narrative, superbly filmed in grainy black and white by A A Englander, was made all the more atmospheric by the weird noises provided by the fledgling BBC Radiophonic Workshop.

The three BBC Kneale and Cartier *Quatermass* sagas were filmed by Hammer for theatrical release. Kneale subsequently wrote numerous film and teleplays, including *The Abominable Snowman* (1957) and *Kinvig* (1981). In 1979 he wrote the Euston films/ Thames TV serial reprise of *Quatermass*, with Sir John Mills in the title role.

Red Dwarf

UK 1988– 30+ × 30m col BBC2. BBC North/A Paul Jackson Production/Grant Naylor Productions Ltd. *cr* Rob Grant and Doug Naylor. *pr* Ed Bye, Rob Grant, Doug Naylor, Hilary Bevan Jones. *dr* Ed Bye, Juliet May, Grant Naylor. *wr* Rob Grant, Doug Naylor. *mus* Howard Goodall (theme). *sfx* Peter Wragg. *cast* **Dave Lister** Craig Charles **Arnold Rimmer** Chris Barrie *Cat* Danny John-Jules *Kryten* David Ross (season 2)/Robert Llewellyn (season 3+) *Holly* Norman Lovett (seasons 1–2)/Hattie Hayridge (season 3+). *Video* BBC.

Space-age sitcom. This tale of intergalactic curry-eating slob Dave Lister, the last human alive, originated as a sketch for BBC Radio 4's *Son of Cliché*, but owed much to such sci-fi screen vehicles as *Dark Star*, >*Quark* and >*Hitchhiker's Guide to the Galaxy*. As incarnated for TV, Dave was a twenty-third-century Liverpudlian with a penchant for derivatives of the expletive 'smeg', and the sole survivor of a radiation leak aboard the mining vessel of the title. Brought out of a three-million-year-long 'stasis' by ship's computer, Holly, Lister was given company in the form of a hologram of his ex-boss, the pompous, doleful Arnold Rimmer (Chris Barrie, also of *The Brittas Empire* and *Spitting Image*). Also on board was Cat, a narcissistic, Little-Richard type dude who had evolved in the ship's hold from Lister's pet feline, and was humanoid except for fangs and six nipples.

Much of the humour of the show, especially in the first two seasons, evolved out of the characters and their inter-relations, but was also schoolboyish ('No way are these my boxer shorts – these bend') and bizarre (the Talking Toaster). Indeed, *Red Dwarf* was a sort of >*The Young Ones* in space. But the comedy was generous and skilful, and it was also more serious than initially appeared. Rimmer was a semi-parody of a Thatcherite – Lister was the proletarian element of the class struggle aboard *Red Dwarf* – and two of the shows from season four, 'Dimension Jump' and 'Meltdown', were held back by the BBC at the time of the Gulf conflict because of their anti-war content.

On its first voyages along the airwaves *Red Dwarf* bumped along the bottom of the ratings (although it scored high in Audience Appreciation). The third season – which opened with the classic 'Backwards' episode – saw changes in format, and the introduction of more recognisably sci-fi situations. The personnel also changed, as stand-up comic Hattie Hayridge replaced Norman Lovett as Holly, while the android Kryten became a regular crew fixture. The production values were also upped, and the series won the World Television Award for its special effects. Subsequent average ratings of over 6 million made *Red Dwarf* one of the most successful shows on BBC2. No less than two attempts to launch *Red Dwarf* on the *US* airwaves – the first, in 1992, featuring Jane Leeves of *Frasier* – proved abortive.

To date the episodes have been: Season 1: The End (GC C P Grogan, ex-singer with Altered Images)/Future Echoes/Balance of Power (GC C P Grogan)/Waiting for God/Confidence and Paranoia/ME/Season 2: Kryten (GC Tony Slattery)/Better Than Life/Thanks for the Memory/Stasis Leak (GC C P Grogan)/Queeg/Parallel Universe/Season 3: Backwards/Marooned/Polymorph (GC Frances Barber)/Body Swap/Timeslides (GC Koo Stark)/The Last Day/Season 4: Camille/DNA/Justice (GC Nicholas Ball)/White Hole/Dimension Jump/ Meltdown/ Season 5: Holoship/The Inquisitor/ Terrorform/ Quarantine/ Demons and Angels/Back to Reality/Season 6: Psirens/ Legion/Gunmen of the Apocalypse/Emohawk – Polymorph II/ Rimmerworld/Out of Time.

Sapphire And Steel

UK 1979–82 34 × 30m col ITV. ATV Network Production. *cr* P J Hammond. *exec pr* David Reid. *pr* Shaun O'Riordan. *dr* Shaun O'Riordan, David Foster. *wr* P J Hammond, Don Houghton, Anthony Read. *mus* Cyril Ornadel. *cast* **Sapphire** Joanna Lumley **Steel** David McCallum **Silver** David Cullings. *Video* ITC.

'All irregularities will be handled by the forces controlling each dimension. Transuranic heavy elements may not be used where there is life. Medium atomic weights are available: Gold, Lead, Copper, Jet, Diamond, Radium, Sapphire, Silver and Steel! Sapphire and Steel have been assigned!'

These words, spoken from an unknown dimension, introduced each episode of British fantasy series *Sapphire and Steel*, a show low in action but high in menace, which premised that the ever-present fourth dimension could rip through the fabric of time and erupt into our world at any moment with terrifying consequences.

Series creator P J Hammond intended *Sapphire and Steel* to be unlike any other sci-fi series: 'There have been plenty of stories of characters who travel in time but none before where time itself actually does the travelling.' Certainly the dangers that called enigmatic agents Sapphire and Steel into being were very different from the usual parade of dinosaurs and silver-clad androids.

The eponymous interdimensional troubleshooters – who would appear magically at the first sign of a rupture in time – were played by David McCallum (>*Man from UNCLE*, >*The Invisible Man*) and Joanna Lumley (>*The New Avengers*, >*Absolutely Fabulous*). McCallum's Steel was like his element: tough, unemotional, dressed in grey, the possessor of enormous strength and a highly analytical mind. Sapphire in contrast was cool and gentle with supersensory powers, dressed all in blue and providing the feminine to complement Steel's masculine. The characters would consult each other in *sotto voce* conversations on the problems before them, sometimes summoning the strength of the hulking Lead (a stereotype black male) or the technical skills of the engaging agent Silver to help them in their task.

The hypnotic, atmospheric series, with its elusive terrors, related six stories about its agents' explorations of the dark side of Time and its attendant perils. Among them were: 'Adventure One', where nursery rhymes triggered the eruption of time into an isolated farmhouse stealing the parents of two young children; 'Adventure Two', in which a long-disused railway station was haunted by ghosts of past wars trapped eternally in the moment of their death; and 'Adventure Four', in which photographs taken long ago unleashed a malevolent Shape into our world. A second series was never made, not because of a lack of audience appreciation, but largely because production company ATV lost its franchise to Central.

Creator P J Hammond, who had previously scripted episodes of *Ace of Wands*, *Shadows*, >*Z Cars* and *Hunter's Walk*, also wrote the scripts for the series, with the exception of 'Adventure Five' – a variation on Agatha Christie's *Ten Little Indians* – which was written by >*Dr Who* writers Anthony Read and Don Houghton.

The Six Million Dollar Man

USA 1973–8 1 × 85m/102 × 60m col ABC. A Universal TV Production. *UK tx* 1974–8 ITV. *cr* Harve Bennett. *exec pr* Harve Bennett, Glen A Larson, Allan Balter, Kenneth Johnson. *dr* Various, including Edward Abrams, Reza Badiyi, Richard Irving, Glen A Larson, Arnold Laven, Earl Bellamy, Cliff Bole, Phil Bondell, Alan Crosland Jr, Richard Moder, Alf Kjellin, Paul Krasny, Christian I Nyby II, Jenny London, Jeannot Szwarc, Jerry Jameson. *wr* Various, including Henri Simoun, Allen Levi, Glen A Larson, Steven de Souza, Lionel E Siegal, Stephen Kandel, Kenneth Johnson, William Driskill, D C Fontana, Mark Frost. *mus* Oliver Nelson, Dusty Springfield (theme vocal). *cast* **Col Steve Austin** Lee Majors **Oscar Goldman** Richard Anderson **Dr Rudy Wells** Alan Oppenheimer/Martin E Brooks.

'Gentlemen. We have the technology . . . We can rebuild him.' Lee Majors, late of >*The Big Valley* and >*The Men from Shiloh*, played Colonel Steve Austin, a handsome NASA pilot who endured a near fatal crash and was refurbished by Dr Rudy Wells, at a cost of six million dollars, with atomic-powered legs, arms and left eye (which came complete with a built-in grid screen). Thus 'bionically' equipped, Austin could perform incredible feats of strength and speed – usually filmed in slow motion – and sallied forth on behalf of the Office of Strategic Investigations (modelled on the Office of Strategic Studies, the forerunner of the CIA), headed by Oscar Goldman, to fight the usual array of meglomaniacs, criminals, aliens which threaten the US of A. The latter included ex- >*Addams Family* Lurch, Ted Cassidy as Big Foot; Meg Foster appeared as a stranded extraterrestrial in 'Straight on Till Morning'.

In season two of *The Six Million Dollar Man*, Austin discovered that he was not bionically alone – a dangerous, out of control seven million dollar man (played by Monte Markham) roamed the Earth, leading to a battle of the titans (Austin, naturally, won). In 1975,

After a near-fatal crash, astronaut Steve Austin (Lee Majors, below in the air) had his body parts replaced with atomic-electronic devices. Thus endowed, he proved more than a match for the gallery of aliens and villains who threatened America in *The Six Million Dollar Man*.

a bionic woman, ex-tennis pro Jamie Summers (Lindsay Wagner) arrived as romantic interest for Austin. Summers – although she was killed off – proved so popular that she was revived and given a series of her own, the Kenneth Johnson-created *The Bionic Woman* (Wagner portrayed her character with depth and won an Emmy in 1976). Not wishing to underplay a good thing, the series also produced a bionic boy, Andy Sheffield (Vincent Van Patten).

Among the series' guest cast were Lee Majors' then-wife Farrah Fawcett of >*Charlie's Angels*, who appeared in three episodes: 'The Rescue of Athena One',

'Nightmare In the Sky' and 'The Golden Pharaoh'. The behind-the-camera personnel included director Jeannot Szwarc ('Population Zero' episode), the maker of the movie *Jaws 2*.

Derived from the Martin Caidin novel *Cyborg*, *The Six Million Dollar Man* started with a pacy, imaginative format and took off in a big way, top-lining the ratings and prompting a wave of merchandising. In later seasons it slowed and was duly terminated in 1978. There have since, however, been two TV bionic movies, *Return of the Bionic Couple* (1987) and *Bionic Showdown* (1989).

Space 1999

UK 1975–8 48 × 60m ITV. ITC/RAI Co-production (season one), Gerry Anderson Production (season two). *USA tx* 1975–8 *syn. cr* Gerry and Sylvia Anderson. *exec pr* Gerry Anderson. *pr* Sylvia Anderson (season one), Fred Freiberger (season two). *dr* Lee Katzin, David Tomblin, Ray Austin, Charles Crichton, Bob Kellett, Tom Clegg, Kevin Connor, Val Guest, Robert Lynn, Peter Medak, Bob Brooks. *wr* Johnny Byrne, Anthony Terpiloff, Christopher Penfold, Elizabeth Burrows, Edward Di Lorenzo, Donald James, Tony Barwick, Jack Ronder, Terence Feely, Lew Schwartz, Charles Woodgrove (alias Fred Freiberger), Tony Barwick, Terrance Dicks, Michael Winder. *mus* Barry Gray (season one), Derek Wadsworth (season two). *sfx* Brian Johnson. *cast **Cmdr John Koenig** Martin Landau **Dr Helena Russell** Barbara Bain **Alain Carter** Nick Tate **Sandra Benes/Sahn** Zienia Merton **Dr Mathias** Anton Phillips; season one only: **Prof Victor Bergman** Barry Morse **Paul Morrow** Prentis Hancock **David Kano** Clifton Jones; season two only: **Maya** Catherine Schell **Tony Verdeschi** Tony Anholt **Yasko** Yasuko Nagazumi. *video* ITC.

The visually stunning and opulent (around $300,000 per episode) successor to >*UFO* – and one of the biggest flops in TV history. Devised by Gerry and Sylvia Anderson as a British >*Star Trek*, the premise of *Space 1999* was simple: in the year 1999 the colonised moon was blown out of orbit by an explosion in a nuclear waste dump on its dark side, sending *Moonbase Alpha* and its crew of three hundred spinning into space. Their consequent great adventure through the galaxy gave them close encounters with such phenomena as a gigantic, man-swallowing squid, living rocks that moved and killed, cosmic gas clouds and new planets, each with a deadly secret or population to threaten *Alpha*'s crew.

The Moonbase staff was headed by Commander John Koenig and chief medical officer, Dr Helena Russell, played by real-life husband and wife team Martin Landau and Barbara Bain, who had previously starred together in >*Mission Impossible*. Other crew members included Prof Bergman (>*Fugitive* hunter Barry Morse), a brilliant scientist handicapped by an artificial heart which reduced his emotional responses, and chief space pilot Captain Carter.

The series producers, the Andersons, split up matrimonially after the first year, and Gerry Anderson brought in Fred Freiberger (producer of the third season of *Star Trek*) to helm the show. Freiberger introduced love interest in the form of science officer Maya, a sensual female alien capable of transforming herself into any form of organic matter, and Tony Verdeschi, the handsome new second in command. But the new characters did not raise any interest from an audience already bored by relentlessly depressing plot lines. For the doomed inmates of *Alpha* no brotherhood was possible with beings from different planets, only distrust, fear or hatred – and in the resulting battles the unprepared crew dropped like flies. Also, the woodenness of, among others, Martin Landau and Barbara Bain's acting became infamous, suggesting that the producers were happier with their usual stringed actors than human ones (the same problem was evident in the Andersons' earlier >*UFO* series).

One thing that could not have caused *Space 1999*'s failure was lack of guest actors; these included Ian McShane, Brian Blessed, Joan Collins, Christopher Lee, Peter Cushing, Billie Whitelaw, Lionel Blair and Pamela Stephenson.

Space Precinct

US 1994 24 × 60m col. Mentorn Films/Gerry Anderson Production/Grove Television Enterprises. *UK tx* 1995 Sky1.

cr Gerry Anderson. *exec pr* Tom Gutteridge. *pr* Gerry Anderson. *dr* Various, including Alan Birkinshaw, John Glen, Sidney Hayers, Piers Haggard. *wr* Various, including Larry Carroll, David Carren, Paul Mayhew-Archer. *sfx* Richard Gregory (animatronics). *cast* **Lt Patrick Brogan** Ted Shackelford **Officer Jack Haldane** Rob Youngblood **Officer Jane Castle** Simone Bendix **Sally Brogan** Nancy Paul **Liz Brogan** Megan Olive **Matt Brogan** Nic Klein **Podly** Jerome Willis **Orrin** Richard James **Took** Mary Woodvine **Fredo** David Quilter. *Video* Polygram.

Risible police-in-space drama from Gerry Anderson. Although Anderson is on record as declaring 'I'd seen every cop on TV but I'd never seen a space cop', the show is disarmingly similar in concept to Chris Boucher's >*Star Cops*.

Set in the twenty-first century (naturally), *Space Precinct* follows the fortunes of veteran NY policeman Patrick Brogan (Ted Shackelford, *Knot's Landing*), transferred to Demeter City on the planet Altor via the officer exchange scheme. Although assisted by human officers, the beautiful Jane Castle and boorish Jack Haldane, most of Demeter's population is composed of alien Creons and Tarns. Creons are superstitious and large; Tarns are telepathic and small. The look of the aliens was often a small child's idea of extra-terrestrial, purple-headed and saucer-eyed – Muppets in latex. Characterisation was slight, plots even slighter, with the baddie inevitably the 'legitimate businessman' of the episode. If little of the $36 million budget went on scriptwriting and the imaginative creation of alien life forms, the show's sfx were occasionally spectacular, despite a shooting schedule of ten days per episode and each episode having as many as 100–plus effects. Directors numbered John Glen of *Bond* fame.

The original pilot, *Space Police*, was shot in 1987 (with Anderson stock voice-actor Shane Rimmer as Brogan) and then aborted, only to be rescued from the television dumpbin by a US–UK partnership of Grove Television and Mentorn Films. With jokes like 'Raise your hands. All of them!' and central characters entitled V. Lann and E. Vile, the pilot was clearly targeted at kids. The series aimed up the age-scale to adults, but never quite left childish things behind.

Star Cops

UK 1987 9 × 55m col BBC2. A BBC Production. *cr* Chris Boucher. *pr* Evgeny Gridneff. *dr* Christopher Baker, Daniel Benzali, Graeme Harper. *wr* Chris Boucher, Philip Martin, John Collee. *mus* Justin Haywood and Tony Visconti (theme). *sfx* Robin Lobb (video). *cast* **Nathan Spring** David Calder **David Theroux** Erick Ray Evans **Pal Kenzy** Linda Newton **Colin Devis** Trevor Cooper **Alexander Krivenko** Jonathan Adams **Anna Shoun** Sayo Inaba. *Video* BBC.

The thinking person's sci-fi drama. In 2027, irascible, balding career policeman Nathan Spring is assigned – against his will – to the command of the International Space Police Force (alias the 'Star Cops'), a bevy of part-timers who maintain law and order in the bases and stations which have begun to inhabit the firmament. Spring's job is to lick the amateurish, multi-national Star Cops into shape; there may be no aliens in space, but human crime is rife. Despite an attachment to Box, an electronic 'intelligent listening device', Spring was a quintessentially old-fashioned intuitive detective, suspicious of technology in general, computers in particular; in the opening episode, 'An Instinct For Murder', he solved two crimes which the computer judged accidents. Assisting Spring was black American David Theroux, and other prominent Star Cops were abrupt, corrupt (initially) female Australian Pal Kenzy and corpulent Colin Devis. It was the chauvinistic womaniser Devis who provided most of the show's humour, including the immortal line 'Fancy a quick game of Hide the Sausage?'.

Star Cops was devised by Chris Boucher, whose previous sci-fi credits numbered teleplays for >*Dr Who* and >*Blake's 7*, for which he had also acted as script editor. As in *Blake's 7*, much of the interest of *Star Cops* derived from its developing characters and the intelligence of the stories. The other scriptwriters were Philip Martin and John Collee, sometime novelist and *Observer* medical correspondent. The series was also, *pace Blake's 7*, coldly realistic about the future. Episode two, as if to emphasise the series' hard-hearted credentials, saw Spring's girlfriend Lee Jones (Gennie Nevinson) cruelly murdered.

Alas, *Star Cops* was bedevilled by problems. Boucher resented the introduction of the female Japanese star cop Anna Shoun ('I hated the whole concept. I don't think the show did it well'), and the low budget was painfully obvious. For one scene in a Chinese restaurant in 'An Instinct to Murder' a portable television on a trolley served implausibly as futuristic personal video/communications screen. A derisory theme tune, 'It Won't Be Easy', was the contribution of Justin Haywood (of the Moody Blues) and Tony Visconti. More damaging still, the BBC seemed uncertain whether to market the show as sci-fi or crime drama – Boucher had also been a stalwart on >*Shoestring*, *Bergerac* and >*Juliet Bravo* – eventually plumping for 'a futuristic police series'. As a final ignominy, the Corporation transmitted the fifty-minute show on BBC2 at 8.30pm (on Mondays), where its end time did not synchronise with other programme schedules to the annoyance of prospective viewers.

Ratings were low. Yet a video release of the series proved a surprise hit, showing that the show's low BARB figures hid a great deal of affection.

Star Trek

USA 1966–9 79 × 50m col NBC. Desilu/A Norway Production/Paramount Television. *UK tx* 1969–70 BBC1. *cr* Gene Roddenberry. *exec pr* Gene Roddenberry. *pr* Gene Roddenberry, Gene L Coon, John Meredyth Lucas, Fred Freiberger. *dr* Various, including Marc Daniels, Lawrence Dobkin, James Goldstone, Leo Penn, Harvey Hart, Vincent McEveety, Joseph Sergent, Robert Butler, Joseph Pevney, Michael O'Herlihy, Ralph Senensky, John Newland, Herschel Daugherty, Gene Nelson, John Meredyth Lucas, Jud Taylor, Marvin Chomsky, David Alexander, John Erman, Herb Wallerstein, Herb Kenwith. *wr* Various, including Gene Roddenberry, George Clayton Johnson, D C Fontana, Gene L Coon, Sam Peebles, John D F Black, Richard Matheson, Steven Kandel, Robert Bloch, Adrian Spies, Shari Lewis, Shimon Wincelberg, Jerry Sohl, Paul Schneider, Harlan Ellison, Theodore Sturgeon, Don Mankiewicz, Boris Sobelman, Carey Wilber, Gilbert Ralston, John Meredyth Lucas, Jerome Bixby, Max Ehrlich, Norman Spinrad, Margaret Armen, Robert Sabaroff, Edward J Lakso, Jean

'Highly illogical, Captain!' Pointy-eared Mr Spock (Leonard Nimoy, left) and Captain Kirk (William Shatner, right) prepare to meet another alien life form in Gene Roddenberry's *Star Trek*. Now one of the world's most popular shows, the series flopped on its original sixties transmission.

Lisette Aroeste, Rick Vollaerts, Judy Burns, Chet Richards, Meyer Dolinsky, Arthur Heinemann. *sfx* Jim Rugg, William Ware Theiss (costumes). *mus* Alexander Courage, Gerald Fried, George Dunning. *cast* **Captain James T Kirk** William Shatner **Mr Spock** Leonard Nimoy **Dr Leonard 'Bones' McKoy** DeForest Kelly **Mr Sulu** George Takei **Lt Uhura** Nichelle Nichols **Montgomery 'Scotty' Scott** James Doohan **Yeoman Janice Rand** Grace Lee Whitney **Ensign Pavel Chekov** Walter Koenig **Nurse Christine Chapel** Majel Barrett. *Video* CIC.

It might now be one of the most successful programmes in the history of TV, but *Star Trek* almost never got made: the original pilot ('The Cage', featuring Jeffrey Hunter, co-star of Western film *The Searchers*) was dismissed by the American network NBC as 'too cerebral'. An unprecedented second pilot was commissioned and the series went ahead – but never upwards in the ratings. Only a campaign by fans of the show (not yet 'Trekkies') and such sci-fi writers as Poul Anderson and Philip José Farmer ensured a third season. Not until it was repeated in the seventies did *Star Trek* become a viewer phenomenon and a multi-million-pound industry.

The series was the creation of Gene Roddenberry, a former WWII pilot, Los Angeles policeman, and writer for such shows as >*Highway Patrol* and >*Dr Kildare*. For several years he had been the headwriter of the TV Western series >*Have Gun, Will Travel* and consciously designed *Star Trek* as a space-age horse opera, even borrowing its episodic format from >*Wagon Train* (in fact, the working title of *Star Trek* was 'Wagon Train to the Stars'). Instead of the Old West, the action was simply switched to the 'final frontier' of space in the twenty-third century.

The new 'pioneers' of *Star Trek* were noble Captain James Tiberius Kirk (played by Canadian actor William Shatner; Hunter left the project after the first pilot) and the 432 officers and crew of the USS *Enterprise*, principal amongst them: pointy-eared half Vulcan, half earthling first officer Mr Spock; black communications officer Lt Uhura (Nichelle Nichols, former singer with Duke Ellington); Chief Engineer Montgomery 'Scotty' Scott; Southern gentleman ship's doctor Leonard 'Bones' McCoy, and helmsman Mr Sulu. At the start of season two, another member was added to the bridge, Russian Mr Chekov (Walter Koenig), reputedly after complaints by the USSR newspaper *Pravda* that the first nation into space was not represented. In fact, the character of Chekov was brought in to temporarily substitute for Sulu (George Takei having taken a brief leave of absence to film *The Green Berets*), but then remained as a permanent part of the cast.

Propelled by a split infinitive, the *Enterprise* – a 190,000–ton Constellation class cruiser belonging to the United Federation of Planets – went forth on a five-year mission to seek out new life forms, new civilisations, 'to boldly go where no man has gone before'. Most notorious of the aliens who attacked the ship along the trail were the Klingons (Tombstone-type outlaws) and the Romulans. The special effects were cheap but ingenious: the transporter effect of dissolving/reassembling atoms was achieved by throwing aluminium dust into a beam of light, while the phaser blasts were animated.

Enjoyable and entertaining though the individual adventures of the *Enterprise* were, the appeal of the show – the first adult space drama, with the exception of the fifties *Space Patrol* – really lay in its characters and its humanistic politics. A fascinating relationship built up between Kirk, Spock and McCoy, with scriptwriters making much of Spock's personality split between logical-alien and emotional-human. Roddenberry always intended *Star Trek* as a vehicle for commentary on social issues, and episodes duly tackled, amongst others, Vietnam ('A Private Little War'), race prejudice ('Balance of Terror'), and totalitarianism ('Patterns of Force'). Numerous segments explored the tension between scientific progress and human ethics. The potential tolerance, meanwhile, of homo sapiens was never better exampled than in the refusal of Kirk to kill the Gorn after the duel in 'Arena'. And, of course, in the everyday racial harmony aboard the bridge of the *Enterprise* itself. Few sci-fi shows have exuded such optimism about the future as *Star Trek*.

It should, though, be pointed out that women did not fare so well in the series. Lieutenant Uhura was little more than an intergalactic telephonist, while other female characters were usually only adornments for the arm of Kirk. And an amazing number of them were willing to die for him: some seventeen in total. Sexism was exacerbated, moreover, by Jerry Finnerman's soft-focus photography of women subjects (including Nurse Christine Chapel, played by Roddenberry's wife, Majel Barrett).

Some *Star Trek* trivia: Captain Kirk was originally to be called Captain April, the *Enterprise* the *Yorktown*; NASA has named a space shuttle after the *Enterprise*; the clothes worn by the SS-style bad guys in 'Patterns of Force' came from the wardrobe of >*Combat; Star Trek* plundered popular and literary classics for its storylines, including *Moby-Dick* (the 'Obsession' segment) and Rider Haggard's *She* ('Mudd's Women'); the merchandising form and repeats of *Star Trek* have earned Paramount over a billion pounds; exasperated by his fan-adulation Leonard Nimoy wrote a book entitled *I Am Not Spock*; NBC wanted to axe Spock in season one in the belief that the character was not sympathetic; Shatner and Nimoy worked together in >*The Man from UNCLE* segment 'The Project Strigas Affair' two years before *Trek*; George Takei has appeared in British panto; *Star Trek* has been translated into over forty-seven languages.

The catchlines were: 'He's dead, Jim' (McCoy); 'Kirk to *Enterprise*'; 'We need more power!', 'She'll not take much more Captain' (Scotty); 'Highly illogical, Captain' (Spock); 'Beam me up, Scotty'.

Since the boom of Trekkie-mania in the seventies has come an animated *Star Trek* (US 1973, 17 × 30m episodes, with some of the original series cast providing the voices) and six *Star Trek* motion pictures. In 1987, a full-scale TV revival of the TV *Trek* began with >*Star Trek: The Next Generation* with Roddenberry as executive producer.

Several of the original TV series episodes won awards, and are detailed in the episode list below, arranged by original American running order: Season 1: The Man Trap/Charlie X/Where No Man Has Gone Before/The Naked Time/The Enemy Within/Mudd's Women/What Are Little Girls Made Of?/Miri/Dagger of the Mind/The Corbomite Maneuver/The Menagerie, Parts I & II (the story, written by Gene Roddenberry won a Hugo Award, and used footage from the original pilot)/The Conscience of the King/Balance of Terror/Shore Leave/The Galileo Seven/The Squire of Gothos/Arena/Tomorrow is Yesterday/Court Martial (GC Elisha Cook Jr)/Return of the Archons/Space Seed (GC Ricardo Montalban as Khan, later to be revived in the second *Star Trek*

movie)/A Taste of Armageddon/This Side of Paradise (GC Jill Ireland)/The Devil in the Dark/Errand of Mercy/The Alternative Factor/The City on the Edge of Forever (Hugo Award winner, written by Harlan Ellison, GC Joan Collins)/Operation Annihilate!/Season 2: Amok Time/Who Mourns for Adonais?/The Changeling/Mirror, Mirror/The Apple/The Doomsday Machine/Catspaw/I, Mudd/Metamorphosis/Journey to Babel/Friday's Child/The Deadly Years/Obsession/Wolf in the Fold/The Trouble with Tribbles/The Gamesters of Triskelion/A Piece of the Action/The Immunity Syndrome/A Private Little War/Return to Tomorrow /Patterns of Force/By Any Other Name/The Omega Glory/The Ultimate Computer/Bread and Circuses/Assignment: Earth/Season 3: Spock's Brain/The Enterprise Incident/The Paradise Syndrome/And The Children Shall Lead/Is There In Truth No Beauty?/Spectre of the Gun/Day of the Dove/For the World is Hollow and I Have Touched the Sky/The Tholian Webb (Emmy Award winner)/Plato's Stepchildren/Wink of an Eye/The Empath/Elan of Troyius/Whom Gods Destroy/Let That Be Your Last Battlefield/Mark of Gideon/That Which Survives/Lights of Zetar/Requiem for Methuselah/The Way to Eden/The Cloud Minders/The Savage Curtain/All Our Yesterdays/Turnabout Intruder.

Star Trek: Deep Space Nine

USA 1993– 2 × 120m/70+ × 30m col. A Paramount Production. *UK tx* 1993– Sky 1. *cr* Rick Berman, Michael Piller. *exec pr* Rick Berman, Michael Piller, Ira Steven Behr. *pr* Ronald D Moore, Rene Echevarria, Robert Hewett Wolfe. *dr* David Livingstone, James L Conway, Alexander Singer, Les Landau, Corey Allen, Robert Scheerer, Robert Wiemer, Winrich Kolbe, David Carson, Paul Lynch, Robert Legato, Cliff Bole, Jonathan Frakes, Kim Friedman, Avery Brooks, Reza Badiyi. *wr* Michael Piller, Rick Berman, Peter Allan Fields, Mark Gehred-O'Connell, Ira Steven Behr, Robert Hewitt Wolfe, Frederick Rappaport, Gabe Essoe, Kelley Miles, Joe Menosky, Jim Trombetta, Bill Dial, Morgan Gendel, Paul Robert Coyle, Jeff King, Richard Manning, Hans Beimler, James Crocker, Robert Hewitt Wolfe, Flip

Kobler, Cindy Marcus, Peter Allan Fields, Jeri Taylor, Gerald Sanford, Kathryn Powers, Tim Burns, Hannah Louise Shearer, Dorothy C Fontana, Lisa Rich, Jeanne Carrigan-Fauci, Sam Rolfe, Richard Danus, Evan Carlos Somers, Hilary Bader, Kurt Michael Bensmiller, Nell McCue Crawford, William L Crawford, Don Carlos Dunaway, John Whelpley, Steven Baum, Mike Krohn, Tom Benko, Rene Echevarria, Christopher Teague, Thomas E Maio, Steve Warneck, Toni Marberry, Jack Trevino, David Mack, John J Ordover, Ronald D Moore, Robert Gillan. *mus* Jerry Goldsmith (theme). *sfx* Glenn Neufeld, Gary Hutzel, Bob Blackman (costume). *cast* **Commander (later Captain) Benjamin Sisko** Avery Brooks **Lt Worf** Michael Dorn **Odo** Rene Auberjonois **Major Kira Nerys** Nana Visitor **Lt Jadzia Dax** Terry Farrell **Chief Operations Officer Miles O'Brien** Colm Meaney **Dr Julian Bashir** Siddig El Fadil **Jake Sisko** Cirroc Lofton **Quark** Armin Shimerman **Keiko O'Brien** Rosalind Chao **Kai Opaka** Camile Saviola **Vedek Winn** Louise Fletcher. *Video* Paramount.

If the original >*Star Trek* was a sci-fi take on >*Wagon Train*, the third *Trek* series owed something to >*Gunsmoke* and the Chuck Connors Western series *The Rifleman*. The eponymous desolate space station, reluctantly commanded by Benjamin Sisko (played by ex-*Spenser: For Hire* actor and professor of theatre Avery Brooks) was located at the back end of the universe in the orbit of the planet Bajor, surrounded by hostile tribes and outlaws. A 360–degree promenade on *DS9* – only recently freed from Cardassian rule – was the twenty-sixth-century version of Dodge City's Main Street. Like Connors' Lucas Cain character, Sisko was a lone father trying to bring up a son (Jake) on the far frontier.

Much of the outlawry aboard DS9 was traced by the shape-shifting chief of security Odo (Rene Auberjonois of *Benson*) to Quark, a Ferengi who ran the entertainment concessions, including a holographic brothel. Though exhibiting the same social concerns as the earlier *Treks*, the creators of *DS9*, Michael Piller and ex-Paramount vice-president Rick Berman, had a darker vision than Trekmaster Gene Roddenberry (who died in 1991, playing no part in the execution of the new series). Squabbles and sins among the DS9 crew were endemic. Sisko blamed *Star Trek: The Next Generation*'s Captain Jean-Luc Picard for the death of his wife, a deed committed when Picard had fallen under the influence of the Borg. Chief Operations Officer Miles O'Brien, promoted from the *Enterprise* to *DS9*, spatted domestically with his wife Keiko, forced to abandon her own career aboard the starship to accompany him to his new posting. Major Kira Nerys, a former Bajoran freedom fighter assigned to *DS9* as first officer, was virulently patriotic, disliked the epochal peace with the Cardassians and crossed swords regularly with her commander. Science officer Lieutenant Jadzia Dax (former model Terry Farrell, also the abortive *Red Dwarf USA* pilot) had little need for others to spar with; she was a member of the joined species known as Trill, the main element of which was a 300–year-old slug-like form which lurked inside her delectable humanoid host body, making her simultaneously male-female, young-old. Dax's essentially mollusc nature, however, did nothing to diminish the interest of naive physician Dr Julian Bashir, who suffered paroxisms of unrequited passions for her. Meanwhile, Odo – who was obliged to return to his base state of liquid every sixteen hours – caught the romantically inclined eye of the Lawaxana Troi (played by Roddenberry's widow, Majel Barrett).

DS9 was *Star Trek*, Jim, but not as audiences knew it. Denuded of the 'to boldly go' questing-exploratory element of the first two *Trek* series, *DS9* was insipid, soap-opera-ish, and low on excitement, despite the fortuitous siting of *DS9* next to a 'wormhole' – a fissure in space through which travellers could, in a nanosecond, be shot to the ends of the galaxy. Faced with fandom unease, even ennui, Paramount used seasons two and three to introduce a new enemy, the Dominion who ruled the unexplored Gamma Quadrant, a fresh prop, the warship *Defiant* (designed by Jim Martin), and a semi-regular bad woman, Bajoran priestess Vedek Winn (Oscar-winning Louise Fletcher, *One Flew Over the Cuckoo's Nest*). Much the biggest revamp, however, was the permanent assignment of *Next Generation* Klingon Starfleet officer, Worf, to *DS9*, an event honoured by a two-hour première which featured nothing less than a full-scale battle with a Klingon armada.

In the USA the series overcame stumbles to secure healthy ratings, a position within the top ten hour-long series on television and three Emmy Awards. Only Trekker enthusiasm eluded it.

Star Trek: The Next Generation

USA 1987–94 42 × 90m/174 × 50m col syndicated.
Paramount TV. *UK tx* 1990–2 BBC2/1992–5 Sky TV. *cr* Gene
Roddenberry. *exec pr* Gene Roddenberry, Rick Berman,
Michael Piller, Jeri Taylor. *pr* Various, including Peter
Lauriston, Ronald D Moore, Wendy Neuss, Ira Steven Behr,
Brannan Braga, Joe Menosky, David Livingston. *dr* Various,
including Chip Chalmers, Jonathan Frakes, Robert Weimer,
Robert Scheerer, Les Landau, Cliff Bole, Patrick Stewart,
Alexander Singer, Winrich Kolbe, David Livingston, David
Carson, Gabrielle Beaumont, Timothy Bond, Adam Nimoy,
Robert Legato, LeVar Burton, Gales McFadden, Corey
Allen, Adam Nimoy. *wr* Various, including Gene
Roddenberry, D C Fontana, Rene Echevarria, Ronald D
Moore, Jeri Taylor, Brannon Braga, Frank Abatemarco,
Allison Hock, Pamela Gray, Adam Belanoff, Rene Balcer,
Michael Piller, Michael Wagner, Sam Rolfe, Melinda M
Snodgrass, Ira Steven Behr, Richard Manning, Rick
Berman. *mus* Jerry Goldsmith and Alexander Courage
(theme), Dennis McCarthy, Jay Chattaway, Ron Jones. *sfx*
Robert Legato, Dan Curry, Ron Moore, David Stipes. *cast*
Captain Jean-Luc Picard Patrick Stewart **William T Riker**
Jonathan Frakes **Lt Geordi LaForge** LeVar Burton **Lt Tasha
Yar** Denise Crosby **Lt Worf** Michael Dorn **Lt Cmdr Data**
Brent Spiner **Dr Beverly Crusher** Gates McFadden
Counsellor Deanna Troi Marina Sirtis **Wesley Crusher** Wil
Weaton **Dr Katherine 'Kate' Pulaski** Diane Muldaur
Guinan Whoopi Goldberg **Transporter Chief Miles
O'Brien** Colm Meaney **Ensign Ro Laren** Michelle Forbes.
Video CIC.

These then were the new voyages of USS *Enterprise*. Set
seventy-eight years after the original mission, the sequel
featured an upgraded ship (Galaxy Class) and a new crew
on the bridge. The captain was reserved Jean-Luc Picard
(British Shakespearian actor Patrick Stewart), less
inclined to heroic action than his predecessor, a man who
often allowed the outboard crises to be dealt with by
'Away Teams' led by Commander William Riker ('No 1'),
the closest of the Next Generation to Kirk in looks and
persona (hence the similarity of their surnames). Other
prominent ship's officers were the half-Betzoid
counsellor, empathic Deanna Troi; Lt Cmdr Data, a
whey-faced android who desired to be human; Lt Worf,
the security officer (the Federation had achieved peace
with the Klingons since the original series); Lt Cmdr
Geordi LaForge, blind helmsman who saw with the use
of VISOR glasses; Chief Medical Officer Beverly
Crusher; her son, Ensign Wesley Crusher, and
Transporter Chief Miles O'Brien (played by Colm
Meaney, ex->*Z Cars*). Hollywood actress Whoopi
Goldberg played Guinan, the mysterious bartender in the
Enterprise's Ten Forward lounge. The new bad guys of
the Universe were the big, bald Ferengi, the lizard-necked
Cardassians and the cybernetic Borg.

The initial involvement of *Star Trek's* creator, the late
Gene Roddenberry, ensured that *The Next Generation*
was as concerned to make moral points as the original.
(It was noticeable that Roddenberry had taken
complaints about *Star Trek's* sexism on board, and the
1000–person crew of the new *Enterprise* counted several
women in leading positions). Yet the sequel lacked
warmth and charm, and Roddenberry's liberalism sat ill
at ease with the designer sci-fi sets. The cast was earnest,
less interesting, and humour was rare (although Worf's
desire to photon-torpedo everything in sight could be
amusing, so too Guinan's trick on him that prune juice
was a 'warrior's drink'). Yet, viewed on its own terms,
The Next Generation was often watchable, with
exemplary special effects. It won numerous Emmy
Awards – a number for technical achievements – and
became the highest-rated non-networked show in the
USA. Several of the first *Star Trek* cast appeared in the
sequel, including Majel Barrett, DeForest Kelley, James
Doohan and Leonard Nimoy. (Nimoy's son Adam also
directed on *TNG*). The guest stars have included Kelsey
Grammer and Bebe Neuwirth from >*Cheers*, and also
Samantha Eggar, Carolyn Seymour (of >*The Survivors*)
and Stephanie Beacham.

On the back of the success of *The Next Generation*,
Paramount TV launched a third *Star Trek* series, *Star
Trek: Deep Space Nine*, and then a fourth, *Star Trek:
Voyager*, as well as sending the *TNG* cast into the
movies.

Let's see what's out there . . .

Star Trek: Voyager

USA 1995– 32 × 60m col UPN. Paramount. *cr* Rick Berman, Michael Piller, Jeri Taylor. *exec pr* Rick Berman, Michael Piller, Jeri Taylor. *dr* Various, including Winrich Kolbe, Kim Friedman, Les Landau, David Livingston, LeVar Burton, Robert Scheerer, Jonathan Frakes, Jim Conway. *wr* Michael Piller, Jeri Taylor, Brannon Braga, Jim Trombetta, David Kemper, Skye Dent, Timothy DeHaas, Bill Dial, Hilary J Bader, Evan Carlos Somers, Michael Perricone, Greg Elliott, David R George III, Eric Stillwell, Chris Abbott, Paul Robert Coyle, Naran Shankar, Joe Menosky, Jonathan Glassner, Adam Grossman, Ronald Wilkerson, Jean Louise Matthias, Jack Klein, Karen Klein, Scott Nimerfro, Jim Thornton, Jimmy Diggs, Steve J Kay, Kenneth Biller, Arnold Rudnick, Rick Hosek. *mus* Jerry Goldsmith (theme). *sfx* Dan Curry, David Stipes, Ron B Moore. *cast* **Captain Kathryn Janeway** Kate Mulgrew **First Officer Chakotay** Robert Beltran **Lieutenant Tom Paris** Robert Duncan McNeill **Tactical/Security Officer Tuvok** Tim Russ **Ops/ Communications Officer Harry Kim** Garrett Wang **Chief Engineer** Roxann Biggs-Dawson **Neelix** Ethan Phillips **Kes** Jennifer Lien **Doctor** Robert Picardo. *Video* Paramount.

'. . . it's a fine crew . . . and I've got to get them home'
Captain Kathryn Janeway

No sooner had *Star Trek: Deep Space Nine* been manufactured in the Paramount yards, then the dilithium crystals of the *Trek* franchise were powered up to produce a fourth TV series, *Star Trek: Voyager*. Airing on the fledgling United Paramount Network on 16 January 1995 with a two-hour première 'Caretaker', the concept of the new show was that in the twenty-fourth century a ship crewed by Maquis – outlaw resistance fighters opposed to the peace treaty signed between the Federation and the Cardassians – disappeared into the Badlands. A Federation ship, USS *Voyager*, dispatched as rescue discovered the lost Maquis but not before being swept up by a mysterious energy wave which blasted them all 70,000 light years into an uncharted region of the far galaxy called the Delta Quadrant. The Federation and Maquis crews then joined together aboard the *Voyager* to try to find their long way home.

On their way home. Captain Kathryn Janeway (former Mrs Columbo Kate Mulgrew) and crew in *Star Trek's* fourth television enterprise, *Star Trek: Voyager*.

While *Voyager* incorporates the journeying theme of the original *Trek*, it evidences some notable differences. *Star Trek* was the televisual metaphor of JFK's new, bold expansionist America of the sixties; *Voyager* is the small screen reflection of the USA in isolationist, end-of-the-century, minding-its-own-business mode. But the most obvious variation from classic *Trek* is that the captain's chair in *Voyager* is occupied by a double XX chromosome, Kathryn Janeway. The final frontier in the Roddenberrian universe has been broken. Unlike the swashbuckling Kirk, and the reserved Picard and abrasive Sisko, Janeway is a conspicuously nurturing leader, though equally adept at rasp-throated, hands-on-hips authority. Academy Award nominee Geneviève Bujold was initially slated to play Janeway (variously christened Elizabeth and Nicole, before the producers and Paramount legal department settled on Kathryn) but bowed out after only a day and a half of shooting, apparently unprepared for the rigours of conveyor-belt TV. The part then went to Iowa-born actress Kate Mulgrew, previously best known as *Kate Columbo* (aka *Kate Loves a Mystery*) and her roles as Dr Joanne Springstein in ABC drama *Heartbeat* and Sam Malone's love interest in a sequence of >*Cheers* episodes.

Under Mulgrew's Janeway served a crew who were studiedly different, but ultimately unoriginal. The first officer Chakotay (played by Mexican Indian Robert Beltran, Soto in *Models Inc.*), a former Starfleet lieutenant commander turned Maquis, was of Native American descent and had a spirit guide in the form of a timber wolf.

Lieutenant Tom Paris (Robert Duncan McNeill) was from a family of legendary Starfleet officers, but was discharged from the service after placing the blame for a fatal mistake on a dead man. (The backstory is based on *The Next Generation* episode 'First Duty' in which Wesley Crusher must decide whether to lie about an accidental death; his classmates included Ensign Lecarno, played by McNeill). After joining the Maquis, Paris was captured by the Federation, and finally hauled out of prison by Janeway and given a second chance in Starfleet.

Tuvok, a Vulcan male (and Spock clone), was the Starfleet Tactical/Security Officer for USS *Voyager*, and also the cool-headed peacekeeper aboard ship. Harry Kim, a recent graduate from the Starfleet Academy, was the nervous, wide-eyed, squeaky clean Operations/Communication Officer. Chief Engineer was B'Elanna Torres, a half-Klingon female and another former Maquis. Also aboard were two previously unseen life-forms, Neelix, a male Talaxian serving as cook and handyman, and his Ocampa lover Kes; both were unfeasibly cute. The holographic Doctor made for a curmudgeonly counterweight.

The ship they sailed was leaner and sleaker than its *Trek* ancestors, ideal for flight as well as fight. Designed by Richard James and Rick Sternback, *Voyager* was organic, replete with new technology and had an advanced warp drive system which allowed it to exceed warp speed limit (imposed in the *Star Trek: The Next Generation* episode 'Force of Nature') without polluting the space continuum. An intrepid-class vessel, *Voyager* was capable of holding 200 crew members.

The show's technology might have gleamed, but the narratives borrowed shamelessly from *Star Trek*. Few protested, however, and *Voyager* did well enough in ratings to survive UPN's swingeing mid-1995 cull. For many 'Trekkers' it, rather than the stationary space-station show *Deep Space Nine*, was the true torchbearer of the *Star Trek* TV franchise.

The Survivors

UK 1975–7 38 × 50m col BBC. BBC. *cr* Terry Nation. *pr* Terence Dudley. *dr* Pennant Roberts, Gerald Blake, Terence Williams, Eric Hills, Peter Jeffries, Tristan de Vere Cole, George Spenton Foster, Terence Dudley. *wr* Terry Nation, Jack Ronder, M K Jeeves (aka Clive Exton), Ian McCulloch, Martin Worth, Roger Parkes, Roger Marshall, Terence Dudley, Don Shaw. *mus* Anthony Isaac. *cast* **Abby Grant** Carolyn Seymour **Jenny Richards** Lucy Fleming **Greg Preston** Ian McCulloch **Vic Thatcher** Terry Scully **Tom Price** Talfryn Thomas **Arthur Russell** Michael Gover **Charmian Wentworth** Eileen Helsby **John** Stephen Dudley **Lizzie** Tanya Ronder **Paul Pitman** Christopher Tranchell **Mrs Emma Cohen** Hana-Maria Pravda **Charles Vaughn** Denis Lill **Pet** Lorna Lewis **Hubert** John Abineri.

This Terry Nation (>*Dr Who*, >*Blake's 7*) series is something of an underrated, seldom seen treasure. The nightmarish premise, effected in the opening episode, 'The Four Horsemen of the Apocalypse', was that an oriental scientist dropped a test-tube containing a deadly virus which wiped out 95 per cent of the Earth's population. Subsequent episodes followed the fortunes of a small group of British survivors – principally Abby Grant, Greg Preston, architect Charles Vaughn and Jenny Richards – as they tried to adapt, rebuild communities and re-invent skills and technologies. Their trials were made all the harder by widespread lawlessness and disease. Nation's recurring interest in the misuse of power was widely evidenced, particularly in the segment 'Genesis', in which George 'Inspector Wexford' Baker played Wormly, a trade union boss attempting to impose a miniature military dictatorship.

As a dramatic exploration of the question: could humanity endure if it had to start over again?, *Survivors* was intelligently done. It was noteworthy, too, for having a woman (Abby) as the lead character, which was particularly unusual in a sci-fi serial. Nation himself – a Welsh ex-gag-writer for Tony Hancock – left the project after season one, and this coupled with the fact that as civilisation was rebuilt the series lost its *froideur* (if not its *raison d'être*) meant a drop in quality. Filmed on location in the Welsh Marches and Herefordshire, many of *Survivors* behind-camera personnel came from another BBC sci-fi series with its optimism on horizontal hold, >*Doomwatch*.

The Time Tunnel

USA 1966–7 30 × 50m col ABC. 20th Century Fox Television. *UK tx* 1968 BBC; 1970 ITV. *cr* Irwin Allen. *exec pr* Irwin Allen. *dr* Irwin Allen, Harry Harris, Sobey Martin, William Hale, Murray Golden, Jerry Hopper, Paul Stanley, Jerry Briskin, Herschel Daugherty, Jerry Juran. *wr* Harold Jack Bloom, William Welch, Peter Germano, Ellis St Joseph, Bob and Wanda Duncan, William Read Woodfield, Allan Balter, Carey Wilbur, Theodore Apstein, Leonard Stadd, Barney Slater, Robert Hamner. *mus* Johnny Williams. *sfx* L B Abbott. *cast* **Dr Tony Newman** James Darren **Dr Doug Phillips** Robert Colbert **Dr Ann Macgregor** Lee Meriwether **Dr Raymond Swain** John Zaremba **Lt Gen Heywood Kirk** Whit Bissell.

It all started when young scientists Tony Newman and Doug Phillips were working on a top-secret government project miles beneath the surface of the Arizona desert. Their goal was to build a tunnel to launch mankind into time past and future. Forced to demonstrate their as yet untested invention to the US senator who controlled funds for the project, Tony Newman found himself successfully hurled back in time. The only snag was that the machine was not able to bring him back. Horrified colleagues monitored Tony's progress on a viewing screen back at the lab and brave comrade Doug Phillips jumped in after him – leaving both men trapped on the *Titanic* just before it went down.

The two scientists were then doomed to travel from one historic hot spot to another, knowing the horrible outcome of the moment they were witnessing but powerless to alter events, while colleagues contrived to bring them back in the nick of time. Viewers received a crash course in decisive moments of history from Krakatoa ('The Crack of Doom') to the Trojan War 500 BC ('Revenge of the Gods') from Custer's last stand ('Massacre') to the French Revolution ('Reign of Terror') and from D Day ('Invasion') to the Wild West ('Billy the Kid').

From the first episode our heroes also got caught up in chunks of old Fox movies – 'Rendezvous with Yesterday' used stock footage from Fox's *Titanic* in a special tinted form; 'The Ghost of Nero' used footage from *Farewell to Arms*. Occasionally they were even thrown into the future ('One Way to the Moon') so that the thrifty Mr Allen could re-use >*Lost in Space* outfits. Economies apart however, this was another Irwin Allen extravaganza with deliciously psychedelic effects – in particular the swirling pop-art vortex – and a look created by many of the same production personnel that Allen had used on >*Voyage to the Bottom of the Sea*. It was magnificently photographed by Winton Hoch and its elaborate illusions won Bill Abbott his third Emmy for special photographic effects. The tunnel itself was the most extraordinary effect. It was a drum nine feet in diameter covered with cellophane and Christmas tinsel. When shot through an ultra-wide lens, the result was a dazzling kaleidoscope of 'time fragments' flying through the shaft. The actors, suspended by wires in front of a blue screen, were matted into the scene.

The clean-cut stars of the series (neither their hair-cuts nor their polo necks were ever ruffled) were also sent travelling to future TV careers. Darren later played Officer Jim Corrigan in *T J Hooker* (1982), former Miss America Lee Meriwether played almost simultaneously in >*Mission Impossible* (1966) and then went on to *Barnaby Jones* (1973), while Robert Colbert was already known for his role as Brent in >*Maverick* (1957). Keen eyes would have spotted appearances from guest stars Susan Hampshire ('Rendezvous with Yesterday') and Robert Duvall ('Chase Through Time').

In 1976 Fox made an ill-advised attempt to revive the project with a TV movie called *The Time Travellers* in which an attempt was made to prevent the Chicago fire – using chunks of tinted footage from *In Old Chicago*. The expected series never happened.

Seated before the swirling vortex that transported their characters into the hot spots of history are the stars of Irwin Allen's classic sci-fi show, *The Time Tunnel*. From the Trojan War to the Wild West, no matter how dangerous the action, James Darren never had a hair out of place.

The Time Tunnel's episode titles were as follows: Rendezvous with Yesterday/One Way to the Moon/End of the World/The Day the Sky Fell Down/The Last Patrol/The Crack of Doom/Revenge of the Gods/ Massacre/Devil's Island/Reign of Terror/Secret Weapon/ The Death Trap/The Alamo/The Night of the Long Knives/Invasion/Robin Hood/Kill Two by Two/Visitors from Beyond the Stars/The Ghost of Nero/The Walls of Jericho/Idol of Death/Billy the Kid/Pirates of Deadman's Island/Chase Through Time/The Death Merchant/Attack of the Barbarians/Merlin the Magician/The Kidnappers/ Raiders from Outer Space/Town of Terror.

UFO

UK 1970–1 26 × 60m col ITV. Century 21 Pictures Ltd. *USA tx* 1972 syndicated. *cr* Gerry Anderson, Sylvia Anderson, Reg Hill. *exec pr* Gerry Anderson. *pr* Reg Hill. *dr* Gerry Anderson, David Lane, Ken Turner, Alan Perry, Jeremy Summers, David Tomblin, Cyril Frankel. *wr* Gerry and Sylvia Anderson, Tony Barwick, Alan Patillo, Donald James, Ruric Powell, Alan Fennell, Ian Scott, David Tomblin, Terence Feely, Bob Bell. *mus* Barry Gray. *sfx* Derek Meddings. *cast* **Cmdr Ed Straker** Ed Bishop **Col Alec Freeman** George Sewell **Col Paul Foster** Michael Bilington **Capt Peter Karlin** Peter Gordeno **Joan Harrington** Antonio Ellis **Lt Gray Ellis** Gabrielle Drake **Col Virginia Lake** Wanda Ventham **Lt Nina Barry** Dolores Mantez **Lt Ford** Keith Alexander **SHADO Operative** Ayshea Brough **General Henderson** Grant Taylor. *Video* Polygram.

1980. The Earth. Aliens in spinning, pyramid-shaped UFOs raid the planet to secure human body parts to maintain their sterile race. Trying to stop them is SHADO (Supreme Headquarters Alien Defence Organisation) a secret, international outfit with a base underneath the Harlington-Straker Film Studios on the edge of London. Boss of SHADO is divorced, ex-USAAF pilot Ed Straker (Ed Bishop, formerly the voice of Captain Blue in >*Captain Scarlet and the Mysterons*). His chief aides are Colonel Alec Freeman (pock-faced George Sewell from >*Special Branch*), and Colonel Paul Foster. To enable it to combat the UFOs, SHADO has an impressive range of futuristic technology: a satellite early-warning system SID (Space Intruder Detector), a submarine/aircraft called *Skydiver*, and tank-like SHADOmobiles to pursue any UFOs which land. The rarely seen alien pilots of the UFOs wear bulky space suits and helmets filled with a viscous liquid.

UFO was Gerry Anderson's first TV series without puppets (although >*Secret Service* had presaged the move, and his 1969 cinema film *Doppelganger* had been stringless) and the first explicitly aimed at adults. The ITV stations disliked it – a number aired it in graveyard slots – and one episode ('The Long Sleep') was held back because of an LSD sequence. Season two was cancelled to produce >*Space 1999*.

This was unfortunate because *UFO* was superior space drama, high-tensioned and exciting, with the approach of the alien spacecraft heralded by an unforgettably spooky whirring noise. The writing was almost uniformly imaginative and gripping, with David Tomblin's 'Reflections in the Water' (where the aliens built an underwater replica of SHADO HQ) being one highlight amongst many. The cast's acting, though, was on a par with Anderson's puppets (although >*Space 1999* would provide worse); some of the worst offenders were the extraordinarily pneumatic, purple-haired women who staffed Moonbase (among them actress Gabrielle Drake, later to beam down to Earth as the manager of >*Crossroads*). Lower down the cast list, avant-garde theatre writer and director Steven Berkoff appeared several times as a SHADO astronaut. The subsequent work of Anouska Hempel, *UFO* radio operative, included a celebrated whip-wielding plantation mistress in the Russ Meyer movie, *Slaves* (1973). Patrick Mower ('The Square Triangle') and Stephanie Beacham ('Destruction') also figured on the *UFO* guest cast.

V (The Mini-series)

USA 1984 5 × 110m col NBC. Kenneth Johnson Production/Warner Bros TV. *UK tx* 1984. *cr* Kenneth Johnson. *ex pr* Kenneth Johnson. *pr* Chuck Bowman. *dr* Kenneth Johnson. *wr* Kenneth Johnson. *mus* Joe Harnell. *cast* **Diana** Jane Badler **Julie Parrish** Faye Grant **Mike**

An alien-fighting SHADO operative (Ayshea Brough) in the
Andersons' underrated live-action series *UFO*.

Donovan Marc Singer **Robert** Michael Durrell **Robin**
Maxwell Blair Tefkin **Willie** Robert Englund **Ham Tyler**
Michael Ironside **Martin** Frank Ashmore. *Video* Warners
Home Video.

The V of the title did not stand for Vile, but it might have
done. This $50 million blockbuster space opera about an
alien invasion of Earth in the late 20th century contained
some of the most deliciously disgusting moments in
telefantasy. In one scene the alluring leader of the
humanoid-alien Visitors, Diana (Jane Badler), 'ate' a live
rat (a clever trick with a mechanical head designed by
make-up artist Leo Lotito). In another, Robin, a seducee
of an alien called Brian, gave birth to their love children.
Since the aliens were actually lizards underneath their
assumed human exteriors, one baby was born a reptile,
the other a human with a forked tongue.

Ostensibly the alien 'Visitors' of V who arrived in
thirty-one five-mile wide spaceships, came in peace and
need of minerals. But no sooner had they touched down
than they launched a totalitarian-style takeover,
disseminating propaganda ('The Visitors Are Our
Friends') and herding scientists into concentration
camps. Even worse, as intrepid TV newsman Mike
Donovan discovered when he sneaked aboard the
Visitors' Mother Ship, their real mission was to transport
humans back to Sirius for food. With scientist Julie
Parrish, mercenary Ham Tyler and alien fifth columnists
Willie (Robert 'Freddy Kruger' Englund) and Martin,
Donovan formed a Resistance Movement – which
adopted the 'V' for Victory sign of the Allies in World
War II – with an HQ at the Creole club, Los Angeles. In
a climactic showdown the aliens were defeated by using
'red dust' poison, manufactured from the cells of
Elizabeth, the human/reptile baby.

V was, of course, a thinly veiled liberal parable about
the rise of Nazism in Germany in the thirties. (The
producers, however, took no chances on audience
intelligence and scripted a Jewish member of the
Resistance to make explicit how similar the experiences
were.) The series might not have been sophisticated, but
it was fast-moving, resplendent with glossy special effects
and had, on stages twenty-five and twenty-six of the
Burbank Studios in California, one of the most elaborate
sets ever constructed for TV.

Diana (Jane Badler), leader of the alien visitors reveals her
true reptilian nature in *V*, a thinly veiled allegory of the Nazis'
rise to power.

Inevitably, the success of *V* – in Britain alone it was watched by 10 million viewers per night – spawned a full series (nineteen episodes), with most of the cast reprising their mini-series' roles. The Nazi parallel was dropped, and *V: The Series* turned out a routine space actioner.

Voyage To The Bottom Of The Sea

USA 1964–8 110 × 50m (32 bw/78 col) ABC. An Irwin Allen Production for 20th Century Fox. *UK tx* 1964–6. *cr* Irwin Allen. *exec pr* Irwin Allen. *dr* Various, including Irwin Allen, John Brahm, Alan Crosland, James Goldstone, Sobey Martin, Gerd Oswald, Harry Harris, Leo Penn, Jerry Hooper, Abe Biberman, Sutton Roley, Tom Gries, Robert Sparr, Jus Addiss, Bruce Fowler, James Clark, Jerry Juran. *wr* Various, including Irwin Allen, Richard Landau, Anthony Wilson, Don Brinkley, Rik Vollaerts, Simon Wincelberg, Arthur Weiss, Arthur Browne Jr, Harlan Ellison, Allan Balter, William Read Woodfield, Robert Hamner, Sidney Marshall, Allan Caillou, Sheldon Star. *mus* Lionel Newman. *cast* **Adm Harriman Nelson** Richard Basehart **Cmdr Lee Crane** David Hedison **Lt Cmdr Chip Morton** Robert Dowdell **Chief Petty Officer Curley Jones** Henry Kulky **Chief Sharkey** Terry Becker **Stu Riley** Allan Hunt **Kowalsky** Del Monroe **Crewman Patterson** Paul Trinka **Crewman Sparks** Arch Whiting **Doctor** Richard Bull.

A television spin-off from Irwin Allen's 1961 block-buster movie of the same title, *Voyage to the Bottom of the Sea* followed the exploits of the all-male crew of the *Seaview*, the most extraordinary submarine in the seven seas: 600 feet long, glass-nosed and atomic powered. Ostensibly an instrument of scientific research for the California-based Nelson Institute of Marine Research, the *Seaview* was, in fact, a secret weapon dedicated to combating threats to world peace from villains both human and alien.

The movie-land origins of *Voyage* meant (initially at least) that the series was able to achieve outstanding production values. Props, sets – including the main sections of the *Seaview*, worth $400,000 – and costumes all came straight from the film, as did thousands of feet of underwater scenes. Allen himself was accustomed to working to high standards, and for the first episode of the TV *Voyage*, 'Eleven Days to Zero', brought in Maurice Zuberano, Hollywood's top production illustrator, to prepare 1,100 sketches of the upcoming action as a shooting guide. The cameraman for the series was three-time Oscar-winner Winton Hoch (who had also worked on the movie version). Also on board the production team was 20th Century Fox photographics chief Billy Abbott, whose visual effects for the TV *Voyage* earned him a brace of Emmys.

The cast was also culled from Hollywood, and included Richard Basehart as brilliant sailor-scientist Admiral Harriman Nelson, USN (Ret), and David Hedison, star of the classic submarine feature *The Enemy Below* and the 1959 movie *The Fly*, as sidekick Commander Lee Crane, captain of the *Seaview*. (Hedison later appeared in the Bond films *Live and Let Die* and *Licence to Kill*.)

Voyage started out as an extension of science fact, and was thrilling because it was plausible. But as the episodes multiplied, credibility soon became stretched. And stretched. Season two specialised in gadgetry (the *Seaview* gained a flying mini-sub) and horror-show gimmicks ('Terror on Dinosaur Island', 'Graveyard of Fear'). By season three the show was sinking fast – it featured such weirdities as 'The Plant Man' and 'The Heat Monster' – and with season four the depths were finally plumbed, as the show ran out of ideas – and apparent budget (in one episode the crew was attacked by toy mechanical robots). Also, the crew's inability to remember that the aliens/monsters/psychopaths who routinely attacked the *Seaview* always hid in the large air ducts became tiresome.

Creator Irwin Allen, however, continued his highly commercial career in sci-fi undaunted. His credits include the films *Lost World* (1960) and *The Poseidon Adventure* (1972), the latter responsible for launching the disaster movie cycle of the seventies. His TV *Voyage* was the first of a quartet of sixties small-screen sci-fi series from Allen. The others were >*Lost in Space*, >*The Time Tunnel* and *Land of the Giants*. Allen also produced *The Return of Captain Nemo* (1978) and *Swiss Family Robinson* (1975–6) for TV.

Wonder Woman

USA 1976–9 1 × 90m/45 × 45m ABC/CBS. Warner Bros Television/Douglas S Cramer Co. *UK tx* 1978–80 BBC1. *exec pr* Douglas S Cramer. *pr* Wilfred Lloyd Baumes. *dr* Various, including Alan Crosland, Michael Caffey, Seymour Robbie. *wr* Various, including Stephen Kandel, Anne Collins, Alan Brennert, Bruce Shelley. *mus* Charles Fox. *cast* **Wonder Woman/Yeoman Diana Prince** Lynda Carter **Maj Steve Trevor/Steve Trevor, Jr** Lyle Waggoner **Gen Blankenship** Richard Eastham **Corp Etta Candy** Beatrice Colen **Joe Atkinson** Normann Burton **Eve** Saundra Sharp. **Voice of IRA (IADC Computer)** Tom Kratochzil.

Wonder Woman was pure comic-strip – as indeed it should have been, based as it was on Charles Moulon's forties comic-book superheroine. Wonder Woman hailed from a 'lost' island peopled by a band of Amazon women who had fled there in the year 200 BC to escape male domination. On Paradise Island they found Feminum – a magic substance which when moulded into a golden belt or bracelets gave them superhuman strength and deflected bullets.

The superheroine's first TV outing was as *The New Original Wonderwoman* (ABC, 1976–7), aka Diana Prince, bespectacled secretary to handsome Major Steve Trevor of the US Army. Major Trevor had crash-landed on the island during World War II and Prince had fallen in love and returned with him. Major Trevor however was unaware that, when trouble threatened, his love disappeared, twirled and transformed into Wonder Woman with the help of knee-length zip-up boots, tights and star-spangled bodice and tiara. Her red, white and blue costume signalled her commitment to freedom and democracy and the heroine's superpowers were engaged to help America in its fight against the Nazis.

In 1977 the series moved to CBS where it was retitled *The New Adventures of Wonder Woman* and updated to the seventies where the Amazon was given gutsy speeches to fit the times and won the backing of women's groups. (In one scene a woman confided 'I've learned my lesson; I'll rely on myself, not on a man' and Wonder Woman replied approvingly 'Don't forget that'). Nowadays the heroine was required to fight terrorists and subversive elements for undercover organisation Inter-Agency Defense Command (IADC). Working closely with her was Steve Trevor Jr, the son of Major Trevor. Since Wonder Woman had not aged at all (residents of Paradise Island lived for centuries) and Steve Trevor Jr bore an uncanny resemblance to his departed father (as well he might since he was played by the same actor) the couple were to all intents and purposes unchanged. Eve filled the now vacant post of Steve's secretary.

New adversaries included a rock musician who hypnotised young women into stealing for him ('The Pied Piper') and Roddy McDowall as a crazy scientist who used a laser weapon to create volcanic eruptions across the globe ('The Man Who Made Volcanoes').

In this clean, all-action, all-American series former Miss World and 1973 Miss USA Lynda Carter was well fitted to the title role. Not six feet tall as claimed by over-eager publicists, but five feet ten inches, athletic and pneumatic in true comic-strip style, she was ideally equipped to fight evil and champion all that was good.

Wonder Woman made its début as a made-for-TV movie, with Cathy Lee Crosby in the lead role. Low ratings led to the recast, a second TV movie starring Carter and the two television series. From 1976, Diana's younger sister Drusilla, Wonder Girl, played by Debra Winger (star of film *An Officer and a Gentleman*, 1981), occasionally aided the superheroine in her efforts.

The X-Files

US 1993– 72+ × 50m col Fox. Ten Thirteen Productions/20th Century Television. *UK tx* 1994– Sky 1. *cr* Chris Carter. *exec pr* Chris Carter, James Wong, Glen Morgan, R W Goodwin. *pr* Howard Gordon, Alex Gansa. *dr* Various, including Robert Mandel, Daniel Sackheim, Harry Longstreet, Joe Napolitano, Michael Katleman, Jerrold Freedman, David Butler, William Graham, Larry Shaw, Fred Gerber, David Nutter, Rob Bowman, Michael Lange, R W Goodwin. *wr* Various, including Chris Carter, Glen Morgan, James Wong, Alex Gansa, Howard Gordon, Kenneth Biller, Chris Brancato, Larry Barber, Paul Barber, Scott Kaufer, Marylin Osborn, Chris Ruppenthal. *mus* Mark Snow. *cast* **Fox Mulder** David Duchovny **Dana Scully** Gillian Anderson

Deep Throat Jerry Hardin **Assistant Director Skinner**
Mitch Pileggi **Cigarette-Smoking Man** William B Davis.
Video Fox.

'The Truth is out there . . .'

A scary, unsettling drama about a pair of charismatic FBI
agents who investigate weird phenomena which became
a minor institution in the US and UK. The brainchild of
ex-surfing writer Chris Carter, the series was inspired by
his childhood viewing of *The Twilight Zone, Alfred
Hitchcock Presents* and, especially, *>Kolchak: The Night
Stalker.* (Carter has declared *The X Files* to be a '*Kolchak*
for the nineties'.) For subject matter, Carter drew heavily
on allegedly real instances of strange occurrences ('the
following story is inspired by actual documented
accounts'), while the dark paranoic air of government
conspiracy which permeated the show owed something
to the John F Kennedy assassination and Watergate
affair.

Investigating the so-called X-files, the FBI's convenient
shorthand for unexplained, unsolved cases, was Fox
Mulder. A brilliant criminal psychologist, 'Spooky'
Mulder was motivated – some said obsessed – by a belief
in the paranormal, occasioned by his apparent witnessing
of the abduction of his sister by aliens when he was a boy.
Dana Scully was the power-dressed sceptic, medically
trained, and sidelined into the department initially in order
to keep an eye on her partner. Aiding – and sometimes
hindering – Mulder in season one was a high-placed
government informer called Deep Throat, who also
protected the investigator from obstructive FBI superiors
whose *raison d'être* seemed to be the neat, official cover
up. When Deep Throat was murdered at the close of the
first season (his last words to Scully being 'trust no one'),
a group of unofficial advisers called the Lone Gunmen
came to the fore. Other supporting characters included
Assistant Director Skinner, Cigarette-Smoking Man (later
Cancer Man), the Well-Manicured Man, Mr X and
traitorous Agent Alex Kycek.

Cast as Mulder was Yale postgraduate David
Duchovny, whose most famous TV role prior to *The X-
Files* was as a transvestite FBI agent in David Lynch's
>Twin Peaks. For the part of Scully, Gillian Anderson
had to overcome considerable opposition. Primarily a

stage actress, Anderson's small-screen career had been
limited to a single appearance in *The Class of '96*. More
than this, the network, Anderson later recalled, was
'interested in getting a typically marketable beauty' such
as her *>Baywatch* namesake. Yet, with applications of
lip-gloss and judicious lighting, the Fox network
eventually created a sex symbol out of Anderson to rival
any on the small screen; her image was one of the most
popular on the Internet, where the series flourished –
thanks to self-styled 'X-Philes' – from its beginning.
Although the relationship between Anderson's Scully and
Duchovny's Mulder was professional rather than
romantic, the producers were astute enough to let old-
fashioned sexual tension smoulder beneath the
investigations of UFO sightings, out-of-body homicides,
parasitic alien life forms, genetic mutations, poltergeists,
hibernating serial killers (the classic connected episodes
'Squeeze' and 'Tooms') and assorted weirdities.

Dramatic quality was high, although not consistently
so. Season two jittered in a sequence of 'Scully abducted'
stories (necessitated by Anderson's maternity leave; her
husband was *X-File* show designer Clyde Klotz, whom
she married in 1994) before ending with the highly rated
'Anasazi' segment. This cliffhanger left Mulder seemingly
dead in the desert, only to be revived by Native American
religious practice in season three opener 'The Blessing
Way', and thus able to carry on his inexorable quest to
discover the truth about the existence of the supernatural
and the extra-terrestrial. In particular, the factory-like
demands of TV resulted in a tendency to narrative
cannibalism and cliché. A segment entitled 'Firewalker'
was a reworking of the episode 'Ice', itself derived from
the thriller theatrical feature *The Thing*. The episode
'Dod Kalm', in which Mulder and Scully suffer rapid
ageing aboard a latterday *Marie Celeste*, was
commissioned largely because the producers wanted to
get their money's worth from the ship used in 'Colony'
and 'End Game'. (Reasons of economy also caused the
programme to be shot in Vancouver.) The duo's endless
lighting up of darkened sets with flashlights was
parodied by *Spitting Image*, while Scully's persistent
denials of alien life – despite all evidence to the contrary
– were easily burlesqued by British comedians *Punt &
Dennis* in a 'Z-Files' sketch that saw her devoured by
extra-terrestrials. The same show also replaced the

original's fuzzy title shot of a UFO with a fuzzy shot of a flying paper plate. They looked uncannily similar.

This spoof notwithstanding, *The X-Files*' ultimate 'turn on' factor was its ability to articulate late twentieth-century fears and phobias. With its quasi-documentary feel (complete with computer date and place lines), it appeared to inform Us about the secret things that They, the government, wanted kept hidden. The end scene from the pilot lingered over the entire series: an unwholesome government official placing evidence of an alien visitation in a box, next to thousands of such evidence boxes, in a secure basement room in the Pentagon.

Crime and Mystery

The Avengers

UK 1961–9 161 × 50m bw/col ITV. An ABC Television Production. *US tx* 1966–9 seasons four to six only ABC. *cr* Sydney Newman, Leonard White. *exec pr* Albert Fennel (season 4), Julian Wintle (season 5), Gordon L T Scott (season 6). *pr* Leonard White, John Bryce (seasons 1–3), Albert Fennel, Brian Clemens (seasons 4–6). *dr* Don Leaver, Charles Crichton, Bill Bain (all seasons); Peter Hammond, Robert Tronson, Guy Verney, Richmond Harding, Jonathan Alwyn, Kim Mills, Raymond Menmuir (seasons 1–3); Roy Baker, Sidney Hayers, James Hill, Peter Graham Scott, Gerry O'Hara, Robert Day, Gordon Flemyng, John Krish, John Moxey, John Hough, Cyril Frankel, Ray Austin, Don Chaffey, Robert Fuest, Don Sharp (seasons 4–6). *wr* Brian Clemens, Malcolm Hulke and Terrance Dicks, John Lucarotti, Roger Marshall, Martin Woodhouse, Richard Harris, Dennis Spooner (all seasons); Terence Feely, Geoffrey Bellman and John Whitney, Fred Edge, Peter Ling and Sheila Ward, Berkley Mather, James Mitchell, John Kruse, Eric Paice, Jeremy Scott, Anthony Terpiloff, Geoffrey Orme, Reed de Rogsen (seasons 1–3); Philip Levene, Robert Banks Stewart, Tony Williamson, Michael Winder, Jeremy Burnham, Leigh Vance, Terry Nation, Dennis Spooner, Donald James, Dave Freeman (seasons 4–6). *mus* Johnny Dankworth (seasons 1–3), Laurie Johnson (seasons 4–6). *cast* **John Steed** Patrick Macnee **Dr David Keel** Ian Hendry **Catherine Gale** Honor Blackman **Venus Smith** Julie Stevens **Dr Martin King** Jon Rollason **Emma Peel** Diana Rigg **Tara King** Linda Thorson **One-Ten** Douglas Muir **Charles** Paul Whitsun Jones **Quilpie** Ronald Radd **Mother** Patrick Newell **Carol Wilson** Ingrid Hafner **One-Twelve** Arthur Hewlett.

The quintessential 'British' spy series. Known in France as *Chapeau Melon et Bottes de Cuir* (Bowler Hat and High Leather Boots) and in West Germany as *Mit Schirm, Charm und Melone* (With Umbrella, Charm and Bowler Hat), watched by tens of millions in seventy countries round the world, *The Avengers* was set in a picture-postcard Britain of castles, stately homes, old pubs and cricket greens. Wry and stylish it starred a sophisticated agent who out-Bonded James Bond, drove a vintage Bentley, enjoyed polo, archery and fencing and fought in a bowler hat with a furled umbrella.

The Avengers began life in 1961 when Dr David Keel (Ian Hendry), hero of the successful *Police Surgeon*, given a new vehicle, enlisted the help of secret agent John Steed to find his wife's murderers. Played to exquisite perfection by Old Etonian Patrick Macnee, Steed stole the show and when Hendry left after an Equity strike in 1962 he took over as the show's lead character.

To assist him he was given the first in a line of elegant but lethal female partners. Catherine Gale, played by Honor Blackman (Pussy Galore in the James Bond movie *Goldfinger*, 1964) was a widow, Doctor of Anthropology, judo expert and the original girl on a motorcycle (Blackman had trained as a motorbike despatch rider during the war). For her all-action role Gale wore a leather combat suit, high boots and a flick-up hairstyle

Lethal action-woman Emma Peel (Diana Rigg) dons the trademark bowler hat of partner John Steed (old Etonian Patrick Macnee) in the quintessentially British spy show *The Avengers*. Mrs Peel's outfits, designed by John Bates, were marketed at home and abroad as The Avengers Collection.

that, like her, never lost its composure however hot the situation. To complement Gale's outfit Steed became even more of a dandy with a penchant for braided Savile Row suits, embroidered waistcoats and handmade Chelsea boots.

In 1964 Blackman announced her departure and Steed acquired a new partner, Emma Peel (Diana Rigg). Once again Peel was a sleek, sexy all-action widow, this time with a preference for sixties mod fashion, a wicked karate chop and a love of adventure. Not the first choice for the part (actress Elizabeth Shepherd was signed up but dropped halfway through shooting episode one), Rigg's famous outfits were by designer John Bates and sold in shops throughout Britain and abroad as 'The Avengers Collection' – three dozen items plus relevant accessories. These included stretch jersey catsuits, hipster pants and exotic get-ups with flesh-revealing keyholes or suspenders. Dominant themes were the colours black and white and the pop-art target motif.

But Steed was soon to lose his second female accomplice. In 1968 after a row over wages Diana Rigg, who had come to the series from the Royal Shakespeare Company, left to concentrate on stage acting. In a plot-line worthy of any soap, her test pilot husband was promptly discovered alive in a Brazilian jungle, and Mrs Peel, no longer widowed, left the agency to join him. She was replaced by twenty-year-old Tara King (Linda Thorson), a single girl with no martial arts skills, though she could floor villains with a punch or a swipe from her handbag. But the Tara King/Steed relationship lacked the chemistry so evident with previous partners and Mother, Steed's portly wheelchair-bound controller (played by Patrick Newell) was introduced to fill the gap.

Indeed, after Peel left, one partner was never again enough for Steed. The show was cancelled in 1969 but its loss was so mourned around the world that offers of co-finance came from France and Canada, and *The New Avengers* came into being with episodes set in those countries. By then Macnee was fifty-four and far from lithe so the action was left to a new, younger pair, Gareth Hunt as Mike Gambit, an ex-army major who had served in the parachute regiment and the SAS, and Joanna Lumley (>*Absolutely Fabulous*, >*Sapphire and Steel*) as Purdy (named after the guns), an ex-ballerina with a much copied hairstyle, whose fighting style was high kicks – performed, unlike Steed's earlier partners, in skirts that allowed fetching glimpses of leg.

At its height – generally considered to be the filmed seasons starring Emma Peel (the Americans never saw Honor Blackman as Cathy Gale; the series was only sold to the States after it moved into colour) *The Avengers* had superb scripts, written by among others Dennis Spooner, Brian Clemens, Terence Feely and Terry Nation and stylish direction from Peter Hammond and Charles Crichton. A brief glance at the list of guest stars shows the series to have been a training ground for actors of pukka Englishmen (Peter Bowles, Paul Eddington), arch villains (Philip Madoc, Christopher Lee), comedians (John Cleese, Ronnie Barker), character actors (Warren Mitchell, Roy Kinnear), and cool female beauties with brains (Charlotte Rampling, Kate O'Mara). The series also sported famous tongue-in-cheek humour – cover agencies came with names such as PURRR (The Philanthropic Union for Rescue, Relief and Recuperation of Cats) or GONN (The Guild of Noble Nannies) – and similar exuberance was shown in episode titles such as Dennis Spooner's 'Look (Stop Me If You've Heard This One) But There Were These Two Fellers', guest starring John Cleese.

This escapist, fantasised espionage series was unique. Performed with consummate panache, the key to its success was a carefully created and maintained illusion: this was a Britain with no factories, no poverty, and no sex – the partners may have shared adventures featuring man-eating plants and steel robots but Steed still addressed his colleague as Mrs Gale. Brian Clemens, creator of >*The Professionals* and producer of the later seasons astutely laid down the following rules for the series: 'No woman should be killed, no extras should populate the streets. We admitted to only one class . . . and that was the upper. As a fantasy we would not show a uniformed policeman or a coloured man. And you would not see anything as common as blood in *The Avengers*.'

Certainly not, old boy.

Episode titles were as follows: Season one: 26 monochrome videotaped episodes starring Ian Hendry and Patrick Macnee: Hot Snow/Brought to Book/Square Root of Evil/Nightmare/Crescent Moon/Girl on the Trapeze/Diamond Cut Diamond/The Radioactive Man/ Ashes of Roses/ Hunt the Man Down/Please Don't Feed the Animals/Dance with Death (GC Geoffrey Palmer)/ One for the Mortuary/The Springers/The Frighteners/ The Yellow Needle/Death on the Slipway/Double Danger/Toy Trap/The Tunnel of Fear/The Far Distant Dead/Kill the King/Dead of Winter/The Deadly Air/A Change of Bait/Dragonsfield/Season two: 26 monochrome videotaped episodes starring Patrick Macnee, Honor Blackman, Julie Stevens and Jon Rollason: Mr Teddy Bear/Propellant 23 (GC Geoffrey Palmer)/The Decapod (GC Philip Madoc)/Bullseye/Mission to Montreal/The Removal Men/The Mauritius Penny/Death of a Great Dane/The Sell-Out/Death on the Rocks/ Traitor in Zebra (GC William Gaunt)/The Big Thinker/ Death Dispatch/Dead on Course/Intercrime/ Immortal Clay (GC Paul Eddington)/Box of Tricks/ Warlock/The Golden Eggs/School for Traitors/The White Dwarf/Man in the Mirror/Conspiracy of Silence/A Chorus of Frogs/Six Hands Across a Table/Killerwhale/Season three: 26 monochrome videotaped episodes starring Patrick Macnee and Honor Blackman: Brief for Murder/The Undertakers/The Man with Two Shadows (GC Geoffrey Palmer)/The Nutshell/Death of a Batman (GC Philip Madoc)/November Five/The Gilded Cage/Second Sight (GC Peter Bowles)/The Medicine Men/The Grandeur That Was Rome/The Golden Fleece (GC Warren Mitchell)/Don't Look Behind You/Death A La Carte/Dressed to Kill (GC Leonard Rossiter)/The White Elephant (GC Geoffrey Quigley, Judy Parfitt)/The Little Wonders/The Wringer/Mandrake (GC John Le Mesurier)/The Secrets Broker/The Trojan Horse/Build a Better Mousetrap/The Outside-in-Man/The Charmers (GC Warren Mitchell, Fenella Fielding)/Concerto/Esprit De Corps (GC John Thaw, Roy Kinnear)/Lobster Quadrille (GC Corin Redgrave)/Season four: 26 monochrome filmed episodes starring Patrick Macnee and Diana Rigg: The Town of No Return/The Gravediggers/The Cybernauts/Death at Bargain Prices/ Castle De'ath/The Masterminds/The Murder Market (GC Patrick Cargill)/A Surfeit of H_2O/The Hour That Never Was (GC Gerald Harper, Roy Kinnear)/Dial A Deadly Number/The Man-Eater of Surrey Green/Two's A Crowd (GC Warren Mitchell)/Too Many Christmas Trees/Silent Dust/Room Without A View/Small Game For Big Hunters/The Girl From Auntie (GC Bernard

Cribbins)/The 13th Hole/The Quick-Quick-Slow Death/The Danger Makers (GC Nigel Davenport)/A Touch of Brimstone (GC Peter Wyngarde)/What the Butler Saw (GC John Le Mesurier)/The House That Jack Built/A Sense of History (GC Patrick Mower)/How to Succeed At Murder/Honey For the Prince (GS Ron Moody)/Season five: 25 colour filmed episodes starring Patrick Macnee and Diana Rigg: From Venus With Love (GC Jon Pertwee)/The Fear Merchants (GC Patrick Cargill)/Escape in Time (GC Peter Bowles, Judy Parfitt)/The See-Through Man (GC Warren Mitchell, Roy Kinnear, Moira Lister)/The Bird Who Knew Too Much (GC Ron Moody)/The Winged Avenger/The Living Dead/The Hidden Tiger (GC Ronnie Barker)/The Correct Way to Kill/Never, Never Say Die (GC Christopher Lee)/Epic (GC Peter Wyngarde)/The Superlative Seven (GC Donald Sutherland, Charlotte Rampling)/A Funny Thing Happened on the Way to the Station/Something Nasty in the Nursery (GC Yootha Joyce, Geoffrey Sumner)/The Joker/Who's Who? (GC Freddie Jones)/The Return of the Cybernauts (GC Peter Cushing)/Death's Door/The £50,000 Breakfast/Dead Man's Treasure (GC Arthur Lowe)/You Have Just Been Murdered/The Positive-Negative Man (GC Ray McAnally)/ Murdersville/ Mission . . . Highly Improbable/The Forget-Me-Knot/ Season six: 32 colour episodes starring Patrick Macnee and Linda Thorson: Game/The Super-Secret Cypher Snatch/You'll Catch Your Death/Split (GC Nigel Davenport)/Whoever Shot Poor George Oblique Stroke XR40?/False Witness/All Done With Mirrors (GC Dinsdale Landen)Legacy of Death/Noon-Doomsday/ Look (Stop Me If You've Heard This One) But There Were These Two Fellers (GC John Cleese)/Have Guns . . . Will Haggle (GC Nicola Pagett)/They Keep Killing Steed (GC Ray McAnally, Ian Ogilvy)/The Interrogators (GC Christopher Lee, David Sumner)/The Rotters (GC Gerald Sim)/Invasion of the Earthmen/Killer/The Morning After (GC Joss Ackland, Brian Blessed)/The Curious Case of the Countless Clues/Wish You Were Here (GC Robert Urquhart)/Stay Tuned (GC Kate O'Mara)/Take Me To Your Leader (GC Michael Robbins)/Fog/Homicide and Old Lace (GC Joyce Carey, Gerald Harper)/Love All/Get-a-Way (GC Peter Bowles)/Thingumajig (GC Iain Cuthbertson)/Pandora (GC Peter Madden)/Requiem/ Take-Over/Who Was That Man I Saw You With?/My Wildest Dream (GC Edward Fox)/Bizarre (GC Fulton Mackay, Roy Kinnear).

Banacek

USA 1972–4 16 × 90m col NBC. A Universal Television Production. *UK tx* 1975–7 ITV. *cr* Richard Levinson, William Link. *exec pr* George Eckstein. *pr* Howie Horowitz. *dr* Lou Antonio, Herschel Daugherty, Daryl Duke, Theodore J Flicker, Richard T Heffron, Bernard L Kowalski, George McCowan, Bernard McEveety, Andrew McLaglen, Jimmy Sangster, Jack Smith. *wr* Mort Fine, Theodore J Flicker, Stephen Kandel, Richard Levinson, William Link, Harold Livingston, Stephen Lord, David Moessinger, Paul Playdon, Robert Presnell Jr, Del Reisman, Stanley Roberts, Stanley Ralph Ross, Jimmy Sangster, Lee Stanley, George Sheldon Smith, Jack Turley, Robert Van Scoyk. *mus* Billy Goldenburg. *cast* **Thomas Banacek** George Peppard **Jay Drury** Ralph Manza **Felix Mulholland** Murray Matheson **Carlie Kirkland** Christine Belford **Penniman** Linden Chiles.

Shrewd Polish-American investigator Thomas Banacek's was a lucrative line of work: he recovered stolen goods for the Boston Insurance Company, collected ten per cent commission on the goods tracked down, and he never went after anything cheap. Not that he needed the money. He rode around in a chauffeur-driven limo and lived in the exclusive Beacon Hill section of Boston. He had impeccable taste in clothes, food, art and women and he was a connoisseur of difficult cases: an aeroplane that disappeared, and a missing three-ton statue.

Mostly a solo operator, Banacek did get occasional help from native New Yorker Jay Drury who drove his car and from his up-market bookshop proprietor friend Felix Mulholland. At the end of each episode it was the mystified viewer's turn for help as Banacek revealed how he cracked the case. Other series regulars were rival investigators Penniman and, from the second season, Carlie Kirkland, who fell for his charms.

The show's gimmick was ethnic. Polish proverbs were sprinkled through the shows and Banacek's cool, successful character, who was able to make it in the States without abandoning his roots, won the series an award from the Polish-American Congress for positive portrayal of Polish-Americans.

Banacek (played by George Peppard, later to lead >*The A-Team* as John 'Hannibal' Smith) was one of the rotating elements of NBC's *The Wednesday Mystery Movies*. It was introduced by a ninety-minute made-for-TV movie, then moved into the slot when previous occupants >*Columbo*, >*McCloud* and >*McMillan and Wife* were shifted to Sunday. *Banacek's* creators, producer-writer team Levinson and Link, were also the power behind TV successes including *Mannix*, >*Columbo*, *Ellery Queen* and >*Tenafly*.

Baretta

USA 1975–8 80 × 60m col ABC. Roy Huggins/Public Arts Productions, in association with Universal Television. *UK tx* 1978–9 ITV. *cr* Stephen J Cannell. *exec pr* Bernard L Kowalski, Anthony Spinner. *pr* Charles E Dismukes, Alan Godfrey, Robert Harris, Howie Horowitz, Robert Lewis, Jo Swerling Jnr, Ed Waters. *dr* Reza S Badiyi, Robert Blake, Burt Brinkerhoff, Robert Douglass, Charles S Dubin, Douglas Heyes, Bruce Kessler, Bernard L Kowalski, Russ Mayberry, Don Medford, Sutton Roley, Charles Rondeau, Michael Schultz, Vincent Sherman, Jeannot Szwarc, Don Weis. *wr* Nick Alexander, Richard Bluel, Michael Butler, Stephen J Cannell, Paul Casey, Robert Crais, Don Carlos Dunaway, Sidney Ellis, Rift Fournier, Alan Godfrey, John Thomas James (Roy Huggins), Edward J Lakso, Alan J Levitt, Norman Liebman. *mus* Dave Grusin, Tom Scott; theme, 'Keep Your Eye on the Sparrow' sung by Sammy Davis Jnr. *cast* **Detective Tony Baretta** Robert Blake **Lt Hal Brubaker** Edward Grover **Rooster** Michael D Roberts **Inspector Schiller** Dana Elcar **Billy Truman** Tom Ewell **Fats** Chino Williams.

Cop Tony Baretta was streetwise and single with a low-down lifestyle. The orphaned son of poor Italian immigrants, he slept in a run-down old hotel, The King Edward, lived for his job and was known for his trademark outfit of T-shirt, jeans and a cap pulled down over his forehead. He worked alone out of Los Angeles 53rd Precinct, paid scant attention to his boss and undercover work was easy – his rough look and Mob-style accent blended naturally with pimps, gangs or gangsters.

Baretta started life as *Toma* in 1973, a series starring Tony Musante and based on the adventures of a real-life cop who used his wits and imaginative disguises. But Musante left after one season, leaving a show with reasonable ratings and nowhere to go. It was revived in 1975 with ex-child star Robert Blake as Baretta, faring badly at first despite the name change in *Toma's* old slot. Then its slot was changed from Friday to Wednesday night, ratings soared and *Baretta* demolished >*Cannon* over on rival network CBS to become an ABC mainstay – as well as earning Blake an Emmy for Best Actor.

This was a hard, action series, despite Blake's public protestations that he was opposed to violence on TV. But it was also a show with humour, in common with its predecessor >*Columbo*, with comedy supplied by Tony's fast-talking pimp informant friend Rooster and by Fred, Tony's cockatoo with whom the hero held rambling one-sided conversations. Blake's real-life wife Sondra Blake – as well as having a hand in creating the Baretta character background – was an occasional guest star. Other characters included crabby Inspector Schiller, Baretta's original boss, later succeeded by Lt Brubaker and Billy Truman, a retired cop who combined the job of manager and house detective at The King Edward Hotel.

Producer/writer Stephen Cannell – one of TV's top hit-makers in the eighties – specialised in action adventure. He polished his reputation on >*The Rockford Files*, created and produced *Tenspeed and Brownshoe* and *The Greatest American Hero* for ABC and won an exclusive agreement with the network to produce one series a year, among them *Hunter*, *Wiseguy* and *21 Jump Street*.

Robert Blake (real name Michael Gubatosi) had mostly played Indians until he hit fame with *Baretta*. He failed to go on to much greater things, but did star in NBC's *Hell Town* (1985–6) as Father Noah 'Hardstep' Rivers, an ex-con turned Catholic priest and guardian angel in a tough East Los Angeles neighbourhood.

The Baron

UK 1966–7 30 × 50m col ITC. An ITC Production. *US tx* 1966 ABC, syndicated. *cr* Robert Baker, Monty Berman. *pr* Monty

Berman. *dr* Leslie Norman, John Moxey, Cyril Frankel, Jeremy Summers, Roy Baker, Gordon Flemyng, Robert Asher, Don Chaffey, Quentin Lawrence, Robert Tronson. *wr* Dennis Spooner, Terry Nation, Michael Cramoy, Brian Degas, Tony O'Grady (aka Brian Clemens), Harry H Junkin. *mus* Edwin Astley. *cast* **John Mannering, The Baron** Steve Forrest **Cordelia** Sue Lloyd **Templeton Green** Colin Gordon **David Marlowe** Paul Ferris.

The origins of John Mannering, aka *The Baron*, lay in the novels of John Creasey, wherein the handsome, Jensen-driving and firmly British hero, owner of fine antique shops in London, Paris and Washington, had reformed from his one-time profession of gentleman jewel thief into unofficial Scotland Yard aide. That was the book. But at the behest of ATV boss Lew Grade and his push for American success, Mannering's television embodiment was as a Texan-born ranch owner based in London whose nickname, far from having aristocratic connections, was acquired from the Baron-brand cattle he reared back home. Steve Forrest (later to star as Lt Dan 'Hondo' Harrelson in ABC's crime series *S.W.A.T.*, 1975–7) was enlisted to help play this transatlantic hero.

For The Baron, examining priceless *objets d'art* for his exclusive clientele played second place to the pursuit of dangerous missions around the world – now on behalf of British Intelligence. His British contact was John Templeton-Green, to whom beautiful secret agent Cordelia Winfield of the Special Branch Diplomatic Service also reported – unsurprisingly, Cordelia was soon drafted in as The Baron's full-time assistant.

Plots usually involved priceless antiques and jewels – a series of large-scale art robberies behind the Iron Curtain in 'Diplomatic Immunity', a plan to steal the Crown Jewels in 'Masquerade', a curse on a valuable cameo in 'Time to Kill', Nazi art treasures on the British antiques market in 'A Memory of Evil' – although trusty plot favourites such as dope-smuggling rackets, imposters and the Mafia also played their part.

The creative team behind *The Baron* was a star-studded list of the greats of British TV: creator/producers Robert Baker and Monty Berman were behind most of ATV's filmed adventure series such as >*The Saint* and >*The Persuaders*; script editor for the series was Terry Nation (>*The Saint*, >*Dr Who*, >*Blake's 7*); and writers included Dennis Spooner and Brian Clemens (>*The Avengers*, >*The Persuaders*). Filmed at Elstree Studios and on location, this was a high-gloss action series with enjoyably implausible plots, extended in Britain beyond its intended run of twenty-six to thirty episodes. For all Lew Grade's ambitions, though, the series was pulled early in the USA.

Guest stars in the series included Peter Wyngarde, Sylvia Sims, Philip Madoc, Peter Bowles and Robert Hardy.

Cagney and Lacey

USA 1982–8 125 × 60m col CBS. A Mace Neufeld/Barney Rosenzweig Production/Orion. *UK tx* 1982–8 BBC1. *cr* Barney Rosenzweig, Barbara Corday, Barbara Avedon. *exec pr* Barney Rosenzweig. *pr* Steve Brown, Terry Louise Fisher, Peter Lefcourt, Liz Coe, Ralph S Singleton, Patricia Green, P K Knelman, Georgia Jeffries, Jonathan Estrin, Shelley List. *dr* Various, including Arthur Karen, Georg Stanford Brown, Bill Dukes, Jackie Cooper, Michael Vijar. *wr* Various, including Patricia M Green, Terry Louise Fisher, Alison Hock, Larry Kenner, Ronie Wenker-Konner. *mus* Bill Conti (theme), Ron Ramin. *cast* **Det Mary Beth Lacey** Tyne Daly **Det Christine Cagney** Meg Foster (season one), Sharon Gless **Harvey Lacey** John Karlen **Lt Samuels** Al Waxman **Det Petrie** Carl Lumbly **Det Isbecki** Martin Kove **Det LaGuardia** Sidney Clute **Det Esposito** Robert Hegyes **Sgt Dory McKenna** Barry Primus **Harvey Lacey Jr** Tony La Torre **Michael Lacey** Troy Slaten **Desk Sergeant Coleman** Harvey Atkin **Charlie Cagney** Dick O'Neill.

The long-awaited female buddy show. US TV had fielded a (sexy) lone female >*Police Woman* and a team of three pin-up detectives working for a male boss (>*Charlie's Angels*), but here were two women characters with a strong bond, flat shoes and sensible hairdos, pulling their weight as detectives. *Cagney and Lacey* ran for six Emmy-studded years, winning audiences and plaudits rounds the world – but it took nearly a decade to make it happen.

The series was conceived way back in 1974 by producer Barney Rosenzweig, his then-wife Barbara

Corday and co-creator Barbara Avedon. Corday, a writer for American daytime soaps such as *The Days of our Lives*, wanted to score a first with a series starring two equal women in partnership. The fact that *Cagney and Lacey* were police officers was just a way to get the concept on television.

All three networks turned *Cagney and Lacey* down as a series and it was not until October 1981 that CBS aired it as a made-for-TV movie starring Tyne Daly and Loretta Swit. Huge audience response led to a short-run series which, because Swit was still playing Major 'Hotlips' Houlihan in >*M*A*S*H*, starred Meg Foster in her part. Subsequent poor ratings for the mini-series, a CBS executive explained, were because the American public 'perceived them as dykes'. Enter beautiful blonde Sharon Gless to set the record straight and get gay groups protesting. Still the ratings were low, and the series was cancelled after the 1982–3 season. But not for long – loyal viewers inundated CBS with letters and that September the series won its first Emmy. In 1984 *Cagney and Lacey* were back to stay and *TV Guide* proclaimed: 'You Want Them! You've Got Them!'

What they got was a tough, human series that dealt head-on with difficult issues. At its centre was a real relationship – hard times, arguments and all – between two believable women. They were different – Christine Cagney was ambitious, single and hard-headed at work, Mary Beth Lacey wore her heart on her sleeve and had a husband and kids to go home to – but they were united by the .38s they carried on duty, an ability to drive like saloon car racers and a total commitment to putting villains behind bars by any means just within the law.

Not all of their cases worked out. Like >*Hill Street Blues* and other 'reality' shows, *Cagney and Lacey* reflected the rough world of the big city cop. The two women made mistakes, made wrong judgements, and let feelings get in the way. And the place they discussed all this was the ladies' room.

Storylines could be overtly political – Mary Beth was arrested off-duty for demonstrating against nuclear waste transportation in 'Special Treatment' – or straight cops and robbers – Mary Beth was gunned down on a dirty tenement roof by a teenage robbery suspect in 'Happiness is a Warm Gun'. As the series went on, however, the women's personal lives became more

The first female buddy cop show, *Cagney and Lacey*, featured Sharon Gless (right) and Tyne Daly as New York's finest. Initially a ratings disaster only kept alive by fan pressure (adverts in the *TV Guide* declared, 'You want them! You've got them!'), the show went on to run for six Emmy-studded years.

prominent. Chris' life as a single woman became a means of exploring difficult issues – she struggled with alcoholism and at one point she was the victim of date rape.

Series regulars at work included tough-but-caring boss Lieutenant Samuels, earnest Det Mark Petrie and womanising Det Victor Isbecki. At home Mary Beth's supportive husband Harvey, sons Harvey Jr and Michael, and later daughter Alice, were mainstays.

Both Gless and Daly had done service in a number of TV series before winning lead roles in *Cagney and Lacey*. Gless played secretary to the PI in the ex-cop-and-ex-con series *Switch* (CBS 1975–8) starring Robert Wagner, and had roles in *Clinic on 18th Street*, *Faraday and Company*, *House Calls*, >*Marcus Welby M.D.*, >*McCloud*, *Palms Precinct*, and *Turnabout*. Daly's past work included the role of Jenny Lochner, wife of Dr Paul Lochner, hero of CBS's long-running series *Medical Center* (1969–76).

Producer Barney Rosenzweig went on to produce *The Trials of Rosie O'Neill* (1990–) for CBS, also starring Sharon Gless, whom he later married.

Cagney and Lacey won the following Emmy awards: Outstanding Drama Series: 1985, 1986; Outstanding Lead Actress: Tyne Daly 1983, 1984, 1985, 1988; Sharon Gless 1986, 1987; Outstanding Directing in a Drama Series (single episode): Arthur Karen, 'Heat' 1985, Georg Stanford Brown, 'Parting Shots' 1986; Outstanding Writing for a Drama Series (single episode): Patricia M Green, 'Who Said It's Fair – Part II' 1986; Outstanding Supporting Actor: John Karlen 1986.

Callan

UK 1967–72 21 × 60m bw/22 × 60m col ITV. ABC Network Production/Thames Television Network Production. *cr* James Mitchell. *exec pr* Lloyd Shirley (season one). *ass pr* Terence Feely (season one), John Kershaw (season two). *pr* Reginald Colin. *dr* Bill Bain, Toby Robertson, Peter Duguid, Robert Tronson, Guy Verney, Piers Haggard, Mike Vardy, Peter Sasdy, James Goddard, Reginald Collin, Voytek, Jonathan Alwyn, Shaun O'Riordan. *wr* James Mitchell, Robert Banks Stewart, Ray Jenkins, Hugh D'Allenger,

Trevor Preston, William Emms, Michael Winder, Bill Craig, Peter Hill, George Markstein. *mus* Jack Trombey (seasons three and four). *cast* **Callan** Edward Woodward **Lonely** Russell Hunter **Hunter MK1** Ronald Radd **Hunter Mk 2** Michael Goodliffe **Hunter Mk 3** Derek Bond **Hunter Mk 4** William Squire **Hunter MK 5 (Wet Job)** Hugh Walters **Meres (TV Play)** Peter Bowles **Meres Mk 2** Anthony Valentine **Cross** Patrick Mower **Hunter's secretary** Lisa Langdon.

David Callan, cold-blooded secret service agent, worked for British Secret Intelligence. The section's top hitman, his brief was to ensure the enemies' silence – by whatever means necessary. Played by the tough and intransigent Edward Woodward, Callan was a far cry from the glamorous tongue-in-cheek James Bond. His was a violent, bleak world where if you didn't kill first they killed you. Callan was an outsider – isolated, often in direct conflict with his superior Hunter, a codename given to all Heads of Section. Doubly on the run, Callan had more in common with close contemporary Patrick McGoohan's Prisoner than with the insider Bond. These were late sixties, anti-Establishment days.

Viewers first met secret agent Callan in a one-off Armchair Theatre play *A Magnum for Schneider*, in which the disgraced former top agent was given an opportunity to redeem himself with one more liquidation. So successful was his hitman that author James Mitchell was asked to write a series. In future episodes Callan was pitted against a former mentor turned mercenary (Michael Robbins from >*On the Buses*) in 'Goodbye Nobby Clarke'; against an oriental villain in 'The Death of Robert Lee'; against the enemy behind the Iron Curtain in 'Heir Apparent'; against a neo-fascist party in 'The Running Dog'; against the KGB in 'Death of a Hunter'; and against every hazardous location that could be dreamed up, from Canadian atomic power stations to deep-sunken ships.

Callan made stars of its two central performers, Woodward as the disaffected agent and Russell Hunter, who played snivelling, smelly petty thief Lonely, the spy's accomplice. Other notable characters were Meres and, from the third season, Cross, Callan's fellow agents and rivals. Woodward and Hunter reprised their roles in the feature film *Callan* (1973) and the one-off television drama *Wet Job* (1981) and Woodward made good use of his TV past as ex-secret agent Robert McCall aka *The Equaliser* in CBS's 1985–9 New York-based detective series.

James Mitchell went on to write the BBC's acclaimed *When the Boat Comes In* (1975), set in the North-east of England during the Depression.

Cannon

USA 1971–6 120 × 60m col CBS. A Quinn Martin Production. *UK tx* 1972–8 BBC1. *cr* Quinn Martin. *exec pr* Quinn Martin. *pr* Alan A Armer, Harold Gast, Anthony Spinner. *dr* Various, including Corey Allen, John Badham, Michael Caffey, Hershel Daugherty, Richard Donner, Alf Kjellin, George McGowan, Don Medford, Michael O'Herlihy, Virgil Vogel. *wr* Various, including George Bellak, Harold Gast, Edward Hume, Stephen Kandel, Robert W Lenski, Worley Thorne. *mus* John Parker, John Cannon. *cast* **Frank Cannon** William Conrad.

An archetypal early seventies private eye drama, down to the one-word title and the disadvantaged hero. (In shameless exploitation of the social liberation movements of the day the US small screen came up with a wave of minority PIs with tough names, viz. the Polish-American >*Banacek*, the black >*Shaft*, and the paraplegic *Ironside*). Frank Cannon's handicap was that he was plain obese, weighing in at nineteen stones. In *Cannon* episodes the villain would inevitably run, leaving the balding, moustachioed Los Angeles PI wheezing gamely far behind. Handicapped by his considerable morphology, Cannon relied on smarts to solve his cases. His fees were at the top end of the scale, his interest in justice tempered by his need for money to pay for gourmet cooking and the upkeep on his luxury Lincoln Continental. The mysteries themselves were often a slow plod, but Cannon was a genuine TV PI creation.

The part was specifically created for William Conrad by Quinn 'The Fugitive' Martin. Conrad had first come to prominence as the voice of Matt Dillon in the radio version of >*Gunsmoke* in the mid fifties, but had not been chosen to play the role on screen; in his own words

he had been 'too fat and unattractive'. Before *Cannon*, most of Conrad's TV work had been as a director and producer of shows such as >*Gunsmoke*, >*Naked City*, >*77 Sunset Strip*. After *Cannon*, most of his TV work was acting as . . . a fat detective. In 1981 he played Rex Stout's *Nero Wolfe*. More recently he was the co-star of *Jake and the Fatman*.

The series *Cannon* was first developed as 100–minute CBS TV movies, aired in 1970. It had a close relationship with another Quinn Martin detective show, *Barnaby Jones* (1973–80, 176 × 60m col), and Cannon occasionally appeared in *Barnaby Jones* episodes. The latter show featured Buddy Ebsen (>*The Beverly Hillbillies*) as the eponymous gun-toting oldster and master criminologist PI, retaking over the family firm on the murder of his son. He was assisted by his daughter-in-law Betty, played by Lee Meriwether (>*The Time Tunnel*).

C.A.T.S. Eyes

UK 1985–7 1 × 90m/30 × 60m col ITV. A TVS Network Production. *cr* Terence Feely. *pr* Dickie Bamber, Frank Cox (season one), Raymond Menmuir (seasons two and three). *dr* William Brayne, James Hill, Ian Toynton, Robert Fuest, Tom Clegg, Dennis Abbey, Ian Sharp, Raymond Menmuir, Carol Wiseman, Anthony Simmons, Terry Marcel, Edward Bennett, Gerry Mill, J B Wood, Alan Bell, Claude Whatham, Francis Megahy. *wr* Terence Feely, Ray Jenkins, Martin Worth, Don Houghton, Ben Steed, Anthony Skene, Ray Jenkins, Jeremy Burnham, Paul Wheeler, Gerry O'Hara, Barry Appleton, Reg Ford, Jenny McDade, Andy De La Tour, Francis Megahy. *mus* John Kongos (season one), Barbara Thompson (seasons two and three). *cast* **Pru Standfast** Rosalyn Landor **Maggie Forbes** Jill Gascoine **Fred Smith** Leslie Ash **Nigel Beaumont** Don Warrington **Tessa Robinson** Tracy-Louise Ward.

>*Charlie's Angels'* all-women action team was a runaway success on TV screens from 1977–82, but it was not until 1985 that ITV chiefs realised that a similar formula was missing from home-grown product. Enter the stiff-upper-lipped British version, *C.A.T.S Eyes*: three gun-toting

action women with a suitable history and sufficiently sensible hairstyles for native taste.

The trio worked for the Eyes Enquiry Agency – on the surface a run-of-the-mill investigation outfit, but actually a cover for the top-secret Home Office security squad known as C.A.T.S. (Covert Activities Thames Section). Leader of the three was Pru Standfast, a tall Oxford University graduate (and ex-student union president) with a War Office background. Also on board was Maggie Forbes, played by Jill Gascoine. Widowed ex-detective Forbes – with eighteen years' police experience under her belt, five of them in CID – had been Britain's first policewoman star in her own ITV series *The Gentle Touch* (1980–4). As well as her all-action job, as loyal viewers knew, Forbes had plenty of problems at home bringing up a teenage son single-handedly. The third member of the team, and the youngest, was Frederica 'Fred' Smith. Her dual talents were driving at breakneck speed and a precocious flair for computers which had attracted attention in the Civil Service. Helping the women with their investigations was 'man from the ministry' Nigel Beaumont, their link to those in command.

The series was set up by a ninety-minute pilot *Goodbye Jenny Wren*, written by creator Terence Feely, in which Maggie Forbes joins the team on the day Jenny Cartwright, another team member is killed. From then on jewels, foreign scoundrels, the Mafia and Triads routinely supplied the cases, with specifically female interest supplied by a marriage racket using Asian girls, a woman terrorist, and the need for Tessa (who replaced Pru in season two), to go undercover as a club barmaid while Maggie took the spotlight and sang the blues.

C.A.T.S. Eyes' ratings never compared with glitzy precursor the *Angels*, although season one was quality fare with high-calibre writers, directors and theme music (composed by John Kongos). From season two on, however, there were major changes both in front of the camera (Maggie Forbes was promoted to leader and Pru Standfast was replaced by Tessa Robinson) and behind. Producers relied on an inferior creative team (and even a different theme tune), and the compromise was all too apparent on screen.

Charlie's Angels

USA 1976–81 109 × 60m col ABC. A Twentieth Century Fox Production. *UK tx* 1977–82 ITV. *exec pr* Aaron Spelling, Leonard Goldberg. *pr* Rick Huskey, David Levinson, Edward J Lasko, Barney Rosenzweig. *dr* Various, including Richard Benedict, Don Chaffey, Phil Bondelli, John Moxey, Bernard McEveety, Bill Bixby. *wr* Various, including John D F Black, David Levinson, Rick Huskey, Lee Sheldon. *mus* Jack Elliott, Allyn Ferguson, Henry Mancini (theme). *cast* **Sabrina Duncan** Kate Jackson **Jill Munroe** Farrah Fawcett-Majors **Kelly Garrett** Jaclyn Smith **Kris Munroe** Cheryl Ladd **Tiffany Welles** Shelley Hack **Julie Rogers** Tanya Roberts **John Bosley** David Doyle **Charlie Townsend** John Forsythe (voice only).

'Once upon a time there were three girls who went to the police academy and they were each assigned very hazardous duties, but I took them away from all that and now they work for me. My name is Charlie.' Charlie was Charlie Townsend, wealthy head of Townsend Investigations who was heard but never seen (his voice was lent to the series by John Forsythe, who later played Blake Carrington in >*Dynasty*) in a show that was blatant in its appeal – glamour and girls. The three Angels who received instructions from the invisible, all-knowing boss on high may have been action women but their main function on our screens was to titillate – an Angel for every male taste – and no star landed a part unless her image was as flawless and glossy as Farrah Fawcett's teeth. Costume was the all-important department in this production, and executive producer Aaron Spelling (>*Dynasty*, >*The Colbys*, >*Beverly Hills 90210*) made no secret of the fact that he was 'more concerned with hairdos and gowns than the twists and turns of the plot'. Henry Mancini's theme music was also appropriately lavish, and was a hit single in 1977. The plots, for what they were worth, always revolved around an assignment relayed by phone from boss Charlie. Charlie's assistant John Bosley meanwhile was on hand to keep an eye on the girls, the costs and other less glamorous details.

Sabrina Duncan (Kate Jackson) was the cool, multi-lingual leader, Jill Munroe (Farrah Fawcett-Majors, later

'More concerned with hairdos and gowns than twists and turns of the plot', producer Aaron Spelling selected a woman for every male taste in his female private eye show *Charlie's Angels*, starring Farrah Fawcett-Majors, Kate Jackson and Jaclyn Smith. The gumshoettes' boss Charlie Townsend, who was heard but never seen, was voiced by John Forsythe, who later played Blake Carrington in Spelling's oily melodrama *Dynasty*.

to drop the Majors after her divorce from Lee Majors, star of the >*Six Million Dollar Man*) was the athletic type and Kelly Garrett (Jaclyn Smith) the former show-girl who had 'been around'. They usually worked as an undercover team, each taking a different role to suit a situation: when they were looking into the death of a roller-derby queen, Sabrina posed as an insurance investigator, Kelly as a magazine writer and Jill as a derby competitor. More often than not, though, cases involved health spas or Las Vegas nightclubs where the girls would be required to pose as strippers or nightclub singers, or don shorts or bikinis.

Farrah Fawcett-Majors was the last of the Angels to be cast (the show required a blonde) and when the series began was less well known than the lead, Kate Jackson. However, Farrah and her flowing hair, flashing smile and

fabulous limbs became an overnight sensation, which soon led to the marketing of Farrah Fawcett-Majors dolls, T-shirts and other gimmicks. She left after a year to pursue a career in film.

Thereafter the introduction of a new Angel became an almost annual occurrence. First Farrah was replaced by Cheryl Ladd, playing her spunky younger sister Kris Munroe (1977). Two years later Sabrina left and was replaced by Tiffany Welles (Shelley Hack) daughter of a Connecticut police chief. A year after that Tiffany was out and replaced by street-wise Julie Rogers (Tanya Roberts). When the series ended in 1981 Jaclyn Smith was the only survivor from the original cast.

Seven years later, in 1988, an attempt was made to revive the formula and *Angels 88* was launched, this time with a team of four girls, chosen from 2,000 applicants desperate to land the parts. It fell to earth with a thud.

CHiPS

USA 1977–83 138 × 60m col NBC. Rosner TV/An MGM Television Production. *UK tx* 1979–87 ITV. *cr* Rick Rosner. *exec pr* Cy Cermak *pr* Rick Rosner, Ric Rondell. *dr* Various, including Michael Caffey, Don Weis, Gordon Hessler, Nicholas Colasanto, Barry Crane, Paul Krasny, Christian Nyby II, Don Chaffey, Larry Wilcox, John Florea. *wr* Various, including Jim Carlson, Marshall Herskowitz, Stephen Kandel, Ivan Nagy, Mort Thaw, James Schmerer, Jerry Thomas. *mus* Mike Post, Pete Carpenter, John Parker (theme). *cast* **Officer Jon Baker** Larry Wilcox **Officer Frank 'Ponch' Poncherello** Erik Estrada **Sgt Joe Getraer** Robert Pine **Officer Sindy Cahill** Brianne Leary **Harlan** Lou Wagner **Officer Bonnie Clark** Randi Oakes **Officer Bobby 'Hot Dog' Nelson** Tom Reilly **Officer Turner** Michael Dorn **Officer Grossman** Paul Linke.

The freeways and byways of Los Angeles provided the beat for Officers Jon Baker and Frank 'Ponch' Poncherello, a pair of clean-cut, good-looking cops who rode motorcycle for the California Highway Patrol (CHiPS). Jon Baker was pure country, 'Ponch' a barrio kid good old Jon boy had persuaded to join the force. The body-count was low (indeed, zero) for a cop series, but there were plenty of high-speed chases of hot rodders, hijackers and Hell's Angels, with an enormous death rate amongst automobiles. Off duty and on, the guys kept their teeth white and their eyes peeled for 'foxy ladies'.

Complex CHiPS was not. The stars were Erik Estrada, a Spanish-American actor who came to prominence in the do-gooder film *The Cross and the Switchblade* (1970), and blond Vietnam veteran and professional cowboy, Larry Wilcox (also >*The Adventures of Lassie*). In 1981 Bruce Jenner, ex-Olympic decathlete, rode with Wilcox (as Officer McCleish) while Estrada was involved with the production company in a salary dispute. During the last season Wilcox left the show after refusing to work with Estrada any longer, and was replaced by Tom Reilly. Other actors who came and went were Randi Oakes, as glamorous 'Chippie' Bonnie Clark, and Robert Pine, who played the cop duo's long-suffering superior, Sergeant Getraer. Michael Dorn, later Worf in >*Star Trek: The Next Generation*, played Officer Turner.

The series was a top-rated hit in both the USA and UK, and Estrada and Wilcox became pin-ups on countless teen bedroom walls. At the show's peak, Estrada alone received 3,000 fan letters a week.

In 1992 Estrada and Wilcox revealed an unforeseen sense of irony when they obliged with a CHiPS guest spot in the spoof police film, *National Lampoon's Loaded Weapon 1*.

Columbo

USA 1971–7, 1989–90, 27 × 90m/36 × 20m col NBC. Universal Television. *UK tx* 1972–9 ITV. *cr* Richard Levinson, William Link. *exec pr* Richard Levinson, William Link, Roland Kibbee, Dean Hargrove, Richard Alan Simmons. *pr* Douglas Benton, Everett Chambers, Dean Hargrove, Richard Alan Simmons, Edward K Dodds, Roland Kibbee, Robert F O'Neill. *dr* Various, including Hy Averback, Robert Butler, Jonathan Demme, Peter Falk, Bernard L Kowalski, Patrick McGoohan, Leo Penn, Steven Spielberg, Jeannot Szwarc, Sam Wanamaker, Edward M Abroms, Robert Douglas, Alf Kjellin. *wr* Various, including Myrna Bercovici, Robert Bless, Steven Bochco, Steven J Cannell, Larry Cohen, Dean Hargrove, Roland Kibbee, Richard Levinson, William Link,

Barney Slater, Robert Malcolm Young. *cast* **Lt Columbo** Peter Falk.

The shambolic Lt Columbo, everybody's folk hero, drove a beaten-up old Peugeot, wore a shabby, rumpled raincoat (he was once told he looked like an unmade bed) and went about his work with an air of naive puzzlement which threw the upper-class killers against whom he pitted his wits off guard. One of the many pleasures of this series was watching the idiosyncratic commoner detective getting the better of members of society's élite. 'Look, I don't mean any offence,' he would explain, 'I'm just trying to tie up loose ends' – and wealthy art collectors, powerful politicians and talented poets would fall prey to his indefatigable desire to find out the truth.

Unusually for a detective show, *Columbo* was not a whodunnit, but a howdunnit: the viewer knew the identity of the killer, and was witness at the beginning of each episode to the planning and execution of what would have been the 'perfect' murder. Thereafter the satisfaction was watching the Lieutenant meticulously put each piece of the puzzle into place, 'Just one more thing,' he would say, then snare his quarry. Even the villains had to applaud his methods.

Starring the charismatic Peter Falk, *Columbo* was the most popular segment of NBC's *Mystery Movie* package which also featured >*McMillan and Wife* and >*McCloud*. Created by Richard Levinson and William Link (>*Mannix*, *Ellery Queen*, >*Tenafly* and *Murder She Wrote*), the character was modelled on Petrovitch, the detective in Dostoevski's *Crime and Punishment*. It was only Falk's reluctance that prevented this multiple award-winning show (the series won eight Emmy's, four for Falk as lead actor) running as a series in its own right; the original run ended in late 1977 on NBC, after which only the occasional new episode was filmed. In 1989, more than a decade later, Falk returned with some new films for ABC's *Mystery Wheel* and then came back periodically in the form of TV movies.

Loath to lose the ratings of the series when its original run ended, NBC decided to invoke the oft mentioned but never seen wife of the detective for a spin-off. They first cashed in on the well-loved name with *Mrs Columbo*, running February to June 1979 and dealing with the life of pretty Kate Columbo (Kate Mulgrew, later >*Star Trek:*

Voyager), journalist for the *Weekly Advertiser* in San Fernando, California. Next they tried to sever the links and ran *Kate Loves a Mystery* which took up the story after Kate's divorce from the Lieutenant, when Kate resumed her maiden name Callahan and moved on to a job as reporter for the *Valley Advocate* in San Fernando. This series lasted from October to December 1979, after which Columbo's missus was laid to rest. The lead role, Peter Falk (actually the producers' second choice for *Columbo* – the first actor approached was Bing Crosby), began as a stage actor, starting out in TV in programmes such as *Studio One* (1957) and *The Dick Powell Show* (1962) or playing gangster roles in such shows as >*The Untouchables* and >*Naked City*. The charm, wisdom and naivety of his screen persona *Columbo* however later led to a major part as an angel-made-mortal in Wim Wenders 1987 feature film *Wings of Desire*.

Columbo's reputation pulled in guest stars of considerable calibre – Patrick McGoohan won two Emmys for his guest appearances as well as directing an episode of the series and Donald Pleasance cropped up as guest star in both *Columbo* and ill-fated spin-off *Mrs Columbo*. *Columbo* also boasted a star-studded list of directors which included Peter Falk himself, Steven Spielberg, Sam Wanamaker and Jonathan Demme, while writers included Steven 'Hill Street Blues' Bochco and Larry Cohen, creator of >*The Invaders* and >*Branded*.

Crime Story

USA 1986–8 48 × 60m col NBC. *UK tx* 1989 ITV. *cr* Chuck Adamson, Gustave Reininger. *pr* Michael Mann. *dr* Various, including Michael Mann. *wr* Various. *mus* Del Shannon (theme). *cast* **Lt Michael Torello** Dennis Farina **Pauli Taglia** John Santucci **Ray Luca** Anthony Denison **Atty David Abrams** Stephen Lang **Det Danny Krychek** Bill Smitrovish **Det Joey Indelli** William Campbell **Det Walter Clemmons** Paul Butler **Det Nate Grossman** Steve Ryan **Frank Holman** Ted Levine **Manny Weisbord** Joseph Wiseman **Cori Luca** Johann Carlo **Max Goldman** Andrew Clay **Julie Torello** Darlanne Fluegel **Inga Thorson** Patricia Charbonneau **Ted Kehoe** Mark Hutter **Chief Kramer** Ron Dean **Phil Bartoli** Jon Polito **Steven Kordo** Jay O Sanders.

Mob-buster Lieutenant Torello (Dennis Farina) in Michael Mann's stylish neo-noir *Crime Story*. At an estimated $1.5 million per sixty-minute episode it was one of the most expensive cop shows ever made for network TV.

This police drama series set in Chicago in the early sixties was the next step for Michael Mann after >*Miami Vice*. A hit among crime aficionados, though not a big ratings success, it told the story of Lt Michael Torello, chief of the city's MCU (Major Crime Unit), and his fight against gangster Ray Luca and his mob. Joining Torello in his struggle were Danny, Joey, Walter and Nate, his team of hard-bitten but honest detectives. Julie was his estranged wife. Initially mobster's son attorney David Abrams was also on the side of law and order, but by season two Abrams had returned to his roots and joined Luca's camp. The action moved cities when Luca transferred his base to Los Angeles and Torello followed, but the squad was no match for the young gangster and Luca's empire continued to prosper with the help of old-time mobsters Manny Weisbord and Phil Bartoli.

A kind of latter-day >*Untouchables*, authenticity was guaranteed for *Crime Story* by the fact that series co-creator Chuck Adamson had served seventeen years with the Chicago police force, and Dennis Farina, also an ex-cop, had actually been a member of the unit on which the squad was based. The villains' pock-marked feel, meanwhile, was enhanced by the choice of unknown actors from the right background – Anthony Denison (Luca) was a one-time professional gambler and John Santucci (Taglia) was a former jewel thief.

With a budget of around $1.5 million per episode, the series was one of the most expensive ever made for network TV, and mixed in the essential Mannian manner speed, visuals and music. Of particular note were the stark night-time scenes, the low-life period look, and a medley of sixties pop sounds (Del Shannon's 'Runaway' was the theme music) which pulsed forcefully through the action and got the emotions flowing.

Mann's work subsequent to *Crime Story* includes the feature film, *The Last of the Mohicans*.

Danger Man

UK 1960–8 39 × 30m bw/45 × 60m bw/2 × 60m col ITV. ITC. *USA tx* 1961 CBS. *cr* Ralph Smart. *exec pr* Ralph Smart. *pr* Ralph Smart, Aida Young, Sidney Cole. *dr* Various, including Ralph Smart, Peter Graham Scott, Terry Bishop, Patrick

McGoohan, Seth Holt, Charles Crichton, Don Chaffey, Quentin Lawrence, Peter Yates. *wr* Brian Clemens, Ralph Smart, Jo Eisinger, John Roddick, David Stone, Philip Broadley, Tony Williamson. *mus* Edwin Astley. *cast* **John Drake** Patrick McGoohan **Hobbs** Peter Madden. *Video* ITC.

Superior early spy thriller, and the series which made Patrick McGoohan an international name. McGoohan played John Drake, a suave loner operative for NATO's Washington DC Secret Service branch, whose assignments to defeat Treaty enemies were invariably successful, if violent. As would become customary with TV series of similar type (>*The Saint*, >*The Persuaders*, >*Man in a Suitcase*), *Danger Man* was often filmed in exotic locations, from Arabia to Venice, with the scenery improved by beautiful women. However, unlike his rivals, in particular The Saint, Drake was not a philanderer, but the ultimate dedicated action man, a small boy's ideal of an hero. Not once did Drake fall for the charms of the many women he encountered in eighty-six adventures. As McGoohan said, 'Drake was the only secret agent who never carried a gun and never went to bed with a girl.' The same ascetic professionalism inhabited McGoohan's Number Six in >*The Prisoner*, a series co-developed with *Danger Man* script editor George Markstein and heavily derived from the *Danger Man* episode, 'Colony Three'. (The *Danger Man* segment 'View From the Villa' also gave McGoohan his introduction to the Italianate folly, Portmeirion, which formed the setting for *The Prisoner*.)

Danger Man changed in 1964 when segments were expanded to sixty minutes, and Drake himself was 'transferred' to the British Secret Service's M19 branch, where he received his orders from boss Hobbs. The action-intrigue content, though, remained undiminished and the only discernible change to the formula was a new emphasis on gadgetry (this some three years before Bond hit the screens). The last two *Danger Man* episodes 'Koroshi' and 'Shinda Shima', were shot in colour as part of a projected fourth season which ended abruptly because McGoohan had lost interest in playing John Drake, and wanted to make progress with *The Prisoner*. In the USA, where it topped the ratings, the series was syndicated under both its British title and the title *Secret Agent*.

The series proved a training school for many British screen personnel, including the Hungarian-born director Peter Medak, whose later work included the movies, *A Day in the Death of Joe Egg* (1970), *The Krays* (1990) and *Let Him Have It* (1991).

Department S

UK 1969–70 28 × 60m col ITV. ITC. *USA tx* 1971 syndicated. *cr* Monty Berman, Dennis Spooner. *pr* Monty Berman. *dr* Ray Austin, John Gilling, Cyril Frankel, Paul Dickson, Gill Taylor, Roy Ward Baker, Leslie Norman. *wr* Gerald Kelsey, Philip Broadley, Terry Nation, Tony Williamson, Harry H Junkin, Leslie Darbon, Donald James. *mus* Edwin Astley. *cast* **Jason King** Peter Wyngarde **Stewart Sullivan** Joel Fabiani **Annabelle Hurst** Rosemary Nichols **Sir Curtis Seretse** Dennis Alaba Peters. *Video* ITC.

Moustachioed Australian actor Peter Wyngarde played the flamboyant Jason King ('Whenever I feel the need for exercise I lie down until it passes'), head investigator of Department S, an Interpol branch which specialised in 'unsolvable' crimes. A spare-time detective author, King's *modus operandi* was to approach each Department S case as though he himself were Mark Caine, his own ace detective creation – a somewhat fanciful methodology which continually irked his co-workers, the prosaic Stewart Sullivan and computer expert Annabelle Hurst. The trio's boss was Sir Curtis Seretse (played by black actor Dennis Alaba Peters), and it was he who gave them their international assignments. These were usually murder or kidnapping mysteries which had a strong element of the fantastic: 'The Pied Piper of Hambledown' concerned the mass abduction of an English village, 'One of Our Aircraft is Empty' a pilotless plane, and 'The Man in the Elegant Room' a killing in a palatial chamber in an otherwise abandoned factory. The scripts were highly polished, and no matter how seemingly implausible the plots they were usually convincingly resolved. The guest cast included Kate O'Mara – a trooper in a range of sixties action series – and Alexandra Bastedo (>*The Champions*).

Less successful, though, was the spin-off *Jason King* (1971–2, 26 × 60m col) in which Wyngarde reprised his

'Evenin' all!' Jack Warner as kindly British bobby George Dixon in *Dixon of Dock Green*. The series, which ran on the BBC for twenty-one years, was penned by Ted Willis, who was entered in the *Guinness Book of Records* as TV's most prolific writer.

King character but this time as a solo, non-Department S, crime-busting operative. King was as urbane and dandyish as ever, with his turned-up shirt cuffs, but the plots were standard stuff, slowed down by bed-to-bed girls, and demanded not so much the suspension of disbelief as its drawing and quartering.

Dixon of Dock Green

UK 1955–76 367 × 25m/45m bw/col BBC1. A BBC TV Production. *cr* Ted Willis. *pr* Various, including Douglas Moodie, Ronald Marsh, Philip Barker, Joe Waters. *dr* Various, including A A Englander, David Askey, Robin Nash, Vere Lorrimer, Michael Goodwin, Douglas Argent, Mary Ridge. *wr* Various, including Ted Willis, Arthur Swinton, Eric Price, Gerald Kelsey, N J Crisp, Jack Trevor Story, P J Hammond, Robert Holmes, Tony Williamson, David Ellis, Peter Ling, Richard Waring. *cast* **PC George Dixon** Jack Warner **Det Sgt Crawford** Peter Byrne **Mary Crawford** Billie Whitelaw (1955) Jeannette Hutchinson (from 1955) **PC Lauderdale** Geoffrey Adams **Desk Sgt Flint** Arthur Rigby **PC Willis** Nicholas Donnelly **PC Tubb Barrell** Neil Wilson **Sgt Grace Millard** Moira Mannion **Cadet Jamie MacPherson** David Webster **PC Bob Penney** Anthony Parker **WPC Kay Shaw** Jocelyn Rhodes.

'Evenin' all.' Avuncular PC George Dixon was the first British copper to tread the TV beat and, running for twenty-one years, the longest-lasting. The character was first seen in the J Arthur Rank movie *The Blue Lamp* (1950) where he was famously killed by young Dirk Bogarde's villain in the climax. But so popular was the kindly, tea-drinking copper that the BBC unashamedly brought him back to life, with co-creator Ted Willis penning most of his early small-screen appearances. The character of PC Dixon was based by Willis on a real policeman from Leman Street in the East End, and on an archetype of the English bobby. Keen to have an air of reality about the series, Willis kept on his payroll 250 real-life policemen who would pass on anecdotes about their job.

The emphasis in the series, which was reassuringly cosy and quaint even in the fifties, was on small, everyday human experiences, not major-league crime and sensationalism, with Dixon a benevolent father figure to the local community. 'Murder cases are not so frequent as some crime writers would have us imagine,' the *Radio Times* primly introduced the first episode, 'PC Crawford's First Pinch'. But no matter what the crime, justice was always done, and each episode ended with a summation and a homily from Dixon standing outside the station.

Other characters at Dock Green who made the move from the movie along with Dixon included Andy Crawford, later to become a Detective Sergeant and to marry Dixon's daughter Mary, PC 'Laudy' Lauderdale, and Desk Sergeant Flint (Arthur Rigby), who lodged with Dixon's mother.

In 1964 Dixon was promoted to Sergeant and became more desk-bound, too old to pound the beat any more. He finally retired in 1976, as the show was beginning to pale in comparison to such energetic vehicles as >*The Sweeney*. Jack Warner died five years later aged eighty-five. His coffin was borne by police officers from Paddington Green and the show's theme tune 'An Ordinary Copper' played over the PA. It was the end of an era and a British institution. Lord Ted Willis, who created *Dixon*, was somewhat of a British monument himself. Made a Labour peer by Harold Wilson in 1963, his output included thirty-four stage plays, thirty-nine films and forty television series and he earned a place in the *Guinness Book of Records* as TV's most prolific writer. Credited as the pioneer of the 'kitchen sink' dramas of the fifties, he made a controversial start to his career as a radio writer for *Mrs Dale's Diary*, writing an episode in which Mrs Dale and friends plunged to their deaths after reversing a car over Beachy Head. He was promptly fired. Lord Willis died in 1992.

One of the small screen's most flamboyant and rakish characters ('Whenever I feel the need for exercise, I lie down until it passes'), Peter Wyngarde as Interpol detective and author Jason King in *Department S*. A sequel, *Jason King*, was less successful.

Dragnet

USA 1952–8 263 × 30m bw/1967–70 98 × 30m col NBC. MCA TV/Mark VII/Universal TV. *UK tx* 1955–9 ITV. *cr* Jack Webb, Richard L Breen. *exec pr* Jack Webb. *pr* Robert A Cinader, William Stark, Jack Webb. *dr* Jack Webb. *wr* Various, including James Moser, Richard L Breen, Henry

Irving, Sidney Morse, Jerry D Lewis, Robert Soderburg. *mus* Walter Schumann. *cast* **Sgt Joe Friday** Jack Webb **Sgt Ben Romero** Barton Yarborough **Sgt Ed Jacobs** Barney Philips **Officer Frank Smith** Herb Ellis/Ben Alexander **Officer Bill Gannon** Harry Morgan.

'The story you are about to see is true. Only the names have been changed to protect the innocent.' This dramatic warning introduced every episode of Jack Webb's hyper-realistic *Dragnet*, one of the most popular and influential police series in TV history. While other cop shows traded in superheroic detectives who carried a blonde in one hand and a stuttering machine-gun in the other, Webb – as director, producer and star – played it low-key, with documentary-style photography and laconic voice-over narration. Authenticity was assured by using cases actually pulled from files of the Los Angeles Police Department, with many of the walk-on parts played by those involved in the real crime. Webb spent two years riding in LAPD patrol cars to learn police jargon and behaviour. Sergeant Joe Friday, too, was suitably downbeat, not given to loquaciousness, emotion, shoot-outs (Webb only allowed one bullet to be fired every four episodes) or fights, only hard plodding policework. 'Just the facts, Ma'am', 'That's my job' and 'I carry a badge' were Friday's standard lines for every eventuality.

The hero may have been uncharismatic and the style *verité*, but *Dragnet* was far from boring. Webb's direction was taut, with lots of close-ups, while Walter Schumann's music provided dramatic changes of pace and mood. (Schumann's famous 'dum-de-dum-dum' theme became a hit record in 1953). The programme's fault was the occasional lapse into sententious moralising on behalf of the fine, decent, upstanding nature of American law enforcement.

Like several other small-screen hit dramas of the fifties, *Dragnet* began life as a radio series. It was first transmitted as a segment in *Chesterfield Sound Off Time* in 1951, before going independent in the following year. In 1955, it became the first US police show to be screened in Britain (and one of ITV's first hits), where it ran against the infinitely tamer native >*Dixon of Dock Green*. *Dragnet*'s prime-time run in the USA came to an end in 1959, by which time Friday had been promoted to lieutenant and had had three sidekicks (Romero, Jacobs and Smith). But you cannot keep a good TV series down, and Webb resurrected *Dragnet* as a colour 60-minute show in 1967. Friday was back to a sergeant again and his new partner was Officer Bill Gannon, a married hypochondriac played by Harry Morgan (later to be promoted to Colonel Sherman Potter in >*M*A*S*H*). Around the same time, the original *Dragnet* was syndicated under the title *Badge 714* (Friday's warrant number).

Since Webb's death in 1982, yet another *Dragnet* (an Arthur Company Production for WWOR-TV, 1989–90) has appeared, with the leads played by Jeffrey Osterhage and Bernard White. There was also a 1987 film feature *Dragnet*, directed by Tom Mankiewicz, with Dan Ackroyd playing Friday as an amusingly starched, cleaner-than-clean parody of the original.

The Fugitive

USA 1963–6 90 × 60m bw/30 × 60m col ABC. A Quinn Martin Production. *UK tx* 1963–6 ITV. *cr* Roy Huggins. *exec pr* Quinn Martin. *pr* Alan A Armer, Wilton Schiller. *dr* Various, including Robert Butler, Sydney Pollack, Ralph Senensky, Jerry Hopper, James Goldstone, Walter Grauman, Sutton Roley, Alexander Singer, Don Medford, William A Graham. *wr* Various, including George Eckstein, Harry Kronman, William Link, Richard Levinson, Larry Cohen, Philip Saltzman, William D Gordon, Dan Ullman. *mus* Peter Rugolo. *cast* **Dr Richard Kimble** David Janssen **Lt Philip Gerard** Barry Morse **Fred Johnson (aka The One-Armed Man)** Bill Raisch **Donna Taft** Jacqueline Scott.

A phenomenally popular sixties TV series, in which Dr Richard Kimble (David Janssen) was on the run for a crime he did not commit, the murder of his wife Helen. Over four seasons Kimble evaded the ruthless manhunt by Lt Gerard – who had accidentally let Kimble escape during a train derailment – at the same time criss-crossing the USA in search of the real killer, a mysterious one-armed man. To subsist he took a variety of odd jobs, while his only confidante was his sister-in-law, Donna Taft.

Inspired by both the real-life Dr Sam Shepard case of 1954 (in which an Ohio physician was wrongly imprisoned for the murder of his wife) and Victor Hugo's novel *Les Miserables*, *The Fugitive* maintained constant tension and was constructed with almost Aristotelian perfection, reaching a climactic two-part resolution where Kimble confronted the one-armed man on top of a water tower. The killer confessed and the Javert-like Lt Gerard arrived in time to shoot him and save Kimble's life. The conclusion was watched by a then-record TV audience around the world, a record not surpassed until >*Dallas*'s 'Who Shot JR?' cliffhanger in 1980. Robert Duvall, Angie Dickinson, a very young Kurt Russell ('Nemesis' episode), Warren Oates and Telly Savalas were among *The Fugitive*'s guest cast. The voice of the narrator who introduced each episode was William 'Cannon' Conrad.

The show made Janssen one of TV's first superstars, and only ended in 1966 because Janssen, who appeared in over 80 per cent of scenes, was suffering from exhaustion. Janssen – real name David Meyer – later starred in >*Harry O*, a downbeat private eye series from Warner Bros. He died in 1980 aged fifty.

Inevitably, the success of *The Fugitive* led to a run of similar manhunt shows, including *Run For Your Life* and >*The Invaders* (also a Quinn Martin production). In 1993 The Fugitive ran again, this time in a motion picture starring Harrison Ford and Tommy Lee Jones.

Gangsters

UK 1975–8 1 × 110m/12 × 50m col BBC1. BBC Birmingham. *cr* Philip Martin. *pr* David Rose. *dr* Philip Saville, Alistair Reid. *wr* Philip Martin. *mus* Dave Greenslade. *cast* **John Kline** Maurice Colborne **Khan** Ahmed Khalil **Anne Darracott** Elizabeth Cassidy **Dermot Macavoy** Paul Antrim **Malleson** Paul Barber **Sarah Grant** Albie Parsons **Rafiq** Saeed Jaffrey.

This BBC serial remains one of British TV's few underworld thrillers, an account of the profession of villainy in multi-racial, boomtown Birmingham circa 1975. Episodes – or 'Incidents' as they were termed – related the internal and external politicking of top-ranking white, Asian and West Indian gangdom, together with the gangsters' attempts at money-making through drug-smuggling, prostitution and the like. Stylish, edgy and electric at times, it veered too close to melodrama overall to be entirely successful. Its violence quotient provoked such an outcry that a special TV discussion was screened. Nonetheless, it deserved a footnote in British small-screen history for sheer chutzpah.

The twelve-part serial was developed from a 1975 *Play for Today*, directed by Philip Saville, whose subsequent career includes the film features *The Fruit Machine* and *Fellow Traveller*.

The Green Hornet

USA 1966–7 26 × 30m col ABC. Greenway Productions. 20th Century Fox Television. *UK tx* 1996 Bravo. *cr* George W Trendle. *exec pr* William Dozier. *pr* Richard Bluel. *dr* Various, including Leslie Martinson, Allen Reisner, Darrel Hallenbeck, Norman Foster, William Beaudine. *wr* Various, including Art Weingarten, William L Stuart, Lorenzo Semple, Ken Pettus, Charles Hoffman. *mus* 'Flight of the Bumble Bee' by Rimsky-Korsakov, updated by Al Hirt (theme), Billy May. *cast* **The Green Hornet/Britt Reid** Van Williams **Kate** Bruce Lee **Leonore 'Casey' Case** Wende Wagner **Mike Axford** Lloyd Gough **District Attorney F P Scanlon** Walter Brooke.

'. . . to protect the lives and right of decent citizens rides the Green Hornet'

Flying high on the success of >*Batman*, producer William Dozier decided to introduce another daring masked crime-buster to the small screen – The Green Hornet. Accompanied by faithful Oriental chauffeur Kato ('Faster Kato!'), the Hornet sped to the scene of crime in the 'rolling arsenal' known as the Black Beauty (a customised 1966 Chrysler Imperial), and then set about sleuthing the villain of the piece. When identified, the baddie would be immobilised by the Green Hornet's non-lethal Sting Gun, which used high-pitched soundwaves, or dealt with by Kato's dashing martial arts. Only Kato, Reid's secretary Casey, and the DA knew that the Hornet was really Britt Reid, crusading editor-publisher of *The*

Daily Sentinel and TV station owner. Considered criminal by the police, the Green Hornet and Kato always disappeared before the authorities arrived to take over.

The series was a flop. It was simultaneously too similar to *Batman*, yet had none of its knowing camp. Probably its sole interest was the extraordinary kung fu-fighting character of Kato, played by Bruce Lee in his first appearance on an American screen. Born in 1940 in San Francisco to theatrical-touring Chinese parents, Lee Jun Fan – as Lee was named in Mandarin – was brought up in the British colony of Hong Kong, where he became an expert in the wing chun ('Beautiful Springtime') style of kung fu as well as a child actor. Returning to America in 1959, aged nineteen, Lee made a sensational appearance at the International Karate Championship at Long Beach, California, in 1964, where his stylish, dynamic kicking and punching was witnessed by Hollywood hair stylist Jay Sebring. Some time later when Sebring (who would evenually be murdered by the Manson gang when they invaded the home of Sharon Tate) was cutting the hair of TV producer Dozier he mentioned Lee. Dozier, at that stage looking for someone to play Charlie Chan's Number-One-Son in a TV series, sent for a film of Lee's demonstration at Long Beach. Dozier liked what he saw and optioned Lee for $180. Scratching the Charlie Chan series, Dozier installed Lee as the black-suited, black-masked Kato in *The Green Hornet*, Lee joking that he got the part because he was 'the only Chinaman in all California who could pronounce Britt Reid'. So quick were Lee's martial arts movements, that he was forced to slow them down for the show's cameras. Audiences were appreciative of their first taste of kung fu, and Lee went on to spice up episodes of >*Ironside*, *Blondie*, *Longstreet*, and *Here Come the Brides*. Lee also helped develop the idea of a wandering Shaolin monk which became >*Kung Fu*, and was bitterly disappointed when Warner Bros and ABC-TV gave the lead role to the more experienced – and Caucasian – David Carradine. However, unknown to Lee *The Green Hornet* had become a television phenomenon in the Far East – where it was retitled *The Kato Show* – and he had ascended to celestial celebrity. In 1971 the Golden Harvest studios of Hong Kong sent a senior producer to the USA to sign up Lee for a movie deal; Lee

then returned East to make a cycle of kung fu films which would include *The Big Boss*, *Fists of Fury* and *Enter the Dragon*. The rest is legend.

By way of footnote, *The Green Hornet* was created as a radio character in 1936 by George W Trendle, who also invented >*The Lone Ranger* with whom the Hornet has obvious clean-cut and be-masked similarities. Britt Reid first appeared on the wireless waves as the son of Dan Reid, the Lone Ranger's nephew.

Harry O

USA 1974–6 2 × 120m/43 × 60m col ABC. A Warner Bros Television Production. *UK tx* 1974–7 BBC1. *cr* Howard Rodman. *exec pr* Jerry Thorpe. *pr* Robert E Thompson, Robert Dozier, Buck Houghton, Alex Beaton, Rita Dillon. *dr* Barry Crane, Richard Bennett, Daryl Duke, Harry Falk, Richard Lang, Robert Michael Lewis, Jerry London, Joe Manduke, Russ Mayberry, John Newland, Jerry Thorpe, Don Weiss, Paul Wendkos. *wr* Various, including John Meredyth Lucas, Michael Adams, Dorothy Blees, Larry Forrester, Robert Dozier, Susan Glasgow, Ron Jacoby, Stephen Kandel. *mus* Jerry Goldsmith. *cast* **Harry Orwell** David Janssen **Det Lt Manny Quinlan** Henry Darrow **Lt K C Trench** Anthony Zerbe **Lester Hodges** Les Lannom **Dr Fong** Keye Luke.

While responding to a burglary in progress, LA Police Officer Harry O (for Orwell) is shot in the back and disabled when the bullet lodges in his spine. He retires from the force and becomes one of TV's more bohemian private eyes, living in a beachfront cottage near San Diego. Here the dour ex-marine takes on only those cases that interest him. These usually involve luscious girls – Harry's girl-next-door Sue Ingham was played by pre-*Charlie's Angels* Farrah Fawcett – but Harry O shows little desire to pursue them.

Harry's sometimes nemesis, sometime ally, was his contact Lt Manny Quinlan of the San Diego Police Department (played by TV veteran Henry Darrow whose credits include >*Invisible Man*, >*Tarzan*, >*Lone Ranger* and >*Zorro*). But Manny was killed off in a February 1975 telecast, after which Harry moved his base of operations to Santa Monica and inherited a new official nemesis, Lt Trench, plus occasional unsolicited help with his cases from amateur criminologists Lester Hodges and Dr Fong. The series needed two pilots – *Harry O* and *Smile Jenny You're Dead* (featuring twelve-year-old Jodie Foster) – before it got off the ground, and when it did it lost out to NBC's rival Californian PI, James Rockford. Starting out at the same time, >*The Rockford Files* far outran the disabled Orwell, lasting until 1980.

In fact *Harry O* had little to recommend it apart from the gimmick that Orwell's car was in an almost permanent state of disrepair, leaving him to bus to the scene of the crime, and its star, David Janssen, well known to viewers as >*The Fugitive* and with a track record in TV crime which included producer Jack Webb's *O'Hara, United States Treasury* (1971–2) and *Richard Diamond Private Detective* (1957–60).

Hart to Hart

USA 1979–81 110 × 60m col ABC. Spelling-Goldberg. *UK tx* 1980–5. *cr* Sidney Sheldon. *exec pr* Aaron Spelling, Leonard Goldberg. *pr* David Levinson, Matt Crowley. *dr* Various, including Bruce Kessler, Earl Bellamy, Tom Mankiewicz, Stuart Margolin, Leo Penn, Peter Medak, Reza S Badiyi, Seymour Robbie, Ralph Senensky, Sam Wanamaker. *wr* Various, including Catherine Bacos, Earl Bellamy, Allan Folsom, Stephen Kandel, David Levinson, Anthony Yerkovich, Edward Martino, Martin Roth, Lana Sands. *mus* Mark Snow. *cast* **Jonathan Hart** Robert Wagner **Jennifer Hart** Stefanie Powers **Max** Lionel Stander.

He was a handsome self-made millionaire. She was a famous journalist. Their hobby was murder.

Stalwart good-looking lead Robert Wagner (*It Takes a Thief, Colditz, Switch*) and ex-*Girl from UNCLE* Stefanie Powers starred in this popular Aaron Spelling series about a husband and wife amateur sleuthing duo, Jonathan and Jennifer Hart, who discovered corpses galore as they jet-setted around the world. A particular peril for the Harts was that Jennifer Hart was peculiarly prone to being kidnapped. The other cast regulars were Lionel Stander as the Harts' rasp-voiced, cigar-smoking retainer Max, and a dog, Freeway.

The programme credits listed bestselling novelist Sidney Sheldon as the programme's creator, but the series was merely an update of popular *Thin Man* movies of the thirties, which in turn were derived from the novels of Dashiell Hammett. (A previous TV series using Hammett's characters, *The Thin Man*, had been made by MGM in the fifties.) *Hart to Hart* lacked the urbane, sophisticated wit of the films – which starred William Powell and Myrna Loy – not to mention their passable plots. The Harts were also indecently gooey, always ending the day with pyjamas, milk and cookies, before turning off the light for another honeymoon. Unfortunately, their sheer good spirits and a certain self-mockingness made them curiously watchable.

Hawaii Five-O

USA 1968–80 270 × 50m col CBS. Leonard Freeman Productions. *UK tx* 1970–82 ITV. *cr* Leonard Freeman, Jack Lord. *exec pr* Leonard Freeman, Philip Leacock, Douglas Greene. *pr* Bill Finnegan, Bob Sweeney, Richard Newton, Gene Levitt, B W Sandefeur, Stanley Kallis, Leonard Katzman, Leonard B Kaufman, Jack Lord. *dr* Various, including Michael O'Herlihy, Gordon Hessler, Sutton Roley, Alvin Ganzer, Corey Allen, Herschel Daugherty, Alf Kjellin, Marvin Chomsky, Reza S Badiyi, Nicholas Colasanto, Paul Krasny, Philip Leacock, Jerry Thorpe, Irving J Moore, Jerry Jameson, Jack Lord, John Moxey, Robert Butler, Harvey S Laidman, Barry Crane, William Hale, Ernest Pintoff, Sutton Roley, Brad Van Ecker. *wr* Various, including Robert Lewin, Leonard Freeman, Arthur Bernard Lewis, Robert C Dennis, Stephen Kandel, Norman Lessing, John D F Black, Shirl Hendryx, Edward J Lask, Glen Olson, Martin Roth, Robert Hamner, Dean Tait, William Robert Yates. *mus* Morton Stevens (theme), Peter Rugolo. *cast* **Steve McGarrett** Jack Lord **Det Danny 'Dan-O' Williams** James MacArthur **Det Chin Ho Kelly** Kam Fong **Det Kono Kalakaua** Zulu **Governor Philip Grey** Richard Denning **Doc Bergman** Al Eben **Jenny Sherman** Peggy Ryan **Wo Fat** Khigh Dhiegh **Lt Lori Wilson** Sharon Farrell **Det Ben Kokua** Al Harrington **Che Fong** Harry Endo **Det Duke Lukela** Herman Wedemeyer.

The longest-running cop series in the history of American TV. Ex->*Stoney Burke* star Jack Lord played detective Steve McGarrett of the Hawaii State Police, head of a special squad working out of the Iolani Palace which reported directly to the governor. Too important for everyday crime-busting, the team – principally McGarrett himself, boyish Danny 'Dan-O' Williams and native islanders Chin Ho Kelly and Kono Kalakaua – concentrated on psychopathic killers and Triad-like forces from the Hawaiian underworld. A particularly cunning and elusie Mr Big was Wo Fat (Khigh Dhiegh). Fighting Wo Fat and his ilk was a full-time mission for McGarrett; he had no apparent life outside the office, save for an occasional sail in his dinghy.

The kindest thing to say of the acting of the principals in *Hawaii Five-O* is that it was constant: Lord never

Steve McGarrett (Jack Lord, second from right), Danny 'Dan-O' Williams (right) and the team from Honolulu's special police squad plan the capture of another baddie in paradise in *Hawaii Five-O*. 'Book 'em, Dan-O!'

registered an emotion, MacArthur never looked anything other than surprised. The rank-and-file police, played by off-duty cops, were often more accomplished. And the stories were frequently flimsy. However, few shows have looked more stunning than *Hawaii Five-O*, which was shot entirely on location in Hawaii. Even when plot and character dragged, viewer attention was taken by the exotic setting, enhanced by exquisite photography.

For a series of such longevity, cast changes were few (presumably the working conditions were too good to give up). Zulu departed in 1972, but Kam Fong and MacArthur played McGarrett's assistants until the end of the seventies. With the departure of MacArthur, the show's famous catchphrase, 'Book 'em, Danno', had to go too, and somehow things were never the same. The ratings were falling anyway, and the introduction of a new woman detective in 1979, Lori Wilson, played by Sharon Farrell, did nothing to halt them. No doubt, however, it was some satisfaction to Lord/McGarrett that in the last episode before the series was unplugged he finally caught Wo Fat ('Woe to Wo Fat').

The memorable theme music, played over the stylish opening and ending credits (the latter showing Polynesians powering an outrigger canoe) was composed by Morton Stevens.

Despite the murder rate of the series it did much to promote Hawaiian tourism. Hawaii now has a 'Jack Lord Day' on its calendar.

Hazell

UK 1978–80 22 × 60m col ITV. A Thames Television Network Production. *cr* Gordon Williams, Terry Venables. *pr* June Roberts (season one), Tim Aspinall (season two). *dr* Don Leaver, Alistair Reid, Jim Goddard, Moira Armstrong, Peter Duguid, Colin Bucksey, Brian Farnham. *wr* Richard Harris, Gordon Williams, Tony Hoare, Peter Ransley, Trevor Preston, Terry Venables. *mus* Andy McKay. *cast* **James Hazell** Nicholas Ball **'Choc' Minty** Roddy McMillan **Cousin Tell** Desmond McNamara.

'Hazell is divorced, ex-police, big, good-looking, slightly battered . . . He has mass tastes – *Daily Mirror*, slightly old-fashioned pop music, films, paperbacks . . . His accent is variable, basically cockney.' These were novelist Gordon Williams' notes for the TV production team translating his PI creation, James Hazell, to the small screen. Aged thirty-three, cockney Jack-the-lad Hazell worked seedy suburban London like Chandler's Marlowe worked downtown Los Angeles. Down at heel, invalided out of the police with a dodgy ankle, with a penchant for saying 'kin'ell!', he had a drink problem that put an end to his marriage and a streak of disillusion beneath his East End humour. Always on the lookout for reasons to withdraw Hazell's PI licence was dour Scottish CID man 'Choc' Minty.

Hazell was the product of Thames Television's policy of producing contemporary drama with a London flavour. Under the guidance of Verity Lambert – brought in as head of drama by Programme Controller Jeremy Isaacs in 1974 – the series was developed by the *Hazell* novels of P B Yuill, aka journalist Gordon Williams (who wrote *The Siege of Trencher's Farm* which formed the basis of the film *Straw Dogs*) and Terry Venables, ex-star football player for Chelsea, Spurs, Queen's Park Rangers and England, then manager of Crystal Palace FC and England. In particular, Lambert approved of the books' 'cockney sense of humour' and potential to show 'the underbelly of London'. Thames' hope was that *Hazell* would help ITV regain the ground it had been losing in its ratings battle against the BBC.

At £80,000 per episode, the series was comparatively cheap. Unlike its predecessor in the same slot, >*The Sweeney*, *Hazell* was shot in studio on tape with only ten or fifteen minutes per episode shot on film. Like the novels, the TV *Hazell* harked back to Chandler, but interpretations of this differed. For June Roberts, the script executive, Chandler's Los Angeles was a state of mind, and she showed series writers the *film noir* classics *The Big Sleep* and *Double Indemnity* as a guide. For script editor Kenneth Ware (ex->*Z Cars* and >*Softly Softly*) and co-creator Gordon Williams, the 'real' London was to be a star of the series. The resulting mix had a Marlowe-style voice-over, stylish location filming in Soho and scenes of seedy reality shot in Acton, the East End, or Clapton dog stadium. Time pressures led to an absence of the *film noir*-style strong women characters June Roberts had hoped for; even Hazell's ex-Rodean debt-collector girlfriend (or rather, the East London Romeo's main girlfriend) turned out to be a passive onlooker. Another compromise was made on the theme tune. In keeping with the cockney feel of the series the producers had asked Ray Davies of The Kinks to write a theme tune along the lines of *Dead End Street*, but Davies pulled out at the last minute and Roxy Music's Andy McKay, who wrote the music for earlier Thames success >*Rock Follies* stepped in.

Too violent for some tastes *Hazell* was a top-grade series, but it never achieved Jeremy Isaacs' stated goal of thirty-nine episodes. The BBC dealt the series a fatal blow by scheduling a season of Robert Redford films in the same time slot. After twenty-two memorable, idiosyncratic episodes, *Hazell* was a goner.

Highway Patrol

USA 1955–9 156 × 30m bw syndicated. A Ziv Production. *UK tx* 1960–2 ITV (London 1956–8). *exec pr* Vernon E Clark. *asst pr* Joe Wonder. *mus* Richard Llewellyn. *cast* **Chief Dan Matthews** Broderick Crawford **Narrator** Art Gilmore.

Burly, gravel-voiced Broderick Crawford was Dan Matthews, chief of the *Highway Patrol* in a series that was one of the most popular syndicated programmes in television history.

The action took place on the sprawling highway system of an unidentified Western state with plenty of hardware to help it along – patrol cars, motorbikes, helicopters. Story-lines were straight crime dramas from a time when good was good and bad was bad, with the chief and his uniformed officers nailing hijackers, smugglers and robbers. But it was the way fast-talking Dan Matthews leant against his patrol car to radio to headquarters that really captured the public imagination. 'Ten-four' (message received and understood) and 'Ten-twenty' (report your position) became catchphrases around the world.

The programme's opening announcement thundered: 'Whenever the laws of any state are broken, a duly authorised organisation swings into action. It may be called the State Police, State Troopers, Militia, the Rangers or the Highway Patrol. These are the stories of the men whose training, skill and courage have enforced and preserved our state laws.' In one episode a young newlywed couple were hunted when they were sole witnesses to a café hold-up and murder, in another a bank messenger absconded with $50,000, took it home and his wife made off with the money. But a chase here, an all-points bulletin there, and Chief Matthews won every time in the name of the law.

Hill Street Blues

USA 1980–7 145 × 60m col NBC. MTM Productions. *UK tx* ITV 1981–4; C4 1984–9. *cr* Michael Kozoll, Steven Bochco. *exec pr* Steven Bochco, Gregory Hoblit (season three and four). *assoc pr* Scott Brazil, David Anspaugh. *dr* Robert Butler, Georg Stanford Brown, Arnold Laven, Jack Starrett, Robert C Thompson, Gregory Hoblit, Corey Allen, David Anspaugh, Rod Holcomb, Randa Haines, Jeff Bleckner, Thomas Carter, Lawrence Levy, Robert Kelljan, Christian Nyby II, Oz Scott, David Rosenbloom, Rick Wallace, Alexander Singer, Bill Duke, Arthur Seidelman, Gabrielle Beaumont, Richard Compton. *wr* Various, including Steven Bochco, Michael Kozoll, Anthony Yerkovich, Lee David Zlotoff, Geoffrey Fischer, Bill Taub, E Jack Kaplan, Gregory Hoblit, Alan Rachins, Robert Crais, Jeffrey Lewis, Michael Wagner, David Milch, Karen Hall, Robert Earll, Mark Frost, Peter Silverman, Dennis Cooper, Roger Director. *mus* Mike Post. *cast* **Capt Frank Furillo** Daniel J Travanti **Sgt Phil Esterhaus** Michael Conrad **Officer Bobby Hill** Michael Warren **Det Mick Belker** Bruce Weitz **Lt Howard Hunter** James B Sikking **Sgt Henry Goldblume** Joe Spano **Fay Furillo** Barbara Bosson **Det Neal Washington** Taurean Blacque **Det Johnny 'J.D.' La Rue** Kiel Martin **Lt Ray Calletano** Rene Enriquez **Officer Lucy Bates** Betty Thomas **Officer Andy Renko** Charles Haid **Joyce Davenport** Veronica Hamel **Officer Joe Coffey** Ed Marinaro **Leo** Robert Hirschfeld.

'And hey, let's be careful out there.' From its familiar early morning roll call episode-opener, *Hill Street Blues* looked different. Part soap opera, part cop-action melodrama, its first season left viewers quizzical and

They were careful out there. The cast of Steven Bochco's mould-breaking American police series *Hill Street Blues*. Daniel J. Travanti (bottom row, second from right) starred as Capt Frank Furillo and Veronica Hamel (bottom row, second from left) as public prosecutor Joyce Davenport, Furillo's secret lover, and later, wife.

critics elated (it scooped a record nine Emmys in 1980). *Hill Street Blues* not only mixed its genres, it had an unwieldy regular cast number of around thirteen, ran up to half a dozen storylines and subplots in each episode and then left them dangling, and was shot *verité*-style, with hand-held camera, choppy cuts and an eight-track sound previously only glimpsed in >*M*A*S*H*.

The officers who received their duties from Sgt Phil Esterhaus each morning worked out of Hill Street Station in the run-down inner city area of a large unnamed Eastern city (Maxwell House precinct in Chicago provided the station exterior). Quietly forceful Capt Frank Furillo was in charge of a bunch of officers of assorted ethnic mix (Hill Street gave a number of talented black actors and actresses a chance for challenging work) and personal habit. Down-at-heel Det Mick Belker's forte was undercover work as a tramp, and he had a line in terrorising offenders: 'Would you like to sit down, hairball, or would you prefer internal bleeding.' Henry Goldblume was the station's liberal and anti-racist, while Howard Hunter was the team's redneck and trigger-happy leader of the precinct's SWAT team. Each episode ended late at night after a day that witnessed all the problems of the ghetto – drugs, prostitution, burglary, murder – entangled with the messy personal lives of the precinct's warts'n'all cops.

It was not long before each episode also ended with Furillo unwinding in public prosecutor Joyce Davenport's bed or bath. The object of many viewers' desires as well as Capt Frank Furillo's, Davenport ably fulfilled the demands of her profession as well as those of soap opera, first becoming Furillo's secret lover and later, in a lunchtime ceremony, his wife. But for a would-be soap opera *Hill Street* had few women in its regular cast and two of these featured only as ongoing problems – Furillo's ex-wife and thorn-in-his-side Fay who constantly badgered him for more alimony, and the maniacal Belker's mom at home, experienced only through irritating phonecalls. In other respects the series was unfashionably liberal, although unlike its MTM stablemate >*Lou Grant* episodes were not 'about' social problems. Instead a storyline about a brutal policeman posted to the precinct became a personal story about a man under stress, and rather than making racism an 'issue' *Hill Street* wrote racists (Renko) and anti-racists (Goldblume) into its cast.

After the first ground-breaking season, there were some changes and in season two audiences went up and quality went down. At the start of *Hill Street* NBC had guaranteed no network interference in storylines, but for the second season NBC demanded producers MTM tie up at least one storyline per episode. Co-creator Michael Kozoll distanced himself to the role of creative consultant and storyline composer and by the end of the second series he was gone. What's more, a Writers' Guild strike in 1982 used up the backlog of scripts so that episodes had to be churned out at one a week instead of one a fortnight. As a result *Hill Street* had more fights, shoot-outs, car wrecks and chases, and less creativity. The new formula, however, was a network's dream: it attracted those all-important young urban adults in the eighteen to forty-nine age range (rated first among men, third among women), that meant NBC could charge advertisers more for slots in *Hill Street* than for higher-rated top ten hits. Mercedes Benz became a regular *Hill Street* advertiser in 1983 and Thorn EMI chose the slots for their first network ads for video software.

The second of the series' creators, Steven Bochco, left in 1985, supposedly fired by MTM for going over budget. Bochco had brought with him a wealth of experience (*Sarge* 1971–2, >*Six Million Dollar Man* 1974, *Griff* 1973–4, *Delvecchio* 1976–7). Many of *Hill Street*'s cast and technical personnel had worked together on Bochco's previous series *Paris* 1979–80 (actors Michael Warren, Kiel Martin and Joe Spano were all from the previous team). While Bochco went on to create >*L.A Law*, *Doogie Howser M.D.* (1989–), *Hooperman* (1987–9) and costly musical flop *Cop Rock* (1990), *Hill Street* continued until Travanti refused to do an eighth season in 1987.

Honey West

USA 1965–6 30 × 30m ABC. A Four Star Production. *UK tx* ABC Midlands 1966. *pr* Jules Levy, Arthur Gardiner, Arnold Laven. *mus* Joseph Mullendore. *cast* **Honey West** Anne Francis **Sam Bolt** John Ericson **Aunt Meg** Irene Hervey.

Honey West was a blonde, judo-kicking, leather-clad private eye created by husband and wife writing team 'G G Fickling' in a series of late fifties/early sixties novels. She made her first television appearance in an episode of *Burke's Law*, in which she succeeded in outwitting Capt Amos Burke himself (no small feat).

Honey turned to detective work after inheriting the family agency, complete with employee Sam Bolt, from her father. And she was spectacularly well equipped for the job. Not only a martial arts expert, she was also the owner of a positive arsenal of gadgetry which included such items as a radio transmitter concealed in a lipstick. Her undercover operations were undertaken from a specially equipped van labelled 'H.W. Bolt and Co, TV Service' and, like many PIs after her, her constant companion was a pet – Bruce the ocelot.

Inevitably compared to British series >*The Avengers*, *Honey West* did not match up. The concept was good and Honey deserves credit for working in a man's world in such prehistoric TV times, but the half-hour slots lacked much in their execution – the blonde was not brassy enough and the storylines were unimaginative. All this, plus poor production values and casting problems meant the series only lasted one season in the States and made it to just one brief airing on ABC Midlands in Britain. Intended to be noteworthy for its gusty heroine, it was in fact mostly memorable for the fight scenes in which a man with a blond wig was quite obviously wheeled in to do the stunts.

Ironside

(British title: A Man Called Ironside)

USA 1967–75 188 × 60m/7 × 120m col NBC. Harbour Productions/Universal TV/NBC. *UK tx* 1967–75 BBC. *cr* Collier Young. *exec pr* Cy Chermak, Joel Rogosin, Frank Price, Collier Young. *pr* Albert Aley, Douglas Benton, Norman Jolley, Paul Mason, Jerry McAdams, Winston Miller, Lou Morheim, Collier Young. *dr* Abner Biberman, Michael Caffey, Richard Colla, Charles S Dubin, John Florea, David Friedkin, William Graham, Daniel Haller, Leonard Horn, Jerry Jameson, Bruce Kessler, Alf Kjellin, Russ

Mayberry, Don McDougall, James Neilson, Christian I Nyby II, Leo Penn, Daniel Petrie, Allen Reisner, David Lowell Rich, Boris Sagal, Jimmy Sangster, Robert Scheerer, Ralph Senensky, Barry Shear, James Sheldon, Jeannot Szwarc, Don Weis. *wr* Don Mankiewicz, Collier Young, Albert Aley, Michael Philip Butler, Francine Carroll. Cy Chermak, James Doherty, William Gordon, Norman Jolley, Ken Kolb, William Douglas Langsford, Lou Morheim, Sy Salkowitz, Lane Slate, Christopher Trumbo. *mus* Monty Paich, Oliver Nelson. *cast* **Chief Robert T Ironside** Raymond Burr **Det Sgt Ed Brown** Don Galloway **Eve Whitfield** Barbara Anderson **Mark Sanger** Don Mitchell **Fran Belding** Elizabeth Baur **Commissioner Dennis Randall** Gene Lyons **Lt Carl Reese** Johnny Seven **Diana Sanger** Joan Pringle.

San Francisco Chief of Detectives Ironside, member of the force for twenty-five years, is paralysed from the waist down when a would-be assassin's bullet tears through his spinal column. Such was the premise of *Ironside*, initially intended as a two-hour made-for-TV movie. But this unusual hero proved so popular that an unplanned series took up where the movie left off.

Two hundred and fifteen-pound, wheelchair-bound Ironside (played by ex->*Perry Mason* star Raymond Burr) was duly given a permanent post as special consultant to the SFPD by Police Commissioner Randall, along with an operations base in the converted attic of Police Headquarters. Helping him wage his war against crime were top-flight police officers Sgt Ed Brown, policewoman Eve Whitfield and Mark Sanger, a black man with a history of run-ins with the law, who became Ironside's aide, bodyguard and driver of his customised van, specially equipped with telephone, tape-recorder and hydraulic lift.

Whitfield (played by Barbara Anderson of >*Mission Impossible)* left the series at the end of the 1970–1 season over a contract dispute and was replaced by Elizabeth Baur as policewoman Fran Belding. Sgt Brown and Sanger were given expanded roles – Brown took on more undercover work, and Mark went to law school, graduating at the start of the 1974–5 season and getting married.

The appeal of this solid, old-fashioned police series in which the robbers and murderers were always caught lay in the commanding, magnetic presence of Raymond Burr, who was so convincing in his role that viewers believed that Burr himself was paraplegic. Burr regarded the part as both a challenge and an eye-opener. 'There are many people incapacitated in many ways, not just paraplegics, who are being ignored,' he said. 'We kind of push them away into the dark.'

The series, consistently rating in the top twenty-five for most of its eight-year run, was only finally terminated due to Burr's ill-health. In 1974 he suffered first a heart attack and then further illness requiring a spell in hospital. Burr then retired to the Pacific Island Naitauba, near Fiji, that wages from his previous role as *Perry Mason* had earned him, and laid the law book to rest.

I Spy

USA 1965–8 82 × 60m NBC. NBC/Sheldon Leonard. *exec pr* Danny Thomas, Sheldon Leonard. *pr* Mort Fine, David Friedkin. *dr* Various, including Tom Gries, Paul Wendkos, Mark Rydell, David Friedkin, Mort Fine, Richard Sarafin, Sheldon Leonard. *wr* Various, including Mort Fine, David Friedkin, Arthur Dales. *mus* Earle Hagen (theme). *cast* **Kelly Robinson** Robert Culp ***Alexander Scott*** Bill Cosby.

Espionage entertainment of some slickness, but chiefly interesting as the first major series to star a black actor and a white actor on equal footing. NBC worried about Southern reaction to this innovation and producers lost sleep over such questions as whether the two stars should sit together in the front of a car or occupy the same room in a hotel. *I Spy* told, with an edge of subversive humour, of the exploits of US government undercover agents Kelly Robinson, a former Princeton law student posing as a top-seeded tennis player, and Alexander Scott, graduate of Temple, Rhodes scholar and consummate linguist who posed as his trainer and travelling companion.

Solutions to the delicate points of black/white relations were overcome in many ways: Culp's Kelly tended to be in command (as Don Johnson would be in >*Miami Vice* some twenty years later when working with black actor Philip Michael Thomas); the series took place not in the States but always in foreign lands; and Cosby's Scott was well dressed, well spoken and easily

Bill Cosby was the first black actor to receive equal billing with a white star in the 1960s thriller series *I Spy*. Cosby and Robert Culp played international espionage agents, Alexander Scott and Kelly Robinson, who went undercover as a tennis coach and ace player.

assimilated. He was also presented as less sexual and less of a ladies' man than Culp although he did appear opposite black women such as Cicely Tyson, Nancy Wilson and Gloria Foster.

Competently made, with good scripts and some excellent locations, the series was a ratings success and Cosby won three Emmys for his role. Arriving during an era of intense racial turmoil, *I Spy* projected a vision of black and white harmony. It set a precedent for televisual inter-racial male bonding – which had previously come no closer than the master/servant relationship of Jack Benny and Rochester – which was to recur regularly in shows such as *NYPD Blue*, *Enos*, *Stir Crazy*, *The Insiders* and of course >*Miami Vice*. The black man had now come into American homes as a trusted friend, and was soon seen in this guise in network series as diverse as >*Mission Impossible*, >*Daktari*, >*Star Trek* and >*Mannix*.

Cosby himself of course was to become a national institution with his liberal values and a series of comedy-variety shows that led to his monster hit >*The Cosby Show*.

Series director Richard Sarafian went on to direct feature film *Vanishing Point* (1971), while in 1972 Culp and Cosby teamed up again as a pair of down-at-heel private eyes in the movie *Hickey & Boggs*, which Culp also directed.

Johnny Staccato (aka Staccato)

USA 1959–60 27 × 25m bw NBC/ABC. MCA/Universal. *UK tx* 1960 ITV. *cr* John Cassavetes. *pr* William Freye. *dr* John Cassavetes, Bernard Girard, Robert Parrish, Joseph Pevney, Boris Sagal, John Brahm, Paul Henreid. *wr* Various, including John Cassavetes. *mus* Elmer Bernstein (theme). *cast* **Johnny Staccato** John Cassavetes **Waldo** Eduardo Cianelli.

Much criticised on its original US release for being a carbon copy of >*Peter Gunn*, this John Cassavetes series actually had a dynamic style all its own. Cassavetes played Johnny Staccato, a jazz musician turned private detective, working out of Waldo's club in downtown New York and taking whatever cases came along. The series was *noir*-ishly shot and lit, performances were sharp, and the stylish visuals were underscored by pulsating jazz rhythms. The theme was composed by Elmer Bernstein, while scenes in Waldo's club often included background playing by such jazz luminaries as Barney Kessel, Red Mitchell, Red Norvo and Johnny Williams. (The latter composed the music for the film *Star Wars* among other high-profile projects.)

John Cassavetes used the money he earned from this popular and too-brief series to finance his directorial début film, *Shadows* (1959). As with his subsequent movies as director – which include *Husbands*, 1970, and *Gloria*, 1980 – the film was experimental and controversial, and Cassavetes remains one of the biggest influences on American avant-garde film. He is probably most familiar, however, for his starring role in the movie *The Dirty Dozen* (1967) and as Mia Farrow's betraying husband in *Rosemary's Baby* (1968).

Paul Henreid, one of the stars of the classic movie *Casablanca*, directed the *Staccato* episode, 'The Mask of Jason'.

Juliet Bravo

UK 1980–5 82 × 50m col BBC1. BBC. *cr* Ian Kennedy Martin. *pr* Terence Williams, Peter Cregeen, Geraint Morris. *dr* Various, including Adrian Shergold, Derek Lister, Paul Ciappessoni, Jan Sargent, Carol Wilks, Jonathan Alwyn, Pennant Roberts, Brian Finch, Tristan De Vere Cole. *wr* Various, including Ian Kennedy Martin, Wally K Daly, Susan Pleat, Paula Milne, John Foster, Tony Parker, Ewart Alexander, Don Webb, Tony Charles. *cast* **Insp Jean Darblay** Stephanie Turner **Insp Kate Longton** Anna Carteret **Tom Darblay** David Hargreaves **Sgt Joe Beck** David Ellison **Sgt Joe Parrish** Noel Collins **PC Danny Sparks** Mark Botham **PC Brian Kelleher** C J Allen.

Although it came from the creator of actioner >*The Sweeney*, this Lancashire-based police series was reminiscent of >*Z Cars* – low-key Northern, but full of realistically human drama. The opening episode,

'Fraudulently Uttered', about a charlady stealing the boss's profits (but not for her own benefit) set the tone for the whole series. What distinguished *Juliet Bravo* from *Z-Cars* was that the central figure was a woman police officer, Inspector Jean Darblay (played by Stephanie Turner, one-time *Z-Cars* WPC, also George Carter's wife in >*The Sweeney*), and the series limelighted the sexism she faced from the male officers at the fictional Hartley police station. In the fourth season Darblay was promoted upstairs and Inspector Kate Longton (Anna Carteret from *The Raving Beauties* feminist cabaret) took over her post.

Unsurprisingly perhaps, *Bravo* – which débuted in the same year as another British policewoman series, *The Gentle Touch* with Jill Gascoine – was particularly popular amongst female viewers. The series' title came from the radio call sign for Hartley's station's woman commander.

'Who loves ya, baby?' Telly Savalas as lollipop-sucking, hard-nosed but soft-hearted New York homicide cop *Kojak*.

Kojak

USA 1973–8 112 × 60m/2 × 120m/1 × 180m col CBS. A Universal Television Production. *UK tx* 1974–8 BBC1. *cr* Abby Mann. *exec pr* Matthew Rapf. *pr* James McAdams, Jack Laird, Chester Krumholz. *dr* Edward M Abroms, Richard Donner, Charles S Dubin, Jerrold Freedman, David Friedkin, Daniel Haller, Jerry London, Russ Mayberry, Sigmund Neufeld Jr, Christian I Nyby II, Joel Oliansky, Ernest Pintoff, Allen Reisner, Telly Savalas, Nicholas Sgarro, Paul Stanley. *wr* Various, including Donald P Bellisario, Ray Brenner, Robert Earll, Jerrold Freedman, Mort Fine, Rift Fournier, Robert Foster, Gene Kearney, Chester Krumholz, Marvin Kupker, Jack Laird, John Meredyth Lucas, Harriet Margulies, James McAdams, Joel Oliansky, Don Patterson, Joseph Polizzi, Eugene Price, Matthew Rapf, Albert Ruben, Bill Schwartz, Robert Swanson, Ross Teel, Michael Wagner. *mus* Billy Goldenberg (theme). *cast* **Lt Theo Kojak** Telly Savalas **Frank McNeil** Dan Frazer **Lt Bobby Crocker** Kevin Dobson **Det Stavros** George Savalas **Det Saperstein** Mark Russell **Det Rizzo** Vince Conti.

'Who loves ya baby?' Until he starred in *Kojak*, the answer for Telly Savalas was 'No one'. He had played the baddie in over seventy films (he first shaved his head for Burt Lancaster's 1962 film *Birdman of Alcatraz*) but it was not until he played the lollipop-sucking, shaven-headed Greek-American cop at the age of forty-nine that Savalas got famous.

The character audiences fell for worldwide was loud, straight-talking Theo Kojak. A snazzy dresser with fancy waistcoats and an eye for the women, Kojak worked out of New York City's Manhattan South precinct and was a tough, cynical cop for a tough cynical town. But that was just on the surface – inside he had a tender streak. He cared about his job and he cared about people getting a rough deal and he was prepared to break the rules if it meant he got justice.

Kojak had a failed marriage and twenty years in the force behind him. His partner in the NYPD when he started out was Frank McNeil, but Frank had worked his way up while Kojak had done things his way, so now Frank McNeil was chief of detectives and his boss. They were still friends but Frank was never entirely sure about his old pal's methods. Kojak's new partner was young plainclothes detective Lt Bobby Crocker and plump, easy-going Det Stavros – whose name at first appeared on cast lists as 'Demosthenes' but who was actually played by Telly's younger brother George Savalas.

Police applauded *Kojak* for being true to life, while anti-violence lobbies complained about the violence, although violence was always a last resort in the series. Extensive use of location footage gave *Kojak* edge and flavour. But what gave the series its realism and its huge appeal was Savalas himself. Savalas played the part with gusto and identified strongly with his on-screen persona ('You tell me the difference between Kojak and Telly and I'll tell you the difference between apples and apple pie.' he declared). Unashamedly larger than life himself he acquired a home in Paul Newman's one-time Beverly Hills estate, a Rolls Royce Silver Cloud – numberplate TELLY S – and six other foreign sports cars, cut a best-selling LP and got paid $100,000 a week to headline a Las Vegas hotel show. But just like Kojak, there was another side to Savalas. Awarded the Purple Heart as a war hero he had worked as a senior director for ABC News before turning to acting in his thirties, and continued to work behind the camera for *Kojak*, directing episodes of the series.

Theo Kojak made his first appearance in a three-hour Emmy Award-winning TV movie *The Marcus-Nelson Murders*. This case established the cop's ethics, as he defended a black Brooklyn kid who had been pushed by the police into confessing to a crime he had not committed. The series was an instant hit, number seven in the ratings in its first season and second only to >*Hawaii Five-O* out of all cop and detective shows.

Kojak returned to rival ABC late in 1989 – after an eleven-year absence. The reprised series was one of four rotating elements in the network's *Mystery Movie* package along with >*Columbo*, Kojak's old adversary, also enjoying a reprise. By this time Telly Savalas was sixty-five, and Kojak was an Inspector with a bright young assistant called Winston Blake and a secretary called Pamela.

LA Law

USA 1986– 140+ × 60m col NBC. Twentieth Century Television. *UK tx* 1987–1992 ITV. 1992– BSkyB. *cr* Stephen Bochco, Terry Louise Fisher. *exec pr* Steven Bochco, Gregory Hoblit, Rick Wallace, David E Kelley, William Finkelstein, Mark Tinker, Elodie Kene. *pr* Various, including Terry Louise Fisher, Ellen S Pressman, James C Hart, Philip M Goldfarb, David E Kelley, Scott Goldstein, Michele Gallery, William M Finkelstein, Judith Parker, Elodie Keene, Michael M Robin, Patricia M Green. *dr* Various, including Gregory Hoblit, Elodie Keene, Mervin Bennett Dayan, Rick Wallace, Steve Robman, Mimi Leder, Janet Greek, Philip M Goldfarb, E W Swackhammer, Donald Petrie, Eric Laneuvile, Kim Friedman, Sam Weisman. *wr* Various, including Terry Louise Fisher, D Keith Mano, David E Kelley, John Masius, John Tinker, Julie Martin. *mus* Mike Post. *cast* **Leland McKenzie** Richard Dysart **Douglas Brackman Jr** Alan Rachins **Michael Kuzak** Harry Hamlin **Grace Van Owen** Susan Dey **Arnie Becker** Corbin Bernsen **Ann Kelsey** Jill Eikenberry **Victor Sifuentes** Jimmy Smits **Abby Perkins** Michele Greene **Roxanne Melman** Susan Ruttan **Jonathan Rollins** Blair Underwood **Stuart Markowitz** Michael Tucker **Benny Stulwicz** Larry Drake **Rosalind Shays** Diana Muldaur **Tommy Mullaney** John Spencer **C J Lamb** Amanda Donohoe **Zoey Clemmons** Cecil Hoffmann

Corrine Hammond Jennifer Hetrick, **Gwen Taylor** Sheila Kelley **Tommy Mulkiney** John Spencer **Daniel Morales** A Martinez.

Stylish and sexy legal drama. Co-devised by Steven Bochco, *LA Law* won both viewer popularity and critical acclaim with its formula of strong ensemble acting, layered stories, humour and social awareness; it won Emmy Awards for Outstanding Drama Series in 1987, 1989, 1990 and 1991.

Soapier than Bochco's earlier hit show >*Hill Street Blues*, *LA Law* concerned the ambitious and attractive attorneys of prestigious Los Angeles firm McKenzie Brackman Chaney & Kuzak, devoting as much time to their byzantine internal sexual affairs as to their external professional casework. Kuzak (played by Harry Hamlin, voted the sexiest man alive by *People* magazine in 1987) lusted after idealistic DA Grace Van Owen, but she became pregnant by the firm's token Hispanic, Sifuentes, while Markowitz had the hots for Kelsey . . . In one of the most famous episodes, 'Venus Butterfly' (which won a best teleplay Emmy in 1987 for co-creator Terry Louise Fisher) Markowitz was taught a sexual technique by a client which meant that Kelsey succumbed to his charms overnight. Other main members of the practice were fatherly senior partner Leland McKenzie, egotistical Brackman, and sleazy divorce lawyer Arnie Becker. In 1989 Roz Shays joined McKenzie Brackman and almost destroyed it – after an affair with McKenzie – in a boardroom power-struggle. A later addition was Cara Jean ('C J') Lamb, played by Golden Globe-winning English actress Amanda Donohoe (also the film *Castaway*).

The series' liberal airing of 'problem' issues generated almost as much interest as its sex life. The cases taken by the firm's legal eagles frequently reflected topical social problems such as Aids, racial discrimination, sexism, persistent vegetative syndrome and Tourette's syndrome. The American media went into frenzy when C J enjoyed an on-screen lesbian kiss with Abby, and the show was notable for being one of the few ever to feature a retarded person, Benny Stulwicz, portrayed by two-time Emmy-winner Larry Drake.

In 1991 several of the main characters left the show, including Kuzak (Hamlin), and the show slid somewhat in critical and popular affection.

To put the chutzpah back in the show, William Finkelstein was drafted in as executive producer. Finkelstein, a former attorney, had been *LA Law*'s original supervising producer, but had left to create and oversee *Civil Wars*. Returning to *LA Law* he brought with him *Civil Wars* actors Alan Rosenberg and Debi Mazar, who reprised their *Civil Wars* characters – Eli Levinson and Denise Iannello – on *LA Law*. Their addition to the cast was the first time in prime-time TV history that characters from one **series** had been transplanted to another network's non-spin-off series.

The Man From UNCLE

USA 1964–7 105 × 50m bw/col NBC. MGM/Arena. *UK tx* 1965–8 BBC1. *cr* Norman Felton, Ian Fleming, Sam Rolfe. *exec pr* Norman Felton. *pr* Sam Rolfe, David Victor, Anthony Spinner. *dr* Various, including John Brahm, Barry Shear, E Darrell Hallenbeck, Don Medford, Alf Kjellin, Sherman Marks, Richard Donner. *wr* Various, including Peter Allen Fields, Dean Hargrove, Harlan Ellison, Robert Towne. *mus* Jerry Goldsmith. *cast* **Napoleon Solo** Robert Vaughn **Ilya Kuryakin** David McCallum **Mr Alexander Waverly** Leo G Carroll. *Video* MGM/UA.

'Open Channel D.' A legendary spy spoof conceived over lunch in London between producer Norman Felton and James Bond's creator, Ian Fleming. Felton wanted to do a TV series which mixed elements of MGM's 1959 feature starring Cary Grant, *North by North-West*, and the Bond films. Fleming thought it was a good idea, and chipped in the name 'Solo' for the character and the series. The US NBC network bought the show but Fleming was forced to drop out of the project by the Bond producers, who considered it too much like their movies. (They also prevented the series being called *Solo*, the name of a character in *Diamonds Are Forever*.) In his place, Felton hired Sam Rolfe, previously the writer-producer of >*Have Gun – Will Travel*. And it was Rolfe, from Felton and Fleming's sketchy beginnings, who developed the product which became *The Man From UNCLE*. Rolfe begat the idea that Solo should belong to an international organisation called UNCLE (initially a meaningless collection of letters, but later to stand for United Network Command for Law Enforcement), as well as inventing Solo's sidekick, Ilya Kuryakin.

The part of the suave, womanising Napoleon Solo, super-spy, ex-Korean War veteran and philosophy graduate, was turned down by Harry Guardino and by Robert Culp. Third choice, Robert Vaughn, one of the stars of *The Magnificent Seven* film, accepted. Meanwhile blond-haired British David McCallum, at the time a virtual unknown in America, got the part of austere Ilya Kuryakin because he happened to be wandering the *The Man From UNCLE* lot with his friend, Charles Bronson, and was introduced to one of the series' directors, Don Medford. Although only a minor role to begin with, the character of Kuryakin was essential to the success of *The Man From UNCLE*. His black polo-necked cool and long(ish) hair became much admired amongst middle-class youth, while his Russian nationality enabled *The*

Born over a lunchtime conversation with 007's creator Ian Fleming, *The Man From UNCLE* was a spy spoof which became a craze. From left to right are UNCLE operatives Ilya Kuryakin (David McCallum) and Napoleon Solo (Robert Vaughn) with their boss Mr Waverly (Leo G Carrol).

Man From UNCLE to be the first TV spy series of the 1960s to transcend the Cold War. Utopian and escapist, *The Man From UNCLE* perfectly fitted the new mood of the Kennedy years.

This notwithstanding, Solo and Kuryakin still needed villains to vanquish. In a refinement of the Bond film's SPECTRE organisation, *The Man From UNCLE* introduced THRUSH, an international criminal organisation, as Solo and Kuryakin's principal enemy. This was dedicated to achieving world power, and used many dastardly means to this end, among them a formula for anti-matter ('The Suburbia Affair'), a death ray ('The Maze Affair') and a volcano detonator ('The Cherry Blossom Affair'). Occasionally, Solo and Kuryakin fought non-THRUSH villains, such as crazy Nazis ('The Deadly Game Affair'). But whoever the bad guys were the episodes – or 'Affairs' – were highly formulaic. The agents would be briefed at UNCLE's HQ, behind Del Floria's tailorship in New York, by tweedy boss Alexander Waverly (Leo G Carroll, who had appeared in *North by North-West*), and the case would involve an ordinary person in trouble – a housewife or lorry driver, for instance – and nothing less than the fate of the world. After life-threatening setbacks, the agents would triumph, and Solo would get the girl.

There were other standard elements too. Each episode featured at least two high-profile guest stars. Appearing over the seasons were, among others, Vincent Price (as a THRUSH bad-guy in 'The Fox and Hounds Affair'), Boris Karloff (in drag in 'The Mother Muffin Affair'), Sharon Tate ('The Girl of Nazarene Affair'), Jill Ireland (then McCallum's wife, in 'The Tigers Are Coming Affair'), and Joan Crawford ('The Concrete Overcoat Affair'). William Shatner and Leonard Nimoy appeared in 'The Project Strigas Affair' two years before they were on the bridge of the USS *Enterprise* together. *The Man From UNCLE* also featured an impressive display of gimmickry and techno-hardware. Apart from radio-receiver pens, there was the Man from UNCLE car, a blue two-seat Piranha sports coupé, complete with rocket launchers and machine guns, and the famous 'UNCLE Special' gun. This state-of-the-art weapon was a pistol which could be converted by attachments into a machine-gun or rifle. It was designed by resident *UNCLE* props men Reuben Klemmer and Richard Conroy.

The gadgetry undoubtedly added to the appeal of the show (especially amongst small boys), which by its third season had developed a fan club of some half-million members. Unfortunately, the same season saw the show flip into outright comedy, while the gadgets descended to the ridiculous, including, in 'The Suburbia Affair', popsicle grenades. The show also met with an anti-TV violence campaign of some influence.

However, during its heyday (when show scriptwriters included Robert Towne, later to win an Oscar for *Chinatown*) some eight films edited from TV episodes, including *To Trap a Spy*, *One of Our Spies Is Missing*, *The Helicopter Spies*, and *How to Steal the World* were produced. There was also a spin-off series, *The Girl From UNCLE*, in 1967, with Stefanie Powers as title character April Dancer, and Noel 'son of Rex' Harrison playing Mark Slade. (Dancer was first played by Miss America, Mary Ann Mobley, in a *Man From UNCLE* episode entitled 'The Moonglow Affair', but she was dropped for the series.) In 1983 Robert Vaughn – a PhD and author of a study of Hollywood blacklisting, *Only Victims* – and David McCallum reprised their super-spy roles in *The Return of the Man From UNCLE*, a made-for-TV movie.

Man In A Suitcase

UK 1967–8 30 × 60m col ITV. An ITC Production for ATV. *USA tx* 1968 28 × 60m ABC, syndicated. *cr* Richard Harris, Dennis Spooner. *pr* Sidney Cole. *dr* Charles Crichton, Gerry O'Hara, Pat Jackson, Robert Tronson, Freddie Francis, Herbert Wise, Peter Duffell, Don Chaffey, John Glen, Jeremy Summers, Charles Frend. *wr* Francis Megahy and Bernie Cooper, Edmund Ward, Philip Broadley, Stanley R Greenberg, Wilfred Greatorex, Jan Read, Roger Parkes, Vincent Tilsley, Reed de Rouen. *mus* Albert Elms, Ron Grainer (title). *cast* **MacGill** Richard Bradford. *Video* ITC.

Bounty hunter McGill, modern adventurer, was an ex-CIA man turned private investigator. Falsely accused of a treasonable offence (failing to stop an eminent scientist defecting to Russia) and kicked out of his job, he was forced to take up a new life and became the *Man in a Suitcase* – a British-based investigator willing to take on any job that paid him $500 a day (plus expenses).

McGill, played by Richard Bradford, was the latest in a string of ATV boss Sir Lew Grade's mid-Atlantic heroes. Sir Lew had been aiming series at the American market with considerable success since >*The Saint*, and was looking for more of the same. McGill neatly fitted the bill. Following close on the heels of ATV's >*The Baron*, McGill was a rugged loner searching Europe for clues to clear his name. His only companions were a battered leather suitcase containing a change of clothes and a gun, and the fear of his shady background catching up with him. Old romances occasionally flickered back into his life, only to be left behind as a new mission called. Always ready to pull a gun, he would win his fights without so much as taking the cigarette out of his mouth. And he needed to be tough because he could expect no help from the authorities against his never-ending stream of ruthless adversaries. In 'Day of Execution' he faced an unknown assassin's threat to eliminate him; in 'Dead Man's Shoes' he became the target for a group of vicious gangsters; in 'No Friend of Mine' his job as a mercenary in Africa got him sandwiched between white settlers and native; and in 'Three Blinks of the Eyes' he faced the guillotine unless he could find the woman who had hired him to bring her playboy husband to heel.

Man In A Suitcase was a superior thriller series. Thanks to Sir Lew Grade's lust for US sales some of the best production personnel and guest stars were engaged. Directors included John Glen (now better known as director of the Bond films *For Your Eyes Only*, *Octopussy* and *A View to a Kill*), Charles Crichton (respected director of comedy films from *Lavender Hill Mob* and *The Titfield Thunderbolt* to *A Fish Called Wanda*) and Freddie Francis (who made his name in feature films of a more gruesome nature, such as *Dracula Has Risen from the Grave* and *The Creeping Flesh*). Guest stars included Colin Blakely, George Sewell, Robert Urquhart, Donald Sutherland, Judy Geeson, Peter Vaughan, Patrick Cargill, Philip Madoc, Felicity Kendal, Ray McAnally and Edward Fox.

Mannix

USA 1967–75 191 × 60m col CBS. Paramount Television. *UK tx* 1971, 1980–3 ITV. *cr* Richard Levinson, William Link *exec pr* Bruce Geller. *pr* Ivan Goff, Ben Roberts. *dr* Various, including Corey Allen, Michael Caffey, Reza S Badiyi, Richard Benedict, Marvin Chomsky, Barry Crane, Harry Harvey Jr, Alf Kjellin, John Llewellyn Moxey, Paul Krasny, Seymour Robbie, Arnold Laven, Michael O'Herlihy, Allen Reisner, Sutton Roley, Jud Taylor, Bruce Geller, Fernando Lamas. *wr* Various, including Richard L Breen Jr, Don Brinkley, Howard Browne, Ric Vollaerts, John Kneubuhl, Robert Pirosh, John Meredyth Lucas, Edward J Lasko, Shirl Hendryx, Robert Lewin, Don M Mankiewicz, James Surtees, Lionel L Siegel. *mus* Lalo Schifrin. *cast* **Joe Mannix** Mike Connors **Peggy Fair** Gail Fisher **Lou Wickersham** Joseph Campanella **Lt Adam Tobias** Robert Reed **Lt Arthur Malcolm** Ward Wood **Lt George Kramer** Larry Linville **Lt Daniel Ives** Jack Ging.

Some like 'em tough. Joe Mannix, played with muscular professionalism by Mike Connors, was a private detective of some brains, but more considerable brawn. Initially an operative with the hi-tech Los Angeles agency Intertect, Mannix left after disagreements with boss Lou Wickersham (over Mannix's violent methods) to set up his own solo operation. From season two onwards, Mannix rented a Marlowesque office on the ground floor of his own apartment block at 17 Paseo Verde, with secretarial help from black Peggy Fair, widowed wife of a former cop buddy. (Part of the series' draw was undoubtedly the thrill of possible miscegenation.) Away from the restraining influence of Wickersham, Mannix was even more routinely involved in fight action and car chases. As his clients found to their relief, there was nothing – absolutely nothing – that scared iron Joe Mannix.

Naturally though, a heart of gold beat beneath the armour-plated exterior. A small child or a pretty girl needed only to ask and Joe Mannix would perform his services for free. His sleuthing efficiency was improved by occasional favours from LAPD lieutenants Tobias (Robert Reed) and Kramer (played by Larry Linville, later Frank Burns in >*M*A*S*H*).

Mannix is almost certainly the most violent crime series ever to appear on TV. Every episode was replete with bloody fisticuffs and deadly gun action. The wonder is not that *Mannix* was popular – in 1971 it was the top-rated crime show of the season in America – but that it lasted eight years before being cancelled.

In 1981 Mike Connors – real name Kreker Ohanion – starred in the revival of Quinn Martin's *FBI*, *Today's FBI*.

Mark Saber

(US title The Vise)

UK 1957–9 52 × 30m bw ITV. ABC. *US tx* ABC 1955–7. *pr* Edward and Harry Lere Danziger. *wr* Brian Clemens. *cast* **Mark Saber** Donald Gray **Stephanie Ames** Diane Decker **Barney O'Keefe** Michael Balfour **Insp Brady** Patrick Holt **Insp Chester** Colin Tapley.

Saber of London

UK 1959–61 83 × 30m bw ITV. *US tx* NBC 1957–60. *pr* Edward and Harry Lee Danziger. *cast* **Mark Saber** Donald Gray **Bob Page** Robert Arden **Peter Paulson** Neil McCallum **Eddie Wells** Jerry Thorne **Insp Parker** Colin Tapley.

Mark Saber graced the small screen in many guises, but was most famous in his incarnation as the British, one-armed PI. Played by South African Donald Gray – who had actually lost an arm in World War II – Saber was one of the earliest British private eyes to gain transatlantic fame and his movie-idol looks won him devoted fans in the US. One of the BBC's first postwar television announcers, Gray made over 100 *Saber* adventures in which he was joined by other series regulars Stephanie Ames, his secretary, and right-hand man Barney O'Keefe. The series saw the dapper Saber and friends leave their London base to track blackmailers, and murderers and other crooks through glamorous locations in Paris, the Riviera and elsewhere.

A second series, *Saber of London*, produced by the same team for syndication in the States, followed hot on the heels of the first and found our hero assisted by a different team. Secretary Stephanie found her services no longer required and a series of male assistants including Canadian associate Peter Paulson stepped in to replace O'Keefe. Colin Tapley stoically remained an Inspector, though curiously under a change of name.

After the series Gray found himself unable to escape typecasting and had to work almost exclusively in radio and commercials until his death in 1978.

The first time the Saber character was seen on TV was actually in a US production *Inspector Mark Saber*. Even in this version Saber was thoroughly British, with pinstriped suits and pencil-thin moustache and it starred Tom Conway, with James Burke as sidekick Sergeant Tim Maloney. This half-hour detective series, originally titled *Mark Saber Mystery Theatre* had transferred from radio and ran for seventy-eight episodes from 1951–4. It was produced by Roland Reed Productions for ABC.

McCloud

USA 1970–7 6 × 60m/19 × 90m/21 × 120m col NBC. Universal. *UK tx* 1972–6 ITV. *cr* Herman Miller, Glen A Larson. *exec pr* Glen A Larson, Leslie Stevens, Richard Irving. *pr* Michael Gleason, Dean Hargrove, Winrich Kolbe, Ronald Gilbert Satloff, Lou Shaw. *dr* Various, including Glen A Larson, Richard A Colla, Douglas Heyes, Bruce Kessler, Lou Antonio, Nicholas Colasanto, Jerry Paris, Harry Falk, Jimmy Sangster, Russ Mayberry, Hy Averback, Boris Sagal, Noel Black, Jerry Jameson. *wr* Various, including Leslie Stevens, Dean Hargrove, Nicholas Baehr, Sidney Ellis, Robert Hamner, Glen A Larson, Stephen Lord, Michael Gleason, Sy Salkowitz. *mus* Richard Clements. *cast* **Deputy Marshal Sam McCloud** Dennis Weaver **Police Chief Peter B Clifford** J D Cannon **Sergeant Joe Broadhurst** Terry Carter **Chris Coughlin** Diana Muldaur, **Sergeant Maggie Clinger** Sharon Gless.

The exploits of a cowboy-laymen-in-the-big-city, loosely based on the 1968 Clint Eastwood feature *Coogan's Bluff*. Dennis Weaver played Sam McCloud, a New

Mexican in New York ostensibly studying the ways and methods of the cops of the 27th Precinct. In fact, Deputy Marshall McCloud studiously ignored local *modus operandi* and treated Manhattan like the Wild West, wore a stetson and cowboy boots, and talked in a homily-laden, down-home-on-the-range manner. Occasionally, he even rode his horse.

McCloud was not a cop show which was very serious about itself; indeed, it usually had its tongue in both cheeks. It also worked the idea of a Western-set-in-a-city effortlessly well, with New York's skyscrapers doing a good job as substitute canyons. And a good number of McCloud's cases were uncannily pure frontier: cattle rustling at the meat market, banks robbed by villains in Old West outfits and the like. Leslie Stevens, one of the series' main producers, had a long history in TV Westerns (including the creation of >*Stoney Burke*), as did Dennis Weaver himself, onetime Deputy Chester from >*Gunsmoke*.

The other cast members were J D Cannon as long-suffering Chief Peter B Clifford, Terry Carter as black Sergeant Joe Broadhurst (dragged into constant trouble by McCloud), and Diana Muldaur as McCloud's love interest, Chris Coughlin. Sharon Gless got in some early practice for >*Cagney and Lacey* as Sergeant Maggie Clinger.

The series originated as part of American NBC's *Four-in-One* series, moving to the *Mystery Movie* slot in 1971, where it rotated with >*Columbo* and >*McMillan and Wife*. There you go.

McMillan and Wife

USA 1971–7 1 × 120m/39 × 90m NBC. Talent Associates-Norton Simon Inc/Universal TV. *UK tx* 1972–9 ITV. *cr* Leonard B Stern. *exec pr* Leonard B Stern. *pr* Jon Epstein, Paul Mason, Ted Rich. *dr* Various, including Edward A Abroms, Lou Antonio, John Astin, Hy Averback, Harry Falk, Mel Ferber, Leonard J Horn, Lee H Katzin, Alf Kjellin, Barry Shear, James Sheldon, E W Swackhamer, Roy Winston. *wr* Various, including Howard Berk, Steven Bochco, Oliver Hailer, Robert Lewin, Leonard B Stern, Don M Mankiewicz. *cast* **Police Commissioner McMillan** Rock Hudson **Sally** **McMillan** Susan Saint James **Sgt Charles Enright** John Schuck **Mildred** Nancy Walker **Agatha** Martha Raye **Sgt Steve DiMaggio** Richard Gilland **Police Chief Paulsen** Bill Quinn **Maggie** Gloria Stroock.

Like >*Hart to Hart*, *McMillan and Wife* was a TV crime show which owed much to the Nick and Nora Charles *Thin Man* films of the thirties and forties. Hollywood star Rock Hudson, in his first small-screen series, played Stewart McMillan, debonair San Francisco Police Chief whose sexy-but-scatty wife, Sally (Susan Saint James), had an uncanny knack of finding corpses in the libraries of the glitzy mansions to which they were invited for cocktails every weekend. Sally usually also found herself kidnapped or in some form of life-threatening danger. The mysteries themselves owed much to the traditional or 'cosy' English whodunnit, but the series' most entertaining quality was the frolicsome relationship between Sally and Mac.

In the USA, *McMillan and Wife* rotated as part of the *NBC Mystery Movies* slot, reaching its highest US Nielsen position, number five, in 1972–3. The show changed format in 1976 when Saint James left over a contract dispute. Her character was killed off in a plane crash, leaving Hudson to detect alone as plain *McMillan*. Nancy Walker, who did scene-stealing stuff as the McMillans' acid housekeeper also left at the same time. The magic was gone, and the new version lasted only one season.

The episode directors included John Astin, better known as Gomez from >*The Addams Family*.

Miami Vice

USA 1984–9 108 × 60m/3 × 120m col NBC. A Universal Television Production. *UK tx* 1985–90 BBC. *cr* Anthony Yerkovich, Michael Mann. *exec pr* Michael Mann, Anthony Yerkovich. *dr* Various, including Michael Mann, David Soul, Don Johnson, Lee Katzin, Virgil W Vogel, Paul Michael Glaser, Michael O'Herlihy, Edward James Olmos, Paul Krasny. *wr* Various, including Miguel Pinero. *mus* Jan Hammer. *cast* **Det James 'Sonny' Crockett** Don Johnson **Det Ricardo Tubbs** Philip Michael Thomas **Lt Martin**

Castillo Edward James Olmos **Det Ginma Navarro
Calabrese** Saundra Santiago **Det Trudy Joplin** Olivia Brown
Det Stan Switek Michael Talbott **Det Larry Zito** John Diehl
Izzy Moreno Martin Ferrero **Caitlin Davies** Sheena Easton.
Video CIC.

Miami Vice was conceived in response to a single two-
word memo sent by NBC boss Brandon Tartijoff to
creators Yerkovich and Mann. It read: 'MTV Cops' and
the resulting series with its hyper-real colour, blue, blue
skies, Art Deco glitz, and throbbing rock soundtrack hit
the instruction on target.

Launching two relative unknowns in starring roles,
Miami Vice had a pair of male drug squad cops patrolling
the glamorous but sleazy Southern city. Sonny Crockett
(Don Johnson), an ex-football star, was the rough-edged,

Don Johnson (right), *sans* socks and with designer stubble,
gets his badge out as Sonny Crockett in Michael Mann's
colour co-ordinated *Miami Vice.* Philip Michael Thomas, as
partner Ricardo Tubbs, looks on.

designer-stubbled, bare-ankled vice cop who lived alone (after a failed marriage) save for pet alligator Elvis on a boat called *St Vitus Dance*; his partner Det Ricardo Tubbs (Philip Michael Thomas) had come to Miami from New York to search out the Colombian drug dealer who had killed his brother, and stayed. The audience knew little else about the duo save their jobs, but that didn't matter. The inter-racial buddy combo bonded and went undercover on the glamorous beaches and in the seedy back alleys of Miami, tracking pimps, drug-rackets and hookers amongst the seamy ethnic mix. From then on it was more form than content, but there were few complaints.

Scenes were colour co-ordinated – lime green and hot pink neon, bright white suits for sunshine and sand, pastels for daytime interiors, deep blues and purples for skylines at night. Clothes were from Uomi and Gianni Versace. These were the state-of-the-art production values of pop video, with high tech and rapid edits. If the plots sometimes wore thin the thickly woven music propelled the viewer on to the next piece of action with a soundtrack that was either specially commissioned or brought in from established stars to fit the action – among them were tracks by Tina Turner, Lionel Ritchie, the Pointer Sisters and the Rolling Stones. With the top cops driving Ferraris and speedboats this was TV as a ride in a fast car with stereo system blaring.

The hip, hip series was a smash hit and celebrities not normally seen in TV queued for cameo and guest roles, including singers from the fifties to the eighties – Little Richard, James Brown, Phil Collins, Ted Nugent and the Fat Boys. British stars making an appearance included Sheena Easton as singer Caitlin, who briefly became Mrs Crockett until she was gunned down by scriptwriters fearful that she would disturb the boys' relationship. As with much of the series, this black/white friendship was more fashion than social statement and there was no subversion involved – Crockett was always in control, leader of the two-man team. That said, at least a black man was in a lead role in a major weekly series and ex-*Hair!* star Thomas emerged as TV's first black male sex symbol.

But the glossy accessories and props took their toll on budgets. To attain the lush look Michael Mann was spending $1.2 million per episode. He was amply rewarded with a top ten hit in the first two seasons and fifteen Emmy nominations in the series' first year. But then NBC programmed it against >*Dallas*, and *Miami Vice* proved no match for the other high-life series. By its fifth and final season it had fallen to fifty-third place and the series was cancelled.

Executive producer Michael Mann meanwhile took his distinctive style on to the big screen with *Manhunter* (1986), a tense thriller that, long before *Silence of the Lambs*, had Dr Hannibal Lecter as its hero. Mann went on to hit box office success and critical acclaim with *Last of the Mohicans* (1992), starring Daniel Day Lewis and once again distinguished by vivid photography and a heart-pumping soundtrack.

Mission: Impossible

USA 1966–73 171 × 50m col CBS. Paramount TV. *UK tx* 1967–74 ITV. *cr* Bruce Geller. *exec pr* Bruce Geller. *pr* Stanley Kallis, Lee H Katzin, Joseph E Gantman, Laurence Heath. *dr* Various, including Bruce Geller, Alexander Singer, Allen H Miner, Bernard Kowalski, Alvin Ganzer, Lee H Katzin. *wr* Various, including Bruce Geller. *mus* Lalo Schifrin (theme) Shorty Rogers, Richard Hazard. *cast* **Daniel Briggs** Steven Hill **Jim Phelps** Peter Graves **Cinnamon Carter** Barbara Bain **Rollin Hand** Martin Landau **Willie Armitage** Peter Lupus **Barney Collier** Greg Morris **Voice on Tape** Bob Johnson **Paris** Leonard Nimoy **Dana Lambert** Lesley Ann Warren **Doug** Sam Elliot **Mimi Davis** Barbara Anderson **Lisa Casey** Lynda Day George.

'Your mission, Jim, should you decide to accept it . . .' Spoken on a tape-recorder that self-destructed five seconds later these words introduced each week's instalment of *Mission: Impossible*, a glossy actioner about the high-dramatic activities of the IMF (Impossible Missions Force), an élite American government espionage agency. Head of the IMF was Jim Phelps (Peter Graves, although Steven Hill as Dan Briggs held the post for season one), under whom worked a team of skilled agents: Rollin Hand (Martin Landau) was a master of disguise, Willie Armitage provided the muscle-power, Cinnamon Carter (Barbara Bain) was the female seductress and Barney Collier the electronics whizz-kid.

Although towards the end of its run the IMF tackled

such baddies as Organised Crime, its initial assignments nearly always involved saving some small country from Communism. To say that *Mission: Impossible* was pro-CIA would be an understatement; at times it might have served as a recruiting advertisement for Fort Langley. The programmes' saving graces were tight, fast-moving scripts and an array of neat gadgetry. And it did assume a certain level of viewer intelligence. Consequently it picked up a clutch of Emmy Awards: Outstanding Dramatic Series (1967, 1968); Outstanding Dramatic Writing (1967); and Outstanding Continued Performance by an Actress in a Leading Role (Barbara Bain, 1967, 1968, 1969). It also sold to seventy-one countries. Lalo Schifrin's jazzy theme music entered record charts on both sides of the Atlantic.

In 1969 Barbara Bain left the series, along with husband Martin Landau (the pair later starred together in >*Space 1999*). Their shoes were filled variously by Lesley Ann Warren, Lynda Day George, Barbara Anderson, and Leonard 'Spock' Nimoy as Paris. A notable aspect of the cast list for its time was that it included a black actor, Greg Morris, in a major role. Indeed, Morris' Barney Miller was something of a breakthrough character for African-Americans on TV in the sixties, being portrayed as the equal of the series whites in intelligence and professionalism.

In 1988 the American ABC network revived (badly) *Mission: Impossible*, producing episodes in Australia to avoid the American Writer's Guild strike. In a technological update, the details of the mission were given to Jim on a laser-disk that self-destructed.

Moonlighting

USA 1985–9 1 × 120m/66 × 60m col ABC. Picturemaker Productions. *UK tx* 1986–9 BBC2. *cr* Glenn Gordon Caron. *exec pr* Glenn Gordon Caron. *pr* Jay Daniel. *dr* Various. *wr* Various, including Glenn Gordon Caron. *mus* Lee Holdridge and Al Jarreau (theme), sung by Al Jarreau. *cast* **Maddie Hayes** Cybill Shepherd **David Addison** Bruce Willis **Agnes Dipesto** Allyce Beasley **Herbert Viola** Curtis Armstrong **Virginia Hayes** Eva Marie Saint **Alex Hayes** Robert Webber **MacGilicuddy** Jack Blessing. *Video* V-COL/ABC.

The epitome of postmodern TV, *Moonlighting* starred two beautiful people and tricksy self-referential technique. For all its crime plots and action, it was ultimately a romantic comedy with one old-fashioned and enduring question: 'Will they or won't they?'

This glamorous series – which rescued Cybill Shepherd's flagging career and shot Bruce Willis to Hollywood stardom – was one of ABC's few major hits in the mid-eighties, replete with in-jokes as well as detective elements. The plot revolved around cool one-time international model Maddie Hayes who after being swindled by embezzlers decides to turn the small detective agency among her assets from tax-dodge to profit-making concern. Along with the newly named Blue Moon Detective Agency she inherits brash, lascivious, wisecracking private eye David Addison whom she promotes to partner. Together they became LA's unlikeliest detective team and their love-hate relationship was the stuff of the show. Sexual chemistry sparked on screen. He lusted and wolf-whistled after her but elegant Maddie resisted – until the end of the second season that is, when the producers and the two characters gave in to the inevitable with a bed scene generating massive advance publicity and correspondingly huge ratings. Receptionist Miss Dipesto also added her own daffy, special charm to the proceedings.

There was considerable crossover between the stars and their on-screen characters (although if Shepherd's off-screen statements were to be believed, this did not stretch to the sexual chemistry). Cybill Shepherd was indeed an ex-model (in 1968 she was Model of the Year) and came to *Moonlighting* as one-time star of feature film *The Last Picture Show* (1971) and NBC's Texan rancher series *The Yellow Rose* (1983–4). Willis had previously landed only one role as a crook in *Miami Vice* and turned up among 3,000 hopefuls to read for the part of David Addison with a punk haircut, khaki army trousers and three earrings. He was the last to read and he got the part.

The show's aficionados loved it for its quirkiness and knowing games with TV conventions. One episode, for example, dealing with an unsolved forties mystery was shot in black and white. Another, 'Atomic Shakespeare' was written in iambic pentameter. Most featured one style-trick or another – asides to camera, shows within a show or comments on the show itself before the story began. The show pleased male and female audiences alike and the series won the ratings battle with the male-appeal show *Riptide* scheduled against it on NBC.

Inspired by the 1940 film *His Girl Friday*, *Moonlighting* was created by Glenn Gordon Caron (previous credits as producer-writer include *Breaking Away*, *Remington Steele* and >*Taxi*) and produced by his own company, Picturemaker Productions. Its much publicised production and personality problems – there was a running three-way battle between Shepherd, Willis and Caron that forced its creator off the series for its final season – only added a frisson for its devoted audience. But the problems were real. Episodes often ran over budget and over time and repeats were frequent during the regular season. *Moonlighting* was hastily cancelled in 1989. This proved no hardship to Bruce Willis, however, whose future was secure in movie stardom with lead roles in movies such as *Die Hard I* and *II*.

Murder One

USA 1995 23 × 60m col ABC. Steven Bochco Productions/20th Century Fox. *UK tx* 1996 Sky Movies, BBC2. *cr* Steven Bochco, Charles H Eglee, Channing Gibson. *exec pr* Steven Bochco, Charles H Eglee, Michael Fresco. *pr* Various, including Joe Ann Fogle, Ann Donahue, Geoffrey Neigher, Mark Buckland. *dr* Various, including Charles Haid, Michael Fresco, Nancy Savoca, Jim Charleston. *wr* Various, including Charles H Eglee, Steven Bochco, Geoffrey Neigher, Charles D Holland, Gay Walch, Channing Gibson, David Milch. *mus* Mike Post. *cast* **Theodore Hoffman** Daniel Benzali **Justine Appleton** Mary McCormack **Chris Docknovich** Michael Hayden **Lisa Gillespie** Grace Phillips **Arnold Spivak** J C MacKenzie **Richard Cross** Stanley Tucci **Det Arthur Polson** Dylan Baker **Lila Marquette** Vanessa Williams **Louis Heinsbergen** John Fleck **David Blalock** Kevin Tighe **Miriam Grasso** Barbara Bosson **Annie Hoffman** Patricia Clarkson **Neil Avedon** Jason Gedrick.

From ten-time Emmy winner Steven Bochco (six for >*Hill Street Blues*, three for >*LA Law*, one for >*NYPD Blue*), the first serialised law drama to follow a single case for an entire season. Hot on the heels of two real-life, long-running trials – the Menendez brothers and O J Simpson – the show took a gamble on art imitating life, hoping to engross a newly law-literate audience. Lest following one case for six months proved arduous for viewers, however, Bochco cannily sugared the pill with a heady mix of Hollywood, drugs, prostitution, and under-age sex: 'You've got your naked fifteen-year-old victim, you've got your presence of drugs, your rumours of sexual depravity and your gorgeous older sister and former alleged prostitute . . .' as character Chris Docknovich succinctly stated in episode one. And from grainy whip-pan *verité* to mannered freeze-frame and slow motion the camerawork helped push up the tension.

Intricately exploring every aspect of the high-profile murder, *Murder One* boasted a tough team of largely unknown actors led by the series' undisputed star – celebrity attorney Theodore 'Teddy' Hoffman played by Daniel Benzali. A theatrical performer citing Laurence Olivier as his hero, shaven-headed Brazilian-born Benzali honed his craft on the British stage (Trevor Nunn's Royal Shakespeare Company, Hal Prince's *Evita*, Andrew Lloyd Webber's *Sunset Boulevard*). Once in Hollywood, a recurring role in *LA Law* was followed by a performance as a mob attorney in *NYPD Blue* powerful enough to land him the role in *Murder One*. Benzali's past credits included a villainous appearance in the 1985 James Bond film *A View to a Kill*, and it was the blend of avenging angel and Machiavellian villain that gave this spock-eared, hawk-eyed man his fascination, his search for truth and justice inevitably compromised by the sleaze and corruption of his clients and milieu.

The world of Hoffman & Co ran the gamut of LA life from media, witnesses and jurors to the team of legal experts: insecure, cuticle-biting attorney Arnold Spivak, veteran investigator David Blalock, receptionist Lila Marquette (played by Vanessa Williams recently of >*Melrose Place*), intrepid legal assistant Louis Heinsbergen, boyish associate Chris Docknovich, and ambitious attorney Justine Appleton. The maestro's chief support on the case came from Lisa Gillespie, the wide-eyed innocent-but-smart attorney (Grace Phillips beat big names such as Claudia Schiffer to this plum part).

Ranged against Hoffman were veteran prosecuting attorney Miriam Grasso played by five-time Emmy nominee Barbara Bosson, Bochco's wife of twenty-six years, and the vengeful Detective Arthur Polson whose ambition to best Hoffman was spiked by a still-smouldering grudge from an earlier case.

Prime suspects, celebrities both, were wealthy Los Angeles philanthropist Richard Cross, owner of the luxurious LA apartment in which the fifteen-year-old girl was found and lover of women including the victim's older sister, and Hollywood brat and heartthrob Neil Avedon, a young star with questionable sexual tastes, once acting big but now running scared.

Sentiment was never too far away in this would-be mainstream production: music, titles and Hoffman's wife and young daughter at home all added a little schmaltz to the show. Fine performances lending a darker, everyone-has-secrets atmosphere and a plot with more twists and turns than an Eszterhas movie gave it a vice-like grip. Even so, when scheduled across America against ratings-topping hospital drama >*ER* poor audiences meant the plug was pulled after episode seven and it was relaunched in a different slot seven weeks later. In Britain, the BBC and Sky paid a record £250,000 for the series and scheduled it more wisely.

Naked City

USA 1958–62 39 × 25m/99 × 55m bw ABC. Shelle Productions/Screen Gems/A Columbia Pictures TV Production. *UK tx* 1962–3 ITV (57 episodes). *cr* Mark Hellinger, Sterling Silliphant. *exec pr* Herbert B Leonard. *pr* Charles Russell. *dr* Various, including Buzz Kulik, Arthur Hiller, Elliott Silverstein, Stuart Rosenberg, William Conrad, Laslo Benedek, Lamont Johnson, Jack Smight, Paul Wendkos, William A Graham, Tay Garnett, Harry Harris, Walter Graumann, Robert Ellis Miller. *wr* Various, including Sterling Silliphant, Herbert Leonard, Gene Roddenberry. *mus* Nelson Riddle, Billy May and Milton Raskin (theme). *cast* **Det Lt Dan Muldoon** John McIntire **Det Jim Halloran** James Franciscus **Janet Halloran** Suzanne Storrs **Lt Mike Parker** Horace McMahon **Det Adam Flint** Paul Burke **Libby** Nancy Malone **Ptlm/Sgt Frank Arcara** Harry Bellaver.

A police procedural out of the >*Dragnet* school of grainy urban realism, *Naked City* had numerous famous leading players – principally John McIntire, also a master of >*Wagon Train* – but the real star of the series was the vast metroplitan city which formed its backdrop: New York. Filmed with a hard, street look, the show made much use of the Big Apple's varied locales from downtown Manhattan to Staten Island, as veteran cop Muldoon taught new boy Halloran lessons on how to catch the city's massed petty villainry. Unlike Jack Webb's >*Dragnet*, *Naked City* did not pretend that all cops were angels in blue clothing, but recognised them as fallible human beings, sometimes little better than the crooks.

Cast changes were numerous. Muldoon's car crashed into a petrol tanker and he was killed in a blaze of glory when McIntire wanted out of the series before the end of the first season, and the role of old hand was taken by Lt Mike Parker. After a sixteen-month break the series returned in 1960 in a sixty-minute format, with tighter, deeper scripts and a new young sidekick for the tough Parker in the shape of Adam Flint, boyfriend of Libby.

The series – based on a 1948 feature *Naked City* directed by Jules Dassin, created and developed by Mark Hellinger – made a particular point of bizarre episode titles, notable among them 'Howard Running Bear Is a Turtle' and 'Today the Man Who Kills Ants Is Coming'. It also gave early parts to a wealth of the not yet famous, such as Dustin Hoffman, Robert Redford and Peter Falk.

The famous endline of each episode, intoned by the narrator, has become something of a cliché: 'There are eight million stories in the Naked City. This has been one of them.'

NYPD Blue

USA 1993– 44+ × 50m col ABC. Steven Bochco Productions. *UK tx* 1994– C4. *cr* Steven Bochco, David Milch. *pr* Steven Bochco, David Milch, Gregory Hoblit. *dr* Various, including Gregory Hoblit, Daniel Sachheim, Michael M Robin, Donna Deitch, Charles Haid, Mark Tinker, Elodie Keene. *wr* Various, including Steven Bochco, David Milch, Ann Biderman, Channing Gibson, Charles H Eglee, Ted Mann, Rosemary Breslin, David Mills, Gardner Stern. *mus*

Mike Post. *cast* **Det John Kelly** David Caruso **Det Andy Sipowicz** Dennis Franz **Lt Arthur Fancy** James McDaniel **Laura Kelly** Sherry Stringfield **James Martinez** Nicholas Turturro **Det Bobby Simone** Jimmy Smits **Det Greg Medavoy** Gordon Clapp **Asst District Attorney Sylvia Costas** Sharon Lawrence **Donna Abandando** Gail O'Grady.

Though much hailed for its originality, *NYPD Blue* owed a debt to Jack Webb's fifties police series >*Dragnet*. Like *Dragnet*, *NYPD Blue* made a virtue of a radical *verité* camerawork and the cityscape of New York.

NYP.D Blue was created by the golden boy of the American small screen, Steven Bochco (>*Hill Street Blues*, >*LA Law*, >*Cop Rock*, *Doogie Howser, M.D.*, *Hooperman*, *Civil Wars*), along with sometime Yale professor of English Literature, David Milch (*Hill Street Blues*, *Beverly Hills Buntz*). Veteran producer/director Gregory Hoblit, winner of ten Emmys, completed the *NYPD Blue* creative partnership. Though ostensibly bleaker than Bochco's other law-based shows, it contained a large degree of schmaltz, concentrating on the romantic liaisons and worktime abrasions of its 15th precinct characters, making it a sort of >*thirtysomething* with handcuffs. The principal protagonists were sensitive, ginger-haired Det John Kelly, who earned his detective shield aged twenty-eight (at the cost of his marriage to attorney Laura), and his long-term partner, the ex-alcoholic and permanently sweating Det Andy Sipowicz (played scene-stealingly by Vietnam vet Dennis Franz, previously >*Hill Street Blues*, >*Beverly Hills Buntz*). Storylines weaved romance, comradeship or competition in the precinct with moral-cum-social-based storylines like wife battering, racism on the streets or Aids victims in the tenements. Yet what held the attention – if not churned the stomach – was the camera work, tight, tense, jerky, hand-held, allowing the viewer fully to feel the precinct's pressure. Authenticity was added to by grainy half-lighting and ear-straining sound. It received a record-breaking twenty-six Emmy nominations at the end of its first season (winning six: Lead Actor for Franz, Writing, Directing, Editing, Art Direction, Casting). In series two a new member was introduced into the precinct, Det Bobby Simone, played by Jimmy Smits (Victor Sifuentes in >*LA Law*), who took over as Sipowicz's partner when Det Kelly's character

Detective John Kelly (David Caruso) in TV wunderkind Steven Bochco's Emmy-winning *NYPD Blue*.

was ruthlessly written out of the story in 'Dead and Gone' (Caruso, to studio ire, had quit for Hollywood). The new pairing was as watchable and nuanced as the old – perhaps no surprise, since Smits was Bochco's original choice for the role of Kelly – with an antagonistic start (Simone telling Sipowicz to 'kiss my French Portuguese ass') giving way to a *modus vivendi*, symbolised by a joint sing-along to 'Duke of Earl'. The other squadroom regulars were: Kelly's amour, Mob-employee Officer Janice Licalsi; streetwise young Det James Martinez (Nicholas Turturro, brother of John Turturro, star of *Barton Fink*), who increasingly took over some of John Kelly's caring, sharing mantle; the by-the-book precinct commander, Lt Arthur Fancy (James McDaniel, previously *Malcolm X*); self-destructive Greg Medavoy (Gordon Clapp, co-star of the cult film *Return of the Secaucus Seven*); the voluptuous-but-sensitive clerk Donna Abandando; and rising Assistant DA Sylvia Costas. At the end of season two Costas and Sipowicz married, ADA Sipowicz becoming pregnant by the opener of the following season, 'ER'.

Perry Mason

USA 1957–66 270 × 60m bw/1 × 60m col CBS. Paisano Productions. *UK tx* 1961–7 BBC1. *cr* Erle Stanley Gardner. *exec pr* Gail Patrick Johnson, Arthur Marks. *pr* Art Seid, Sam White, Ben Brady. *dr* Various. *wr* Various. *mus* Richard Shores, Fred Steiner. *cast* **Perry Mason** Raymond Burr **Della Street** Barbara Hale **Paul Drake** William Hopper **Hamilton Burger** William Talman **Lt Arthur Tragg** Ray Collins **David Gideon** Karl Held **Lt Anderson** Wesley Lau **Lt Steve Drumm** Richard Anderson **Sgt Brice** Lee Miller **Terence Clay** Dan Tobin.

A hugely successful series that made a star of Raymond Burr as Perry Mason, stalwart and near-invincible criminal lawyer. This early, staunchly reliable series with high production values ran in black and white for nine years, only venturing into colour for the final of its 271 episodes. A large part of *Perry Mason's* appeal was its predictability. Plots ran roughly thus: a murder would be investigated by trilby-hatted Lt Arthur Tragg who, with District Attorney Hamilton Burger, would build a watertight case. The accused then went to Perry Mason who would investigate the case along with devoted secretary Della Street and private detective Paul Drake.

Every episode ended in a courtroom trial, and every trial ended either with the witness yielding to Mason's dogged examination or with assistant Paul Drake rushing a vital piece of evidence into the courtroom in the nick of time – leaving Mason's adversary DA Hamilton Burger eternally thwarted, and Perry, Della and Paul to enjoy a leisurely post mortem of their victory. (When Mason lost one case because a defence witness refused to reveal vital information, thousands of viewers' letters signalled the level of audience dissatisfaction.)

Television's longest-running lawyer series was based on lawyer-novelist Erle Stanley Gardner's scores of novels featuring the defence attorney. Created in the 1933 novel, *The Case of the Velvet Claws*, the character was adapted for radio in a CBS series running from 1943–55, which was as much soap opera as detective series. Gardner, unhappy with the adaptation, opted to be creator for the TV series and was closely involved in every aspect from casting through to a cameo role as judge in the final episode 'The Case of the Final Fadeout'.

Burr, who had played a succession of baddies in Hollywood, was originally screentested for the part of Burger, but asked to try out as Mason as well. Gardner spotted him and the rest is history. Burr took his part seriously; he spent six months sitting in court studying real-life attorneys, and consulted throughout the series with six Superior Court judges before delivering his speeches. He was even awarded an Honorary Doctor of Law degree by a law college in Sacramento.

The original *Perry Mason*, with its clean characters welcome in every living room, is one of TV's most enduring series. It has never stopped running in syndication in the US and is a staple of television worldwide. CBS attempted to revive the series in 1973 as *The New Adventures of Perry Mason* with Monte Markham in the title role leading an entirely new cast, but it failed to pick up an audience and was cancelled mid-run. In 1985 NBC aired a reunion movie, *Perry Mason Returns*, once more starring Burr and bringing back Barbara Hale as Della (other regular cast members had since died). This led to a series of feature-length Perry Mason movies.

While *The New Adventures of Perry Mason* was trying to find viewers, Raymond Burr was of course already playing the part of another much-loved television detective. From 1967–75 he was busy as Robert Ironside, crime fighter in a wheelchair and special consultant to the San Francisco Police Department, in NBC's >*Ironside*.

The Persuaders!

UK 1971–2 24 × 60m col ITV. A Tribune Production. *US tx* 1971–2 ABC. *cr* Robert S Baker. *pr* Robert S Baker, Terry Nation, Johnny Goodman. *dr* Basil Dearden, Roy Ward Baker, Roger Moore, Leslie Norman, Val Guest, Peter Hunt, Gerald Mayer, Sidney Hayers, Peter Medak. *wr* Brian Clemens, Terry Nation, Terence Feely, John Kruse, Michael Pertwee, Tony Williamson, Milton S Gilman, Donald James, Tony Barwick, David Wolfe, Walter Black, Peter Yeldham, Harry H Junkin, Donald James. *mus* Ken Thorne, John Barry (theme). *cast* **Lord Brett Sinclair** Roger Moore **Danny Wilde** Tony Curtis **Judge Fulton** Laurence Naismith. *Video* ITC.

Schlock. But enjoyable schlock. *The Persuaders!* was a barely disguised attempt by Sir Lew Grade, head of ATV, to follow up the transatlantic success of >*The Saint* by giving them more of the same under a different name. The small difference was that the suave English adventurer (played by Roger Moore, naturally) in *The Persuaders!* was called Lord Brett Sinclair – and this time out he had a friend, one Danny Wilde (Tony Curtis) from New York.

Sinclair and Wilde, so the premise went, were as different as London gin and Coca-Cola. Sinclair had been to Harrow and Oxford; Wilde had grown up in the Bronx and graduated from the University of Life. Only latterly had he made a million in the oil business. Initially antagonists, the two playboys were brought together at a Riviera party by retired Judge Fulton and blackmailed into cooperating as international fighters against crime. And so they wandered twenty-six glossy international jet-set episodes seeking thrills – and girls, girls, girls.

(Those who served heroically as screen adornments included Joan Collins, Catherine Schell, Susan George, Nicola Pagett, and Diane Cilento in the Terry Nation-written spoof of *Kind Hearts and Coronets* episode, 'A Death in the Family'.) What saved the series from the great TV scrapheap were good scripts, and a sparky, amusing relationship between Sinclair and Wilde, incessant rivals – especially when pursuing the female guest stars – as well as friends.

Despite this and high production values – each episode cost £100,000 – the series failed to sell in the one country it was made for – the USA. The ABC network cancelled it after just twenty-four episodes (130 had been scheduled) following poor ratings. It was judged too jokey for American tastes and Curtis' Wilde, with his bomber jackets and leather gloves, was considered something of a stereotype of the poor, unsophisticated Yankee cousin. The series did enormous business elsewhere, though, was dubbed into over twenty-three languages, and is still a staple of European networks.

Peter Gunn

USA 1958–61 110 × 30m bw NBC, ABC. A Spartan Production. *cr* Blake Edwards. *pr* Blake Edwards. *dr* Various, including Gene Reynolds, Blake Edwards, Lamont Johnson. *wr* Various. *mus* Henry Mancini (theme music). *cast* **Peter Gunn** Craig Stevens **Edie Hart** Lola Albright **Lt Jacoby** Herschel Bernadi **'Mother'** Hope Emerson (season one) Minerva Urecal (season two).

Peter Gunn was one of the first (along with >*77 Sunset Strip*) of a rash of new-style PI series with a cool new feel in the late fifties. These TV private eyes in the late fifties and early sixties had the best of both worlds – plush offices uptown with a list of glamorous clientele and, for their night-time haunts, low-life sleazy jazz clubs where they drank in the atmosphere and music of the beatnik era.

Detective Peter Gunn's well-appointed office was at 351 Ellis Park Road, Los Angeles and his spare time was spent over at 'Mother's' jazz club watching his blonde girlfriend take the stage as resident singer. On the way to getting his clients out of trouble or cracking a case, Gunn might find himself with a fight on his hands, but this man was as cool as he was well-groomed and always came out on top – even if he did need the help of his friend Police Lieutenant Jacoby. Original jazz themes by Henry Mancini punctuated the action and lent the contemporary mood (as well as providing RCA with two memorable and very successful albums). The slick, successful series ran for over 100 episodes and spawned a number of imitators including *Pete Kelly's Blues* and >*Johnny Staccato*. Guest stars included Diahann Carroll, star of >*Julia*.

Peter Gunn helped to launch creator-producer Blake Edwards' glittering career. Edwards' other TV series in the fifties were the similarly jazz-influenced *Mr Lucky* (also with music by Mancini) and *Dante's Inferno*. His feature film credits include *Breakfast at Tiffany's*, *A Shot in the Dark*, the other Pink Panther movies, *10* and *Victor/Victoria*. He returned to TV in 1991–2 as executive producer of the sitcom *Julie*, which starred his wife Julie Andrews. Edwards and Stevens teamed up again in 1967 to make the unsuccessful movie *Gunn*.

Police Woman

USA 1974–8 91 × 60m col NBC. A Columbia Pictures Television Production. *UK tx* 1975–9 ITV. *cr* Robert Collins. *exec pr* David Gerber. *pr* Douglas Benton, Edward De Blasio. *dr* Various, including Robert Collins, Robert Vaughn, Corey Allen, Alvin Ganzer, Alf Kjellin. *wr* Various, including Robert Collins. *mus* Morton Stevens. *cast* **Sgt Suzanne 'Pepper' Anderson** Angie Dickinson **Lt Bill Crowley** Earl Holliman **Det Joe Styles** Ed Bernard **Det Pete Royster** Charles Dierkop **Cheryl** Nichole Kallis **Lt Paul Marsh** Val Bisoglio.

Police Woman was first aired on 26 March 1974 as 'The Gamble', an episode for Joseph Wambaugh's successful show *Police Story* with Angie Dickinson playing policewoman Lisa Beaumont. The pilot achieved good ratings, and the series started up in October of the same year, with Dickinson's character undergoing a name change to the spicier Pepper Anderson. It set a trend in female cops and made a star of Angie Dickinson.

Angie Dickinson as vice detective Pepper Anderson in *Police Woman*.

Although *Police Woman* featured an early leading part for a woman in a traditionally male preserve, it milked star Dickinson's looks and femininity for all they were worth. A sexy, brassy blonde, Sergeant Pepper Anderson was an undercover agent for the criminal conspiracy department of the Los Angeles Police Department. Working on a vice squad team that included two other undercover cops, Det Joe Styles and Det Pete Royster, she was required to pose as anything from a prostitute to a gangster's girlfriend – frequently in short skirts or fishnet tights. The team reported directly to Lt Bill Crowley (Earl Holliman).

But the show was not all high heels. Anderson's personality was rounded out by occasional visits to autistic younger sister Cheryl in the first season while overall the show managed to retain something of the *verité* spirit of its originating series. One month before filming, Dickinson, along with other cast members, went to the Hollywood Division police station to absorb the atmosphere and found herself in the midst of a real-life gun drama ending in the murder of an armed attacker.

Dickinson later starred in another NBC crime series *Cassie and Company* (1982) in which she played Cassie Holland, a beautiful Los Angeles private detective who used her expertise as a former criminologist to solve crimes. Her earlier roles included the part of Mary McCauley in the CBS adventure series *Men into Space* (1959–60), the story of the US government's space programme as seen through the eyes of Air Force Colonel Edward McCauley. Writer, director and creator Robert Collins also worked on >*Marcus Welby MD*, *Police Story* and *Serpico*.

The Prisoner

UK 1967–8 17 × 60m ITV. An Everyman Films Production. *USA tx* 1968. *cr* Patrick McGoohan, George Markstein. *exec pr* Patrick McGoohan. *pr* David Tomblin. *dr* Don Chaffey, Pat Jackson, Patrick McGoohan, Peter Graham Scott, Robert Asher, David Tomblin. *wr* George Markstein (script editor eps 1–12, 16), David Tomblin, Vincent Tilsley, Anthony Skene, Patrick McGoohan, Terence Feely, Lewis Greifer, Gerald Kelsey, Roger Woddis, Roger Parkes, Michael Cramoy. *mus* Ron Grainer. *cast* **Number 6** Patrick McGoohan **Butler** Angelo Muscat. *Video* ITC.

'I am not a number. I am a free man!' – Prisoner Number Six

A British spy abruptly resigns from his job, drives to his flat in a Lotus 7 (registration: KAR 120C), packs a suitcase – but before he can close the lid he is gassed through the keyhole of the door by a man dressed as an undertaker. The spy wakes in a perfect replica of his room; however, outside the window is not London but The Village, a sort of Shangri-La from Hell. The anonymous authorities there use everything from brainwashing to hallucinogenic drugs to discover why the spy – who like the other ex-spy inmates is now known by a number, in his case Six – quit his Ministry job. He refuses to tell the ruler's representative, Number Two (a succession of different people), while at the same time trying to escape from the hermetically sealed colony and discover the identity of Number One, the supreme controller.

Such was the premise of Patrick McGoohan's absurdist espionage series *The Prisoner*, probably the most innovative and analysed show in TV history. The series grew out of McGoohan's dissatisfaction with the hit action series >*Danger Man*, but owed a debt to it. To some extent (how much is the subject of argument) *The Prisoner* was developed by *Danger Man*'s script editor George Markstein (who appears as the Ministry man behind the desk in the opening credits of *The Prisoner*), a reporter for British Intelligence during World War II who had allegedly uncovered an institution where spies who knew too much were isolated. Such an institution had already been sketched out in the *Danger Man* episode 'Colony Three'. And it was while filming *Danger Man* that McGoohan first came across Portmeirion, an Italianate village-folly in North Wales designed by Sir Clough Williams-Ellis, which formed the setting for *The Prisoner*. To make The Village even more bizarre on screen, McGoohan decked out the cast with piped blazers and installed tannoys and surveillance equipment. The soundtrack included snatches of nursery rhymes.

The inevitable question asked about *The Prisoner*, which McGoohan intended to be an 'allegorical

He would not be 'pushed, filed, stamped, indexed, briefed, debriefed or numbered'. Patrick McGoohan as the British spy imprisoned in The Village in the surreal sixties series, *The Prisoner*.

conundrum' (his production company was called Everyman, in a direct reference to the morality plays of the Middle Ages) is what does it all mean? Its main theme is clear, that of individual freedom. Number Six refuses to be 'pushed, filed, stamped, indexed, briefed, debriefed or numbered'. Most importantly, he refuses to tell Number Two why he resigned, purely because in a free society one should not need to explain one's actions. (But Number Six's rebellion, though uncompromising, is limited; it is not a social revolution. At no point does he discard the uniform of The Village, very similar to that of the English gentleman and English public school. His fight is for rights within existing society.)

Unfortunately, the opaque series never pursued all its implications. Markstein left after a dispute with McGoohan, and Sir Lew Grade of ATV refused to bankroll it further than seventeen episodes (out of a planned thirty-six and at a cost of $185,000 per sixty minutes), either because the show was over budget or because its drug references were proving too controversial. The show ended with a hastily written episode of legendary enigma: Number Six captures the elusive Number One, pulls off masks which reveal the face of an ape, and then the face of Number Six himself. Outraged viewers complained about obfuscation, but the message was actually quite simple: we are our own prisoners. Be seeing you.

Some of the more interesting facts about *The Prisoner* series, probably the cultiest of cult TV, are: the white balloon, Rover, which patrolled The Village was an eight-foot weather balloon, and the most expensive special effect in the series; the only person to appear in every episode was the butler, played by Angelo Muscat; the pennyfarthings which appeared throughout the show were an ironic symbol of progress, a visual sign to mankind to slow down; Number Six was born on the same day as Patrick McGoohan, 19/3/28; Markstein intended Number Six to be *Danger Man* John Drake (McGoohan said he was not); McGoohan had always wanted to do a Western, so the episode 'Living in Harmony' was set on the Old Frontier; the identity of Number One was revealed in nearly every episode by a piece of dialogue in which Number Six asked 'Who is Number One?', to which Number Two stonewalled 'You are Number Six'.

The episodes were: Arrival (GC Paul Eddington)/The Chimes of Big Ben (GC Leo McKern as Number Two)/A, B & C (GC Peter Bowles)/Free for All (wr and dr Patrick McGoohan)/The Schizoid Man (GC Anton Rodgers as Number Two)/The General/Many Happy Returns (GC Donald Sinden, Patrick Cargill, dr Patrick McGoohan)/ Dance of the Dead/Checkmate (GC Peter Wyngarde as Number Two)/Hammer into Anvil (GC Patrick Cargill as Number Two)/It's Your Funeral/A Change of Mind/ Living in Harmony (GC Alexis Kanner)/The Girl Who Was Death/Once Upon A Time (GC Leo McKern as Number Two, wr and dr Patrick McGoohan)/Fall Out (GC Leo McKern and Alexis Kanner, wr and dr Patrick McGoohan).

The Professionals

UK 1977–83 57 × 60m col ITV. Avengers Mark I/LWT. cr Brian Clemens. exec pr Brian Clemens, Albert Fennell. dr Various, including Douglas Camfield, William Brayne, Charles Crichton, Anthony Simmons, Peter Medak, Martin Campbell, Pennant Roberts, Tom Clegg, Chris Burt, Gerry O'Hara. wr Various, including Brian Clemens, Dennis Spooner, Gerry O'Hara, Ted Childs, Ronald Graham, Tony Barwick, Christopher Wickling, Roger Marshall. mus Laurie Johnson. cast **William Bodie** Lewis Collins **Ray Doyle** Martin Shaw **George Cowley** Gordon Jackson. Video The Video Collection.

Macho crypto-fascism or clever spoof on hard-boiled police actioners? History is still in judgement on Brian Clemens' seventies hit *The Professionals*, although the interim evidence suggests the former. Bodie and Doyle were action-men members of Criminal Intelligence 5 (CI5), an elite anti-terrorist police unit headed by gruff limping boss, George 'The Cow' Cowley. Bodie was ex-SAS, Doyle an ex-East End cop, Cowley formerly MI5. Episodes consisted mainly of Cowley barking orders (not terribly convincing, since, for most viewers, actor Gordon Jackson was still the butler Hudson from >Upstairs, Downstairs), much rushing around in Doyle's Ford Capri, followed by bouts of violence.

Perhaps the most damning indictment of *The Professionals* was that its own principals disliked it.

Actor Martin Shaw (later *The Chief*), in a belated display of taste, dismissed his character Doyle as a 'violent puppet' (although Doyle's trademark bubble-perm hairstyle made him look more like a violent moppet) and forbade repeats until 1992. The level of violence was so high that one episode had to be pulled completely. (As it happens, the unaired segment, 'The Klansman', was a well-meaning piece of anti-racism, which proves the difficulty of pigeon-holing the show.) Despite the blood-spilling, the National Viewers and Listeners Association pressure group gave *The Professionals* a seal of approval for its lack of swearing and sex. To their credit, Shaw and Collins (once upon a teenage time, the bass player with popsters The Mojos) did their own muscular stuntwork, and at no small cost; between them they sustained twenty-seven stitches, three broken ankles and a fractured collar-bone.

Even if not tongue-in-cheek itself, the show has been remorselessly sent up by others, Keith Allen's *The Bullshitters* being one parody amongst many.

The Protectors

UK 1972–4 52 × 30m col ITV. A group Three Production for ITC. US tx syndicated. cr Lew Grade. pr Gerry Anderson, Reg Hill. dr John Hough, Don Chaffey, Jeremy Summers, Roy Ward Baker, Cyril Frankel, Harry Booth, Michael Lindsay-Hogg, Robert Vaughn, Don Leaver, Charles Crichton, David Tomblin. wr Terence Feely, John Goldsmith, Brian Clemens, Donald James, Ralph Smart, Lew Davidson, Jesse and Pat Lasky, Donald Jonson, Tony Barwick, Sylvia Anderson, Dennis Spooner, Terry Nation, John Kruse, Trevor Preston, Anthony Terpiloff, Shane Rimmer, David Butler, Robert Banks Stewart. mus John Cameron; theme: 'Avenues and Alleyways' by Mitch Murray and Peter Callander, performed by Tony Christie. cast **Harry Rule** Robert Vaughn **Contessa di Contini** Nyree Dawn Porter **Paul Buchet** Tony Anholt **Suki** Yasuko Nazagumi **Chino** Anthony Chinn. Video ITC.

The Protectors: a worldwide, freelance crime-fighting team which hired out its services to whichever government, business or wealthy individual could afford them. Robert Vaughn (>*Man From UNCLE*) played cool professional Harry Rule, based in London, New Zealand actress Nyree Dawn Porter (Irene in >*The Forsyte Saga*) played the Contessa di Contini, a wealthy British noblewoman and widow whose wardrobe lent a touch of >*The Avengers*' style to the series and who ran a high-class detective agency, specialising in art and antiques theft, from her luxury villa in Rome. Tony Anholt played Frenchman Paul Buchet, the youngest of the three, a swinging Parisian whose suave charms attracted a stream of beautiful women. Created by Sir Lew Grade for an international market, *The Protectors* went for the Bond touch with star names, exotic locations and fast cars. Its trio of crime fighters pitted their wits against challenges, kidnappings and diplomatic problems in Rome, Paris, Salzburg, Venice and the Mediterranean. Formula plots included jail-springing, Nazi criminals, jewel thefts, Russian scientists, Vietnam War veterans and atomic secrets.

Other characters, for the first season only, included Eastern martial arts experts Suki, Harry's au pair and judo expert, and Chino, the Contessa's Oriental driver and karate expert. From the second season, *The Protectors* were considered able to fend for themselves.

The Protectors was produced by Gerry Anderson, creator of supermarionation series >*The Thunderbirds* and >*Stingray* and as well as Anderson's wife Sylvia boasted amongst its writers Terry Nation, Dennis Spooner, Brian Clemens and Terence Feely. Directors were equally eminent. Series star Robert Vaughn tried his hand behind the camera for 'It Could Be Practically Anywhere On the Island', and other regular directors included Charles Crichton and Michael Lindsay-Hogg. Guest artists included Patrick 'Dr Who' Troughton, Patrick Mower, Stephanie Beacham, James Bolam, Anton Rodgers, Ian Hendry (star of *Police Surgeon*), Patrick Magee, Sinead Cusack, and Eartha Kitt. Star Robert Vaughn's later credits include *The Lieutenant*, *Washington Behind Closed Doors* (coincidentally also starring *Girl From UNCLE* Steanie Powers), *Backstairs at the White House* and TV movies *The Woman Hunter*, *Centennial*, *City in Fear* and *The Day the Bubble Burst*.

Public Eye

UK 1965–75 28 × 60m bw/59 × 60m col ITV. An ABC Weekend Network Production/Thames Television. cr Roger Marshall, Anthony Marriott. ex pr Lloyd Shirley, Robert Love. pr Don Leaver, John Bryce, Richard Bates, Michael Chapman, Kim Mills, Robert Love. dr Various, including Don Leaver, Robert Tronson, Kim Mills, Jonathan Alwyn, Laurance Bourne, Guy Verney, Quentin Lawrence, Patick Dromgoole, Dennis Vance, Douglas Camfield, Bill Bain. wr Various, including Roger Marshall, Martin Worth, Terence Frisby, Robert Holmes, Julian Bond, Jack Trevor Story, Robert Banks Stewart, Trevor Preston, James Doran, Brian Finch, Richard Harris. mus Robert Earley. cast **Frank Marker** Alfred Burke **Detective Inspector Firbank** Ray Smith **Ron Gash** Peter Childs **Helen Mortimer** Pauline Delany.

Frank Marker was the prototype seedy British PI (>*Hazell* and >*Shoestring* were among his screen heirs). He worked out of dingy offices, wore a raincoat that would have embarrassed Columbo and earned a pittance. A classic, footslogging loner employed on unusually realistic cases (missing persons, thefts, divorce work, blackmail), only towards the very end of the series did he enjoy the company of other characters, namely Ron Gash, a PI who wanted partnership with Marker, manipulative Detective Inspector Firbank, and landlady Helen Mortimer.

Unlike the mid-Atlantic and American private eyes of the time, Marker was far from invincible. In the 1968 episode 'Cross That Palm When We Come To It' he was even caught in possession of stolen jewellery – and went to prison (outraged fans wrote demanding his release). At first Marker was based in London, but later moved on to Birmingham and Brighton.

It is said that Alfred Burke (later >*The Borgias*) was cast as Marker because, thin and forty-six years old, he looked less like a private detective than anyone else who auditioned for the part (he started his acting career as a villain in British films). Certainly, Burke's world-weary, bruised-looking performance was essential to *Public Eye*'s success.

Randall and Hopkirk (Deceased)

UK 26 × 60m 1969–71 col ITV. An ITC Production. *USA tx* 1973 syndicated. *cr* Dennis Spooner. *pr* Monty Berman. *dr* Cyril Frankel, Ray Austin, Paul Dickson, Leslie Norman, Jeremy Summers, Roy Ward Baker, Robert Tronson. *wr* Ralph Smart, Mike Pratt and Ian Wilson, Ray Austin, Tony Williamson, Donald James, Gerald Kelsey. *mus* Edwin Astley. *cast* **Jeff Randall** Mike Pratt **Marty Hopkirk** Kenneth Cope **Jean Hopkirk** Annette Andre. *Video* ITC.

'There's something different about this pair of private eyes . . . one of them is dead!' ran the billing for this typically oddball Spooner/Berman collaboration featuring flesh-and-blood private eye Jeff Randall and his ghostly partner Marty Hopkirk.

The scene for this unnatural pairing was set in episode one, 'My Late Lamented Friend and Partner': Jeff and Marty were partners in detective agency Randall and Hopkirk, until Marty was run down and killed by a car. Grieving Jeff went to his ex-buddy's grave to pay his respects and instead found his ghostly friend paying him a visit to make sure that his killer would be tracked down. Marty made the mistake of staying in the earthly world too long and unwittingly violated an ancient curse: 'Cursed be the ghost who dares to stay and face the awful light of day.' The result was that Marty was forced to roam the earth for 100 years, and Jeff had to endure the company of an invisible partner. The resulting comedy-drama series had plenty of high-speed action, good story-lines and a good gimmick, with Hopkirk visible only to Randall and viewers in an immaculate white suit that symbolised his other-worldliness (although the occasional ghost hunter, psychic or drunk could glimpse him too).

Randall and Hopkirk's was a love-hate relationship. Hopkirk's talents for eavesdropping or slipping through walls could be a considerable asset ('He's standing behind the door with a bottle in his hand' was a typical piece of advice). On the other hand, the long-suffering Randall regularly took the rap for his spiritual companion's actions and got beaten up, thrown down stairs or hospitalised for 'talking to himself'. Hopkirk also proved to be a jealous ghost around his widow Jean, who took on a job at Jeff's office.

The best episodes featured ingenious plots making full use of Hopkirk's supernatural possibilities. In 'But What a Sweet Little Room' written by Ralph Smart, for instance, a greedy financial advisor lured wealthy widows into a sealed room where they were gassed as they helplessly watched him dig their graves through the window. Invisibility also enabled Marty to besport himself at such places as the Queen's tea party or on the pitch at Wembley.

Production values may not have been the highest, with obvious use of stand-ins for location work and some poor editing, but Randall and Hopkirk could be spooky and fun and did not deserve its abysmal reception in the States where its syndication under the title *My Partner the Ghost* failed miserably to attract an audience. Guest stars in the series included Frank Windsor, Peter Vaughan, Philip Madoc and Anton Rodgers, Brian Blessed and George Sewell.

The Rockford Files

USA 1974–80 114 × 60m col NBC. Roy Huggins-Public Arts/Cherokee Productions/Universal TV. *UK tx* 1975–82 BBC1. *cr* Roy Higgins, Stephen J Cannell. *exec pr* Stephen J Cannell, Meta Rosenberg. *pr* Juanita Bartlett, David Chase, Charles Floyd Johnson, Lane Slate. *dr* Various, including Corey Allen, Lou Antonio, Dana Elcar, Reza S Badiyi, Stephen J Cannell, James Coburn, Winrich Kolbe, Jeannot Swarc, Russ Mayberry, Richard Crenna, James Garner, Bruce Kessler, Stuart Margolin, Vincent M McEveety, Juanita Bartlett, Christian I Nyby II, Joseph Pevney, Charles S Dubin, Meta Rosenberg, William Wiard. *wr* Various, including Juanita Bartlett, Howard Browne, Stephen J Cannell, John Thomas James (aka Roy Higgins), Robert Hamner, Edward J Lasko, Eric Kaldor, Mitchell Lindemann, Leroy Robinson, Jo Swerling, Rogers Turrentine, Shel Williams. *mus* Mike Post and C Carpenter (theme). *cast* **Jim Rockford** James Garner **Joseph 'Rocky' Rockford** Noah Beery Jr **Sergeant Dennis Becker** Joe Santos **Beth Davenport** Gretchen Corbett **Evelyn 'Angel'**

Martin Stuart Margolin **John Cooper** Bo Hopkins
Lieutenant Doug Chapman James Luisi **Gandy Fitch**
Isaac Hayes **Lieutenant Alex Diehl** Tom Atkins **Billings**
Luis Delgado **Captain McEnroe** Jack Garner **Lance White**
Tom Selleck.

For someone who is a soldier hero in real life (two Purple Hearts in the Korean War), James Garner has an ironic affinity for cowardly, conniving roles on screen: Bret Maverick in >*Maverick*, the sheriff in the two Burt Kennedy *Support Your Local . . .* Western features – and Jim Rockford, only and eponymous operative of the Rockford Detective Agency, Los Angeles.

Every fictive peeper needs a gimmick and Rockford's – aside from his endearing antipathy to gunplay (he kept his revolver in a biscuit barrel) – was that he was an ex-con, wrongly imprisoned for five years in San Quentin. Consequently, he was no great lover of the police, despite a friendship of sorts with LAPD Sergeant Dennis Becker, and specialised in cases that had them dead-ended. He charged $200 a day ('plus expenses') but was usually cheated out of his fees by clients who were less honest than he. Rockford lived alone in a beachfront trailer, which also doubled as his office. He didn't have a secretary, only an answerphone with the message (played over the opening of every *File*): 'This is Jim Rockford. At the tone leave your name and message. I'll get back to you.'

Despite Rockford's desire to avoid trouble and violence hardly an episode of this wry, atmospheric (even Chandleresque) PI series went past without Jim being beaten up by enormous heavies, giving car-chase in his Gold Pontiac Firebird, or landing in deep jail-sort schtuck, and having to be bailed out by attorney girlfriend Beth Davenport. Not infrequently, Rockford was led astray by former cellmate Angel Martin, a petty criminal of zilch moral fibre but many half-baked scams. (The part was played brilliantly by Stuart Margolin, who won Emmy Awards for Outstanding Supporting Actor in 1979 and 1980.) Rockford's other less than upstanding acquaintances included disbarred lawyer, John Cooper, and tough guy Gandy Fitch, played by Isaac 'Shaft' Hayes. Rockford's retired truck-driving father, 'Rocky' (Noah Berry Jr, *Circus Boy*, *Hondo*), constantly badgered his boy to take up a safer, more honest line of work.

It is often forgotten that Rockford was a good detective – or at least, he got results. He employed extremely dubious means, tricking, bribing and impersonating anybody and anything (he carried a phony ID card for every occasion), but virtually always got his man.

The series came to an abrupt end when Garner quit for health reasons, having badly damaged his legs doing his own stunt work over the *Files'* six seasons. It was never an enormous ratings success – only one breaking into the top twenty in the USA – but few crime shows of the period had better characters, more textured teleplays or finer performances. *The Rockford Files* was made by Roy Huggins (who also created *Maverick*) as a vehicle for Garner and Garner acted the part of the line-shooting gumshoe to a T. He got the just reward of an Emmy for Outstanding Lead Actor in a Drama Series in 1977.

In the final season of the show, Tom Selleck appeared as the irritatingly perfect PI Lance White. The exposure led to him being cast six months later as *Magnum*.

The Saint

UK 1962–9 71 × 60m bw/47 × 60m col ITV. An ATV Production for New World/A Bamore Production for ITC. *USA tx* 1967–9 NBC. *cr* Robert S Baker, Monty Norman. *pr* Robert S Baker, Monty Norman. *dr* Various, including John Ainsworth, Peter Yates, Roger Moore, Jeremy Summers, Robert S Baker, Leslie Noman, Roy Baker, Freddie Francis. *wr* Various, including Gerald Kelsey, Terry Nation, Harry H Junkin, John Kruse, Norman Borisoff. *mus* Edwin Astley. *cast* **Simon Templar, 'The Saint'** Roger Moore **Chief Inspector Teal** Ivor Dean. *Video* ITC.

'. . . a roaring adventurer who loves a fight . . . a dashing daredevil, imperturbable, debonair, preposterously handsome, a pirate or a philanthropist as the occasion demands.' Thus novelist Leslie Charteris defined his most famous creation, Simon Templar, aka 'The Saint' because of his initials and his penchant for helping those (especially damsels) in distress. The character – whose visiting card depicted a stick figure with a halo – first appeared in the 1928 novel *Meet the Tiger* and after becoming a sensation in publishing, comics, on the radio and big screen (played by George Sanders), it was only natural that he would progress to TV. Initially, Charteris himself tried to produce a television version of *The Saint* (with David Niven as the romantic hero), but the project only came to fruition under the guidance of TV tycoon Lew Grade, who considered it ideal for a slick, mid-Atlantic package. Patrick McGoohan (>*Danger Man*, >*The Prisoner*) was offered the title part but turned it down because The Saint womanised too much for his taste, so it was offered to London ex-cardigan model, Roger Moore, already well known to audiences in both the UK and USA for his lead roles in >*Ivanhoe* and >*Maverick*. It turned out to be a good choice: Moore played The Saint with memorable dry style, perfect coiffure, a quizzical arch of his eyebrows, and a wink in his eye.

The TV episodes – initially all adapted from Charteris' stories – were entertaining action-capers in which The Saint roved up-market British and exotic foreign locales (Paris, Rome, Nassau, Athens, Miami) meeting and beating kidnappers, blackmailers, thieves and murderers. The fight sequences, if inevitable, were excellently choreographed. In Britain, The Saint drove around in a yellow Volvo P1800, with a number plate ST 1, a prop much admired by sixties audiences. (The same make of car features in the cult Steve McQueen film *Bullitt*, 1968, the first American movie by ex-*The Saint* director Peter Yates.)

Whatever the setting, every episode involved a beautiful girl; among the actresses featured over the years were Honor Blackman ('The Arrow of God'), Jane Asher ('The Noble Sportsman'), Julie Christie ('Judith'), and Gabrielle Drake ('The Best Laid Plans'). Kate O'Mara appeared in different guises on some four occasions. Apart from The Saint himself, the only other recurring character was Chief Inspector Teal, invariably referred to by Templar in dismissive tones as 'Scotland Yard's finest'. It was Teal's lot to turn up at the often ruthless denouement to find himself once again outsmarted by the modern day Galahad-with-a-gun.

In 1966, filming of *The Saint* switched to colour. Consequently, the budget – the series was the most expensive of its time – in other areas was tightened. Some of the glamour and expensive props went (the radiated,

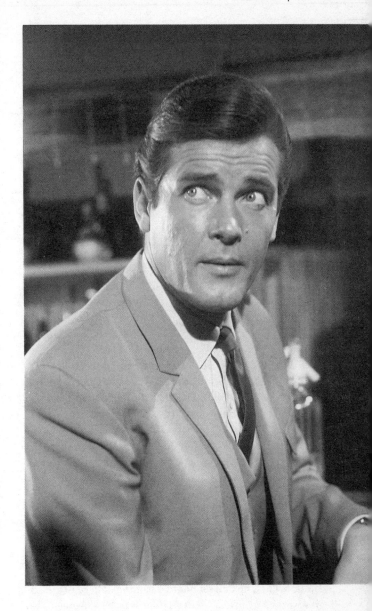

Ex-cardigan model Roger Moore in the title role of *The Saint,* adapted from the best-selling thrillers by Leslie Charteris.

giant ant in 'The House on Dragon's Rock' ranks amongst the lowliest of model creatures ever to appear on screen), but the show continued its triumphant commercial progress. Some estimates put the earnings from world sales as high as £370 million. (Since Roger Moore owns the rights to the forty-seven colour episodes this makes him a man of some wealth.)

A 1978 rehash of the series, *Return of the Saint*, featuring Ian Ogilvy as the suave hero, blessed with perfect taste in all things, was execrable.

77 Sunset Strip

USA 1958–64 205 × 60m bw ABC. A Warner Bros Production. *UK tx* 1958–64 ITV (ABC, Anglia). *cr* Roy Huggins. *exec pr* William T Orr, Jack Webb (season 6). *pr* Howie Horowitz, William Conrad, Fenton Earnshaw, Harry Tatelman, Joel Rogosin. *dr* Various. *wr* Various. *mus* Mack David, Jerry Livingston. *cast* **Stu Bailey** Efrem Zimbalist Jnr **Jeff Spencer** Roger Smith **Gerald Lloyd Kookson III ('Kookie')** Edd Byrnes **Roscoe** Louis Quinn **Suzanne Fabrey** Jacqueline Beer **JR Hale** Robert Logan **Rex Randolph** Richard Long **Hannah** Joan Staley **Lt Gilmore** Byron Keith.

A hip, humorous series with flashy action that ushered in a rash of copycat, new-style private eye shows. *77 Sunset Strip* was set in a glamorous world, Hollywood, with detective partners who were smart in both senses – they had college degrees and they were up-market. Efrem Zimbalist Jr (son of concert violinist Efrem Zimbalist and opera star Alma Gluck, father of *Remington Steele* star Stephanie Zimbalist) starred as Stu Bailey, cultured former OSS officer and expert in languages. An Ivy League PhD, he had set out to become a college professor but turned PI instead. His partner was Jeff Spencer, also a former government agent, who had a degree in law. Both men were judo experts. They worked out of an office at number 77 on Hollywood's world-famous Sunset Strip and their cases took them to all the glamour spots of the world.

Other regulars included Roscoe the racetrack tout and Suzanne the beautiful French switchboard operator. But it was the proto-beatnik teenage would-be PI and parking-lot attendant who worked at posh restaurant Dino's next door that shot the series into the top ten. Constantly combing his glossy, duck-tailed hair and speaking in what was called 'jive talk', Gerald Lloyd Kookson III – 'Kookie' to his friends – helped Stu and Jeff out on their cases and stole the show. Teenage girls went wild for Kookie and his fan mail reached 10,000 letters a week. A glossary was issued for those who wanted to learn his language which included such young dude phrases as, 'let's exitville' (let's go), 'out of print' (from another town), 'piling up the Z's' (sleeping), 'a dark seven' (a depressing week) and 'headache grapplers' (aspirin) – all soon copied by youth worldwide.

Kookie even had a smash hit record with 'Kookie, Kookie, Lend Me Your Comb', a duet with Connie Stevens, star of detective series *Hawaiian Eye*. The show spawned a number of records: the theme music from the show became a best-selling album, while stars Efrem Zimbalist Jr and Roger Smith, both lured into record contracts after Byrnes' success, bombed miserably.

Kookie, a kind of 'Fonzie' of the fifties, fast began to overshadow the principals. At one point Byrnes walked out, angry at his secondary role. He was swiftly brought back and promoted to a fully fledged partnership in the agency by the 1961–2 season. JR Hale took over the job of parking-lot attendant at Dino's.

By 1963 the novelty had worn off and ratings were declining. Drastic changes were made. Jack Webb (>*Dragnet*) was brought in as producer, William Conrad (>*Cannon*) was brought in as director, Efrem Zimbalist Jr became a freelance investigator travelling the world on no-expense spared chases and money was lavished on guest stars and top writers. But it didn't help, and the series left the screens in 1964, with a rash of imitators close behind it.

77 Sunset Strip was introduced by two pilot TV movies – *Anything for Money* (1957, 60m, ABC) and *Girl on the Run* (1958, 90m, ABC) – both starring Efrem Zimbalist Jr. Zimbalist Jr's other TV credits include *FBI*, >*Maverick* and *Remington Steele*.

Creator of the series, action-adventure producer and writer Roy Huggins was also responsible for >*Maverick*, *Colt 45*, >*The Fugitive*, >*The Rockford Files* and *City of Angels*. As executive producer his credits include >*Alias Smith and Jones*, >*Baretta* and *Toma*.

>*The Sweeney* (from the same stable, Thames/Euston in 1975), these policemen were human enough to have faults and flares.

Inspector Jordan was a cop with some of the glamour of a special agent. He was a member of Scotland Yard's Special Branch, a cloak-and-dagger team of spy-hunters whose duties led them into situations that threatened national security. Storylines, though, were standard affairs – Russian VIPs in need of protection, strange thefts at British Embassies, bomb plots against oil sheikhs and the ever-present threat of the KGB (although a nod in the direction of contemporary concerns also brought in hippie encampments and German student revolutionaries).

After the success of its first two videotaped seasons, the series underwent a complete transformation and was revamped, recast and handed over to fledgling production company Euston Films, to become their first ever filmed series. From that time, Euston Films was to prove uniquely influential on British television drama with credits including *Minder*, *Selling Hitler*, *Capital City* and *Shrinks*.

Jordan disappeared in the third and fourth seasons as did his boss Superintendent Eden. In their place came Detective Chief Inspector Alan Craven, played by the distinctive George Sewell (>*UFO*), followed by Detective Chief Inspector Tom Haggerty, played by Patrick Mower. Mower, another modern copper with his own methods, quickly assumed Nesbitt's still-warm role of ladies' man and trendy dresser. Other Euston cast members included Paul Eddington as Strand, a high-powered, toffee-nosed civil servant who kept an unwelcome eye on the detectives and their budgets. Guest stars in the series included Rula Lenska, Dennis Waterman, Patrick Troughton and Michael Gambon.

Patrick Mower was later to resurface in *Target* (1977–8) as unscrupulous Superintendent Steve Hackett, based in a large unnamed port in the South of England. Co-starring Philip Madoc and produced for BBC1 by Philip Hinchcliffe, the series was intended to woo viewers away from Thames/Euston production >*The Sweeney* over on ITV. The BBC series, however, although high on violence was low on *Sweeney*-brand humour and *The Sweeney* triumphed.

Starsky and Hutch

USA 1975–9 88 × 60m col ABC. A Spelling-Goldberg Production for ABC. *UK tx* 1976–81 BBC1. *cr* William Blinn. *exec pr* Aaron Spelling, Leonard Goldberg. *pr* Joseph T Naar. *dr* Earl Bellamy, Georg Stanford Brown, Ivan Dixon, Paul Michael Glaser, Robert Kelljan, Randal Kleiser, Fernando Lamas, Arthur Marks, George McCowan, Dick Moder, Ivan Nagy, Sutton Roley, Barry Shear, David Soul, Jack Starrett, Claude Starrett Jr, Virgil W Vogel, Don Weis. *wr* Tom Bagen, William T Blinn, Jeffrey Bloom, Ron Buck, Robert Earll, Rick Edelstein, Michael Fisher, Steve Fisher, Al Friedman, Sal Green, David P Harmon, Jeff Kanter, Marshall Kauffmann, Edward J Lasko, William Lansford, Tom Maschella, Michael Mann, Ben Masselink, Joe Reb Moffly, Steven Nalevansky, Don Patterson, Parke Perine, Robert Swanson, Anthony Yerkovich. *mus* Tom Scott, Mark Snow. *cast* **Det Dave Starsky** Paul Michael Glaser **Det Ken Hutchinson** David Soul **Huggy Bear** Antonio Fargas **Capt Harold Dobey** Bernie Hamilton.

Dave Starsky and Ken Hutchinson were as different as could be – but they were buddies. Starsky was streetwise, wisecracking and ate junk food; Hutch was educated, preferred health food and practised yoga; Starsky carried an Army .45 automatic, Hutch used a .357 Magnum. But they shared a passion for catching bad guys and for high-speed, tyre-squealing action.

These two swinging bachelor undercover cops worked one of the roughest parts of all Los Angeles, full of pimps, muggers, dope pushers and big-time hoodlums. But they had no problem with that – their contacts all had dubious reputations, their methods were at best questionable, and screeching round town in Starsky's red hot rod 1974 Ford Torino they could catch the worst of the bad guys.

The appeal of this show lay partly in its two young pin-up heroes (David Soul, real name David Solberg, moved on to a career as pop singer with chart toppers such as 'Don't Give Up On Us Baby' among his five British top twenty hits), partly in the gravel-spitting car chases, but mostly in the relationship between Starsky and Hutch. 'Hutchsky' – as they were known to the production team – could count on each other for anything on or off the job.

If one was held hostage the other would stop at nothing in his attempt to free his partner. If one was wounded in the line of duty the other would nail whoever was responsible. If one was upset over a failed relationship the other was there to console him.

But the shoot-outs, brawls and violents methods of death won disapproval from some quarters. In Britain, Kenneth Oxford, Chief Constable of Merseyside, was later to complain that when the series was showing, 'police on duty were adopting sunglasses and wearing their gloves with the cuffs turned down. They also started driving like bloody maniacs.' In the States an anti-violence crusade by churches and America's Parent Teacher Association meant the action was watered down for the 1977–8 season. Instead, in came more romance and more stress on the two buddies' friendship that took it into realms of handkerchief-wringing schmaltz.

Undercover Los Angeles cops Dave Starsky (Paul Michael Glaser, left) and Ken Hutchinson (David Soul) in *Starsky and Hutch*. One British police chief complained that the show influenced UK police officers into 'driving like maniacs'.

Female stars were always temporary in this show (although they included such names as Joan Collins), lest a woman should come between the heroes. But the series featured two talented black actors – Bernie Hamilton (star of the 1964 movie *One Potato Two Potato*) as Capt Dobey, the duo's quick-tempered but understanding boss, and Antonio Fargas as their bar-hopping, jive-talking, flamboyant informant Huggy Bear.

The series, created by Spelling and Goldberg (>*Charlie's Angels*, >*Beverly Hills 90210*), was preceded by one ninety-minute made-for-TV movie simply called *Starsky and Hutch* (1975). Both stars, who harboured ambitions to work behind the camera, directed episodes of the series.

The Streets of San Francisco

USA 1972–80 120 × 60m col ABC. A Quinn Martin Production/Warner Bros. *UK tx* 1973–80 ITV. *cr* Quinn Martin. *exec pr* Quinn Martin. *pr* John Wilder, Cliff Gould, William Yates. *dr* Various, including Walter Grauman, William Hale, Barry Crane, Virgil W Vogel, Barry Shear, Theodore J Flicker, Seymour Robbie, Arthur Nadel. *wr* Various, including Walter Black. *mus* Pat William (theme), John Elizade, Robert Prince. *cast* **Det Lt Mike Stone** Karl Malden **Det Insp Steve Keller** Michael Douglas **Det Insp Dan Robbins** Richard Hatch **Jean Stone** Darleen Carr **Lt Lessing** Lee Harris.

As actor Karl Malden once pointed out, '*The Streets of San Francisco* had three stars – Mike Douglas, me and San Francisco'. Filmed on location with much panache, the series used hilly 'Frisco in the way that >*Naked City* had used New York. The city was more than a back-drop; it was a character, moody and dangerous beneath its urbane charm.

The *Streets'* teleplays were frequently suspenseful – perhaps the best was the William Hale-directed siege story 'Labyrinth' – and the lead performances outstanding. The series, of course, was of some career-launching importance. Although Michael (eldest son of Kirk) Douglas had appeared on the small and big screens before, he had never achieved real notice. Playing young

college-graduate SFPD Inspector Steve Keller opposite veteran Lieutenant Mike Stone changed all that in one short TV season. But the movies soon beckoned and Douglas left in 1975 (his character was said to 'have entered teaching', being replaced by Inspector Dan Robbins) to work as producer on the Oscar-winning *One Flew Over the Cuckoo's Nest*. He has stayed in filmland ever since. One of his best cinema performances was in *Basic Instinct*, in which he played . . . a San Francisco cop.

And yet, no matter how good Douglas or San Fransciso was in *Streets*, it was the wonderful bulbous-nosed, granite-like Malden (real name Mladen Sekulovich) as Mike Stone who stole the show, with a performance every bit as good as his Academy Award-winning performance in *A Streetcar Named Desire*.

The series was based on the novel, *Poor, Poor Orphan* by Carolyn Weston.

The Sweeney

UK 1975–82 52 × 60m col ITV. Euston Films/Thames TV. *cr* Ian Kennedy Martin. *pr* Ted Childs. *dr* Various, including Terry Green, Tom Clegg, Jim Goddard, David Wickes, Douglas Camfield, Mike Vardy, Victor Ritelis, William Brayne. *wr* Various, including Trevor Preston, Troy Kennedy Martin, Roger Marshall, Robert Banks Stewart, Allan Prior, Ronald Graham, Tony Hoare, P J Hammond. *mus* Harry South. *cast* **DI Jack Regan** John Thaw **DS George Carter** Dennis Waterman **CI Frank Haskins** Garfield Waterman.

Developed from a 1974 pilot *Regan*, aired as part of ITV's *Armchair Theatre*, Euston Film's landmark police series eschewed the cosiness of the standard British cop show (notably, the paradigmatic >*Dixon of Dock Green*) in favour of hard-edged realism and visceral action. Its portrait of the police was far from flattering: the series' chief characters, DI Jack Regan (played by John Thaw, *Redcap*, >*Z Cars*, *Thick as Thieves*, *Inspector Morse*) and his young sidekick, East Ender George Carter (Dennis Waterman), routinely ignored the rule book, hit suspects, associated with villains, swore and drank to excess. In one episode, Jack Regan burgled the office of CI Haskins – the man with the unenviable job of keeping the surly Regan under control – in search of his annual report.

Made on a shoestring budget of £40,000 per episode, *The Sweeney* – the title was derived from 'Sweeney Todd', Cockney rhyming slang for Scotland Yard's Flying Squad – was shot on film, with outstanding, often witty, writing. Muscular though the action was, the series' success rested in large part on the matey relationship between Regan and Carter; to enhance this the scriptwriters killed off Carter's wife (played by Stephanie Turner, later >*Juliet Bravo*) so that the detective sergeant could spend his rest hours, as well as his working hours, with his kipper tie-wearing 'guvnor' (Regan being already divorced).

Among the more notable of the large guest cast was George Cole in 'The Tomorrow Man' episode (also with John Hurt), who would later co-star with Dennis Waterman in the hit series *Minder*. The instalment 'Hearts and Minds' featured the English comic duo Morecambe and Wise.

Although the show attracted criticism for its violence and swearing, in retrospect there was an innocence under its bruiser exterior. Invariably, episodes concerned the apprehension of professional villains (preceded by spectacular car chases and the line, 'Yer nicked!'), security van robbers, lorry-hijackers and the like – all bad boys but not murdering psychopaths. Yet even if *The Sweeney* was not as dangerous as supposed, no other British police series has come close on the excitement gauge.

Tenafly

USA 1973–4 5 × 90m NBC. A Universal Television Production. *UK tx* 1974 ITV. *exec pr* Richard Levinson, William Link. *pr* Jon Epstein. *dr* Richard A Colla, Robert Day, Bernard Kowalski, Jud Taylor, Gene Levitt. *wr* Richard Levinson, William Link. *cast* **Harry Tenafly** James McEachin **Ruth Tenafly** Lillian Lehman **Herb Tenafly** Paul Jackson **Lorrie** Rosanna Huffman **Lt Sam Church** David Huddleston.

Harry Tenafly was a rarity among television's private detectives: not only was he black, he was a dedicated and happy family man, living in Los Angeles with his conventional, pretty wife Ruth and their son Herb.

Black private eyes on television enjoyed a brief vogue in the early seventies. The same week in which *Tenafly* featured as a segment of NBC *Wednesday Mystery Movie* – alternating every four weeks with >*Banacek*, *Faraday and Company* and *The Snoop Sisters* – >*Shaft* premièred on CBS as part of an alternating series. But Tenafly was a less romanticised detective than Roundtree's *Shaft* – an ordinary, hard-working man without Roundtree's movie-star looks and sex appeal, he neither chased nor was chased by beautiful women.

Action in the series was divided between Tenafly's home and his office life, where his friend and confidante at the Los Angeles Police Department Lieutenant Sam Church was regularly called upon to get Harry out of jams.

But unfortunately *Tenafly*'s very lack of thrills or glamour proved to be the show's downfall. Television audiences never took to the show and it was taken off the air after six months and only five episodes – just two weeks before *Shaft* was also cancelled.

Twin Peaks

USA 1990–1 2 × 120m/28 × 60m col ABC. A Lynch/Frost Production/Spelling Entertainment. *UK tx* 1990–1 BBC2. *cr* David Lynch, Mark Frost. *exec pr* David Lynch, Mark Frost. *pr* Hayley Payton. *dr* Various, including David Lynch, Duwayne Dunhamn, Diane Keaton, Tina Rathbone. *wr* Various, including David Lynch, Mark Frost. *mus* Angelo Badalamenti. *cast* **Agent Dale Cooper** Kyle MacLachlan **Sheriff Harry S Truman** Michael Ontkean **Leland Palmer** Ray Wise **Audrey Horne** Sherilynn Fenn **James Hurley** James Marshall **Jocelyn 'Josie' Packard** Joan Chen **Laura Palmer/Madelaine Ferguson** Sheryl Lee **Donna Hayward** Lara Flynn Boyle **Catherine Martell** Piper Laurie **Peter Martell** Jack Nance **Big Ed Hurley** Everett McGill **Nadine Hurley** Wendy Robie **Benjamin Horne** Richard Beymer **Shelly Johnson** Madchen Amick **Leo Johnson** Eric Da Re **Dr Lawrence Jacoby** Russ Tamblyn **Deputy Andy Brennan** Harry Goaz **Norma Jennings** Peggy Lipton **Hank Jennings** Chris Mulkey **Lucy Moran** Kimmy Robertson **Gordon Cole** David Lynch **Margaret, the Log Lady**

Catherine E Coulson **Deputy Tommy 'The Hawk' Hill**
Michael Horse. *Video* Screen Entertainment.

An eerie and bizarre murder mystery set in the verdant
US Pacific Northwest, which became an obsession in
America and Britain in 1990. The mastermind behind the
series was avant-garde film-maker David Lynch, with
Twin Peaks continuing his fascination with the dark life
behind the white picket fences of smalltown Ameria, as
exemplified by his 1986 feature *Blue Velvet*.

The TV series, co-developed with >*Hill Street Blues*
stalwart Mark Frost, and set in the fictional lumber town
of the title, hinged around the question: 'Who killed
Laura Palmer?', a beautiful seventeen-year-old High
School student whose grey corpse was washed onto the
lakeside wrapped in a plastic sheet. The main investigator was obsessive FBI Agent Dale Cooper, prone to
ecstasy when drinking coffee and eating cherry pie and
whose detecting methods included quasi-Tibetan
mysticism, dreams and ESP. Gradually, his hunting of the
murderer revealed that Laura Palmer was not the
innocent she seemed; similarly, the town itself was a
black eddying pool of sadism, satanism, pornography
and drugs beneath its still, postcard surface. The finger
of suspicion pointed at most of the town's population
before it was revealed that the culprit was Palmer's own
father, possessed by demonic, long-haired 'Killer BOB'.

As well as the central crime puzzle, there were a
number of sub-plots; a plan by Catherine Martell and
Benjamin Horne to steal the Packard Sawmill from
widow Josie (played by Joan Chen, star of Bertolocci's
The Last Emperor); Big Ed's affair with Double-R Diner
manager Norma; the love triangle betwen Bobby, Shelly
and her thuggish, lorry-driving husband Leo.

There was an almost tangible, sensuous atmosphere to
the series, especially in the episodes helmed by Lynch,
a dream-like mood which was enhanced by self-
consciously weird characters and situations. The most
famous of these were the Log Lady, who carried around a
piece of Ponderosa pine lumber like it was a baby, Cooper's
own narrative through his constant messages to his unseen
secretary Diane via his micro-recorder, and the fish in the
percolator at the Diner. Cooper's one-liners, 'This must be
where pies go when they die' and 'Damn fine coffee – and
hot', became virtual mantras amongst TV watchers.

Sheriff Truman (Michael Ontkean) and Peter Martell (Jack
Nance) discover the body of Laura Palmer in David Lynch's
darkly weird *Twin Peaks*.

The initial ratings were high for such an original TV show (35 million in the USA at its 'peak'), but they tapered off towards the end of the first season, as viewers lost interest in lightweight scripts, not redeemed by some weirdness-for-weirdness'-sake gimmicks.

The large cast featured two of Lynch's stock movie repertory, Kyle MacLachlan (*Dune*, *Blue Velvet*) as Agent Cooper, and Jack Nance (*Eraserhead*) as Peter Martell. Lynch himself appeared occasionally as FBI Chief Cole (it was an open secret that the character of Cooper was a Lynch self-portrait). The series also introduced a gallery of new faces, including Sherilynn Fenn (later to appear in Jennifer Lynch's 1993 film, *Boxing Helena*), who played teenage vamp Audrey Horne, famed for her ability to tie knots in cherry stalks with her tongue. David Duchovny (later >*The X-Files*) appeared as a transvestite FBI agent.

The series was part filmed on location – Hollywood actress Diane Keaton was amongst its directors – in the Washington town of Snoqualmie Falls, which has since become something of a mecca for 'Peakies'. Angelo Badalamenti composed the haunting theme and incidental music.

In 1992 Lynch released a movie based on *Twin Peaks* entitled *Fire Walk With Me*. The series has also spawned a couple of look-alike shows, >*Northern Exposure* and *Eerie Indiana*.

The Untouchables

USA 1959–63 17 × 60m bw ABC. Desilu/Langford Productions. *UK tx* 1966–9 ATV. *exec pr* Jerry Thorpe, Leonard Freeman, Quinn Martin. *pr* Howard Hoffman, Alan A Armer, Alvin Cooperman, Lloyd Richards, Fred Freiberger, Charles Russell. *dr* Various, including Walter Grauman, Tay Garnett, Phil Karlson, Howard Koch, Stuart Rosenberg. *wr* Various. *mus* Wilbur Hatch, Nelson Riddle. *cast* **Eliot Ness** Robert Stack **Agent Martin Flaherty** Jerry Paris **Agent William Longfellow** Abel Fernandez **Agent Enrico Rossi** Nick Georgiade **Agent Cam Allison** Anthony George **Agent Lee Hobson** Paul Picerni **Agent Rossmann** Steve London **Frank Nitti** Bruce Gordon **Narrator** Walter Winchell.

Robert Stack (bottom right) played Eliot Ness, the incorruptible G-Man of the Prohibition era, in *The Untouchables*, one of the most violent series ever to be aired on TV.

In 1960 a television monitoring group based in Los Angeles reported that in one week alone television had shown 144 murders, 143 attempted murders, four attempted lynchings, two massacres or mass murders, fifty-two other killings and eleven planned murders. A ratings war between the major US networks was responsible for this escalating violence in TV crime series, and most notorious amongst the offenders was Quinn Martin's *The Untouchables*. With an eye on the competition, Martin had told his writers early on 'More action, or we are going to get clobbered.' The writers obliged and *The Untouchables*, a fast-action classic amongst crime dramas, soon became known as 'the weekly bloodbath', with the palookas getting mowed down in up to three machine-gun shoot-outs per instalment.

The series was based on the autobiography of Eliot Ness, a Treasury Department crimebuster based in Chicago in Prohibition days. Ness had played a major part in breaking the power of notorious gangster Al Capone in 1931, a story dramatised in two-part TV show *The Scarface Mob*, aired on *Desilu Playhouse* in 1959. The special prompted ABC to run a series – which almost reeked of speakeasy authenticity – with Robert Stack, an accomplished movie actor, starring as Ness. With Capone safely behind bars, action focused on the battle between the gangster's two top lieutenants Jake 'Greasy Thumb' Guzik and Frank 'The Enforcer' Nitti for control of the empire he had left behind, and Ness's attempts to bring the mobsters to justice. The real-life Ness had in fact disbanded his famous band of agents, the Untouchables (so-called by a Chicago newspaper because of their incorruptibility) after the Capone case, but on the small screen *The Untouchables* went after famous gang bosses from Bugs Moran (in whose garage the St Valentine's Day Massacre took place) to Ma Baker, East Coast hoods such as Mad Dog Coll, Dutch Schultz and Philadelphia crime boss Walter Legenza.

The series was a massive hit. Apart from the satisfaction of seeing the Mob get it every week, there was the music, and the stars – it guest-featured some of the medium's heaviest of heavies: William Bendix, Lloyd Nolan, Neville Brand and Neremiah Persoff. The period props and costumes were part of the appeal: *The Untouchables* was all double-breasted suits, flash cars and violin cases. It also had a different, quasi-documentary feel, with a staccato voice-over provided by old-style columnist Walter Winchell. *The Untouchables'* departures from reality attracted complaints from the FBI, Italian-American groups and prison officers, but the producers simply added a disclaimer to the end of each episode and carried on.

Yet success was short-lived. The programme went from forty-three in the charts in its first season, to number eight in its second, then back to number forty-one in the third. In its fourth and final season there was an attempt to win back audiences by making Ness more human and the killings more motivated. New investigators from other government bureaus were brought in, including Barbara Stanwyck as a lieutenant from the Bureau of Missing Persons. But production ended in 1963 after 114 episodes and organised cime didn't feature again on the small screen until J Edgar Hoover gave permission for the series *F.B.I.* (another Quinn Martin production) to be made in 1965.

Z Cars

UK 1962–78 667 × 25m/50 bw/col BBC1. BBC. *cr* Tony Kennedy Martin. *pr* David E Rose, Richard Beynon, Ronald Travers, Ron Craddock. *dr* Various, including John McGrath, Terence Dudley, Paddy Russell, Vivian Matalon, Philip Dudley, Richard Harding, Eric Taylor, Eric Hills, Christopher Barry, Shaun Sutton, Robin Midgeley, Alan Bromly, Michael Hayes. *wr* Various, including Troy Kennedy Martin, John Hopkins, Robert Barr, Alan Plater, Bill Barron, Allan Prior, Keith Dewhurst, John McGrath, Bill Lyons, Elwyn Jones. *mus* played by Johnny Keating. *cast* **Det Insp Charlie Barlow** Stratford Johns **PC Jock Weir** Joseph Brady **PC Bert Lynch** James Ellis **PC David Graham** Colin Welland **Desk Sgt Twentyman** Leonard Williams **Det Supt Miller** Leslie Sands **Det Insp Goss** Derek Waring **Det Con Scatliff** Geoffrey Hayes **PC Quilley** Douglas Fielding **Det Insp Witty** John Woodvine **Det Sgt John Watt** Frank Windsor **PC 'Fancy' Smith** Brian Blessed **PC Bob Steele** Jeremy Kemp **PC Sweet** Terence Edmond **Desk Sgt Blackitt** Robert Keegan **Det Sgt Stone** John Slater **Det Insp Bamber** Leonard Rossiter **PC Newcombe** Bernard Holley **Det Con**

Skinner Ian Cullen **Det Insp Hudson** John Barrie **Det Insp Todd** Joss Ackland. *Video* BBC.

Over in the States audiences were thrilling to machine-gun operas of TV violence, but it took writer Troy Kennedy Martin to notice (when listening to police radio during a bout of mumps) that Britain's >*Dixon of Dock Green* was out of date. With the backing of new BBC Director General Hugh Green and his head of drama Sidney Lawrence, and with help from respected documentarists Elwyn Jones and Robert Barr, Martin set out to create a lifelike, new-style police series for the sixties. The result was *Z Cars*.

The location was the tough Liverpool docklands – Kirby became overspill estate Newtown for the series, and Seaforth became Seaport – and the four young recruits driving around in Ford Zephyr patrol cars Z-Victor-One and Z-Victor-Two, call-sign 'Zulu', encountered harsh urban realities very different from those in *Dixon's* manor. Newtown was a mixed community, displaced by slum clearance, brought together on an estate without amenities or community feeling. The series opened on the grave of PC Farrow, shot down in execution of his duty. The answer was to bring in patrol cars, and the first job was to find the 'crew' – Z-Victor-One was soon in the hands of Northcountryman PC Fancy Smith and Scot PC Jock Weir, Z-Victor-Two held Irishman PC Herbert Lynch and red-haired PC Bob Steele. And in *Z Cars* Liverpool Docklands got the policemen it deserved – these cops were no angels. Constable Lynch was not above a flutter on the horses, Constable Bob Steele was revealed in episode one as a wife-beater and violence on the beat was met by violence from the men in the crime cars. The Police Federation, viewers and even Jack Warner complained, but within two months of the show's first episode in 1962 it was attracting an audience of 14 million. It ran for sixteen years until 1978, when it in turn began to look dated next to new shows like >*The Sweeney*. The two characters who created the most impact were hard and soft men Detective Inspector Charlie Barlow and Detective Sergeant John Watt. Barlow, a huge man not above verbal or physical violence and the gentler Watt, his ideal foil, were so successful that they departed for the Regional Crime Squad and their own spin-off series, *Softly, Softly* (1966–76).

Another early departure was creator Troy Kennedy Martin who left *Z Cars* three months after its first transmision, unhappy with the way the series was going. He had wanted a true-to-life series where the police would lose some of the time but the BBC made sure that the criminal got arrested at the end of every episode.

Even so, the series moved British television police drama on to a new realism. Its all-round high-quality production was the result of a combination of BBC drama-documentary expertise, superb casting – Stratford Johns, Frank Windsor, Leonard Rossiter, Brian Blessed, Colin Welland, who all became household names – and scripts from leading writers such as John Hopkins, Robert Barr, Alan Plater and Allan Prior. Guest stars included such young talents as Judi Dench and among the production team were Julia Smith and Tony Holland who many years later were to be the creators of BBC's *Eastenders*. Actor Brian Blessed's later roles included Caesar Augustus in *I Claudius*, actor and writer Colin Welland starred in Dennis Potter's *Blue Remembered Hills* and wrote the award-winning feature film *Chariots of Fire*, and Stratford Johns fast outgrew his part in *Softly, Softly* to be given his own series *Barlow at Large* (1971–3) and *Barlow* (1974–6) in which he was elevated to Detective Chief Superintendent.

Creator Troy Kennedy Martin later wrote the multiple BAFTA Award-winning nuclear political thriller *Edge of Darkness* (1985) for BBC2.

Westerns

The Adventures of Champion

USA 1955–6 26 × 26m bw. Flying A Productions. *UK tx* 1956–7 BBC1. *cr* Gene Autry. *pr* Gene Autry, Eric Jenson, Louis Gray. *dr* George Archainbaud. *wr* Various. *mus* Frankie Laine (theme vocal). *cast* **Ricky North** Barry Curtis **Sandy North** Jim Bannon **Will Calhoun** Francis McDonald **Sheriff Powers** Ewing Mitchell.

The exploits of Champion, a wild stallion who befriends twelve-year-old Ricky North in the American Southwest in the 1880s. Although Ricky, who lived on his Uncle Sandy's ranch, had a magnetic attraction for trouble he was always rescued by the wonder horse, aided by the boy's other bosom companion, German Shepherd dog Rebel.

In real-life, Champion the wonder horse was owned by the singing cowboy star, Gene Autry, whose production company Flying A made the TV series. Frankie Laine sang the catchy opening and closing theme song.

The Adventures of Rin Tin Tin

USA 1954–9 164 × 26m ABC. Screen Gems/A Herbert B Leonard Production. *UK tx* 1954–9 ITV. *pr* Herbert B Leonard, Fred Briskin. *dr* Various, including William Beaudine, Douglas Heyes, Earl Bellamy, Charles S Gould, Ida Lupino, Robert G Walker. *wr* Various, including Douglas Heyes, Roy Erwin, Frank Moss. *mus* Hal Hopper. *cast* **Rusty** Lee Aaker **Lt Rip Masters** James L Brown **Sgt Aloysius 'Biff' O'Hara** Joe Sawyer **Cpl Randy Boone** Rand Brooks **Col Barker** John Hoyt.

Heroic German shepherd dog Rin Tin Tin ('Yo ho, Rinty!') and his young orphaned master, Rusty, sole survivors of an 1880s 'Injun' raid on a wagon train are found by members of the Fighting Blue Devils of the 101st Cavalry. Brought back to Fort Apache, Arizona, they are unofficially adopted by Lieutenant Rip Masters and made honorary troopers – Rusty is commissioned a corporal in the first episode, Rin Tin Tin a private. They forthwith set about helping the cavalry and townspeople of nearby Mesa Grande to establish law and order on the frontier, which task throws all manner of violent action their way, from gunfights to Indian rampages.

The Rin Tin Tin dog character featured in a series of films between 1916 and 1932 which were among the biggest box office draws of the American silent screen. *Rin Tin Tin* had also been a radio series, once in 1930 and again in 1955. Three different German Shepherd dogs filled the role in the TV series, two of them descendants of the original Rinty (who died in 1932) and the other the offspring of another movie canine, Flame Jr. The all-important role of dog trainer on the series fell to Lee Duncan. The series was filmed at Crash Corrigan's movie ranch in California.

Starting only one month later than rival TV show >*Lassie*, featuring another plucky dog and small boy adventuring team, the show started reruns in September 1959, immediately after the final episode of the series. Further repeats in a new, light brown-tinted version with introductions by original star James Brown were aired in 1976 and, in 1987, The Family Channel made a completely new series, *Rin Tin Tin K-9 Cop*, with the resourceful shepherd dog part of a special canine unit of the Toronto Police Department. In 1958 three episodes of the series – 'Farewell to Fort Apache', 'The White Wolf' and 'The Return of Rin Tin Tin' – were released as a feature film *The Challenge of Rin Tin Tin*.

Alias Smith and Jones

USA 1971–3 1 × 90m/49 × 52m ABC. Universal TV/Public Arts. *UK tx* 1971–3 ITV. *cr* Glen A Larson. *exec pr* Roy Huggins. *pr* Glen A Larson. *dr* Various, including Roy Huggins, Mel Ferrer, Jeffrey Hayden, Gene Levitt, Fernando Lamas, Edward Abroms, Bruce Kessler, David Moessinger, Barry Shear, Alexander Singer, Douglas Heyes, Arnold Laven, Jack Arnold, Jeannot Szwarc, Richard L Bare, Richard Benedict, Mel Ferber. *wr* Various, including Roy Huggins, Matthew Howard, Glen A Larson, Gene Levitt. *mus* Billy Goldenburg. *cast* **Hannibal Heyes (Joshua Smith)** Pete Duel (1971–2)/Roger Davis (1972–3) **Jed 'Kid' Curry (Thaddeus Jones)** Ben Murphy **Clementine Hale** Sally Field **Narrator** Roger Davis (1971–2)/Ralph Story (1972–3).

Inspired by the popularity of the feature film *Butch Cassidy and the Sundance Kid*, this tongue-in-cheek Western series featured ex-outlaws Jed Curry (based on real-life hole-in-the-wall gang member Kid Curry) and Hannibal Heyes who, seeking to end their life of crime, were granted a provisional amnesty by the Governor of Kansas, to be turned into a pardon if the pair led blameless lives for a full twelve months. This ideal, however, was to remain a secret ('Only you and me and

Pete Duel (left) and Ben Murphy (right) starred as Hannibal Heyes and Kid Curry in the TV comedy western *Alias Smith and Jones*. Duel committed suicide during the filming of the show, leaving narrator Roger Davis to take his part.

the governor'll know!') and so the duo accepted the aliases of the title, Thaddeus Jones (Curry) and Joshua Smith (Heyes), and duly roamed the Kansas territory of the 1890s trying their level best to avoid trouble. But with a price still on their heads, a lot of grudges against them and a little larceny still in their hearts, this was no easy proposition. Chased across two TV seasons by posses, bounty-hunters and old outlaw friends who wanted them to revert to their old ways, they never did get their pardon.

The show starred Ben Murphy as Jed 'Kid' Curry and Pete Duel (who spelt his name Deuel on *Love on a Rooftop*) as Hannibal Heyes. On 30 December 1971, Duel, aged 31, shot and killed himself after watching the show at his Hollywood Hills apartment leaving the role of Joshua Smith to be speedily recast. It was taken by Roger Davis, formerly narrator of the series, who continued in the part for another year. Ralph Story took over Davis' previous role as narrator. The occasional role of Clementine Hale, another lovable rogue, was added in October 1971 to give some continuing love interest.

At a time when the TV Western was galloping into the sunset (>*Gunsmoke* was the only traditional Western on the screen in America by the time its production ended in 1975) and with secret agents of all types taking over TV, *Alias Smith and Jones* had good-looking exterior photography, roguish humour and interesting use of voice-over dialogue that succeeded in making it one of the last Western hits.

The Big Valley

USA 1965–9 112 × 52m ABC. Four Star Productions. *UK tx* 1965–8 ITV. *cr* A I Bezzerides, Louis F Edelman. *pr* Louis F Edelman, Arnold Laven, Arthur Gardener, Jules Levy. *dr* Various, including Nicholas Webster, Joseph H Lewis, Ralph Senensky, Michael Ritchie, Ida Lupino, William A Graham, Sutton Roley, Joseph Pevney, Lewis Allen, Arnold Laven, Virgil W Vogel, Richard Sarafian, Paul Henreid, Bernard McEveety. *wr* Various, including Peter Packer, Judith Barrows, Harry Kronman, Ken Trevey. *mus* Lalo Schifrin (theme), George Duning. *cast* **Victoria Barkley** Barbara Stanwyck **Jarrod Barkley** Richard Long **Nick Barkley** Peter Breck **Heath Barkley** Lee Majors **Eugene Barkley** Charles Briles **Audra Barkley** Linda Evans **Silas** Napoleon Whiting. *Video* BRAVE/SMO.

The San Joaquin Valley in the Old West was the setting for this wide-open-spaces family saga of cattle ranching folk. ABC's answer to >*Bonanza*, *The Big Valley* differed from its precusor in being a matriarchal tale starring Hollywood veteran Barbara Stanwyck as widow Victoria Barkley, the iron-willed head of her powerful clan of four sons and a daughter: Richard Long (>*Maverick*, >77 *Sunset Strip*) played level-headed number one son, lawyer Jarrod; Peter Breck played bold, brawling number two son and ranch foreman, Nick; Lee Majors (>*Six Million Dollar Man*, *The Men from Shiloh*) in his first TV role – indeed, the first part he read for after a mere six months of drama instruction – was ruggedly handsome, feisty number three son Heath (the illegitimate half-Indian son of Victoria's late husband); Charles Briles was introspective number four son Eugene; and Linda Evans (later Krystle Carrington in >*Dynasty*) was beautiful daughter Audra. With the help of black servant Silas the Barkleys tried to make a go of it on their 30,000-acre ranch which, though not as large as the Ponderosa, boasted a mine, a vineyard and an orange grove.

Like other settlers, the Barkleys were in a continual fight against the lawless elements of the Old West and *Big Valley* stories were peopled by schemers, murderers, bank robbers, Mexican revolutionaries and con men (one of whom was played by Milton Berle in a guest appearance). But *The Big Valley* also embraced moral and psychological themes in some excellent teleplays: the Joseph H Lewis-directed 'Boots with My Father's Name' and 'Night of the Wolf', for instance, are two above-average segments. Many episodes were directed by female film star Ida Lupino.

Prior to her role as Victoria Barkley, Barbara Stanwyck (real name Ruby Stevens) had portrayed tough, fearsome women of the West in such movies as *The Furies* (1950), *Cattle Queen of Montana* (1954) and *The Maverick Queen* (1956) as well as playing settler women in the TV series >*Wagon Train* and >*Rawhide*. In 1973 she was admitted to the National Cowboy Hall of Fame. She had also put in unsurpassed performances as a *femme fatale* in Billy Wilder's classic *film noir Double Indemnity*

(1944) and King Vidor's *Stella Dallas* (1938). Her TV career also included a period as hostess of the *The Barbara Stanwyck Theatre* (1960–1), NBC's thirty-minute anthology series, the role of Constance Colby in *The Colbys* (ABC 1985–7) and a starring part in the mini-series *The Thorn Birds* (ABC 1983).

Bonanza

USA 1959–73 430 × 52m col NBC. NBC Productions. *UK tx* 1960–73 ITV. *cr* David Dortort. *exec pr* David Dortort. *pr* David Dortort, Thomas Thompson, Richard Collins, Robert Blees. *dr* Various, including Robert Altman, Joseph Sargent, Leon Benson, Virgil W Vogel, William F Claxton, Alan Crosland Jr, Christian Nyby, Charles Rondeau, Paul Henreid, Tay Garnett, R G Springsteen, Jacques Tourneur, Joseph Kane, Gerd Oswald, Ralph Black, Don McDougall. *wr* Various, including Michael Landon, Thomas Thompson, William R Cox, Mort Thaw, Stanley Ellis, Ossie Davis, John T Kelley, Frank Cleaver, William L Stuart, Suzanne Clausner. *mus* Jay Livingston and Ray Evans (theme), David Rose. *cast* **Ben Cartwright** Lorne Greene **Little Joe Cartwright** Michael Landon **Eric 'Hoss' Cartwright** Dan Blocker **Adam Cartwright** Pernell Roberts **Hop Sing** Victor Sen Yung **Sheriff Roy Coffee** Ray Teal **Candy** David Canary **Dusty Rhoades** Lou Frizzel **Jamie Hunter** Mitch Vogel **Griff King** Tim Matheson **Deputy Clem** Bing Russell. *Video* CREAT/VVL.

On 12 September 1959, the Bonanzaland map flamed across the American nation's television screens for the first time. Set in Virginia City, Nevada, during the Civil War years, *Bonanza* was the first of the family formula westerns, more saddle soap than violent actioner, and told the tale of the upright, prosperous Cartwright clan, owners of the thousand-mile square Ponderosa ranch (named after its ponderosa pines) in the post-Comstock silver lode days.

Canadian actor Lorne Greene was plucked from a >*Wagon Train* episode for the role of Ben Cartwright, thrice-widowed patriarch of an all-male family of three sons. David Dortort, creator, writer and producer of the series for its entire fourteen years declared of Ben: 'He is

not led around by the nose by anybody. We do not have any Moms built into our show – or for that matter, any women. We are, as it were, anti-Momism.' The boys that Pa Cartwright had to raise single-handed were half brothers, each the son of a different marriage. Pernell Roberts, from the New York stage, filled the network's demand for a Brando type for the part of introspective eldest son Adam; Dan Blocker, an ex-school teacher from Texas played six feet four inches tall, twenty-one stone gentle giant Eric 'Hoss' and Michael Landon, star of the 1957 film *I Was a Teenage Werewolf*, played youngest son Little Joe – hotheaded, impulsive and destined for heartthrob appeal (*TV Guide* promptly dubbed him a 'Kookie in chaps').

The story of Ben Cartwright's three marriages was told in flashbacks: Adam was born in New England to Ben's first wife Elizabeth, Hoss was the son of second wife Inger, a woman of Norwegian extraction killed by Indians ('Hoss' is Norwegian for 'good luck'), Little Joe was the son of Marie, who died as the result of a fall from her horse. Other regulars included cook Hop Sing, Sheriff Roy Coffee, the Virginia City lawman who frequently called on the Cartwrights for assistance, and various drifters and ranch hands who were taken into the family fold at different times – wanderer Mr Canaday (Candy) who was hired as a ranch hand in the 1967–8 season, and, when he left three years later, Ben's friend Dusty Rhoades who turned up with young orphaned Jamie Hunter.

The four Cartwright men lived for each other, protecting their land, helping the helpless and fighting corruption while Pa Cartwright, owner of the largest expanse of land in Nevada territory, also played the role of benevolent guardian to Virginia City. A host of passers-through meant that the majority of stories revolved around guest characters (guest stars included Yvonne de Carlo of >*The Munsters*) who could be misfits, misunderstood vagabonds or historical characters such as Samuel Langhorne Clemens, Henry T P Comstock and Cochise. And there was comedy aplenty, especially when Little Joe and Hoss got together. But *Bonanza* was also a new kind of thinking person's western and the three holstered sons were for ever being tortured by some ethical conflict that required a fireside chat presided over by Pa Cartwright.

Lorne Greene (above, centre) as *Bonanza* paterfamilias Pa
Cartwright, together with two of his Ponderosa progeny,
Hoss (Dan Blocker, left) and Little Joe (Michael Landon,
right). The series ran from 1959 to 1973, a TV western
longevity only surpassed by *Gunsmoke*.

All this, plus the fact that Dortort (also creator of >*The High Chaparral*) had the foresight to film the stunning Lake Tahoe scenery in colour, meant that, although in its first two seasons *Bonanza* failed in its aim to outdraw CBS's *Perry Mason*, from 1964–7 the series had the highest average ratings in the Nielsen survey, and at the time of cancellation the sage brush saga was being shown in ninety countries to an audience of 400 million viewers. In Britain, where it began in 1960, the series helped to establish the fledgeling ITV as the most popular channel. British homes were named Ponderosa and the Queen confessed to actor Lorne Greene when she met him in Canada in 1964 that she and her children were regular viewers.

There were cast changes over the years. Pernell Roberts left the series at the end of the 1964–5 season, having tired of the role. The series survived this loss and brought in new characters to fill the gap. But before production began for the 1972–3 season, Dan Blocker died. This, plus a scheduling change to Tuesdays brought the *Bonanza* heroic myth to an end halfway through its fourteenth season (reruns, however, under the title *Ponderosa* had begun in summer 1972 even before the original series ended). Only >*Gunsmoke* ran for longer as a small-screen western.

From the outset *Bonanza* had a high standard of camerawork and distinctive look established in no small part by director Robert Altman who executed a number of memorable early episodes such as 'Silent Thunder', 'The Dream Riders', 'The Rival' and 'The Many Faces of Gideon Finch'. Other first-rate directors also worked on the show – Tay Garnett, Jacques Tourneur (the film *Cat People*), Joseph Sargent, William F Claxton and William Witney among them. *Bonanza* made millionaires of the trio that remained after Pernell Roberts left, Greene, Blocker and Landon. The stars also had rich television careers subsequent to the show: Lorne Greene starred in *Griff*, *Battlestar Galactica* and *Code Red*; Pernell Roberts starred as *Trapper John, MD*, in a spin-off from >*M*A*S*H*; and Michael Landon achieved fortune as producer and star of both >*The Little House on the Prairie* and *Highway to Heaven*.

In 1967 a two-part episode from the previous year was released as a theatrical feature under its original title *Ride the Wind*.

In March 1988 the syndicated TV movie *Bonanza: The Next Generation* continued the Cartwright saga with a new cast: John Ireland as Aaron, the late Ben's brother and head of the Ponderosa; Barbara Anderson as Annabelle, the wife of Little Joe (killed in action while serving with the Rough Riders), Brian A Smith as Josh, Hoss's illegitimate son and Michael Landon Jr as Benji, Little Joe's son.

Branded

USA 1965–6 48 × 26m bw (35 col) NBC. Goodson-Todman Productions. *UK tx* 1965–6 ITV. *cr* Larry Cohen. *pr* Andrew J Fenady, Cecil Baker. *dr* Various, including Joseph H Lewis, Lee H Katzin, William Witney, Bernard McEveety. *wr* Various, including Larry Cohen. *mus* A Alch and Dominic Frontiere (theme). *cast* **Jason McCord** Chuck Connors **Joshua McCord** John Carradine.

In the 1880s, West Point graduate Captain Jason McCord (grim-faced Chuck Connors) is unjustly cashiered for cowardice at the Battle of Bitter Creek. In fact, he had been knocked unconscious and left for dead by the Commanche, but the military authorities refused to believe this. *Branded* related the story of McCord's subsequent Western wanderings as he sought to prove his innocence, carrying with him everywhere a broken sword, the symbol of his shame.

A superior adult western – created by Larry 'The Invaders' Cohen, with a pilot directed by Hollywood's Joseph H Lewis – *Branded* had one of the most memorable opening title sequences in small-screen history: McCord stands at the fort, his uniform epaulettes and buttons are ripped off, while drums roll and a solemn voice sings: 'All but one man died, there at Bitter Creek/And they say he ran away. Branded, marked with the coward's chain/What do you do when you're Branded./Well you fight for your name . . .'

Before *Branded* – the persecution theme of which was intended by Larry Cohen to echo McCarthyism – Connors' numerous credits included the film *The Big Country* (1958) and the lead in Sam Peckinpah's frontier-family series, *The Rifleman* (1958–63, so-called because of rancher character Lucas Cain's ability with a modified Winchester). Later, in the comedy western movie *Support Your Local Gunfighter* (1971), he dropped his hard-man persona to show a surprising comic bent.

A three-part episode of *Branded*, 'The Mission', forms the 1965 cinema feature, *Broken Sabre*.

Cade's County

USA 1971–2 24 × 60m col CBS. David Gerber Productions/20th Century Fox TV/CBS TV. *UK tx* 1972 ITV (ATV). *cr* Rick Husky, Tony Wilson. *exec pr* David Gerber. *pr* Charles Lawson. *dr* Martin Chomsky, Robert Day, George Marshall. *wr* Various. *mus* Henry Mancini. *cast* **Sheriff Sam Cade** Glenn Ford **Deputy JJ Jackson** Edgar Buchanan **Joannie Little Bird** Sandra Ego **Pete** Peter Ford **Deputy Arlo Pritchard** Taylor Lacher **Kitty Ann Sundown** Betty Ann Carr **Deputy Rudy Davillo** Victor Campos.

Contemporary western series set in Madrid County, California, with Sheriff Sam Cade policing everything from professional killers to Apache Indians, now riding pick-up trucks rather than painted ponies. Aside from its stunning desertscapes, the series was notable for its positive, unstereotypical attitude to Native Americans, and American Indian actors Sandra Ego and Betty Ann Carr succeeded each other in the role of police dispatcher. The part of Cade himself was taken by Hollywood star Glenn Ford. His son, Peter, also featured in the cast. Three TV movies emerged from the show: *Marshal of Madrid*, *Sam Cade* and *Slay Ride*. Executive producer David Gerber was one of the top independent producers of the 1970s. He was executive producer of, among others, >*Police Story*, >*Police Woman* and *Joe Forrester*. Later he was head of television at MGM-UA and MGM-Pathe.

Casey Jones

USA 1957–8 32 × 30m bw syndicated. Columbia/Birskin. *UK tx* 1958 BBC1. *pr* Harold Green. *dr* Various. *wr* Various. *cast*
Casey Jones Alan Hale Jr **Alice Jones** Mary Lawrence **Casey Jones Jr** Bobby Clark **Red Rock** Eddy Waller **Sam Peachpit** Pat Hogan **Wallie Simms** Dub Taylor **Mr Carter** Paul Keast.

Enjoyable kids' western adventure series set in Tennessee in the 1890s, featuring Alan Hale Jr as the legendary John Luther 'Casey' Jones, engineer-driver with Illinois Central Railroad's Cannonball Express. The storylines invariably involved attempts by rivals, the elements or outlaws to prevent Casey bringing the train in on time – but he always did. There was no discernible character development, but there was lots of narrative excitement and suspense with a likeable hero (whose name now ignominiously graces a railway burger bar chain).

Of Alan Hale Jr it might be said that he was born to play westerns. His father was the rumbustious star of such movie westerns as *Dodge City*, *Sante Fe Trail* and *Colt 45*. Junior himself played the violent outlaw Cole Younger in the 1957 film *The Story of Jesse James*, before relocating genres to become Jonas 'Skipper' Grumby in the Robinson Crusoe-esque *Gilligan's Island* (1964–7).

Cheyenne

USA 1956–63 107 × 60m bw ABC. Warner Bros-TV. *UK tx* 1958–61 BBC1. *exec pr* William T Orr. *pr* Roy Huggins, Arthur Silver. *dr* Various, including Lee Sholem, Richard Sarafian, George Waggner, Joseph Kane, Paul Henreid, Alan Crosland Jr, Leslie H Martinson, Jerry Hopper, Arthur Lubin, Paul Landres, Richard L Bare, Douglas Heyes, Thomas Carr. *wr* Various, including James O'Hanlon, Walker A Tompkins. *mus* William Lara (theme). *cast* **Cheyenne Bodie** Clint Walker **Bronco Layne** Ty Hardin **Smitty** LQ Jones.

Alongside >*Gunsmoke*, probably the show most responsible for TV's stampede into adult westerns in the fifties. Loosely developed from the 1947 movie of the same title, the series starred six foot six, barrel-chested Norman 'Clint' Walker as Cheyenne Bodie, a half-breed loner possessed of an implacable sense of justice who drifted around the 1870s frontier changing jobs (ranch hand, scout, deputy) and women every episode. What set

Cheyenne apart from the juvenile westerns which preceded it was that it had maturity and psychological nuance, as well as gunplay. The stories flowed out of the characters Bodie met on his wanderings. By 1957 the show had entered the top twenty in the Nielsen ratings.

The show's off-screen history is as interesting as its on-screen action. It first appeared on TV as one of three rotation elements in *Warner Bros Presents*. At this stage Cheyenne had a sidekick, mapmaker Smitty (cult western star LQ Jones, aka Justus E McQueen and the director of the classic, low-budget sci-fi film, *A Man and Dog*), but he was quickly dropped to allow Clint Walker to bask in undiluted glory (and become TV's first western hero *sans* pardner). In 1958 Walker walked out on the series over a contract dispute, and the leading character was changed to Bronco Layne, an ex-Confederate officer played by Ty Hardin. Eventually, however, Walker was tempted back to the *Cheyenne* corral by an increased salary. Ty Hardin's popular Layne, meanwhile, was given a show of his own, *Bronco*, in which he encountered such western historical characters as Billy the Kid. In 1960 *Cheyenne* returned to being an anthology series, *The Cheyenne Show*, rotating with *Sugarfoot* (starring Will Hutchens as dude cowpoke Tom Brewster) and *Bronco*.

Despite an often lavish screen look, the making of *Cheyenne* was famously fast; episodes were shot in five days on a budget of $75,000, at a time when a low-grade feature film would cost around $450,000. Warner Bros packed episodes with surplus stampede and bar-room footage from their movies, sometimes even writing *Cheyenne* scripts to fit them. Clint Walker's subsequent TV career has included the lead in the Alaskan police series *Kodiak* (1974, 13 × 25m).

The Cisco Kid

USA 1951–6 152 × 26m col syndicated. Ziv TV. *UK tx* 1954–6 ITV. *pr* Walter Schwimmer. *dr* Various, including Lambert Hillyer. *wr* Various, including Walker A Thomkins. *cast* **The Cisco Kid** Duncan Renaldo **Pancho** Leo Carillo.

Popular juvenile western based on the character created by O Henry in the short story, 'The Caballero's Way'

(1904). Duncan Renaldo played the knight-errant title role, Leo Carillo – then in his seventies – his portly sidekick, Pancho. Cisco and Pancho saw plenty of action as they galloped around 1890s New Mexico on Diablo and Loco meting out justice to black-hearted villains. But the real appeal of the show lay in the characters themselves, especially the rascally Pancho, with his comic malapropisms and fractured English ('Pl-ee-se Ceesco! Let's went!'). The series had the distinction of being the first TV western to be filmed in colour, and is still rerun in syndication.

Davy Crockett

USA 1954–5 5 × 52m bw ABC. Walt Disney Productions. *UK tx* 1956 ITV. *cr* Walt Disney. *exec pr* Walt Disney. *pr* Bill Walsh. *dr* Norman Foster. *wr* Various. *mus* George Bruns. *cast* **Davy Crockett** Fess Parker **Georgie Russell** Buddy Ebsen.

This TV mini-series about the true life and times of the frontiersman, from his days as an Indian-fighter to the stand at the Alamo, led to Crockett-mania in 1954–5, when Americans spent upwards of $100 million in associated merchandising. Walt Disney subsequently claimed that *Davy Crockett*, which developed from ABC's anthology slot *Disneyland*, was the cause of the TV western stampede of the fifties; certainly the series, with its unusually brutal hand-to-hand combat, represented a transition between the era of the kiddie and adult oater.

Two theatrical features were made from re-edited episodes, *Davy Crockett, King of the Wild Frontier* and *Davy Crockett and the River Pirates*, both in 1955.

Actor Fess Parker made something of a speciality of coonskin roles; he went on to star as *Daniel Boone* (1964–9). Buddy Ebsen, who played Crockett's sidekick, Georgie Russell, went on feature in >*The Beverly Hillbillies*.

The episodes of *Davy Crockett* were: Davy Crockett, Indian Fighter/Davy Crockett Goes to Congress/ Davy Crockett at the Alamo/Davy Crockett and the Keelboat Race/Davy Crockett and the River Pirates. (The last two episodes were 'prequels'.)

Gunsmoke

USA 1955–75 233 × 26m/402 × 52m bw/col CBS. Filmaster Productions/Arness & Company. *UK tx* 1956–70 ITV (initially as *Gun Law*). *cr* Charles Marquis Warren. *exec pr* Robert Stabler, Charles Marquis Warren, John Mantley, Philip Leacock. *pr* Philip Leacock, Norman Macdonell, John Mantley, James Arness. *dr* Various, including Charles Marquis Warren, Robert Butler, Arthur Hiller, Andrew V McLaglen,Harry Horner, Marvin Chomsky, Bernard L Kowalski, William Conrad, Joseph Sergeant, Joseph H Lewis, Vincent McEveety, Richard Sarafian, Mark Rydell, Ted Post, Abner Biberman, Philip Leacock, Harry Harris, Bernard McEveety, Christian Nyby, Michael O'Herlihy, Irving J Moore, Victor French, Tay Garnett, RG Springsteen, John Rich. *wr* Various, including Charles Marquis Warren, John Meston, Clyde Ware, Sam Peckinpah, Dick Clark. *mus* Various, including Glenn Spencer and Rex Koury ('Old Trails' theme), Richard Shores. *cast* **Marshal Matt Dillon** James Arness **Kitty Russell** Amanda Blake **'Doc' Galen Adams** Milburn Stone **Deputy Chester Goode** Dennis Weaver **Deputy Festus Hagen** Ken Curtis **Quint Asper** Burt Reynolds **Sam** Glenn Strange.

The grandfather of TV westerns, *Gunsmoke* began life on radio with William Conrad (later >*Cannon*) in the role of frontier lawman Marshal Matt Dillon. Initially the part of the small-screen Dillon was offered to John Wayne who turned it down; he recommended instead his rugged six foot two friend James Arness (previously Howard Hawks' *The Thing*, later the star of TV's *How The West Was Won*). Arness proved perfectly cast, the personification of the western hero.

Set in Dodge City, Kansas, in 1873 – a date chosen arbitrarily by the producers – the show's other notable characters were Kitty Russell (Amanda Blake), the soft-hearted owner of the Longbranch saloon, Dillon's limping deputy Chester B Goode (Dennis Weaver, also >*McCloud*, *Gentle Ben*), and bullet-removing 'Doc' Adams (Milburn Stone). In 1964 Deputy Chester, constant brewer of a 'mean cup of coffee', was replaced by hillbilly deputy Festus Hagen. Half-breed blacksmith Quint Asper (Burt Reynolds) featured for a while, as did gunsmith Newly O'Brien.

Débuting in the same week as >*The Life and Legend of Wyatt Earp*, *Gunsmoke* had an innovative, mature approach which balanced the Marshal's lawkeepin' action with human and social dilemmas and soon began to win a huge viewership. By 1958 it was the most popular show in America, its success, along with that of >*Cheyenne*, causing a TV western boom. By the following year there were over thirty western series per week showing on US television. *Gunsmoke* was still a top thirty hit when, after twenty years, it was cancelled in 1975, the last western on TV. By then, only Arness and Stone were left from the original cast, and the show had subtly changed from its adventure-episode format into a frontier soap, with Marshal Dillon the head of what was, for all intents and TV purposes, a family of characters.

Stylistically, the series – also known as *Gun Law* and syndicated under the title *Matt Dillon* – was often of top calibre, shot with a no-nonsense, spare style. Directors included Andrew McLaglen (son of John Ford's stock actor, Victor), Joseph H 'Gun Crazy' Lewis and double Oscar-winner Harry Horner (the segment 'The Guitar', written by Sam Peckinpah). In 1958 *Gunsmoke* received an Emmy Award for Best Dramatic Series, and Dennis Weaver won the award for Best Supporting Actor the following season.

The revival of the western in the 1980s saw two TV movies based on the series, *Gunsmoke: Return to Dodge* and *Gunsmoke: The Last Apache*, in which Arness and Blake reprised their classic roles as the fictive West's greatest lawman and saloon gal.

Have Gun Will Travel

USA 1957–63 156 × 26m bw CBS. Filmaster Productions. *UK tx* 1959–60. *cr* Herb Meadow, Sam Rolfe. *pr* Frank Pierson, Don Ingalls, Robert Sparks, Julian Claman. *dr* Various, including Andrew V McLaglen, Robert Butler, Seymour 'Buzz' Kulik, Gary Nelson, Sutton Roley, Elliot Silverstein, Ida Lupino, Richard Boone. *wr* Various, including Gene Roddenberry, Sam Rolfe, Bruce Geller, Jack Laird, Sam Peckinpah, Ken Kolb. *mus* theme: Johnny Western, Richard Boone and Sam Rolfe, sung by Johnny

Western. *cast* **Paladin** Richard Boone **Hey Boy** Kam Tong **Hey Girl** Lisa Lu.

Erudite loner Paladin was no everyday gunslinger. Educated at West Point college for a military career, he headed West after the Civil War to become a high-priced gun for hire. His base was the luxurious Hotel Carlton in San Francisco where he dressed in the finest clothes, enjoyed epicurean meals, read the classics and frequented literary company. His assignments arrived courtesy of Oriental servant Hey Boy who, at the start of each episode, bore a message to his master from the prospective client (during the 1960–1 season Kam Tong worked on another series, *Mr Garlund*, and was replaced by Lisa Lu as Hey Girl). Once at work in the Old West, Paladin (the adopted name meant knightly hero) clothed himself in black with a hat to match and became an avenging angel identified by two trade marks – the white chess knight decorating his holster (which held a Colt .45 single action gun with a 7½ inch barrel) and his business card inscribed with the words: 'Have Gun – Will Travel . . . Wire Paladin, San Francisco'.

It was a tough action show. Paladin was no dandy when practising his profession; he neither eschewed violence nor baulked at punishing those who hired him if they proved the guilty party, But it was also a western with sophisticated characterisation and Paladin was a rational hero who served only the cause of the righteous and helpless, free of charge if necessary. One episode, 'Genesis', revealed Paladin's vow, after killing an outlaw as payment for a gambling debt to a land baron, to adopt the villain's guise but use his guns and experience to help those unable to protect themselves.

Have Gun Will Travel was one of the most self-consciously offbeat and successful of the late-fifties wave of different flavour westerns. Richard Boone played the surly, enigmatic character of Paladin with finesse, and adult storylines (from, among others, Sam Rolfe, later creator/producer of >*Man From UNCLE*) and slick direction – notably by Andrew V McLaglen and Seymour 'Buzz' Kulik whose two-parter 'Quiet Night in Town' had Sidney Pollack in an acting role – notched the show above other cowpoke dramas on the network.

Hec Ramsey

USA 1972–4 10 × 90/120m col NBC. Mark VII Ltd/Universal TV. *UK tx* 1973–4 ITV. *exec pr* Jack Webb. *pr* Douglas Benton, Harold Jack Bloom. *dr* Douglas Benton, Nicholas Colasanto, Herschel Daugherty, Andrew McLaglen, Harry Morgan, George Marshall, Alex March, Daniel Petrie, Richard Quine. *wr* S Bar-David, Douglas Benton, William R Cox, John Meston, Richard Fielder, Joseph Michael Calvelli, Brad Radnitz, Mann Rubin, Simon Wincelberg, Harold Swanton. *mus* Fred Steiner, Lee Holdridge. *cast* **Hec Ramsey** Richard Boone **Sheriff Oliver B Stamp** Richard Lenz **Doc Amos B Coogan** Harry Morgan **Arne Tornquist** Dennis Rucker **Norma Muldoon** Sharon Acker **Andy Muldoon** Brian Dewey.

In 1901 grizzled gunfighter-turned-deputy Hec Ramsey tried to keep up with the times by using scientific methods and gadgets (magnifying glasses and the like) to solve crimes. Sensibly, however, as the West was still on the wild side, he kept his gun handy whilst aiding greenhorn Sheriff Oliver B Stamp in the policing of New Prospect, Oklahoma. Richard Boone (>*Have Gun Will Travel*) played Ramsey, while the role of the town's physician, Doc Coogan, was taken by Harry Morgan (>*Dragnet*, >*M*A*S*H*), who narrated the series and directed episodes. Sharon Acker played Norma Muldoon, Hec's love interest.

This popular and original series rotated as part of the *Sunday Mystery Movies* slot on US NBC TV, and was developed from a pilot entitled *The Century Turns*, in which Hec was mistakenly arrested by Sheriff Stamp for a stagecoach hold-up.

The High Chaparral

USA 1967–71 98 × 52m col NBC. Xanadu. *UK tx* 1967–70 BBC1. *cr* David Dortort. *exec pr* David Dortort. *pr* William F Claxton, James Schmerer. *dr* Various, including Seymour Robbie, Harry Harris, William F Claxton, Joseph Pevney, Virgil W Vogel, Leon Benson, William Witney. *wr* Various, including Laird Koenig, Peter L Dix, Lowell Hermstead, Walter Black, William F Leicester, Tim Kelly. *mus* David Rose (theme), Harry Sukman. *cast* **John Cannon** Leif Erickson ***Victoria Cannon*** Linda Cristal ***Buck Cannon*** Cameron Mitchell ***Billy Blue Cannon*** Mark Slade ***Manolito de Montoya*** Henry Darrow ***Sam Butler*** Don Collier ***Don Sebastian de Montoya*** Frank Silvera ***Joe*** Bob Hoy ***Pedro*** Roberto Contreras ***Ted Reno*** Ted Markland ***Wind*** Rudy Ramos.

Western soap from the same creative stable as >*Bonanza*. Set in Arizona in the 1870s, episodes related the attempts of Big John Cannon (Leif Erickson, aka William Anderson) and clan to build a ranch empire, The High Chaparral, in a desertscape beset by rustlers, drought, avaricious Mexicans and Apaches.

The Cannon clan in David Dortort's stylish desert ranch saga, *The High Chaparral*. From left to right, Big John Cannon (Leif Erickson), his son Blue (Mark Slade), wife Victoria (Linda Cristal), brother-in-law Manolito (Henry Darrow) and brother Buck (Cameron Mitchell).

Though the storylines might have occasionally been too thin for fifty-two minutes, THC was one of the most superior sagas to ride the small-screen range. It was more stylish and less old-fashioned than most of its competitors – the two-tone opening credits over David Rose's rousing theme would not have disgraced a Sergio Leone spaghetti western – while the Apaches, in their bandannas, long hair and coloured shirts, were actually the acme of contemporary sixties street fashion. The series' authenticity was heightened by being filmed largely on location in Tucson, Arizona. Moreover THC marked a watershed in TV's political treatment of American Indians, portraying them with dignity and respect. In a key episode, 'Feather of an Eagle', the Cannons rescue a white woman held captive by a band of Apache – but she prefers to return to the American Indians. 'There are things in the Apache culture that we the so-called civilised people might use,' remarks one of the Cannons, perfectly summing up the series' balanced attitude.

Apart from Big John Cannon (the name said it all) the other members of the family were his tremulous second wife Victoria, hard-carousing brother Buck, intellectually challenged son Blue, and brother-in-law Manolito (Henry Darrow, later *Zorro and Son*), wearer of sharp Mexican suits. Occasionally, the trouble besetting *The High Chaparral* was too much even for John Cannon plus family and ranch hands to deal with, in which case they sent for help pronto from Victoria and Manolito's father, grandee rancher Don Sebastian de Montoya.

Among the many guest stars to appear at the ranch was Chief Dan George (*Little Big Man*, *The Outlaw Josey Wales*).

Hopalong Cassidy

USA 1951–2 52 × 26m bw NBC. William Boyd Productions. *UK tx* 1955–6 ITV. *cr* William Boyd. *pr* William Boyd. *dr* Various, including George Archainbaud, Derwin Abbe. *wr* Various, including Doris Schroeder, Harrison Jacobs. *cast* **Hopalong Cassidy** William Boyd **Red Connors** Edgar Buchanan.

Hopalong Cassidy was first introduced on American TV screens in 1945 via edited-down B movies featuring the cowboy character. By 1948 these were proving so successful that William Boyd decided to produce fifty-two low-budget episodes specially made for the small screen. Aside from the fact that Hopalong's sidekick Red Connors was now played by Edgar Buchanan (*The Adventures of Judge Roy Bean*, >*Cade's County*), the TV films were identical to the movie ones, as the saintly cowboy in black chased assorted two-dimensional villains around the Old West on his horse Topper. Like >*The Lone Ranger*, 'Hoppy' was strong on moral codes and clean living (thus bearing little similarity to the characters in Clarence E Mulford's original novels), and never swore or chewed baccy. The show was hugely popular with children, helped by clever merchandising, and was one of TV's first financial bonanzas. A posse of kid-vid westerns followed hard on its TV trail, among them >*The Cisco Kid* and >*Casey Jones*, and these dominated small-screen viewing until the mid fifties. Boyd died in 1972, a multimillionaire.

Johnny Ringo

USA 1959–60 38 × 25m CBS. Four Star/Pamaron/Zane Grey Productions. *UK tx* 1992 Lifestyle. *cr* Aaron Spelling. *pr* Aaron Spelling. *dr* Various. *wr* Various, including Aaron Spelling, Richard Levinson, William Link. *mus* Don Durant (theme vocal). *cast* **Johnny Ringo** Don Durant **Deputy Cully 'Kid' Adonas** Mark Goddard **Cason Thomas** Terence DeMarney **Laura Thomas** Karen Sharpe.

Once upon a time in the West a gunfighter called Johnny Ringo swapped his black hat for a sheriff's star in the Arizona town of Velardi. From then on he kept order amongst locals and passers-through with his smoking LeMat Special (one barrel fired rounds of .45s, the other shotgun shells). Young Deputy Cully offered backup on occasion, Miss Laura Thomas provided overeager love interest and Cason Thomas, Laura's father and store owner, was the stock drunken old timer.

Despite some considerable horse-opera cliché (in one episode Johnny Ringo sang *à la* Roy Rogers), this early

Aaron Spelling (>*Charlie's Angels*, >*Dynasty*, >*Beverly Hills 90210*) series was sometimes top-hand stuff, particularly in the script department. A 1960 instalment entitled 'Black Harvest' contained a chilling account of a man who kept his young wife imprisoned for fear that she would leave him, while Richard Levinson and William Link's 'Shoot the Man' from the same year was an early genre tackling of racism.

An historical footnote: a gunslinger-turned-lawman called Johnny Ringo did actually exist, but Don Durant's clean-cut character bore little relation to him. Durant also wrote and sang the show's theme.

Kung Fu

USA 1972–5 62 × 52m col ABC. WB TV/Jerry Thorpe. *UK tx* 1973–4 ITV. *cr* Ed Spielman. *pr* Jerry Thorpe, Alex Beaton, Herman Miller, Bill Perry. *dr* Various, including Jerry Thorpe, Gordon Hessler, Marvin Chomsky, Richard Lang, Barry Crane, Charles S Dubin, Harry Harris, Robert Butler, Bill Perry. *wr* Various, including Ed Spielman, Howard Friedlander. *mus* Jim Helms (theme). *cast* **Kwai Chang Caine** David Carradine **Caine (as youth)** Radamas Pera/Stephen Manley **Master Po** Keye Luke **Master Kan** Philip Ahn. *Video* Polygram 4 Front.

Chop suey western. David Carradine, son of actor John 'Stagecoach' Carradine, played Kwai Chang Caine, a Chinese-American Shaolin priest wandering the Old West in the 1870s. He sought his long lost brother (and wisdom), but became along the way a champion of Chinese railroad workers' rights. At the same time he was always trying to avoid the bounty hunters stuck on him by the Chinese legation for his self-defence killing of a Ming prince. Episodes also related, by use of flash-back, Caine's training to be a priest in China, where he had affectionately been known as 'Grasshopper'.

Although steeped in gentle mysticism, the shaven-headed, proverb-uttering Caine was also a master of the Chinese martial art of Kung Fu – and this proved to be a lot more useful for fending off the bad guys of the West. In a novel development for TV, the series' fight scenes were filmed in a highly stylised slow-motion. Indeed,

David Carradine assumes fighting pose as Kwai Chang Caine in chop suey western *Kung Fu*. Stunningly filmed by Fred Koenecamp, the show set off a martial arts craze on both sides of the Atlantic.

Fred Koenecamp's stunning photography was one of the many pleasures of this original, mesmeric show. The episode 'Eye for an Eye' won Jerry Thorpe an Emmy for best direction.

The public's interest in the series only increased when Carradine (previously the star of TV's *Shane*) dropped out of the star lifestyle to follow the ways of Confucius himself. Along with the films of Bruce Lee – who was a consultant on the show – *Kung Fu* produced a massive transatlantic craze in the martial arts in the seventies.

At Carradine's instigation, the show was revived in 1992 as *Kung Fu: The Legend Continues*, although with a thoroughly modern setting. Carradine played Caine's grandson, Chris Potter his cop great-grandson. The series was cancelled after four years.

Laramie

USA 1959–63 124 × 52m bw/col NBC. Revue Productions. *UK tx* 1959–62 BBC1. *pr* John Champion, Richard Lewis, Robert Pirosh. *dr* Various, including Lesley Selander, Tay Garnett, Virgil W Vogel, Douglas Heyes, Earl Bellamy, Jesse Hibbs, Joseph Kane, Thomas Carr, William Witney, Hollingsworth Morse. *wr* Various, including Douglas Heyes. *mus* Cyril Mockridge (theme song). *cast* **Slim Sherman** John Smith **Jess Harper** Robert Fuller **Jonesy** Hoagy Carmichael **Andy Sherman** Bobby Crawford Jr **Mort Corey** Stuart Randall **Mike Williams** Dennis Holmes **Daisy Cooper** Spring Byington **Gandy** Don Durant.

Superior domestic western series set in the Wyoming town of the title in the 1880s. After their father is shot by a no-good varmint, young Slim Sherman and his fourteen-year-old brother Andy Sherman (Bobby Crawford, sibling of *The Rifleman's* Johnny Crawford) carry on the family ranch. Saddle tramp Jess Harper (Robert Fuller, >*Wagon Train*) drifted in as a partner, while Jonesy (played by that old music master, Hoagy Carmichael) was the chief ranch hand. In 1961 Dennis Holmes as Mike, a young orphan, and Spring Byington as Daisy Cooper, housekeeper, joined the cast.

The Sherman Ranch also doubled as a stagecoach depot for the Great Overland Mail Stage Line, which allowed a long list of guest actors to mosey through the series, including Charles Bronson and James Coburn. Towards the end of its run, the show was attacked for alleged racism in showing white girls held captive by 'Red Indians'.

The Life and Legend of Wyatt Earp

USA 1955–61 226 × 26m bw ABC. Wyatt Earp Enterprises/Desilu. *UK tx* 1956–7 ITV. *cr* Frederick Hazlitt Brennan. *pr* Louis F Edelman, Robert Sisk, Roy Roland. *dr* Various, including Paul Landres. *wr* Various, including Frederick Hazlitt Brennan, Frank Gruber. *mus* The Ken Darby Singers (theme vocal). *cast* **Wyatt Earp** Hugh O'Brian **Ben Thompson** Denver Pyle **Bat Masterson** Mason Alan Dinehart III **Abbie Crandall** Gloria Talbot **Marsh Murdock** Don Haggerty **Ned Buntline** Lloyd Corrigan **Doc Farbique** Douglas Fowley **Jim 'Dog' Kelly** Paul Brinegar/Ralph Sandford **Doc Holliday** Douglas Fowley **Morgan Earp** Dirk London **Virgil Earp** John Anderson **Old Man Clanton** Trevor Bardette **Sheriff Johnny Behan** Lash LaRue.

The story of how, armed with his trusty long-barrelled Buntline Special .45 pistols, real-life Marshal Wyatt Earp imposed law and order on the West. First he cleaned up Ellsworth, Kansas, before moving on to Dodge City, and finally he tamed Tombstone, Arizona, shooting it out (over five blaze-of-glory episodes) with Old Man Clanton's gang at the OK Corral.

As its title suggested, *Wyatt Earp* mixed fact and myth about the Marshal in roughly equal proportions, but kept its sights set on quality entertainment. It had an unusual semi-serial format, with continuing characters and stories. Playwright-author Frederick Hazlitt Brennan penned nearly all the scripts of the show (borrowing heavily from Stuart N Lake's 1931 biography of the lawman), which premièred almost simultaneously with another adult shoot 'em up, >*Gunsmoke*. Among the regular characters which appeared in the series was Sheriff Johnny Behan, played by the splendidly named Lash LaRue, star of TV's *Lash of the West* and numerous western flicks in which he bullwhipped the baddies into surrender.

As well as Hugh O'Brian (aka Hugh Krampke) other actors to play Earp on the small screen were Med Flory in >*Maverick* and Bruce Boxleitner in *I Married Wyatt Earp*, a TV movie from the Osmond Corporation.

Little House on the Prairie

USA 1974–82 1 × 96m/216 × 52m NBC. NBC Productions/NBC TV. Ed Friendly Productions. *UK tx* 1974–82 BBC1. *cr* Michael Landon. *exec pr* Michael Landon. *pr* Michael Landon, John Hawkins, Winston Miller, B W Sandefur, William F Claxton. *dr* Various, including Michael Landon, Victor French, William F Claxton, Leo Penn, Alf Kjellin, Lewis Allen. *wr* Various, including Michael Landon, Blanche Hanalis, Harold Swanton, Arthur Heinemann. *mus* David Rose. *cast **Charles Ingalls*** Michael Landon ***Caroline Ingalls*** Karen Grassle ***Laura Ingalls Wilder*** Melissa Gilbert ***Mary Ingalls Kendall*** Melissa Sue Anderson ***Carrie Ingalls*** Lindsay Greenbush/Sidney Greenbush ***Lars Hanson*** Karl Swenson ***Nels Oleson*** Richard Bull ***Harriet Oleson*** Katherine MacGregor ***Nellie Oleson Dalton*** Alison Arngrim ***Willie Oleson*** Jonathan Gilbert ***Mr Isaiah Edwards*** Victor French ***Jonathan Garvey*** Merlin Olsen ***Alice Garvey*** Hersha Parady ***Andy Garvey*** Patrick Laborteaux ***Adam Kendall*** Linwood Boomer ***Almanzo Wilder*** Dean Butler. *Video* U-COL NBC.

Based on the Laura Ingalls Wilder books about life in the Old West, *Little House on the Prairie* told the story of the loving, homesteading Ingalls family struggling to eke out a living on a small farm in Walnut Grove, Plumb Creek, Minnesota. Events in the pioneers' lives were related through the sentimental eyes of Laura Ingalls, the second-born daughter and narrator.

The Ingalls moved from the great plains of Kansas to Walnut Grove in search of a future in a young and growing community. Head of the family Charles Ingalls (played by ex >*Bonanza* star and series producer Michael Landon) shared his life with wife Caroline, their two teenage daughters Laura and Mary, the eldest, baby Carrie (played alternately by identical twins Lindsay and

Wyatt Earp (played by Hugh O'Brian) takes a rare rest from cleaning up the West in *The Life and Legend of Wyatt Earp*, ABC's quality fifties western show.

The sentimental series about a frontier 'sod-busting' family, *Little House on the Prairie* was produced by its star, Michael Landon (centre).

Sidney Greenbush) and a dog, Jack. Episodes concerned family life and growing children, struggles against natural disasters and ruined crops, and the trusty frontier types that made up the local community – shopkeepers Nels and Harriet Oleson and their bratty kids Nellie and Willie, Mr Hanson the mill owner, and the gruff but lovable Mr Edwards, a nearby farmer. Over the years the saga fielded a healthy crop of births, marriages and adopted orphans as well as cast changes. Mr Edwards left in 1977 (Victor French moved on to his own series, *Carter Country*, 1977–9, ABC) and Jonathan Garvey (played by former Los Angeles Rams star Merlin Olsen) took his place with wife Alice and young son Andy. Caroline Ingalls gave birth to fourth daughter, Grace, eldest daughter Mary lost her sight and moved to a home for the blind in Dakota where she met her future husband Adam, then the Ingalls left Walnut Grove in hard times only to return again plus adopted orphan Arthur, daughter Laura married Almanzo Wilder in 1980, while Adam regained his sight and joined his father's New York law firm taking Mary with him for ever.

Though famously sentimental, the series also made a point of tackling 'issues', mostly at the behest of Landon who was its chief mover and shaker. After Landon left the series in 1982 changes were made: the title was switched to *Little House: A New Beginning*, Laura and Almanzo became the main stars, economic problems forced Charles to sell the 'little house' and move to Iowa and the former Ingalls home was occupied by the Carter family who ran the town newspaper.

Little House on the Prairie began in September 1974 after a successful two-hour pilot in March of that year. It became a Monday night fixture for NBC and was the network's highest-rated weekly programme during 1978–9. Among the series' directors was Victor French who played Mr Edwards. In 1981–2 Merlin Oleson was spun off to another series, *Father Murphy* (1981–4, NBC), for which Landon was writer, director and executive producer. Landon also (real name Michael Orowitz) worked as creator, writer, director and executive producer of *Highway to Heaven* (1984–9, NBC) in which he starred as probationary angel Jonathan Smith whose mission it was to bring love and understanding into the lives of those in trouble. Landon was also responsible for a number of made-for-TV movies and his last credit was the CBS pilot *Us*, just before he died of cancer in 1991 aged fifty-four.

The Lone Ranger

USA 1952–6 182 × 25m bw (39 col) ABC. Apex Film Corporation/Wrather Corporation. *UK tx* 1956–60 BBC1. *cr* George W Trendle, Fran Striker, James Jewell. *pr* George W Trendle, Jack Chertok, Sherman Harris, Paul Landres, Harry H Poppe. *dr* Various, including George B Seitz, Charles Livingstone, Paul Landres. *wr* Various, including Fran Striker, George G Seitz, Ed Earl Repp, Curtis Kenyon, Walker A Tompkins. *mus* Rossini (theme), Alberto Columbo. *cast* **The Lone Ranger** Clayton Moore (also John Hart) **Tonto** Jay Silverheels **Dan Reid** Chuck Courtney **Jim Blaine** Ralph Littlefield.

Few TV series have had such impact on the popular consciousness as *The Lone Ranger*. More than forty years after it was first broadcast, advertisers still trade on the masked hero's name and legendary moral uprightness to sell their wares ('The Loan Arranger', one presentday financial service terms itself). *The Lone Ranger* is not just a western strip for kids, but an institution. The show began life in 1933 as a radio programme, and was the creation of Detroit WXYZ station-owner George W Trendle, freelance writer Fran Striker and producer James Jewell. Almost overnight, the radio show was taken up nationally, and by 1939 had been turned into two film serials by Republic. In 1949, *The Lone Ranger* débuted as a TV show on America's ABC network, becoming one of the new medium's biggest hits.

Helpfully, the first TV episode explained how the Lone Ranger got his *nom de guerre* and mission to clean up the West. As John Reid he had been one of six Texas Rangers bushwacked by the merciless Butch Cavendish Gang, but had been saved from death by a kindly Indian named Tonto, who said, 'You only Ranger left. You lone Ranger now.' By a tremendous coincidence, the Lone Ranger had saved the life of the selfsame Indian many years before.'You *kemo sabe*,' said Tonto, 'it means "trusty scout". 'And, stopping only to don his mask, the Lone Ranger set off to avenge his comrades and right wrongs in nineteenth-century Texas, accompanied by his Indian companion and his horse Silver.

The plots of the show, themselves mostly cannibalised from Striker's radio scripts, were as standardised as Noh plays: conflict was brought to a settlement by bad men, who in turn were trounced by the Lone Ranger, and thus the community could take its rightful place in civilisation. The Lone Ranger never revealed his identity, leaving the grateful folks to wonder: 'Who was that masked man?' The patriotism and moralism of the series was overt, as was the Lone Ranger's wholesomeness. The production company's list of 'Lone Ranger Don'ts' for potential scriptwriters included: 'At all times, The Lone Ranger uses perfect grammar and speech'; 'The Lone Ranger never shoots to kill . . .'; 'The Lone Ranger does not drink or smoke . . .'; 'the ultimate objective of his story . . . is the development of the west of our Country.'

Parents loved it (especially after FBI head J Edgar Hoover termed it 'one of the greatest forces for juvenile good in the country'). So did children. The Lone Ranger might never have shot to kill, but there was still plenty of stirring action, chases, easily recognisable bad guys, and gunplay in every episode.

Selected to play the part of the daring masked man of the frontier was Clayton Moore, a former trapeze artist and male model who had become the acknowledged 'King of the Serials' at the Republic film studio. When Moore had a contract dispute with *The Lone Ranger's* production company, the part was taken by John Hart for two seasons, but he lacked Moore's gracefulness and presence. Tonto was played by Jay Silverheels, the son of a Mohawk Indian chief from Canada and a former professional lacrosse player and Golden Glove boxer. (Sad to say, however, that his real name was Harold Smith.) Apart from the Lone Ranger and Tonto, the only other recurring characters were their respective horses, Silver and Scout, the Lone Ranger's nephew, Dan Reid and old timer Jim Blaine who ran the Lone Ranger's private silver-mine, the source of the silver for his bullets.

Most of the exterior shooting for the series was done at Corriganville, a movie studio ranch developed by cowboy star Ray Corrigan; observant children noticed that the Lone Ranger and Tonto rode around the same rock every episode. The interiors were filmed at the General Services Studio in Hollywood. *The Lone*

Ranger directors shot up to fifteen minutes of usable footage a day; most movies considered four minutes good going.

The series has been rerun numerous times, most recently in Britain in 1993, where it still garnered audiences of over 2 million. There has also been a cartoon version of *The Lone Ranger* (1966), and some thirteen Lone Ranger TV movies, all edited from existing episodes. It has also been merchandised to the hilt. *The Lone Ranger* was not the first juvenile western to hit the small screen, but it was the most popular. And arguably the best. Hi-Yo Silver! And away!

Maverick

USA 1957–62 124 × 52m bw ABC. Warner Bros Television. *UK tx* 1959–62 ITV. *cr* Roy Huggins. *pr* Roy Huggins. *dr* Various, including Budd Boetticher, Robert Douglas, Richard L Bare, Michael O'Herlihy, Abner Biberman, Alan Crosland Jr, Paul Henreid, Richard Sarafian, Douglas Heyes. *wr* Various, including Roy Huggins. *mus* David Buttolph. *cast* **Bret Maverick** James Garner **Bart Maverick** Jack Kelly **Samantha Crawford** Diane Brewster **Cousin Beauregard Maverick** Roger Moore **Brent Maverick** Robert Colbert.

A dust-covered stranger rides into a seedy mining town, enters a hotel, surreptitiously cuts a stack of bill-sized pieces from an old newspaper, takes a $1,000 bill from the lining of his coat and tucks the whole pile into an envelope. He approaches the sniffy desk clerk, demands the best room in the hotel and, on being refused, asks to put his envelope of 'money' in the safe. Before so doing he removes the lone $1,000 bill – letting the clerk get a good look – and reseals the newspaper-filled envelope. The clerk, now paying the 'rich' stranger fawning respect, personally escorts his guest to the penthouse suite.

This was the first of many tricks executed by western anti-hero Bret Maverick, perfectly incarnated by James Garner (>*The Rockford Files*) in the pilot for *Maverick*. One of the small-screen western classics this clever, subversive series turned the late fifties TV western on its

head, featuring as it did a devious, cowardly card-sharp hero who relied on guile rather than guns and drifted from one easy opportunity to the next. Creator Roy Huggins intended to turn conventional westerns inside out: 'I wanted to see how many rules we could break and get away with it,' he said. The result was that Bret Maverick was more interested in himself than high ideals or justice. As far as he was concerned the poor could fight their own battles.

Fast-talking ladies' man Bret was joined by his strait-laced brother Bart in November 1957 to keep the series from straying too far from the traditional western mould. But neither of the brothers Maverick were heroes in the usual sense. The untrustworthy duo roamed the west on the search for rich prey and, when faced with violence would unhesitatingly follow their 'pappy's' advice: in the face of overwhelming odds, run. Bret and Bart alternated as leads and sometimes appeared together, but Bret was more visible. Their exploits took them to frontier towns such as Hounddog, Apocalypse and Oblivion and sometimes out of the country as when Bret sailed to the South Pacific. Putting in occasional appearances were Bart's friend Dandy played by Efrem Zimbalist Jr (>*77 Sunset Strip*) and Gentleman Jack Darby played by Richard Long (>*Big Valley*). During the second season female interest was introduced when Bret had a running feud with rival con-artist Samantha Crawford.

Maverick delighted in satirising other well-known TV shows such as >*Gunsmoke*, >*Dragnet* (in one episode Bret gave a deadpan, Joe Friday-style narration) and >*Bonanza*, in a spoof of which Bart encountered a ranching baron named Joe Wheelwright, owner of the vast Subrosa Ranch who was trying to marry off his three idiot sons Moose, Henry and Small Paul. In another segment Bart, looking for help in a tight spot, ran into Clint ('Cheyenne') Walker, John Russell and his deputy Peter Brown (*Lawman*), Will ('Sugarfoot') Hutchins, Ty ('Bronco') Hardin and Edd ('Kookie') Byrnes.

In 1960 James Garner walked out on Warner Brothers demanding a better contract. In a virtual rerun of the confrontation between Warner Brothers and >*Cheyenne* star Clint Walker two years earlier, the studio refused to give in and instead hired a new actor to replace him. Enter Cousin Beau Maverick – played by a young Roger

Moore – an expatriate Texan who had fought with valour in the Civil War, moved to England and returned as a cultured Englishman to further the family fortunes in America. Unlike Walker on *Cheyenne* Garner never returned to *Maverick* and only went back to TV production on his own terms through his company Cherokee Productions (which made Garner's cult, personal project *Nichols*, 1971, in which he starred in a *Maverick*-style role as the title character). Cousin Beau and Bart alternated for the rest of the 1960–1 season and in spring 1961 another brother, Brent, entered the fray. In the final season Bart was seen alone, along with reruns of earlier episodes starring Bret.

In 1979 Warners attempted to revive the series with a made-for-TV movie, *The New Mavericks*, also starring James Garner. Instead it resulted in a short-run spin-off series *Young Maverick* featuring Beau's son and Bret's nephew Ben Maverick played by Charles Frank. In 1981 after the *Rockford Files* Garner himself returned when Cherokee Productions produced a season of *Bret Maverick* with Maverick finally settling down in Arizona as a rancher and saloon owner. Thirteen years later a movie version of *Maverick* was released with, incongruously enough, Australian Mel Gibson as the West's ultimate comic anti-hero. Garner himself played Maverick's pa.

Much of *Maverick*'s success can be attributed to the calibre of its creators and producers. Noted western director Budd Boetticher handled *Maverick*'s pilot, made it a hit and directed the first two episodes of the resulting series, 'Point Blank' and 'According to Hoyle', before returning to his motion picture career. Robert Altman (*Come Back to the 5 & Dime Jimmy Dean, Jimmy Dean*, *M*A*S*H*, *The Player*, *Prêt à Porter*) directed the episode 'Bolt from the Blue', Richard Sarafian (*Vanishing Point*) directed 'The Forbidden City' segment. Roy Huggins, who created the show, also wrote many of the segments and produced all of them for the first two years. A prolific TV creator, writer and producer, Huggins was responsible for >*The Fugitive* and was executive producer of >*Alias Smith and Jones* and >*Baretta*, as well as >*The Rockford Files* on which he and Garner were reunited. *Maverick* made James Garner a star, won Huggins an Emmy and remains a landmark in TV.

Rawhide

USA 1959–66 217 × 52m bw CBS. CBS TV. *UK tx* 1961–6 ITV. *cr* Charles Marquis Warren. *exec pr* Charles Marquis Warren. *pr* Vincent M Fenelly, Bruce Geller, Bernard L Kowalski, Endre Bohem. *dr* Various, including Charles Marquis Warren, Jack Arnold, Bernard Girard, Tay Garnett, R G Springsteen, Laslo Benedek, Earl Bellamy, Christian Nyby, Gene L Coon, Charles Rondeau, Alan Crosland Jr, Ted Post, Michael O'Herlihy, Andrew V McLaglen, Joseph Kane, Jesse Hibbs, Harry Harris, Vincent McEveety. *wr* Various, including Charles Marquis Warren, Elliott Arnold, Clair Huffaker, Al Ward, Clyde Ware, Bernard Girard, Archie L Teglend. *mus* theme: Ned Washington, Dimitri Tiomkin sung by Frankie Laine. *cast* **Rowdy Yates** Clint Eastwood **Gil Favor** Eric Fleming **Pete Nolan** Sheb Wooley **Wishbone** Paul Brinegar **Jim Quince** Steve Raines **Joe Scarlett** Rocky Shahan **Harkness 'Mushy' Mushgrove** James Murdock **Hey Soos Patines** Robert Cabal **Clay Forrester** Charles Gray **Ian Cabot** David Watson **Jed Colby** John Ireland **Simon Blake** Raymond St Jacques **Pee Jay** L Q Jones **Teddy** John Erwin **Yo Yo** Paul Comi.

'This is the landscape of Rawhide: desert, forest, mountain and plains. It is intense heat, bitter cold, torrential rain, blinding dust, men risking their lives, earning small reward – a life of challenge – Rawhide.'

So intoned the voice which introduced each episode of *Rawhide*, like >*Wagon Train* a western on the move. The series featured events in the lives of the men who worked on the great cattle drives between San Antonio, Texas, and Sedalia, Kansas, during the rugged and lawless days of the 1860s and the constant travelling allowed the series to tell stories of people met along the way. Created by Charles Marquis Warren (>*The Virginian*) and based on material from an 1866 diary by drover George Dutfield, *Rawhide* had similarities with Howard Hawks' feature film *Red River* (1948). Warren had directed the film *Cattle Empire* before *Rawhide* and originally planned to call the series *Cattle Drive*.

The team of men who regularly risked their lives to keep the cattle on course to Kansas included trail boss Gil Favor, supervisor of the operation. His right-hand man and second in command was ramrod Rowdy Yates,

Before he was cast as 'The Man with No Name' in a fistful of spaghetti westerns, Clint Eastwood guarded the herd as cowhand Rowdy Yates in *Rawhide*.

played by a young Clint Eastwood (one of the few regulars to remain with the show for its entire run, taking over the role of trail boss in autumn 1965 when Fleming left the show). The rest were cantankerous cook Wishbone, trail scout Pete Nolan, played by country music comedian Sheb Wooley, and drovers including good-natured Mushy, Quince, Hey Soos and Civil War veteran Simon Blake, played by Raymond St Jacques (real name James Arthur Johnson) who was the first black actor regularly featured in a western series.

Contrary to popular myth, they did finish their original drive and went on to other cattle drive-related adventures. Eastwood himself, needless to say, went on to fame and fortune – spaghetti western director Sergio Leone spotted the young actor as Rowdy Yates and rocketed him to superstardom on the big screen as 'The Man with No Name'.

Move 'em on, head 'em up, head 'em up, move 'em on . . . Rawhide.

The Roy Rogers Show

USA 1952–7 100 × 26m bw CBS. Roy Rogers Productions/Frontier Productions. *UK tx* 1955–7 ITV. *cr* Roy Rogers. *pr* Roy Rogers, Jack Lacey, Bob Henry, Leslie H Martinson. *dr* Various, including Leslie H Martinson. *wr* Various. *mus* Roy Rogers and Dale Evans (theme vocal). *cast* Roy Rogers, Dale Evans, Pat Grady, The Sons of the Pioneers.

A modern-era western for kids in which the singing cowboy played himself in a fight for law and order. Other regulars at crusade HQ, the Double R Bar Ranch in Paradise Valley, were Roger's horse, Trigger, his wife, Dale Evans, her horse, Buttermilk, bumbling pardner, Pat Grady (who drove a jeep, Nellybelle) and dog, Bullet. Episodes frequently involved abandoned children, to whom Rogers and Evans would become surrogate parents. Evans sang the 'Happy Trails to You' theme song.

Stoney Burke

USA 1962–3 32 × 52m bw ABC. United Artists/Daystar. cr
Leslie Stevens. pr Leslie Stevens. dr Various, including
Leslie Stevens, Leonard Horn. wr Various, including Leslie
Stevens. mus Dominic Frontiere. cast **Stoney Burke** Jack
Lord **Cody Bristol** Robert Dowdell **EJ Stocker** Bruce Dern
Ves Painter Warren Oates.

Stoney Burke (Jack Lord) was a young rodeo rider
champing at the bit to be the world's number one bronco
buster, possessor of the Golden Buckle Award. Filmed on
location in the US South West, this contemporary
western series had strong stories – but could never decide
whether it was an actioner or something more cerebral.
Before Burke could win the big prize the show ended. It
did, however, kick off a number of careers: Jack Lord
went on to swap blue denims for a shiny blue suit in
>*Hawaii Five-O* three years later, while cast regulars
Bruce Dern (father of actress Laura) and Warren Oates
landed in Hollywood. Creator-producer Leslie Stevens
went on to helm the production of >*The Virginian* and
>*McCloud*.

Tales of Wells Fargo

USA 1957–61 167 × 25m/34 × 50m bw NBC. MCA/
Universal/Overland/Juggernaut. UK tx 1959–62 BBC1. cr
Frank Gruber. pr Earle Lyon, Nat Holt. dr Various, including
Earl Bellamy, William Witney. wr Various, including Frank
Bonham, William R Cox, D B Newton, Frank Gruber. mus
Stanley Wilson. cast **Jim Hardie** Dale Robertson **Beau
McCloud** Jack Ging **Jeb Gaine** William Demarest **Ovie**
Virginia Christine.

Jim Hardie was a strong-but-silent troubleshooter for
transport company Wells Fargo in the 1860s, his job
being to protect the company's gold and passenger
shipments from no-good outlaws. Originally aired as the
segment 'A Tale of Wells Fargo' on *Schlitz Playhouse of
Stars* in 1956, the show was expanded in 1961 from a
thirty-minute to a sixty-minute format, and storylines
began to include Hardie's adventures as a rancher in San
Francisco. The cast was also increased to include Jack
Ging as Beau McCloud, another Wells agent, William
Demarest as Hardie's ranch foreman Jeb Gaine, and
Virginia Christine as the widow-rancher neighbour.

Jack Nicholson appeared in one of his first TV roles
in the 1961 episode, 'The Washburn Girl'.

The Virginian

USA 1962–70 208 × 90m col NBC. Universal/Revue
Productions. UK tx 1965–72 BBC1. cr Charles Marquis
Warren. exec pr Charles Marquis Warren, Roy Huggins,
Frank Price, Norman Macdonnell, Leslie Stevens. pr
Howard Christie, James McAdams, Paul Freeman, Richard
Irving, Winston Miller, Herbert Hirschman, Glen A Larson.
dr Various, including Sam Fuller, Andrew McLaglen, Robert
Butler, Richard A Colla, Burt Kennedy, Stuart Heisler, Gene
L Coon, Daniel Friedkin, John Florea, Charles S Dubin,
Bernard L Kowalski, Jeannot Swarc, John Brahm, Ted Post,
Abner Biberman, Joseph Pevney, William Witney, Bernard
McEveety, Charles S Dubin, Ida Lupino. wr Various,
including Roland Kibbe, Glen A Larson, Daniel Friedkin,
Samuel Fuller, William R Cox. mus Percy Faith (theme),
David Shire, Bernard Herrman. cast **The Virginian** James
Drury **Trampas** Doug McClure **Emmett Ryker** Clu Gulager
Judge Henry Garth Lee J Cobb **Steve** Gary Clarke **Molly
Wood** Pippa Scott **Betsy** Roberta Shore **Randy** Randy
Boone **John Grainger** Charles Bickford **Clay Grainger** John
McIntire **Belden** L Q Jones **Alan McKenzie** Stewart
Granger **Sheriff Abbott** Ross Elliott **Jim Horn** Tim
Matheson **Roy Tate** Lee Majors **David Sutton** David
Hartman **Morgan Starr** John Dehner.

The Virginian first rode the range in Owen Wister's
classic 1902 novel of that name, before being thrice
filmed by Hollywood, including a 1929 version which
launched the career of Gary Cooper. But for most horse-
opera aficionados, *The Virginian* will always and forever
be a TV series with James Drury as the eponymous ranch
foreman.

Drury first played *The Virginian* in a 1958 TV pilot
which flopped, largely because of its interpretation of

Based on Owen Wister's classic western novel, *The Virginian* featured James Drury (above) as the mysterious foreman of the Shiloh Ranch.

Wister's hero was perversely dude-ish (including ruffles, and slinky breeches). Despite the pilot failure, the American NBC network was eventually persuaded to buy a series, with Drury reprising his role in more suitable garb.

TV's *Virginian*, the first western at ninety minutes, was set on the Shiloh Ranch, near Medicine Bow in rugged Wyoming, and mainly concerned the fortunes of the 'mysterious' Virginian himself, his impetuous cowpoke friend Trampas (a much sanitised version of Wister's character), top hand Steve, and the successive owners of the ranch, Judge Henry Garth, John Grainger and Clay Grainger (John McIntire, also >*Wagon Train*). Some of the series' photography was inspirational, while the directors' list included Sam Fuller, Andrew McLaglen and Burt Kennedy ('The Woman from White Wing'). In time-honoured Western TV tradition, the show boasted a posse of guest stars, among them George C Scott ('The Brazen Bell'), Lee Marvin ('It Tolls for Thee') and Robert Redford ('The Evil That Men Do'). And yet nobody ever quite eclipsed the *Virginian* prominence of James Drury, with Clu Gulager and Doug McClure riding at his side.

In retrospect, the series can be seen as part of the same strand of clan-saga westerns as >*Bonanza* and >*High Chaparral*, with the ranch hands of Shiloh forming a quasi-extended family. The saddle-soap element of *The Virginian* became most pronounced in its final season, when its name was retitled *The Men from Shiloh* and the setting was moved up in time to the 1890s. Here Stewart Granger played the new English owner of Shiloh, Colonel Alan Mackenzie, and Lee Majors (also >*The Six Million Dollar Man*, >*The Big Valley*) was introduced as Roy Tate. The spaghetti western composer Ennio Morricone (*The Good, The Bad, and The Ugly, Once Upon a Time in the West*) contributed the new theme music.

The Virginian was the last of the classic western TV series (for thirtysomethings who grew up in the sixties it was *the* oater series of blessed memory, what >*Gunsmoke* was to the generation before). Although the comic outlaw saga >*Alias Smith and Jones*, the sod-buster-saga *Little House on the Prairie* and the chop suey western >*Kung Fu* all enjoyed success in the seventies, the traditional TV oater spent twenty years in the sunset after *The Virginian*. Not until the very end of the eighties with *Young Riders*, *Paradise* and the outstanding *Lonesome Dove* mini-series did the genre make a real return to the small screen.

Wagon Train

USA 1957–65 252 × 52m bw/32 × 90m col NBC/ABC. Universal/MCA/Revue Productions. *UK tx* 1958–64 ITV/BBC1. *cr* Bert Glennon. *exec pr* Howard Christie. *pr* Richard Lewis, Richard Irving. *dr* Various, including Allen H Miner, Virgil Vogel, Richard H Bartless, Tay Garnett, Ted Post, William Witney, John Ford, Jesse Hibbs, Russell Simpson, Jerry Hopper, Joseph Pevney, Herschel Daugherty, Earl Bellamy, Sidney Lanfield, Jack Arnold. *wr* Various, including Robert E Thompson, Jean Holloway, William Fay, Aaron Spelling, Gene L Coon, Thomas Thompson, Harry von Zell, D B Newton. *mus* David Buttolph (theme). *cast* **Major Seth Adams** Ward Bond **Flint McCullough** Robert Horton **Chris Hale** John McIntire **Bill Hawks** Terry Wilson **Charlie Wooster** Frank McGrath **Duke Shannon** Scott Miller **Cooper Smith** Robert Fuller **Barnaby West** Michael Burns.

The true epic amongst TV westerns, the story of pioneers trekking their way in Conestogas (covered wagons) from St Joseph to Sacramento in the 1860s. Initially the wagon train was led across the Plains and Rockies by Ward Bond as Major Seth Adams, with Robert Horton as scout Flint McCullough. After five seasons, however, Horton quit to work in films (though he returned to TV as the amnesiac *A Man Called Shenandoah*) and was replaced by >*Laramie* star Robert Fuller as Cooper Smith. When Bond died of a heart attack on location in Texas on 5 November 1960, John McIntire took over the reins as wagon master Chris Hale.

Stylistically, the series had a distinctive format: each episode featured the problems of one of the pioneers, usually a newcomer. Invariably, the story was of some moral complexity (executive producer Howard Christie insisted absolutely on scripts which allowed performers to 'love, hate, cry or express some other definite feeling'). For inspiration *Wagon Train* writers raided everything from stocks of western clichés (pesky warpathing Redskins, rampaging outlaws) to British literary classics (*Pride and Prejudice* appeared as 'The Steel Family Show').

Production values were notably high. The entire *Wagon Train* cast and crew were moved periodically to panoramic locations such as Monument Valley, Utah and New Mexico. For 'The Gus Moran Story', the wagon train was transported to the top of California's Mount Witney. Another large chunk of the budget was spent on the weekly guest stars. Ernest Borgnine, Barbara Stanwyck, Henry Fonda, Mickey Rooney, Ronald Reagan and Joseph Cotton were among those who appeared on the *Wagon Train*'s nine-year trail. Dennis Hopper and Clint Eastwood played some of their first bit parts, while Aaron Spelling (later blockbuster producer of >*Charlie's Angels* and >*Beverly Hills 90210*) was one of its principal writers.

Based loosely on John Ford's film *Wagon Master* (1950) the series itself was perhaps the closest TV has come to the Hollywood director's particular democratic, mytho-poetic vision of the American West. Gruff Ward Bond was one of Ford's regular company of actors, and had appeared in *Wagon Master* itself. (The two first met when Ford was at the University of Southern California's football park looking for extras, saw Ward Bond and said: 'Get me that one with the ugly face.') John Ford himself even directed an episode of *Wagon Train*, the 1960 'The Colter Craven Story'. Ford's lead man, John Wayne, appeared in an uncredited cameo role as General Sherman – his only dramatic appearance in a TV show.

Among the most successful western series ever, *Wagon Train* dominated ratings on both sides of the Atlantic on its initial release. In Britain it was in the top ten from 1958–60, not infrequently in pole position. (Labour leader Hugh Gaitskell wanted the General Election of 1959 held on a day when *Wagon Train* wasn't screened, in case it kept his voters at home.)

In 1962, series episodes were expanded to seventy-five minutes and shot in colour. Somehow *Wagon Train* wasn't the same. Thankfully, classic Bond–Horton *Wagon Train* episodes are regularly repeated on networks everywhere, sometimes under the title *Major Adams* and *Major Adams, Trailmaster*.

'Wagon Train, Keep on Rolling . . .'

TV's epic series about pioneers crossing the west, *Wagon Train*, featured Ward Bond as the wagonmaster and Robert Horton (pictured) as chief scout Flint McCullough. A ratings hit in both the USA and UK, the show was the unlikely inspiration for *Star Trek*.

Wanted: Dead or Alive

USA 1958–61 94 × 26m bw CBS. Four Star/Malcolm
Enterprises. *UK tx* 1985 ITV. *exec pr* John Robinson. *pr*
Harry Harris, Ed Adamson, Vincent M Fennelly. *dr* Various,
including Thomas Carr, R G Springsteen, Donald
MacDougall, Richard Donner, Murray Golden. *wr* Various,
including Charles Beaumont, William Loose, Frank D Gilroy,
John Robinson, Ed Adamson. *mus* Rudy Schrager (theme
song). *cast* **Josh Randall** Steve McQueen **Jason Nichols**
Wright King.

The series which made Steve McQueen a star, and created
the mould for his loner screen image. McQueen played
Josh Randall, a bounty hunter in the 1870s who pursued
those with a reward on their heads with a 'Mare's Leg',
a sawn-off carbine used like a pistol. McQueen observed
about the violent character he played, 'He isn't always a
nice guy – you didn't stay alive long in the Old West by
being nice.' Developed from a segment called 'Bounty' in
the *Trackdown* series, the pacy and stylish *Wanted: Dead
or Alive* was computer-colourised in the eighties for US
syndication.

The Westerner

USA 1960 13 × 25m bw NBC. Fourstar/Winchester
Productions. *cr* Sam Peckinpah. *pr* Sam Peckinpah, Hal
Hudson. *dr* Sam Peckinpah, Tom Gries, Bruce Geller, Andre
de Toth. *wr* Various, including Sam Peckinpah, Tom Gries,
Bruce Geller. *cast* **Dave Blassinghame** Brian Keith
Burgundy Smith John Dehner.

The story of Dave Blassinghame, a working but
wandering ranch hand in the American South West of the
1890s, helping out pioneers in their troubles. Intelligent,
devoid of clean-cut heroes and easy gunplay, *The
Westerner* was unlike almost any other western show of
its day. Essentially a character study of a cowboy set
against a bitterly realistic period backdrop, the series was
beautifully, even lyrically, shot. In retrospect the special
quality of *The Westerner* should be no surprise for it was

the creation of Sam Peckinpah, the most talented of the
directors to come up through the mill of the fifties TV
western. Peckinpah had already written and directed
episodes of >*Gunsmoke* and >*Have Gun Will Travel*, and
went on to write and direct much of *The Rifleman* series,
but *The Westerner* was his greatest legacy to the small
screen.

The series grew out of a segment 'Trouble at Tres
Cruces', which Peckinpah directed for *Dick Powell's
Zane Grey Theatre* in 1954, and was developed via a
pilot entitled *Winchester*. Not only did Peckinpah write,
produce and direct much of *The Westerner*, he was also
responsible for the inspired casting of the burly but
sensitive Keith as Blassinghame (a composite of
westerners Peckinpah knew personally), an *hombre* who
was tough but inclined to muse on the complexities of
life. Apart from Keith Blassinghame, the only other
recurring characters were his mongrel dog, Brown (star
of the Walt Disney movie *Old Yeller*), and Burgundy
Smith (John Dehner), an itinerant con man.

For viewers in 1960, however, the series was 'too
adult' lamented Peckinpah, its stories of drifter-killers
('Dos Pinos') and masochistic prostitutes ('Jeff') not the
fibreless oater fare they were used to. Minimal ratings
ensured its death after just one season, and it was buried
in the vault of obscurity. It has never been shown in
Britain.

With the finish of the series Peckinpah directed his
first feature *The Deadly Companions* (1961, also with
Brian Keith), returned to TV for *The Rifleman* and
isolated episodes of such series as >*Route 66* and *Pony
Express*, before decamping to Hollywood for good and
the making of some of the last great film Westerns: *Ride
the High Country* (1962), *Major Dundee* (1964), *The
Wild Bunch* (1969), and *Pat Garrett and Billy the Kid*
(1973). As for Keith, he starred in his own *The Brian
Keith Show* and guested in countless Western and TV
projects, among them >*The Virginian*, >*Wagon Train* and
Centennial. At the end of the seventies he starred in the
best forgotten *Zoo Gang*.

In 1963 an attempt was made to revive *The Westerner*
as *The Losers* (with Lee Marvin) but it failed to make it
past the pilot stage. A more successful resurrection – and
for most people the only way to glimpse the magnificence
of *The Westerner* – was Tom Gries' feature film *Will*

Armed with a sawn-off carbine, the charismatic bounty hunter Josh Randall (played by a youthful Steve McQueen in his first starring role) tracked down those with a price on their head in *Wanted: Dead or Alive*.

Penny (1967, starring Charlton Heston) based on Gries' *Westerner* segment 'Line Camp'.

The Wild, Wild West

USA 1965–9 104 × 60m bw/col CBS. A Michael Garrison Production. *UK tx* 1968 ITV. *cr* Michael Garrison. *exec pr* Michael Garrison. *pr* Gene L Coon, Paul Playdon, Fred Freiberger, Collier Young, Bruce Lansbury, John Mantley. *dr* Various, including Paul Wendkos, Irving J Moore, Richard Sarafian, Mark Rydell, Marvin Chomsky, Alvin Ganzer, Bernard McEveety, William Witney, Don Taylor, Harvey Hart, Alan Crosland Jr, Richard Whorf, Jesse Hibbs. *wr* Various, including Gene L Coon, Paul Playdon, Stephen Kandel, Oliver Crawford, John Kneubuhl, Edward J Lasko. *mus* Richard Markowitz. *cast* **Major James T West** Robert Conrad **Artemus Gordon** Ross Martin **Dr Miguelito Loveless** Michael Dunn **Jeremy Pike** Charles Aidman **Tennyson** Charles Davis.

Take an Old West setting, an arsenal of sci-fi gadgetry, a pinch of comic-strip violence, a dash of James Bond and you have *The Wild, Wild West*, a bizarre but wholly original TV series. In the 1870s, so the premise went, the Wild Frontier of America was menaced by megalo-maniacal supervillains, possessors of such deadly armaments as volcano-detonators, robots, A-bombs and submarines. To protect the USA, President Ulysses S Grant despatched his top secret agents, macho swashbuckling James T West and sidekick Artemus Gordon, an inventor and master of disguise. To aid them in their task, they were equipped with a mobile HQ in the form of a luxury train in which they secreted weapons (the pool cue was a rifle) in case of surprise attack.

The Wild, Wild West was outrageous, but it worked. The props were a cleverly contrived marriage of hi-tech and Victorian Gothic (steam-powered robots, for instance), while the villains behind the pieces of evil weaponry were worthy enemies, particularly the charismatic miniature Professor Moriarty, Miguelito Loveless (played by dwarf Michael Dunn). The thing Loveless had least love for – apart from people taller than himself – was the United States.

Ultimately, though, *The Wild, Wild West* was a success because it was a spoof. Not only of the genres it raided – western, sci-fi and, especially, spy – but, most cleverly of all, of itself. In 1969 the high-style series was cancelled by the head of CBS, Dr Stanton, to appease a periodic moral panic by the US Congress concerning violence on TV. A thawing in the climate saw two movies based on the series: *The Wild, Wild West Revisited* (directed by Burt Kennedy) in 1979, and *More Wild, Wild West* in 1980.

Zorro

USA 1957–9 70 × 26m bw ABC. Walt Disney Productions. *UK tx* 1958–60 ITV. *cr* Johnston McCulley, Walt Disney. *exec pr* Walt Disney. *pr* William H Anderson. *dr* Various, including Norman Foster, Hollingsworth Morse, William Witney. *wr* Various. *mus* George Burns (theme), William Lauar. *cast* **Don Diego de la Vega ('Zorro')** Guy Williams **Bernado** Gene Sheldon **Sgt Garcia** Henry Calvin **Capt Monastario** Britt Lomond **Anna Maria Verdugo** Jolene Brand **Don Alejandro** George J Lewis.

Zorro, masked swordsman of the Old Californian frontier, first appeared in a 1919 short story 'The Curse of Capistrano' by Johnston McCulley, and was the hero of several motion pictures (played by, among others, Douglas Fairbanks Sr and Tyrone Power) before Walt Disney put him on TV. Zorro was the Superman of his time. Summoned home by his father Don Alejandro to fight Captain Monastario, tyrant of the Pueblo de Los Angeles, young Spanish-Californian aristocrat Don Diego de la Vega pretended to be a lazy fop. Secretly, though, he was Zorro, and donned a black outfit at every available opportunity and set out to defend the oppressed *peons*. Zorro's sidekick was the mute Bernado, his horses were Phantom and Tornado. Trying to capture him was the hapless, corpulent Sergeant Garcia. Plots were simple, with plenty of dashing action, but overall this was splendid western stuff for juveniles. The theme from the show ('Zorro – the fox so cunning and free/Zorro – make the sign of the Z!') was recorded by Henry Calvin (Sgt Garcia) and was later a hit for the Chordettes.

Two cinema features were made from episodes, *Zorro the Avenger* and *The Sign of Zorro*, both released in 1958. In 1983 a Walt Disney sequel appeared, *Zorro and Son*, but this played it for laughs rather than thrills, the premise being that the masked man (Henry Darrow, also >*The High Chaparral*, >*Harry O*) was now too aged to swing from the chandeliers.

A more traditional interpretation was offered by a new *Zorro* series aired in the US in 1990 with Duncan Regehr as Zorro and Efrem Zimbalist Jr (>*77 Sunset Strip*) as Don Alejandro.

Children's

The Adventures of Superman

USA 1953–5 104 × 25m bw/col syndicated. Lippert/National Periodical Productions. *UK tx* 1956–7 ITV (as *Superman*). *cr* Jerry Siegel, Joe Shuster. *pr* Robert Maxwell, Bernard Luber, Whitney Ellsworth. *dr* Thomas Carr, Lee Sholem, George Reeves, George Blair, Harry Gerstad, Howard Bretherton, Lew Landers, Phil Ford. *wr* Various, including Jackson Gillis, Whitney Ellsworth, David Chantler. *sfx* Thol (Si) Simonson. *cast* **Superman/Clark Kent** George Reeves **Lois Lane** Phyllis Coates (1952)/Noel Neill (1953–7) **Jimmy Olson** Jack Larson **Perry White** John Hamilton **Inspector William Henderson** Robert Shayne. *Video* Warner Home Video.

'Look up in the sky . . . it's a bird . . . it's a plane . . . it's Superman!' Following his career in comic books (where he was created by teenagers Jerry Siegel and Joe Shuster), radio and theatrical features, the being from planet Krypton zoomed on to TV in the fifties, becoming one of the medium's biggest hits of the decade.

In case any viewer was unaware of Superman's ancestry, episode one of the TV series helpfully provided a resumé. Moments before the destruction of doomed planet Krypton, the baby Kal-El was placed in a rocket by his father (Jor-El) and mother (Lara). The space vehicle landed on Earth, where the infant was found by kindly farm couple Eben and Martha Kent, who named him Clark. As he grew up Clark discovered he had amazing powers, and later, aged twenty-five, moved to Metropolis, where he posed as a bespectacled journalist for *The Daily Planet*. This was edited by brusque Perry White, and Lois Lane (played initially with admirable acid by Phyllis Coates, who was replaced by marshmallow Noel Neill) was the star reporter. Mild-mannered he may have seemed, but when danger loomed Kent nipped into a dazzling red-and-blue costume (with a big 'S' on the front) and flew off to fight for 'truth, justice and the American way'. The only substance to which superstrong, X-ray-eyed Superman was vulnerable was Kryptonite, fragments of green rock from his home planet. Naturally, this mineral commodity was much prized by the melodrama's bad guys, usually mafia-type palookas, but occasionally sci-fi aliens like 'Mr Zero'.

Production was low budget ($15,000 per episode) and the special effects were crude but believable: Superman's flying was achieved by wires, or by filming him lying on a glass table. One of the series' principal directors, Thomas Carr, had also directed on the movie serials about the 'Man of Steel'. George Reeves – who made his screen début in *Gone with the Wind* – became so typecast that he was unable to get other acting work. It seems this was a factor in his suicide in 1959.

The fictional Superman, however, has proved immortal. Since the TV series there have been, amongst others, a CBS cartoon *Superman*, a CBS cartoon *New*

'Whatever has happened to Looby Loo?' Andy and Teddy and their visible strings in the BBC's classic *Andy Pandy*, Tuesday's slot in *Watch with Mother*.

Adventures of Superman, a new TV show >*Lois and Clark* and four big-budget movies starring Christopher Reeve as the superhero with his underwear outside his trousers.

Andy Pandy

UK 1950–7 Approx 300 × 15m bw BBC. BBC. *cr* Freda Lingstrom, Maria Bird. *wr* Freda Lingstrom. *mus* Maria Bird. *narr* Vera McKechnie. *Video* BBC.

Andy Pandy's much loved – and much spoofed – style of earnest narration, tinkling songs, and nursery rhymes set the tone for the fifties golden age of BBC children's television.

With his visible strings, blue and white striped all-in-one suit, ruffle collar and hat, Andy had started life as a solo performer. Some months passed before he was joined first by trusty playmate Teddy and later by Looby Loo, a rag doll introduced as one of many playthings but given a regular spot after insistent demand from the young. Looby, with her fetching spotted skirt and yellow plaits led a rather lonely life, only coming to life when Andy and Teddy were elsewhere, but when alone she would dance, play, clean and dust and even had her own special song, 'Here we go Looby Loo', with which children were exhorted to sing along.

The stories were as simple as the means by which the puppet trio were moved. Sometimes Andy Pandy would swing on his swing ('Children, you swing your arms backwards and forwards and pretend you're on a swing just like Andy!'), sometimes Andy and Teddy would see-saw or trampoline, or even play at engine driving ('All engines can go backwards, but I don't think the children watching ought to go backwards because they couldn't see where they were going and they might bump into things!').

Watch with Mother, created by Freda Lingstrom, artist, novelist and pioneering head of the Children's Department at the BBC from 1951, was a major innovation – the first coherently planned combination of education and entertainment specifically for very small children, each day with its own flavour. *Andy Pandy* was the first segment produced and ran on Tuesdays at 3.45pm, next came *The Flowerpot Men* which filled the

Wednesday slot. *Rag, Tag and Bobtail*, Louise Cochrane's stories about a hedgehog, a mouse and a rabbit arrived in the Thursday slot in 1953, and in 1955 the last two slots were filled by *Picture Book* on Monday (with Patricia Driscoll as principal storyteller, later Maid Marion in *The Adventures of Robin Hood*) and >*The Woodentops* in the Friday slot.

Andy Pandy was first screened as a two-week experiment in 1950 and proved so popular that programmes were made up to 1957 and repeated up to 1969. By 1970 the black-and-white prints of *Andy Pandy* had become too poor to use and thirteen new colour episodes were made in the famous Abbey Road Studios. In the late 1980s, the BBC had a surprise hit with *Watch with Mother* on video and it topped the bestseller lists.

'Time to go home, time to go home, Andy is waving goodbye, goodbye.'

Astroboy

Japan 1963 26 × 30m bw. Mushi Productions. *UK tx* 1964 ITV. *USA tx* 1963 syndicated. *cr* Fumiro Suzuki. *pr* Fumiro Suzuki, Osamu Tekuka. *cast* (voices) **Astroboy** Billie Lou Watt **Dr Elefun** Ray Owens.

When his wife and son are killed in a car crash in the year 2000, scientist Dr Boynton builds a robot, Astroboy, for company. Dismayed by the failure of the robot to mature, Boynton sells it to a circus troupe, from whom it is purchased by Dr Pachedyrum Elefun. Dr Elefun gives Astroboy human qualities – and an assignment to combat space monsters and mad scientists.

The first Japanese animation to become a hit in Britain and America, *Astroboy* made up what it lacked in animation technique with exemplary characterisation and storylines.

Bagpuss

UK 1974 13 × 20m col BBC. Smallfilms. *cr* Peter Firmin, Oliver Postgate. *dr* Peter Firmin. *wr* Oliver Postgate. *mus* John Faulkner, Sandra Kerr. *narr* Oliver Postgate. *Video* BBC.

'Bagpuss, oh Bagpuss,
Oh fat, furry cat puss,
Wake up and look at this thing that we bring,
Wake up be bright be golden and light.'

These were the magic words that woke Bagpuss, the pink-and-white-striped lugubrious cloth puppet cat that belonged to Emily. Emily had a 'shop', Bagpuss and Co, in which nothing was for sale and whose window was filled with things that she found and brought home to her beloved cat. Bagpuss – 'the most magical saggy old cloth cat in the whole wide world' – slept on a cushion in the window until aroused into action (and colour) by his young mistress' voice. Then he would blink, yawn and stir into life together with the various small animals and curiosities displayed in the old-fashioned shop front. The toy mice awoke on the mouse organ, Madeleine the doll sat up in her chair, Gabriel the banjo-playing toad began to strum and Professor Yaffle, a very distinguished wooden woodpecker bookend, came down from his shelf.

Once brought to life this motley crew would all investigate Emily's found object in their own way. The mice would play and sing a song, working their mouse organ all the while with the bellows, Professor Yaffle would tut, find fault and exclaim 'fiddlesticks' and Madeleine would solve the problem, get out her sewing kit and mend the homeless item ready for display in the window and collection by its owner. Bagpuss, 'baggy and a bit loose in the seams', would then give a big yawn and settle back down until woken for the next adventure.

Bagpuss came from Smallfilms, the prolific stable of Oliver Postgate and Peter Firmin who worked with Associated Rediffusion from the late fifties and were pioneers in both stop-frame puppet animation and drawn animation techniques (*Bagpuss* made use of both methods). Smallfilms operated from Firmin's eighteenth-century farmhouse in a village near Canterbury where both the cowshed and the pigsty were brought into service as the duo's studios. The company created and produced a list of animated classics including *Ivor the Engine*, the little Welsh railway engine from the Merioneth and Llantisilly Rail Traction Company

Limited fired by Idris the dragon who lived in Ivor's boiler, driven by Jones the Steam and overseen at stations by Dai Station. Also from the pens and doodle of Postgate and Firmin came >*Noggin the Nog*, >*Pogle's Wood*, >*The Clangers* and *Pingwings*.

Batman

USA 1966–8 120 × 30m col ABC. A Greenaway Production for Twentieth Century Fox TV. *UK tx* 1966–8 ITV. *cr* Bob Kane. *exec pr* William Dozier. *pr* Howie Horowitz. *dr* Robert Butler, Don Weiss, Tom Gries, Norman Foster, Murray Golden, William A Graham, James Sheldon, Les Martison, James B Clark, Richard C Sarafian, Charles R Rondeau, Larry Peerce, Sherman Marks, Oscar Rudolph, James Neilson, George Waggner, Jeff Haydn, Robert Sparr, Sam Strangis. *wr* Lorenzo Semple Jr, Robert Dozier, Max Hodge, Fred De Gorter, Charles Hoffman, Stephen Kandel, Stanley Ralph Ross, Lee Orgel, John Cardwell, Jack Paritz & Bob Rodgers, Francis and Marian Cockrell, Robert C Dennis and Earl Barret, Rik Vollaerts, Dick Carr, Sheldon Stark, Henry Slesar, Bill Finger and Charles Sinclair, Ed Self, Stanford Sherman, Jay Thompson and Charles Hoffman, Ellis St Joseph, W P D'Angelo, Peter Rabe, Robert Mintz, Dwight Taylor, Elken Allan. *mus* Neal Hefti (theme), Nelson Riddle. *cast* **Batman/Bruce Wayne** Adam West **Robin/Dick Grayson** Burt Ward **Alfred** Alan Napier **Aunt Harriet** Madge Blake **Commisioner Gordon** Neil Hamilton **Chief O'Hara** Stafford Repp **Batgirl** Yvonne Craig. *narr* William Dozier.

Whenever trouble brewed in Gotham City, Police Commissioner Gordon and Chief O'Hara would race to their red phone and call Batman. 'I don't know who he is behind that mask of his,' Gordon would declare. 'But I know we need him and we need him now!' Meanwhile at Wayne Manor the beeping batphone alerted the playboy millionaire's loyal butler Alfred. Alfred delivered the message to his master and Wayne and his ward Dick Grayson would disappear without delay down the batpoles hidden behind the drawing-room bookcase. Seconds later they emerged as famed crime fighters Batman and Robin, jumped into the batmobile and blasted through the camouflaged batcave exit to Gotham City.

'ABC bought the Batman concept without the slightest idea what to do with it,' recalls executive producer William Dozier. 'Camp solved that problem. What we had on Batman was an exaggerated seriousness that became amusing to adults and provided high adventure for the youngsters.' Camp it certainly was. Dozier and Lorenzo Semple Jr, his story editor, made Batman the squarest hero ever. Borrowing heavily from the radio serials, each show was produced as a two-part serial (broadcast on Wednesday and Thursday evenings in the USA). The first episode ended with a cliff-hanger and the 'voice of doom' (William Dozier) which exhorted everyone to tune in 'same bat-time, same bat-channel' next day. During the episode that completed the bat-adventure the Caped Crusader and the Boy Wonder would escape from their hideous predicament, enter into a splendidly choreographed fight sequence with their fiendish enemies and put the world to rights once more. Perils into which the plucky duo were plunged, at first simple, became ever more baroque, including such horrors as having the caped crusaders frozen or grilled alive ('Holy Inferno, Batman,' cried Robin. 'Is this the end?' 'If it is,' replied Batman, 'let us not lose our dignity').

No expense was spared on creating a success. For *Batman*'s début ABC staged a lavish première in a theatre in Manhattan attended by such celebrities as Andy Warhol and Roddy McDowall. For the pilot, 'Hi Diddle Diddle' and its follow-up 'Smack in the Mouth', a fortune was spent on sets, props and bat paraphernalia, including a giant papier-mâché elephant large enough to hold two crime fighters in the final sequence.

Creating a 'comic strip' look was of prime importance to Dozier – *Batman* was originally created by Bob Kane for Detective Comics in 1939 – and was achieved in part by use of coloured lights on the sets. Catwoman's office and lair was bathed in 'cat colour' amber, greens were used for the Riddler and purple was used for the Penguin. Tilted camera angles added an evil warped effect in the lairs of the villains. Most clever of all were the animated comic-book titles, ZAP! POW! BAM!, which were synched with the appropriate action and superimposed on the fight scenes.

The series was an overnight smash, audience ratings went through the roof and the show even earned a special commendation from the National Safety Council for the shot of the heroes buckling up for safety in the batmobile. The Caped Crusader's nifty dancing in a swinging discotheque with the treacherous Molly ('You swing a pretty mean cape,' she declared) led to a 'batusi' dance craze which swept the nation.

Batman boasted a panoply of fiendish villains played by star names – Burgess Meredith as The Penguin, 'that pompous, waddling perpetrator of foul play', Cesar Romero as The Joker, the nefarious 'clown prince of crime', the cold-blooded Mr Freeze played first by George Sanders, later Otto Preminger and then Eli Wallach, the Riddler played by John Astin and alluring feline fiend Catwoman played first by Julie Newmar, then by Lee Meriwether and later Eartha Kitt. Dozier's choice of little-known actor Adam West to play Batman baffled many and West, a far cry from the well-muscled hero of the comics, became the butt of many editorial jokes. (A virtual unknown outside the industry before Batman, West's credits include roles in 77 *Sunset Strip*, *Cheyenne*, *Maverick*, *Perry Mason*, *Bonanza*, *Bewitched* and *The Virginian*.) Burt Ward as Robin was more suitable. He held a brown belt in karate and convinced producers he was right for the part by cracking a brick with his bare hand at the screen test. The extraordinary success of the series meant Hollywood's finest would plead for parts in the show. Guest stars included Victor Buono (as King Tut), Roddy McDowall, Art Carney, Shelley Winters, Vincent Price (as Egghead), Liberace, Carolyn Jones, Bruce Lee, Tallulah Bankhead, George Raft, Joan Collins, Milton Berle, Anne Baxter, Ida Lupino, Glynis Johns, Ethel Merman and Zsa Zsa Gabor. William Dozier and Howie Horowitz also stepped in front of the camera for the last episode, 'Minerva, Mayhem and Millionaires'.

After a season and a half, though, the fad faded. In an attempt to rekindle interest, Dozier and producer Howie Horowitz introduced female crime fighter Batgirl played by ballerina turned actress Yvonne Craig (also in Horowitz's earlier series >77 *Sunset Strip*) who, in a close-fitting purple outfit with cowl and gold-lined cape gained the series another season from ABC. But it was a temporary reprieve. The Caped Crusader was no match

'Holy mackerel, Batman, we've got our underpants on outside our trousers!' Adam West (right) as the caped crusader of Gotham City, and Burt Ward as his sidekick Robin in *Batman*. Adam West later blamed the high-camp show for ruining his acting career.

for low ratings and the cancellation notice came in February 1968. Kerpow!

But *Batman* lives on. As recently as 1988 the shows were still playing in 106 countries with a worldwide audience of 400 million and the Caped Crusader has starred in a flight of recent movies, to join the 1969 *Batman* feature directed by Leslie Martinson. These are *Batman* (1989, directed by Tim Burton, starring Michael Keaton and Kim Basinger), *Batman Returns* (1992, *dr* Burton, with Keaton and Michelle Pfeiffer), and *Batman Forever* (1995, *dr* Joel Schumacher, starring Val Kilmer).

Camberwick Green

UK 1966 13 × 15m col BBC1. Gordon Murray Puppets. *cr* Gordon Murray. *pr* Gordon Murray. *wr* Gordon Murray. *mus* Freddie Phillips. *narr* Brian Cant. *Video* BBC.

Camberwick Green was a village idyll of picturesque shops and neat little houses in which puppet-people lived happily ever after. At the start of each episode a musical box would play, rotate and open to reveal its 'secret' – the character around whom the episode was based. This might be village gossip Mrs Honeyman, Windy Miller who made the flour, Micky Murphy who baked the cakes, Tommy Tripp the milkman or Mr Carraway the fishmonger. But one thing you could be sure of – something would go awry and word would be sent to Pippin Fort for help. Here Sergeant Major Grout exercised his soldiers and prepared them for inspection by Captain Snort or the minor village emergencies that required their skills. With a little help from Privates Higgins or Lumley all the other villagers – Dr Mopp, Mrs Barley, Peter Hazel the Postman, Mrs Dingle at the post office, Packet the post office puppy and Farmer Bell – could rest assured that things would be well in Camberwick Green before the musical box played again at the episode end. Animation was by Bob Bura and John Hardwick.

Gordon Murray, creator of *Camberwick Green* was also the man behind that other puppet tale *Trumpton* (1967) in which we met the redoubtable Captain Flack of the Trumpton Fire Brigade and his plucky firefighters

Hugh, Pugh, Barney McGrew, Cuthbert, Dibble and Grubb. *Trumpton* was introduced each week by the Trumpton clock ('telling the time steadily, sensibly, never too quickly, never too slowly') and all small-town life dwelt in harmony beneath its tower. Murray was also creator and producer of *Chigley* (1968).

Captain Pugwash

UK 1957–6, 1974–5 90+ × 5 m bw/col BBC. A John Ryan Production for BBC. *cr* John Ryan. *pr* John Ryan. *dr* John Ryan. *wr* John Ryan. *mus* Johnny Pearson. *narr* Peter Hawkins. *Video* BBC.

'Plundering porpoises! Jumping jellyfish! Harrowing hurricanes!' blustered pirate Captain Pugwash to the work-shy crew of his ship the *Black Pig* as they sailed the Seven Seas and encountered adventures. The rotund Captain, always bold before the event, with a tendency to get into scrapes (and make a speedy exit forthwith) was star of this very basic animated programme, in which speech was simulated by moving a piece of card behind the characters' open mouths. The good Captain was a simple man and no match for his various shiver-me-timbers foes but fortunately he was regularly rescued from the clutches of black-bearded arch villain Cut Throat Jake by the cunning and courage of the *Black Pig*'s cabin boy Tom.

All the characters were voiced by Peter Hawkins (who also spoke for *The Flowerpot Men* and some of the Daleks) and the catchy sea-shanty signature tune became a firm children's favourite. Author-artist John Ryan, creator of Captain Pugwash and of *The Adventures of Sir Prancelot* recorded the Captain's adventures for over twelve years through four TV series, three books and many miles of strip cartoon. Pugwash, unkempt and sinister in his original incarnation, with an ugly shrewish wife, put on weight and grew jollier for his TV appearances.

Captain Pugwash, first broadcast in 1957, was guaranteed adult audiences by rumours of deliberate sexual puns and innuendoes, something strenuously denied by both its maker and the BBC.

Captain Scarlet and the Mysterons

UK 1968 32 × 25m col ITV. A Century 21
Production/ATV/ITC. *USA tx* 1968 syndicated. *cr* Gerry and
Sylvia Anderson. *exec pr* Gerry and Sylvia Anderson. *pr* Reg
Hill. *dr* Desmond Saunders, David Lane, Brian Burgess,
Alan Perry, Bob Lynn, Ken Turner, Leo Eaton. *wr* Gerry
Anderson, Tony Barwick, Peter Curran, David Williams,
Richard Conway, Stephen Mattick, Ralph Hart, Shane
Rimmer, Alan Patillo, Bill Hedley, Bryan Cooper, Leo Eaton,
David Lee. *mus* Barry Gray. *sfx* Derek Meddings. *cast*
Captain Scarlet Francis Matthews **Colonel White/Captain
Black/The Mysterons** Donald Gray **Captain Grey/World
President** Paul Maxwell **Captain Blue** Ed Bishop **Captain
Ochre** Jeremy Wilkin **Captain Magenta** Gary Files
Lieutenant Green Cy Grant **Doctor Fawn** Charles Tingwell
Melody Angel Sylvia Anderson **Symphony Angel** Janna
Hill **Rhapsody/Destiny Angel** Liz Morgan **Harmony Angel**
Lian-shin. *Video* Polygram.

After a landing on Mars in 2065 AD by Earth's Spectrum
police force, the planet's Mysteron inhabitants mistakenly
believed that an invasion was under way and unleashed a
war of attrition. They taunted the Earthlings with their
superior powers (each episode began with a warning) and
killed Spectrum's top agents, Captains Scarlet and Black,
intending to 'retrometabolise' (resurrect) them as
Mysteron agents. This indeed was the fate of Captain
Black who became the series' villain, but Scarlet, now
immortal, regained his humanity and became the series'
hero, the Mysterons' only indestructible adversary.

A colour-coded cast of Spectrum puppets was
assembled to aid Englishman Scarlet in the great fight
against the invisible Martian enemy: Colonel White, ex-
Royal Navy and Spectrum's commander-in-chief;
Captain Blue, US ex-test pilot and Scarlet's usual combat
partner; Captain Grey, American ex-World Aquanaut
Security Patrol; Captain Ochre, US flyer and previously
a squad leader with the World Government Police Corps;
Lieutenant Green, Colonel White's Trinidadian aide-de-
camp; Doctor Fawn, Australian medic; and Captain
Magenta, Irishman and sometime New York gangster.

The Angels – Melody, Symphony, Rhapsody, Destiny and
Harmony – were the quintet of beautiful female pilots
who flew for Spectrum.

Gerry Anderson's fifth Supermarionation series was
the acme of puppet sophistication, with the machinery
that worked the limbs, eyes and lips hidden in the body,
so ending the 'big-headed' look. Moreover, the
marionettes were designed to look like the actors who
gave them voice and the puppet's lifelike eyes were
achieved by superimposing film of real eyes onto plastic
balls. As with >*Thunderbirds*, there was model hardware
aplenty, including Spectrum's flying aircraft-carrier,
Cloudbase, the ten-wheeled Spectrum Pursuit Vehicles
(SPV), the bullet-proof Maximum Security Vehicles
(MSV) and the 300mph Angel Aircraft.

Among the voice cast were Ed Bishop (Captain Blue)
later to play Straker in >*UFO*, Paul Maxwell (previously
>*Fireball XL5*'s Steve Zodiac) as Captain Grey, and
>*Emergency Ward 10*'s Charles Tingwell as Dr Fawn. A
series which was strictly SIG (Spectrum is Green).

The episodes were: The Mysterons/Winged Assassin/
Big Ben Strikes Again/Manhunt/Point 783/Operation
Time/Renegade Rocket/White as Snow/Seek and Destroy/
Spectrum Strikes Back/Avalanche/The Shadow of
Fear/The Trap/Special Assignment/Lunarville 7/Heart of
New York/The Traitor/Model Spy/Fire at Rig 15/Flight
to Atlantica/Crater 101/Dangerous Rendezvous/ Noose
of Ice/Treble Cross/Inferno/Flight 104/Place of the
Angels/ Expo 2068/The Launching/Codename Europa/
Attack on Cloudbase/The Inquisition.

Captain Video

USA 1949–55 60+ × 30m & 15m bw syndicated.
Dumont/Columbia. *pr* James L Caddigan. *dr* Larry White. *wr*
Arthur C Clarke, Jack Vance, Damon Knight. *cast* **Captain
Video** Richard Coogan (1949–50), Al Hodge (1951–55) **The
Ranger** Don Hastings **Dr Pauli Bram Nossen** Hal Conklin.

'Captain Video! Master of Space! Hero of Science!
Captain of the Video Rangers! Operating from his secret
mountain headquarters on the planet Earth, Captain
Video rallies men of good will everywhere. As he rockets

from planet to planet, let us follow the champion of justice, truth and freedom throughout the universe!'

Captain Video was TV's very first blast-off to the stars. Long before men walked on the moon, the tiny Dumont network took their cue from the space serials pulling in audiences on radio and film (*Flash Gordon* and *Buck Rogers*) and launched its new live TV serial. The TV show became all the rage for kids and the Captain was responsible for helping to sell TV sets in the medium's early years.

It was 2254 AD and all-American Captain Video, the greatest scientist in history, who hated all evil and was given to such expletives as 'Jumpin' Saturnian Salamanders!', patrolled the universe in his spaceship *The Galaxy*. This moral paragon operated from a secret mountain headquarters and was an inventor extraordinaire. Although he had no superpowers, the Captain had created such an arsenal of incredible superweapons as to make himself near-invincible. There was the Cosmic Vibrator, a ray-gun which could shake a man into submission, the Radio Scillograph, a two-way radio the size of a pack of cigarettes, the Remote Tele-Carrier which enabled Video to see anything anywhere in the world on a television screen and the Captain's main weapon, his trusty Opticon Scillometer, with which he was able to see through walls or any other solid objects. And the Captain had good need of these weapons in his fight against arch-rival Doctor Pauli, Head of the Asteroidal Society, an evil scientist as brilliant as Video, inventor of the Cloak of Invisibility, the Trisonic Compensator (which made bullets turn corners) and the Barrier of Silence (which made all sound cease, enabling the evil doctor to sneak up to Captain Video's secret mountain top headquarters). Video's other chief adversary was I Tobor, a voice-activated giant indestructible robot (Tobor is robot spelt backwards) who fell into the hands of the evil Atar. The Captain was assisted on Earth by a legion of Video Rangers, many of whom patrolled the Old West on horseback (actually old cowboy films inserted to save production expense), and later a youngster known only as The Ranger, the Captain's fifteen-year-old sidekick, the idol of every young television fan in America.

Captain Video had the lowest special effects budget of any major TV show in history – only $25 a week – which even in 1950 did not go far. This meant that the *Galaxy*'s control panel was just a painted board, the rest of the ship's interior was made of cardboard, pilots wore leather football helmets and business suits in space and the Captain's snappy uniform was World War II military surplus. Toy space ships soared through a void of black velvet decorated with sequins and, to simulate space-travel, the crew would affix a sparkler to the space ship and throw it. Scripts were equally cardboard and the actors had to work at containing their laughter. 'We have to run through it to get the laughs out,' admitted Coogan. 'The lines are so corny that we always break up in rehearsal.' After a year Coogan left to star in a Broadway play with Mae West. From 1950, Video was played by Al Hodge, a Sunday school teacher who believed the show taught the young people of America 'the importance of courage, character and a sense of moral values'.

But Captain Video was aimed at children and they loved it. The programme was responsible for propelling a whole generation of American children into space. Video's popularity led to Fawcett Publications putting the Captain between the covers of a comic book, and Columbia Pictures filming a fifteen-minute serial based on Captain Video's adventures.

Despite being the idol of millions of American children, however, Al Hodge was unable to get work as an actor after the show folded. After living in obscurity for over a decade he was rediscovered in the late seventies and had just announced his comeback when he was found dead in a New York hotel in 1979.

Catweazle

UK 1970–1 26 × 25m col ITV. London Weekend Television. *cr* Richard Carpenter. *exec pr* Joy Whitby. *pr* Quentin Lawrence, Carl Mannin. *dr* Quentin Lawrence, David Reed, David Lane. *wr* Richard Carpenter. *cast* **Catweazle** Geoffrey Blaydon **Carrott** Robin Davies **Cedric** Gary Warren **Groome** Peter Butterworth **Lord Collingford** Moray Watson **Lady Collingford** Elspet Gray.

Comedy fantasy about a ragged eleventh-century wizard who becomes accidentally trapped in the twentieth century. Inevitably, Catweazle was somewhat bemused by the gadgets of the nuclear age and thought that electric light was the sun trapped in a bottle. He was helped in his first series of misadventures by farmer's boy Carrot Bennett, who finally managed to return him to Norman times. Somewhat carelessly, Catweazle got lost in time again, and in his second visit was befriended by Cedric, son of Lord and Lady Collingford.

The Clangers

———

UK 1969–74 27 × 9m col BBC1. Smallfilms. *cr* Oliver Postgate. *pr* Oliver Postgate. *wr* Oliver Postgate. *mus* Vernon Elliott. *sfx* Peter Firmin (set and puppet designer). *Video* BBC.

The Clangers were small, pink, knotted mouse-like creatures who lived on a blue moon, and whose neighbours included a Soup Dragon and the Froglets. They wore little gold suits of armour and communicated by musical whistles. Major Clanger was head of the Clanger family, their name deriving from the noise the metal dustbin-lid entrances to their burrows made when the animals dived below ground to avoid the meteorites which landed with impunity because of the blue moon's thin atmosphere.

The series was by Oliver Postgate and Peter Firmin, who also made and created >*Pogle's Wood*, >*Bagpuss*, *Ivor the Engine* and >*Noggin the Nog*.

Daktari

———

USA 1966–9 89 × 60m col CBS. MGM/Ivan Tors. *UK tx* 1966–9 BBC. *cr* Ivan Tors. *exec pr* Ivan Tors. *pr* Leonard Kaufman. *dr* Otto Lang, Paul Landres, Andrew Marton, John Florea, Richard (Dick) Moder, Marshall Thompson, Alan Crosland, Art Arthur. *wr* Various, including Robert Lewin, Stephen Kandel, William Clark, Arthur Weiss, Marvin Wald, Richard Carlson, J E Selby, Stanley H Silverman, Alan Caillou, Ted Herbert, Robert E Smith, Richard Tuber, Jack Jacobs, Marshall Thompson. *cast* **Dr Marsh Tracy** Marshall Thompson **Paula Tracy** Cheryl Miller **Jack Dane** Yale Summers **Hedley** Hedley Mattingly **Mike Makula** Hari Rhodes **Bart Jason** Ross Hagen **Jenny Jones** Erin Moran.

A piece of animal magic from Hungaro-American producer Ivan Tors (*Sea Hunt*, >*Flipper*, *Ripcord*), featuring Marshall Thompson as Dr Marsh Tracy, a veterinary surgeon based in deepest Africa. Helping Dr Tracy – 'Daktari' is Swahili for doctor – at his Wameru Game Preserve Centre was teenage daughter Paula, handsome assistant Jack Dane and native worker Mike Makula (played by black American actor Hari Rhodes). Hedley Mattingly was the blimpish British warden of the game preserve. The other stars were Clarence the cross-eyed lion – in fact, the series was derived from a Tors cinema feature called *Clarence, the Cross-Eyed Lion* – and Judy the chimp (who simultaneously appeared in >*Lost in Space*). Occasional use of trick photography allowed the viewer to see the world through the crossed eyes of Clarence. Episodes mainly told of Tracy's efforts in dealing with the poaching of endangered wild species by native and white hunters.

In 1968 Erin Moran – later to play Joanie in >*Happy Days* and *Joanie Loves Chachi* – joined the cast as seven-year-old orphan Jenny Jones, while Ross Hagen was added as safari guide Bart Jason. Somewhat incredibly, given its apparent darkest African setting, the adventure series was filmed in a safari park outside Los Angeles.

Danger Mouse

———

UK 1981–91 50 × 30m col ITV. Cosgrove Hall/Thames TV. *USA tx* 1984 Nickleodeon. *exec pr* John Hambley. *pr* Brian Cosgrove, Mark Hall. *dr* Brian Cosgrove, Chris Randall. *wr* Brian Trueman, Mike Harding. *mus* Mike Harding. *cast* (voices) **Danger Mouse/Narrator/Nero/Colonel K** David Jason **Penfold** Terry Scott **Baron Greenback** Edward Kelsey **Stiletto** Brian Trueman. *Video* Thames/Video Collection.

The comic episodes of Danger Mouse, ever so serious superhero of the British Secret Service, aided by small and bespectacled friend, Penfold. Chief enemy of the eye-patch-wearing, recklessly brave cartoon rodent was toad

Baron Greenback, whose plans to take over the world incorporated everything from a soundgun made from bagpipes to a giant mechanical cat. Another series fiend was Count Duckula, a vegetarian vampire who was spun-off to a show of his own in 1988.

David Jason (*Do Not Adjust Your Set*, *Open All Hours*, *A Sharp Intake of Breath*, *Only Fools and Horses*, *A Bit of a Do*, *The Darling Buds of May*) voiced the 'greatest secret agent the world has ever known'. Terry Scott (>*Terry and June*) acted his sidekick. Singer-comic Mike Harding contributed the music. The series was made by Brian Cosgrove and Mark Hall whose Manchester-based Cosgrove Hall company, a subsidiary of Thames TV, was also responsible for *Count Duckula*, and the model animations *Wind in the Willows* and *The Pied Piper of Hamlyn*.

Dogtanian and the Three Muskehounds

Spain 1981 12 × 25m col. BRB International SA, Madrid. *UK tx* 1985 BBC1. *cr* Claudio Biern Boyd. *exec pr* Claudio Biern Boyd. *dr* Tom Wierner, Robert Barron, Byrd Ehlmann. *wr* Claudio Biern Boyd. *mus* Guido and Maurisio de Angelis. *sfx* Luis Castro. *Video* Video Collection.

Animation based on Dumas' classic *The Three Musketeers* in which all the characters are metamorphosed into canines. Dogtanian, an endearingly gauche puppy from Gascony, travels to Paris to join the King's Own Guard, falling in love *en route* with the beautiful Juliette, but eventually teaming up with swordsters Athos, Porthos and Aramis. Together they become famous throughout France as Dogtanian and the Three Muskehounds (motto: 'One for all, and all for one').

Earthworm Jim

USA 1995– 13 × 39m col WB Network. TCC/MCA/Universal Family Entertainment. *UK tx* 1995 TCC. *cr* Doug TenNAPEL.

pr Kathi Castillo, Roy Allen Smith. *dr* Various. *wr* Various, including Doug Langdale. *mus* William Anderson. *cast* (voices) Charlie Adler, Jeff Bennett, Dan Castellaneta, Jim Cummings, Edward Hibbert, John Kassir, Andrea Martin, Kathi Soucie.

Not so long ago, and not so far away on the planet Insectika, lived a slimy despot named Queen Slug-for-a-Butt, whose bad sense of humour and lust for power were a danger to life forms everywhere. Who could save the earth, the universe? Crawl forward Jim, a happy, innocent multi-celled organism who, one day as he burrowed happily through some topsoil, was transformed by a supersuit which fell out of the sky. No longer was Jim a humble worm but a mega-superhero, greater even than the >*X-Men*, the pizza-eating >*Teenage Mutant Ninja Turtles*, or the Daemonite-battling *Wild C.A.T.S* of Jim Lee.

Earthworm Jim's breathless, lunatic adventures to defeat Queen Slug-for-a-Butt (and save her nice sister, the rightful occupant of the Insectika throne, Princess What's-Her-Name) took him to places alternatively disgusting and weird, like Evil's Funhouse, where the universe's worst performers forced alien captives to watch really bad performances. The colourfully named supporting cast of bad guys was: megalomaniac Professor Monkey-for-a-Head; Bob, the Killer Goldfish (a comic take on the murderer in >*Twin Peaks*); Psy-Crow, a bounty hunter with bad breath, retained by Slug-for-a-Butt for the express purpose of retrieving Jim's supersuit; and Evil, the Cat from Heck. Meanwhile, Jim was aided by Peter Puppy, playful and housetrained, but a fanged monster when provoked.

Originally a video game, *Earthworm Jim* was animated for television by The Children's Channel/MCA/Universal at the cost of $5 million for thirteen instalments. The voice cast numbered among them Don Castellaneta, Homer in >*The Simpsons*.

Fireball XL5

UK 1963 39 × 30m bw ITV. An AP Films Production/ATV/ITC. *USA tx* 1963–5 NBC. *cr* Gerry Anderson. *pr* Gerry Anderson. *dr* Gerry Anderson, Alan Patillo, David Elliott, Bill Harris,

John Kelly. *wr* Gerry Anderson, Sylvia Anderson, Alan Fennell, Anthony Marriott, Dennis Spooner. *mus* Barry Gray. *sfx* Derek Meddings (visuals). *cast* **Col Steve Zodiac** Paul Maxwell **Prof Matic/Lieut 90/Zoonie** David Graham **Venus** Sylvia Anderson **Robert the Robot** Gerry Anderson **Commander Zero** John Bluthal. *Video* ITC.

The futuristic exploits of 'brave and fearless' Steve Zodiac, commander of 300-foot long rocketship *Fireball XL5* (with detachable nose-cone), as he patrolled Sector 25 of the Solar System in the year 2067 AD. The other *XL5* crew were beautiful female space doctor Venus, bespectacled scientist-navigator Prof Matt Matic and transparent auto-pilot Robert the Robot. Zoonie was the crew's strange pet, a Lazoon which had a passion for Martian Delight confectionery and a mynah-like talent for mimicry.

XL5 was part of the World Space fleet based at Space City, a Pacific Island. Assigning Zodiac and crew to their dangerous missions – on which they encountered alien invaders and human villains, notably Mr and Mrs Spacespy – was Commander Zero and his aide Lieutenant 90.

Fireball XL5 was Gerry Anderson's second supermarionation and his breakthrough into the American market, where it was networked by NBC. In particular, the set and model work was more detailed than >*Supercar*.

The Flintstones

USA 1960–6 166 × 30m col ABC. Hanna Barbera. *UK tx* 1961–6 ITV. *cr* Joseph Barbera, William Hanna. *pr* William Hanna, Joseph Barbera. *dr* Various, including William Hanna, Joseph Barbera, Charles A Nichols, Ray Patterson. *wr* Joseph Barbera, William Hanna, Warren Foster, Mike Maltese, R Allen Saffian, Barry Blitzer, Tony Benedict, Herb Finn, Jack Raymond, Sydney Zelinka, Arthur Phillips, Joanna Lee. *mus* (theme) Hoyt S Curtin, William Hanna, Joseph Barbera. *cast* (voices) **Fred Flintstone** Alan Reed **Wilma Flintstone** Jean Vander Pyl **Barney Rubble** Mel Blanc **Betty Rubble** Bea Benaderet (1960–4) Gerry Johnson (1964–6) **Dino the Dinosaur** Mel Blanc **Pebbles** Jean Vander Pyl **Bamm Bamm** Don Messick. *Video* Video Collection.

'Yabba-dabba-doo!' Fred Flintstone (left) and Bedrock neighbour Barney Rubble from Hanna Barbera's Stone Age hit *The Flintstones*. Modelled on Jackie Gleason's *The Honeymooners*, the 'kidult' series was the first prime-time cartoon show.

The life and times of Stone Age suburban family the Flintstones and their best friends and neighbours the Rubbles who lived in the prehistoric city of Bedrock, 250 miles below sea level in Cobblestone Country. Fred Flintstone, operator of a dinosaur-powered crane at the Rock Head & Quarry Cave Construction Co. (slogan: 'Own Your Own Cave and Be Secure') and his wife Wilma had a split-level cave replete with such ingenious Stone Age gadgetry as Wilma's Stoneway piano, a hi-fi on which Fred played his 'rock' music (for which a bird with a long beak served as the needle), a vacuum cleaner (a baby elephant with a long trunk) and an automatic garbage disposal unit (a famished buzzard stashed under the sink). Favourite foods included brontosaurus cutlets, lizards' gizzards and swamp roof soufflé. They travelled in the Cavemobile, propelled by the passengers' own feet. At first Fred and Wilma Flintstone had only Dino, their pet dinosaur, around the cave to play with. Then, in February 1963, they were blessed with a baby daughter, born in Bedrock's Rockapedic Hospital, whom they called Pebbles. Not to be outdone the Rubbles adopted the baby boy found on their doorstep, Little Bamm Bamm, an infant possessed of alarming strength (the two later had a spin-off series of their own, *Pebbles and Bamm Bamm*).

The Flintstones (originally to be called 'The Flagstones' until the name ran into copyright problems) were dreamed up in response to a request for a prime-time, half-hour animated sitcom with 'kidult' appeal from executive producer John Mitchell. Hanna-Barbera started by taking *The Honeymooners* as their model (the hugely successful series starring Jackie Gleason as bus driver Ralph Kramden, his long-suffering wife Alice and neighbours the Nortons), then artist and storyboard man Dan Gordon came up with characters out of the Stone Age dressed in leopard skins and the concept fell into place.

Like Ralph Kramden of *The Honeymooners* Fred Flintstone was a well-meaning know-all who fancied himself capable of carrying out get-rich schemes. Like Ralph, Fred had a long-suffering wife (Wilma) and neighbours (Barney and Betty Rubble) who became involved in his antics. Genial but none too intelligent Barney, in the style of Ralph Kramden's neighbour Ed Norton, acted as a foil to Fred. *The Flintstones* also drew

on all the old jokes of sitcom – Fred had an ogre of a boss (Mr Slate or Mr Rockhead), forgot his wedding anniversary and was always having mother-in-law problems. More comedy came from the showbiz in-jokes – Lollobrickida featured as a beautiful cook, Ann-Margrock (voiced by actress Ann Margret herself) as a baby-sitter, attorney Perry Masonry who never lost a case turned up, as did actor Stony Curtis (voiced by Tony Curtis) and Weirdly and Creepella Gruesome, a parodic fusion of the then popular >*Addams Family* and >*The Munsters*.

The Flintstones was not easy to sell. CBS and NBC both turned it down (a prime-time animated programme was too much of an unknown factor) but after eight weeks ABC said yes, Reynolds Tobacco Company bought half the show for Winston Cigarettes, Miles Laboratories bought the other half for their One-a-Day vitamins and the show was ready to go ahead. It premièred on 30 September 1960 and instantly assumed historic status as the first animated TV sitcom, the first animated series longer than the standard six or seven minutes and the first animated series to feature human characters. Reviews were largely hostile (Jack Gould of the *New York Times* dubbed the programme 'an inked disaster') but the programme was given an Emmy nomination, won a Golden Globe Award, was voted the most original new series by *TV Radio Mirror* and pulled in the punters in their hordes.

As well as being the longest-running animated series in prime-time history *The Flintstones* and its spin-offs have re-run on CBS and NBC. *The Flintstone Kids* ran on ABC from September 1986 to 1989. A 1994 movie based on the show, directed by Brian Levant, starred John Goodman (>*Roseanne*) as Fred Flintstone, Elizabeth Perkins as Wilma, Rick Moranis as Barney Rubble, Rosie O'Donnell as Betty Rubble and Kyle Maclachlan (>*Twin Peaks*) as Chief Vandercave. 'Yabba-Dabba-Doo!'

Flipper

USA 1964–8 88 × 60m col NBC. MGM-TV/Ivan Tors Films. *UK tx* 1966–9 ITV. *cr* Ivan Tors. *exec pr* Ivan Tors. *pr* Leon Benson, James Buxbaum. *dr* Various, including Ivan Tors, Leon Benson, Herman Hoffman, Ricou Browning, Stanley Z

tales are cautiona[...] [w]hatever the attitude of adults,
teenagers love it: [...] [re]gularly watched by twenty-five
per cent of the fift[...] [to] eighteen age group. Techniques
such as special low [...] [camer]a angles all help give ownership
of the show to you[...] [peo]ple.

Numerous of [...] [Grange] Hill's child actors have
graduated to othe[...] [sho]ws. The programme's first star
was Todd Carty [...] [(Pet]er Jenkins) later the lead in
Tucker's Luck, [...] [and more] recently Mark Fowler in
EastEnders. Susa[...] [...] [was] also made the walk from
Grange Hill to E[...] [...] (playing Michele Fowler).

The Guyver

Japan 1989 6 × 30m col. Takaya Productions. *USA tx* 1995
syndicate[...] [U]K *tx* 1996 Paramount. *cr* Takaya. *pr* Osamu
Shimizu[...] [Ka]tsutoshi Sasaki, Yutaka Maseba. *dr* Masachiro
Otami, [...] [M]oto Hashimoto. *wr* Motonori Tachikawa (Brother
Noppo). *mus* '[...] [R]ock' (theme) Mad Dog Winston. *cast*
(English voices) **Sho Fukamachi** Tom Charles **Agito
Maksehima** Steve Blum **Tesuro Sagawa** Victor Garcia
Mizuky Sagawa Melissa Charles **Murakami** Steve Areno
Fumia Fuksmachi Sonny Byrkett **Apton** Gary Michaels
Onuma Dan Martin **Secretary** Susan Byrkett **Narrator** Hal
Cleveland **Zoanoid Data** Dougary Grant.

Stylishly violent 'Japanimation' or *animé* (pronounced
ah-nee-may). The Guyver is the ultimate weapon, a 'bio-
armor' mechanism which interfaces with humans – in
this case, several teenagers – and turns them into
awesome combatants. At the command 'Guyver', the
select few become futuristic robot-like warriors of
awesome strength. And they need it in the titanic battle
against the evil Kronos syndicate, whose main leader, Dr
Balkus, has the ability to transform innocent humans
into hulking beasts called zoanoids. Aiding the Guyver
was Murakami, a mysterious, sunglass-wearing journalist
with telepathic powers – strong enough to intercept and
freeze those of Dr Balkus – and a very large gun.

Like most pre-teen and teen sci-fi the show tapped
into youthful paranoia (there's something out there that
hates me) and power fantasies (I too might be a
megahero). But it was also visually stunning, even

overwhelming. Some of the narrative was decently
complex and moving, too. In one episode the hero Sho
was forced to fight (to the death) his father who had been
transformed into a zoanoid.

Based on the Manga comic strip of the same name,
The Guyver was one of a number of *animé* shows to
break into the English-language market from the mid
eighties onwards, thanks to US producer Carl Macek. In
1985, Macek packaged three totally unconnected *animé*
shows into a syndicated series called *Robotech*. A huge
underground fandom built up, although it took the
international release of the theatrical feature *Akira*
(1987, *dr* Katsuhiro Otomo) for networks really to
interest themselves in 'Japanimation'.

Hector's House

France 1967 50 × 60m col. *UK tx* 1968. *cr* Georges Croses.
Video Polygram.

Known in France, where it was created by Georges
Croses, as *La Maison de Tu Tu*, *Hector's House* starred
sad-eyed dog Hector, breathy Zaza the cat (voiced by
Joanna Lumley) and giggling Mrs Kiki the frog.
Adventures, such as they were, took place mostly in
Hector and Zaza's garden where Hector would busy
himself with odd jobs until Kiki appeared over the high
wall by ladder and he was inevitably called upon to help
the two ladies in some way. Hector, a dog with 'a touch
of old world courtesy' would willingly oblige. Episodes
began and ended with a bird singing in a tree and Hector
would always describe himself appropriately to camera
as each adventure closed. 'It's lucky for me I'm such a
great big sensible old Hector,' he would declare after he
had come to the rescue once again. Occasionally Hector
tried to better himself; once he took a correspondence
course on guard-dogging, donning a smart navy uniform
for the occasion ('I'm a big old ambitious Hector'). Now
and then Zaza and Kiki would cook up a joke between
them, but Hector would take it all in his stride ('I'm a big,
ridiculous old Hector'). All in all relationships were
traditional with Hector dressed in dungarees, Zaza,
dressed in a red apron, showing off her sewing skills and

chiding him for his bad manners and Kiki, whose talent was weather forecasting, wearing a pink gingham frock and hat, whilst coyly asserting 'Mr Hector's such a gentleman!'

Hector's House was successor to the BBC's 5.40pm slot after it was vacated by >*The Magic Roundabout*, also a French import. Filling this prime pre-news slot, it aimed to appeal across the generations – and succeeded. Children and adults alike voted its dog star 'a big old loveable Hector' and made sure they tuned in.

The Herbs

UK1970–2 40 × 15m col BBC1. Filmfair. *cr* Michael Bond. *exec pr* Graham Clutterbuck. *dr* Ivor Wood. *wr* Michael Bond. *mus* Tony Russell, Brenda Johnson. *cast* (storyteller) Gordon Rollings. *Video* Abbey/Video Collection.

Created by Michael 'Paddington' Bond, *The Herbs* was set in the walled English country garden of Sir Basil and Lady Rosemary. The other Herb characters were the young lion with a large head, Parsley, daffy Dill the Dog, Sage the owl, Bayleaf the Gardener, Constable Knapweed, Mr Onion, Aunt Mint, The Chives, Tarragon, Pashana Bedhi and Belladonna. Parsley was the undoubted luminary of the show and ended up in his own series, *Parsley the Lion*. Although *The Herbs* was part of a long list of BBC puppet shows with rural settings, such as >*Camberwick Green*, >*Trumpton* and >*Pogle's Wood*, it was pleasantly off-beat. It was directed by Ivor Wood (also *Postman Pat*), who had worked in Paris with Serge Danot on >*The Magic Roundabout*.

Here Come The Double Deckers

UK 1971 17 × 20m col BBC. TCF. *USA tx* 1970–1 ABC. *cr* Roy Simpson, Harry Booth. *pr* Roy Simpson. *dr* Harry Booth, Charles Crichton, Jeremy Summers. *wr* Harry Booth, Glyn Jones, Melvyn Hayes, Peter Miller, Jan Butlin. *mus* Ivor Slaney. *cast* **Albert** Melvyn Hayes **Billie** Gillian Bailey **Brains** Michael Audreson **Doughnut** Douglas Simmonds **Scooper** Peter Firth **Spring** Brinsley Forde **Sticks** Bruce Clark **Tiger** Debbie Russ.

Zany seventies comedy series featuring a gang of seven young heroes, the Double Deckers, who congregated in a disused London Transport double decker bus which served as their base, clubhouse and location for plotting and hatching weekly adventures involving anything from robots to celebrities, TV studios and fundraising charity shows. The wacky, singing, dancing, game-for-anything gang were the leader of the gang, Scooper, the podgy Doughnut, bespectacled Brains, American Sticks who played the drums, sensible Billie and little Tiger who was inseparable from her cuddly toy.

There were guest appearances from, among others, Clive Dunn, Sam Kydd and James Seymour. Two of *Double Deckers'* stars went on to greater fame – Peter Firth (Scooper) grew up to star in feature films including *Aces High* (1976) and Brinsley Forde (Spring), is now a member of reggae band Aswad. Melvyn Hayes (Albert) was later to be seen in *It Ain't Half Hot Mum*.

Initially turned down by ITV, the series was snapped up by American giant ABC for immediate nationwide broadcast before it was bought and screened by the BBC.

Series creators Booth and Simpson's previous TV work included writing credits on >*The Adventures of Robin Hood*, >*Danger Man* and >*The Avengers*.

Hong Kong Phooey

USA 1974–6 16 × 22 m col ABC. Hanna-Barbera. *UK tx* 1975–6 BBC1. *pr* William Hanna, Joseph Barbera, Iwao Takamoto. *cast* (voices) **Penrod 'Penry' Pooch** Scatman Crowther **Sgt Flint** Joe E Ross **Rosemary** Kathi Gori **Spot** Don Messick. *Video* Hanna-Barbera.

Penry Pooch (voiced by black actor Scatman Crowther) was the meek police station janitor who, at the drop of a bucket and a leap into the filing cabinet, turned into Hong Kong Phooey, the Mutt of Steel, 'America's secret weapon against crime'. Phooey was accompanied on his exploits by Spot, a horizontally-striped cat, perpetually smacking his head in exasperation at the antics of the long-eared, would-be inscrutable dog hero.

An amusing cartoon spoof of *Superman* and the Kung Fu craze of the seventies. >*Sergeant Bilko* veteran Joe E Ross played the station's Sergeant Flint.

The Huckleberry Hound Show

USA 1958–62 195 × 30m bw, syndicated. Hanna-Barbera. *UK tx* 1960–4 ITV. *cr* William Hanna, Joseph Barbera. *pr* William Hanna, Joseph Barbera. *wr* Joseph Barbera, Warren Foster. *mus* Bill Hanna, Joseph Barbera and Hoyt Curtin (theme song). *cast* (voices) **Huckleberry Hound** Daws Butler. *Video* Brave/SMO.

Cartoon anthology show featuring the eponymous dog with a corn pone voice. Every week 'Huck' turned up in a different guise – medieval knight, snake charmer, mailman, swashbuckling Purple Pumpernickle – and set forth on slapstick adventure. Although it always ended in comic disaster, the old hound dog remained infuriatingly noble and naive. *Huckleberry Hound* was the first animation series to receive an Emmy Award (for Outstanding Achievement in Children's Programming, 1959). The other segments of the show were *Pixie and Dixie* (two mice who tortured a cat, Mr Jinks), *Hokey Wolf* and >*Yogi Bear*.

The series' creators Bill Hanna and Joseph Barbera had risen to fame as the team behind Warner Bros' *Tom & Jerry* film shorts and had moved to TV when the studio began to wind down its animation department. For the new medium they developed a cheaper technique of cartoon production, which reduced lip movements to a simple vowel-to-vowel cycle, and kept body movement and artistic detail to a minimum. Their initial TV show was *Russ and Ready*, but *Huckleberry Hound* marked their popular breakthrough. They went on to create, amongst others, >*The Flintstones*, >*The Jetsons*, >*Wacky Races* and >*Scooby Doo*.

The Jetsons

USA 1962–3/1984–7 75 × 35m col ABC/syndicated. Hanna-Barbera/MGM. *UK tx* 1963 ITV. *cr* William Hanna, Joseph Barbera. *exec pr* William Hanna, Joseph Barbera. *dr* William Hanna, Joseph Barbera. *wr* Warren Foster, Mike Maltese, Harvey Bullock, Larry Markes, Tony Benedict. *mus* Hoyt Curtin, William Hanna, Joseph Barbera (theme). *cast* (voices) **George Jetson** George O'Hanlon **Jane Jetson** Penny Singleton **Judy Jetson** Janet Waldo **Elroy Jetson/Cogswell/ Henry** Daws Butler **Rosie/Mrs Spacefly** Jean Vander Pyl **Astro** Don Messick **Mr Spacefly** Mel Blanc **Orbity** Frank Welker.

The Jetsons was >*The Flintstones* gone space age. In an attempt to repeat the success of their Stone Age cartoon smash hit, Hanna-Barbera Studios reversed the formula and transported a contemporary middle-American family not into the past, but way into the future: the year 3000 AD. Head of the futuristic sitcom Jetson family was George Jetson, holder of the post of 'digital index operator' at Spacely Space Sprockets (Prop: Mr Cosmo G Spacefly, voiced by Mel 'Barney Rubble' Blanc). George's nuclear family comprised shopaholic wife Jane, rock-and-roll teenager Judy (voiced by Janet Waldo, also Penelope Pitstop in >*The Wacky Races*) and nine-year-old Elroy (Daws Butler, >*Yogi Bear*). Astro was the family pooch.

While most space shows were full of scary aliens and morbid existen... ...oncerns, *The Jetsons* was a reassuring fantas... ...future. Not least because the Jetson family had ... ...out every convenience and gadget any Westerner ... ...nt. Their flat in Skypad Apartments – raised ... ...d according to the weather – was kept clea... ...maid Rosie (Jean Vander Pyl, also Wilma... ...food came automatically out of the 'fo... machine, and they nipped aro... ...-button powered airmobile. George work... ...mic- day (even if it was, according to Ge... ...went ...a many). ...Dalek... Despite disappointing ratings on p... ...Bird, the series proved phenomenally durable... ...also th To capitalise on this, in 1985, forty-one...

(which included a new alien household pet, Orbity) were added to the original twenty-four and the series was resyndicated.

The original episodes were: Rosie the Robot/A Day with Jet Screamer (in which Judy wins a date with rock star, Jet Screamer)/The Space Car/The Coming of Astro/Jetson's Night Out/The Good Little Scouts/The Flying Suit/Rosie's Boyfriend/Elroy's TV Show/Uniblab/Visit from Grandpa/Astro's Top Secret/Elroy's Pal/Test Pilot/Millionaire Astro/The Little Man/Las Venus (in which George and Jane visit the gambling town of that name, where the nightclub singer at the Supersonic Sands Hotel is 'Dean Martian')/Jane's Driving Lesson/GI Jetson/Miss Solar System/TV or Not TV/Private Property/Dude Planet/Elroy's Mob.

Joe 90

USA 1968 30 × 30m col. A Century 21 Production in association with ATV for ITC World-Wide. *UK tx* 1968 ITV. *cr* Gerry and Sylvia Anderson. *exec pr* Reg Hill. *pr* David Lane. *dr* Desmond Saunders, Alan Perry, Leo Eaton, Ken Turner, Peter Anderson. *wr* Gerry and Sylvia Anderson, Tony Barwick, Shane Rimmer, David Lane, Des Saunders and Keith Wilson, Donald James, John Lucarotti, Pat Dunlop. *mus* Barry Gray. *cast* (voices) **Joe 90** Len Jones **Mac** Rupert Davies **Shane Weston** David Healy **Sam Loover** Keith Alexander **Mrs Harris** Sylvia Anderson. *Video* Polygram.

The stuff of a young boy's fantasy. A nine-year-old boy, equipped only with intelligence-denoting black-rimmed spectacles and all too visible strings gets to be an air force pilot, aquanaut, astronaut, President of the World Bank, a Monte Carlo rally driver and much, much more. Every week the earnest-faced, plucky Joe 90 would step into another crisis and save the day.

The premise of this puppet series from the prolific Anderson stable – it was Gerry Anderson's ninth puppet show and sixth of the Supermarionation series – was this: Brilliant electronics engineer Professor Ian 'Mac' McClaine, Joe 90's guardian, invents BIG RAT (Brain Impulse Galvanascope Record and Transfer), a machine capable of transferring brain patterns from one person to another. Mac shows his invention to Shane Weston, Deputy Director and head of the London office of the World Intelligence Network (WIN), an organisation based in America dedicated to maintaining the world balance of power. Shane realises the machine's potential to create a new and deadly form of secret agent able to make use of the skills and experience of any living person. Who better to perform this role, suggests Weston, than Mac's nine-year-old adopted son Joe who could slip into – and out of – any situation without arousing suspicion? Young Joe agrees, and WIN's most special secret agent Joe 90 goes into action.

From then on each nail-biting episode required Joe 90 – outwardly an innocent boy, inwardly equipped with invincible brain power – to save the day and rescue WIN, its agents and even his adopted father. In 'International Concerto' Joe stands in for a top WIN agent and international concert pianist in danger of kidnap; in 'Operation McClaine' a world-famous writer is about to undergo a major brain operation when the surgeon is seriously injured in an accident – and young Joe steps in as brain surgeon; in 'Lone Handed 90' Joe is a fast-shooting sheriff who saves Mac from an evil gang and in 'The Professional' Joe uses the brain patterns of a (jailed) professional safecracker to recover stolen gold from an evil dictator.

All secret agents must have their gadgets, cunningly concealed from the enemy, and Joe 90 hid his in his very special school case. One half contained his usual school kit, but secret catches opened to reveal his WIN badge and code book, transceiver, report book and automatic pistol as well as his BIG RAT adapted glasses which activated the brain patterns transferred to him in the BIG RAT cage in his father's hidden laboratory.

But all good things must come to an end and even Joe could not be nine years old for ever. Episode 30, 'The Birthday', found Joe celebrating his tenth birthday over a huge birthday cake reminiscing about his daring missions on behalf of WIN, while Mac, Sam (Deputy Head of WIN's London Office) and Shane gave a final toast to Joe 90, WIN's most special agent!

Series regulars included Mrs Ada Harris, the McClaine housekeeper, unaware of their secret, who was voiced by Sylvia Anderson, the series' co-creator. Other voices behind the puppets were TV's *Maigret*, Rupert

(superhero) show, *Zyu Ranger*. Such cost-cutting had some bizarre results: although in the American version the Yellow Ranger was female, in the masked Japanese sequences the character was played by a male. The series might have been made on the cheap, but it created a merchandising gold-rush ($350 million in 1993), encouraged the making of a 1995 *Morphin* movie, and spun-off a companion show, *VR Troopers*. This drew footage from no less than two *sentai* shows from Japan's Toei Company, *Metalder* (1987) and *Spielvan* (1986).

The original five Rangers were karate black-belt Jason, gymnast Kimberly, reflective Trini, brainy Billy and exuberant Zack. The sixth Ranger, Tommy, was initially the tool of Rita, before being saved by the gang, who made him the Green Ranger, then promoted him to White Ranger, complete with enchanted white sabre. Later, Trini was replaced by Aisha, Jason by Rocky, and Zack by Adam.

Notwithstanding Saban's promotion of the show as an 'excellent role model for today's youth', there were concerns over its apparent glorification of the martial and person-to-person violence. (Actually, the villains of the series were robotic; violence between humans was of quite... or transmission in Canada the series was cut.

Benn

3 × 15m col BBC1. Zephyr Film Productions/BBC. McKee. *dr* Pat Kirby. *wr* David McKee. *mus* Don arr Ray Brooks. *Video* WL/Polygram.

...ries of animated films about bowler-hatted Mr Number 52 Festive Road, London, who visited a costume shop. There, 'as if by magic', the r appeared and allowed Mr Benn to try on a hough viewers never saw Mr Benn in anything ly as his underwear) in the magic changing room. Mr Benn went through the door 'that always led re' (shades of Hesse's *Steppenwolf*) and emerged rld of whichever costume he had tried on. There, a very nice man, would help solve problems, rom assisting an Arabian boy mistreated by his o reinstating an unemployed dragon. The

'As if by magic', a costume shop yielded weekly adventures for bowler-hatted Mr Benn of Number 52 Festive Road, London.

adventure was always ended by the appearance of the shopkeeper, who escorted Mr Benn back to the changing room of the shop. Afterwards, Mr Benn returned home (doing his famous stiff-legged walk) to Number 52 with a souvenir to remind him of his magic travel.

Mr Benn was the 1969 creation of David McKee, a prolific writer and illustrator of children's books and shows (including *King Rollo* and *Not Now, Bernard*). Festive Road was modelled on Festing Road in Putney, London, where McKee lived at Number 52. Since its original 1971 transmission, the series has been shown every year on BBC, making it the UK's longest-running children's TV show after *Blue Peter*. It has been translated into languages as diverse as Gaelic and Japanese. *Mr Benn* fan clubs exist in institutions from banks to universities. Series narrator, Ray Brooks, has starred in the TV series *Cathy Come Home* and *Big Deal*.

Mr Benn's thirteen adventures are: Red Knight/ Hunter/Cook/Caveman/Balloonist/Zoo Keeper/Diver/ Wizard/Cowboy/Clown/Magic Carpet/Spaceman/Pirate.

Muffin the Mule

UK 1946–56 Approx 300 × 16m bw BBC1. A Parthian Production. *cr* Annette Mills. *dr* Jan Bussell. *wr* Ann Hogarth, Annette Mills (dialogue). *mus* Annette Mills. *Video* BBC.

Here comes Muffin, Muffin the Mule,
Dear old Muffin, playing the fool,
Here comes Muffin, everybody sing
Here comes Muffin the Mule.

Introductory jingle to *Muffin the Mule*

Muffin the Mule was undoubtedly the first star of British children's TV. Originally bought by puppeteer Ann Hogarth for fifteen shillings and already an experienced performer in the theatres of the land, the piebald wooden animal was first put on TV by Annette Mills in a 1946 edition of *For the Children*. Afterwards Muffin got his own show, capering around on a piano top, kissing the personable and awfully English Annette Mills as they

sang songs together. Muffin's friends included Sally the sea-lion, Peregrine the penguin, Oswald the ostrich, Monty the monkey, Louise the lamb and the frocked kittens Prudence and Primrose. The puppet was worked by Ann Hogarth ('who pulls the strings'), who stood behind a striped screen on the piano top. Hogarth also wrote the scripts. Mills – sister of movie actor John Mills, and a onetime rival for Mistinguett's title of 'woman with the most beautiful legs' – provided the dialogue, lyrics and songs. In 1949 she was awarded the Television Society's Silver Medal for outstanding TV personality of the year.

Noggin the Nog

UK 1965 20 × 10m col BBC. Smallfilms. *cr* Peter Firmin. *pr* Oliver Postgate. *wr* Oliver Postgate. *dr* Peter Firmin. *mus* Vernon Elliott. *cast* **Narrators** Oliver Postgate, Ronnie Stevens. *Video* BBC.

'Listen and I will tell you more of the saga of Noggin the Nog . . .' intoned a Viking bard, introducing each ten-minute tale of the gentle Noggin, Prince of the Nogs, his small son Knut, the mighty Thor Nogson, and Olaf the Lofty, inventor extraordinaire. Together with Noggin's Eskimo bride Nooka, and weird bird the Graculus, these cartoon Norse folk ran into many mystifying matters and fearsome foes including Noggin's evil uncle Nogbad the Bad.

Noggin's conception dated back to 1952 when art student Peter Firmin encountered a set of twelfth-century Norse chessmen in the British Museum. The figures haunted him – a phenomenon he described as 'Nogmania' – until 1959 when he wrote the first saga telling how Noggin built a long ship and sailed to find his bride Nooka. Firmin showed the results to scriptwriter Oliver Postgate and Postgate too was gripped. He turned the tale into film scripts and the BBC commissioned a series. 'Noggin' was a word dreamed up by its creator, but turned out to have the appropriate meaning of a small barrel or block of wood, which suited Noggin's square little character.

Noggin's appeal lay in clever storylines and in its villain – Nogbad's style of ruthless pillaging gained a firm following among youthful iconoclasts (and indeed Postgate claimed Nogbad as his own alter ego). And *Noggin* sales overseas mean Nogmaniacs are found as far afield as New Zealand and Hong Kong.

Noggin the Nog was produced by Smallfilms, Postgate and Firmin's prolific studio based in the village near Canterbury where the two men both live. Smallfilms also produced animated successes >*Bagpuss* and >*The Clangers*.

Pinky and Perky

UK 1957–70 220 × 30m bw/col BBC1/ITV. BBC North/ Thames TV. *cr* Jan and Vlasta Dalibor. *pr* Various, including Trevor Hill, Stan Parkinson. *dr* Various. *wr* Various, including Margaret Potter, Don Nichols. *mus* Norman Newell and Philip Green (theme). *Video* Polygram.

The exploits of twin porker puppets, the creation of Czech emigrants Jan and Vlasta Dalibor. Identical except for the fact that Perky wore blue (and a hat) while Pinky wore red, the pig duo spoke in a speeded-up fashion, danced to pop music, and made cover versions of records. Their human partners were: Jimmy Thompson, Roger Moffat, John Slater, Brian Burdon and Fred Emney. At the height of their fame, the puppets received more fan mail than the Beatles. To cash in on Pinky-Perkymania, the BBC transmitted them at a more adult viewing hour. Among the other puppet characters to appear on the show were The Beakles, Ambrose Cat and Bertie the baby elephant.

After their long career with the BBC, Pinky and Perky (theme song: 'We belong together') appeared briefly on Thames TV before their final retirement in 1970 to the great sty in the sky.

Pogle's Wood

UK 1966–7 13 × 15m BBC1. BBC. *cr* Oliver Postgate. *pr* Oliver Postgate. *wr* Oliver Postgate. *mus* Vernon Elliott. *sfx* Peter Firmin (set and puppet design). *cast* (voices) Olwen Griffiths, Steve Woodman, Oliver Postgate. *Video* BBC.

If you went down to the woods in the late sixties you would have been sure to bump into Mr and Mrs Pogle ('wife'), Pippin and squirrelly Tog, a family of puppets who lived in the root of a tree. (Initially, the series was called *Pogle* and featured a witch, but the BBC thought this might scare younger viewers so she was sent on her broomstick and the title was changed.) The Pogles spoke with thick yokel accents, but were clearly intended to be of educational value as their adventures frequently uncovered the marvels of nature. Footage of the puppets was intercut with film of countryside scenery and humans.

The series was transmitted as part of *Watch with Mother*, and made by the Smallfilms firm of Oliver Postgate and Peter Firmin (>*Clangers* and >*Noggin the Nog* etc.). Puppet manipulation was by Peter Firmin.

Press Gang

UK 1990–2 36 × 30m col ITV. Richmond Film and TV for Central Television. *pr* Sandra Hastie. *dr* Bob Spiers, Lorne Magory, Gerry O'Hara, Bren Simpson, Bill Ward, John Hall. *wr* Steven Moffat. *cast* **Lynda Day** Julia Sawalha **Spike Thomson** Dexter Fletcher **Kenny Phillips** Lee Ross **Sarah Jackson** Kelda Holmes **Matt Kerr** Clive Ward **Danny McColl** Charles Creed-Miles **Tiddler** Joanna Dukes **Billy Homer** Andy Crowe **Julie Craig** Lucy Benjamin **Frazz Davies** Mmoloki Chrystie **Colin Mathews** Paul Reynolds **Jennie Eliot** Sadie Frost **Sam Black** Gabrielle Anwar **Matt Kerr** Clive Wood.

School newspaper drama, based in the offices of the *Junior Gazette*, an offshoot of the local newspaper run by GCSE students at Norbridge High. The *Gazette* may be a mere school rag, but it has all the glamour, crises and conflict of any other newsroom – cluttered desks, ringing phones, clattering typewriters, a meddling proprietor in the shape of the headmaster and the thrill of news-gathering to impossible deadlines.

Junior Gazette newshounds comprise hard-nosed editor Lynda Day – 'I can give you till yesterday evening, ok?' – ace wisecracking reporter Spike, nice-guy deputy editor Kenny, Billy, in a wheelchair and with a razor-sharp mind (played by real paraplegic actor Andy

Crowe), dependable Sarah, and glamorous Julie. Colin is the would-be Thatcherite capitalist – 'To you seven pounds, reduced from five pounds' – head of advertising on the paper and always cooking up another (unsuccessful) scam. At the centre of newsroom relationships lies the will-they-won't-they tease between Lynda and Spike.

In true TV series newsroom style *Press Gang* contains all human life within the *Junior Gazette* walls. Funny, touching and not afraid to deal with difficult issues, it has much in common with American series such as >*LA Law*, >*Lou Grant* or >*Hill Street Blues*, with humorous, ensemble scenes from a gang of attractive young people with shifting alliances, smart brains and quick wits.

Though much of the show revolves around getting that scoop, the *Junior Gazette*'s relationship with the outside world also enables the series to tackle issues such as teenage suicide, drugs, council corruption and sexual abuse. In the two-parter 'Something Terrible' Colin gradually pieces together the facts when a girl from the lower school flinches when touched and is afraid of her father. The programme even gave a follow-up number at Childline.

For its third series *Press Gang* made some changes. The *Junior Gazette* went independent (its editorial staff had to leave school) and computer terminals replaced some of the romantic manual typewriters.

Actress Julia Sawalha has since achieved greater fame in the award-winning comedy series >*Absolutely Fabulous*. Thespian Dexter Fletcher's credits include roles as Al Pacino's son in *Revolution*, the young Caravaggio in Derek Jarman's film of the same name, as well as a criminal in *The Bill* and a disc jockey in *Boon*. The series won a BAFTA Award for producer Sandra Hastie (Head of Richmond Films and Television) and writer Steven Moffat (whose father, Bill, a Glasgow headmaster, created the series). *Press Gang* director Bob Spiers is a leading figure in TV comedy and has also worked on >*Absolutely Fabulous*.

Ren & Stimpy

USA 1980– 30 × 25m col Nickelodeon. Carbunkle/Spumco/ Nickelodeon. *UK tx* 1991 Sky1. *cr* John Kricfalusi. *exec pr* Vanessa Coffey. *pr* Various, including Bob Camp, Jim Smith, John Kricfalusi, Jim Ballentine, Frank Sapperstein. *dr* Various, including John K, Bob Camp, Vincent Waller, Greg Vanzo. *wr* Various, including John K, Vincent Waller, Bob Camp, Richard Pursel, Elinor Blake, Jim Smith. *cast* (voices) **Ren** John Kricfalusi **Stimpy** Billy West.

Launched in 1979, the Nickelodeon cable-TV channel aimed at kids' programming – from a kid's point of view. Accordingly, its ethos was rude and crude. It also promoted creator-based cartoons, several of which became big hits: *Doug*, *Rugrats* and, especially, *Ren & Stimpy*. A direct descendant of Tex Avery, *Ren & Stimpy* featured the physically gross, nuclear-fried chihuahua (with cod Mexican voice) and cat of those names, and was replete with lateral jokes, high production values and outlandish stories ('The Rubber Nipple Salesmen'). And satire. Notably, the show bit the hand that fed it and sent up kids' TV, seen to best effect in *R&S*'s parodies of toy adverts. It also sank its teeth into America, its history and its culture, with such episodes as the Western spoof 'Out West', which not only featured red-necked townsfolk going lynch-crazy to the tune of 'The Lord Loves a Hanging', but a talking horse that was mighty tired of being rustled: 'It's that old steal-a-horse bit, is it? Well, let's get on with it . . .'

Some parents were not amused, even if their prodigy were. In particular, the blood-spurting violence caused outrage. A number of child psychologists and politicians issued dire warnings. The TV industry, however, jumped aboard the gravytrain, rushing out a number of imitations (usually toned down). One was *The Shnookums & Meat Funny Cartoon Show*, which came, improbably enough, from the Disney studios. The crossover appeal of the original irritable dog and the superbly stupid, fat cat was testified to by *R&S*'s place in the late-night programming of cable/satellite stations in several countries.

Roobarb and Custard

UK 1974 30 × 5m col BBC. Bob Godfrey's Movie Emporium. *cr* Grange Calveley. *pr* Bob Godfrey. *dr* Bob Godfrey. *wr*

Grange Calveley. *mus* Johnny Hawksworth.*narr* Richard Briers. *Video* Polygram.

A witty animation series starring green dog Roobarb and bright pink cat Custard whose relationship of eternal, loving rivalry ranks alongside such classics as *Krazy Kat* and *>Hancock*. Director Bob Godfrey saw the series like this: 'It has a basic triangular structure: Roobarb is the Hancock figure, a kind of holy fool, then there is the Sid James character, an odious pink cat, and on the fence sit the lunatic birds, who will always go with whoever is winning.'

Each story, narrated in the unmistakable tones of Richard Briers, told of either the dog or cat getting the upper hand over his rival, and grinning a huge, toothy grin. The action never left the back garden, the writing was inspired and the tightly structured plots were admirably simple: in 'When Custard Stole the Show' the pink cat dubs himself 'Jacques Coostard, deep pond diver' and decides to eat all the fish in the pond, but Roobarb gets there first and removes them; in 'When Roobarb Wasn't as Pleased as Punch' Roobarb decides to stage a play which he thinks is hilarious, but the audience is silent because Custard tricks him with a dummy crowd. Each tale required lengthy preparation of the requisite equipment inside the shed at the end of the garden – suit of armour, deep diving gear, masks – while the assembled wildlife audience of birds, animals, psychedelic butterflies and other exotic insect life awaited the fantastic results. The series was inspired by Calveley's own dog, also called Roobarb, which habitually attempted to climb trees and behave in other un-dog-like ways. Co-protagonist Custard was not part of the original concept but after a first appearance in episode two proved to be such a strong character that the cat was made a key player in the series.

Roobarb and Custard, the product of Bob Godfrey's Movie Emporium, was highly distinctive for its rough-drawn, 'wobbly' style which was invented to make a creative virtue out of a low-budget necessity. When dog-lover Monica Simms finally commissioned *Roobarb and Custard* for the BBC (it had taken Godfrey and creator Calveley one year to arouse interest from the Corporation) the Movie Emporium was only given a small loan with which to make the series. Undeterred,

Godfrey saved money by creating the first animation series drawn on paper rather than using the traditional cell method in which drawings on transparent acetate are placed over prepared backgrounds. This, plus the fact that the team decided to use the then-new magic markers which advertising man Calveley had discovered at work, gave *Roobarb and Custard* lines and characters that shimmered constantly against a plain white background. The bouncy, twangy guitar music – composed and performed by Johnny Hawksworth, double bass player in the Ted Heath Band – added to the effect and made the series a whole new experience for young animation fans. The thirty episodes were produced in a year in small studios – to which fellow animator Terry Gilliam was a regular visitor – without the help of modern technology such as video scanners. Despite the shoestring budget, *Roobarb and Custard* did not break even for ten years although it is now a favourite around the world.

Series director Bob Godfrey, who also brought his unique TV cartoon style to *Noah and Nellie* (1976) and the long running *Henry the Cat*, is one of the most respected and original figures in British animation. Born in 1921, his first animated cartoon film was *The Big Parade* made in 1952. In 1965 he formed his own company Bob Godfrey's Movie Emporium which later became Bob Godfrey Films and his long list of productions include *Polygamous Polonius* (1958), *Morse Code Melody* (1963), *Marx for Beginners* (1978) and *Wicked Willie* (1990). He has had two Oscar nominations, for cartoons *Dream Doll* (1979) and *Kama Sutra Rides Again* (1972), an Oscar for *Great* (1975) and BAFTA Awards for, among others, *Henry's Cat* (1983). Oscar-nominated *Kama Sutra Rides Again* was a far less outrageous animation than its title implies, however. What Bob Godfrey refers to as his 'little sex films' had their roots in the sixties and 'flower power' and, because they were only ever hired and screened by film clubs, the titles were deliberately chosen to entice cinema programmers. The animated shorts which included such titles as *Dear Marjorie Boobs* and *Instant Sex* were, declares Godfrey 'about as sexy as plum pudding'. Godfrey won a Lifetime Achievement Award at the Zagreb International Festival in 1992.

Episode titles: When Roobarb made a spike/When Roobarb didn't see the sun come up/When Roobarb was

Green dog Roobarb picnics with pink cat Custard while
birds and assorted wildlife look on. The series was by
Oscar-winning animation wizard Bob Godfrey whose other
work includes *Kama Sutra Rides Again* and *Instant Sex*.

being bored, then not being bored/When the tree fell to pieces/When Roobarb found sauce/When it was night/When it was Christmas/When the sun was just right/When the opera wasn't a phantom/When there wasn't treasure/When it wasn't Thursday/When Roobarb was cheating/When Custard was sorry/When Roobarb mixed the paint/When Roobarb's heart rules his head/When you're going to fly – fly high/When the day didn't arrive/When Roobarb did the lion's share/When Roobarb was at the end of his tether/When there was a dance at Foxes Dale/When Custard stole the show/When Roobarb wasn't as pleased as punch/When Roobarb turned over a new leaf/When there was someone else/When the day wouldn't keep still/When Roobarb got a long break/When the pipes call the tune/When a night lost his day/When Custard got too near the bone/When there was a big mix up.

Scooby Doo, Where Are You?

USA 1969–72 72 × 22m col ABC. Hanna-Barbera. *UK tx* 1970–2 BBC1. *cr* Ken Spears, Joe Ruby. *pr* Joseph Barbera, William Hanna. *dr* Oscar Dufau, George Gordon, Charles A Nichols, Ray Patterson, Carl Urbano. *wr* Ken Spears, Joe Ruby. *cast* (voices) **Scooby Doo** Don Messick **Shaggy** Casey Kasem **Freddy** Frank Welker **Velma** Nicole Jaffe **Daphne** Heather North. *Video* Video Collection.

Had Fred Silverman, head of Daytime Programming for CBS, not been listening to Frank Sinatra on the radio one fateful night, Scooby Doo might have been no more than a nameless sidekick to his four teenage friends. Asked to create a comedy adventure for Silverman's new-look Saturday morning, Hanna-Barbera's writers had dreamed up a gang of four teenage detectives and their pet great dane who roamed the countryside in a van called the Mystery Machine solving supernatural mysteries. Silverman knew something was missing with this package – but then he happened to tune in to Frank Sinatra singing 'Strangers in the Night', was struck by the phrase 'scooby-dooby-doo' and the rest is history. The

Self-confessed member of the American Cowards' Association, Scooby Doo. The dog-hero's name was lifted from a line in Frank Sinatra's song 'Strangers in the Night'. Scooby, dooby, doo . . .

dog became Scooby Doo, the show was renamed *Scooby Doo, Where Are You?* (it was first known as *Mysteries Five* and then as *Who's Scared?*), the goofy ungainly great dane with the scratchy voice and foolish laugh (courtesy of Don Messick) was made star of the show, and the series was an instant hit.

Trembling, fearful Scooby (self-confessed member of the American Cowards' Association and often to be found trembling in human arms) travelled the roads seeking spooky situations, clues and solutions with teenagers Shaggy, Freddy, Velma and Daphne. Scooby and the aptly named unkempt Shaggy formed a comic double act, united by their tendency to panic attacks and their constant search for food while stalwart blond Freddy, brainy, bespectacled Velma and trouble-prone red-head Daphne got down to business. The show had loveable characters and exciting mysteries but it was Scooby and Shaggy's comic reactions and antics that were the ratings grabbers.

Despite his cowardice, Scooby proved to be a character with staying power, a great dane to identify with. After all, despite his imperfections and human foibles he always landed on his four feet and came out unscathed. Between 1972 and 1974 the big unbrave dog featured in *The New Scooby Doo Comedy Movies*, which had the same gang and basic format but added the voices and likenesses of such stars as Laurel and Hardy and the Addams Family. After a seven-year run on CBS Scooby and friends moved over to ABC, first as part of the ninety-minute *Scooby Doo/Dynomutt Hour* and then in a two-hour show under the title *Scooby's All-Star Laff-a-lympics*. For these shows Scooby acquired two canine cohorts, clumsy country cousin Scooby Dum and flirtatious female Scooby Dear. In 1979 *Scooby and Scrappy Doo* brought Scooby's feisty little nephew Scrappy ('I may be small but I'm tough') to his uncle's aid, complete with battle cry 'Puppy Power!'.

Secret Service

UK 1969 13 × 30m col ITV regions (ATV Midlands, Granada, Southern). Century 21/ITC Production for ATV. *cr* Gerry and Sylvia Anderson. *exec pr* Reg Hill. *pr* David Lane. *dr* Alan Perry, Leo Eaton, Brian Heard, Ian Spurrier, Alan Perry, Peter Anderson, Ken Turner. *wr* Gerry and Sylvia Anderson, Donald James, Tony Barwick, Shane Rimmer, Pat Dunlop, Bob Keston. *mus* Barry Gray, The Mike Sammes Singers (theme). *cast* **Father Unwin** Stanley Unwin **Yokel Matthew** Keith Alexander **Agent Matthew** Gary Files **Mrs Appleby** Sylvia Anderson **The Bishop** Jeremy Wilkin. *Video* ITV/Polygram.

This bizarre, short-lived series is far from the Andersons' best but has a certain oddity appeal in its transitional blend of live action and Supermarionation techniques. *The Secret Service* (1969) falls between the last of the Andersons' pure Supermarionation series, >*Joe 90*, 1968, and the first of their live TV action series, >*U.F.O.*, 1970. (The Andersons had already branched out into live action on the big screen with feature film *Doppelganger*, 1969.) Always seeking to overcome the short-comings of his puppets' physical movements, Anderson hit on the idea of using a human star for long shots and location work and a puppet double for close-ups and studio work, thus allowing characters to walk and stand realistically. Consequently double-talk comedy actor Stanley Unwin acted and voiced both hero Father Unwin and his puppet double.

The Secret Service had a folksy appeal. Lacking futuristic hardware and set in picture-book England it was rather more in >*The Avengers* mould than >*Thunderbirds* or >*Captain Scarlet*. Its central character, Father Stanley Unwin, was an amiable fifty-seven-year-old vicar whose life was suddenly changed when a late member of his parish bequeathed him a suitcase containing the Minimiser, a miniaturisation device capable of shrinking objects or people to a third of their normal size, with instructions that the vicar use it for the good of mankind. Father Unwin duly decided to use this gift in the service of British Intelligence where his contact was the Bishop (British Intelligence Service Headquarters Operation Priest). The Vicarage was transformed into operation headquarters for the purpose, complete with gardener Matthew Harding who posed as a slow-witted country bumpkin but was really a top agent ready to be miniaturised whenever a case demanded. Totally unaware of their covert activities was kindly housekeeper Mrs Appleby, voiced by Sylvia Anderson. The series' other 'star' was Gabriel, Father Unwin's 1917 vintage Model

'T' Ford. The genuine article was used on location while a radio-controlled replica was used by the puppet Unwin.

Any time British security was threatened the vicar could be relied upon to smuggle his reducible friend (even smaller and less conspicuous than predecessor >*Joe 90*) into the thick of the action in his briefcase headquarters equipped with chair, drawers, periscope and miniature tool kit. The plots were standard special agent fare: sabotage ('A Question of Miracles'), train robbery ('Last Train to Bufflers Halt'), stolen secrets ('A Case for the Bishop'), Russian agents ('The Cure') and Arabian royalty in need of protection ('May-Day, May-Day!'). The special agent buddies, however, were unusual – Stanley Unwin's double-talking talents were fully used as he sprayed gobbledygook over evil agents. Returning to his peaceful parish after each mission Father Unwin would exploit the moral lessons of his adventures in his Sunday sermons.

Unfortunately, for all his efforts and on his country's behalf, Father Stanley Unwin lacked appeal. *The Secret Service* was never networked by ITV – only ATV Midlands, Granada and Southern screened the show – and ATV chief Lew Grade had reservations about the programme's high cost – £20,000 per episode. After six episodes Grade limited the series to a maximum of thirteen, leaving Anderson to abandon the limitations of puppet movement and try his hand at live action (>*U.F.O.*, >*The Protectors*, >*Space 1999*).

Script editor for the series was Tony Barwick, and Derek Meddings was visual effects supervisor.

Skippy the Bush Kangaroo

Australia 1966–8 91 × 25m col. Norfolk International. *UK tx* 1967–9 ITV. *exec pr* John McCallum, Bud Austin. *pr* Lee Robinson, Dennis Hill. *dr* Max Varnel. *wr* Ross Napier, Ed Devereaux. *mus* Eric Jupp. *cast* **Matt Hammond** Ed Devereaux **Sonny Hammond** Garry Pankhurst **Mark Hammond** Ken James **Jerry King** Tony Bonner **Clarissa 'Clancy' Merrick** Liza Goddard **Dr Anna Steiner** Elke Neidhardt.

Whose heart could remain unmoved at the sight of Skippy, bounding through the undergrowth of Waratah National Park, Australia, and towards his adoring young owner Sonny Hammond to the words of the jaunty theme song: 'Skippy, Skippy, Skippy the bush kangaroo'? Making good use of the Australian landscape as well as the allure of such down-under animals as wombats, emus and koala bears, *Skippy the Bush Kangaroo* starred the eponymous marsupial, lovable and plucky pet of Sonny Hammond, son of the park ranger of Waratah National Park. Stories related the duo's adventures as together they helped protect the game reserve from all manner of evil and danger, Skippy ever watchful and ready to alert his young friend with his distinctive tut-tutting, or to lead him to the scene of a crime. Tearful moments would also come when Skippy fell ill, victim of a villainous plot or a disease sweeping the park. Other characters were Sonny's father Matt, brother Mark and long-legged, long-haired blonde Clarissa 'Clancy' Merrick, a friend staying with the all-male family – played by a young Liza Goddard in one of her first appearances.

Fame had its downside for the lead kangaroo however. In 1970 vandals tried to kill the real Skippy in Australia's Waratah National Park.

The legendary *Skippy* continues to play in regular repeats worldwide and was syndicated in the US under Kellogg Co. sponsorship in 1969.

Spiderman

USA 1969–70 52 × 25m col ABC. A Marvel Production. *UK tx* 1969–70 ITV. *cr* Stan Lee. *pr* Robert L Lawrence. *cast* **Peter Parker/Spiderman** Bernard Cowan, Peter Soles **Betty Brandt** Peg Dixon **J Jonah Jameson** Paul Kligman.

While attending a demonstration of radioactivity, New York Central High School student Peter Parker is bitten by a spider that has been exposed to radiation. Later, Peter realises that the spider's venom has become a part of his bloodstream and that he has absorbed the proportionate power and ability of a living spider. Developing a special costume, and acquiring a job as a reporter for the *Daily Bugle*, Peter wages a war on crime, dispensing justice as the mysterious *Spiderman*. His extra-sensory perception, strength and wall-scaling arachnid skills afford him a certain advantage over his merely human foes. A bigger swinger than >*Tarzan*, Spiderman kept his magic web concealed in a wrist band when it wasn't flying him from skyscraper to skyscraper in the name of all that is Good.

Television has screened several adaptations of the adventures of Marvel comic's half-spider superhero. The first animated series appeared in America in 1967 and hit TV schedules in Britain in 1969 with Peter Parker, college freshman, donning his superguise whenever supervillains threatened. Spin-off *Spiderwoman* appeared on ABC in 1979–80 in sixteen twenty-five-minute episodes produced by DePatie/Frelang and shown in Britain on ITV in 1983, with Joan Van Ark as Jessica Drew who is bitten by a poisonous spider in her father's lab. The only way that Dr Drew can save her life is to inject her with spider serum which endows her with extraordinary powers which turn her into the superheroine. Also in 1983 BBC1 began showing *Spiderman and his Amazing Friends*, a spoof series set in a small college town and featuring Spidey, his cool roommate Bobby Drake, the Iceman and beautiful Angelic Jones as Fire-Start. Together they save Earth from outlandish do-badders such as the Goblin, Swarm and Dr Doom. A TV movie, *The Amazing Spiderman*, was broadcast on CBS in 1978–9 and followed by thirteen fifty-minute live action episodes under the same title, with Nicholas Hammond as Peter Parker/Spiderman and Fred Waugh doing the stunt sequences. Charles Fries and Daniel Goodman were executive producers.

Stingray

UK 1964–5 39 × 30m col ITV. AP Films/ATV/ITC. *USA tx* 1965 syndicated. *cr* Gerry Anderson, Sylvia Anderson. *pr* Gerry Anderson. *dr* Alan Patillo, John Kelly, Desmond Saunders, David Elliott. *wr* Gerry and Sylvia Anderson, Alan Fennell, Dennis Spooner. *mus* Barry Gray. *sfx* Derek Meddings. *cast* (voices) **Troy Tempest** Don Mason **Phones/Agent X20** Robert Easton **Atlanta** Lois Maxwell **Commander Shore/Titan/Sub-Lieutenant Fisher** Ray Barrett. *Video* Polygram.

'Stand by for action . . . We're about to launch *Stingray!*' After land (>*Supercar*) and air (>*Fireball XL5*), Gerry

Puppets on a string: Captain Troy Tempest (left), a chip off the matinee-idol block, with green mermaid Marina and drawling 'Phones' Sheridan in the Andersons' submarine Supermarionation *Stingray*. Sheridan shared with fellow Anderson puppet Lady Penelope of *Thunderbrids* the distinction of being a marionette who smoked. *Stingray* was the first British television series to be filmed in colour.

Anderson went undersea for his third Supermarionation, which related the exploits of the World Aquanaut Security Patrol (WASP). *Stingray* was also the first British TV series to be filmed in colour.

In the twenty-first century the job of WASP, a sort of ocean police force, was to keep the seas free from the forces of evil, principally the megalomaniacal, green-skinned overlord of Titanica, Titan. Inept bug-eyed Agent X20 was Titan's spy on land, while the Aquaphibians in their gothic *Terror Fish* formed his underwater army. Fortuitously, WASP had *Stingray* on its side, an atomic-powered submarine equipped with sixteen Sting missiles and based at Marineville, WASP's inland HQ (connected to the sea by a tunnel). The captain of *Stingray* was Troy Tempest, dashing, blue-eyed and square-jawed. Also on board was drawling Southern gentleman George 'Phones' Sheridan (who, along with >*Thunderbird's* Lady Penelope, was one of the few puppets on a string to smoke) and Marina. She was the silent green-haired mermaid daughter of Aphony, benevolent ruler of Pacifica, rescued from the clutches of Titan by Troy and Phones in episode one. WASP itself was headed by paraplegic, hovercrafting Commander Shore, assisted by daughter Atlanta who soapily vied with Marina for Troy's affections.

Even when measured against Anderson's later puppet works, *Stingray* stands up well. There was plenty of kiddie-time exciting narrative action, while the more sophisticated could enjoy its proclivity to spoof virtually everything which passed its periscope. Troy himself, his eyebrow permanently stuck in quizzical mode, was a caricature of a movie idol. One of the best episodes, 'Raptures of the Deep', ruthlessly burlesqued flower-powered hippies. The series was filmed with flair; the effect of *Stingray* moving underwater was achieved by the simple method of shooting the model through a thin aquarium full of guppies. Lois Maxwell, Miss Money-penny of the James Bond films, provided the voice for sexy Atlanta. Despite being filmed in colour, at a cost of £1 million, the series was originally broadcast in black and white.

The episodes were: Stingray/Emergency Marineville/The Ghost Ship/Subterranean Sea/Loch Ness Monster/Set Sail for Adventure/The Man from the Navy/An Echo of Danger/Raptures of the Deep/Titan Goes Pop/In Search of the Tajmanon/A Christmas to Remember/Tune of Danger/The Ghost of the Sea/Rescue from the Skies/The Lighthouse Dwellers/The Big Gun/The Cool Caveman/Deep Heat/Star of the East/Invisible Enemy/Tomb Thumb Tempest/Eastern Eclipse/Treasure Down Below/Stand By for Action/Pink Ice/The Disappearing Ships/Secret of the Giant Oyster/The Invaders/A Nut for Marineville/Trapped in the Depths/Count Down/Sea of Oil/Plant of Doom/The Master Plan/The Golden Sea/Hostages of the Deep/Marineville Traitor/Aquanaut of the Year.

Supercar

UK 1961–2 39 × 30m bw ITV. An AP Films Production for ATV/ITC World-Wide Distribution. *USA tx* 1962 syndicated. *cr* Gerry Anderson, Reg Hill. *pr* Gerry and Sylvia Anderson. *dr* David Elliott, Alan Patillo, Desmond Saunders, Bill Harris. *wr* Reg Hill, Gerry and Sylvia Anderson, Hugh and Martin Woodhouse. *mus* Barry Gray. *cast* (voices) **Mike Mercury** Graydon Gould **Doctor Beaker** David Graham **Mitch the Monkey** David Graham **Professor Popkiss** George Murcell **Masterspy** George Murcell **Zarin** David Graham **Jimmy Gibson** Sylvia Anderson **Other female voices** Sylvia Anderson. *Video* ITC/Polygram.

The time is the present. *Supercar*, a futuristic multi-terrain vehicle is a one-of-a-kind experimental model, brainchild of fatherly mid-European Professor Popkiss and balding British boffin Doctor Beaker, his assistant. From their isolated laboratory in the middle of the Nevada desert the eccentric scientists hire daredevil Mike Mercury, a fearless and courageous test pilot, to put *Supercar* through its paces. In numerous exciting adventures the astounding vehicle travels the world by land, air, sea or space.

Supercar was Gerry Anderson's fourth puppet series (after *Twizzle*, >*Torchy the Battery Boy* and >*Four Feather Falls*) but the first of the Supermarionation sci-fi shows that made his name. Supermarionation was Anderson's term for the realistic style of puppetry he had developed since setting up his company AP Films in 1956. The technique featured a cast of eighteen-inch-high marionettes that blinked, moved their eyes and seemed to speak their own dialogue. They were suspended by control wires that triggered machinery hidden inside them. Through the wires, for instance, Anderson could transmit recorded speech to a mechanism that moved the marionette's mouth to achieve synchronisation between dialogue and lip movement. The only problem that remained was to simulate realistic walking, and this was solved in *Supercar* by seating the characters in the futuristic car which became the star of the show. The resulting series was staggeringly successful and led to a whole run of Supermarionation sci-fi series (>*Fireball XL5*, 1962, >*Stingray*, 1964, >*Thunderbirds*, 1965, and *Captain Scarlet*, 1968).

Supercar had eight rockets which could be controlled from a distance by a special remote control. On land it hovered just above the surface, it had folding wings for flight and when underwater it had a periscope and sonar. Its unique 'Clear-vu' system allowed its pilot to 'see' on a display screen in the cockpit through clouds, fog or storms.

Regular characters were Jimmy Gibson, a ten-year-old boy rescued by *Supercar* who became part of the team, and Jimmy's pet Mitch, a talking monkey. The arch-villain of the show was a big Sydney Greenstreet-style character, the devious, deep-voiced mercenary Master-spy, an evil villain out to steal *Supercar* at any opportunity. Zarin was his bungling accomplice who provided comic relief (and gave rise to the line 'Zarin, you fool . . .') and their British counterparts Harper and Judd completed the quartet of treachery. Adventures included capture by headhunting tribesmen ('Amazonian Adventure'), sabotage ('Grounded'), pirates ('Pirate Plunder'), underwater excavations and giant fish ('Trapped in the Depths') and a famous TV gorilla and jazz drummer ('King Kool'), but none of these perils was a match for the amazing *Supercar*'s abilities on land, sea, underwater and in the air.

Supercar was dreamed up in 1959 but Anderson's previous backers, Granada, did not take the project, leaving it to be rescued by Lew Grade's ITC. Director of photography was John Read, the puppeteers were Christine Glanville and Mary Turner, special effects were by expert duo Derek Meddings (*Superman I* and *Superman II*) and Brian Johnson (*Aliens*) who pioneered the use of 'lived in' models – spaceships with discolouration from rocket blasts and characters who had shadows under their eyes when they were tired. *Supercar* itself, a seven-foot craft made mostly of lightweight balsa wood was designed by Reg Hill and cost £1,000 to build – a fortune for the fledgeling company, but one that soon paid off. *Supercar*'s thirty-nine episodes turned the tide for Anderson, selling into more than 100 US television stations and more than forty countries.

Sweet Valley High

USA 1994– 50+ × 30m col syndicated. Teen Drama Productions/Saban Entertainment Inc. *UK tx* 1995 Nickelodeon. *cr* Francine Pascal. *exec pr* Lance H Robbins, Haim Saban, Francine Pascal. *pr* David Garber, William G Dunn Jr, Ronnie Hadar. *dr* Various, including Harvey Frost. *wr* Various, including David Garber. *cast* **Jessica Wakefield** Brittany Daniel **Elizabeth Wakefield** Cynthia Daniel **Patty Gilbert** Amarilis **Todd Wilkins** Ryan James Bittle **Bruce Patman** Brock Burnett **Enid Rollins** Amy Danles **Lila Fowler** Bridget Flanery **Winston Egbert** Michael Perl **Manny Lopez** Harley Rodriguez.

Made by Saban Entertainment, the world's largest independent purveyor of kiddie entertainment, *Sweet Valley High* is based on the mega-selling *Sweet Valley* novels by Francine Pascal. (The title of the eponymous school was to have been Sweet Apple High – until Pascal's brother, Michael Stewart, pointed out that this was the title of the pedagogical institution in his play *Bye Bye Birdie*.) Set in the permanently sunny Californian town of Sweet Valley, the series revolves around the lives and loves of blue-eyed, blond-haired twins, Jessica and Elizabeth Wakefield. Though physically identical, the two sixteen-year-olds differ predictably in their personalities: Elizabeth is the studious goody-goody; Jessica, the mischievous, boy-chasing socialite. Their implausibly perma-tanned, white-toothed classmates (who presumably graduate to *Baywatch*) include: Patty Gilbert, the cheerleader captain; Todd Wilkins, basketball hero and Elizabeth's boyfriend; Bruce Patman, the sultry, spoilt hunk; brainy redhead Enid Rollins, who hides a dark secret; rich bitch Lila Fowler; class clown Winston Egbert; and gold-hearted track star Harley Rodriguez.

As educational establishments go, Sweet Valley is the school of teen fantasy. Lessons are apparently non-existent, while dating is mandatory. Typical dialogue is: 'Who *is* that guy? I've not seen him in school before.' Romantic revenge is the plot staple, along with worries over who's popular and who's not. Unlike >*Beverly Hills 90210* and >*Melrose Place*, both of which are pitched at an older age base, *SVH* assiduously avoids social issues in favour of sweet-sixteen crushes and adolescent angst.

Playing the Wakefield sisters are twins, Cynthia and Brittany Daniel, who previously starred in the Wrigley chewing gum print and TV ads as the 'Double Twins'. Unusually, the series is shot on film (at Saban's Valencia, California, studios), giving it an appearance closer to a TV movie than to a soap. The first flight of episodes was helmed by Harvey Frost, Emmy Award-winning director of Disney Channel's *Avonlea*.

Tarzan

USA 1966–8 58 × 60m col NBC. Banner Productions. *UK tx* 1967–9 ITV. *exec pr* Sy Weintraub. *pr* Jon Epstein, Maurice Unger. *dr* Robert Day, Paul Stanley, Earl Bellamy, Robert L Friend, Lawrence Dobkin, Alan Crosland Jr, Hollingsworth More, Tony Leader, R G Springsteen, Alex Nicol, Harmon Jones, James Komack, William Witney, William Wiard, Gerald Mayer, Ron Ely, Barry Shear, Darrell Hallenbeck. *wr* George F Slavin, Don Brinkley, Oliver Crawford, S J Loy, Robert Sabaroff, Lee Erwin and Jack H Rohm, Sam Roeca, James Leighton, Robert L Goodwin, Sid Saltzman, G Joshua David, Cornelius Hallard, Wells Root, Norman Lessing, Samuel Newman, Carey Wilbur, S S Schweitzer, Jackson Gillis, Arnold Belgard, Lawrence Dobkin, James Menzies, Terence Maples, Al Martin, Edmund Morris, Lee Loeb, William Driskill and Jerry Adelman, Donn Mullally, Richard and Esther Shapiro, Lee Erwin, Richard Landau. *mus* Nelson Riddle. *cast* **Tarzan** Roy Ely **Jai** Manuel Padilla Jr **Jason Flood** Alan Caillou **Rao** Rockne Tarkington **Tall Boy** Stewart Raffill.

The story of *Tarzan*, created by Edgar Rice Burroughs in 1914, runs thus: Lord John Greystoke and his wife Alice, put ashore by a mutinous crew, are marooned in Africa. One year later a baby boy is born to them, but they are killed by bull apes and a female ape raises their young son as Tarzan, King of the Jungle. Twenty years later Tarzan meets a Frenchman on safari who teaches him English and persuades him to return to the land of his parents where the young Earl of Greystoke is educated at the finest schools. Unable to adjust, however, Tarzan returns to this native jungle with its open and honest life and lives among the wild creatures with whom he can communicate. Here, possessed of great strength and incredibly acute senses, he fights evil wherever he encounters it. Friend to all the creatures of the wild, his closest companion is the chimp Cheetah. Other series regulars include a small orphan boy called Jai, Jai's tutor Jason Flood, Rao the village veterinarian and his assistant, Tall Boy. Guest stars included Diana Ross and The Supremes who in 'The Convert' made a rare acting appearance as three nuns.

Threats which brought Tarzan swinging into action, helped by his animal friends, were many and various in this eventful jungle. Often the forest had to be protected from those who would plunder its ritches as in 'Pearls of Tanga' where a German U-Boat Commander is using his submarine to raid pearl beds. Madmen and villains also abounded – in the two-parter 'The Deadly Silence' the paradise of nature is in danger from a maniacal ex-colonel who wants to be its ruler. And many beautiful young women were in need of defending, whether missionaries, archaeologists, plane crash survivors or princesses. In 'The Three Faces of Death' Tarzan's manly strength underwent three dreaded tests of courage – a crocodile pool, the Dive of Death and the Cage of Spears – to help tribal Queen Laneen retain her right to rule.

Manly, athletic Ron Ely was the fourteenth actor to play the King of the Jungle since *Tarzan of the Apes* was made as a silent movie almost half a century earlier. Ely did many of his own stunts for this series (although he was not equal to the famous Tarzan yell which was actually recorded by another Tarzan, Olympic swimmer Johnny Weissmuller) and was called upon to ride a zebra bareback, wrestle a lion and, of course, to swing from vine to vine. On one occasion he lost his hold and fell twenty-eight feet. The scene remained in and was explained by having Tarzan shot. The character of Jane and the famously crude English Tarzan had used in the movie versions ('Me Tarzan, you Jane') were dropped for the TV version, deemed inapplicable for the young Earl.

CBS aired reruns of the NBC series during the summer of 1969 and some episodes were shown together as full-length features. Other TV Tarzans included a cartoon version shown on CBS as part of an adventure hour together with >*The Lone Ranger* and >*Zorro* from 1981–2, *Tarzan: Lord of the Jungle*, a thirty-minute cartoon series on CBS, 1976–8, and a syndicated, environmentally sound *Tarzan* released in 1991 starring Wolf Larsen as Tarzan and Lydie Denier as Jane. This Tarzan had had no formal schooling and spoke only halting English; Jane was restored to the cast list but as a French environmental scientist running an African wildlife institute.

Film incarnations of *Tarzan* proliferate. There were scores of Tarzan titles dating from 1918. In 1932 came the first of the long line of MGM pictures starring Johnny Weissmuller as Tarzan and Maureen O'Sullevan as Jane. *Tarzan the Ape Man* arrived in 1981, directed by John Derek and starring Bo Derek as Jane and Miles O'Keeffe as Tarzan. And *Greystoke – the Legend of Tarzan Lord of the Apes* screened in 1984, directed by Hugh Hudson and starring Christopher Lambert as the noble ape man and Andie MacDowell as Jane.

Warner Brothers 'own whirling dervish', the teenage party animal Taz plus the other members of The Devil clan father Hugh, mother Jean and siblings Molly and Jake, in *Taz-Mania*. The antipodean family lived in a cave tastefully furnished in Danish Modern. The all-star voice cast included Dan Castellaneta of *The Simpsons* and John Astin of *The Addams Family*.

Taz-Mania

USA 1991– 28 + x 30m col Fox Television Network. Warner Bros. *UK tx* 1991– ITV. *exec pr* Tom Ruegger, Jean MacCurdy. *pr* Art Vitello. *dr* Various, including Art Vitello, Doug McCarthy, Keith Baxter, Lenord Robinson, Garry Hartle. *wr* Various, including Bill Kopp, Mark Saraceni. *mus* Richard Stone. *cast* **Taz/Buddy Boar/Wendel T Wolf/Bushwacker Bob** Jim Cummings **Mr Thickly** Dan Castellaneta **Molly Devil** Kellie Martin **Bull Gator** John Astin **Hugh Devil/Daniel Platypus/Bush Rat** Maurice LaMarche **Jean Devil** Miriam Flynn **Jake Devil** Debi Derryberry **Dog/Didgeri Dingo/Francis X**

Bushlad/Ax/Timothy Platypus Rob Paulsen
Matilda/Constance Koala Rosalyn Landor. *Video* Warner.

Warner Brothers' cartoon Tasmanian Devil first appeared in their 'Looney Tunes' anthology show, before spinning-off to his own series after just six short, but frenetic, appearances. Taz, the ultimate teenage party animal, waits tables and bellhops at Hotel Tasmania, a small resort hidden away on a distant island in an antipodean sea. He also eats virtually everything in sight. The ramshackle hotel is run by dumb but egotistical Bushwacker Bob, son of owner Matilda, the wealthiest women in Tasmania. Other employees at the hotel include giant Constance Koala and the not very handy handymen, Timothy and Daniel Platypus.

Also resident on the island are Taz Devil's family – Jean, Hugh, Molly and Jake – all of whom live in a cave furnished in Danish Modern; Mr Thickly, a harmless but offensive wallaby; Buddy Boar, a narcissistic wild pig; Didgeri Dingo, a con man; Wendel, a neurotic wolf; Bull Gator, the last of the great green hunters, who is aided by sidekick, Axl; and Francis X Bushlad, crown prince of the Mud Men tribe.

The voice cast of this off-the-wall show includes such distinguished names as Dan Castellaneta (also Homer in >*The Simpsons*), John Astin (better known as Gomez in >*The Addams Family*), and Jim Cummings, winner of two Emmys for his voicing of Winnie the Pooh.

Teenage Mutant Hero Turtles

USA 1987– 80 × 30m col syndicated. Murakami Wolf Swenson, Inc./Group W Productions. *UK tx* 1988– BSkyB/BBC1. *cr* Kevin Eastman, Peter Laird. *pr* Various, including Fred Wolf, Walt Kubiak. *dr* Various, including Bill Wolf. *wr* Various, including Michael Reaves, Brynne Stephens, Dave Bennett Carren, J Larry Carroll. *cast* **Donatello** Barry Gordon **Leonardo** Can Clarke **Michelangelo** Townsend Coleman **Raphael** Rob Paulsen **April** Ranae Jacobs **Irma** Jennifer Darling **Splinter** Peter Renaday **Shredder** James Avery **Krang** Pat Fraley. *Video* Tempo.

'Teenage . . . Mutant . . . Ninja . . . Turtles Heroes in half shell . . . Turtle power!'

The Turtles – Donatello, Raphael, Michelangelo and Leonardo – were originally pet-store turtles who accidentally fell into the New York sewer system. There, they were exposed to the mysterious radioactive 'Mutogen' – and began to walk upright and talk. With aid of a martial arts guru, Splinter the rat, the magnificent green four began a fearless crusade for justice, sustained in their endeavours by copious quantities of pizza. Helped by TV reporter April O'Neil, the turtles combated in particular the evil designs of arch foe, the Shredder.

The *Teenage Mutant Ninja Turtles* may go down in TV history as one of the most profitable jokes of all time. They were conceived in 1983 as a napkin doodle by Kevin Eastman and Peter Laird as a parody of the Japanese samurai-type heroes then preoccupying comic books. To continue the joke, Eastman and Laird gave their unlikely warrior heroes the names of refined Italian Renaissance artists. A *Turtle* comic book was hugely successful, and the characters were picked up by Group W for a TV animated series, syndicated in 1987. A live action movie released in 1990, *Teenage Mutant Ninja Turtles* (*dr* Steve Barron), was a box-office hit, and that year CBS took the series from syndication for its Saturday morning line-up. A follow up theatrical feature, *Teenage Mutant Ninja Turtles II: The Secret of the Ooze* (1991, *dr* Michael Pressman) was scarcely less successful. In Britain concerns about the Turtles' use of 'Ninja' fighting techniques, resulted in both the series and the movies being retitled 'Teenage Mutant *Hero* Turtles'.

Among those lending their voices to the Turtle show was James Avery, also the well-to-do uncle in *The Fresh Prince of Bel Air*. Voicing gadget-expert Donatello was President of the Screen Actors' Guild, Barry Gordon.

Thunderbirds

UK 1965–6 32 × 60m col ITV. An AP Films Production for ATV/ITC. *cr* Gerry Anderson, Sylvia Anderson. *pr* Gerry Anderson, Reg Hill. *wr* Gerry Anderson, Sylvia Anderson,

Alan Fennell, Alan Patillo, Donald Robertson, Dennis Spooner, Martin Clump, Tony Barwick. *dr* Alan Patillo, Desmond Saunders, David Elliott, David Lane, Brian Burgess. *mus* Barry Gray. *cast* (voices) **Jeff Tracy** Peter Dyneley **Scott** Shane Rimmer **Virgil** David Holiday **Alan** Matt Zimmerman **Gordon** David Graham **John** Ray Barrett **Brains** David Graham **Tin Tln** Christine Finn **Lady Penelope Creighton-Ward** Sylvia Anderson **Parker** David Graham **The Hood** Ray Barrett **Kryano** David Graham. *Video* Polygram.

'5,4,3,2,1 – Thunderbirds are go!' The year is 2063 and International Rescue, a secret organisation based somewhere in the Pacific, always on the lookout for trouble and dedicated to saving those in perilous situations, is dynamically overseen by Jeff Tracy, ex-astronaut and self-made millionaire whose private South Pacific island is International Rescue's secret HQ. Tracy's five sons, Scott, Virgil, Alan, Gordon and John (named after the first five American astronauts in space), are also dedicated to the cause, as are shy young boffin designer Brains and female engineer and electronics expert Tin Tin. Arch-villain of the piece is mysterious master of disguise The Hood, a supercriminal with hypnotic powers and a determination to undermine International Rescue and learn the secrets of the *Thunderbirds* craft. The Hood, who lives in an Eastern temple is half-brother to Kryano, Tin Tin's father and Jeff's loyal butler, and exercises a curious mental control over him. Rounding up the regulars is ever-doting and ever-cooking Grandma. But the two puppets who steal the show are International Rescue's London agent, blonde, bouffanted Lady Penelope Creighton-Ward and her 'cor-blimey' East End Butler 'Yus, m'lady' Parker. Lady Penelope has the cool action-woman persona of >*The Avengers'* Emma Peel, an impeccable upper-class English accent and the distinction of being one of the few puppets on TV to have mastered the art of smoking (with a cigarette holder, of course). Parker doubles as chauffeur of her pink, gadget-laden – it boasts TV and radio transmitters, retro-rocket brakes and a machine gun hidden behind the radiator – six-wheeled Rolls Royce, number plate FAB 1 (FAB 2 is Lady Penelope's rather more conventional yacht).

For each Tracy son there is a super-secret hi-tech craft equipped by Brains and ever ready to spring into action – the *Thunderbirds!* Silver-grey *Thunderbird 1*, manned by decisive eldest son Scott is a vertical take-off rocket plane capable of speeds of 7,000 mph and always first at the scene of the crisis; *Thunderbird 2*, piloted by the steady Virgil, is a huge green carrier whose job it is to haul vital machinery such as the Mole and the Thunderizer to the danger zone in six interchangeable pods; orange spaceship *Thunderbird 3* is used primarily for near-space travel and crewed by handsome, impetuous one-time racing driver Alan; *Thunderbird 4* is a yellow submarine, transported to rescues whenever necessary by *Thunderbird 2* and manned by jocular youngest son Gordon. These four craft were based at the island HQ, where nature had been adapted to aid secrecy. The cliff face moved, trees fell back and a swimming pool disappeared so that the craft could enter and leave their hiding place. *Thunderbird 5* was a space satellite, the organisation's eyes and ears in outer space where it monitored every frequency on earth and transmitted SOS signals back to earth. It was manned by the patient, solitary John Tracy.

Together the dauntless siblings and their supercraft stepped in as troubleshooters. Some problems were technological: in episode one, 'Trapped in the Sky', The Hood places a bomb aboard the new atomic airliner *Fireflash*; in 'Pit of Peril' a revolutionary new army vehicle disappears beneath the ground; in 'Sun Probe' a research ship loses its direction. Sometimes the Thunderbirds team protected the innocent: in 'The Uninvited' Scott is kidnapped by lost race the Zombites; in 'The Perils of Penelope' Lady Penelope is kidnapped and tied directly in the path of an oncoming express train. Sometimes they would recover stolen, highly sensitive secret equipment: in 'The Mighty Atom' The Hood steals the robot rat programmed by the organisation to take photographs and attempts to gather information on the Thunderbirds.

Anderson spent between $60,000 and $70,000 for each of the thirty-two episodes and used more than two hundred different models of the five *Thunderbird* vehicles. One person was hired simply to make and upholster model chairs. Each model cost £300 to make and had a selection of heads to suit different moods. Lady Penelope even had her own personal costume designer, Zena Relph. The special effects on *Thunderbirds* were by

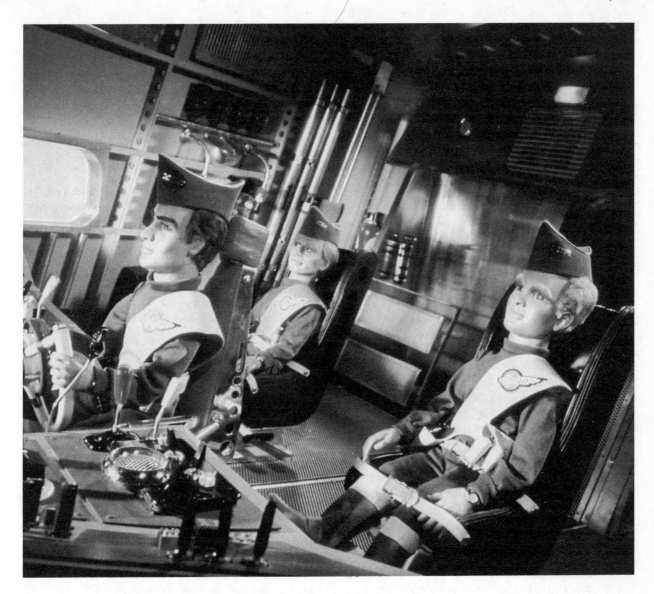

'5,4,3,2,1 – Thunderbirds are go!' International Rescue on another daredevil mission against nemesis The Hood in puppet classic *Thunderbirds*, a series that was strictly FAB. First a hit in the sixties, the show became a hit all over again in the nineties.

Derek Meddings, a regular member of the Anderson team who later worked on James Bond films and *Superman I* and *Superman II*. By the time of *Thunderbirds*, Anderson's pioneering Supermarionation technique was highly sophisticated (*Thunderbirds* was the fourth Supermarionation series and followed >*Supercar*, >*Fireball XL5* and >*Stingray*), the marionettes moved more naturally than ever with only a rare glimpse of controlling wires and the realism of the series was enhanced by director of photography John Read's mobile camerawork.

Despite the obvious allure of these puppets and fantastic craft for children – no child's toy set in the sixties, or indeed during *Thunderbirds*' repeats in the nineties, was complete without one or more *Thunderbirds* craft, comics or records including 'The Thunderbirds Are Go!' EP by Cliff and the Shadows – the success of the series was largely an accident. *Thunderbirds* was originally intended as a half-hour adventure, but when Lew Grade, head of ITC, saw the rushes he declared: 'This is too damned good for half an hour,' and instructed Gerry Anderson to make the shows fifty minutes each. Anderson solved the problem by inserting padding dialogue which allowed the puppets to develop real personalities. The Tracy sons in particular became highly individual characters and even had hobbies: Virgil, *Thunderbird 2*, played piano, Alan, pilot of *Thunderbird 3*, raced cars and had a romantic liaison with Tin Tin (Malaysian for 'Sweet'). This, together with the Andersons' perennial optimism about the future – humankind living in peace with itself and its servant, technology – sealed the show's crossover appeal to adults as well as children.

The series spawned two 120–minute movie spin-offs, *Thunderbirds Are Go*, 1966, and *Thunderbird Six*, 1968, both written by Gerry and Sylvia Anderson and directed by David Lane. In 1986 a Japanese-made cartoon series *Thunderbirds 2086* cashed in on the name. The thirty-two episodes have been seen in sixty-six countries and are still being transmitted. In Britain, repeats of the series run in 1991 achieved unprecedented ratings, members of *Fanderson*, the official *Thunderbirds* fan club, doubled, and manufacturers of *Thunderbirds* toys were caught on the hop by demand.

FAB.

Timeslip

UK 1970–1 26 × 30m col ITV. ATV Midlands. *cr* Ruth Boswell, James Boswell. *pr* John Cooper. *dr* John Cooper, Peter Jeffries, Ron Francis, Dave Foster. *wr* Bruce Stewart, Victor Pemberton. *cast* **Simon Randall** Spencer Banks **Liz Skinner** Cheryl Burfield **Frank Skinner** Derek Benfield **Jean Skinner** Iris Russell **Commander Traynor** Dennis Quilley. *Video* ITC.

'Have you ever had the feeling that you've been here before and yet everyone tells you you can't have been? Or perhaps you've felt that this has all happened to me before just like it's happening now, and I know what's going to happen next. Well, a lot of people do get these sensations and nobody can yet explain them.' *Timeslip* proclaimed its intention to educate loud and clear with this opener to its first episode, 'The Wrong End of Time', introduced by none less than Peter Fairley, the ITN and *Look In* science correspondent, who went on to elaborate on the concept of time travel. Part adventure story, part puzzle and part horror, the intelligent series told in four separate stories the tale of plucky Liz Skinner and shy but courageous Simon Randall, two children who discovered a Time Barrier that enabled them to travel into their own past and future, helping others but exposing themselves to danger. Time travel itself was painless. Encountering an invisible barrier in a Midlands village Liz and Simon simply fell through a 'hole' into another time and sometimes another location. When beyond the barrier Liz and Simon were able to see into the present, but were not themselves visible to those they had left behind. The contradictions of time travel could have perplexing results – when Liz was shot for instance she felt pain and saw blood but there was no wound because she did not exist in that time.

Also heavily involved in the adventures were Liz's parents Frank and Jean (whose telepathic link with her daughter enabled her alone to see Liz's experiences in other times) and the sinister figure of Commander Traynor, played by Dennis Quilley (also *The Tomorrow People*), a government scientist with hidden secrets and a greed for knowledge. Traynor, who rapidly emerged as star of the series, was seen altogether in five incarnations including as a clone.

Although it was a children's series, *Timeslip* took on adult themes such as the destruction of the Earth's climate, the dangers inherent in the progress of science and the inevitable interdependence of past and future. In story one (episodes 1–6), 'The Wrong End of Time', first Sarah, an educationally subnormal girl, and then Simon and Liz discover the hole in the Time Barrier and find themselves caught up in the middle of the Second World War, in a German raid on a secret radar establishment. In the second story, 'The Time of the Ice Box' (episodes 7–12) Liz and Simon find themselves in the Ice Box, an Antarctic research base in the year 1990 where a series of experiments is being carried out on humans including trials of longevity drug HA57. Liz meets her mother, an older version of herself (whom she dislikes) and her father – preserved in an ice block, the result of an earlier failed experiment. The most horrific discovery, which gave a whole generation of children sleepless nights, was the body of Australian Dr Edith Joynton who took a faulty dose of HA57 and aged dramatically to 100 years old. In story three, 'The Year of the Burn Up' (episodes 13–20), Simon and Liz find themselves in a future tropical jungle-style England in 1990, the scene of a project to alter world climates that is going disastrously wrong. They meet another, future friendly Beth and also Simon's future self, a clone known only as 2957. In the final story, 'The Day of the Clone' (episodes 21–6), Simon and Liz fall into a cloning experiment in the year 1965 – of which Traynor is the resulting clone (the real Traynor is found imprisoned).

The effect of the Time Barrier itself was achieved using a split-screen process whereby the same film was used twice, each time with a different half masked, thus allowing a character apparently to vanish into thin air. Acting, from such distinguished performers as Dennis Quilley and John Baron, was of a high standard. Among the regular cast, Spencer Banks who played Simon went on to star in two further ITV series, *Tightrope*, 1972, and a spy drama, *The Georgian House*, 1976, another time adventure. He also appeared in >*Crossroads*. Derek Benfield, who played Frank Skinner, became a familiar face to adult TV audiences in BBC's >*The Brothers* while Iris Russell had been 'Father' in one episode of >*The Avengers*.

Ruth Boswell, creator of the series together with her husband James, was later script editor and co-producer of the time-travel drama >*The Tomorrow People*.

The Tomorrow People

UK 1973–9 68 × 30m col ITV. Thames Television. *cr* Roger Price. *pr* Ruth Boswell, Roger Price, Vic Hughes. *dr* Paul Bernard, Roger Price, Stan Woodward, Vic Hughes, Leon Thau, Peter Webb, Peter Yolland. *wr* Roger Price, Brian Finch, Jon Watkins. *mus* Dudley Simpson, Brian Hodson. *cast* **John** Nicholas Young **Stephen** Peter Vaughn-Clarke **Elizabeth** Elizabeth Adare **Carol** Sammie Winmill **Kenny** Stephen Salmon **Tyso** Dean Lawrence **Mike Bell** Mike Holloway **Hsui Tai** Misako Koba **Andrew Forbes** Nigel Rhodes **Voice of TIM** Philip Gilbert **Jedekiah** Dennis Quilley.

'Let's jaunt, TIM!' The Tomorrow People were a precocious group of seventies children who had reached the next stage of evolution, Homo Superior, and consequently enjoyed special powers. These included telekinesis and telepathy, but most sensational of all the Tomorrow kids had the ability to teleport ('jaunt') themselves around the universe. Based in the 'lab' in a disused tunnel of London Underground, the Tomorrow persons protected planet Earth on behalf of the Galactic Federation. Conspicuously pacifistic, their most extreme measure against enemies terrestrial and alien (Jedekiah, a shape-changing robot, being the most original of them) was a stun-gun. A talking biotronic computer, TIM, helped the Tomorrow People access state information networks.

Over six seasons, membership of *The Tomorrow People* changed considerably, although John remained leader for the duration. Other longtime digital watch-wearing People were Elizabeth, Stephen and Mike (played by ex-*Flintlock* popster, Mike Holloway). In season one, actress Lynne Fredericks, later wife of Peter Sellers and David Frost, was beaten for the part of Carol by Sammie Winmill (*Doctor at Large*).

Intended by Roger Price (also *Pauline's People*) as an intelligent, entertaining juvenile series, *The Tomorrow People* developed a remarkable teen following in the seventies, despite tinfoil-type sets and, in later seasons, naff special effects (the show was hit by a fire on set and reduced production budget). Price got the idea for *The Tomorrow People* after meeting Dr Christopher Evans, author of psychic tome *The Mind in Chains* and, allegedly, a long talk with musician David Bowie. The show's plus points were a determinedly optimistic multi-ethnicity – the cast featured Far Eastern and black actors (Elizabeth Adare, in fact, stayed until the final curtain because of her awareness of her position as a role model for African-British youth) – and the sense of empowerment it offered: all teenagers, it suggested, could 'breakout' into being a Tomorrow person during adolescence.

The Tomorrow People, intended as ITV's answer to >*Dr Who*, ironically provided the TV début of actor Peter Davison, later to become the fifth incarnation of the BBC Time Lord. Davison appeared in the infamous 1975 'A Man for Emily' episode as Elmer, an alien who ran around London in silver briefs. Playing his wife, Emily, was actress Sandra Dickinson (he met her for the first time on the set) who later became his real-life spouse.

In 1992 *The Tomorrow People* was revived by an American cable company, Nickelodeon, in association with Roger Price and Tetra films. In a calculatedly shrewd piece of casting, Kristian Schmid, star of >*Neighbours*, was installed as the new leading Homo Superior.

Top Cat

USA 1961–2 30 × 22m col ABC. Hanna-Barbera. *UK tx* 1963 BBC1 (as *Boss Cat*). *cr* Joseph Barbera. *exec pr* William Hanna, Joseph Barbera. *pr* Berny Wolf, Jeff Hall. *dr* Ray Patterson. *wr* Various, including Barry Blitzer, Harvey Bullock and Ray Allen. *cast* (voices) **Top Cat** Arnold Stang **Benny the Ball** Maurice Gosfield **Choo Choo** Marvin Kaplan **Spook/The Brain** Leo DeLyon **Fancy-Fancy** John Stephenson **Officer Dibble** Allen Jenkins **Goldie** Jean Vander Pyl. *Video* Hanna-Barbera.

Top Cat, the indisputable leader of a gang of New York alley cats, was a feline cartoon version of Nat Hiken's *Sergeant Bilko* character. 'TC', as he was known to his close friends, was an irrepressible smart-alec con artist, who lived in a customised dustbin, stole milk from doorsteps, and used the local police phone for his own calls. He was always on the lookout for new money-making scams including, memorably, passing off tone-deaf sidekick Benny to the Carnegie Hall as the world-famous violinist Lazlo Lazlo ('The Violin Player'). Officer Dibble (voiced by B-movie regular tough guy Allen Jenkins) was the beat cop from the 13th Precinct who had the unenviable job of trying to keep TC and his five cohorts in check. The full line-up of the gang – all loosely based on the members of *Bilko*'s entourage – were: TC; fat Benny the Ball (voiced by Maurice Gosfield, the actor who played his human model Private Doberman); earnest Choo Choo; hip cat Spook; dim-witted Brain; and Fancy-Fancy, a ladies' tom. Since the series ended its original US broadcast, TC has been a running character on *The Fantastic World of Hanna-Barbera* and in 1987 appeared in a TV special entitled *Top Cat and the Beverly Hills Cats*. In Britain the series was transmitted as *Boss Cat*, since *Top Cat* was the brand name of a UK cat food.

The theme song: 'Top Cat/The most effectual Top Cat/Whose intellectual close friends get to call him 'TC'/Providing it's with dignity/Top Cat/The indisputable leader of the gang/He's the boss/He's a VIP/He's a championship/He's a most tip top Top Cat . . ./Yes – he's the boss/He's the king/But above everything/He's the most tip top . . . Top Cat!'

Torchy the Battery Boy

UK 1960 26 × 15m bw ITV. An AP Films Production for Associated Rediffusion Network. *cr* Roberta Leigh. *wr* Roberta Leigh. *dr* Gerry Anderson. *Video* Polygram.

Torchy the Battery Boy is a wind-up clockwork toy with a battery-powered lamp on his helmet. Helped by Mr Bumbledrop, Torchy has been sent by rocket to Topsy Turvy Land, a land where all mistreated or neglected toys from Earth can walk and talk as if they are human. The ruler of Topsy Turvy Land is King Dithers who lives in the Orange Peel Palace. Torchy lives in Frutown with his toy friends, except when he returns to Earth on one of his trips. Only Torchy and Pom-Pom, the French poodle, can return to Earth because they are clockwork, moving toys, although if Torchy's battery is too low he sometimes has trouble with the return trip.

Other characters included Flopsy the rag doll, Pilliwig the toy clown, Sparky the baby dragon, Squish the space boy, Pongo the rag doll pirate and Bossy Boots the Earth girl who is rude to everyone including Torchy but especially grown ups.

Creator Roberta Leigh was also creator of Anderson's first series *Twizzle*, 1957, which featured a boy doll of that name who could 'twizzle' his legs and arms longer and who, accompanied by cat Footso, set up a sanctuary for mistreated toys. Leigh went on to produce a series of her own, *Space Patrol*, set in the year 2100 and recounting the deeds of members of the peacekeeping United Galactic Organisation. Art director for *Torchy* was Reg Hill (later co-creator of >*Supercar*) and the show's puppetry supervisor was Anderson regular Christine Glenville.

The Tripods

UK 1982–5 22 × 30m col BBC1. BBC. *cr* John Christopher. *pr* Richard Bates. *dr* Graham Theakston, Christopher Barry, Bob Blagden. *wr* Alick Rowe, Christopher Penfold. *mus* Ken Freeman. *sfx* Robin Lobb, Steven Drewett, Kevin Molly, Steve Bowman, Simon Taylor, Michael Kelt. *cast* **Will Parker** John Shackley **Henry Parker** Jim Baker **Beanpole (Jean-Paul)** Ceri Seel **Fritz** Robin Hayter **Master 468** John Woodvine.

Tripods was one of the most expensive (£1 million plus) BBC sci-fi serials ever made, only to be ignominiously terminated in mid run by BBC1 Controller Michael Grade due to poor ratings and reviews. This was unfortunate because *Tripods* was actually superior kiddie-vid space opera. Based on the trilogy of novels of the same title by John Christopher (adapted for TV by Alick Rowe), *Tripods* was set in 2089 AD, when the Earth was ruled by aliens who travelled around in giant laser-firing three-legged machines. The aliens – bug-eyed monsters from Trion – had enslaved humanity, and ensured its docility by 'capping', a mind-control technique which involved the attaching of a triangular plate to the top of the head. English teenager Will Parker and his cousin Henry desired to remain free and, aided by a vagrant named Ozymandias, escaped to the White Mountains in Switzerland, where they joined a resistance to the Tripods known as The Network. Later, as members of The Network, they infiltrated the aliens' City of Gold, discovered vital information, hot-footed back to HQ, only to find it destroyed . . . at which point the BBC pulled the plug.

If the serial had a fatal flaw it was a handful of duff scripts (notably a tedious sojourn for the teenage heroes in a French château) in season one. Otherwise, *Tripods* was intelligent, commendably acted with well above average BBC special effects.

The Wacky Races

USA 1968–70 52 × 25m col CBS. Hanna-Barbera. *UK tx* 1969–70. *cr* William Hanna, Joseph Barbera. *pr* William Hanna, Joseph Barbera. *dr* Iawo Takamoto. *cast* **Dick Dastardly** Paul Winchell **Muttley** Don Messick **Penelope Pitstop** Janet Waldo **Red Max/Rufus Ruffcut/Rock and Gravel/Peter Perfect** Daws Butler **Luke and Blubber Bear/The General** John Stephenson **The Ant Hill Mob** Mel Blanc **Narrator** Dave Wilcock. *Video* First/SMO.

Cartoon saga of a madcap cross-country car race in which villainous Dick Dastardly machinated to win the title of The World's Wackiest Racer. Aside from Dastardly – and sniggering canine sidekick Muttley – in The Mean Machine, the other contestants and bizarre autos were: The Slag Brothers in the Bouldermobile; The Gruesome Twosome in the Creepy Coupé; Professor Pat Pending in the Convert-A-Car; Red Max in the Crimson Haybailer; 'glamour girl' Penelope Pitstop in The Compact Pussycat; Sarge and Meekly in the Army Surplus Special; The Ant Hill Mob in The Roaring Plenty; Luke and Blubber in the Arkansas Chugga-Bug; Peter Perfect in the Varoom Roadster; and Rufus Ruffcut and Sawtooth in The Buzz Wagon.

Dastardly never did win. The series was derived from the Lemmon–Curtis theatrical feature the *The Great Race* and marked a new, more anarchic phase of Hanna-Barbera output, with animation which was less technically complex. A massive and enjoyable hit none the less, the show led to two spin-offs: *The Perils of Penelope Pitstop* and *Dastardly and Muttley in their Flying Machines,* 1969, in which double-dealing Dastardly appeared as an incompetent World War I spy.

The Wombles

UK 1973 60 × 5m col BBC. Filmfair. *cr* Elisabeth Beresford. *dr* Ivor Wood. *mus* Mike Batt. *narr* Bernard Cribbins. *Video* Polygram.

'Underground, overground, wombling free,
The Wombles of Wimbledon Common are we,
Making good use of the things that we find,
Things that the everyday folks leave behind.'

Each week the furry, long velvety-nosed Wombles – pioneers on the ecology and recycling front – would exit from their burrow under Wimbledon Common and 'get wombling'. Wombling consisted of using brooms, bags and sheer Womble-force and ingenuity to rid the Common of those objects left behind by thoughtless humans. Sent on their eternal battle against litter by bespectacled Great Uncle Bulgaria in his tartan hat and shawl, dozy flowerpot-hatted Orinoco, industrious bespectacled Wellington, busy tweed-hatted Bungo and greedy bare-headed Tomsk would waddle engagingly over grass and past trees, white soles of their feet flapping, and carry home all manner of objects. There Tobermory, who wore mechanic's dungarees, would convert them in a twinkling into the very thing that was needed in the burrow that day. Week by week the Womble burrow was transformed into a veritable recycler's paradise, with newspaper-covered walls, old car doors, Womble telephone system and Tobermory's other Heath Robinsonesque contraptions. Womble possessions, clothing and bags all carried the distinctive 'W' in a circle logo. Presided over the wise and elderly Uncle Bulgaria and cooked and cared for by the French Madame Cholet these, together with Miss Adelaide, were a happy household leading fruitful and fulfilled lives. The only danger was that these foot-high creatures would be spotted by humans (only ever seen Womble-eye view to knee height) and have to appear on TV.

The Wombles were the creation of Elisabeth Beresford – she wrote all of the series episodes as well as twenty Womble books – and the stories were narrated with droll humour and in London twang by Bernard Cribbins. In 1974 Mike Batt brought the Wombles into the *Top of the Pops* studio with a series of eight chart-topping Wombles records and four top ten records – among them 'The Wombling Song', 'Remember You're a Womble' and 'Wombling Merry Christmas', with later records including 'Super Womble' and 'Let's Womble to the Party Tonight'. Merchandising aplenty followed. So successful were these bizarre puppets that they even got to star in their own feature film, *Wombling Free.*

In 1991 *The Wombles* were brought back in a new, half-hour adventure *The Wandering Wombles* from the original team of Beresford, Cribbins and Batt in which the furry conservationists went global. Tackling such ambitious matters as the destruction of Brazilian rainforests and the conservation of Kenyan elephants required the talents of new characters including Serengeti, the Womble on the spot in Kenya, and Brazilian Womble Obidos. Those Wombles left at home had to content themselves with a visit to aristocratic old Womble Osborne at a Royal Garden Party, where they found that even the Royals discarded Womble-friendly litter.

The Woodentops

UK 1955–8 Approx 160 × 15m bw BBC1. BBC. *cr* Freda Lingstrom, Maria Bird. *wr* Maria Bird. *mus* Maria Bird. *cast* (voices) Peter Hawkins, Eileen Brown, Josephina Ray.

For fifteen minutes every Friday *The Woodentops* filled the final segment of *Watch With Mother*, relating an eventful slice of middle-class life down on the farm, with the adventures of Mummy, Daddy and Baby Woodentop, twins Willie and Jenny, Mrs Scrubit the daily char, Sam the wellington-wearing farmhand, Buttercup the cow and, of course, the scene-stealing Spotty Dog, 'the biggest spotty dog you ever did see'. All the cast came with wires clearly attached. The original series lasted only three years, but repeats kept *The Woodentops* on the air until 1973. Audrey Atterbury and Molly Gibson pulled the family's strings.

The puppets – along with *Bill & Ben* – made headline news when they were stolen on the way to an exhibition for children in Edinburgh, and later turned up in a London auction room.

The X-Men

US 1992– 60+ × 30m col Fox. GRAZ Entertainment, Inc./Saban International Services, Inc. *UK tx* 1993– Sky1. *cr* Stan Lee, Jack Kirby. *exec pr* Stan Lee, Joe Calamari, Avi Arad. *pr* Scott Thomas, Larry Houston. *dr* Various, including Larry Houston. *wr* Various, including Martha Moran. *mus* Shuli Levy, Kussa Mahchi. *cast* (voices) Cedric Smith, Norm Spencer. Catherine Disher, Alison Sealy-Smith, Lenore Zann, Chris Potter, Cal Dodd, Alyson Court, George Buza.

Cyclops. Storm. Rogue. Gambit. Beast. Jubilee. Wolverine. Human mutants who have superpower (the 'X' refers to their X-tra capabilities) to fight the gallery of villains and dark forces who threaten to dominate the world in the chaotic twentieth century. Among the X-Men's chief foes are the maverick 'Master of Magnetism', Magento, and the Sentinels, vast Mutant-apprehending robots.

Although the X-Men (and women) are humanity's only hope for survival they are, perversely enough, persecuted by that selfsame humanity for their mutancy. No one chooses to be a mutant; it is a genetic accident which lies dormant until the subject reaches puberty, when the amazing powers emerge. Some mutants try to live quietly with the stigma; others strike out angrily and join mutant gangs such as the underground Morlocks; some take the third path and become X-Men, under X-Men mentor Professor Charles Xavier, whose dream is that someday humans and mutants might live in peace.

(And presumably X-Men with X-Men; the angst-ridden superheroes were studiedly prone to inter-personal conflict.)

It took thirty years for the X-Men to make the giant leap from the printed page of Marvel Comics (where they were created by Stan Lee and Jack Kirby) to TV, initially showing as guest stars in *Spiderman and his Amazing Friends*. On being given their own series they became the nineties rocket-powered, mega-hit of Fox's Saturday morning programming. *X-Men* was produced by Saban Entertainment (also >*Mighty Morphin Power Rangers*, >*Sweet Valley High*), with the animation provided – for reasons of cost – by studios in the Far East, such as Philipline Animation Studios and Hung Ying Animation. Marvel legend Stan Lee served as executive producer.

Yogi Bear

USA 1958–62 123 × 25m col. Hanna-Barbera. *UK tx* 1960–4 ITV. *cr* Joseph Barbera, William Hanna. *pr* Joseph Barbera, William Hanna. *wr* Warren Foster, Mike Maltese. *mus* Joseph Barbera, William Hanna. *cast* (voices) **Yogi Bear** Daws Butler **Ranger John Smith** Don Messick **Boo Boo** Don Messick.

Artful, genial, pork pie-hatted Yogi Bear ('I'm smarter than the average bear') was consumed by one overriding goal: to purloin the 'pic-a-nic' basket from the picnickers, who swarmed into his home territory of Jellystone National Park, by whatever ingenious means necessary. The merest whiff of blueberry pie and Yogi's brain would begin conjuring up fanciful and elegant schemes.

Aided and nervously abetted by faithful and admiring bear cub Boo Boo, the nonconformist bear's other aim in life was to torment his perpetual adversary Ranger John Smith by narrowly avoiding being caught or punished for his deeds. Warnings and punishments proved of no avail. Such was the pleasure for the viewer – and indeed for Yogi – of this enduring, traditional cartoon-style conflict that when the Ranger threatened to disappear from Yogi's life the bear acted speedily to lure him back. In one episode, 'Home, Sweet Jellystone', Ranger Smith inherits

He was smarter than the average bear, Boo Boo, and the scourge of picnickers in Jellystone National Park. He was Yogi Bear, Hanna Barbera's ratings-topping cartoon superstar.

his uncle's estate and leaves Jellystone Park, but Yogi, missing 'his worthy opponent' pretends to go on hunger strike. The dismayed Ranger returns and the old disorder is happily restored. Yogi's other ongoing relationship was a recurring romantic attachment in the form of Southern belle girlfriend Cindy Bear whose breathlessly girlish exclamation 'Ah do declare' became another of the show's catchphrases.

Yogi Bear started life as the third segment of *The Huckleberry Hound Show* (along with >*Huckleberry Hound*, *Pixie and Dixie* and *Hokey Wolf*) but proved to be the most popular and durable of the four. By 1960 Yogi and Boo Boo were ratings-topping superstars and in 1961 they were given a series of their own, Hanna-Barbera's third half-hour series *The Yogi Bear Show*. In 1964 Yogi became the star of Hanna-Barbera's first feature-length cartoon *Hey There It's Yogi Bear*, in 1973 the boisterous bear was joined by Huckleberry Hound and Snagglepuss and travelled round the country in a balloon called the Ark Lark in the hour-long series *Yogi's Gang;* Yogi also featured in various TV specials – *Yogi's First Christmas*, 1980, *Yogi's Great Escape*, 1987, and *Yogi and the Magical Flight of the Spruce Goose*, 1987.

Daws Butler and Don Messick who between them voiced the *Yogi Bear* characters were Hanna-Barbera cartoon voice stalwarts. Daws Butler spoke, among others, for Snagglepuss and Huckleberry Hound. Messick lent his oral skills to Scooby Doo, Bamm Damm, Rubble and Dino.

Melodrama & Adventure

The A-Team

USA 1983–7 4 × 120m/90 × 60m col NBC. Stephen J Cannell Productions/Universal TV. *UK tx* 1984–8 ITV. *cr* Brandon Tartikoff, Frank Lupo, Stephen J Cannell. *exec pr* Stephen J Cannell, Frank Lupo, John Ashley. *pr* Gary Winter. *dr* Various, including Bernard McEveety, Christian I Nyby Jr, Ron Satlof, Arnold Laven, Dennis Laven, Michael O'Herlihy, Tony Mordente, David Hemmings, Bruce Kessler. *wr* Various, including Stephen J Cannell, Frank Lupo, Thomas S Szollosi and Richard Christian Matheson, Stephen Katz, Mark Jones, Bill Nuss. *mus* Mike Post, Pete Carpenter. *cast* **Col John 'Hannibal' Smith** George Peppard **Lt Templeton 'Faceman' Peck** Dirk Benedict (Tim Dunnigan in pilot episode) **Capt HM 'Howling Mad' Murdock** Dwight Schultz **Sgt Bosco 'B A' Baracus** Mr T **Amy Amanda 'Triple A' Allen** Melinda Culea **Gen Hunt Stockwell** Robert Vaughn **Frankie 'Dishpan' Sanchez** Eddie Velez. *Video* CIC/SMO.

In 1972 an elite US Special Forces unit, or A-Team, in Vietnam robs the Bank of Hanoi. Unfortunately, an accident back at HQ means that they are not able to prove this was a legitimate act of war, and they are imprisoned by their own government for larceny. However, they escape back to the USA, spending the next ten years underground, hiring themselves out as benevolent mercenaries. Leader of the A-Team was cigar-chewing Colonel 'Hannibal' Smith (George Peppard), a master of disguise. 'Faceman' Peck (Dirk Benedict, also >*Battlestar Galactica*) was the Number Two and a handsome con man. 'Howling Mad' Murdock was their

pilot, while giant black sergeant B A ('Bad Attitude') Baracus provided the driving and engineering skills plus the musclepower. As B A was less than keen on flying, it was necessary to dope him whenever the team needed to plane it on an assignment. In their first season the vigilante combo was aided by a woman journalist, Amy Allen; in their last they were joined by 'Dishpan' Sanchez.

The A-Team was unquestionably one of the most meretricious and soporific shows ever made. The story-lines never changed: each episode ended with the team assembling an awesome array of firepower (made out of bits of old junk) and a battle which made Khe Sahn look like a village fireworks party. Yet, nobody ever got hurt – even the baddies – despite the explosions and whizzing bullets. The US flag flew high and wide over the series, although few bothered to notice the paradox of saluting lawlessnes in the name of maintaining order. None of this dissuaded millions (14.6 million at its 1984 British peak) from tuning in. Many of these were pre-teens who idolised actor Mr T (Lawrence Tero, born Lawrence Tureaud), whose grunting, comic-book version of B A (catchphrase: 'Watch it, sucker') was the show's main attraction. In fact, *The A-Team* was virtually created for Mr T after NBC programme chief Brandon Tartikoff saw him as Clubber Lang in the movie *Rocky III*. Mr T earned around $1 million per year for his work on *The A-Team*, and was assiduous in building his kiddie following with merchandise opportunities such as his autobiography, *Mr T: The Man with the Gold*, and a Mr

T doll. Despite this, as the eighties progressed Mr T's career went inexorably downhill. *The A-Team* slipped in the ratings – in Britain it was taken off the air after complaints about its violence – and cast members began to object to Mr T's arrogance. Increasingly, Mr T's unsophisticated strong-arm act came to be seen as an undesirable role model for black youths.

Adam Adamant Lives!

UK 1966–7 26 × 50m BBC. *cr* Verity Lambert, Tony Williamson. *pr* Verity Lambert. *dr* Various, including Leonard Lewis, Laurence Bourne, Moira Armstrong, Anthea Browne-Wilkinson, Ridley Scott, Philip Dudley, Paul Ciappessoni, William Slater, David Proudfoot. *wr* Various, including Tony Williamson, Vince Powell and Harry Driver, John Pennington, Richard Harris. *mus* David Lee (theme), Hal Sharper and David Lee, performed by Kathy Kirby. *cast* **Adam Adamant** Gerald Harper **Georgina Jones** Juliet Harmer **William E Sims** Jack May. *Video* BBC/TECHN.

'Bold as a knight in white armour,
Cold as a shot from a gun,
If you should look for a man who loves danger
To whom Love is a stranger – this man is the one'
Adam Adamant theme song.

From its Bond-style signature tune and swirling sixties title graphics onwards, *Adam Adamant* was a child of its time. Made a few years after >*The Avengers* it had the same male/female dynamic partnership at its core, the same slick production and a similar tongue-in-cheek humour (co-creator Tony Williamson was a writer on *The Avengers*). But while the earlier series looked back to rural picture-book Britain, *Adam Adamant* was firmly rooted in a beatnik jazz-age London of Soho strip joints, protection rackets and scooter-riding youths armed with flick knives.

Dashing Adam Adamant, England's gallant defender ('Not dancing Adam?' 'Not while my country is at stake!'), however, was actually from the Edwardian age – he had been kidnapped and entombed in a block of ice back in 1902 by evil fiend The Face. Sixty-four years later the bemused adventurer thawed out in Soho. Now aged ninety-nine, though still with the body of a thirty-five-year-old, and armed only with a sword, antique clothing and archaic language, he was forced to adjust to the high-speed new age, aided by swinging, boyish chick-about-town Georgina Jones. Georgie (as she called herself) worked as a DJ in a disco and was the quintessential mod girl with 'gear' to match. Each episode provided her with a minimum of three costume changes. She also just happened to have long been a fan of Adamant (her grandfather had been an acquaintance of his). Together Adam Adamant and Georgie took on assorted gangsters, foes of the nation and military fanatics, none of whom proved a match for the hero's individual style. Adam was a rum old cove who quickly picked up the new lingo ('Piece of the action? Yes, I like that!') although he never quite adjusted to Georgie's new-fangled, unfeminine behaviour.

Inspired in concept, *Adam Adamant* proved to be just as good in its execution. Witty and stylish, with some experimental photography – directors included Philip Dudley and, for the segment 'The League of Uncharitable Ladies', Ridley Scott (later to direct features *Alien*, *Blade Runner*, *Someone to Watch over Me*) – it cleverly cashed in on the dual appeals of *fin de siècle* gallantry and sixties hip, melded together with good old-fashioned adventure plots.

The Adventures of Robin Hood

UK 1956–60 143 × 30m bw ITV. A Sapphire Films Production for ITC. *USA tx* 1955–8 CBS, syndicated. *exec pr* Hannah Weinstein. *dr* Ralph Smart, Dan Birt, Bernard Knowles, Arthur Crabtree, Terence Fisher, Lindsay Anderson, Bernard Knowles, Terry Bishop, Don Chaffey, Anthony Squire, Robert Day, Gerry Bryant, Peter Maxwell, Ernest Borneman, Peter Seabourne, Compton Bennett, Gordon Parr. *wr* Ralph Smart, Eric Heath, Anne Rodney, John Dyson, Paul Symonds, James Aldridge, C Douglas Phipps, Paul Dudley, Neil R Collins, Arthur Baer, John Cousins, Albert G Ruben, Norma Shannon, Warren Howard,

Norman Best, Peter Kay, Charles Early, Francis Nesbitt, Ernest Borneman, Milton S Schlesinger, Alan Moreland, Basil Dawson, Sidney Wells, Clare Thorne, Aileen Hamilton, Leighton Reynolds, James Carhart and Nicolas Winter, Michael Connor, Carey Wilbur, Leslie Poynton, Shirl Westbury, Robert Newman, Oliver Skene, Leon Griffiths, Samuel B West, George and Gertrude Fass, R W Bogany, Arthur Dales, Peter Yeldham, Philip Bolsover, Raymond Bowers, Louis Marks, Jan Read, William Templeton, Owen Holder, Alan Hackney, Palmer Thompson, Wilton Schiller. *mus* (theme) Dick James. **cast** **Robin Hood** Richard Greene **Maid Marian** Bernadette O'Farrell/Patricia Driscoll **Little John** Archie Duncan/Rufus Cruikshank **Friar Tuck** Alexander Gauge **Will Scarlett** Ronald Howard/Paul Eddington **Derwent** Victor Woolf **Alan-a-Dale** Richard Coleman **Prince John** Hubert Gregg/Brian Haines/Donald Pleasance **Sheriff** Alan Wheatley **Deputy Sheriff** John Arnatt **Prince Arthur** Pete Asher/Richard O'Sullivan/Jonathan Bailey **Joan** Simone Lovell. *Video* ITC/POL-R.

This dashing tale of combat in a noble cause was Britain's first costume series – the knights and soldiers were kitted out in chain-mail made of knotted string sprayed with silver paint – and one of fledgeling ITV's first successes. It went straight into the top ten in the ratings, ran to 143 episodes and was the first of TV tycoon Lew Grade's transatlantic sales (it was shown on the CBS network within days of its opening in Britain). Even the stirring title music was ITV's first hit theme.

TV's first *Robin Hood*, with Richard Greene as the swashbuckling hero, was faithful to legend. It was set in the Nottingham area in the last years of the twelfth century when noble King Richard the Lionheart was away on crusades in the Holy Land and evil Prince John schemed to usurp the throne. One nobleman, Robin of Locksley, remained loyal to King Richard and, outlawed by Prince John, became Robin Hood the rebel hero. From their home in Sherwood Forest he and the Merry Men set about thwarting the Prince and the Sheriff, by robbing the rich to give to the poor. Robin's true love, the lovely Lady Marian Fitzwalter, helped him in his noble crusade. Threats facing this early radical figure included ambushes and traps set by the no-good Sheriff, unscrupulous moneylenders, the necessity of hiding in wine barrels to rescue Friar Tuck from an evil Abbot, the forced marriage of Maid Marian to an untrustworthy knight and the burning of an innocent woman at the stake as a witch.

Those travelling to Sherwood Forest to find the series' locations, though, would be sorely disappointed. Shot at Nettlefold Studio, Walton-on-Thames, *Robin Hood* pioneered new techniques in film making which enabled the unit to change an entire set in six minutes and turn out a twenty-six minute programme every four and a half days. Rather than use cinema-style permanent sets, art director Peter Proud substituted interchangeable props on wheels – mobile baronial fireplaces, staircases, corridors and entrance halls, speedily moved into position, were all used again and again from different angles. Two trees-on-wheels – one a real twenty-foot-high hollow tree-trunk on a fake mossy bank, the other a wood and plaster fabrication with an overhanging branch – served as the majority of the famed Sherwood Forest.

Many of the series' guest stars went on to become the greats of British TV. They included Leo McKern, Thora Hird, Joan Sims, Nicholas Parsons, Jane Asher, Ian Bannen, John Schlesinger, Sidney James, Leonard Sachs, Patrick Troughton, Irene Handl, Lionel Jeffries, Wilfred Brambell, Patrick Cargill, Harry H Corbett, Billie Whitelaw and Nigel Davenport. Richard Greene was made rich enough by the series to retire to Ireland and breed horses.

Robin Hood has since returned to British TV in a variety of incarnations. In 1977 Martin Potter portrayed the green-garbed hero as an early freedom fighter in *The Legend of Robin Hood*, BBC. In 1984 Richard Carpenter's *Robin of Sherwood* (HTV/Goldcrest) starred Michael Praed (>*Dynasty*, *Riders*) and then Jason Connery as the legendary outlaw. This was a mystical sword-and-sorcery epic in which a young and virile Robin was called into action by Herne the Hunter, stag-headed god of the forest. The multi-award-winning comedy series *Maid Marian and her Merry Men* (BBC1, 1991), meanwhile, written by and starring Tony 'Baldrick' Robinson as the Sheriff of Nottingham, unearthed the 'true story' of what happened in Sherwood Forest – Maid Marian (Kate Lonergan) did all the work and Robin Hood (Wayne Morris) took all the credit, with occasional help from Danny John-Jules (the ship's cat in >*Red Dwarf*) and Patsy Byrne (better known as 'Nursey' in >*Blackadder*). On the wide screen Douglas

Fairbanks donned tights for the 1922 silent version, Errol Flynn played a romantic lead in *The Adventures of Robin Hood*, 1938, in 1964 *Robin and the Seven Hoods*, set in gangland Chicago, starred Frank Sinatra, Dean Martin, Bing Crosby, Sammy Davis Jnr and Peter Falk; Walt Disney made an animated version, *Robin Hood*, in 1973, and *Robin and Marian* (1976) starred Sean Connery and an all-star cast including Audrey Hepburn as Maid Marian.

The story of a blacklisted Hollywood writer Asa Kaufman arriving in London to work anonymously on episodes of the series formed the backdrop for the film *Fellow Traveller* (Philip Saville, 1989) and most recently Kevin Costner (*Robin Hood: Prince of Thieves*, 1991) and Patrick Bergin (*Robin Hood*, 1990) have struggled for box office dominance.

The Adventures of Robin Hood spawned a whole series of imitators and its influence can be seen on >*The Buccaneers* (1956) which starred Robert Shaw as a reformed seventeenth-century pirate, >*The Adventures of William Tell* (1957), once described as 'Robin Hood in the Alps', and *Sword of Freedom* (1957) which starred Edmund Purdom as as fifteenth-century Italianate version of the character.

The Adventures of Sir Lancelot

UK 1956–7 30 × 25m bw ITV. A Sapphire Films Production for ITC. *USA tx* 1956–7. *exec pr* Hannah Weinstein. *pr* Sidney Cole, Dallas Bower, Bernard Knowles. *dr* Ralph Smart, Bernard Knowles, Arthur Crabtree, Anthony Squire, Terry Bishop, Laurence Huntington, Peter Maxwell, George More O'Farrell, Desmond Davies. *wr* Leslie Poynton, Ralph Smart, Leighton Reynolds, John Ridgley, Peggy Philips, Harold Kent, H H Burns, Selwyn Jepson, Peter Key. *mus* Edwin Astley. *cast* **Sir Lancelot du Lac** William Russell **Queen Guinevere** Jane Hylton **King Arthur** Bruce Seaton/Ronald Leigh-Hunt **Merlin** Cyril Smith **Brian** Robert Scroggins.

This costume actioner owed much to >*The Adventures of Robin Hood* and was filmed on the neighbouring set at Nettlefold Studios. William Russell (who cropped up thirty years later as Rita Fairclough's lover in >*Coronation Street*) played a brilliantined Sir Lancelot du Lac, King Arthur's bravest knight and Queen Guinevere's champion. As the theme song put it, 'he rode the wilds of England, adventures for to seek'. These usually consisted of rescuing kidnapped knights, kidnapped queens and, preferably, kidnapped princesses in towers. Though fondly remembered, in truth the series was unexceptional, save for the dramatic fight scenes and the seventh-century period detail, which was based on specially commissioned research from Oxford University. Probably the series' greatest legacy was that it provided actor Patrick McGoohan with an early role in 'The Outcast' episode and so introduced him to one of *Sir Lancelot*'s mainstay directors and writers, Ralph Smart. When Smart later came to devise >*Danger Man*, he cast McGoohan in the lead part and so propelled him to stardom and, eventually, >*The Prisoner*.

The Adventures of William Tell

UK 1957 39 × 25m bw ITV. ITC. *USA tx* 1958, syndicated. *cr* Leslie Arliss. *pr* Leslie Arliss, Ralph Smart. *dr* Ralph Smart, Peter Maxwell, Terry Bishop, Quentin Lawrence, Anthony Squire, Ernest Morris. *wr* Various, including Rene Wilde, Leslie Arliss, Doreen Montgomery, John Kruse, Ralph Smart, Lindsay Galloway, Larry Forester, Michael Connor, Martin Worth, Max Savage, Paul Christie, Ian Stuart Black, Arnold Abbott, Roger Marshall. *mus* Harold Durrell (theme song). *cast* **William Tell** Conrad Phillips **Hedda** Jennifer Jayne **Walter** Richard Rogers **Gessler** Willoughby Goddard **Fertog (The Bear)** Nigel Greene. *Video* ITC.

Tights and arrows epic, set in fourteenth-century Switzerland, and based on Johann von Schiller's famous story about the freedom fighter against Austrian occupation. Conrad Phillips played William Tell (whose legendary act of marksmanship, shooting an apple off his son's head, was relived in episode one) and Willoughby Goddard the thoroughly perfidious and corpulent

Austrian Governor, Landburgher Gessler. To capture and kill Tell, Gessler (wonderfully overhammed by Goddard) used every dirty trick conceivable, including assassins disguised as resistance heroes and kidnapping Tell's wife, Hedda. Gessler even once 'framed' Tell for a crime against the Swiss in an effort to make them renounce their outlaw leader.

Given the decade of its production, it is tempting to see anti-McCarthyite references in *William Tell* (as there certainly are in >*The Adventures of Robin Hood*), but the series is more obviously a commentary on World War II, concerning as it does an hegemonic Germanic power which organises slave-labour camps and takes mass hostages (Landburgher Gessler was definitely not an adherent of the Geneva Convention). One episode, 'The Magic Power' is a retelling of the Albert Einstein–Atom bomb story.

Filmed on location in Snowdonia (a surprisingly convincing stand-in for the Swiss Alps) and the National Studio, Elstree, the series had a quiverful of yet-to-be-famous British actors in early appearances: Michael Caine ('The Prisoner' and 'The General's Daughter' episodes), Christoper Lee ('Manhunt'), and Donald Pleasence (the torturing Austrian commander in 'The Spider'). Imaginative scripts, shining performances, and virile fight sequences all made this one of the peaks of fifties adventure TV. Conrad Phillips – who appeared in the 1989 TV version of the Tell story, *Crossbow*, as the hero's avuncular mentor – even looked good in hose.

Baywatch

USA 1989– 100+ × 30m col NBC/All American Television/The Baywatch Production Company. *UK tx* 1990– ITV. *cr* Gregory Bonann. *exec pr* Douglas Schwartz, Michael Berk, Gregory Bonann, David Hasselhoff. *dr* Various. *wr* Various. *cast* **Lt Mitch Bucannon** David Hasselhoff **Shauni McLain** Erika Eleniak **Eddie Kramer** Billy Warlock **Lt Stephanie Holden** Alexandra Paul **C J Parker** Pamela Anderson-Lee **Matt Brody** David Charvet **Police Sergeant Garner Ellerbee** Greg Allan-Williams **Hobie Bucannon** Brandon Call/Jeremy Jackson **Caroline Holden** Yasmine Bleeth **Logan Fowler** Jaason Simmons.

On every continent of the globe, with the exception of Antarctica, a total of one billion viewers in more than 110 countries kept a weekly appointment with the men and women of *Baywatch*.

Made by the aptly named All American TV *Baywatch* did not overly trouble its pretty head with subtlety or complexity. After all, it was set on the ultra-filmic sun-kissed shoreline of Southern California, where beautiful bodies glistened and flexed against a background of rolling surf. Who needed more?

Such narratives as the show contained centred on a corps of Los Angeles County Lifeguards, who patrolled a mile-long beat near Malibu and whose courage and compassion was clear and as deep as their tans. At work, their hours were packed with action and danger (in one *Jaws*-inspired episode lifeguard Jill Riley was eaten by a shark); off-duty their time was filled with love, relationships and hokey emotions.

Baywatch was conceived by Californian Gregory J. Bonann who, aged seventeen, got a summer job as a lifeguard to help pay for business school. Bonann's idea was for a show with spectacular scenery and breath-stopping (and starting) lifeguard adventure where each one of the victims had a story and so did each one of the guards. It took him ten years to find a taker for his dream but, as luck would have it, his sister married a TV producer called Douglas Schwartz. In 1987 Schwartz, Bonann and Schwartz's cousin Michael Berk collaborated on a script for a two-hour movie, *Baywatch: Panic at Malibu Pier* which was sold to NBC and broadcast in spring 1989. NBC decided to commission a season of prime-time episodes – which flopped; given mouth-to-mouth resuscitation by Bonann and star David Hasselhoff (who put up his own money), however, it aired an off-network syndication from September 1990, and became the most watched show in the world.

The show's nominal star was caring hunk Lt Mitch Bucannon, a life-long lifeguard and single father, played by David Hasselhoff (6 foot 4; 185 lbs), late of >*Knight Rider*, who also served as executive producer on the series. Mitch was the father of junior lifeguard Hobie, aged thirteen, but also father to the whole 'Baywatch family'. An early storyline followed earnest Mitch's custody battle with his ex-wife, Gayle (he won). After a decent interval, Mitch – curiously unmoved by the

David Hasselhoff, star of lifeguard melodrama *Baywatch* – dubbed 'Barewatch' on account of its acres of revealing tanned flesh. Cancelled after its first season, it was resuscitated by an injection of Hasselhoff's own cash and went on to become one of the most popular shows in the history of global TV.

mountains of female flesh around him – began dating newspaperwoman Kay Morgan (played by Hasselhoff's real-life wife, Pamela Bach). Later, Mitch began an affair with Lt Stephanie Holden, who would become supervisor of the Will Rogers lifeguard station.

But the real celebrity of *Baywatch*, however, was C J Parker, played by Pamela Anderson, blonde stereotype made flesh. Canadian Pamela Anderson was 'discovered' at a British Columbia Lions football game. Dressed in a Labatt's Beer T-shirt, her pneumatic image was transmitted on the stadium's wide screen and when appreciative fans cheered she was brought down and introduced to the crowd. From there a commercial contract with Labatt's led on to two seasons in the top-ten ABC Television hit series *Home Improvement*, as Lisa, the Tool Time Girl, which she left to go full-time on *Baywatch*. She has now been immortalised as 'Baywatch Barbie', complete with mandatory plunge-line bikini.

With ratings so dependent upon the desirability of its performers, *Baywatch* took care to offer a full range of physical appeal (if a narrow range of acting skills). Thus, among those joining the *Baywatch* rookie lifeguard programme vying for a chance to join the elite corps was Shauni McLain (Erika Eleniak, like Anderson a former *Playboy* Playmate) and later dark-haired athletic Caroline Holden, impressionable younger sister of Lt Stephanie Holden. Women viewers, meanwhile, could variously admire Matt Brody, played by French-born ex-model (Bugle Boy, Levi's, Coca-Cola) David Charvet or cocky Australian lifeguard Logan Fowler, the bad boy of *Baywatch* played by Tasmanian Jaason Simmons, star of *Paradise Beach*. Tough but lovable police sergeant Garner Ellerbee lent racial diversity while Hobie Bucannon, played by Brandon Call and then Jeremy Jackson, gave young viewers a would-be lifeguard to identify with. Jackson, like the show's star, had pretensions to sing. A recording artist on David Hasselhoff's record label Hassechits, he opened for his co-performer's highly successful European concerts.

After five years the seemingly invincible *Baywatch* formula began to show signs of fatigue. A spin-off detective series, *Baywatch Nights*, only generated modest success. In 1996 it was revealed that Hasselhoff had ordered a *Baywatch* paycut in the face of sinking ratings and spiralling costs.

Beverly Hills 90210

USA 1990– 100+ × 50m col Fox. Twentieth Century Fox/Torand Productions/Spelling Entertainment Inc. *UK tx* 1991– ITV/Sky One. *cr* Darren Star. *exec pr* Charles Rosin. *pr* Aaron Spelling, Darren Star, Sigurjon Sighvatson. *dr* Various, including Tim Hunter, Charles Braverman, D Attias, Burt Brinckerhoff, Darren Star, Corey Allen, Paul Lazarus, Michael Katleman, David Carson, Bill D'Elia, Eric Laneuville. *wr* Various, including Charles Rosin, Darren Star, Steve Wasseman, Jessica Klein, Amy Spies. *mus* John E Davis. *cast* **Brenda Walsh** Shannen Doherty **Brandon Walsh** Jason Priestley **Jim Walsh** James Eckhouse **Cindy Walsh** Carol Potter **Kelly Taylor** Jennie Garth **Steve Saunders** Ian Ziering **Dylan McKay** Luke Perry **Andrea Zuckerman** Gabrielle Carteris **David Silver** Brian Austin Green **Donna Martin** Tori Spelling **Scott Scanlon** Douglas Emerson **Nat** Joe E Tata **Chris Suiter** Michael St Gerard **Henry Thomas** James Pickens Jr **Emily Valentine** Christine Elise. *Video* V-COL Cinema Club/Video collection.

Attractive sixteen-year-old twins Brenda and Brandon Walsh have just moved to glamorous Beverly Hills with their parents Jim and Cindy. Once settled they start at exclusive West Beverly Hills High where all the kids are rich and beautiful (or if they're not they get a nose job), have houses like film sets, cars to die for and wardrobes straight out of style magazines. Beverly Hills, it might be said, is totally cool. The Walshes, on the other hand, are from Minneapolis and they have old-fashioned values. Jim is an executive with an accounting firm and he and his home-making wife Cindy are still very much in love. They have a respectable house, an adequate car and all the clothes they need.

This is the premise of megahit *Beverly Hills 90210*, number one show amongst American viewers aged twelve to seventeen. Originally titled *Class of Beverly Hills*, but changed to incorporate the ZIP code of the area, the show was given a clear brief from the Fox Broadcasting Network to appeal to teenagers, but to take them seriously. It was to foreground the difficult issues that today's teens face: Aids, date rape, cancer, addiction, divorce and teenage sexuality. (Each episode in the US ends with a public service announcement about the week's problem and a list of helpful phone numbers.) Consequently, viewers soon learned that the kids of West Beverly High might be rich but they had their problems. Kelly, leader of the hippest brat pack at the school and Brenda's snobby best friend, had an alcoholic mother; Steve, Kelly's jaded ex-boyfriend, communicated with his TV star mom Samantha Saunders only via intercom; rebel Dylan, Brandon's best friend and Brenda's boyfriend, had a father who was indicted for corporate financial fraud; over-achiever Andrea, bespectacled poor-girl editor of the school newspaper, actually lived in the downtown San Fernando Valley but used her grandmother's address in Beverly Hills to enrol; Donna, Kelly's shopaholic sidekick, had a learning difficulty.

The pill of good intent and social realism, though, was sugared by *90210*'s opulent background and by the fact that the teens acting out the traumas were an ensemble of young heartthrobs – primary amongst them Jason Priestley (later to use his sensuous appeal to good effect in Pepe Jeans ads), Luke Perry and Shannen Doherty (the most-watched relationship in *90210* was that between Brenda and Dylan whose affair took a major turn at the end of the first season when they made love in the episode 'Spring Dance'). Fan clubs sprang up from Minnesota to Memphis, sixteen million people tuned in and grateful producers indulged their viewers with merchandising ranging from sheets and pillows stamped with pictures of Perry and Priestley to beach towels, notebooks, coffee mugs and even Sindy-sized dolls of *90210* characters.

There were some cast losses over the years. Shannen Doherty left, followed by her erstwhile screen lover, Luke Perry, whose character Dylan McKay departed in a 1995 episode entitled 'One Wedding and a Funeral'. This saw his cliff-top marriage to gangster's daughter Toni Marchette (Rebecca Gayheart) end in a bloodbath only topped by that of >*Dynasty*'s Amanda Carrington to Prince Michael of Moldavia, which came complete with post-nuptial terrorists.

Most of the young stars had TV credits behind them before the show. Shannen Doherty played roles in *Father Murphy, Little House: A New Beginning, Highway to Heaven, Our House*, and (as Heather Duke) the movie *Heathers*. Luke Perry appeared in the daytime dramas *Loving* and, with co-star Gabrielle Carteris, *Another World*; Jason Priestley starred in the Disney Channel TV

California dreaming, the cast of teenage hit *Beverly Hills 90210*. Originally titled *Class of Beverly Hills*, but changed to incorporate the area's elite zip code, the show paraded pecs and Porsches but also an array of pubescent problems. A telephone helpline ran after each episode broadcast in the States. Twins Brandon (Jason Priestley, centre) and Brenda (Shannen Doherty, far right) were the series' main pin-ups.

movie *Teen Angel Returns* (where his co-star was fellow 90210er Jennie Garth) and motion pictures *Watchers*, *The Boy Who Could Fly* and *Nowhere to Run*. His TV credits include appearances in >*Quantum Leap* and >*McGyver* and the role of orphan Todd Mahaffey in NBC's sitcom *Sister Kate*. Brian Austin Green played Brian Cunningham, Donna Mills' son, in *Knots Landing*, and Tori Spelling, daughter of producer Aaron Spelling, played Violet Bickerstaff in NBC series *Saved by the Bell*.

Beverly Hills 90210 producer Aaron Spelling was also producer of >*Charlie's Angels*, >*Starsky and Hutch*, >*Dynasty* and *The Colbys*. In 1991 *Beverly Hills 90210* launched a spin-off series with similar success. Called *Melrose Place*, the show was essentially *90210* with an older cast list.

The Boat (Das Boot)

West Germany 1985 1 × 90m/4 × 55m col. Bavaria Atelier.
UK tx 1984 BBC2. *cr* Lothar Gunther-Bucheim. *pr* Gunther
Rohrbach. *dr* Wolfgang Petersen. *wr* Wolfgang Petersen.
mus Klus Doldinger. *cast* **Der Kapitan** Jurgen Prochnow **Lt
Werner** Herbert Grunemeyer **Chief Engineer** Klaus
Wennemann **First Lt** Hubertus Bengsch **Second Lt** Martin
Semmelrogge **Bridge Officer** Bernd Tauber **Ullmann** Martin
May **Johann** Erwin Leder.

Made simultaneously with the abridged, and inferior,
movie version, *The Boat* recorded the lupine missions of
German submarine U-96 on patrol in the Atlantic and
Mediterranean in 1941. Directed with skill and panache
by Wolfgang Petersen, who used Steadicam to capture the
interior claustrophobia of the U-boat, it gave a rare, but
far from propagandist, view of World War II from the
other side. Of his cast Petersen said: 'I didn't want
recognisable faces, for that destroys credibility.'
However, in Jurgen Prochnow who played the young but
wily Kapitan, he found a screen charismatic, one whose
subsequent appearances include the Madonna feature
Body of Evidence. Equally unforgettable was the narrow,
sinister *Boot* itself (a life-size, seventy-metre model,
accurate down to the last bolt). The visceral score was by
Klaus Doldinger. With a handful of exceptions –
>*Combat*, and comedies like >*M*A*S*H* and >*Dad's
Army* – war has not been well served by the small screen.
The Boat was TV at its most sublime.

Developed from Lothar Gunther-Bucheim's 1974
autobiographical novel, *Das Boot*, the series was
transmitted in Britain before its German release.

The Borgias

UK 1981 10 × 50m col BBC2. BBC *cr* Mark Shivas. *pr* Mark
Shivas. *dr* Brian Farnham. *wr* John Prebble, Ken Taylor. *mus*
Georges Delerue. *cast* **Roderigo Borgia** Adolfo Celi **Cesare
Borgia** Oliver Cotton **Guiliano della Rovere** Alfred Burke
Lucrezia Borgia Anne Louise Lambert **Juan Borgia** George
Camiller.

Adolfo Celi as Pope Alexander VI in the unintentionally
hilarious fifteenth-century dynastic saga *The Borgias*. The
show received a letter of complaint from the Vatican for its
portrait of the pontiff as a mumbling lover of orgies and
incest.

Unintentionally hilarious dynastic drama – and blatant attempt to reproduce the success of the classic *I Claudius*, 1976 – about fifteenth-century Roderigo Borgia, also known as Pope Alexander VI. Roderigo was famously impious, being the sire of seven bastard offspring, the most unpleasant of which was Cesare Borgia (the model for Machiavelli's *The Prince*), closely followed by the poisoning Lucrezia. What reduced the serial to 'Carry On' levels of farce was Sicilian actor Adolfo Celi's fractured, mumbling command of English (frequently reduced to an exasperated, 'Cesare, Cesare, Cesare'), plus several orgy scenes, one of which required the cast to crawl half-naked on the floor picking up chestnuts with their mouths. The show has the distinction of a formal note of censure from the Vatican. A Borgia music album and cassette were released to accompany the serial.

The Brothers

Uk 1972–6 52 × 45m col BBC1. BBC. *cr* Gerald Glaister, N J Crisp. *pr* Various, including Gerald Glaister, Bill Podmore. *dr* Various, including Ronald Wilson, Quentin Lawrence. *wr* Various, including N J Crisp. *mus* Dudley Simpson. *cast* **Mary Hammond** Jean Anderson **Edward Hammond** Glyn Owen/Patrick O'Connell **Brian Hammond** Richard Easton **David Hammond** Robin Chadwick **Jennifer Kingsley** Jennifer Wilson **Ann Hammond** Hilary Tindall **Carol Hammond** Nicola Maloney.

In his will Robert Hammond, owner of the Midlands-based Hammond Transport Services, left mistress Jennifer Kingsley a sizeable shareholding in the firm. This proved irksome to his wife Mary and three rivalrous sons, brusque Edward, boring Brian, and young David. Episodes related the subsequent struggle between dragon-like Mary and prim, sensitive Jennifer as well as the inter-filial strife. The producers astutely kept the grimy intricacies of the haulage business in the background, and concentrated on large measures of bedroom affairs and boardroom wranglings. It was one of the first family feud soaps, an early British version of >*Dallas*. Playing the baddie was Brian's wife Ann, bitchy

and ambitious. Actress Kate O'Mara (>*Triangle*) vamped it up as the boss of an airfreight business, and Gabrielle Drake (>*UFO*, >*Crossroads*) was one of David's several girlfriends. Towards the end, though, *The Brothers* ran out of fuel.

The Buccaneers

UK 1956–7 39 × 30m ITV. A Sapphire Films Production for ITC. *USA tx* 1956–7 CBS. *exec pr* Hannah Weinstein. *pr* Sidney Cole, Ralph Smart, Pennington Richards. *dr* Ralph Smart, Terry Bishop, Leslie Arliss, Robert Day. Pennington Richards, Peter Maxwell, Bernard Knowles, Peter Hammond. *wr* Thomas A Stockwell, Terence Moore, Zacary Weiss, Peter C Hodgking, John Cousins, Peggy Philips, Alan Moreland, Roger McDougall, Basil Dawson, Alec G Ruben, Peter Rossano, Marion Myers, Neil R Collins, Phillis Miller. *mus* Edwin Astley, Albert Elms and Kenneth V Jones. *cast* **Captain Dan Tempest** Robert Shaw **Lieutenant Beamish** Peter Hammond **Governor Woodes Rogers** Alec Clunes **Blackbeard** Terence Cooper **Crewman Benjy** Hugh David **Crewman Armando** Edwin Richfield **Crewman Taffy** Paul Hansard **Crewman Gaff** Brian Rawlinson **Crewman Van Bruch** Alex Mango **Crewman Dickon** Wilfrid Downing.

Television's first pirate series, featuring swashbuckling adventure on land and high seas. Set in the West Indies in the 1720s (although shot, like its predecessor >*The Adventures of Robin Hood*, in a studio in Walton-on-Thames), *The Buccaneers* told the rousing tale of reformed pirate Dan Tempest as he battled against buccaneers and Spanish attack. The story began with the arrival of Governor Woodes Rogers at the Caribbean pirate stronghold, New Providence island (the series, unusually, did not introduce its hero, played by actor Robert Shaw, star of *The Dam Busters*, 1955, *From Russia with Love*, 1963, *A Man for all Seasons*, 1966, *Jaws*, 1975, until episode three). The new governor pardoned all those who swore allegiance to the King – among them legendary adventurer Dan Tempest. He, after Rogers had left New Providence in the hands of young Deputy Governor Lt Beamish, went on to sail his ship *The Sultana* in the service of the Crown, braving constant threats of attack from arch-rival Blackbeard and Spanish warships, encountering stowaways, deserted galleons, ghost ships and women in need of protection. Still a rebel at heart, though, Tempest stopped at nothing to defend the weak, poor and needy, bending rules wherever necessary to bring meat to families dying of starvation or to save innocent men unjustly sentenced to hanging.

This seafaring drama proved an obvious audience winner for ITV, and *Sir Francis Drake* (1961–2 ABC/ATV) soon followed in *The Buccaneers'* wake. It featured the adventures of the eponymous sailor, adventurer and confidant of Queen Elizabeth I aboard his ship *The Golden Hind*, and starred Terence Morgan as Drake, Jean Kent as Queen Elizabeth I. Michael Crawford (also *Some Mothers Do 'Ave 'Em*) played John.

Combat

USA 1962–7 127 × 60m bw/25 × 60m col ABC. Selmur Productions. *exec pr* Selig Seligman. *pr* Gene Levitt, Robert Blees, Robert Altman, Burt Kennedy. *dr* Robert Altman, Vic Morrow, Gene Levitt, Dick Caffey, Burt Kennedy. *wr* Robert Altman, Robert Blees, Robert Pirosh, Gene Levitt, Burt Kennedy, Vic Morrow, John F D Black. *mus* Leonard Rosenman. *cast* **Lt Gil Hanley** Rick Jason **Sgt Chip Saunders** Vic Morrow **PFC Paul 'Caje' Lemay** Pierre Jalbert **Pvt William G Kirby** Jack Hogan **Littlejohn** Dick Peabody **Doc Walton** Steven Rogers **Doc** Conlan Carter **Pvt Braddock** Shecky Greene **Pvt Billy Nelson** Tom Lowell.

Two of the great TV series about war, >*M*A*S*H* and *Combat*, benefited from the influence of director Robert Altman (also *Whirlybirds*, >*Maverick*, >*Route 66*, >*Bonanza* and the feature films *Come Back to the Five and Dime, Jimmy Dean, Jimmy Dean, The Long Goodbye, McCabe and Mrs Miller, Nashville, The Player*). While M*A*S*H was absurdist comedy, *Combat* – following the exploits of a US Army platoon fighting its way across Europe during World War II following D-Day – was a stark, *verité* drama which drew on Altman's own World War II experiences. Not only did the series provide Altman with his first opportunity to direct 'mini movies' for TV, he also helped cast, write and produce it.

If the stories of *Combat* ranged from straight war action to human interest to occasional humour, the overall tone was uncompromisingly anti-war, and emphatic in its realism, with original World War II battle footage included in some of its episodes. Its characters were portrayed as martyrs to the whimsical fortunes of war, condemned to agonise over their own moral responsibilities while others were sent to die useless deaths under orders from incompetent officers. *Combat*'s platoon regulars included Private Braddock, joker and resident hustler, Caje, the sly Cajun, Doc Walton, sensitive medical orderly, 'Wild Man' Kirby and Littlejohn. Out in front were the stars of the show – tough, rugged leaders Sergeant Chip Saunders (Vic Morrow) and Lieutenant Gil Hanley (Rick Jason).

Combat was not a high-gloss production (each episode cost only $110–115 thousand) and the team would film one episode while preparing another, editing a third and preparing the script of two or three for the future. The series was filmed at MGM's famous Lot Two which had a French village complete with lakes, bridges, forest and train stations remaining from previous productions. Its 'look', however, was outstanding, the natural accompaniment to its gritty story material: scenes were deliberately cobwebbed, obscured by smoke or fog, dazzled by sunlight, cloaked in moonlight or glimpsed in heavy weather. As often as not the camera was mobile. (This naturalistic visual style won cameraman Hauser an Emmy nomination in the first season.) The first episode, 'Forgotten Front', directed by Altman, told of a German POW captured by the Combat squad behind enemy lines. When he became a liability they were forced to face the moral dilemma of how to dispose of him. 'Off Limits' dealt with a complex personal triangle and was an essay on love and guilt; 'The Volunteer' was about a French boy whose hero-worship of the American platoon led him to a deadly meeting with a German officer; this last was shown at the Venice Film Festival.

But the most memorable of the first season's segments was the final one directed by Altman before he left the series. The episode was 'Survival', which had previously been blocked, but which Altman pushed through when the production office was in a period of confusion; the script, by John F D Black, had virtually no dialogue or plot, concentrating on Vic Morrow's character wandering crazed and wounded through an hour of intense reverie against a background of smoke and fire, fallen timber and desolate battlefields. Much of it was filmed by Altman in harrowing, extreme close-up with mobile camera. The soundtrack was reduced to the sounds of a babbling brook, howling wind, thunder, and inchoate sobbing. The episode ended with Morrow carrying the body of a dead German whom, in his hallucinatory state he had mistaken for his brother, stumbling into the path of an oncoming tank brigade. (Morrow won an Emmy nomination for Best Actor for this segment.) Executive producer Seligman's anger on finding out that the episode had been filmed led to a row in which Altman was either fired directly or left before he was fired. Altman told an American TV guide, 'Seligman wanted action. I wanted to do the war stories you couldn't do in 1946.' He had directed thirteen of the first season's twenty-six episodes.

Combat won huge critical respect – actors such as Charles Bronson, James Caan and Dennis Hopper queued up to appear in it – and was solid in the Nielsen ratings for five and a half years. In its fifth year the show moved to colour photography, but was cancelled shortly afterwards by the studio, so that it could be sold to syndication.

Star Vic Morrow (who also wrote and directed episodes of *Combat*) had previously won attention in feature *The Blackboard Jungle* (1955). After the series, he directed and co-produced the film of Jean Genet's *Deathwatch*, 1966, co-written with wife Barbara Turner, but never directed another film and only acted sporadically. He died on 23 July 1982 in an accident on the set of *The Twilight Zone* movie.

Coronation Street

UK 1960– 4000+ 30m bw/col ITV. Granada TV. *cr* Tony Warren. *pr* Various, including H V Kershaw, Bill Podmore, Tim Aspinall, Susi Hush, Eric Prytherch, Mervyn Watson, Carolyn Reynolds, Pete Eckersley, Stuart Latham, David Liddiment, Derek Granger, Jack Rosenthal, Richard Everitt. *dr* Various, including Quentin Lawrence, Lawrence Moody, June Wyndham-Davies, Cormac Newell, Richard Argent, Gareth Morgan, Joe Boyers, Carol Wilks. *wr* Various, including Tony Warren, H V Kershaw, Vince Powell, John Finch, George Reed, Cyril Abraham, Adele Rose, Peter Tomkinson, Harry Driver, Kay McManus, Malcolm Lynch, Susan Pleat and Les Duxbury, Ken Blakeson, Geoffrey Lancashire, Esther Rose, John Temple, Jack Rosenthal, John Stevenson, Barry Hill, Peter Eckersley, Paula Milne, Julian Roche, Kay Mellor. *mus* Eric Spear. *cast* **Ena Sharples** Violet Carson **Elsie Tanner** Pat Phoenix **Annie Walker** Doris Speed **Hilda Ogden** Jean Alexander **Stan Ogden** Bernard Youens **Minnie Caldwell** Margot Bryant **Ken Barlow** William Roache **Bet Gilroy (Lynch)** Julie Goodyear **Len Fairclough** Peter Adamson **Albert Tatlock** Jack Howarth **Ray Langton** Neville Buswell **Jack Walker** Arthur Leslie **Leonard Swindley** Arthur Lowe **Martha Longhurst** Lynne Carol **Rita Fairclough** Barbara Knox **Emily Bishop (Nugent)** Eileen Derbyshire **Ernie Bishop** Stephen Hancock **Billy Walker** Kenneth Farrington **Betty Turpin** Betty Driver **Maggie Clegg** Irene Sutcliffe **Mike Baldwin** Johnny Briggs **Eddie Yates** Geoffrey Hughes **Mavis Wilton** Thelma Barlow **Derek Wilton** Peter Baldwin **Alf Roberts** Bryan Mosley **Audrey Roberts** Sue Nicholls **Valerie Barlow** Anne Reid **Gail Platt (Tilsley)** Helen Worth **Brian Tilsley** Christopher Quinten **Ivy Brennan** Lynn Perrie **Don Brennan** Geoff Hinsliff **Alma Sedgewick** Amanda Barrie **Vera Duckworth** Elizabeth Dawn **Jack Duckworth** William Tarmey **Alec Gilroy** Roy Barraclough **Curly Watts** Kevin Kennedy **Ernie Bishop** Stephen Hancock **Suzie Birchall** Cheryl Murray **Raquel Wolstenhulme** Sarah Lancashire **Terry Duckworth** Nigel Pavaro **Percy Sugden** Bill Waddington **Phyllis Pearce** Jill Summers **Reg Holdsworth** Ken Morley **Des Barnes** Philip Middlemass **Steph Barnes** Amelia Bullmore **Maureen Holdsworth** Sherrie Hewson **Jim McDonald** Charles Lawson **Liz McDonald** Beverly Callard **Kevin Webster** Michael Le Vell **Sally Webster** Sally Whitaker. *Video* Windsong 'Granada'.

'Mondays and Wednesdays, I live for them. Thank God, half past seven tonight and I shall be in Paradise.'
Sir John Betjeman, Poet Laureate, on *Coronation Street*.

Originally to be titled *Florizel Street* – until Agnes, a Granada TV tea lady, pointed out that Florizel sounded like a disinfectant – this nostalgic look at the inhabitants of a terraced working-class backstreet in the fictional

Manchester suburb of Weatherfield is the world's longest-running TV serial. It is also, with 18 million plus viewers per episode, Britain's most popular. Created by Tony Warren (also writer of the film, *Ferry Across the Mersey*), the *Street* has changed markedly since its first episodes, which were kitchen-sink dramas, with grim-up-north characters (curler-wearing char Hilda Ogden, hairnet harridan Ena Sharples) and storylines. In 1964 the show was given a lighter tone which has continued until today, despite a brief brush with social realism under the reign of producer Susi Hush (later >*Grange Hill*). Of the major British soaps, it is the least interested in 'issues'. Indeed, the *Street*'s time-trapped fiftiesness virtually precludes them; hence the rareness of black and Asian characters in Weatherfield.

Aside from its reassuring good-old-days proletarian cosiness, the *Street* provides the TV equivalent of over-the-fence neighbourhood gossip, telling 'everyday' tales of petty scandals, local adulteries (most famously that between Mike Baldwin and Deirdre Barlow in 1983, which was actually reported in *The Times*), and family strife. Although the show's highest viewing figure, 27 million, was for the 1987 episode in which Alan Bradley tried to murder lover Rita Fairclough, owner of the Kabin newsagents, such high drama is rare. In a shrewd pitch at the main viewing base of soap operas, *Coronation Street* has made something of a speciality of strong women characters: cut-glass Annie Walker, landlady of The Rovers Return, home-maker Gail Platt, gossipy Martha Longhurst (sadly killed off), dithering Mavis Wilton, brassy barmaid Bet Gilroy, and the queen of the street, tarty Elsie Tanner (Pat Phoenix). The *Street*'s women, though, have noticeably softened over the years. Rita Fairclough's past as an exotic dancer has been successfully shaken off, while the man-eaters Audrey Roberts (Sue Nicholls, also >*Crossroads*) and Alma Sedgewick (Amanda Barrie, previously Cleopatra in the film *Carry on Cleo*) have become tamed. Even Elsie Tanner ended up being almost respectable.

Despite its resolutely Northern English setting, *Coronation Street* has sold around the world, from Hong Kong to Nigeria. The only country which proved immune to its charms, initially at least, was the USA, where Lord Bernstein of Granada TV could not give it away. Nonetheless, the US ABC network was so envious of the *Street*'s success that it created a neighbourhood soap of its own: >*Peyton Place*.

Although they may now be embarrassed by the fact, many well-known acting names started out with minor roles in the Weatherfield drama. They number: Joanna Lumley (Ken Barlow's girlfriend in 1973), Prunella Scales, Mollie Sugden, Martin Shaw (as hippie Robert Croft), Arthur Lowe (whose portrait of Leonard Swindley was made into a short series, *Pardon the Expression*, 1965), Joanne Whalley-Kilmer, Davy Jones, Michael Elphick, Gordon Kaye, Stephanie Turner, Kenneth Cope and Richard Beckinsale.

Crossroads

UK 1964–88 4510 × 25m bw/col ITV. ATV/Central TV. *cr* Hazel Adair and Peter Ling. *pr* Reg Watson, Eric Fawcett, Jack Barton, Phillip Bowman, William Smethurst, Michele Buck. *dr* Various, including Alan Coleman, Kenneth Carter, Jack Barton, Michael Hart, Dennis Vance, Rollo Gamble, Tim Jones, Jonathan Wright-Miller, Sid Kilbey. *wr* Various, including Peter Ling, Hazel Adair, Andrew Hill, Ted Dicks, Jon Rollason, Michaela Crees, David Garfield, Arthur Schmidt, Evadne Price, Ken Attiwill, Paul Erickson, Malcolm Hulke, Keith Miller, Barbara Clegg, Stewart Farrar, Paula Milne, Gerald Kelsey, Julian Spilsbury. *mus* Tony Hatch (theme), Max Early and Raf Ravenscroft (1987 theme). *cast* **Meg Richardson** Noele Gordon **Kitty Jarvis** Beryl Johnstone **Dick Jarvis** Brian Kent **Jill Harvey (née Richardson)** Jane Rossington **Sandy Richardson** Roger Tonge **Penny Richardson** Diane Grayson **Brian Jarvis** David Fennell **David Hunter** Ronald Allen **Barbara Hunter** Sue Lloyd **Vince Parker** Peter Brookes **Paul Ross** Sander Eles **Diane Parker (Lawton)** Susan Hanson **Benny Hawkins** Paul Henry **Carlos Rafael** Anthony Morton **Josephine Rafael** Gillian Betts **Amy Turtle** Anne George **Mr Lovejoy** William Avenell **Myrtle Cavendish** Gretchen Franklin **Marilyn Gates** Sue Nicholls, Nadine Hanwell **Adam Chance** Tony Adams **Hugh Mortimer** John Bentley **Paul Stevens** Paul Greenwood **Shughie McFee** Angus Lennie **Sid Hooper** Stan Stennett **Nicola Freeman** Gabrielle Drake **Tommy 'Bomber' Lancaster** Terence Rigby **John Maddington** Jeremy Nicholls.

The Queen of Soap Opera, Noele Gordon as tragic motel owner Meg Richardson in *Crossroads*. Infamously poor in scripts, acting and sets, the show was parodied by comic Victoria Wood as *Acorn Antiques*.

A Midlands-based soap of infamously poor quality. The Crossroads Motel first opened its doors in 1964 as ATV's answer to Granada's Northern soap, >*Coronation Street*. Although savaged by the critics (ATV's production chief Bill Ward was so embarrassed by the show's reception he petitioned for its closure), it soon developed a large, loyal following, even challenging *Coronation Street* for ratings supremacy in the late seventies (its highest viewing figure, 17.6 million, came in January 1987). The Midlands drama, however, remained dogged by criticism of its poor production values, which became a byword for cheap television. Not until 1972 could ATV supremo Sir Lew Grade persuade the other ITV companies to network the show. On a 'better fewer but better' basis the number of *Crossroads* episodes was reduced from five – it began life as the UK's first daily serial – to four per week. The IBA, still aghast at the dire state of *Crossroads* scripts and acting, ordered a further cut to three episodes per week in 1980. It was in vain.

Set in King's Oak on the edge of an industrial conurbation, the eponymous motel was ruled over for most of its existence by matriarch Meg Richardson (played by ex-*Lunch Box* performer Noele Gordon) and her family. Even by the standards of soap opera, the Richardsons were a tragic clan: undoubtedly, the motel's most frequent visitor was Misfortune. Meg herself was blasted out of the hotel in 1967 by an accidentally detonated wartime bomb, and was subsequently imprisoned for dangerous driving. Then her amour Hugh Mortimer married another woman, leaving Meg to the devices of Malcolm Ryder, who tried to poison her. On an uncharacteristically happy note, Meg and Hugh finally got hitched to each other in 1975 – but then Hugh was kidnapped by terrorists, and died of a heart attack. In 1981 the motel burned to the ground. Meg was presumed to be inside, but was later discovered on the *QE2* liner sailing to a new life Down Under and thus out of the serial. Outraged viewers campaigned for her return, leading to a phenomenon one newspaper called 'Megomania'; actress Noele Gordon, despite being so unceremoniously removed from *Crossroads*, graciously referred to her tenure as a 'long and lovely velvet rut'.

Meg's daughter Jill was even more of an unfortunate. Over *Crossroads'* near twenty-four years Jill was married three times (once to a bigamist), had a baby by her stepbrother, became a drug addict, became an alcoholic, had two miscarriages and a nervous breakdown. Surprisingly perhaps, Jill was the only member of the original cast (indeed, she uttered the show's immortal first words, 'Crossroads Motel, may I help you?') to endure until the final episode. Her brother Sandy, meanwhile, was disabled in a motor accident.

After Misfortune, the most regular guest at Crossroads was Inconsistency. Characters came and went without explanation. The dim-witted, woollen hat-wearing Benny, for example, once disappeared for six months from the series after 'going to fetch a spanner'. The staff failed to notice in 1984 that the layout of the motel changed completely over forty-eight hours without the intervention of a builder. And the mole on the face of Barbara Hunter, wife of sometime motel manager David Hunter (Ronald Allen, also *Compact* and *United*), he of the cavernous 'hellos', moved from episode to episode.

It has been estimated that 20,000 actors and actresses passed the portals of *Crossroads*. Among those who also served were Diane Keen, John Finch, Arthur Marshall, Larry Grayson (as Meg's wedding chauffeur), Gretchen Franklin (later Ethel in *Eastenders*) and Stephanie de Sykes, whose motel rendition of 'Born with a Smile on my Face' reached number two in the record charts in 1974. And de Sykes was not the only singing member of the cast; Sue Nicholls, who subsequently moved to *Coronation Street*, released a single, 'Where Will You Be When I Need You?'. Of the show's backroom staff, the initial producer Reg Watson went on to create Australian supersoap, >*Neighbours*, and the classic melodrama >*Prisoner: Cell Block H*.

With hindsight, the motel fire storyline can be seen as marking the beginning of the end of *Crossroads*. Without Meg Richardson the show lost its focus, even its *raison d'être*. The serial's producers in the eighties – Phillip Bowman, William Smethurst and Michele Buck – tried various devices to boost the show's post-Meg appeal, most of which involved taking the soap upmarket, even retitling it *Crossroads, King's Oak*. Gabrielle Drake (>*UFO*) was brought in as sexy, sophisticated motel manager Nicola Freeman. All this was to misunderstand *Crossroads'* allure: it was popular precisely because it *was* cheap, tacky and utterly unbelievable. Of the British soaps, *Crossroads* has been the closest to the original American daytime model. The series was created by *Compact* writers Hazel Adair and Peter Ling.

Dallas

USA 1978–91 356 × 60m col CBS. Lorimar Studios. *UK tx* 1978–91 BBC1. *cr* David Jacobs. *exec pr* Philip Caprice. *pr* Leonard Katzman. *dr* Various, including Larry Hagman, Patrick Duffy, Leonard Katzman, Michael Preece, Corey Allen, Barry Crane, Linda Gray. *wr* Various, including David Jacobs, Arthur Bernard Lewis, Camille Marchetta, Rena Down, D C Fontana, Richard Fontana. *mus* Jerrold Imel (theme), John Parker. *cast* **John Ross (J R) Ewing** Larry Hagman **Eleanor Southworth (Miss Ellie) Ewing** Barbara Bel Geddes/Donna Reed (1984–5) **John Ross (Jock) Ewing** Jim Davis **Bobby Ewing** Patrick Duffy **Pamela Barnes Ewing** Victoria Principal **Lucy Ewing Cooper** Charlene Tilton **Sue Ellen Ewing** Linda Gray **Ray Krebbs** Steve Kanaly **Cliff Barnes** Ken Kercheval **Gary Ewing** David Ackroyd/Ted Shackleford **Valene Ewing** Joan Van Ark **Kristin Shepard** Mary Crosby **Dusty Farlow** Jared Martin **Donna Culver Krebbs** Susan Howard **Mitch Cooper** Leigh McCloskey **John Ross Ewing III** Tyler Banks/Omri Katz **Afton Cooper** Audrey Landers **Rebecca Wentworth** Priscilla Pointer **Clayton Farlow** Howard Keel **Katherine Wentworth** Morgan Brittany **Mickey Trotter** Timothy Patrick Murphy **Mark Graison** John Beck **Jenna Wade** Morgan Fairchild/Francine Tacker/Priscilla Presley **Christopher Ewing** Joshua Harris **Peter Richards** Christopher Atkins.

Dallas, the tale of a rich and powerful Texan family who lusted after power, money and sex. Created by David Jacobs (who wrote the drama without ever visiting the oil-rich state), it was produced by Lorimar, and was a sort of inversion of the studio's earlier show, the homily-laden, >*The Waltons*.

The Ewings were a fabulously wealthy family who had built their empire on cattle and oil. They had also been feuding with the Barnes for over forty years, ever since Ewing patriarch Jock had manoeuvred partner Digger Barnes out of his oil fortune and his true love, Eleanor Southworth. In 1978, however, Jock and Miss Ellie's youngest son Bobby brought his beautiful young bride home to Southfork Ranch, the Ewing's sprawling home in Braddock, Texas. Her name was Pamela Jean Barnes and she was Digger's daughter. But if Romeo Bobby and Juliet Pamela were prepared to let bygones be bygones, other members of their families still wanted to feud – principally Pam's brother, Cliff, and Bobby's brother, stetson-hatted J R. The eldest of the three Ewing brothers and the central figure in Ewing Oil, J R was ruthless, power-hungry and continually unfaithful to his wife, Sue Ellen, even after she had borne him a son, John Ross Ewing III. Brother Bobby, who had all the morals and integrity his older brother lacked, was a particular thorn in J R's side. Middle Ewing brother Gary, meanwhile, was unable to compete with his strong-willed siblings, and only occasionally appeared in *Dallas* to visit his petite blonde daughter Lucy who resided under the Southfork roof. (He did, though, get his own spin-off series, *Knot's Landing*.) Lucy spent much of her time seducing a queue of men, among them ranch manager Ray Krebbs, later revealed to be Jock's illegitimate son and therefore a Ewing.

Dallas was originally known as 'The Linda Evans Project' and was created as a vehicle for the star, who was under contract to CBS. But as the project progressed, her designated role as Pamela was seen as 'unworthy' of her talent and she dropped out of the show. (By the time of >*Dynasty*, though, the star's thoughts on such soapy roles had changed.) Robert Foxworth, the handsome star of *The Black Marble*, was offered the part of J R, but wanted the character softened. This didn't fit with the producers' plans and so Larry Hagman, the long-suffering straight man of sixties comedy series >*I Dream of Jeannie* got the role. At the time Patrick Duffy, fresh out of the water from >*The Man from Atlantis* was thought to be the star male attraction as Bobby, but Hagman turned in a virtuoso performance as evil J R, making him one of the most memorable villains in TV history.

Once up and running, *Dallas* pushed audience credulity to the very limit. Tragedy, murder, corruption, adultery, alcoholism and illegitimate offspring were apparently the norm above a certain income down south. Jock had a heart attack, Miss Ellie (Barbara Bel Geddes, also the Hitchcock film, *Vertigo*) found she had cancer, Pam discovered that Digger was not her dear old dad, but an imposter who had murdered her real father. Marriages and divorces proliferated. J R and Sue Ellen separated

The man they loved to hate, J R Ewing, in *Dallas*, a torrid tale of Texan oil folk. The villainous part was originally offered to Robert Foxworth before Larry Hagman, the son of singer Mary Martin and previously star of *I Dream of Jeannie*, made it his own.

and later remarried. After her failed union with Mitch, Lucy had an ill-fated affair with Mickey Trotter, but Mickey was seriously injured in a car accident caused by a drunken Sue Ellen. While he was lying brain-dead in hospital, Ray Krebbs (Steve Kanaly, a Vietnam veteran whose experiences were used by John Milius in the writing of the movie *Apocalypse Now*) pulled the plug on his life-support system. Then Pam, after telling Bobby on her carphone that she could have children, died as she drove into a lorry.

Such seething Southern melodrama proved addictive viewing. By early 1980 *Dallas* was the most popular television series in the world (members of Turkey's parliament even cut short a meeting in order to catch an episode). And the best was still to come, the cliff-hanging 'Who Shot J R?' episode. (Actually occasioned by the fact that Larry Hagman was in contract dispute, and Lorimar were uncertain as to whether he would return.) Viewers the globe over had to wait all summer 1980 to discover who the arch-villain's unseen assailant had been. The episode that opened the 1980–1 autumn season was the highest-rated individual show in history, and the answer to the question was Kristin Shepard, his wife's sister, who was pregnant with his child.

It was not only J R who survived near-death in *Dallas*. The show's stars had a habit of being born again. Miss Ellie apparently had the world's first successful head transplant in 1984 when Donna Reed stepped into the part, only to return to her former self a year later. Meanwhile Gary Ewing looked at different times like both Ted Shackleford and David Ackroyd, and Jenna Wade was characterised by three actresses: Morgan Fairchild, Francine Tacker and Priscilla Presley. The greatest of all the *Dallas* rebirths, however, was Bobby Ewing's. Bobby was killed in a hit-and-run car accident in 1985 (his last words, 'Be a family'). But ratings sagged and star Larry Hagman made a personal appeal to Patrick Duffy to rejoin the cast. A full season later Pam had remarried and was on her honeymoon when the formerly deceased Ewing emerged from the shower asking for a towel. The happenings of the previous series, it transpired, had been nothing but a bad dream.

By the end of the eighties, though, despite the import of such stars as Gayle Hunnicut (as Vanessa Beaumont) and Lesley-Anne Down (as Stephanie Rogers), the ratings began to fall and the show was cancelled after the 1990–1 season. In the final episode, 'Conundrum', J R's world seemed to have crashed down around him. His business was gone – Ewing Oil now belonged to Cliff – his family was dispersed, even Southfork had been turned over to Bobby by Miss Ellie. As J R drank and contemplated suicide, an apparition named Adam (Joel Grey of *Cabaret* fame) appeared to show him what life would have been like if he had never been born (*It's a Wonderful Life* turned upside down). Finally the 'angel' Adam's eyes flashed red, J R raised a pistol and a shot rang out. Bobby burst into the room and only he, not the viewer, saw what had happened.

Dr Kildare

USA 1961–6 142 × 60m bw/58 × 30m col NBC. Arena Productions in association with MGM-TV. *UK tx* 1961–6 BBC. *exec pr* David Victor. *pr* Norman Felton, Herbert Hirschman, David Victor. *dr* Leonard Horn, Alf Kjellin, Don Medford, Ralph Senensky, Lawrence Dobkin, Michael Ritchie, James Goldstone. *wr* Various. *mus* Jerry Goldsmith. *cast* **Dr James Kildare** Richard Chamberlain **Dr Leonard Gillespie** Raymond Massey **Dr Simon Agurski** Eddie Ryder **Dr Thomas Gerson** Jud Taylor **Receptionist Susan Deigh** Joan Patrick **Nurse Zoe Lawton** Lee Kurty.

Dr Kildare brought bit-part actor Richard Chamberlain to TV stardom in the role of the handsome, dedicated intern of large, metropolitan Blair General Hospital. The young doctor, eager to learn about his profession, was given guidance and inspiration in his efforts by crusty father figure Dr Gillespie (Raymond Massey), senior medic in Kildare's speciality of internal medicine. The action-packed series (with dramatic freeze-frame titles) featured realistic portrayals of hospital life and tense dramatisations of life-and-death struggles, all attended by the fully committed, idealistic hero.

Dr Kildare built up an audience of 15 million within a year and Richard Chamberlain attracted a legion of young female fans and over 35,000 letters a month. The actor's image was closely guarded during the series' run, antiseptic, clean-living Richard Chamberlain, it was claimed, never drank, smoked or swore (facts that Chamberlain, once free of the part, refuted). So closely was the actor identified with his role that viewers believed Chamberlain himself was a physician and used to ask his advice on medical problems. Over the course of the series Kildare progressed from intern to newly promoted resident to mature, self-assured doctor. His stern colleagues from the first season, Doctors Agurski and Gerson, were absent from later seasons and the programme focused more closely on the patients and their families. (Observant viewers would also have noticed that Kildare's promotion brought a change in hairstyle; once qualified, as the British *Radio Times* noted, the doctor's hair was lightened and coiffured with 'a long professional lock swept back on the left side'.)

Dr Kildare was first aired on television in 1961 (the same year also saw the début of American channel ABC's rival medical series *Ben Casey*, starring Vince Edwards as the neurosurgeon). Having started out as a once-weekly, one-hour programme, in 1965 it moved to a twice-weekly, half-hour format and began to develop more of a serial nature, with stories running up to seven episodes in length. After five years in the role Chamberlain felt he had exhausted its possibilities and the series ended production in 1966.

The character of Dr Kildare was based on the short stories written by Frederick Schiller Faust under the pen name of Max Brand (also the pseudonym used by the prolific Faust for hundreds of Western novels including his classic *Destry Rides Again*). The character of Dr Kildare was first seen on the screen in over fifteen successful feature films from 1937, where the part was taken by Lew Ayres (dropped from the role in 1942, after declaring himself a conscientious objector). Gillespie was played by Lionel Barrymore. A radio series was broadcast in 1939. The Kildare stories were also seen in a 1972 syndicated TV series called *Young Doctor Kildare* (MGM, 1972) starring Mark Jenkins as Kildare and Gary Merrill as Gillespie.

The Duchess of Duke Street

UK 1976–80 31 × 50m col BBC1. BBC-TV/Time-Life Television. *cr* John Hawkesworth. *pr* John Hawkesworth. *dr* Bill Bain, Cyril Coke, Simon Langton, Raymond Menmoui, Gerry Mill. *wr* Julian Bond, Jack Rosenthal, John Hawkesworth, Rosemary Ann Sisson, David Butler, Bill Craig, Julia Jones, Jeremy Paul, Maggie Wadey. *mus* Alexander Faris. *cast* **Louisa Trotter** Gemma Jones **Charlie Tyrell (Lord Haslemere)** Christopher Casanove **Major Toby Smith-Barton** John Vernon **Merriman (Head Waiter)** John Welsh **Starr (Head Porter)** John Cater **Mary** Victoria Plunkett.

John Hawkesworth's Edwardian TV drama to follow >*Upstairs, Downstairs* was a fictionalisation of the life of Rosa Lewis, the owner-dictator of the exclusive and eccentric Cavendish Hotel in Jermyn Street. By any standards, but especially those of snobbish, chauvinist early 1900s Britain, Lewis' story was exceptional: born in poverty in London's East End in 1869, she became the best French chef in the capital and managed, through unstinting labour, to buy the Cavendish Hotel. This she turned into a private home-from-home for the society in-crowd. She died in 1952.

In *The Duchess of Duke Street* Hawkesworth renamed Lewis Louisa Trotter (played with folded-arms, aitch-dropping Cockney formidability by Gemma Jones) and relocated the Cavendish half a block and retitled it The Bentinck. Here Trotter had a turbulent relationship with handsome lover, Lord Haslemere (Christopher Casanove, also >*Dynasty*), the father of her secret daughter. Less staid than most BBC period dramas, the series had top-drawer writers – among others, Jack Rosenthal and Julian Bond contributed teleplays – and a strong circle of lead characters. The period detail was lavish and scrupulous. Inevitably, the theme of class difference (and whether Trotter and Haslemere would surmount it) was an intriguing constant.

The Dukes of Hazzard

USA 1979–85 147 × 60m col CBS. Lou-Step Productions/Warner Bros TV. *UK tx* 1979–85 BBC1. *cr* Guy Waldron. *pr* Paul Picard, Joseph Gantman, Hy Averback, Rod Amateau. *dr* Various, including Guy Waldron, Herman Groves, Denver Pyle, Sy Rose, Paul Savage, William Raynor,

Myles Wilder. *wr* Various, including William Raynor, Myles Wilder, Martin Roth. *mus* Waylon Jennings. *cast* **Luke Duke** Tom Wopat **Bo Duke** John Schneider **Daisy Duke** Catherine Bach **Uncle Jesse Duke** Denver Pyle **Sheriff Rosco P Coltrane** James Best **Jefferson Davis 'Boss' Hogg** Sorrell Booke **Cooter** Ben Jones **Deputy Enos Strate** Sonny Schroyer **Vance Duke** Christopher Mayer **Coy Duke** Byron Cherry.

In which Southern country cousins Luke and Bo Duke sped around Hazzard County in a souped-up car *The General Lee*, getting themselves into trouble with the law. They may have been moonshining outlaws but 'them Duke boys' were good guys, latter-day knights in a Dodge Charger. Trying to catch the dynamic duo was corpulent, corrupt politician, Boss Hogg, and his cronies, inept Sheriff Rosco P Coltrane and Deputy Enos Strate. Occasionally, the Dukes halted the frantic chase'n'crash car action (300 Dodge Chargers were wrecked during the show's course) to refuel on food and homilies back at the old homestead, which they shared with Uncle Jesse (Denver Pyle, who also directed on the show) and cousin Daisy Duke, she of the minimal attire. Country music star Waylon Jennings provided the music and narration.

In 1982 stars John Schneider and Tom Wopat walked out in the perennial salary dispute, and Warner Bros held a nationwide contest to find their replacements. The lucky winners from the 2,000 screen-tested applications were Christopher Mayer and Byron Cherry, who were subsequently introduced to Hazzard as returning home Duke Cousins Coy and Vance. In practice Mayer and Cherry were lacklustre, and Wopat and Schneider returned to the show – after a pay rise – in 1983.

The hit show spun off a cartoon version, *The Dukes* (1983, Hanna-Barbera) and a short-lived series, *Enos* (1980–1), in which the grinning Georgia deputy was seconded to the Los Angeles PD.

Dynasty

USA 1981–9 169 × 50m col ABC. Aaron Spelling Productions/Fox. *UK tx* 1982–9 BBC1. *cr* Richard and Esther Shapiro. *exec pr* Aaron Spelling, Douglas Kramer, Richard and Esther Shapiro. *pr* Various, including Elaine Rich. *dr* Various, including Alf Kjellin, Philip Leacock. *wr* Various, including Richard Shapiro, Esther Shapiro, Edward Deblasio, Leah Markus, Eileen Mason Pollock, Robert Mason Pollock. *mus* Bill Conti (theme), Peter Myers. *cast* **Blake Carrington** John Forsythe **Krystle Jennings Carrington** Linda Evans **Alexis Carrington Colby** Joan Collins **Fallon Carrington Colby** Pamela Sue Martin/Emma Samms **Steven Carrington** Al Corley/Jack Coleman **Adam Carrington/Michael Torrance** Gordon Thomson **Jeff Colby** John James **Claudia Blaisdel** Pamela Bellwood **Sammy Jo Dan** Heather Locklear **Farnsworth 'Dex' Dexter** Michael Nader **Amanda Carrington** Catherine Oxenburgh/Karen Cellini **Dominique Devereaux** Diahann Carroll **Prince Michael** Michael Praed **Ben Carrington** Christopher Casanove **Caress Morell** Kate O'Mara **Krystina Carrington** Jessica Player **Sable Colby** Stephanie Beacham **Monica Colby** Tracy Scoggins.

Like >*Dallas*, the supersoap it set out to emulate, *Dynasty* featured an American Western oil family (in fact, the series was originally to be titled *Oil*), but this time the setting was Denver, Colorado. Head of the dynasty was smooth, silver-haired Blake Carrington (John Forsythe, aka John Lincoln Freund, previously the star of *Bachelor Father*, *The John Forsythe Hour*, and the voice of Charlie in >*Charlie's Angels*), who married secretary Krystle Jennings (Linda Evans, >*The Big Valley*) in the first episode. Fallon was Blake's spoiled daughter, Steven his gay son. And so began a cat's cradle of plot twists, of varying degrees of improbability.

In the beginning ratings were modest, but at the end of the first season Blake was put on trial for the murder of son Steven's boyfriend. Into the courtroom swept a mysterious figure, witness for the prosecution. She turned out to be Alexis Carrington, Blake's former wife, a vengeful do-badder of man-eating, shoulder-padded proportions. *Dynasty* now not only had its villain, but it had one who was even more wicked and comic-strip than >*Dallas*'s J R. (Sophia Loren had originally been up for the part, but English Joan Collins got it largely because of her performance in *The Bitch*.) By the end of 1982, *Dynasty* was watched by 22.4 per cent of America's prime-time audience, only 3.1 per cent behind its prototype. In 1984 *Dynasty* topped the Nielsen ratings.

After Alexis Carrington's arrival, *Dynasty* came to centre more and more on her schemes either to woo back or demolish Blake Carrington (and his empire). After he rejected her, she married his arch-rival Cecil Colby, who promptly died leaving her a multi-millionairess and a major oil player. And if Alexis hated Blake, she positively loathed his new wife, limpid-eyed Krystle ('that blonde tramp'), causing her to lose her baby. Krystle in turn slugged it out with Alexis in a lily pond, later in a burning cabin. Meanwhile, back at Blake Carrington's sumptuous mansion, Steven became bisexual and married Sammy Jo, before disappearing to Indonesia and reappearing with a face altered by plastic surgery (a script measure necessitated by the fact that he was now played by Jack Coleman). Then saturnine Michael Torrance washed up at the door, and turned out to be Blake's long lost son, an unexpected arrival only eclipsed later by that of black singer Dominique (Diahann Carroll, >*Julia*), who was actually Blake's half-sister. Fallon, meanwhile was bedding everything that passed by her boudoir's doorway, including good-guy Jeff, whom she briefly married. The most memorable wedding of the series, though, was that of Alexis's daughter, Amanda (naturally, she was long lost too), who married Prince Michael (Michael Praed, >*Robin of Sherwood, Riders*) of the European Ruritanian kingdom of Moldavia in the 1984–5 season. The happy event was interrupted by the arrival of revolutionaries who machine-gunned the guests.

By this stage in its screen life, *Dynasty* was becoming more and more kitsch and fantastic. Major storylines of its later seasons included a scheme by Sammy Jo and accomplice, producer Joel Abrigore (George Hamilton), to kidnap Krystle, substituting her with actress Rita; the appearance of Alexis' sister Caress (Kate O'Mara, *Weavers Green*, >*Triangle*) who wrote a muckraking biography of her elder sister; Blake's attack of amnesia in which he thought he was still married to Alexis; the abduction of Blake and Krystle's baby, Krystina; and a murder investigation at the Carrington estate, after the discovery of a mummified body (the killer was Fallon, many years before). In the final episode, Fallon and Krystina were buried in a tunnel with a Nazi art hoard and a psychopath, while Blake shot it out with the crooked murder squad cop who was trying to blackmail

him, and Adam Carrington pushed Alexis and husband Dexter off a balcony. The outcome of this balcony hanger was revealed to the world in the 1991 TV movie, *Dynasty: The Reunion*. Alexis managed to turn in the air and land on Dexter – and walk away.

Dynasty certainly lacked realism, even real characterisation, but few soap operas have had more glamour. Each episode cost $1.2 million and to add to its idea of class it imported a gallery of English actors: Joan Collins, Emma Samms (who played the second incarnation of Fallon), Kate O'Mara, Michael Praed and Stephanie Beacham (previously the rag-trade tycoon, *Connie*). The series' ultimate touch of gloss, though, was guest appearances from former US President, Gerald Ford, and former Secretary of State, Henry Kissinger.

A spin-off from the series, *The Colbys* (1985–7), featured Charlton Heston as Jason Colby, head of the multinational Colby Enterprises, Stephanie Beacham as wife Sable Scott Colby, and Katherine Ross as her much-married sister, Francesca. Barbara Stanwyck played Constance Colby, Jason's elder sister and company co-owner.

Emergency Ward 10

UK 1957–67 966 × 30m/50 × 60m bw ITV. An ATV Network Production. *cr* Tessa Diamond. *pr* Anthony Kearey, Cecil Petty, Josephine Douglas. *dr* Various, including Anthony Kearey, Rex Firkin, Royston Morley, Robert D Cardona, Philip Dale, Eric Price, Kevin Shine, Bill Stewart, David Reid, Dickie Leeman, Christopher Morahan. *wr* Various, including Tessa Diamond, Rachel Grieves, Hazel Adair, Don Houghton, Rosemary Ann Sisson, Basil Dawson, William Emms, Bill Strutton, Pat Dunlop, Stewart Farrar, Jan Read, William Hood, Roger Marshall. *cast* **Nurse Pat Roberts** Rosemary Miller **Nurse Carole Young** Jill Browne **Sister Cowley** Elizabeth Kentish **Nurse Stevenson** Iris Russell **Patrick O'Meara** Glyn Owen **Alan Dawson** Charles Tingwell **Potter** Douglas Ives **Mrs Hill** Dandy Nichols **Home Sister** Catherine Salkeld **Simon Forrester** Frederick Bartman **Dr Brook** William Wilde **Nurse Wilde** Tricia Money **Dr Richmond** Noel Coleman **Chris Anderson** Desmond Carrington **Richard Moone** John Alderton.

Britain's first twice-weekly serial was a drama about the staff of bustling fictional Oxbridge General Hospital, in particular those who worked behind the white swing-doors of *Ward 10*. Actress Jill Browne played the main character, blonde, flirtatious Nurse Carole Young, who arrived in the first episode as a probationer and stayed at Oxbridge General for the full ten years. Other featured players were Rosemary Miller as Nurse Young's room-mate and fellow probationer, fifteen-year-old farmgirl Nurse Pat Roberts, Glyn Owen as Irish Casualty Officer Patrick O'Meara, Charles Tingwell as chip-on-his-shoulder Australian House Surgeon Alan Dawson, Frederick Bartman as upper-class heartthrob Simon Forrester and veteran Douglas Ives as porter Potter (reprising his roles in *Doctor in the House* and *The Happiest Days of Your Life*). John Alderton (also >*Please Sir!, No Honestly*), Joanna Lumley, Ian Hendry, Dandy Nichols, Paul Darrow and Albert Finney also played doctors, nurses and patients in the series. Episodes regularly featured heartrending tales of patients whose fight for life required all the skills of the team.

Created by Tessa Diamond, *Emergency Ward 10* was the first script sold by the twenty-seven-year-old as a freelance. Born in Johannesburg and educated in England, Diamond had started her career in a commercial radio station in South Africa then moved to Britain where she was employed by ATV as a promotions writer. Originally scheduled to run twice a week for only six weeks, the series was so popular (it was ITV's first hit soap, and reached the ratings top twenty in its first year) that its run was extended, forcing a series of changes in the production process. Tessa Diamond, sole writer for the first series of twelve episodes, was given help by two new female writers, successful West End playwright Rachel Grieves and Hazel Adair (previously writer of *Mrs Dale's Diary*, ATV's *Sixpenny Corner* and later co-creator of >*Crossroads*). Anthony Kearey, initially both producer and director, was joined by directors Rex Firkin and Christopher Morahan. Because of the punishing shooting schedule – rehearsal time for a half-hour play was usually ten days, while *Ward 10* only had three or four – scripts were henceforth written so that two or three characters were left out of each instalment.

Shown on Tuesdays and Fridays from 19 February 1957 to 1 October 1966 in a half-hour format, *Ward 10*

Nurse Carole Young (Jill Browne) at the centre of another unfolding drama in Britain's first medicated soap *Emergency Ward 10*, set in bustling Oxbridge General Hospital. Also playing doctors and nurses in the series were the young John Alderton, Joanna Lumley and Albert Finney.

did a final year of hour-long episodes before production was halted. ATV's Lew Grade later decided that it had been a mistake to cancel the show and launched another twice-weekly medical soap, >*General Hospital*, in 1972. A film, *Life in Emergency Ward 10*, was made in 1959.

ER

USA 1994– 1 × 90/30+ × 60m col NBC. Michael Crichton Productions/Amblin Television/Warner Bros. *UK tx* 1995– C4. *cr* Michael Crichton. *exec pr* Michael Crichton, John Wells. *pr* Mimi Leder, Robert Nathan, Lydia Woodward, Chris Chulack, Paul Manning. *dr* Various, including Rod Holcomb, Mimi Leder, Eric Laneuville, Felix Alcala, Dean Parisot, Lesli Linka Glatter, Christopher Chulack, Thomas Schlamme, Donna Deitch, Whitney Ransick, Richard Thorpe, Barnet Kellman, Lance A Gentile. *wr* Various, including Michael Crichton, Lance Gentile, Neal Baer, John Wells, Lydia Woodward, Paul Manning, Carol Flint, Anne Kenney, Tracy Stern, Belinda Casas-Wells, Joe Sachs. *cast* **Dr Mark Greene** Anthony Edwards **Dr Susan Lewis** Sherry Stringfield **Dr Douglas Ross** George Clooney **Nurse Carol Hathaway** Julianna Margulies **Dr Peter Benton** Eriq La Salle **John Carter** Noah Wyle **Jeanie Boulet** Gloria Reuben **Kerry Weaver** Laura Innes.

ER began life in 1974 as a movie script, before creator Michael Crichton got sidetracked by a succession of projects which culminated with the thriller *Jurassic Park*, later filmed by Steven Spielberg. It was under the auspices of Spielberg's Amblin Company that *ER* was at last sold and made, débuting on NBC in September 1994, where it became the highest-rated new network drama for nearly a decade. It was also the first American medical soap to be a hit since >*M*A*S*H*.

ER's key gimmick was a fast, emotionally wringing tempo, intended by Crichton – who had served time as a medical student at Massachusetts General Hospital – to imitate life in a real Emergency Room. This 'rock 'em – sock 'em' (Crichton) pace was also founded on Crichton's personal belief that 'most television is too slow'. The result was channel-surfing without touching the button, as stories, crises and patients rushed through the ER room of the Cook County General Memorial Hospital in Chicago at frantic rate. The opening ninety-minute pilot had no less than forty-five medical stories, ranging from a pregnant child to lung cancer, from a drunk paediatrician to an eight-year-old with an ulcer. To ensure that the viewer identified with the perspective of the overworked, adrenaline-pumped staff, the interior sets and shooting angles were intentionally claustrophobic (just as the grim surgical procedures were queasily close-up). Only occasionally did *ER*'s jerky, rushing cameras wander outside the hospital precincts.

Not that the sole, or even main, arc light of *ER* was directed at the staff's workload. The personalities, personal lives and multitudinous professional conflicts of the doctors were examined in full clinical detail. Dr Mark Greene (Anthony Edwards, *Top Gun* and the lawyer Mike Monroe in >*Northern Exposure*) was the balding conscientious practitioner whose ex-wife fought him bitterly for the custody of their daughter. Susan Lewis (Sherry Stringfield, >*NYPD Blue*) was an ambitious high achiever, burdened by her family's expectations and then the care of her baby niece, Chloe. Douglas Ross (George Clooney, nephew of singer Rosemary Clooney) was the handsome paediatrician given to destructive drinking, who rescued his peer esteem with the saving of a young boy from drowning ('Hell and High Water'). Peter Benton was the tough-guy surgeon, seemingly foreign to emotion until he punched an obnoxious salesman after Jeanie Boulet ended their affair. Nurse Hathaway attempted suicide in episode one – to be cheesily revived an episode later – a storyline from whose shadow she never quite crawled clear. John Carter was the hapless medical student for whom things always seemed to go wrong; typically, when he got to do his first unsupervised surgery ('Do One, Teach One, Kill One') he perforated the patient's liver, indirectly causing his death.

The Forsyte Saga

UK 1967 26 × 50m bw BBC2. BBC/MGM-TV. *USA tx* 1969–70 National Educational Television. *cr* Donald Wilson. *pr* Donald Wilson. *dr* David Giles, James Cellan Jones. *wr*

Various, including Lennon Philips, Constance Cox, Lawrie Craig, Vincent Tilsey, Anthony Stevens. *mus* Marcus Dods. *cast* **Jolyon 'Jo' Forsyte** Kenneth More **Soames Forsyte** Eric Porter **Irene Forsyte (née Heron)** Nyree Dawn Porter **Jolyon Forsyte** Joseph O'Connor **James Forsyte** John Welsh **Winifred Forsyte** Margaret Tyzack **Ann Forsyte** Fay Compton **Monty Dartie** Terence Alexander **Helene Hilmer** Lana Morris **Philip Bosinney** John Bennett **Frances Forsyte** Ursula Howells **Mrs Heron** Jenny Laird **Fleur Forsyte** Susan Hampshire **Annette Forsyte** Dallia Penn **Jolyon 'Jon' Forsyte** Martin Jarvis **June Forsyte** Susan Pennick/June Barry **Jolyon 'Jolly' Forsyte** Michael York. *Video* BBC.

A classic of sixties TV, based on John Galsworthy's chronicle of the upper-middle-class Forsyte family from 1879 to the 1920s, and produced by Donald Wilson (also *The First Churchills, Anna Karenina*). Although sold as period drama, *The Forsyte Saga* was near pure sex-scandal soap; consequently, it was much favoured by the urban middle classes, who could enjoy its salaciousness without denting their chintzy respectability. Set amongst the comfortable drawing rooms of Victorian London, the saga opened as the heir to the family's building-industry fortune, Jo Forsyte (played by Kenneth More), left his wife Frances for his pregnant mistress, the Austrian governess Helene Hilmer, and a struggling life as an artist. This so broke the family code of propriety and respectability that he was excommunicated by his ageing father, Old Jolyon. Meanwhile, cousin Soames (Eric Porter of the Royal Shakespeare Company), a calculating, possessive lawyer, met the beautiful Irene Heron (Nyree Dawn Porter, ex-Miss Cinema of New Zealand, later >*The Protectors*), an aspiring musician. But no sooner had Soames and Irene married than their relationship began to cool. Unloved Irene later had an affair with Philip Bosinney, the architect of Soames' country mansion, Robin Hill. In the nadir of their marriage, Soames raped Irene (one of the most infamous scenes in television history). The couple divorced and Irene fell in love with Jo Forsyte, married him, and produced a son, Jon. Soames, in turn, married Annette and forced her to have a child – which turned out to be not the long-hoped for boy, but a girl, Fleur (Susan Hampshire, later >*The Pallisers*). The impetuous Fleur

was the main focus of the *Saga* as it moved into its final phase, the Flapper Age.

The last major British serial to be made in black and white, *The Forsyte Saga* was watched by 160 million across the world (it was even sold to the Soviet Union), earning a small fortune for the BBC, and prompting it to produce a string of period dramas. In America the show was screened on National Educational Television, the forerunner of Public Service Broadcasting, where its success encouraged TV companies previously allergic to dramas with finite stories to create the 'mini-series'. The serial received the Silver Medal of the Royal Television Society and a BAFTA for Best Drama.

General Hospital

UK 1972–9 110 × 30m/54 × 60m col ITV. ATV. *pr* Ian Fordyce, Royston Morley. *dr* Various, including Shaun O'Riordan, David Foster, John Scholz-Conway, Pembroke Duttson. *wr* Various, including David Fisher, Brian Finch, Allan Prior, Patrick Alexander. *mus* Derek Scott (theme). *cast* **Dr Matthew Armstrong** David Garth **Dr William Parker-Brown** Lewis Jones **Dr Martin Baxter** James Kerry **Dr Peter Ridge** Ian White **Dr Robert Thorne** Ronald Leigh-Hunt **Doctor Neville Bywaters** Tony Adams **Sister Ellen Chapman** Peggy Sinclair **Nurse Hilda Price** Lynda Bellingham **Student Nurse Katy Shaw** Judy Buxton.

In 1972 the lifting of broadcasting restrictions brought afternoon TV to Britain for the first time and with it the first British-made romantic melodramas already known in the States as soap operas, or 'soaps'. Aimed at a housewife audience they were often sponsored by soap companies such as Proctor & Gamble and Lever Bros and were conceived to run with no end in view. The casts of soaps were large and ever-changing, the substance a complex tapestry of interwoven dramas and crises. To please its new *postmeridian* female viewers, Yorkshire Television produced *Emmerdale Farm*, while ATV produced *General Hospital* to fill the prescription.

General Hospital had much in common with ATV's earlier medical drama, >*Emergency Ward 10*, whose demise five years earlier had been regretted by boss Lew

Grade and featured surgery, romance and upset among doctors, nurses and patients twice-weekly at lunchtime for half an hour. The set, initially tiny, was swapped for a larger, specially built stage at Elstree in 1975 when the series changed to a weekly, one-hour slot.

Over the years on the wards of *General Hospital*, women viewers dreamed about the bedside manner of Doctor Baxter and Doctor Bywaters (Tony Adams, later of >*Crossroads*) and thrilled to the power struggles between Doctor Armstrong and difficult Doctor Parker-Brown. West Indian Sister Washington was also a great favourite and two of the best-loved nurses were played by Lynda Bellingham (later in *All Creatures Great and Small, Faith in the Future*) and Judy Buxton.

General Hospital took the same title as the successful American soap opera which ran on ABC from April 1963.

Hadleigh

UK 1969–74 24 × 60m col ITV. Yorkshire TV. *pr* Terence Williams. *dr* Various, including Brian Parker, Tony Wharmby, Peter Creegen. *wr* Various, including Anthony Couch, Leslie Sands, Stephen Rich, Ian Kennedy Martin. *mus* Tony Hatch. *cast* **James Hadleigh** Gerald Harper.

Film director Carl Foreman once described Gerald Harper as 'the world's idea of a gentleman', and the actor (also >*Adam Adamant Lives*) was at his most languidly aristocratic as divorced Yorkshire squire James Hadleigh, owner of stately home Melford Park. The mansion and the problems posed by its upkeep provided the main storylines, with frequent breaks for romantic action. Hadleigh's innate physical pulling power was only added to by his white Monteverdi 375L sports car and thoroughbred horse, The Drummer. Towards the end of the series Hadleigh remarried, the new Mrs H (played by Hilary Dwyer) being of an altogether lower class. At its peak, the nostalgic brew was watched by 17 million viewers.

The character of Hadleigh originated in Yorkshire TV's *Gazette*, a soap about a weekly newspaper owned by Hadleigh's father.

Ivanhoe

UK 1958–9 39 × 30m bw ITV. A Sydney Box Television Presentation. *USA tx* 1959 syndicated. *cr* Walter Scott. *exec pr* Peter Rogers. *pr* Bernard Coote. *dr* Lance Comfort, David McDonald, Pennington Richards, Bernard Knowles, Arthur Crabtree. *wr* Joel Carpenter, Saul Levitt, Thomas Law, Richard Fiedler, Larry Forrester, Geoffrey Orme, Shirl Hendryx, Bill Strutton, Felix Van Lieu, Aubrey Feiest, Anthony Verney, M L Davenport, George Baxt, Sheldon Stark, Lawrence Hazard, Tania Lawrence, Alan Reeve Jones, Samuel B Wells. *mus* Albert Elms. *cast* **Ivanhoe** Roger Moore **Gurth** Robert Brown **Bart** John Pike **Prince John** Andrew Keir.

Given British TV's penchant for swashbuckling sagas in the fifties (>*The Adventures of Robin Hood*, >*The Adventures of William Tell*, >*The Adventures of Sir Lancelot*, >*The Buccaneers*), it was inevitable that Sir Walter Scott's novel about the knightly scourge of evil King John would sooner or later be adapted. Cast in the role of the medieval chivalric-hero-on-a-white-charger was policeman's son, Roger Moore, then an unknown, but destined to follow up the sizeable transatlantic success of *Ivanhoe* with >*Maverick*, >*The Saint*, >*The Persuaders* and numerous theatrical features, including several in the James Bond cycle. Robert Brown and John Pike played Gurth and Bart, Ivanhoe's ex-serf retainers. Two of the more noteworthy guest appearances were Christopher Lee in 'The German Knight' episode, and youthful actor-director John Schlesinger in 'The Masked Bandits'. As the theme song had it: 'Ivanhoe, Ivanhoe to adventure, bold adventure watch him go/There's no power on earth can stop what he's begun/With Bart and Gurth, he'll fight till he has won/Ivanhoe, Ivanhoe . . .'

Lou Grant

USA 1977–82 113 × 60m CBS. MTM. *UK tx* 1979–82. *cr* Allan Burns, James L Brooks, Gene Reynolds. *exec pr* Gene Reynolds, Allan Burns, James L Brooks. *pr* Seth Freeman, Gary David Goldberg. *dr* Gene Reynolds, Mel Damski,

Charles Dubin, Jay Sandrich, Richard Crenna, Alexander Singer, Jud Taylor, Harry Falk, Irving J Moore, Jim Burrows, Harvey Laidman, Corey Allen, Burt Brinckerhoff, Roger Young, Michael Zinberg, Gerald Mayer, Paul Leaf, Peter Levin, Alan Cooke, Donald A Baer, Ralph Senensky, Allen Williams, Bob Sweeney, Seth Freeman, Paul Stanley, Georg Stanford Brown, Neil Cox, Jeff Bleckner, Roy Campanella, Peter Bogart. *wr* Leon Tokatyan, Seth Freeman, Gordon Dawson, Leonora Thuna, Robert Schlitt, Del Reisman, Gene Kearney, David Lloyd, Charles Einstein, Bud Freeman, Ken Trevey, Michele Gallery, Gary David Goldberg, Gina Frederica Goldman, Steve Kline, Eliot West, Gene Reynolds, Johnny Dawkins, Michael Vittes, Shep Greene, Allan Burns, April Smith, Paul Ehrmann, Joanne Pagliaro, Patt Shea and Harriet Weiss, William Hopkins, Everett Greenbaum and Elliott Reid, Rogers Turrentine, Jeffrey B Lane. *mus* (season one) Patrick Williams, Michael Melvoin; (season two) Hod David; (seasons three to five) Patrick Williams. *cast* **Lou Grant** Edward Asner **Billie Newman McCovey** Linda Kelsey **Joe Rossi** Robert Walden **Charlie Hume** Mason Adams **Margaret Pynchon** Nancy Marchand **Dennis 'Animal' Price** Daryl Anderson **Adam Wilson** Allen Williams **Carla Mardigian** Rebecca Balding **Art Donovan** Jack Bannon.

Much-respected newspaper drama from MTM (producers of >*Rhoda*, *Remington Steele*, *Paris*, >*Hill Street Blues*) and a spin-off from one of their most successful series. In the final episode of >*The Mary Tyler Moore Show*, Lou Grant, gruff, soft-hearted boss of the newsroom, had been fired from WJM-TV in Minneapolis. But the popular fifty-year-old newshound was promptly given his own series, *Lou Grant*, and moved to Los Angeles to work as crusading city editor of the *Los Angeles Tribune*, a fictional newspaper under the autocratic rule of owner-publisher Margaret Pynchon. In the new, one-hour format Lou (played by Ed Asner) grew from a comic to a dramatic character.

Though officially Lou worked for managing editor and old friend Charlie Hume, newsroom storylines usually revolved around a battle of wills with widowed Mrs Pynchon whose stubborn style was not dissimilar to Lou's. Other main players chasing the scoops included hotshot Joe Rossi, talented young investigative reporter Carla Mardigian (soon replaced by a new character, Billie

There was considerable overlap between actor and political activist Ed Asner (below right) and his on-screen persona, campaigning newspaper editor Lou Grant. As leader of the Screen Actors' Guild, he clashed showily with President Reagan over US policy in Central America.

Newman), assistant city editor Art Donovan and staff photographer 'Animal'. Punchy one-word episode titles meanwhile gave clues to the *Trib*'s – and the series' – social conscience. 'Hooker', for instance, focused on prostitution, 'Poison' dealt with radioactive contamination, 'Vet' with the ever-present Vietnam War and 'Rape' brought its subject matter close to home, when one of the paper's own reporters was the victim of a rape attack. The characters' personal lives also made their presence felt in episodes such as 'Wedding' (season five), which saw a proposal for Billie, and 'Lou' (season three), which saw the strain of his single-minded devotion to his job finally taking its toll on the newspaper editor.

For all Asner's popularity, *Lou Grant* didn't establish itself as a firm hit until its third season, but it became one of TV's most critically acclaimed shows. The series had both humour and conviction, the latter due in no small part to the overlap between the charismatic Asner and his screen persona. While Lou Grant the crusading editor took on humane causes on screen, Asner himself became controversial off screen as a liberal political activist during the Reagan years, involving himself in the Equal Rights Amendment, opposition to American involvement in El Salvador and opposition to nuclear arms. During the actors' strike of 1980 Asner became a leading spokesman for the workers' cause and a year later was elected president of the Screen Actors' Guild, the post that had started Ronald Reagan on his political career. The series ended its US run amid controversy not dissimilar to that which served as material for *Lou Grant*. Despite CBS's statement that the show was cancelled due to poor ratings, many felt that star Ed Asner's political statements were the real reason. Asner himself accused CBS of dropping *Lou Grant* because of his highly publicised condemnation of US involvement in Central America. Asner resigned as SAG president in 1985 but remained active in political and social issues.

Lou Grant won a total of eleven Emmys over its five-year run, including two for Ed Asner, three for supporting actress Nancy Marchand and two as Outstanding Drama Series. The episodes 'Dying' and 'Cop' were singled out for particular attention, with Michele Gallery winning an Emmy for writing the first and Roger Young winning an award as director on the second.

Asner's other TV credits include *Naked City*, 1963, *Slattery's People*, 1965, *Roots*, 1977, *A Small Killing*, 1981, *Off the Rack*, 1985, and *The Trials of Rosie O'Neill*, 1991. He was also featured in the film *Fort Apache, the Bronx* (1981).

Marcus Welby MD

USA 1969–76 172 × 50m col ABC. Universal TV. *UK tx* 1969–76 ITV. *cr* David Victor. *exec pr* David Victor. *pr* David O'Connell. *dr* Various, including Jeannot Szwarc, Joseph Pevney, Robert Collins, Leo Penn, Arnold Laven, Marc Daniels, Randal Kleisner, Charles Haas, Philip Leacock, Daniel Petrie, Jerry London, Richard Benedict, Rick Edelstein, Bernard McEveety, Russ Mayberry, Dennis Donnell. *wr* Various, including Robert Collins, Don Mankiewicz, Lionel Siegel. *mus* Leonard Rosenman (theme song). cast **Dr Marcus Welby** Robert Young **Dr Steven Kiley** James Brolin **Nurse Consuelo Lopez** Elena Verdugo **Nurse Kathleen Faverty** Sharon Gless **Janet Blake** Pamela Hensley.

Aged sixty-two, actor Robert Young – previously best known as Jim Anderson in the fifties hit series *Father Knows Best* – stepped out of retirement to accept the title role in this long-running show about a kindly Santa Monica general practitioner. James Brolin played his young heartthrob assistant, Doctor Steven Kiley, who made his housecalls on a motorcycle. The two doctors often clashed over methods, as Welby's by-the-gut sympathetic approach was diametrically opposed to Kiley's academic, med-school views. The wise, warm Welby invariably diagnosed the patient's problems as stemming from something beyond the illness, so giving himself the opportunity to concern himself with the patient's psychological well-being. Such uplifting drama soon achieved healthy ratings, and *Marcus Welby MD* became American network ABC's biggest hit to date. It also earned the approval of the TV industry, winning the 1970 Emmy for Outstanding Dramatic Programme, though it declined in quality in later years.

In addition to Young and Brolin, also featured were Anne Baxter in season one as Welby's romantic interest,

Elena Verdugo as Nurse Lopez, and Pamela Hensley as Janet Blake, the public relations director of the Blake Memorial Hospital, whom Kiley married in 1975. Sharon Gless (later >*Cagney and Lacey*, >*McCloud*, and *The Trials of Rosie O'Neill*) appeared as Nurse Faverty.

Developed from a 1968 pilot, *Marcus Welby MD* (with Young, Brolin, Baxter and Lew Ayres), the series was retitled *Robert Young, Family Doctor* in syndication.

Melrose Place

USA 1992– 40+ × 60m col Fox TV. Darren Star Productions/Spelling Television Inc. *UK tx* 1993– BSkyB. *cr* Darren Star. *exec pr* Aaron Spelling, E Duke Vincent, Darren Star. *pr* Various, including Fred Rappaport, Chip Hayes, Chuck Pratt. *dr* Various, including Mel Ferber, Barbara Amato, Charles Braverman, Chip Chalmers, Victoria Hochberg, Paul Lazarus, Jefferson Kibbee, Janet Greek, David Rosenbloom, Charles Corell, Daniel Attias, Steve Robman, Nancy Malone, John Nicolla. *wr* Various, including Darren Star. *cast* **Billy Campbell** Andrew Shue **Amanda Woodward** Heather Locklear **Jane Mancini** Josie Bissett **Michael Mancini** Thomas Calabro **Matt Fielding** Doug Savant **Jake Hanson** Grant Show **Alison Parker** Courtney Thorne-Smith **Jo Reynolds** Daphne Zuniga.

Following the runaway success of his >*Beverly Hills 90210*, wunderkind creator Darren Star penned a spin-off, *Melrose Place*, based loosely on his own youthful experience of living in a West Hollywood condo complex (actually a few blocks north of the real Melrose Place). Although Star has likened himself to Charles Dickens and has defended the night-time soap as having 'a tiny strain of reality', *MP* was easily and ruthlessly lampooned for its over-the-top depiction of yuppie life: almost without exception the residents who tanned themselves around the courtyard pool were libidinous, neurotic and infinitely ambitious. The quintessential *MP* character was double-crossing Amanda Woodward (played to bitchy perfection by ex-*Dynasty*, ex-*T J Hooker* actress Heather Locklear, wife of Bon Jovi musician Richie Sambora), invented by Star after the first year's episodes – which were morally/socially aware in the early *Beverly Hills* mode – generated disappointing ratings. No sooner in place as artistic director of D&D advertising agency, Woodward began seducing most of Melrose's men, even the token nice-guy, writer Billy Andrew, and the boyfriend of her mother, Hilary (played by >*Dallas'* Linda Gray). Almost as outrageous as Woodward was Sydney Andrews, younger sister of Jane Mancini (Josie Bissett, wife of Rob Estes), who had an affair with her brother-in-law, Michael Mancini, then blackmailed him into marriage. Previous to being Mrs Mancini, Sydney had been a call girl and exotic dancer with a drug addiction. The most improbable plot turn saw photographer Jo Reynolds in a custody battle for her son – after she had killed his father, the drug smuggler Reed Carter – then lose the child to her sister, get him back, hire the babysitter from Hell, before eventually giving him away. Much the biggest ratings-grabber, however, was the story in which Dr Kimberley Shaw ran a car over lover Michael Mancini (alas, not fatally) while disguised as his ex-wife. The motive was revenge: Kimberley had been disfigured (but only on the top of her pretty head) by a previous car accident, which she blamed on Mancini.

Such melodramatic characters and storylines made *Melrose Place* the second top drama series amongst the eighteen to twenty-five age group in the US. Fox used the series to spinoff *Model's Inc.* based around Linda Gray's Hillary Michaels character, on which Star received a production credit, but was not creatively involved. Instead Star, son of an East Coast orthodontist and a *Washington Post* journalist, directed his sudster energies into the birth of *Central Park West*, set amidst New York's publishing scene. Somewhat immodestly, the launch episode was transmitted on a giant screen in Times Square.

Neighbours

Australia 1985– 600+ × 25m col Channel 7/Channel 10. Grundy Television Productions. *UK tx* 1986– BBC1. *cr* Reg Watson. *exec pr* Marie Trevor, Don Battye. *pr* Various, including Sue Masters, Philip East, Margaret Slarke. *dr* Various, including Judith John-Story, Chris Adshead. *wr*

Various, including Christine Madafferi, Betty Zuin, Geoffrey Truman. *mus* Tony Hatch (theme), Jackie Trent (theme lyrics), Barry Crocker (theme singer). *cast* **Madge Bishop** Anne Charleston **Helen Daniels** Anne Haddy **Jim Robinson** Alan Dale **Charlene Robinson** Kylie Minogue **Scott Robinson** Darius Perkins, Jason Donovan **Henry Ramsey** Craig MacLachlan **Paul Robinson** Stefan Dennis **Joe Mangel** Mark Little **Mrs Mangel** Vivean Gray **Shane Ramsey** Peter O'Brien **Mike Young** Guy Pearce **Des Clarke** Paul Keane **Gail Robinson** Fiona Corke **Kerry Bishop** Lynda Hartley **Sky Mangel** Miranda Fryer **Toby Mangel** Ben Geurens **Caroline Alessi** Gillian Blakeney **Christina Alessi** Gayle Blakeney **Harold Bishop** Ian Smith **Dorothy Burke** Maggie Dence **Melissa Jarrett** Jade Amenta **Todd Landers** Kristian Schmid **Melanie Pearson** Lucinda Cowden **Doug Willis** Terence Donovan **Pam Willis** Sue Jones **Cody Willis** Amelia Frid, Peta Brady **Lucy Robinson** Melissa Bell, Kylie Flinker, Sascha Close **Josh Anderson** Jeremy Angerson **Rick Alessi** Dan Falzon **Lou Carpenter** Tom Oliver **Mark Gottlieb** Bruce Samazan **Annalise Hartman** Kimberley Davies **Brad Willis** Scott Michaelson **Libby Kennedy** Kym Valentine **Malcolm Kennedy** Benji McNair **Sam Kratz** Richard Grieve **Cheryl Stark** Caroline Gillmer **Danni Stark** Eliza Szonert **Brett Stark** Brett Blewitt. *Video* BBC/TECHN.

The TV tale of everyday Australian folk, created by Reg Watson (also >*Prisoner: Cell Block H*, *Sons and Daughters*, *The Young Doctors*) who learned his sudster craft as the first producer of Britain's >*Crossroads*. Although now an international success, the early history of *Neighbours* was troubled. First screened on Australia's 7 Network, it was axed after just six months, until Grundy Productions persuaded rival Channel 10 to buy it. There it was injected with a dose of light humour and 'yoof' appeal, including the addition of bronzed, blonde teenagers Jason Donovan and Kylie Minogue. Eventually it caught on, but only after a massive publicity campaign. To restore its lost soap honour, 7 Network had to create *Home and Away*. Imported to Britain in 1986 as a cheap daytime filler, *Neighbours* did tolerably well until schoolgirl Alison Grade complained to her father that she and her friends had to miss the lunchtime episodes during term time. So her father, who happened to be Michael Grade, Controller of BBC1, arranged for the repeat to be shown in the 5.35pm timeslot. Within months it was challenging the soaps *Eastenders* and >*Coronation Street* at the top of the ratings.

Neighbours is set in Ramsey Street, in the invented Melbourne suburb of Erinsborough (although based on the Brisbane Street where Watson grew up). Initially the leading families in the show were the Ramsey–Mitchell–Bishops and the Robinsons. Madge Bishop (née Ramsey) was the matriarch of the former, barmaid at the Waterhole and mother to Charlene (Kylie Minogue) and Henry (Craig MacLachlan, who subsequently moved soaps to play Grant Mitchell in *Home and Away*). Later, Madge married fuddy duddy Harold Bishop (Ian Smith, formerly associate producer on >*Prisoner: Cell Block H*). Heading the Robinson clan was ever-understanding Helen Daniels (Anne Haddy, also >*Prisoner: Cell Block H*), mother-in-law to Jim Robinson and grandmother of Paul, the ambitious, J R-like, owner of the Lassiters hotel complex. Paul Robinson's business affairs and turbulent marriages (including to identical twin, Christina Alessi) were frequent providers of storylines. As the series progressed, the Willis and Alessi families took over the spotlight, only to be succeeded in turn by the Starks and the Kennedys.

Like >*Crossroads*, the show has a high level of human tragedy; at times the death rate in Ramsey Street has threatened to rival that of Bogota (among those killed off have been Joe Mangel's trendy wife, Kerry, Harold Bishop and Jim Robinson). The street's population, however, is kept stable by a constant stream of long-lost never-before-heard-of relatives. Often these are teenagers (like adopted Robinsons Todd and Katie), allowing much young love interest. Overall, though, the melodrama is cleverly tempered by blue Australian skies, good-looking people, an apparently free-and-easy surfing lifestyle, and some near comic characters, most outstandingly Joe Mangel and his gossipy mother.

Around the world the show's most fervent viewers are teenagers, and numerous of the cast have used their exposure on *Neighbours* to launch careers in the pop music industry: Kylie Minogue, Jason Donavan (whose father played Ramsey Street's Doug Willis), Craig MacLachlan, and the Blakeney sisters.

Northern Exposure

USA 1990– 88+ × 60m col CBS. A Falsey-Austin Street Production. *UK tx* 1991– C4. *cr* Joshua Brand, John Falsey. *exec pr* John Falsey, Andrew Schneider, Rob Thompson. *pr* Various, including Cheryl Bloch, Matthew Nodella, Diane Frolov, Robin Green, Jeff Melvoin, Rob Thompson. *dr* Various, including Nick Marck, Bill D'Elia, Miles Watkins, David Carson, Sandy Smolan, Jack Bender, Max Tash, Tom Moore, Eric Laneuville, Charles Braverman, Win Phelps, Daniel Attias, Lee Shallat, Rob Thompson, Josh Brand. *wr* Various, including Martin Sage, Sybil Adelman, Ellen Herman, Robi Green, Craig Volk, Henry Bromwell, Dennis Koenig, Diane Frolov, Andrew Schreider, Jeff Melvoin, David Assael. *mus* David Schwartz. *cast* **Dr Joel Fleischmann** Rob Morrow **Maggie O'Connell** Danine Turner **Ed Chigliak** Darren E Burrows **Chris Stevens** John Corbett **Maurice Minnifield** Barry Corbin **Marilyn Whirlwind** Elaine Miles **Holling Vincoeur** John Cullum **Shelly Tambo** Cynthia Geary **Ruth-Anne** Reg Phillips.

The goings-on in the remote Alaskan town of Cicely (pop. 215) and the comi-tragic attempts by confirmed New Yorker Joel Fleischmann to come to terms with the rugged, check-shirt local lifestyle. To repay the $125,000 cost of his medical tuition Fleischmann has to practise medicine in Cicely for four years, a placement he regards as a 'sentence'. Quirky, humorous, filled with odd-ball characters – not to mention a moose, Mort, which likes to stroll down mainstreet – and with a strong sense of place, the show is frequently likened to David Lynch's >*Twin Peaks*, although *Exposure*'s creators have claimed, 'We hadn't heard of *Twin Peaks* when we wrote the pilot episode.' But Cicely is a far gentler American timber town than that created by Lynch, and is almost idyllically free of racism, crime and social evils. Indeed, Cicely is not so much a place as a New Age state of mind.

Among the other townsfolk are token baddie Maurice Minnifield, an ex-NASA astronaut whose capitalist dream is to pave Cicely with Burger Kings and mini-malls; the eighteen-year-old film-obsessed American Indian, Ed Chigliak (IQ: 180); Chris Stevens, the resident DJ on KBHR radio, whose patter is smattered with cosmic thoughts, Jung, and Walt Whitman; Ruth Anne,

Half-baked Alaska. Mystical Marilyn Whirlwind (Elaine Miles), a moose's head and film buff Ed Chigliak (Darren E Burrows) from the quirky new age series *Northern Exposure*. The programme won the 1992 Emmy for Outstanding Dramatic Series.

the right-on seventysomething who runs the local store; Shelley Tambo, a beautiful young blonde brought to town by Minnifield, whom she promptly dumped for Holling Vincoeur, owner of The Brick diner; and Marilyn Whirlwind, Fleischmann's inscrutable, mystical receptionist. Maggie O'Connell is the local air pilot, and possessor of something of a love curse, since five of her boyfriends have suffered untimely deaths. She has a love-hate relationship with Fleischmann, which has come close on occasion to consummation. Also popping up from time to time is Chris Steven's African-American half brother Bernard with whom he has a telepathic relationship. Adam is a surly backwoodsman with a hypochrondriac wife, Eve.

Filmed in the town of Roslyn, Washington, in the Cascade Mountains of the Northwest USA (about 1,000 miles from Alaska), the series is from the same team that produced *St Elsewhere*.

The success of >*Twin Peaks* and *Northern Exposure* has led to a third TV exercise in smalltown bizarreness, *Eerie Indiana* (1992, Unreality Inc/Cosgrove-Meurer Productions) featuring Omri Katz, formerly John Ross Ewing in >*Dallas*, as Marshall Teller, a teenager who discovers that the settlement of the title is 'the centre of weirdness for the entire planet'. Among the show's directors is Joe Dante, whose Hollywood credits include *Gremlins*, *Innerspace* and *The 'Burbs'*.

The Onedin Line

UK 1974–80 50 × 50m col BBC1. BBC. *cr* Cyril Abraham. *pr* Peter Graham Scott. *dr* Various, including Darrol Blake. *wr* Various, including Cyril Abraham, David Weir. *mus* Khachaturyan (theme). *cast* **James Onedin** Peter Gilmore **Robert Onedin** Brian Rawlinson **Elizabeth Onedin** Jessica Benton **Anne Onedin (née Webster)** Anne Stallybrass **Baines** Howard Lang **Callon** Edward Chapman **Albert Fraser** Philip Bond **Margarita Juarez** Roberta Iger. *Video* BBC.

Captain James Onedin was a poor nineteenth-century ship's master with just twenty-five pounds to his name – the family ship's chandlers business had been bequeathed

to brother Robert – and a vaulting ambition to own a fleet of sailing vessels. Step number one in the building of the Onedin Line was to form a partnership with the owner, Webster, of the neglected three-masted schooner, the *Charlotte Rhodes* (each episode of the series opened with a stirring shot of the *Charlotte Rhodes* in full scud, to the chords of Khachaturyan's *Spartacus*), an arrangement cemented by Onedin's marriage to Webster's daughter, Anne. A wine contract in his pocket, the gruff Onedin began his ruthless empire-building. Anne, though, died in childbirth and in the bleak years that followed, Onedin relied increasingly on faithful, whiskered Baines. Meanwhile, Onedin's sister Elizabeth married shipowner Albert Fraser, inheriting a line of her own on his untimely death. To complete his misery, all James Onedin's fortune was lost in a rash South American venture and his second wife, Letty, died childless.

Part of the BBC's enduring fascination with matters nautical (>*Triangle*, *Howard's Way*), *The Onedin Line's* calculated blend of boudoir, boardroom, costume drama and family history made it almost the quintessence of seventies Sunday evening soap opera. The location sequences were filmed off Dartmouth.

The Pallisers

UK 1974 26 × 50m col BBC1. BBC. *USA tx* 1975. *cr* Martin Lisemore. *pr* Martin Lisemore. *dr* Hugh David, Ronald Wilson. *wr* Simon Raven. *mus* Herbert Chappell, Wilfred Josephs. *cast* **Lady Glencora Palliser (née McCluskie)** Susan Hampshire **Plantagenet Palliser** Philip Latham **Duke of Omnium** Roland Culver **Countess Midlothian** Fabia Drake **Marchioness of Auld Reeke** Sonia Dresdel **Lizzie Eustace** Sarah Badel **George Vavasor** Gary Watson **Alice Vavasor** Caroline Mortimer **Phineas Finn** Donal McCann **Laura Kennedy** Anna Massey **Lord Fawn** Derek Jacobi **The Earl of Silverbridge** Anthony Andrews **Lady Mabel Grex** Anna Carteret **Burgo Fitzgerald** Barry Justice.

Sub-*Forsyte Saga* series (down to the importation of actress Susan Hampshire) about a Victorian aristocratic family with political ambitions and scandalous lives.

Made on a modest £500,000 budget, it was adapted from one-time Liberal candidate Anthony Trollope's Palliser novels by Simon Raven. Hampshire was suitably flighty – including a dalliance with rakish Burgo Fitzgerald – as Lady Glencora, wife of greying Plantagenet Palliser (who eventually became Prime Minister), but overall the show failed to fly the artistic or popular heights. It did, however, do good business in the USA, where its nostalgic air of olde England was much admired. Anthony Andrews (*Brideshead Revisited*), Derek Jacobi, Anna Massey and Anna Carteret (*The Gentle Touch*) were all to be found in the minor reaches of the cast list.

The Pallisers was part of a wave of upper-crust costumeries inspired by the success of >*The Forsyte Saga*, namely *The First Churchills* (again starring demure Susan Hampshire), *Edward and Mrs Simpson* (also written by Simon Raven), *Edward the Seventh*, *Jennie*, *Lady Randolph Churchill* and *Lillie*.

Peyton Place

USA 1964–9 514 × 30m ABC. Twentieth Century Fox TV. *UK tx* 1965–70 ITV. *cr* Paul Monash. *exec pr* Paul Monash. *pr* Everett Chambers. *mus* Franz Waxman. *cast **Constance Mackenzie** Dorothy Malone **Allison Mackenzie** Mia Farrow **Doctor Michael Rossi** Ed Nelson **Matthew Swain** Warner Anderson **Leslie Harrington** Paul Langton **Rodney Harrington** Ryan O'Neal **Norman Harrington** Christopher Connelly **Julia Anderson** Kasey Rogers **George Anderson** Henry Beckman **Steven Cord** James Douglas **Elliott Carson** Tim O'Connor **Rita Jacks** Patricia Morrow **Martin Peyton** George Macready/Wilfred Hyde-White (temporary replacement 1967).

Based on Grace Metalious' steamy best-selling novel, this tempestuous romantic drama (dubbed TV's first 'sexial'), was set in the small New England town of Peyton Place, a community seething with extramarital affairs, dark secrets and skulduggery of every kind. The saga told of the lives and loves of the Harringtons and Carsons, Mackenzies and Andersons. Top of the cast list was Dorothy Malone as bookshop proprietress Constance Mackenzie whose particular dark secret involved the circumstances surrounding the birth of her illegitimate daughter Allison eighteen years earlier. The fragile Allison meanwhile (played by an unknown, nineteen-year-old Mia Farrow) formed a romantic entanglement with wealthy Rodney Harrington but then mysteriously 'disappeared' in a fog (when Farrow wanted to quit the series). Allison was not forgotten, however, and from time to time young girls would appear with clues to her disappearance. Other major storylines centred on Rodney Harrington (played by blond, boyish, twenty-three-year-old Ryan O'Neal) who was on trial for murder and defended by young lawyer Steven Cord. By the series' end another resident, handsome young physician Doctor Michael Rossi, would face trial for the murder of his lover Marsha Russell's husband, while the arrival of Dr Harry Miles (played by black Canadian actor Percy Rodrigues) also caused a stir in the strictly WASP community. The town was named after patriarch Martin Peyton who owned Peyton Mill, grandfather of Rodney Harrington but not so aged that he was not set to marry young Adrienne Van Leyden – until her untimely killing in a struggle with Betty Anderson.

Over its five years of production *Peyton Place* employed over 100 actors and actresses and twenty writers who each took responsibilities for specific characters. The set grew from a few houses around a square to include shops, a factory, a hospital, a fire station and a wharf, while the plots grew so complex that new viewers could no longer follow them. It sold to fifty countries, with 8 million viewers in Britain alone, but the change to thrice-weekly instalments proved a mistake and it was cancelled. (Dutch viewers, frustrated that Doctor Rossi's murder charge was left unresolved flew a few cast members to Holland to film their desired happy ending.)

Peyton Place owed its existence to Britain's >*Coronation Street*. In the early sixties America considered soaps worthy only of low budgets and daytime slots, but the success of the *Street* in a prime-time position led producer Paul Monash to search for a similar product for the States. Aiming for the same appeal but with richer, more glamorous characters, he settled on *Peyton Place*, which had already seen service as a lavish 1957 feature starring Lana Turner. The main characters reappeared in 1973 in *Return to Peyton Place*

(NBC), a daytime soap with an entirely different cast, but audiences were unimpressed and it ended after fifty episodes.

Poldark

UK 1976–7 29 × 50m col BBC1. London Films/BBC. *cr* Winston Graham. *pr* Tony Coburn, Richard Beynon, Morris Barry. *dr* Paul Annett, Kenneth Ives, Christopher Barry, Philip Dudley, Roger Jenkins. *wr* Paul Wheeler, Peter Draper, Jack Pulman, Alexander Baron, John Wiles, Martin Worth. *cast* **Ross Poldark** Robin Ellis **Demelza** Angharad Rees **Elizabeth** Jill Townsend **Warleggan** Ralph Bates **Francis Poldark** Chris Francis. *Video* BBC.

Arriving home to brooding eighteenth-century Cornwall after service against the Americans in the Revolutionary War, squire Ross Poldark (Robin Ellis, also *Blue Remembered Hills*, *The Good Soldier*) found his father dead, his estate run down, and his copper mines about to be sold to the scheming Warleggan. Over the following twenty-eight episodes, Poldark, never without his tight breeches and riding boots, fought for his birthright, fought the perfidious French, fought Warleggan (played by Ralph Bates, later to feature in the sitcom *Dear John*), and fought to break the local Parliamentary rotten borough. In between the derring-do, Poldark tried to resolve his feelings for old flame, aristocratic Elizabeth, and his passion for urchin servant girl, the ambitious Demelza. Demelza won.

At its peak this Sunday evening bodice-ripper serial attracted 12 million viewers, many of them women drawn by the romantic hero's pony-tailed dashingness. In a nineties survey of *Radio Times* readers, *Poldark* was voted the drama they most wanted repeated.

Based on the novels by Winston Graham.

Prisoner: Cell Block H

Australia 1979–87 692 × 60m col O-TEN. Grundy. *UK tx* 1989– ITV. *cr* Reg Watson. *exec pr* Reg Watson, Godfrey Philip. *pr* Ian Bradley, Philip East, John McRae, Sue Masters, Marie Trevor. *dr* Various, including Graeme Arthur, Rod Hardy. *wr* Various, including Reg Watson, Ian Bradley, Denise Morgan, Michael Brindley, Ian Smith, Marie Trevor. *mus* (theme) Allan Caswell. *cast* **Karen Travers** Peta Toppano **Lynnette Warner** Kerry Armstrong **Frieda 'Franky' Doyle** Carol Burns **Bea Smith** Val Lehman **Marilyn Anne Mason** Margaret Laurence **Doreen Anderson** Colette Mann **Jeannie 'Mum' Brooks** Mary Ward **Lizzie Birdsworth** Sheila Florance **Chrissie Latham** Amanda Muggleton **Anne Yates** Kristy Child **Noelene Burke** Jude Kuring **Barbara Davidson** Sally Cahill **Sharon Gilmour** Margot Knight **Pixie Mason** Judy McBurney **Rita Connors**. Glenda Linscott **Erica Davidson** Patsy King **Meg Jackson (née Morris)** Elspeth Ballantyne **Vera Bennett** Fiona Spence **Joan Ferguson** Maggie Kirkpatrick **Terri Malone** Margot Knight **Anne Reynolds** Gerda Nicholson **Doctor Greg Miller** Barry Quinn **Jean Vernon** Christine Amor **Jim Fletcher** Gerard Maguire **Eddie Cook** Richard Moir **Steve Wilson** Jim Smillie **Bill Jackson** Don Barker **Steve Faulkner** Wayne Jarratt **Jock Stewart** Tommy Dysart. *Video* NTV/TBD 'Grundy'.

Los Angeles, 10 January 1980. Around fifty leather-clad women bikers congregate outside TV station KTLA-5 on Hollywood's famous Sunset Boulevard. The night before, TV character Franky Doyle, lesbian bikie inmate of the fictitious Wentworth Jail, setting of Australian drama series *Prisoner: Cell Block H*, had been killed by a police bullet while trying to ecape. In total across Los Angeles more than 3,000 Doyle fans assembled to pay homage.

Such were the passions aroused by *Prisoner: Cell Block H*, created for the Grundy organisation by Reg Watson, previously producer of British ITV series >*Crossroads*, and later creator of >*Neighbours*. Watson had been inspired by *Within These Walls*, the British series about a women's prison, to create a similar jail-based show, but one which focused on inmates rather than staff. When Australian Network O-Ten announced they were looking for a hard-hitting, contemporary series it was just the package they wanted. From the outset the series was radically different, with the emphasis on realism; Australia's longest-serving female prisoner, murderess Sandra Wilson, acted as series advisor, while a fact-gathering team visited prisons interviewing staff and inmates. Series art director Ian Costello used more than 350 reference photographs and sketches of Melbourne and Sydney prisons to build sets that ranged from claustrophobic cells and corridors to the Wentworth Detention Centre laundry, the recreation room, the library, the governor's office and the hospital.

Nor did the show eschew violence or sensation. The first few scripts featured a fatal stabbing, a suicide, a hanging and an assault with a hot iron. Lesbian relationships recurred between inmates and staff and violence and brutality were constant themes. Bullying, tattooed lesbian Franky Doyle (in for nine years for armed robbery) regularly slugged it out with stocky dual-killer Bea Smith and, later in the series, sadistic Warder Joan 'The Freak' Ferguson – a lesbian who was to have a relationship with fellow Warder Terri Malone – joined in the mêlées. Even the most apparently sweet-natured inmates had terrifying pasts behind them. Frail, chain-smoking Lizzie Birdsworth had poisoned four sheep shearers with arsenic when they insulted her cooking, beautiful schoolteacher Karen Travers had stabbed her husband to death (and was the unwilling object of Franky Doyle's desire), Doreen Anderson who sucked her thumb was in for forgery (and paired off with the rebuffed Franky), and winsome country girl Lynn Warner (played by Kerry Armstrong, later a much-publicised guest star in >Dynasty) had been convicted of kidnapping a baby and trying to bury him alive.

The staff were almost as colourful, from authoritative, open-minded Governor Erica Davidson to second in charge Warder Vera 'Vinegar Tits' Bennett, the head 'screw' who had a hand of steel and an acid tongue, and Warder Meg Morris. After five years Meg was the only remaining member of the original cast and had suffered a catalogue of ill-treatment which included: the fatal stabbing of her husband jail psychiatrist Bill Jackson (one of the few token men allowed into *Block H*, along with electrician Eddie Cook) by inmate Chrissie Latham, pack-rape by female inmates, a knifing, being shot at and being locked in a booby-trapped building about to explode.

Such heady material made *Block H* one of TV's rare instant hits, and the series, originally scheduled for just sixteen episodes, ran and ran. In 1980 *Prisoner* screened its 100th episode in Australia and won two *TV Week*

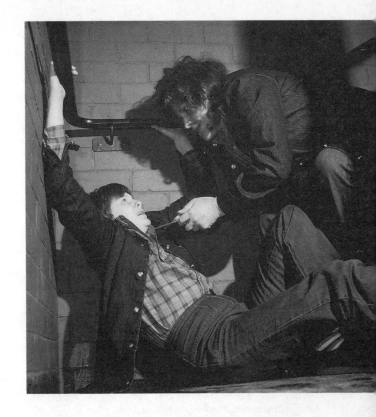

An everyday scene of fighting inmates from Australian jail-house schlock series *Prisoner: Cell Block H*. The show, which has won a worldwide lesbian audience, was created by former *Crossroads* producer Reg Watson.

Logie awards (Australia's equivalent to the US Emmys) for Best Drama Series and Best Actress in a Drama Series (Carol Burns). Sixty-four-year-old Sheila Florance won a Sammy Award for Best Actress in a Series (awarded by votes from actors and actresses within the industry). In 1982 Val Lehman won a Logie for her portrayal of Bea Smith.

In America *Prisoner: Cell Block H* aired on KTLA-5, Los Angeles, from August 1979, and soon outrated all other programmes in its timeslot except >*Charlie's Angels*. By late 1980 the show was on thirty-eight stations across America, and had been sold to Canada. The following year it was sold to New Zealand. Britain, though, did not catch on to the phenomenon until 1989, after the runaway success of Australian teen shows >*Neighbours* and *Home and Away*.

The show spun off a two-hour special, *The Franky Doyle Story*, made up from edited episodes, about the lesbian biker. It was said to be the most VCR-copied telemovie of its time. Grundy TV also attempted a male version of the show. Entitled *Punishment* it was screened over Christmas and New Year 1981–2, but was a failure, despite numbering a young Mel Gibson and Barry Crocker (later to sing the >*Neighbours* theme song) amongst the inmates of Longridge Jail.

'On the Inside', the theme song for the closing Cell *Block* credits sung by Lynne Hamilton was a number one hit in the Australian charts in 1979, and hit the British charts ten years later when the series started gaining millions of regular viewers on the ITV network. Originally titled *Prisoner*, the show was retitled *Prisoner: Cell Block H* for sale to America because of fears that viewers would confuse it with Patrick McGoohan's >*The Prisoner*. In Canada the series was aired as *Caged Women*.

Rock Follies

UK 1976 6 × 60m col ITV. Thames Television. *US tx* 1977 PBS. *cr* Howard Schuman. *exec pr* Verity Lambert. *pr* Andrew Brown. *dr* Brian Farnham, Jon Scoffield. *wr* Howard Schuman. *mus* Andy Mackay, Howard Schuman (lyrics). *cast* **Anna Ward** Charlotte Cornwell **Nancy 'Q' Cunard de Longchamps** Rula Lenska **Devonia 'Dee' Rhoades** Julie Covington **Derek Huggin** Emlyn Price.

Rock Follies was an eccentric and original fusion of music, drama, comedy, satire, fantasy and dance, its roots were as much in the American musicals of the thirties and forties (*42nd Street*, *Babes on Broadway*, *The Gold Diggers of '33*) as in seventies glam rock and women's liberation. Scripts and lyrics were by American Howard Schuman and his idea was simple: six plays about three girls who decide to form themselves into a rock group, The Little Ladies. It was about trying to make it rather than making it – the rehearsals, the hard times, the compromises and the gigs. Gutsy, sassy 'Q', Anna and Dee wore anything from T-shirts and leather jackets to the obligatory metallic jump suits and curly wigs of the period as they went through the mill of clubs, pubs and porn and belted out around fifty songs composed by Andy Mackay of Roxy Music. The Little Ladies were the victims of managers and bankers, publishers, gramophone producers and Golden Disc seducers but they kept on fighting, as numbers such as 'I'm going to live on Sugar Mountain', 'On the Road' and 'Climbing up the Stairway' testified. The songs were germane to the action. Gigging away from home the girls sang, 'I washed my kids and called them pet, I dragged their nappies to the launderette, I've served my sentence so now I get some time off for Good Behaviour.' It was in the fantasy sequences that the links with film musicals were strongest, as the budding rockettes dreamed of being the 'Greatest Rock Group in the World' entertaining screaming fans at Wembley with the number 'Little Ladies' or strutting their stuff for the troops in Northern Ireland with 'Glen Miller is Missing'.

Rock Follies won the BAFTA for Best Drama Series in 1977 and a clutch of craft awards. Its production team was tight and talented, with Verity Lambert (>*Dr Who*, >*Adam Adamant*, *The Sweeney*, *Minder*, >*Hazell*, *GBH*, *Eldorado*), imaginative Controller of Drama at Thames, the person responsible for giving the series the go-ahead. Produced on tape entirely in studio – and sometimes requiring up to fifteen different sets in one episode – *Follies* was shot to look like film with a fast pace and fast edits. Resources were piled into the more spectacular sets such as the ones used in 'The Black and White Idols

Nightclub' and 'The Blitz' while other scenes were shot with little or no background.

A second series was called *Rock Follies of '77*, although a strike at Thames meant most of the run was held up until the following year, and brought with it the ample person of Kitty Schreiber (played by Beth Porter) a high-powered American agent and packager.

Three actresses who sang together as the group Rock Bottom claimed *Rock Follies* was about them and won half a million pounds in compensation.

Route 66

USA 1960–3 116 × 50m bw CBS. Screen Gems/Columbia. *exec pr* Herbert B Leonard. *pr* Jerry Thomas, Sam Manners. *dr* Various, including Robert Altman, Elliot Silverstein, Sam Peckinpah, Richard Donner, Philip Leacock, Ted Post, Arthur Hiller, William Conrad, David Lowell Rich, Tom Gries, Alvin Ganzer, Allen Miner. *wr* Various, including Stirling Silliphant, Howard Rodman, Leonard Freeman, Gill Ralston, William R Cox, Shimon Wincelberg. *mus* Nelson Riddle (theme). *cast* **Tod Stiles** Martin Milner **Buzz Murdoch** George Maharis **Linc Case** Glenn Corbett.

Get your kicks on Route 66. Made some nine years before the film *Easy Rider* hit the road, this picaresque series featured buddies Tod Stiles and Buzz Murdoch cruising the 2,200-mile Chicago–LA Route 66 in an open-top Chevvy in search of adventure, thrills, romance and a place eventually to lay their hats. Tod was a rich man's son, Buzz a poor boy from Hell's Kitchen, New York, who had worked for Tod's deceased father. *En route* they found guest stars galore: Lee Marvin, Robert Duvall, Darren 'Kolchak: The Night Stalker' McGavin, Robert Redford, Boris Karloff, Rod Steiger, Ed Asner, Gene Hackman, Alan Alda, William Shatner and James Coburn amongst them. For some of the series' directors – Robert Altman, Sam Peckinpah, Richard 'Superman' Donner amongt them – the eventual terminus of *Route 66* was Hollywood.

In 1962 George Maharis left the show, allegedly because of hepatitis, although the rumour-mill blamed strained relations with his co-star. He appeared intermittently until March 1963 when he was replaced by Glen Corbett as existentially anguished ex-soldier Linc(oln) Case. The show, with its freewheeling, on-the-road drifter characters was near revered by American teenagers in conformist middle America.

Tenko

UK 1981–6 30 × 55m/1 × 110m col BBC1. BBC. *cr* Lavinia Warner. *pr* Ken Riddington, Vere Lorrimer. *dr* Pennant Roberts, David Askey, David Tucker, Jeremy Summers, Michael Owen Morris. *wr* Jill Hyem, Anne Valery, Paul Wheeler. *mus* James Harpham. *cast* **Marion Jefferson** Ann Bell **Minah** Pauline Peters **Colonel Jefferson** Jonathan Newth **Vicky Armstrong** Wendy Williams **Rose Millar** Stephanie Beacham **Bernard Webster** Edmund Pegge **Corporal Jackson** Colin Dunn **Major Sims** David Gooderson **Sister Ulrica** Patricia Lawrence **Nun** Betsan Jones **Saunders** Gregory de Polnay **Milne** Andrew Sharp **Father Lim** Ric Young **Nellie Keene** Jeananne Crowley **Kate Norris** Claire Oberman **Beatrice Mason** Stephanie Cole **Tom Redburn** Daniel Hill **Jack Armstrong** Ivor Danvers **Simon Treves** Jeffrey Hardy **Christina Campbell** Emily Bolton **Dolah** Ronald Eng **Major Yamauchi** Burt Kwouk **Mrs Van Meyer** Elizabeth Chambers **Dorothy Bennett** Veronica Roberts **Sally Markham** Joanna Hole **Joss Holbrook** Jean Anderson **Debbie Bowen** Karin Foley **Verna Johnson** Rosemary Martin **Miss Hasan** Josephine Welcome **Shinya** Takashi Kawahara **Kasaki** Takahiro Oba **Maggie Thorpe** Elizabeth Mickery **Alice Courtenay** Cindy Shelley **Edna** Edna Dore **Yukio** Peter Silverleaf **Sato** Eiji Kusuhara **Timmy** Nigel Harman **Joan** Dawn Keeler.

In the panic following the fall of Singapore in 1942 hundreds of British women, trying to escape by sea, were captured by the Japanese and interned in makeshift camps where they were forced to come to terms with overcrowding, malnutrition, violence, disease and death. *Tenko* – the word is Japanese for roll-call – told the story of a fictional camp and the women imprisoned in it. It was a series with no stars, no make-up other than boils, bruises, cuts, bites and dirt, no shaved armpits and hardly any men. Research was meticulous and stereotypes avoided, with real-life survivor Molly Smith acting as series advisor throughout. As the series progressed the actresses became more and more ragged, filthy and emaciated as they struggled to survive from day to day. *Tenko* also dealt, without sensationalism, with abortion, suicide, lesbian love, stillbirth, prostitution and euthanasia.

There was a wide range of women – some Dutch, some British (which was a constant source of conflict) – with different backgrounds and characters: Marion Jefferson, wife of a Colonel, soon had leadership of the camp forced upon her; Dr Beatrice Mason (played by Stephanie Cole, *Waiting for God*) did not suffer fools gladly; Sister Ulrica was the formidable leader of the more privileged Dutch contingent; Rose Millar (Stephanie Beacham) was an independent 'man's woman'; 'Joss' Holbrook was an Oxford graduate and suffragette; genteel Verna Johnson had her own maid, orphaned Daisy; Miss Hasan worked for the second camp's commandant; and Dorothy Bennett lost both husband and child and turned to prostitution with the Japanese guards.

Tenko's women endured much in the series' three seasons: the degradation and despair – and comradeship – of camp one; a gruelling march through the jungle to the old mission school that became camp two; a direct hit in an allied attack; and, for those who made it to the end of the war – Marion, Beatrice, Joss, Dorothy, Mrs Van Meyer, Kate and Christina – the problems that came with freedom. Nonetheless, five years after their release (Christmas 1986 for viewers) the women returned to Singapore for the *Tenko Reunion*.

Anne Valery and Jill Hyem were almost the only writers on the series. They had both made the move from acting to scriptwriting and had written episodes of *Angels*, but had never met before. Series creator, Lavinia Warner, went on to form an independent production company, Warner Sisters, which produced another successful 'women-only' series, *Rides*, about a taxi firm of women drivers.

thirtysomething

USA 1987–91 85 × 60m col ABC. MGM. *UK tx* 1989–92 C4.
cr Ed Zwick, Marshall Herskovitz. *pr* Ed Zwick, Marshall Herskovitz, Paul Haggis. *dr* Various, including Marshall Herskovitz, Ed Zwick, Ken Olin, Peter Horton, Tim Busfield, Melanie Myron. *wr* Various, including Ed Zwick, Marshall Herskovitz. *cast* **Michael Steadman** Ken Olin **Hope Murdoch Steadman** Mel Harris **Janey Steadman** Brittany and Lacey Craven **Elliot Weston** Timothy Busfield **Nancy Weston** Patricia Wettig **Ethan Weston** Luke Rossi **Brittany Weston** Jordana 'Bink' Shapiro **Melissa Steadman** Melanie Mayron **Ellyn** Polly Draper **Professor Gary Shepherd** Peter Horton **Miles Drentell** David Clennon **Susannah Hart** Patricia Kalember **Billy Sidel** Erich Anderson **Jeffrey Milgrom** Richard Gilland **Lee Owens** Corey Parker.

Michael and Hope and Elliot and Nancy and Melissa and Ellyn and Gary – two married couples and three singles – were all 'thirtysomething'. The seven yuppie characters, who lived in Philadelphia, shared a relationship of love, tears and a penchant for analysing their problems at length. Surrounded by material comfort, placed in creative or academic jobs, worrying about whether to have children or about the children they already had, they were the essence of the late eighties baby boomers. Michael and Elliot had worked together at a large advertising agency before leaving to form their own. Michael's wife Hope, a dark-haired overachiever from Princeton, wanted to be a superstar in publishing but for now was raising newborn baby Janey. Elliot's wife Nancy, a blonde one-time sixties flower child, had dreams of being an artist but was raising their now school-age children, Ethan and Britanny. Melissa was Michael's photographer want-it-all single cousin; Ellyn was Hope's long-time friend, a worried career woman; and long-haired Gary, an easy-going Assistant Professor of Classics at a nearby college, was Michael's best buddy.

Storylines concentrated on relationships marital and sexual, shared angst, and thwarted creativity. No relationship was simple. By early 1988 Elliot and Nancy were going through a painful separation which took an entire season and then suddenly decided to reconcile. This left young Ethan insecure but worse was to come when Nancy was diagnosed as having cancer. Michael and Hope also hit problems in their marriage with the birth of second child, Leo, in 1990 but Hope compensated by spending time on an environmental campaign. The singles Melissa and Ellyn, meanwhile, searched on for Mr

'Er, um, maybe we should talk about this . . .' The cast of angst-ridden Philadelphians who were *thirtysomething*, a show created by East Coast Jewish writers Marshall Herskovitz (a friend of Woody Allen) and Ed Zwick. From left to right actors Timothy Busfield (holding Jordana Shapiro), Patricia Wettig (holding Luke Rossi), Mel Harris, Ken Olin (holding Brittany Craven), Polly Draper, Melanie Myron and Peter Horton. In real life Ken Olin was married to Patricia Wettig, while Peter Horton was one-time husband of Michelle Pfeiffer.

Right. Ellyn, after extended affairs and shorter flings finally married Billy Sidel whom she had years earlier discarded. Gary moved in with Susannah who bore him a child, Emma, but was fired from his teaching position making it difficult to support his new family. In early 1991 he suddenly died, devastating his circle of friends. And for Michael and Elliot friendship was tested when their small agency went bankrupt and they were forced to work for cold, cunning businessman Miles Drentell.

Sentimental and self-indulgent *thirtysomething* may have been, but it won a devoted following. Filmed in studio, it prided itself on its apparent realism – sets were messy, characters were given real wardrobes of clothes to

mix and match and the series used off-hand filming techniques which gave scenes a spontaneous feel. Conversation, too, was true-to-life with all the confusions of everyday speech. Problems that were difficult to articulate were discussed with, uh, well, all their pauses and fumbles lovingly recreated. Therapists showed the results in their counselling sessions. And the series could be daring. When an episode featured two men in bed it incensed conservative pressure groups and lost the network $1.5 million in cancelled commercials.

But eventually *thirtysomething*'s creators found it increasingly difficult to invent plausible situations to keep the thirtysomethings in dialogue and decided the series had run its course – most of the characters were soon to be fortysomething anyway – and the show ended after eighty-five soul-searching episodes.

Creators Herskovitz and Zwick (also director of the film *Glory*) started out as writers for Spelling/Goldberg's prime-time series *Family* (ABC 1976–80), centring on the lives of a Californian middle-class family, and went on to write, direct and produce NBC TV movies *Special Bulletin* and *Extreme Close-Up*, 1990. Their production company is called Bedford Falls after the town in Frank Capra's heart-searching tear-jerker *It's a Wonderful Life*.

Triangle

UK 1981–3 78 × 25m col BBC1. BBC. cr Bill Sellars. pr Bill Sellars. dr Various, including Marc Miller, Terence Dudley, Darrol Blake. wr Various, including Luanshya Greer, Ben Steed, David Hopkins, Sue Lake. mus Johnny Pearson. cast **Katherine Laker** Kate O'Mara **John Anderson** Michael Craig **Matt Taylor** Larry Lamb **Wally James** Nigel Stock **Charles Woodhouse** Paul Jerricho **Judith Harper** Joan Greenwood **Mrs Landers** Dawn Addams **David West** George Baker **Sarah Hallam** Penelope Horner **Arthur Parker** Douglas Sheldon.

The definitively awful soap opera, so bad that it was mesmeric. The geometric shape of the title was the route taken (exotic Felixstowe to Gothenburg to Rotterdam) by a North Sea ferry. Kate O'Mara starred as chief purser Katherine Laker. As with Bill Sellars' previous series,

>*The Brothers*, also featuring O'Mara, *Triangle* mixed bedroom with boardroom. (O'Mara's purpose as series' sex symbol was made bare in episode one when she appeared semi-naked.) Added to the formula were accidents at sea and customs violations. At the time the series was hailed as a breakthrough in drama production, because new lightweight cameras allowed all the filming to be done on location, the ferry *Tor Scandinavia*. A studio was even built in the ship's hold for editing. Unfortunately, none of the production team understood that the North Sea is amongst the world's roughest and coldest; as a result, the actors always had the green pallor of seasickness, and exterior shots were usually shrouded in mist with the actors buffeted by the wind. Also, the difference in light balance in the cabins between the interior and porthole exterior was so great that curtains had to be kept permanently closed. The result was gloomy claustrophobia. Kate O'Mara jumped the disaster ship after the first season. *Triangle* itself sank just two seasons later.

Upstairs, Downstairs

UK 1971–5 68 × 50m col ITV. London Weekend Television. USA tx 1974–7 PBS. cr Jean Marsh, Eileen Atkins. pr John Hawkesworth. dr Bill Bain, Cyril Coke, Christopher Hodson, Raymond Menmuir, Herbert Wise, Derek Bennett, Lionel Harris, James Ormerod. wr John Hawkesworth, Terence Brady, Charlotte Bingham, Jeremy Paul, Alfred Shaughnessy, Rosemary Anne Sisson, Anthony Skene, Deborah Mortimer, Fay Weldon, Elizabeth Jane Howard. mus Alexander Faris. cast **Rose** Jean Marsh **Sarah** Pauline Collins **Lord Richard Bellamy** David Langton **Hudson** Gordon Jackson **Mrs Bridges** Angela Baddeley **Lady Marjorie Bellamy** Rachel Gurney **Hazel Bellamy** Meg Wynn Owen **Virginia Hamilton** Hannah Gordon **Captain James Bellamy** Simon Williams **Georgina** Lesley-Anne Down **Elizabeth** Nicola Pagett **Edward** Christopher Beeny.

Soapy period drama, about a wealthy Edwardian family and its servants, set in an elegant London townhouse, 165 Eaton Place. Conceived beside a swimming pool in the South of France by resting actresses Jean Marsh and

Elizabeth Walton Kami Cotler ***Jason Walton*** Jon Walmsley ***Erin Walton*** Mary Elizabeth McDonough ***Ben Walton*** Eric Scott ***Grandpa Zeb Walton*** Will Geer ***Grandma Esther Walton*** Ellen Corby ***Ike Godsey*** Joe Conley ***Corabeth Godsey*** Ronnie Claire Edwards ***Aimmee Godsey*** Rachel Longaker ***Sheriff Ep Bridges*** John Crawford ***Emily Baldwin*** Mary Jackson ***Mamie Baldwin*** Helen Kleeb ***Rosemary Fordwicke*** Mariclare Costello ***Rev Matthew Fordwicke*** John Ritter ***Dr Curtis Willard*** Tom Bower/Scott Hylands ***Arlington Westcott 'Jonesy' Jones*** Richard Gilliland ***Narrator*** Earl Hamner Jr.

Sentimental saga about a barefoot-but-happy hick family which operated a sawmill in the Blue Ridge Mountains of Virginia during the Depression of the thirties. Featured were Ralph Waite as John Walton, head of the clan, Michael Learned as ever-loving wife Olivia, and Richard Thomas (in the final seasons, Robert Wightman) as John Boy Walton, the eldest son and a would-be novelist. It was through John Boy's moist eyes that the morally uplifting events on Walton's Mountain were seen. The other Walton children were: Mary Ellen, Jason, Erin, Ben, Elizabeth and Jim-Bob. Grandpa Zeb and Grandma Esther completed the family line-up.

In the 1977 season of the show John Boy achieved his American dream and had his first novel published, allowing him to move to the literary scene in New York. Around the same time his sister Mary Ellen married Dr Curtis Willard, and the series moved up in time to World

to War II. Thereafter, weepiness threatened to drown the
a S¹tons: Grandma became ill, Grandpa died, Curtis
tion d went MIA at Pearl Harbor, and Olivia contracted
amily fr ael Learned, who won three Emmy Awards for
d War I amance as Walton *mère*, wanted out of the
ly's abandortage of materials and manpower obliged
embers and st shut the mill temporarily. Then Mary
al barometer ot with student Jonesy, only to discover
bled scripts to ad been killed after all. (She chose
vement, the General end, John Walton sold the mill to
jazz age. Producer Johrizona to be with Olivia during
tory student, scoured pe.
London *Times*, House o
hemera of all kinds to ensur
ueprint of the five-storey Ea
nstructed in minute detail.

Based on the autobiographical novel by narrator Earl Hamner Jr, the wholesome, heart-warming series piloted as a TV movie, *The Homecoming* (it had already been a theatrical release in 1967, as the rather more rugged *Spencer's Mountain*, starring Henry Fonda). Although *The Waltons* finished production in 1981, it spawned three made-for-TV movies the following year, *A Day for Thanks on Walton's Mountain*, *Mother's Day on Walton's Mountain* and *Wedding on Walton's Mountain*. The series won the Emmy for Outstanding Drama in 1973. Earl Hamner Jr went on to create *Falcon's Crest*.

The Water Margin

Japan 1975 30+ × 45m col NTV. NTV Tokyo. *UK tx* 1976–78 BBC2. *dr* Toshio Masuda, Michael Bakewell (English dubbing). *wr* David Weir (English adaptation). *mus* Masaru Sato. *cast* **Lin Chung** Atsuo Nakamura **Kao Chia** Kei Sato **Wu Sung** Hajine Hana **Hu San-niang** Sanae Tschida **Hsiao Lan** Yoshiyo Matuso (English voices: Michael McClain, Miriam Margoyles, Peter Marinker, Elizabeth Proud, Sean Lynch, Trevor Martin, Bert Kwouk).

Sword-rattling, gloriously theatrical version of the thirteenth-century Chinese epic of the same title by Shih Nai-an which told the tale of the 108 reborn chivalrous knights who fought tyranny and corrupt government from their base in the water margins of the Lian Shan Po. Lin Chung, an inveterate rescuer of damsels in distress (despite being accompanied by his Lotus Blossom wife, Hsiao) and righter of wrongs, was their pony-tailed, charismatic leader. English adapter David Weir followed up this samurai success by translating another Japanese version of a Chinese classic for TV, Wu Ch'eng-en's *Monkey*, a sort of Buddhist *Pilgrim's Progress*. Masaaki Sakai starred as the eponymous god-king.

Comedy

Absolutely Fabulous

UK 1992– 18 × 30m col BBC2/BBC1. BBC. *cr* Jennifer Saunders, Dawn French. *pr* Jon Plowman. *dr* Bob Spiers. *wr* Jennifer Saunders. *mus* (theme) performed by Julie Driscoll, Adrian Edmondson. *cast* **Edina Monsoon** Jennifer Saunders **Patsy** Joanna Lumley **Saffron** Julia Sawalha **Bubble** Jane Horrocks **Mother** June Whitfield.

Edina Monsoon (Jennifer Saunders), a desperately trendy single mother in her very late thirties, has gone through two failed marriages and had a child from each. She runs her own PR/design/fashion business, has recently been through a crystal phase and is now trying her neurotic best to deal with the heavy burden of her career, the sheer social whirl of the fashion world, and the ghastly reality of her teenage daughter Saffron (her son is leading his own life at university). Saffron, poor dear, is hideously unfashionable – she works hard, disapproves of alcohol and talks earnestly to her friends about science projects. When for one brief, wonderful moment, Edina thinks her daughter may be a lesbian, it turns out that Saffron is just more interested in work than boys.

This cannot be said for Edina's best friend, the luscious, mini-skirted Patsy (Joanna Lumley) who provides a running theme for the series by (literally) chasing men. Patsy – to quote Lumley – 'smokes like a chimney, drinks like a fish, dresses like a dream and has a fragile grasp of what work is'. While Edina struggles to conquer life's perpetual problems such as what designer outfit to wear, magazine fashion editor Patsy, whose friendship with Edina dates back to their school days, can be guaranteed to sidetrack her. Meanwhile Bubble (Jane Horrocks), Edina's cheery but totally inefficient secretary, does her best to maintain office operations and Edina's thoroughly sensible mother (June Whitfield) always comes down on Saffron's side.

Absolutely Fabulous was an immediate ratings and critical success – it took number one position in BBC2's viewing figures and won two BAFTA Awards for its first season, one for the series and one for Joanna Lumley's performance. The series was Jennifer Saunders' first major solo project after twelve years performing with partner Dawn French, and was conceived as a response to possible unemployment while French was engaged in her own series *Murder Most Horrid*. The character of Edina (rumoured to be based on real-life fashion PR Lynne Franks) was originally seen as a *French and Saunders* sketch and enlarged upon for Saunders' solo series. Script editor for *Absolutely Fabulous* was Ruby Wax, with whom Saunders co-starred in *Girls on Top* and on whose show she also guested. Saunders' husband, Adrian Edmondson of >*The Young Ones* and >*Bottom*, whose slot *Absolutely Fabulous* took over, performed the series' theme tune, 'Wheels on Fire' together with Julie Driscoll. He also guested in the series as a restaurant critic. Other guest stars have included Alexandra Bastedo, one-time star of >*The Champions*.

Jennifer Saunders is an original member of The Comic Strip and featured in all their productions including *Five Go Mad in Dorset* and *Strike* (winner of the Golden Rose of Montreux). Her TV credits include two series of *Girls on Top* for Central TV with Dawn French, Ruby Wax and Tracy Ullman, *Happy Families*, and *French and Saunders* for the BBC. One-time photographic model Joanna Lumley's TV credits include >*Steptoe and Son, Up the Workers, Darling*, >*Coronation Street*, >*The New Avengers*, >*Sapphire and Steel* and *Lovejoy*. Among her film credits are *On Her Majesty's Secret Service, The Trail of the Pink Panther* and *Shirley Valentine*. Julia Sawalha is best known for her role as newspaper editor in >*Press Gang*. Her other TV credits include *Inspector Morse, Casualty* and *Smith and Jones*. Jane Horrocks starred on the stage in *The Rise and Fall of Little Voice*, specially written for her. Her TV credits include *La Nonna* with Les Dawson, *Came Out, It Was Rainy, Went Inside, Roots* and >*Red Dwarf*. June Whitfield started out in radio in *Take It From Here* and as Eth in *The Glums*. She starred in a series of *Carry On* films and has worked on TV with comedy greats including Hancock, Arthur Askey, Benny Hill, Dick Emery, Frankie Howerd, Ronnie Barker and Leslie Crowther. She is probably best known for her long partnership with Terry Scott, which started with *Scott On*, then *Happy Ever After* and finally >*Terry and June* which ran for thirteen years on BBC1. Jon Plowman produced the award-winning *French and Saunders* and *Smith and Jones*. Bob Spiers has directed some of the best British TV comedy series – among them episodes of >*Fawlty Towers, It Ain't Half Hot Mum*, >*Dad's Army*, >*Are You Being Served?, The Goodies, Comic Strip Presents, French and Saunders, Ruby Wax* and *Alexei Sayle*.

Morticia Frump Addams Carolyn Jones ***Gomez Addams*** John Astin ***Uncle Fester Frump*** Jackie Coogan ***Lurch*** Ted Cassidy ***Grandmama Addams*** Blossom Rock ***Pugsley Addams*** Ken Weatherwax ***Wednesday Thursday Addams*** Lisa Loring ***Cousin Itt*** Felix Silla ***Thing*** Ted Cassidy. *Video* Polygram.

New Yorker magazine cartoonist Charles Addams' macabre family made live. Heading the 'altogether ookie' family were Gomez Addams, a suave lawyer who kept a pet octopus called Aristotle, and his tantalising, black-clad wife Morticia who lovingly cultivated a man-eating plant. The musty household was filled with strange antique objects (moving antlers, stuffed bears, a giant turtle, suits of armour) as well as ghoulish, bald-headed Uncle Fester who lit electric light bulbs by putting them in his mouth, gaunt, imposing family butler Lurch, who was six feet nine inches tall, played the harpsichord and spoke in a cavernous rumble ('You rang?') and haggish Grandmama. The wonderfully weird Addams nurtured two perverse children, daughter Wednesday, who played with a headless doll and a black widow spider named Homer, and son Pugsley, who kept a gallows and an electric chair in his playroom. Fetching, carrying and small tasks around the house such as the lighting of cigarettes or looking up of phone numbers were performed by disembodied hand-in-a-box, Thing (actually Ted Cassidy's hand, unless Lurch was in shot). The extended family included the hirsute Cousin Itt, played by midget Felix Silla. Each episode began with the sombre family group adding percussive finger clicks to the show's catchy theme tune.

A celebration of the bizarre (and so an implied attack on normality), *The Addams Family*'s memorable appeal lay in its sophisticated black humour, the simmering sexual attraction between Gomez and Morticia, who

The 'altogether ookie' members of the *Addams Family*, one of the first of a wave of bizarre sixties sitcoms. The countercultural role models were: standing, left to right: Gomez (John Astin), Uncle Fester (Jackie Coogan), Lurch (Ted Cassidy) and Grandmama (Blossom Rock); seated, front: Morticia (Carolyn Jones) and daughter Wednesday (Lisa Loring). Carolyn Jones landed the role because producers ABC insisted on a named Hollywood actress for the part (she had won an Oscar nomination for a six-minute role as a beatnik in the 1956 film *Bachelor Party*). John Astin originally auditioned for the part of Lurch but was offered the role of wealthy lawyer Gomez – provided he grew a moustache. Post *Addams Family*, Astin has worked mainly behind the TV camera as a director and writer.

the road. The kookie lovebirds even felt obliged to visit their mayor to point out that their council tax was ridiculously low, and worried because they never rowed.

An animated version of *The Addams Family* aired on NBC in 1973. A feature film *The Addams Family*, starring Angelica Houston as Morticia, was a huge box office success in 1991, taking $24 million in its first weekend showing, although its dependence on special effects and lack of subtlety made it inferior to the TV series. It was followed by a second feature, the 1993 *Addams Family Values*.

Actor John Astin played Harry Dickens in *I'm Dickens . . . He's Fenster* and Candy's Uncle Jack in the controversial all-star sex satire *Candy*, 1969. He was also an accomplished director, making his début with *Prelude* in 1968, a short film which he wrote, produced and starred in and which won him an Oscar nomination. His subsequent TV work included, among others, episodes on the series >*Macmillan and Wife* and *Night Gallery*, for which he directed two particularly interesting segments, 'The House' and 'The Dark Boy'.

'Allo, 'Allo

UK 1982–92 Approx 55 × 30m col BBC1. BBC1. *cr* David Croft, Jeremy Lloyd. *pr* David Croft, Mike Stephens. *dr* David Croft, Mike Stephens, Sue Longstaff. *wr* David Croft, Jeremy Lloyd, Paul Adam. *cast* **René Artois** Gordon Kaye **Edith** Carmen Silvera **Yvette** Vicki Michelle **Maria** Francesca Gonshaw **Michelle** Kirsten Cooke **Lieutenant Gruber** Guy Siner **Mme Fanny** Rose Hill **Flying Officer Fairfax** John D Collins **Flying Officer Carstairs** Nicholas Frankau **Colonel Von Strohm** Richard Marner **Von Klinkerhoffen** Hilary Minster **Captain Hans Geering** Sam Kelly **Helga** Kim Hartmann **M Leclerc** Jack Haig, Derek Royle, Robin Parkinson **Herr Flick** Richard Gibson (1984–91), David Jansen (1992) **Mimi** Sue Hodge **Von Smallhausen** John Louis Mansi **Alfonse** Kenneth Connor **Crabtree** Arthur Bostrom **Bertorelli** Gavin Richards, Roger Kitter.

A send-up of *Secret Army* and the long line of films and television serials in which plucky Brits and French Resistance fighters give their all for their country against

'Leesten very carefooly, I weel say zees ernly wernce . . .'
Some failed to see the joke in Croft and Lloyd's slapstick
wartime spoof *'Allo 'Allo*, but Britain's Northern Examining
Board chose to put it on the GCSE syllabus. Featured were:
top, standing, left to right: Yvette (Vicki Michelle), Herr Flick
(Richard Gibson), Helga (Kim Hartman), Lt Gruber (Guy
Siner), Capt Hans Geering (Sam Kelly), Col von Strohm
(Richard Marner): middle row: Maria (Francesca Gonshaw),
Mme Fanny (Rose Hill), René Artois (Gordon Kaye), Edith
(Carmen Silvera); front: second from left: Michelle (Kirsten
Cooke).

the dastardly Germans. The time is 1940, the place a café in the small town of Nouvion in occupied Northern France. While the patron waits on German officers and Madame entertains the customers with a selection of songs, there is a girl from the Resistance waiting in the back room, two British airmen hiding upstairs in a cupboard in grandmother's bedroom, and a radio transmitter hidden under the bed. But this is 'Allo, 'Allo and consequently René is less frightened of the Germans than he is of his wife Edith finding out about his peccadillos with waitresses Yvette and Maria, Gestapo officer Herr Flick gets a headache if people raise their voices and Madame's voice is so bad that the customers plug their ears with cheese.

More panto than drama and heavy with *Carry On*-style *double entendres*, 'Allo 'Allo outraged and scandalised many. But that is to miss the rollicking, knock-about farce of it all – the elaborate and ridiculous escape plots, the eternal stupidity of the Germans who fail to smell a rat, the implausibility of plump, balding René as an object of ceaseless desire. With a long list of running jokes and catchphrases – The Fallen Madonna with the Big Boobies, the earnest repetition by the raincoat- and beret-sporting Michelle in every episode of the Resistance's latest instructions: 'Leesten very carefooly, I weel say zees ernly wernce', Herr Flick's passion for Helga who hides a whalebone corset and black suspenders under her SS uniform, Secret Serviceman Crabtree's preposterous French accent which he sincerely believes renders him invisible in the small French town and the need for eternal subterfuge with entries and exits regularly accomplished through windows. 'Allo 'Allo poked fun at all the stereotypes.

Of course there were complaints. Co-creator David Croft answered those who saw 'Allo 'Allo as an insult to those who fought in the war by pointing out how evenly the series poked fun: 'Our Germans are insensitive, nest-feathering and kinky, the French are devious, nest-feathering and immoral and the British are real twits. No nation should feel it's been singled out!' he claimed.

And somebody must have seen the joke because 'Allo 'Allo was loved throughout Europe for a full ten years after its pilot episode was aired and even the French bought it in 1989, although a deal with the Americans fell through. The final series bowed out as the war drew to an end and the Colonel and Gruber headed for the Spanish border dressed as flamenco dancers.

David Croft, who produced as well as wrote the first series, liked to reuse his comic actors. Gordon Kaye, first seen on TV as Elsie Tanner's nephew Bernard Butler in >*Coronation Street* (1968) has also played in Croft's >*Are You Being Served?*, and *It Ain't Half Hot Mum*. Carmen Silvera (who was the subject of *This Is Your Life* in 1990) played Captain Mainwaring's fling in an early episode of >*Dad's Army*. Arthur Bostrom featured in >*Hi de Hi!*

Co-creators Croft and Lloyd have a string of TV credits between them. Actor and writer Jeremy Lloyd is co-author of *Rowan and Martin's Laugh In* and, with David Croft, of >*Are You Being Served?* Producer and writer David Croft is holder of television's highest accolade, the Desmond Davies Award. Son of musical comedy star Anne Croft, he joined first Tyne Tees Television as a producer and later went to the BBC. He has written and produced over 100 stage and television shows including >*Dad's Army*, *It Ain't Half Hot Mum* and >*Hi de Hi!* with co-writer Jimmy Perry. In 1979 he was awarded the OBE for services to television.

Are You Being Served?

UK 1974–84 60 × 30m col BBC1. BBC. *cr* Jeremy Lloyd and David Croft. *pr* David Croft. *dr* Various, including Bob Spiers, Bernard Thompson. *wr* Jeremy Lloyd and David Croft. *cast* **Mrs Slocombe** Mollie Sugden **Mr Humphries** John Inman **Miss Brahms** Wendy Richards **Captain Peacock** Frank Thornton **Mr Granger** Arthur Brough **Mr Lucas** Trevor Bannister **Mr Rumbold** Nicholas Smith **Mr Harman** Arthur English **Young Mr Grace** Harold Bennett. *Video* BBC.

The doors of Grace Brothers department store first opened in 1974 as part of the BBC's *Comedy Playhouse*, launching the disaster-prone staff of Ladies and Gentleman's Ready to Wear on an eleven-year career of bargain basement jokes (customers stuck in lifts, innuendos such as 'There's my pussy to consider'). As with David Croft's other shows, which include >*Dad's*

Army and >Hi de Hi! the atmosphere was quaintly old-fashioned. John Inman's portrayal of camp, mincing menswear assistant Mr Humphries, who volunteered to measure an inside leg with alacrity and a cry of 'I'm free', made him a household name. (Inman said he based the character on shop assistants he had known during a brief employment as a window dresser for Austin Reed.) Also appearing were Wendy Richards (later Pauline Fowler in *EastEnders*) as tottering blonde Miss Brahms, Mollie Sugden (*That's My Boy, My Husband and I*) as lacquered, pompous Mrs Slocombe, Frank Thornton as clipped floorwalker Captain Peacock and Trevor Bannister as menswear assistant Mr Lucas. In America the show had a successful run on PBS, although a US version entitled *Beane's of Boston* never caught on. A film version of *Are You Being Served?* was released in 1977.

In 1992 the main cast of the show, save for Trevor Bannister, was reunited in a spin-off, *Grace and Favour*, based in a country house hotel bequeathed them them by store owner, young Mr Grace (who had bought it with their pension fund).

Barney Miller

USA 1975–82 168 × 25m col ABC. Columbia TV. *cr* Danny Arnold, Theodore Flicker. *pr* Danny Arnold, Chris Hayward. *dr* Various, including John Rich, Tony Sheehan, Robert Day, Danny Arnold, Noam Pitlik. *wr* Various, including Danny Arnold, Chris Hayward, Reinhold Weege, Bob Colleary, Jordan Moffat, Nat Mauldin, Tony Sheehan, Jeff Stein, Frank Dungan. *mus* Jack Elliott, Ally Fergusson. *cast* **Capt Barney Miller** Hal Linden **Det Sgt Phil Fish** Abe Vigoda **Det Sgt Chano Amenguale** Gregory Sierra **Det Sgt Stan Wojciehowicz** Maxwell Gail **Det Sgt Nick Yemena** Jack Soo **Det Sgt Ron Harris** Ron Glass **Insp Frank Luger** James Gregory **Det Sgt Arthur Dietrich** Steve Landesburg **Off Carl Levitt** Ron Carey **Elizabeth Miller** Abby Dalton (pilot)/Barbara Barrie.

After airing the pilot of this comedy about a compassionate New York cop and his confederates, the American ABC network promptly binned the idea, which they considered too 'busy'. It was only resurrected to please hot director John Rich (of *All in the Family* fame) whom ABC were desperate to recruit, and who was a personal friend of *Barney Miller*'s co-creator Danny Arnold. Shot on videotape, the celebrated downbeat look of the series' squad room – where virtually all the action took place – was achieved by a complex lighting arrangement, adjusted for each scene (as is done in movie-making). As a result, the shooting schedule often lasted far into the night. To play the varied Twelfth Precinct cops, ABC brought in a fine ensemble cast, headed by Hal Linden (aka Harold Lipschitz) as Barney Miller, but the episodes were frequently made good by the guest cast who acted the eccentrics (including a werewolf), prostitutes, vandals, crooks and other forms of street life who passed through the station house. The humour was sardonic, taking a rare prime-time wit, intelligence and humanism to such taboo subjects as mental illness, arson and teenage pregnancy. After eight seasons, the crew and cast decided to close the New York cop shop for the simple reason that they were running out of topics to deflate, and they wanted to bow out with artistic standards intact. In the last episode, a three-parter called 'Landmark', the station house was declared a site of historic significance (it had been the campaign HQ of Theodore Roosevelt), and the Twelfth was disbanded.

Barney Miller was awarded an Emmy for Outstanding Writing (Bob Colleary's 'The Photographer' episode) in 1980, and an Emmy for Outstanding Comedy Series in 1982. So enamoured with the show was the Mayor of Los Angeles that on its fifth anniversary he instituted 'Barney Miller Week'.

One of the show's most popular characters, the worn-down, ever-complaining Detective Phil Fish (played by Abe Vigoda, also the Mafia don Tessio in the film *The Godfather*) was given his own series, *Fish*, in 1977.

Beavis & Butt-Head

USA 1992– 66+ × 30m col MTV. MTV Networks. *UK tx* 1993– MTV/C4. *cr* Mike Judge. *exec pr* Abby Terkhule. *pr* John Andrews. *dr* Various. *wr* Various, including Mike

Judge, Sam Johnson, Chris Marcil, David Felton, Tracy Grandstaff. cast **Beavis/Butt-head** Mike Judge (voices).

Huh-huh, huh-huh, huh-huh. Beavis and Butt-Head were two ugly, pubescent cartoon males variously regarded as 'the latest link in the Darwinian descent of the American adolescent' (*New York Times*) or *'idiots savants'* (*Rolling Stone*), even 'the first truly modern attempt at TV' (*Time*). Moronically stupid, vicious, anal- and genital-fixated, Beavis (blond hair, Metallica T-shirt, shorts, distended lower jaw) and Butt-Head (brown hair, AC/DC T-shirt, short upper lip) spent half of their thirty-minute show critiquing pop music videos. Their philosophy of aesthetics was simple: explosions, thrash metal (accompanied by the playing of air guitars), 'chicks' with 'thingees', and death, were 'cool'. Almost everything else was greeted with the judgement: 'this sucks'. They remorselessly jeered the manhood of high-voiced heavy metal hopefuls ('wusses') and cruelly pricked pop pretensions, once memorably claiming that the straining, anguished singer Edie Bricknell looked like she was 'pinching a loaf'. Occasionally, they mooned at the screen, while the vaguest double-entendre ('He said come . . .') would set off a breathy stuttering chorus of 'huh-huh, huh-huh, huh-huh'.

Away from the couch, the glue-sniffing duo wandered a suburban, parentless wasteland of shopping malls and monster truck rallies, embarking on sordid adventures which sometimes proved controversial. Amongst other outrages, they played baseball with a live frog, sniffed paint thinner, deep-fried a rat, put a vomit-coated poodle in a washing machine, graffitied 'MEGADEATH' on the side of a teacher's house, and blew up a locust with a firecracker. In one episode they shot down an aircraft, but failed to call the emergency services after becoming distracted by flatulence. After an Ohio mother claimed that the pyromaniacal pair caused her five-year-old son to burn down their trailer home, killing his two-year-old sister, the ensuing controversy led MTV to give the show a late night time-slot and a disclaimer to the effect that *B&B* were not real people and their pranks should not be tried at home. This did not stop former TV producer and California state lottery winner, Dick Zimmerman, campaigning to ban *B&B* and setting up a hotline for irate and concerned parents.

Beavis and Butt-Head were the creation of Mike Judge, an American born (in 1963) in Ecuador. A sometime musician and physics student at the University of California at San Diego, Judge based the characters of Beavis and Butt-Head on 'people I knew in junior high and kids I just see everywhere', developing them for the screen with the help of a $300 animation kit. Though Judge claimed only to be 'sending up the kids who watch MTV', the humour of the show – written mostly by Judge and *National Lampoon* alumni Sam Johnson and Chris Marcil – had a subversive, as well as a puerile, edge; in one episode, the metalheads did a school report on the *Challenger* disaster, destroying a toy rocket in science class, an act which tastelessly but effectively burlesqued government and NASA propaganda.

Although *B&B* sent up the MTV generation of 'blank heads', the show ironically debuted on MTV's *Liquid Television* series in September 1992 with 'Frog Baseball'. *B&B* got their own show on the station just three months later, with MTV rushing sixty-five episodes into production. Conspicuously running counter to MTV's self-consciously politically correct ethos, *Beavis & Butt-Head* became the station's most popular show, earning over $15 million in ad revenue in 1994 alone. As is the way of all television, the metalhead teenagers eventually graduated to a major cinema feature, the ultimate sign of societal acceptance and commercial success.

The Beverly Hillbillies

USA 1962–70 216 × 25m bw/col CBS. Filmways. *UK tx* 1964–70 ITV. cr Paul Henning. pr Paul Henning, Al Simon, Joseph DePew, Mark Tuttle. dr Various, including Joseph DePew. wr Various, including Paul Henning. mus Jerry Scoggins (theme), Lester Flatt, Earl Scruggs. cast **Jed Clampett** Buddy Ebsen **Granny (Daisy Moses)** Irene Ryan **Elly May Clampett** Donna Douglas **Jethro Bodine** Max Baer Jr **Milburn Drysdale** Raymond Bailey **Jane Hathaway** Nancy Kulp.

The adventures of the hillbilly Clampett family who discovered oil on their backwoods ranch, and then decamped to Beverly Hills to live the high life.

The backwoods Clampett family went to live the high life in Southern California in the CBS sitcom *The Beverly Hillbillies*. Though panned by the critics, it was the fastest success in the history of American television, shooting to the top of the ratings in record time. It also spawned a string of 'rustic' comedies. The stars were, from left to right: ex-dancer and *Davy Crockett* star Buddy Ebsen (Pa Clampett), Irene Ryan (Granny Moses), Max Baer Jr (Jethro Bodine) and Donna Douglas (Elly May).

Unfortunately, their attempt to do so was doomed, partly because they still yearned for their old tarpaper shack, and partly because they might have had every luxury that $25 million could buy, but they did not always know what to do with it. Granny even had trouble telling the TV set from the washing machine. The uncouth Clampetts were the bane of socially prominent Mrs Drysdale, who lived in the mansion next door. In one ignominious episode her pampered poodle gave birth to a litter of pups by patriarch Jed Clampett's old coondog, Duke.

At its best, *The Beverly Hillbillies* was an attack on consumer culture, at its worst it ridiculed rural folks. It was universally lambasted for lowbrowness by the critics, but jumped to the top of the Nielsens and stayed there until 1964. A good proportion of the audience were males tuning in to see young Elly May Clampett in the tightest jeans west of the Ozarks. Anxious to capitalise on its success, CBS developed two other 'rustic' sitcoms, *Petticoat Junction* and *Green Acres*. By 1971 a change of president at the network, and advertisers' concern that the show's viewers were too heavily concentrated in country states, led to all shows 'with trees in' being cancelled.

Star of *Beverly Hillbillies*, ex-dancer Buddy Ebsen, had previously featured in *Barnaby Jones* and >*Davy Crockett*. Actress Sharon Tate, later infamously to be murdered by the Charles Manson gang, appeared as Janet Trego. In 1981 creator Philip Henning produced *The Return of the Beverly Hillbillies*, with Imogene Coca replacing the late Irene Ryan as Granny. A 1993 movie, *The Beverly Hillbillies*, based on the TV series starred Dabney Coleman, Erica Eleniak (>*Baywatch*), and Cloris Leachman. Penelope Spheeris directed.

Bewitched

USA 1964–72 254 × 30m col ABC. Screen Gems. *UK tx* 1964–72 BBC1. *cr* Sol Saks. *exec pr* Harry Ackerman. *pr* William Asher. *dr* William Asher, Alan Rafkin, Sidney Miller, Ida Lupino, David McDearmon, Sherman Marks, Joseph Pevney, William D Russell, E W Swackhamer, Howard Morris, Jerry Davis, R Robert Rosenbaum, Alan Jay Factor, Paul Davis, Richard Kinon. *wr* Sol Saks, Barbara Avedon, Danny Arnold, Jerry Davis, Bernard Slade, Paul David and

With just a wiggle of her nose, suburban witch Samantha Stephens (Elizabeth Montgomery) could break up her housewifely day by having lunch with Napoleon or Julius Caesar in *Bewitched*. Merely mortal husband Darrin was not amused by the antics of his wife or the rest of his supernatural household, mother-in-law Endora (five times Oscar nominee Agnes Moorehead) and subsequent offspring Adam and Tabitha (above). The latter was the only baby born to a sitcom mom to be given a show of her own. In *Tabitha* (1977–8) she appeared as a young adult working at TV station KXLA. But while the child witch was played by twins Erin and Diane Murphy, the adult Tabitha was played by Lisa Hartman.

John L Greene, Fred Freeman and Lawrence J Cohen, Jack Sher, Roland Wolpert, Herman Groves, Tom and Frank Waldman, Earl Barrett, Richard and Mary Sale, Joanne Lee, Ken Englund, Richard Baer, Ted Snerdeman and Jane Klove, Ruth Brooks Flippen, Mort R Lewis, Paul Wayne, Howard Leeds, Ron Friedman, Lee Erwin, James Henerson, Syd Zelinka, Doug Tibbles, David V Robinson, Ed Jurist, Robert Riley Crutcher, David Braverman and Bob Marcus, Coslough Johnson, Jerry Devine and Izzy Elinson. *cast* **Samantha Stephens/Serena** Elizabeth Montgomery **Darrin Stephens** Dick York (1964–9)/Dick Sargent (1969–72) **Endora** Agnes Moorehead **Maurice** Maurice Evans **Larry Tate** David White **Louise Tate** Irene Vernon (1964–6)/Kasey Rogers (1966–72) **Tabitha Stephens** Heide and Laura Gentry (1966), Erin and Diane Murphy (1966–72) **Adam Stephens** David and Greg Lawrence **Abner Kravitz** George Tobias **Gladys Kravitz** Alice Pearce (1964–6)/Sandra Gould (1966–72) **Aunt Clara** Marion Lorne **Uncle Arthur** Paul Lynde **Esmerelda** Alice Ghostley **Dr Bombay** Bernard Fox. *Video* C-VIS/BMG.

Pretty young witch Samantha Stephens shocked her mortal husband Darrin on their wedding night by confessing her more than mortal powers. *Bewitched* made gentle comedy from her earnest attempts to abandon her craft after he begged her to refrain. Sometimes the challenge – and the encouragement of a bevy of witchly relatives – proved too great. A mere twitch of the nose from Samantha could make a flower bloom or clean a room in an instant and objects habitually moved and floated around the marital home. But despite all their trials and tribulations Samantha and her ad man husband loved each other. Good writing made the most of this simple premise, with each episode running the same theme: Samantha – or one of her relatives – would get Darrin, or another mortal, into trouble and then have thirty minutes to restore the happenings to normality and the mortal to sanity. Neighbours and in-laws alike would be given elaborate excuses for the weird events in the unusual household.

Samantha was played by Elizabeth Montgomery, daughter of Robert who took on the role in order to work with her husband, William Asher, who directed the first fourteen episodes. Samantha's relatives included her mother Endora (whose threats to turn Darrin into an artichoke put a whole new twist on the mother-in-law joke), her father Maurice, practical-joking Uncle Arthur and forgetful Aunt Clara, witches and warlocks all. Esmerelda the housekeeper, who came along in 1969 was also a witch, although a timid soul with declining powers, and Samantha's mischievous lookalike cousin Serena (also played by Montgomery) cropped up too from time to time. Darrin and Samantha were themselves responsible for increasing the population of hexes with first child Tabitha (born in the episode of 13 January 1966), and second child Adam (October 1969), a warlock. Other characters included nosy neighbours Gladys and Abner Kravitz, Larry Tate, Darrin's long-suffering boss at the New York Advertising Agency of McMann and Tate, and Larry's wife Louise. More extraordinary visitors to the Stephens household included Julius Caesar (summoned up by mistake when Samantha asked Esmerelda to make a Caesar salad), George Washington and Henry VIII.

Another star of the series, albeit an invisible one, was special effects man Dick Albain, who invented Samantha's 'magic' self-operating vacuum cleaner (it was remote controlled) and suitcases that packed and unpacked themselves (invisible wires were pulled). Other effects were rather more prosaically achieved. When objects had to disappear in Samantha's hand, Montgomery would freeze, Albain would remove the object, and the footage of Albain would be edited out. Samantha's nifty cleaning of the kitchen by witchcraft was achieved by the young witch saying 'swoosh', raising her arms and then holding her hands absolutely still while the crew swept and dusted to get the kitchen immaculate before the next shot.

Bewitched was an imaginative and well-written show that earned several Emmys. Extremely popular, it was the biggest hit series produced by the ABC network up to that time (it ranked number two among all programmes on air in its first season).

Black Adder

UK 1983–9 24 × 30m col BBC1. BBC. *cr* Richard Curtis, Rowan Atkinson. *pr* John Lloyd. *dr* Martin Shardlow, Mandie Fletcher. *wr* Richard Curtis, Rowan Atkinson, Ben Elton. *mus* Howard Goodall. *cast* **Edmund Blackadder** Rowan Atkinson **Baldrick** Tony Robinson. *Video* BBC.

From the really dark part of the Dark Ages came the viperous Edmund, Duke of Edinburgh, alias the *Black Adder* (Rowan Atkinson, above). Regarded as too expensive, the series was nearly axed by the BBC. But the clammy anti-hero escaped and returned to the small screen thrice more.

A cycle of comedy shows which began with *The Black Adder*, in which Rowan Atkinson played Edmund Blackadder, a venomous young aristocrat in Dark Age Britain, who was accompanied on his exploits by wretched, foul-smelling retainer, Baldrick. Reincarnations of Blackadder and Baldrick subsequently appeared in Elizabethan times (*Black Adder II*), in the reign of George III (*Black Adder the Third*), and the First World War (*Black Adder Goes Forth*). Though the production values declined somewhat after the first series (when the budget was slashed by the BBC), the show steadily improved its high-grade mix of schoolboy humour, convoluted and clever wordplay, historical parody and ruthless lampooning of the sort of costume dramas that were once so beloved by the BBC itself. Moreover, the gags were delivered faultlessly by rubber-faced Atkinson (*Not the Nine O'Clock News*, *Mr Bean*) and the other performers. The series bowed out in 1989, after burlesquing the trench madness of World War I with a celebratedly moving and uncompromisingly bleak finale.

One of the most successful British comedies of the eighties (not a great decade for UK TV humour), *Black Adder* was the creation of Rowan Atkinson and Richard Curtis, and developed by them in association with John Lloyd. The trio met when working on *Not the Nine O'Clock News*. From *Black Adder II* onwards the show was written by Curtis and alternative comedian Ben Elton.

Also featured in the cast of the *Black Adder* series were Tim McInnerny (Lord Percy in *Black Adder* and *Black Adder II*, and Captain Darling in *Black Adder Goes Forth*), Stephen Fry (Lord Melchett in *Black Adder II*, the General in *Black Adder Goes Forth*), Miranda Richardson (Queenie in *Black Adder II*), Patsy Byrne (Nursie in *Black Adder II*), and Hugh Laurie (The Prince Regent in *Black Adder the Third*, and Lieutenant George in *Black Adder Goes Forth*).

Bless This House

UK 1971–6 36 × 25m col ITV. Thames TV. *pr* William G Stewart. *dr* William G Stewart. *wr* Various, including Vince Powell, Harry Driver, Carla Lane, Dave Freeman, Myra Taylor. *mus* Geoff Love. *cast* **Sid Abbott** Sidney James **Jean Abbott** Diana Coupland **Mike Abbott** Robin Stewart **Sally Abbott** Sally Geeson. *Video* Video Collection.

Traditional British domestic sitcom, the main themes of which were 'The Generation Gap' (the title of the opening episode) and the battle of the sexes. Sid Abbott was a sales rep for a stationery firm, a man who alphabetically listed his pleasures as 'Ale, Birds and Chelsea'. He was much perplexed, even exasperated, by his workshy ex-art college son, Mike, and teenage schoolgirl daughter, Sally. Meanwhile, wife Jean long-suffered.

In the shape of Sid Abbott, veteran comic actor Sidney James received one of the better roles of the twilight of his screen career. Born in South Africa in 1913, James came to Britain in 1946 after being demobbed from the South African Army, and began his acting career in rep theatre. He appeared in more than 250 films (including most of the *Carry On* cycle). It was his partnership with Tony Hancock in >*Hancock's Half Hour* that first made him a household name, and after the duo parted James starred in several TV comedies, *East End, West End*, *George and the Dragon* (with John Le Mesurier and Peggy Mount) and *Citizen James*. Actress Sally Geeson, who played James' daughter in *Bless This House* is the sister of film actress Judy Geeson. The show's writers included Vince Powell and Harry Driver (also *Love Thy Neighbour*, *Never Mind the Quality, Feel the Width*), and Carla Lane (*The Liver Birds, Bread*).

Bottom

UK 1991–2 12 × 30m col BBC2. BBC. *cr* Adrian Edmondson, Rik Mayall. *pr* Ed Bye. *dr* Ed Bye. *wr* Adrian Edmondson, Rik Mayall. *cast* **Ritchie** Rik Mayall **Eddie** Adrian Edmondson. *Video* BBC.

Originally conceived under the title *Your Bottom* to allow the tantalising prospect of viewers declaring 'I saw *Your Bottom* on television last night', *Bottom* was the story of two bachelors on the bottom of the heap.

Here the sex-starved flatmates sat and sniped at each other in time-honoured sitcom fashion, a pair of disgusting characters in an unsavoury Hammersmith bedsit containing little of interest other than a fetid fridge.

Written, created by and starring Rik Mayall and Adrian Edmondson who shot to fame in >*The Young Ones*, the series had much in common with the earlier series although it lacked *The Young Ones'* originality and surrealism. Jokes, as the series title and episode titles such as 'Smells' indicated, mostly dealt with farting, vomiting, vile male habits – dirty socks, festering food – and sex. Rik Mayall as Richard Richard (lifetime ambition to have sex) and Adrian Edmondson as Eddie Hitler sneered and snivelled throughout, and Ritchie idled away his sexless days by hitting Eddie with sharp instruments. Storylines mostly featured the duo's woefully inadequate attempts to impress women ('I wish someone would sleep with me, I mean stay awake with me').

Bottom, however, had its moments, with the pair repeatedly failing to understand why their crass tactics failed to pay off. Belonging, along with such series as >*Men Behaving Badly*, to a new genre of post-New Man ladcom, *Bottom* did much to point up the absurdities of the male ego. It won a devoted following and the bulk of its viewers, according to director Ed Bye, were young empathising males aged between fifteen and twenty.

Adrian Edmondson and Rik Mayall first performed together as 20th Century Coyote when at Manchester University in 1976 and have continued to work together since then. Regular performers at London's Comedy Store and Comic Strip in the late seventies and early eighties, they have starred on television in *The Comic Strip Presents*, *The Dangerous Brothers* and *Filthy Rich and Catflap* and in feature films such as *Supergrass* (Edmondson). Rik Mayall has also starred as odious politician Alan B'Stard in Laurence Marks and Maurice Gran's comedy series *The New Statesman* and in the short series of dramas *Rik Mayall Presents*.

Bottom's BBC2 slot was later home to >*Absolutely Fabulous*, a comedy series created by and starring Jennifer Saunders, another member of the talented and prolific Comedy Strip team and Edmondson's wife.

Cheers

USA 1982–93 273 × 25m/1 × 90m col NBC. A Charles Burrows Charles Production/Paramount TV. *UK tx* 1983–93 C4. *cr* Les Charles, James Burrows, Glen Charles. *exec pr* James Burrows, Les Charles, Glen Charles, Tom Anderson, Dan O'Shannon, Rob Long, Dan Stalley. *pr* Various, including Tim Berry, David Isaacs, Ken Levine. *dr* Various, including James Burrows. *wr* Various, including James Burrows, Les Charles, Glen Charles, Ken Levine, David Isaacs, David Angell, Earl Pomerantz, Sam Simon, Heide Perlman, David Lloyd, Kathy Ann Strumpe. *mus* Judy Hart Angelo and Gary Portnoy (theme song, 'Where Everbody Knows Your Name'), Craig Safan. *cast* **Sam Malone** Ted Danson **Diane Chambers** Shelley Long **Coach Ernie Pantuso** Nicholas Colasanto **Norm Petersen** George Wendt **Cliff Clavin** John Ratzenberger **Carla Tortelli** Rhea Perlman **Frasier Crane** Kelsey Grammer **Woody Boyd** Woody Harrelson **Rebecca Howe** Kirstie Alley **Lilith Crane** (née **Sternin**) Bebe Neuwirth **Eddie LeBec** Jay Thomas **Robin Colcord** Roger Rees **Kelly Gaines** Jackie Swanson **Paul** Paul Wilson **Nick Tortelli** Dan Heydaya **Harry** Harry Anderson **John Allen Hill** Keene Curtis. *Video* CIC.

Set in the Boston bar (est. 1895) of the title, this single-set show was one of the most popular and critically acclaimed comedies of recent decades. The regulars were womanising owner Sam 'Mayday' Malone, a reformed alcoholic and one time relief pitcher for the Red Sox, dense barman Ernie 'Coach' Pantuso, promiscuous acid-tongued waitress Carla Tortelli, corpulent barfly Norm, prim English Literature graduate Diane, and anally retentive mailman Cliff Clavin, a veritable fountain of trivia. The storylines of the first seasons were dominated by Sam and Diane's love-loathing relationship; eventually she left him to marry pompous psychologist Frasier Crane. However, unable to forget Sam she jilted Frasier and returned to bussing tables at Cheers. Then Coach died (as had actor Nicholas Colasanto, who was also one of US TV's principal directors). His place was taken by Woody, a farmboy of awesome simpleness from Hanover, Indiana. At around the same time the dejected Frasier pulled up a stool at the bar, and later married the

The regulars of the Boston 'charactercom' bar where everybody knows your name – NBC's *Cheers*. Back row, from left to right: Cliff Clavin (John Ratzenberger), Robin Colcord (Roger Rees), Woody Boyd (Woody Harrelson); middle row, left to right: Carla Tortelli (Rhea Perlman), Sam Malone (Ted Danson), Rebecca Howe (Kirstie Alley), Norm Petersen (George Wendt); front, left to right: Frasier Crane (Kelsey Grammer), Lilith Crane (Bebe Neuwirth).

acerbic, night-creaturish Lilith (when she once asked the bar 'Where can I sleep tonight?', Carla said, 'I've got an attic you can hang upside down in').

In 1987 Diane left the bar to write a novel, and a saddened Sam sold the business to a large corporation, and set off to sail the world. But his yacht sank and he had to slink back to Cheers to beg a job off the new manager, gold-digging Rebecca Howe. Meanwhile, Carla married hockey player Eddie LeBec (who was subsequently killed in an ice rink accident) and had two more children, making her the mother of eight. Though Sam set out to seduce Rebecca, and she had to fight her attraction to him, ultimately she was more interested in rich corporate raider Robin Colcord – until he ended up in jail. Eventually Sam regained ownership of the bar from the corporation, making the supercilious Rebecca *his* underling. Subsequent storylines included Woody's marriage to Kelly Gaines (an occasion which produced a rare *Cheers* exercise in physical comedy), Lilith's sojourn with an eccentric scientist in an underground pod, the revelation that Sam wore a hairpiece, and the culmination of the bar's long rivalry with Gary's Old Time Tavern, where the *Cheers* gang finally got one over the smug Gary. It was a sweet moment, one which had been eleven years in the waiting.

Although it was replete with brilliant one-line gags, the wit of *Cheers* came from its characters, who were types but not stereotypes. 'How's life in the fast lane?' Sam asked Norm, an almost permanent bar fixture. 'Don't ask me, Sammy,' replied Norm, 'I can't find the on ramp'. Such jokes were all the better for the fact that the characters were not portrayed with sentimentality; on the contrary, they were almost painfully inadequate. It is a testament to the brilliance of *Cheers'* characters, and the wit of the series' writers, that only one of the main cast, Shelley Long, ever left to do other things (although Ted Danson, Kirstie Alley and Woody Harrelson combined *Cheers* with active film careers). The guest list included John Cleese, in an Emmy-winning performance as a deranged marriage guidance counsellor, and Tom Berenger.

The final episode, transmitted in America in May 1993, gained an audience of 150 million, making it the most watched show in TV history. By that time it had won twenty-six Emmy Awards, just three fewer than the record held by the >*Mary Tyler Moore Show*. A spin-off, *Frasier*, featuring Kelsey Grammar, premièred in 1993.

Cheers was created by >*Taxi* producer-writer James Burrows, Les Charles and Glen Charles. The *Cheers* bar is based on a real Boston tavern, the Bull and Finch.

Citizen Smith

UK 1977–80 Approx 32 × 30m col BBC1. BBC. *cr* John Sullivan. *pr* Dennis Main Wilson. *dr* Ray Butt. *wr* John Sullivan. *cast* **Wolfie Smith** Robert Lindsay **Shirley** Cheryl Hall **Ken** Mike Grady **Mrs Johnson** Hilda Braid **Charlie Johnson** Peter Vaughan/Tony Steedman **Tucker** Tony Millan **Harry Fenning** Stephen Greif **Speed** George Sweeney. *Video* BBC.

Written by BBC scene-shifter John Sullivan and based on a person he once encountered in a public house, *Citizen Smith* was a gentle burlesque of the Marxist Left, in the shape of the fictional Tooting Popular Front. Leader of the 'Party' was megalomaniacal suburban guerilla Wolfie Smith, a busker who wore a Che beret, an afghan coat, rode a scooter and shouted 'Power to the People!' on the high street. A socialist Walter Mitty he may have been, but his occasional victories over the narrow-minded adult world and his love of life made him one of situation comedy's most engaging creations. Wolfie's proselytising was also tempered by a tendency towards con-artistry. The other Front regulars were weedy sidekick Ken, diffident (but fecund) Tucker, and greaser Speed. Shirley was Wolfie's long-suffering girlfriend, while her parents, scowling right-winger Mr Johnson ('bloody yeti') and nice but dim Mrs Johnson (who always mistakenly called the anti-hero 'Foxie') eventually became Wolfie's landlords. By the fourth and last season, the series had lost actress Cheryl Hall (Shirley) while the evilly brilliant Peter Vaughan (Mr Johnson) was replaced by Tony Steedman. Classic episodes include Wolfie's invasion of Parliament and his sabotage of a nobs' party.

The series established John Sullivan as one of the UK's most popular small-screen writers (his subsequent shows include *Only Fools and Horses*, the title of a *Citizen Smith* episode, and *Dear John*), and made Robert

Lindsay (later *GBH*, and >*Nightingales*) one of the medium's brightest stars.

The Cosby Show

USA 1984–93 200+ × 25m col NBC. A Carsey-Werner Production in Association with Bill Cosby. *UK tx* 1986–94 C4. *cr* Ed Weinberger, Michael Leeson, William H Cosby Jr. *exec pr* Marcy Casey, Tom Werner, Earl Pomerantz, Bernie Kukoff. *pr* Various, including Caryn Sneider Mandabach, Carmen Finestra, Terri Guarnieri, Steve Kline. *dr* Various, including Jay Sandrich. *wr* Various. *mus* Stu Gardner and Bill Cosby (theme). *cast* **Cliff Huxtable** Bill Cosby **Clair Huxtable** Phylicia Rashad (Phylicia Ayers-Allen) **Denise Huxtable** Lisa Bonet **Sondra Huxtable** Sabrina LeBeauf **Vanessa Huxtable** Tempestt Bledsoe **Theodore Huxtable** Malcolm Jamal-Warner **Rudy Huxtable** Keshia Knight Pulliam **Russell Huxtable** Earle Hyman **Anna Huxtable** Clarice Taylor **Pam Turner** Erika Alexander.

Although Bill Cosby (>*I Spy*, *The Bill Cosby Show*, *Fat Albert and the Cosby Kids*) had been a popular TV fixture for nearly two decades, few industry executives gave this show any chance of success when it premièred in 1984. It had two counts against it; it was a situation comedy at a time when the genre was thought to be in decline, and it was about a black family. Whites, it was believed, would not watch it. The show's immediate and enormous success turned TV wisdom upside down. Episodes have been watched by as many as 38.8 million viewers in America, a third of the total audience. It triggered a number of imitations, such as *Charlie and Company*, and placed the NBC network at the top of prime-time ratings. Most important, it proved that all-black shows could be popular with white audiences.

The series related the events in the life of the black, middle-class Huxtable family, headed by fallible Cliff (Cosby's most sensitive, skilful performance to date), an obstetrician, and his lawyer wife, Clair (Phylicia Rashad, sister of Debbie Allen from TV's *Fame*). Their children were Denise (Lisa Bonet, voted one of the ten most beautiful women in America by *Harpers Bazaar* magazine), Theo, Vanessa, Rudy and Sondra. All were intelligent, urbane and charming.

The series has won, in addition to three Emmys, three Image Awards from the National Association for the Advancement of Colored Peoples, although some black groups have criticised it as unrealistic and idealised. With massive overseas sales, and syndication deals fetching record prices of around $1 million per episode, *The Cosby Show* has made William H Cosby Jr, Doctor of Education (as he proudly credited himself in early episodes), one of the richest men in entertainment.

In 1987 there was a spin-off focusing on Denise Cosby's college experience, entitled *A Different World*.

Dad's Army

UK 1966–77 80 × 30m col BBC1. BBC. *cr* Jimmy Perry. *pr* David Croft. *dr* David Croft, Bob Spiers. *wr* Jimmy Perry. *mus* Ivor Novello (theme), Bud Flanagan (theme singer). *cast* **Captain Mainwaring** Arthur Lowe **Sergeant Wilson** John Le Mesurier **Corporal Jones** Clive Dunn **Private Frazer** John Laurie **Private Pike** Ian Lavender **Private Godfrey** Arnold Ridley **Private Walker** James Beck **ARP Warden Hodges** Bill Pertwee **Verger Yateman** Edward Sinclair **The Vicar** Frank Williams **Mavis Pike** Janet Davies. *Video* BBC.

The archetypal English TV comedy, a gentle and nostalgic look at the misadventures of a Home Guard platoon in the fictional South Coast town of Walmington-on-Sea during World War II. Based by writer Jimmy Perry on his own youthful experiences in the local defence corps, the series was initially rejected by the BBC for fear that it would denigrate the wartime heroes. This was to miss the point gloriously; the Walmington platoon, led by pompous bank manager Captain Mainwaring, may have been bumblers of the first rank, but there was never any doubt that if the feared 'Nazi paratroopers' had actually landed they would have fought to a man. Much of the humour of the show came from the mixing of the social classes that war occasioned, and from the inspired characters. Alongside Mainwaring ('Right then. Pay attention, men'), the other platoon members were eternally volunteering Corporal Jones ('Don't panic!'), spivvy Private Walker (whose shiftiness was perfectly captured in the end credits, as he sneaked a 'gasper' on duty), the wild-eyed coffin-maker Private Fraser ('We're doomed, I say. Doomed'), the diffident public school-educated Sergeant Wilson ('Is that really wise, sir?'), young mummy's boy Pike, and ageing Private Godfrey. The ARP warden, the vicar and the verger were constant irritations to the platoon, endlessly competing with them for use of the church hall.

So identified did the distinguished cast become with their *Dad's Army* roles, that their other achievements are often forgotten. Arthur Lowe, for instance, was previously Mr Swindley in >*Coronation Street* (he even had his own spin-off series, *Pardon the Expression*), while the distracted John Le Mesurier had previously starred in the TV series *George and the Dragon*, and numerous cinema films. (First married to *Carry On* actress Hattie Jacques, his air of good breeding hid an irreverent nature; he once famously smoked a cannabis joint at a BAFTA Awards ceremony.) Arnold Ridley OBE was a well-known West End playwright, with thirty-eight plays to his name.

Filmed on location in Thetford, Norfolk, the classic episodes of *Dad's Army* include 'The Deadly Attachment' (with Philip Madoc as the captured German officer who demands the name of the young Walmington Home Guardsman who mocked him; 'Don't tell him, Pike,' shouts Captain Mainwaring), 'The Gorilla' and 'The Day the Balloon Went Up'. The series won the BAFTA for Best Comedy in 1971. A theatrical feature based on the series was released in the same year.

Producer David Croft, formerly a wartime major in the Royal Artillery, went on to oversee and create many other successful shows, including >*'Allo 'Allo* and >*Hi-de-Hi!*, but *Dad's Army* remains his – and arguably English comedy's – finest half-hour.

'They don't like it up 'em . . .' Clive Dunn as panicking Corporal Jones (left) and John Laurie as mutinous Private Frazer in *Dad's Army*. Creator Jimmy Perry based the comedy about Walmington-on-Sea's finest – if most inept – Home Guard platoon on his youthful misadventures with the wartime volunteer service.

Desmond's

UK 1990–94 52 × 30m col C4. Humphrey Barclay Productions. *USA tx* 1990– Black Entertainment Television. *cr* Trix Worrell. *dr* Trix Worrell, Charlie Hanson, Nic Phillips,

Liddy Oldroyd, Mandie Fletcher. *wr* Trix Worrell, Joan Hooley. *cast* **Desmond Ambrose** Norman Beaton **Shirley Ambrose** Carmen Munroe **Pork Pie** Ram John Holder **Matthew** Gyearbuor Asante **Lee** Robbie Gee **Tony** Dominic Keating **Michael Ambrose** Geff Francis **Sean Ambrose** Justin Pickett **Gloria Ambrose** Kim Walker **Louise** Lisa Georghan. *Video* CIC.

Channel 4's most successful home-grown comedy, starring Norman Beaton as Desmond Ambrose (a rare black hero on British television), proprietor of a barber's shop, coping with the everyday struggles of a family in South London and foiled at every turn by his wife, Shirley. Desmond's barber shop is at the centre of Peckham's social scene – it serves food, plays videos and organises domino matches and sometimes even gives haircuts. As well as Desmond's immediate family – sons Michael and Sean, daughter Gloria – *Desmond's* almost entirely black cast features an extended family of regulars including Pork Pie, Matthew, Lee, Tony and Gloria's friend Louise.

Desmond's has won critical plaudits and awards for its successful blend of black, British and intergenerational comedy. Much of its humour comes from the conflict between the young black characters who grew up in Britain and the values of the older generation from the West Indies. The show has fans in Canada, Israel and the Netherlands and is a massive success in the West Indies and America where it attracts millions of viewers on the Black Entertainment Television cable network. It was created by St Lucia-born Trix Worrell (and commissioned by Channel 4's multicultural editor Farrukh Dhondy).

Robbie 'Buck' Gee, who plays Lee, is a member of the all-black comedy team 'The Posse' and stars in BBC2's black comedy sketch show *The Real McCoy*. Norman Beaton starred in the earlier British TV series *The Fosters*, 1976, London Weekend TV's sitcom which followed the fortunes of a black family in London, and *Empire Road*, 1978, the BBC's first popular drama based around a multicultural family.

Black American star Bill Cosby was so impressed with *Desmond's* that he invited Norman Beaton to guest on two episodes of >*The Cosby Show*, in which the British star played a cricket-loving West Indian doctor.

The Dick Van Dyke Show

USA 1961–6 158 × 25m bw CBS. Calvada Productions/T & L Productions. *UK tx* 1963–6 BBC1. *cr* Carl Reiner. *exec pr* Sheldon Leonard. *pr* Various. *dr* Various, including Carl Reiner, Jerry Paris, John Rich, Theodore J Flicker. *wr* Various, including Carl Reiner, Bill Persky, Sam Denoff, Garry Marshall. *mus* Earle Hagen. *cast* **Rob Petrie** Dick Van Dyke **Laura Petrie** Mary Tyler Moore **Ritchie Petrie** Larry Matthews **Alan Brady** Carl Reiner **Jerry Helper** Jerry Paris **Millie Helper** Ann Morgan Guilbert **Buddy Sorrell** Morey Amsterdam **Sally Rogers** Rose Marie **Mel Cooley** Richard Deacon.

Classic sixties sitcom about Rob Petrie, the head TV comedy writer for the fictional *The Alan Brady Show*. For the most part, the plots involved shenanigans at the office, where Petrie worked with the wise-cracking Sally Rogers and Buddy Sorrell (plus pompous balding producer, Melvin Cooley), and at his home in the New York suburb of New Rochelle. There Petrie lived with his perky wife, the former dancer Laura, and son Ritchie. Jerry and Millie Helper were the next-door neighbours.

Originally creator Carl Reiner intended to play the lead part of Rob Petrie himself, but was persuaded to stand down by veteran executive producer Sheldon Leonard (although Reiner got to play the often heard but rarely seen Alan Brady). In his stead Sheldon cast one-time game show host and Broadway actor Dick Van Dyke. After much searching, unknown actress Mary Tyler Moore (whose most substantial role hitherto had been the secretary – seen only from the hips down – in *Richard Diamond, Private Eye*) was chosen for the part of Laura.

As if to prove the truth of Sheldon Leonard's axiom 'the higher the quality of the show, the longer it will take to catch on with the general public', the sitcom took two seasons to become a hit, but was never out of the ratings top twenty thereafter. In part, the slow start of *The Dick Van Dyke Show* was caused by the obstruction of CBS chief, Jim Aubrey (nicknamed 'The Smiling Cobra'), who took a perverse and inexplicable dislike to the show, and had to be pressurised into airing it by sponsors Proctor and Gamble. Famously liberal in its worldview, the show was financed initially by money from the Kennedy clan, via John F Kennedy's brother-in-law, Peter Lawford.

Among the fifteen Emmy Awards bestowed on *The Dick Van Dyke Show*, a yardstick in the development of adult TV comedy for the sophistication of its scripts, were Emmys for Outstanding Comedy Series in 1963, 1964 and 1966. The show came to an end in 1966 when Van Dyke, 'the male Julie Andrews' as he called himself, left to pursue movie work full-time. He returned to TV in 1971 with *The New Dick Van Dyke Show* playing Dick Preston, the host of a TV chat show. Meanwhile, Mary Tyler Moore went on to star in her own successful >*Mary Tyler Moore Show*, also set in TV land.

Episodes of *The Dick Van Dyke Show* are repeated to this day, its timeless appeal helped by being filmed originally without any slang expressions.

Dream On

USA 1990–2 30 × 30m col. Home Box Office. Kevin Bright Productions in association with MCA Television Entertainment. *UK tx* 1991– C4. *cr* David Crane and Marta Kauffman. *exec pr* Kevin Bright, John Landis. *pr* Robb Idels, David Crane, Marta Kauffman. *dr* Various, including John Landis, Eric Laneuville. *wr* David Crane, Marta Kauffman. *cast* **Martin Tupper** Brian Benben **Judith Tupper** Wendie Malick **Toby Pedalbee** Denny Dillon **Jeremy Tupper** Chris Demetral **Eddie Charles** Jeffrey Joseph.

Adult comedy relating the troubled life of midly neurotic New York book editor Martin Tupper, aged thirty-six, a TV child of the fifties and soon-to-be-single guy of the nineties. Martin is trying to cope with an impending divorce at the same time as maintaining a relationship with his eleven-year-old son Jeremy and (after an absence of twelve years) re-entering the world of modern dating and sex with a selection of beautiful women. Though he's still good friends with his wife, Martin is unsettled by his divorce, and the fact that Judith is about to marry the perfect man and all-round hero. At work he gets little sympathy from straight-talking secretary Toby Pedalbee and at play he gets confusing advice from womanising stud and chat show host friend Eddie.

Martin, though, does not face the battleground that is his life alone; he shares the small screen with a plethora of old black-and-white movie clips that are his thought bubbles. Martin is a baby boomer who was put in front of a TV at an early age and never tore himself away. As a result his brain is bursting with images which push themselves into his life. His fears, fantasies and self-delusions are all illustrated by brief appearances from such classic performers as George Burns, Lee Marvin, Jack Benny, Vincent Price, Joan Crawford, Shelley Winters, Bette Davis, Groucho Marx and Ronald Reagan. When his wife wants a divorce we cut to Lee Marvin delivering a knock-out blow.When he has to break the news of the divorce to his son, Groucho Marx pops up to say, 'Marriage is a very serious thing.' When a young college student tries to seduce him, handsome Hollywood star Cornel Wilde tells him, 'Age has nothing to do with it, it's performance that counts.' In short, all Tupper's feelings come courtesy of long-lost television comedies, dramas, romances, varieties and suspense tales including the *Jane Wyman Show*, *Alcoa Premiere*, *G. E. Theatre*, *Ford Startime*, *Pepsi-Cola Playhouse* and *Revlon Mirror Theatre*.

The man responsible for the blending of old and new was executive producer John Landis who was approached by Home Box Office to come up with a concept that would use over 800 half-hour episodes of MCA television footage that could not be syndicated. Landis brought in writers David Crane and Marta Kauffman to create the situation and storyline. Crane and Kauffman watched fifty-five half-hour vintage episodes to write the pilot for *Dream On* and 200 more to write the first series. Three researchers chronicled all the material in a computer, cross-referencing by individual dialogue lines and emotions. Sometimes the *Dream On* story came first, sometimes the vintage clip. 'In the case of the story coming first, we'd ask ourselves "How is Martin feeling?" then search for a clip showing the appropriate emotion,' note Crane and Kauffman. 'Other times, we'd write around a clip. For example, we realised that the characters were drinking coffee in many of the anthology shows, so we decided to utilise the clips and wrote the episode "Death Takes A Coffee Break", where Martin must give up caffeine.'

Dream On provoked some complaints about its perpetual topic of sex – most of its humour came from hilarious sex scenes punctuated by wise comment from TV stars of old – and an episode in which Martin and friend Eddie smoked a joint. But the risky formula worked perfectly and built up a devoted following.

John Landis is best known as the director of feature films including *The Blues Brothers*, *Trading Places*, *Coming to America*, *An American Werewolf in London*, *National Lampoon's Animal House* and the Michael Jackson *Thriller* video.

Drop the Dead Donkey

UK 1990– 33+ × 25m col C4. Hat Trick. *cr* Andy Hamilton, Guy Jenkin. *exec pr* Denise O'Donoghue. *pr* Andy Hamilton, Guy Jenkin. *dr* Libby Oldroyd. *wr* Andy Hamilton, Guy Jenkin. *cast* **Gus Hedges** Robert Duncan **George Dent** Jeff Rawle **Alex Pates** Haydn Gwynne **Damien Day** Stephen Tomkinson **Dave Charnley** Neil Pearson **Henry Davenport** David Swift **Sally Smedley** Victoria Wicks **Joy** Susannah Doyle **Helen** Ingrid Lacey.

In the beginning this sitcom set in the fictional newsroom of Sir Royston Merchant's Globelink TV was heavily topical in its humour, with a steady stream of up-to-the-minute one-liners about real-life events. As the seasons passed, however, the current events gags were much reduced in number (from around twenty-five per episode to around twelve per episode), and the humour came to centre on the caricatured characters who were the staff of Globelink. These were : Gus Hedges, the craven, jargon-spouting chief executive ('could we interlock brain spaces in my office'); Alex, his acerbic prime mover, later replaced by lesbian Helen; Damien (Stephen Tomkinson, *Ballykissangel*), the amoral, thrusting cub reporter, constantly looking for (and prepared to invent) telegenic disasters; Henry, the irascible anchorman who was constantly at war with the snobbish but dim newsreader, Sally Smedley; George, the be-cardiganed hypo-chondriac, divorced senior news editor; Dave Charnley (played by Neil Pearson, also *Between the Lines*), the indefatigable philanderer, and Joy, the cynical PA. Transmuted into what was essentially a conventional comedy, the show became a massive international hit,

selling to such diverse countries as Turkey and Iceland. In 1992 the series was awarded the Emmy for International Popular Arts with an episode about the office Christmas party. This contained the classic gag of the John-Major-a-gram, when a man looking like the British PM enters the room, but nobody notices and he goes away again. Series guest stars included the Labour Party's Neil Kinnock and Ken Livingstone.

Fawlty Towers

UK 1975–9 13 × 30m col BBC2. BBC. *US tx* 1976 PBS. *cr* John Cleese, Connie Booth. *pr* John Howard Davies, Douglas Argent. *dr* Bob Spiers. *wr* John Cleese, Connie Booth. *mus* Dennis Wilson. *cast* **Basil Fawlty** John Cleese **Sybil Fawlty** Prunella Scales **Polly** Connie Booth **Manuel** Andrew Sachs **Major Gowen** Ballard Berkeley **Miss Tibbs** Gilly Flower **Miss Gatsby** Renee Roberts. *Video* BBC.

The origins of *Fawlty Towers* are well known: in 1972 the *Monty Python* team stayed in a hotel in Torquay which gave them a somewhat jaundiced view of Britain's hotel industry. The following year Cleese wrote six scripts for *Doctor at Large*, setting one of them in just such a seedy hotel, and two years later he wrote the first six-episode series of *Fawlty Towers* together with his then-wife Connie Booth.

Fawlty Towers starred John Cleese as manic, blustering hotelier Basil Fawlty, Prunella Scales as his long-suffering wife Sybil and Connie Booth as pert maid Polly, apparently the only sensible person in the hotel. Spanish waiter Manuel (Andrew Sachs) meanwhile darted about imcompetently, much bullied by his employer and hampered by his inadequate grasp of English. Manuel's usual response to an order was an uncomprehending 'Que?', whereupon Fawlty would explain to his guests 'You'll have to excuse him – he comes from Barcelona.' (Spanish TV actually bought the series, but avoided offending its viewers by transforming the waiter into an Italian in the dubbing.)

Plots were based on misunderstandings and Basil's tireless efforts to impress those guests he believed were important while mercilessly insulting those he considered inferior. When Polly and the kitchen staff went out for the evening, a solo Basil attempted to pretend to his American guests that the hotel was actually fully staffed. A visit by German tourists ('Don't mention the war!') ended with Basil goose-stepping around his dining room making a finger-moustache above his upper lip. Imagined romantic intrigues behind the hotel's bedroom doors led Basil into paroxysms of indignation and ill-fated attempts to spy through keyholes and from wardrobes. And when a woman complained that her half-eaten prawn cocktail was inedible the hotelier responded with 'Well, only half of it is inedible, apparently' and agreed to refund the full price only if she brought it up during the night. Through all of this Basil and Sybil maintained a relationship based entirely on mutual irritation.

Much of the humour of *Fawlty Towers* came from the performances, with John Cleese in particular the master of comic movement. According to series director Bob Spiers, Cleese wrote every detail of his performance into the scipt with no move or gesture, however apparently spontaneous, the result of last minute improvisation. Scripts were superb and closely packed and tight production schedules led to high-pressure deadlines (the episode in which a dead body was trundled all over the hotel was so complicated it was barely finished). Cleese and Booth took six weeks to write each script (the norm is ten days) and while most half-hour shows have about sixty-five pages of script, *Fawlty Towers* ran to around 120 pages. (Cleese and Booth met on the set of *Monty Python* and first collaborated on a sketch for that series.)

Prunella Scales' previous comedy credits include *Marriage Lines* with Richard Briers and *Seven of One* with Ronnie Barker. Ex-Python John Cleese has gone on to international acclaim in such feature films as *Clockwise* and *A Fish Called Wanda*. Series director Bob Spiers has worked on a number of British TV comedy series, among them >*Dad's Army*, >*Are You Being Served?*, *The Goodies* and >*Absolutely Fabulous*.

A US made show, *Amandas*, starring Bea Arthur (>*The Golden Girls*), tried to duplicate the formula, but failed to achieve either the same comic brilliance or critical success, even when it appropriated some episodes word for word.

The Fresh Prince of Bel Air

USA 1990– 90+ × 30m col NBC. A Stuffed Dog Company and Quincy Jones Entertainment Production in Association with NBC Productions. *UK tx* 1991– BBC2. *cr* Benny Medina. *exec pr* Susan Borowitz, Andy Borowitz, Quincy Jones, Kevin Wendle. *pr* Werner Wallan, Samm-Art Williams, Cheryl Gard, Benny Medina, Jeff Pollack. *dr* Debbie Allen, Jeff Melman, Rita Rogers Blye. *wr* Susan Borowitz, Andy Borowitz, Samm-Art Williams, Shannon Gaughan, Cheryl Gard, Rob Edwards, Lisa Rosenthal, John Bowman, Sandy Frank. *cast* **Will Smith** Will Smith **Philip Banks** James Avery **Vivian Banks** Janet Hubert-Whitten **Carlton Banks** Alfonso Ribeiro **Hilary Banks** Karyn Parsons **Ashley Banks** Tatyana M Ali **Geoffrey the Butler** Joseph Marcell **Jazz** Jeff Townes (DJ Jazzy Jeff).

Funky comedy co-produced by multi-Grammy-winning musician Quincy Jones and starring real-life rap star Will Smith as Will, an innocent, fun-loving black rapper from a tough West Philadelphia neighbourhood who is sent west by his mother to live with rich relatives in Bel Air, California. In Bel Air, Will is confronted by Uncle Philip and family who live in a huge, ornate mansion, speak a refined language and even have a liveried butler, Geoffrey. When needed, though, pompous attorney Philip can tell Will a thing or two about black experience and Geoffrey may seem to be uptight, but he's just an efficient person with a hidden sense of humour. Preppy son Carlton, a spoiled would-be brat-packer, and Hilary the oh-so-beautiful older daughter are rivals from the start with the newcomer. Youngest daughter Ashley, however, is a friend and confidante. Will soon charms, disarms and alarms members of his adoptive upper-crust family with his streetwise ways, challenging Uncle Philip for forsaking his humble roots and leaving Aunt Vivian to mediate between the two. Will's friend Jazz (among others) periodically brings a little soul to the Banks mansion, as well as to exclusive Bel Air Academy, where Will just does not fit in.

A comedy of clashing cultures, *The Fresh Prince of Bel Air* regularly slipped in comments on the situation of blacks in a white society. Will Smith, who played the lead role with a comic timing and easy enthusiasm largely

Real life rap star Will Smith as Will (left) and Royal Shakespeare Company actor Joseph Marcell as Butler Geoffrey in *The Fresh Prince of Bel Air*. The show was based on an idea by record executive Benny Medina who was himself a poor boy brought up by a Beverly Hills foster family headed by Jack Elliot, composer of music for such TV shows as *Barney Miller*.

responsible for the show's success, previously performed as half of the duo DJ Jazzy Jeff and the Fresh Prince with co-*Bel Air* star Jeff Townes. The duo won a Grammy award for their 1988 hit 'Parents Just Don't Understand'.

The Fresh Prince of Bel Air marked the American début of Joseph Marcell as the butler Geoffrey. A member of the Royal Shakespeare Company, he appeared in a number of their productions as well as in many London stage plays. On British TV he has starred in the series *Empire Road* and >*Juliet Bravo*, and his film credits include *Cry Freedom* and *Playing Away*.

George and Mildred

UK 1976–9 38 × 30m col ITV. Thames TV. *cr* Johnnie Mortimer and Brian Cooke. *pr* Peter Frazer-Jones. *dr* Peter Frazer-Jones. *wr* Johnnie Mortimer and Brian Cooke. *cast* **George Roper** Brian Murphy **Mildred Roper** Yootha Joyce **Jeffrey Fourmile** Norman Eshley **Anna Fourmile** Sheila Fearn **Tristram Fourmile** Nicholas Bond-Owen. *Video* V-COL.

A spin-off from the comedy *Man About the House* (1973–6) with the latter's landlords, George and Mildred Roper, continuing their domestic warfare in the new battleground of a middle-class housing development at Hampton Wick. He was lazy and working class, she was sex-starved (witness her Freudian banana-print trousers) and socially aspirant. Their neighbours were snobbish Jeffrey Fourmile, wife Anne and spectacled son Tristram, who was not allowed to play with 'rough' boys. An element of class conflict was expressed through Fourmile's irritation that Roper and his motor-cycle sidecar was lowering the tone of the neighbourhood. The characters were stereotypical (intentionally so), with George and Mildred merely a TV version of the old music hall hen-pecked husband and nagging wife. The routines may have been Victorian, but they were immaculately performed. Like its predecessor (which starred, in addition to Murphy and Joyce, Richard O'Sullivan, Paula Wilcox and Sally Thomsett), this series was written by the team of Johnnie Mortimer and Brian Cooke, who helped in the creation of an American version of *George and Mildred* called *The Ropers* (transmitted on ABC between 1979 and 1980).

Get Smart

USA 1965–70 138 × 30m col NBC/CBS. Talent Artists and Heyday Productions. *UK tx* 1966–70 BBC. *cr* Mel Brooks, Buck Henry. *exec pr* Arne Sultan, Mel Brooks. *pr* Leonard B Stern, Jess Oppenheimer, Jay Sandrich, Burt Nodella, Arnie Rosen, James Komack. *dr* Various, including Paul Bogart, Richard Donner. *wr* Mel Brooks, Buck Henry, Leonard B Stern. *cast* **Maxwell Smart, Agent 86** Don Adams **Agent 99** Barbara Feldon **Thaddeus, The Chief** Edward Platt **Agent 13** Dave Ketchum **Carlson** Stacy Keach **Conrad Siegfried** Bernie Kopell **Starker** King Moody **Hymie, the C.O.N.T.R.O.L. robot** Dick Gautier **Agent 44** Victor French **Larrabee** Robert Karvelas **99's Mother** Jane Dulo.

A spoof in the inimitable style of Mel Brooks, together with co-creator Buck Henry (*TW3*, >*Quark*, *Captain Nice*), lampooning the rash of spy dramas (>*The Avengers*, >*Man from UNCLE*, >*I Spy*) which graced sixties TV screens in the wake of the James Bond movies.

Get Smart revelled in stereotypes and wordplay and was the tale of Maxwell Smart, enthusiastic but incompetent Agent 86 for Washington-based international intelligence agency C.O.N.T.R.O.L. Headed by 'The Chief', with headquarters in a music hall, C.O.N.T.R.O.L. waged war against the evil agents of K.A.O.S. who, led by mastermind Siegfried and his assistant Starker, planned to take over the world. Max (catchphrases 'Sorry about that, Chief', 'would you believe . . .') went undercover as a greetings card salesman and his equipment included a telephone in one of his shoes which rarely worked. He was aided in his work by Agent K13, a dog named Fang, genius robot Hymie and beautiful and brilliant partner Agent 99. In the 1968–9 season love blossomed between the mismatched Agents 86 and 99 and they married. When NBC cancelled the show in 1969 CBS picked up *Get Smart* for an additional season. The most successful parody in TV history, *Get Smart* won seven Emmies, including three for Don Adams.

Brian Murphy as the hen-pecked husband and Yootha Joyce as the sex-starved wife whose seaside-postcard-style relationship made up *George and Mildred*. A spin-off from *Man About the House*, the later series was sharper and more acerbic and was remade in America as *The Ropers*.

Comedy writer, producer and occasional performer Mel Brooks first attracted attention as a member of the writing stable for *Your Show of Shows*. He was later co-creator and executive producer of ABC series *When Things Were Rotten* which ran for only four months in 1975 and executive producer in 1989 of NBC's *The Nutt House*, another short-lived flop. He is better known as the director of feature films which include *The Producers*, 1967, *Blazing Saddles*, 1974, *Young Frankenstein*, 1974, and *High Anxiety*, 1977.

The Golden Girls

USA 1985–93 180 × 30m col NBC. Witt-Thomas-Harris in association with Touchstone Television. *UK tx* 1986–93 C4. *cr* Susan Harris. *exec pr* Paul Junger Witt, Tony Thomas, Susan Harris. *pr* Various, including Kathy Speer, Terry Grossman, Nina Feinberg, Mitchell Hurwitz, Jim Vallely, Kevin Abbott, John Ziffren, Jamie Wooten, Marc Cherry. *dr* Various, including Jay Sandrich, Paul Bogart, Terry Hughes, Lex Passaris, Peter Beyt. *wr* Susan Harris, Kathy Speer, Terry Grossman, Winifred Hervey, Mort Nathan, Barry Fanaro. *mus* Andrew Gold (theme), George Tipton. *cast* **Dorothy Zbornak** Bea Arthur **Rose Nylund** Betty White **Blanche Devereaux** Rue McClanahan **Sophia Petrillo** Estelle Getty **Stanley Zbornak** Herb Edelman **Miles Webber** Harold Gould.

In 1985 >*Soap* creator Susan Harris followed up her earlier success with *The Golden Girls*, a comedy about four middle-aged to elderly women sharing a house together (and played by four actresses aged fifty-two to sixty-four) in Miami, sunny city of retirees. Harris said she wrote the series to prove that life still went on for women over fifty who, although usually appearing on television only as mad axe-women, could in fact be energetic, fun and sexy. The single 'girls' thoroughly enjoying their golden years were acerbic, outspoken divorcee Dorothy, a substitute teacher who had never forgiven her ex for leaving her for an air hostess after thirty-eight years of marriage; daffy, soft-spoken widow Rose who worked as a grief counsellor and had Norwegian family roots (her mother's maiden name was Gerklelnerbigenhoffstettlerfrau); Blanche, who actually owned the house and was a lusty man-mad Southern belle who took mouth-to-mouth resuscitation classes because she liked kissing; and last but not least Dorothy's diminutive but gutsy eighty-year-old mother Sophia, who moved in when her retirement home, Shady Pines, burned to the ground. Occasional men drifted through the series. Herb Edelman was seen from time to time as Dorothy's ex-husband Stan who now seemed to want her back. Rose, for a while, had a boyfriend called Miles who unfortunately turned out to be a former mob accountant who had to leave town. And Blanche set her heart upon many a passing male but never found lasting love.

The Golden Girls was sharp and witty and the humorous, sometimes poignant relationships between the four single women were the core of its appeal. They may have looked like everyone's favourite aunties or grandmothers, but they traded wicked one-liners over their helpings of cheesecake (over 100 cheesecakes were devoured during the seven-year series) and discussed taboo subjects from dating midgets to drooping breasts, incontinence, flatulence, abortion, artificial insemination and hot flushes. Their surprisingly broad base of fans included the Queen Mother, who personally requested their appearance at the Royal Variety Performance in 1988.

Golden Girls was a smash hit in sixty different countries and highly regarded in the industry. It won sixty-five Emmy nominations, ten Emmy Awards including Best Comedy (twice) and awards for each of its four leads as best actress or best supporting actress (making it the only series on television for which all of its stars have won Emmys), and three Golden Globe Awards. As a result, some of Hollywood's biggest stars have willingly guested on the show including Bob Hope, Burt Reynolds, Don Ameche, Mickey Rooney, Dick Van Dyke and Julio Iglesias.

The show came to the end of its run when Dorothy married Blanche's Uncle Lucas (played by Leslie Nielsen of >*Police Squad* and *The Naked Gun*) and headed off to pastures new in Atlanta. A spin-off of the series *The Golden Palace* (also created by Susan Harris) took over the story, and saw the three remaining Miami matrons enter the hotel trade and buy The Golden Palace and its curious staff of three – manager Roland, young, abandoned Oliver and overworked Chuy, Mexican chef (played by Cheech Marin, one half of seventies comedy duo Cheech and Chong).

The success of *The Golden Girls* on minority Channel 4 in Britain led Carlton Television to develop a British version for mainstream ITV. *The Brighton Belles*, 1993, relocated the 'girls' to Britain's south coast and starred Jean Boht as Josephine (Sophia), Sheila Hancock as Frances (Dorothy), Wendy Craig as Annie (Rose) and Sheila Gish as Bridget (Blanche).

Susan Harris went on to create *Empty Nest*, a comedy starring Richard Mulligan (Burt Campbell in >*Soap*) as widower Doctor Harry Weston who was trying to rebuild his life alone. Harris made full use of her oeuvre by situating Doctor Weston in the same Miami neighbourhood as the Golden Girls with the result that Sophia, Blanche and Rose made visits to his *Nest* and he returned the compliment in *The Golden Girls*.

Hancock's Half-Hour

UK 1956–61 BBC. BBC. *cr* Ray Galton, Alan Simpson. *pr* Duncan Wood. *dr* Duncan Wood. *wr* Ray Galton, Alan Simpson. *mus* Wally Scott. *cast* **Anthony Aloysius Hancock** Tony Hancock **Sid** Sidney James. *Video* BBC.

At 23 Railway Cuttings, East Cheam, the lugubrious Anthony Aloysius Hancock pondered and dreamed of rising above his humble origins with sceptical sparring partner Sid. *Hancock's Half-Hour* had transferred from radio where Hancock's inimitable performance and Galton and Simpson's inspired scripts had combined to produce classic comedy. The bitter-sweet humour lay in acute observations of life's petty frustrations ('The Missing Page' when Hancock reaches the final page of a thriller, only to find it has been torn out), and in Hancock's bitter, paranoid rantings and pompous attempts to impress which always fell flat as he unintentionally revealed his ignorance (in 'Twelve Angry Men' Hancock berates the jurors, 'Does Magna Carta mean nothing to you? Did she die in vain?'). Yet at the same time Hancock's down-at-heel appearance and hang-dog features made him a lovable loser and over 10 million viewers tuned in. Classics such as 'The Blood

Donor' or 'The Radio Ham' are amongst the most famous of Hancock's comic creations (both of them in fact dating from after 1960, when Hancock and Sid James went their separate ways and the series was renamed *Hancock*). After seven series with the BBC Hancock went over to ITV and dispensed with the crucial scripts of Galton and Simpson (who had gone on to write >*Steptoe and Son*). This, plus the fact that he now read his words off cue cards rather than learning his lines, meant that his shows deteriorated badly.

The son of a hotelier and part-time professional entertainer, Hancock made his stage début in the RAF with ENSA (Entertainments National Service Association) and touring gang shows. He moved into pantomimes, cabaret and radio, appearing in *Educating Archie* in 1951. The radio series *Hancock's Half-Hour* began in 1954. Famous as much for his real-life alcoholism and self-doubt as for his comic performances, Hancock finally committed suicide on 25 June 1968 at the age of forty-four in Sydney, Australia.

Sid James went on to star in *George and the Dragon* and >*Bless This House* as well as being a staple cast member of the *Carry On* films.

Happy Days

USA 1974–84 255 × 30m col ABC. Miller-Milkis/Paramount TV. *UK tx* 1975–84 ITV. *cr* Garry Marshall. *pr* Garry Marshall, Edward K Milkis, Thomas L Miller, Jerry Paris. *dr* Various, including Jerry Paris. *wr* Various. *mus* Bill Haley (theme), Gimel and Fox ('Happy Days' theme). *cast* **Ritchie Cunningham** Ron Howard **Arthur 'The Fonz' Fonzarelli** Henry Winkler **Howard Cunningham** Tom Bosley **Marion Cunningham** Marion Ross **Joanie Cunningham** Erin Moran **Potsie Weber** Anson Williams **Ralph Malph** Danny Most **Chachi** Scott Baio.

A sentimental look back at teen life in Milwaukee in the Eisenhower years, part of the wave of fifties nostalgia inspired by the success of the film *American Graffiti*. In the beginning, the series centred on two Jefferson High School students, Ritchie Cunningham (Ron Howard, one of the stars of *American Graffitti*, and later the director of such major Hollywood features as *Cocoon*, *Backdraft* and *Parenthood*) and his friend, Potsie Weber. Ritchie was an innocent, a nice guy ('hum-drum' he called himself), while Potsie was worldly wise. The guys hung out at a malt bar called Arnold's Drive In, invariably with Ralph Malph. It became apparent by the second season, however, that the real star of the show was none of these people but a minor character brought in by creator Garry Marshall to lessen the show's tendency towards middle-American gooeyness: leather-jacketed biker, Arthur 'The Fonz' Fonzarelli. The street-wise Fonz was so cool that he only had to click his fingers and girls came running. To incorporate the Fonz into more of the narrative action, the scriptwriters moved him into the loft-apartment over Ritchie's parents' garage. By 1977 *Happy Days* was the most popular programme on American TV. Kids everywhere imitated the Fonz, his biker look and his gestures, especially his thumbs up 'eeeyyh!'. His iconic nature was only confirmed when the Smithsonian Institute in Washington put his leather jacket on display.

As the show gained in years and stature, it dropped the nostalgia amd became a character-based sitcom, and Ritchie's parents Howard and Marion came increasingly to the fore. (Mrs C's line, 'Are you feeling *frisky* Howard?' became something of a catchphrase.) The cast changed surprisingly little until the eighties, when Ron Howard, Danny Most and Anson Williams all left the show. By that time their characters were far from teenage; they had grown up, gone to college, got jobs and, in the case of Ritchie, got married (to Lori Beth, played by Lynda Goodfriend). The main addition to the cast in the meantime was Chachi, Fonzie's cousin who fell in and out of love with Ritchie's sister Joanie (actors Baio and Moran were also lovers in real life). At one stage the twosome were given their own series, *Joanie Loves Chachi*. It flopped. But two other spin-offs from *Happy Days* became major successes. In 1975 two blue-collar girls, Laverne DeFazio and Shirley Feeney, appeared in *Happy Days* for a double date with Ritchie and the Fonz, and promptly waltzed off to their own >*Laverne and Shirley* series. In 1977 actor Robin Williams, in his first real screen exposure, dropped in to the show as Mork, an extra-terrestrial from Ork. The episode was so successful that he was also given his own series – >*Mork and Mindy* – almost overnight.

Hi-De-Hi!

UK 1980–9 45 × 30m col BBC1. BBC. *cr* David Croft, Jimmy Perry. *exec pr* David Croft. *pr* David Croft, John Kilby, Mike Stephens. *dr* David Croft, Jimmy Perry, John Kilby, Mike Stephens. *wr* Jimmy Perry, David Croft. *mus* (theme) Jimmy Perry. *cast* **Jeffrey Fairbrother** Simon Cadell **Ted Bovis** Paul Shane **Gladys Pugh** Ruth Madoc **Spike Dixon** Jeffrey Holland **Mr Partridge** Leslie Dwyer **Fred Quilly** Felix Bowness **Yvonne Stuart-Hargreaves** Diane Holland **Barry Stuart-Hargreaves** Barry Howard **Peggy** Su Pollard **Sylvia** Nikki Kelly **Betty** Rikki Howard **Mary** Penny Irving **Squadron Leader Clive Dempster** David Griffin **Yellowcoat boys** Terence Creasey, the Webb twins. *Video* BBC.

Good morning campers! It's Maplin's Holiday Camp, 1959, and the staff and entertainers are assembled for *Hi-de-Hi!*, Jimmy Perry and David Croft's affectionate recreation of that peculiarly British institution, the holiday camp. A barely veiled portrait of Butlin's (where series writer Jimmy Perry had once worked), the holiday camp was brought to life by its workers at all levels – portly, spivvy comic Ted, snobby ballroom dancers Barry and Yvonne who tried in vain to inject a little culture into the proceedings, and upper-class, ever-striving entertainments manager Jeffrey Fairbrother. The women, though, were the stars of the show: Welsh Valleys girl Gladys Pugh, the bossy chief yellowcoat and voice of Radio Maplin, who tried in vain to talk posh and had a reckless romantic streak when aroused (her heart was broken first by Fairbrother and then by his replacement, Squadron Leader Clive Dempster) and lovable chambermaid Peggy, who dreamed of being a yellowcoat and constantly had to be rescued from the consequences of her own actions.

The series, which was filmed at a real camp in Clacton, was a big hit for the BBC, attracting around 10 million viewers. Its appeal was part nostalgia, part the warm-hearted characters and part sheer kitsch. Series creators Perry and Croft also collaborated on the comedy series >*Are You Being Served?* Simon Cadell, who played Jeffrey Fairbrother, later married David Croft's daughter Becky.

The Honeymooners

USA 1955–6, 1966–71 39 × 30m, 1971 13 × 60m, 1984–5 68 × 30m CBS. *UK tx* 1987 BBC2. *cr* Jackie Gleason, Joe Bigelow, Harry Crane. *exec pr* Jack Philbin. *pr* Jack Hurdle. *dr* Frank Satenstein. *wr* Marvin Marx, Walter Stone, Andy Russell, Herbert Finn, Leonard Stern, Sidney Zelinka. *mus* Jackie Gleason (theme), Sammy Spear. *cast* **Ralph Kramden** Jackie Gleason **Ed Norton** Art Carney **Alice Kramden** Audrey Meadows (1955–6), Sheila MacRae (1966–71) **Trixie Norton** Joyce Randolph (1955–6), Jane Kean (1966–71).

The saga of Ralph and Alice Kramden, the not-so-newly weds who lived in the grimy, spartan surroundings of a run-down apartment at 328 Chauncey St, Brooklyn, USA. (*The Honeymooners* set was one of the drabbest in the history of television – a kitchen/living-room with an ancient refrigerator, a table in the centre and a window looking out on the bricks of the next building.) The series centred on portly Ralph, an everyday New York City bus driver. Ralph was blustering, avaricious, always on the lookout for a money-making scheme but deep-down lovable. Whether he was trying to foist off a warehouse full of useless can-openers on late-night TV or causing his wife heartache by withholding a five-dollar rent increase, his foolhardy escapades always ended in disaster. Ever willing to help Ralph in his ambitions was wiry, even-tempered best friend Ed Norton, who lived upstairs. Norton, though no better off than 'Ralphie boy', was always full of cheery encouragement, although his incompetence was a constant source of grief and aggravation to Ralph. Continually displeased by the duo's schemes was Ralph's practical wife Alice whose complaints were regularly met by the response, 'One of these days Alice, one of these days . . . pow, right in the kisser.'

Much of *The Honeymooners*' appeal lay in the fact that it was at heart an old-fashioned romance. 'The guy really loves this broad,' creator Gleason maintained. 'They fight, sure. But they always end in a clinch.' And sure enough the curtain would fall on harmony and Ralph proclaiming 'Alice, you're the greatest!' – a moment the scriptwriters dubbed 'kissville'. Added to this was the comic drama of the indefatigable bus driver always keeping his head in the clouds while the rest of him was sinking fast, and the contribution of gifted physical actor Art Carney in whose hands the chalking of a pool cue could become a feat of comic choreography. Although there were only thirty-nine episodes, the show fast became a classic and ran and reran around the world. TV's first animated sitcom >*The Flintstones* was based on the series.

The Honeymooners spent most of its history as a segment in other programmes, running only one season as an independent series. It was first seen in 1951 as a sketch within DuMont's *Cavalcade of Stars*, then on CBS as part of *The Jackie Gleason Show*. *The Honeymooners* finally became a series in its own right in 1955, when The Buick Motor Company sponsored the freestanding sitcom to the tune of over six million dollars – then the largest sponsorship commitment in television's history. One of the first examples of a live-audience, single-set, filmed situation comedy (the first was >*I Love Lucy*), *The Honeymooners* was filmed twice weekly before a live audience of 1,100 people crowded into New York's Adelphi Theatre.

In 1956 *The Honeymooners* – the first TV show to tune in to the frustrations of America's urban blue-collar workers – ended after only one season only to be revived in 1966 in the form of one-hour episodes of Jackie Gleason's then-current variety series (Broadway style musical numbers were added to make the original half-hour up to the required length). A collection of one-hour reruns was aired in 1971 as another *Honeymooner* series, and four 'specials' were shot between 1976 and 1978. In the eighties the 'lost episodes' of *The Honeymooners* were broadcast, but these were actually original fifties sketches edited together to make sixty-eight new *Honeymooner* half-hours.

I Dream of Jeannie

USA 1965–70 139 × 25m col NBC. Columbia. *UK tx* 1966–70 ITV. *cr* Sidney Sheldon. *exec pr* Sidney Sheldon. *dr* Various, including Gene Nelson, Sidney Sheldon, Alan Rafkin, E W Swackhamer, Theodore J Flicker, Larry Hagman, Hal Cooper, Claudio Guzman. *wr* Various, including

Sidney Sheldon, Tom Waldman and Frank Waldman, Arthur Alsberg and Bob Fisher, William Davenport. *mus* Hugh Montenegro. *cast **Jeannie*** Barbara Eden ***Capt Anthony 'Tony' Nelson*** Larry Hagman ***Capt Roger Healey*** Bill Daily ***Dr Alfred Bellows*** Hayden Rorke.

When NASA astronaut Tony Nelson crashes on a desert island he finds a beautiful blonde genie in a bottle. She follows him back to Cape Canaveral in her scanty harem attire, where she proceeds to change his life by magically trying to improve his lot. Unfortunately, Jeannie is both over zealous and petulantly jealous. Still, with just a blink of her eyes she easily undoes the trouble she causes in every episode. The story ends happily ever after when Tony and Jeannie marry in the final season.

Quite apart from its obvious male fantasy nature (the question hanging over every instalment was 'would she really do *anything* for him?'), this supernatural sitcom was a virtual clone of >*Bewitched*. It did, though, have its lightly amusing moments, especially in its early years. Larry Hagman, later to play bad guy J R in >*Dallas*, took the part of Tony Nelson.

I Love Lucy

USA 1951–61 179 × 30m bw CBS. Desilu Productions. *UK tx* 1955–65 ITV. *cr* Jess Oppenheimer, Madelyn Pugh, Bob Carroll, Jr. *exec pr* Desi Arnaz. *pr* Jess Oppenheimer, Desi Arnaz. *dr* Ralph Levy, Marc Daniels, William Asher, James V Kern. *wr* Jess Oppenheimer, Madelyn Pugh, Bob Carroll Jr, Bob Schiller, Bob Weiskopf. *mus* Eliot Daniel (theme), Wilbur Hatch and the Desi Arnaz Orchestra. *cast **Lucy Ricardo*** Lucille Ball ***Ricky Ricardo*** Desi Arnaz ***Ethel Mertz*** Vivian Vance ***Fred Mertz*** William Frawley ***Little Ricky Ricardo*** Richard Keith ***Jerry, the agent*** Jerry Hausner ***Mrs Mathilda Trumbull*** Elizabeth Patterson ***Caroline Appleby*** Doris Singleton ***Mrs MacGillicuddy*** Kathryn Card ***Betty Ramsey*** Mary Jane Croft ***Ralph Ramsey*** Frank Nelson. *Video* Fox.

The supreme situation comedy of the fifties, top in the ratings for most of its years on CBS and popular in almost every country in the world (*I Love Lucy* was one

A rare moment of calm for red-haired, scatterbrained Lucy (Lucille Ball) and her fiery Cuban bandleader husband Ricky (Desi Arnaz) in the classic fifties show *I Love Lucy*. The screen duo were married to each other in real life and founded one of TV's most successful production empires, Desilu. The episode in which Lucy gave birth to son Little Ricky garnered 44 million viewers (President Eisenhower's inaugural address screened the next night managed only 29 million) and was transmitted the same evening that Ball herself gave birth to Desi Arnaz Jr.

of the first ever programmes shown on fledgeling ITV in Britain in 1955). The premise of *I Love Lucy* was not dissimilar to other family sitcoms – a wacky wife making life difficult for a loving but perpetually annoyed husband – but the actors performing them were exceptional. Lucy Ricardo was an American of Scottish ancestry (maiden name MacGillicuddy) married to a Cuban band-leader. Husband Ricky worked at the Tropicana Club and since Lucy was keen to prove to him that she could be in showbusiness too, he spent much of his time trying to keep her off the nightclub stage. Ricky just wanted Lucy to be a simple housewife and, whenever he became particularly frustrated by her schemes, his fractured English would degenerate into a stream of Spanish epithets. Over the years Ricky became more successful. In the 1956–7 season Ricky opened his own club, the Ricky Ricardo Babaloo Club. He also landed a TV show which earned him a country house in Connecticut (and a spin-off series of summer reruns in 1960, *Lucy in Connecticut*).

I Love Lucy had superb plots, inventive gags and brilliant performances from its leads; in particular Ball's clowning (she had perfected her trademark scatter-brained quality and crying fits as the lead in a CBS radio comedy *My Favourite Husband*) made audiences adore her. Watching *I Love Lucy* became a way of life in America.

In the summer of 1958 a collection of reruns entitled *The Top Ten Lucy Shows* revealed the difficulty of selecting an all-time best list – it contained thirteen episodes. Among these was the show in which Lucy manoeuvred her way onto Ricky's TV show to do a health tonic commercial and got drunk sampling the highly alcoholic product. There was the time she tried to bake her own bread, threw in two entire packets of yeast, and ended up pinned to the wall of her kitchen when she opened the oven. And the time when Lucy and neighbour Ethel were looking for mementoes of Hollywood to take home to New York and tried to prise loose the block of cement bearing John Wayne's footprints from in front of Grauman's Chinese Theater.

The success of *I Love Lucy* is unparalleled in the history of television. The decision to film the show rather than use inferior kinescope meant that high-quality prints of each episode were available for rebroadcast.

The appeal of reusable filmed programmes started by *Lucy* eventually led to the shift of television production from New York, where it started, to Hollywood, where the film facilities were. *I Love Lucy* was practically unique at the time for being filmed before a live audience, a practice not commonplace until the seventies, and the simultaneous use of three cameras to allow for editing of the final product was also a *Lucy* first.

Independent Hollywood production company Desilu, a meld of the first names of Lucy and her screen partner and real-life husband (until their divorce in 1960) Desi Arnaz, was created to produce *I Love Lucy* in 1950 and went on to produce numerous other series for the networks, including *December Bridge*, >*Mannix*, >*The Untouchables* and *Whirlybirds* until it was bought out in 1967 for $20 million. Ball was president of Desilu Productions and Desilu Studios, the old RKO lot the company had purchased, from 1960 to 1967.

Julia

USA 1968–71 86 × 30m col NBC. Twentieth-Century Fox. *UK tx* 1969–71 ITV. *pr* Hal Kanter. *cast* **Julia Baker** Diahann Carroll **Corey Baker** Marc Copage **Dr Morton Chegley** Lloyd Nolan **Marie Waggedorn** Betty Beaird **Earl J Waggedorn** Michael Link **Len Waggedorn** Hank Brandt **Melba Chegley** Mary Wickes **Sol Cooper** Ned Glass **Carol Deering** Allison Mills **Hannah Yarby** Lurene Tuttle **Eddie Edson** Eddie Quillan **Steve Bruce** Fred Williamson **Kim Bruce** Stephanie James **Paul Cameron** Paul Winfield.

The first TV series since *Beulah* (ABC, 1950) to star a black woman and, unlike *Beulah's* maid-heroine, the first to star a black woman in a 'prestige' role. *Julia* was a half-hour comedy about a young, black nurse raising her six-year-old son single-handedly after her Air Force pilot husband was killed in Vietnam. Moving to Los Angeles, Julia found a job at the medical office of Astrospace Industries, where life at the office together with her home and social life provided material for the series. The show was totally integrated – a bold move from nervous NBC executives – and after attracting novelty attention became popular with white audiences as well as black. Julia lived in a modern, integrated apartment building with her little boy Corey, whose best friend was white Earl J Waggedorn, one of their neighbours. Other characters in Julia's home life were Earl's dad Leonard, landlord Sol Cooper and mother's helper Carol Deering. At work, the middle-class heroine had equally harmonious relations with her white employer, feisty, kind-hearted Doctor Morton Chegley, his wife Melba, fellow nurse Hannah Yarby and plant employee Eddie Edwards. Romantic partners were, however, strictly black. Paul Cameron was Julia's occasional boyfriend for the first two seasons and was replaced by Steve Bruce, a widower with a four-year-old daughter Kim, during the series' final year.

It soon became apparent, though, that this rather cute, romanticised version of black/white relations was out of step with its time. This was 1968, an era of ghetto riots and new, high-profile black political leaders and Julia's easy, almost colourless integration into the white community and way of life bore little relation to the realities of black urban experience. The liberal white press and young militant blacks criticised and finally denounced the programme as false and distorted and Carroll, in part because of the criticism, decided to leave the series after its third season.

Diahann Carroll, a singer with motion-picture experience, later starred as Dominique Devereaux, Blake Carrington's half-sister, in >Dynasty.

Laverne and Shirley

USA 1976–83 178 × 25m col ABC. Miller-Miklis/Henderson/Paramount TV. *UK tx* 1977–83 ITV. *cr* Garry K Marshall. *exec pr* Thomas L Miller, Edward K Milkis, Garry K Marshall. *pr* Various. *dr* Various. *wr* Various. *mus* Norman Gimble and Charles Fox (theme, 'Making Our Dreams Come True'), Cyndi Grecco (theme vocal). *cast* **Laverne DeFazio** Penny Marshall **Shirley Feeney** Cindy Williams **Andrew 'Squiggy' Squigman** David L Lander **Lenny Kosnoski** Michael McKean **Carmine Raguso** Eddie Mekka **Frank DeFazio** Phil Foster **Edna Babbish** Betty Garrett.

A smash-hit for America's ABC network and, like >*Mork and Mindy*, a spin-off from >*Happy Days*. In its original format the slapstick show concerned two feisty blue-collar fifties girls, Laverne DeFazio and Shirley Feeney, who worked as bottle cappers at the Shotz Brewery in Milwaukee and who roomed together at 730 Hampton Street. After their dismissal from the brewery in the 1980 season, the duo worked for the Bardwell Department Store in California. When a contract dispute forced actress Cindy Williams to leave the show, her character married an army medic and moved overseas, so ending a long-running comedic worry about Shirley retaining her virginity in an increasingly permissive age. Laverne was left alone as a single girl working for the Ajax Aerospace Company and hoping to find romance.

The show was created by Garry K Marshall, who cast his sister in the role of Laverne. More recently Penny Marshall has worked behind the camera, directing such Hollywood features as *Awakenings*, *Big*, *Jumping Jack Flash*, *League of their Own*. Two cartoon versions of the series were made by Hanna-Barbera, *Laverne and Shirley in the Army* (1981–2) and *Laverne and Shirley with the Fonz* (1982–3).

Leave It To Beaver

USA 1957–63 234 × 30m CBS/ABC. Gomalco Productions and Universal. *cr* Bob Mosher, Joe Connelly. *pr* Harry Ackerman, Joe Connelly, Bob Mosher. *dr* Norman Tokar. *wr* Dick Conway, Roland MacLane, Joe Connelly, Bob Mosher. *mus* Dave Kahn (theme), Melvin Lenard. *cast* **June Cleaver** Barbara Billingsley **Ward Cleaver** Hugh Beaumont **Beaver (Theodore) Cleaver** Jerry Mathers **Wally Cleaver** Tony Dow **Eddie Haskell** Ken Osmond **Miss Canfield** Diane Brewster **Miss Landers** Sue Randall **Larry Mondello** Rusty Stevens **Whitey Whitney** Stanley Fafara **Clarence 'Lumpy' Rutherford** Frank Bank **Mr Fred Rutherford** Richard Deacon **Gilbert Bates** Stephen Talbot **Richard** Richard Correll.

Long-running family sitcom – the first to deal with life from a kid's point of view – set within the Cleaver household of 485 Maple Drive, Mayfield, USA. The comfortably off Cleavers were the model to which suburban, middle-American, middle-class families aspired and were much different from the characters of the altogether more modest milieu of >*The Honeymooners*. Ward and June Cleaver were the seemingly perfect partners of offspring Theodore 'Beaver' Cleaver – aged seven when the series began – and his elder brother Wally, aged twelve. Larry, Whitey and Gilbert were Beaver's pals and Wally's buddies were Clarence 'Lumpy' Rutherford (whose father Fred was accountant Ward's boss) and the unctuous, unwholesome Eddie Haskell – sycophantic to adults and a bully to little kids. Miss Canfield and Miss Landers were Beaver's schoolteachers.

Beaver was a typically rumbustious youth, more interested in pet frogs than in girls while Wally was beginning to discover that there were other things in life and the series' storylines dwelt on the good-natured tiffs between these siblings and the necessary chidings and chastisement from their ever-loving elders. Over the six years that the series ran, as Beaver and his brother got older, the stories gradually moved away from the little boy premise until, in the final season, Beaver was about to enter his teens and Wally was ready for college.

Leave It To Beaver premièred on CBS in October 1957 and moved to ABC a year later. In the 1957 pilot for the series Ward Cleaver was played by Casey Adams, Wally by Paul Sullivan, and 'Frankie', an Eddie Haskell-style character, by Harry Shearer, later a regular on *Saturday Night Live*. Creators Mosher and Connelly had written together since 1942 on over 1,500 *Amos 'n' Andy* TV and radio scripts. They went on to create >*The Munsters*.

Twenty years after *Leave It To Beaver* ended its original run the Cleaver family, played by the original cast, were united in a TV movie *Still the Beaver*, 1983. Beaver was now thirty-three and out of work, undergoing a divorce, and had trouble communicating with his two young sons. Wally was a successful attorney, but had troubles at home and Eddie Haskell was a crooked contractor. Dad was no longer around (actor Hugh Beaumont had died) and wife June made regular trips to his grave to ask his advice. Viewers apparently wanted more and so a series *Still the Beaver* ran on the Disney Channel, 1985–6, followed by *The New Leave It To Beaver* on WTBS in 1986.

The Likely Lads

UK 1965–9 26 × 30m bw/col BBC2/BBC1. BBC. *cr* Ian La Frenais, Dick Clement. *pr* Dick Clement. *wr* Ian La Frenais, Dick Clement. *mus* Ronnie Haslehurst. *cast* **Terry Collier** James Bolam **Bob Ferris** Rodney Bewes **Audrey** Sheila Fearn.

Situation comedy set in the British North East, which arose out of a sketch Dick Clement wrote with friend Ian La Frenais for the exam part of his BBC directors course. Terry Collier (ex-trainee chartered accountant James Bolam, also *When the Boat Comes In*, *Only When I Laugh*) and Bob Ferris (Rodney Bewes, *Dear Mother, Love Albert*) were the likely lads, two young workers in an electrical components factory who had markedly different characters and, most importantly, attitudes towards the class system. Terry was brash, aggressive, only interested in girls, and resigned to his proletarian station. Bob was Terry's alter ego, diffident, cautious, scared of authority (particularly if it had a posh accent), with an almost pitiful belief that he could get out of the class trap if only he worked hard enough. Despite their over-a-pint philosophising, the two always viewed the approach of the other with looks of leaden dismay. Not least because their escapades, inevitably initiated by Terry, always ended in disaster.

In 1973 Terry and Bob were brought back for a revival, *Whatever Happened to the Likely Lads?* which, unusually for a sequel, was as well written and acted as the original. And, if anything, it was even sharper on the foibles of the class system. Here the ill-fated pair were four years older, with Terry having spent the intervening time in the army. Bob, meanwhile, had become engaged to the fearsome Thelma (Brigit Forsyth), bought a house of his own and taken to holidays on the Costa Brava and meals in restaurants. Terry's attack on such bourgeois delusions was remorseless.

Ian La Frenais and Dick Clement followed the success of *The Likely Lads* and *Whatever Happened to the Likely Lads?* with the classic shows *Porridge* and *Auf Wiedersehen Pet*. A series about a luxury car-hire company for ITV in 1993 failed, though, to pick up passengers.

Love Thy Neighbour

UK 1972–6 40 × 25m col ITV. Thames TV. *cr* Harry Driver and Vince Powell. *pr* Ronnie Baxter. *dr* Stuart Allen, Ronnie Baxter. *wr* Harry Driver and Vince Powell. *cast* **Eddie Booth** Jack Smethurst **Joan Booth** Kate Williams **Barbie Reynolds** Nina Baden-Semper **Bill Reynolds** Rudolph Walker. *Video* BRAVE/SMO.

One of the first British comedies to deal exclusively with the subject of race relations, placing bigoted white trade unionist Eddie Booth and his wife next door to a black couple, Bill and Barbie Reynolds. Eddie, whose aim was to preserve 'our white heritage', called his neighbour 'Sambo' and 'nig-nog'; in turn, Bill called him 'snowflake' and 'honky'. Co-creator Vince Powell claimed that to expose 'these insults to the public was to take the sting out of them and make them less hurtful'. Meanwhile, as is so often the case in British neighbour sitcoms, the two wives got on like a house on fire. It was never very funny, but its novel subject matter kept it high in the ratings, frequently in the top position, for five years. Viewed from today, the show's politics seem uncomfortably unsophisticated, but it almost certainly helped pave the way for *The Fosters* (1976–7, LWT), Britain's first all-black comedy series, starring Norman Beaton (later >*Desmond's*).

In 1973 a feature film version of *Love Thy Neighbour* was released in the UK, while in the USA an attempt to repeat the show's success, also called *Love Thy Neighbour*, lasted just one season on ABC.

Writers Vince Powell and Harry Driver began their careers as a comedy double act, but turned to scriptwriting when Driver was paralysed from polio. Their series include *Never Mind the Quality, Feel the Width, For the Love of Ada, Spring and Autumn, Nearest and Dearest*. They jointly contributed to the *Harry Worth* and >*Bless This House* shows, while Driver alone was a regular storyliner for >*Coronation Street*. He died in 1973.

The Mary Tyler Moore Show

USA 1970–7 120 × 25m col CBS. MTM Productions. *UK tx* 1972–5 BBC1. *cr* James L Brooks, Allan Burns. *pr* James L Brooks, Allan Burns, David Davis, Stan Daniels, Ed Weinberger. *dr* Jay Sandrich, Marjorie Mullen, James Burrows, Harry Mastrogeorge, Mel Ferber, Doug Rogers, Joan Darling. *wr* Various, including James L Brooks, Allan Burns, Treva Silverman, Ed Weinberger, Stan Daniels, David Lloyd, Bob Ellison. *mus* Sonny Curtis (theme), Pat Williams. *cast* **Mary Richards** Mary Tyler Moore **Lou Grant** Ed Asner **Ted Baxter** Ted Knight **Murray Slaughter** Gavin McCleod **Rhoda Morgenstern** Valerie Harper **Phyllis Lindstrom** Cloris Leachman **Georgette Franklin** Georgia Engel **Sue Anne Nivens** Betty White.

After success in the >*The Dick Van Dyke Show* Mary Tyler Moore spent several years in an ill-fated attempt to emulate Ginger Rogers, before starring in this show about Mary Richards, a career girl about Minneapolis Town, who worked in the newsroom of TV station WJM-TV. The character represented a major breakthrough in TV comedy history, since she was the first small-screen woman who was single by choice. At WJM-TV her boss was irascible-but-gold-hearted Lou Grant ('Oh! Mr Grant!' Richards was to exclaim on many an occasion). Murray Slaughter was the sarcastic head newscaster, and Ted Baxter was the obtuse anchorman. Sue Anne Nivens (Betty White, also >*The Golden Girls*) was the hostess of the station's *Happy Homemaker* show. While many of the laughs in this realistic and polished series came from the workplace antics, it also (like >*The Dick Van Dyke Show*) gave due attention to the main character's homelife. Those featured on the domestic set included Richard's best friend, window dresser Rhoda Morgenstern, and busybody apartment neighbour Phyllis Lindstrom.

The show was created by James L Brooks (>*Taxi*, >*The Simpsons*) and Allan Burns, and developed for television by Moore and her husband, Grant Tinker, via their company Mary Tyler Moore Enterprises. Subsequently, this has become one of the main independent production companies in Hollywood, issuing forth such hits as >*Hill Street Blues* and *Remington Steele*.

Over *The Mary Tyler Moore Show*'s seven-year run, it won a record twenty-seven Emmys, including Outstanding Comedy Emmys in 1975, 1976 and 1977. For many fans and critics alike, the show represents the moment that sitcom achieved the status of art. It also spun off numerous shows. They were: >*Rhoda*, >*Lou Grant*, *The Love Boat* and *Phyllis*.

M*A*S*H

USA 1972–83 250 × 30m/1 × 150m col CBS. 20th Century Fox. *UK tx* 1973–84 BBC2. *cr* Richard Hooker, Larry Gelbart. *pr* Burt Metcalfe, Gene Reynolds. *dr* Various, including Alan Alda, Harry Morgan, Jackie Cooper, Don Weis, Gene Reynolds, Burt Metcalfe. *wr* Various, including Alan Alda, Glen Charles, Les Charles, Jim Fritzell, Everett Greenbaum, Larry Gelbart, Den Wilcox, Thad Mumford. *mus* Johnny Mandel (theme). *cast* **Captain Hawkeye Pierce** Alan Alda **Trapper John** Wayne Rogers **Margaret 'Hotlips' Hoolihan** Loretta Swit **Klinger** Jamie Farr **Colonel Blake** McLean Stevenson **Frank Burns** Larry Linville **Captain B J Hunnicut** Mike Farrell **Walter 'Radar' O'Reilly** Gary Burghoff **Charles Winchester III** David Ogden Stiers **Col Sherman Potter** Harry Morgan **Father Francis Mulcahy** George Morgan/William Christopher.

Developed from Robert Altman's 1970 hit movie about the misadventures of a MASH (Mobile Army Surgical Hospital) during the Korean War, this show was the unlikeliest hit comedy of the seventies. Not only did it satirise war at a time when the US was losing the Vietnam conflict, it also foregrounded such taboo TV subjects as interracial marriage, adultery and homosexuality. On its side it had witty, skilful writers and a likeable collection of oddball characters, prime among them sensitive-but-cynical surgeon Hawkeye Pierce, Trapper John, majorette 'Hotlips' Hoolihan, transvestite assistant Klinger and a telepathic clerk, Radar. Though humorous, the show did not avoid the explicit physical and emotional detail of war. In a key episode, 'Sometimes You Hear The Bullet', a friend of Hawkeye died on the operating table, much to the network's nervousness. The series had high production values, was shot on film, had a top-grade set (left over from Altman's movie) and, unusually for prime-time television, allowed the cast adequate rehearsal time.

In 1976 the show's original writer, Larry Gelbart, left, partly because he was worn out by battling with studio

A patient's-eye view of 4077 surgeons Colonel Sherman Potter (Harry Morgan, left), B J (Mike Farrell, centre) and Hawkeye (Alan Alda, right) from the superlative seventies anti-war satire *M*A*S*H*. Alan Alda, aka Alphonso D'Abruzzo, also wrote and directed on the show. Ironically the one person on record as not liking the liberal series was Richard Hooker, the Republican who wrote the original *M*A*S*H* novel.

executives over the controversial storylines. ('War is hell,' commented Gelbart. 'So is TV.') Thereupon Alan Alda (aka Alphonso D'Abruzzo) took over as the show's creative consultant, and as one of its principal writers and directors. His Hawkeye character became more and more central to the events at the 4077th, which caused actor Wayne Rogers to quit for his own spin-off series, *Trapper John, M.D.* At the end of the third season McLean Stevenson (Colonel Blake) also departed the unit. Their places were taken by Mike Farrell (as B J) and ex-*Dragnet* and ex-*Naked City* star Harry Morgan (as Western-loving Colonel Potter). Under Alda's tutelage, the show came to rely for its humour on the banter between the characters, with fewer madcap antics. It also developed a strong vein of sentimentality, with Hawkeye becoming a 'saint in surgical garb'. In 1983, having earned fourteen Emmys, *M*A*S*H* bowed out with a two-and-a-half-hour special, 'Good-bye, Farewell and Amen', to that date the most watched programme in history. With the signing of the armistice, the medics bid their final adieus, with Hawkeye and B J delivering their first and only salute to Colonel Potter. A sequel, *After Mash*, presented several of the unit adjusting to civilian life.

Ironically, the one man on record as not liking the TV *M*A*S*H* was one Richard Hornberger. Under the pseudonym Richard Hooker he wrote the original *M*A*S*H* novel. He was a conservative Republican, and would not watch the TV version because of its liberal sensibilities.

Men Behaving Badly

UK 1991– 25+ × 30m col ITV/BBC1 (from 1994). Thames TV/Hartswood Films Ltd. *cr* Simon Nye. *pr* Beryl Vertue. *dr* Martin Dennis. *wr* Simon Nye. *mus* Alan Lisk. *cast* **Gary** Martin Clunes **Dermot** Harry Enfield **Tony** Neil Morrissey **Dorothy** Caroline Quentin **Deborah** Leslie Ash **George** Ian Lindsay **Anthea** Valerie Minifie **Les** Dave Atkins.

Politically incorrect – but wonderfully funny – sitcom about a duo of 'lads', who share a squalid flat and a consuming interest in girls. In the first season the two men behaving badly were Gary (jug-eared Martin Clunes, *Staggered*) and Dermot (the ubiquitous Harry Enfield), but then Dermot moved out, leaving Gary to find a new lodger. The successful applicant was Tony (Neil Morrissey, *Boon*) who impressed Gary with his claim to be 'in the music business'. A comic misunderstanding whereby Gary worried that his new flatmate was a 'pillow-biter' (homosexual) was soon ironed out, and the twosome settled down into a soul mateyness, which survived the disclosure that Tony actually ran a secondhand record stall (later abandoned for a career as a busker). For Tony himself, a principal attraction of the flat was the upstairs neighbour, the blonde, Twiggy-like Deborah (Leslie Ash, *Quadrophenia*, >*C.A.T.S. Eyes*) whom he relentlessly lusted after.

Meanwhile, Gary maintained a romantic relationship of sorts with long-suffering State Registered Nurse Dorothy (Caroline Quentin, *An Evening with Gary Lineker*, and wife of comic Paul Merton). By the fourth season, despairing of Gary's adolescent behaviour and lack of commitment, Dorothy's eye began to wander. Her mention of a friend Tim caused Gary to splutter jealously: 'Maybe you'd like to jiggle around on Tim's todger while I bring you a series of tasty snacks?' In fact, Dorothy was having an affair with Jamie, to whom she became afianced, until Jamie called the engagement off – much to Gary's gloating. Gary and Dorothy then recommenced their relationship, although more rockiness ensued in 'Playing Away' when Gary returned home to the flat unexpectedly and found Dorothy *in flagrante* – with Tony. This indiscretion was overcome when Dorothy lied to Gary and told him that Tony was a useless lover. Gary promised not to rub Tony's face in it – and then proceeded to rub Tony's face in it.

Written in its entirety by Simon Nye (also *Frank Stubbs Promotes*, *Is it Legal?*, *True Love*), and based on his novel of the same name, *MBB* is a dextrous balance of the cathartic and the cynical. It allows male viewers to vicariously experience anti-social adolescent behaviour (the show is part of the new TV 'laddism', a minor reaction to feminism which includes such products as Britain's *Fantasy Football League* and America's >*Beavis and Butt-Head*). At the same time, it pleases and appeases women viewers through its resigned, knowing ridicule of the bad but lovable Gary and Tony. Above this, it is a genuine sitcom in that the humour comes from the characters and their context. 'I don't do mad, plot-driven farragoes,' Nye has remarked. 'You have to allow your characters time to talk.' A garland of prizes has been bestowed on *MBB*, including the Comedy Awards' Best ITV Comedy, and the first National Television Award for Situation Comedy.

The behind-the-scenes mover and shaker of *MBB* is the venerable Beryl Vertue. Originally an artists' agent, Vertue moved into production with the Eric Sykes silent comedy *The Plank* and the movie version of *Till Death Us Do Part*. As deputy chairman of the Robert Stigwood Group, Vertue pioneered the selling of basic formats of British TV comedies to other countries, among them >*Till Death Us Do Part* (which became *All in the Family* in the USA), *Steptoe and Son* (*Sanford and Son* in the USA) and >*Upstairs, Downstairs* (*Beacon Hill*). When, inexplicably, ITV decided not to film a second series of *MBB*, Vertue then sold the show to the BBC. An American version is in development.

The Monkees

USA 1966–7 28 × 25m col NBC. Columbia TV. *UK tx* 1966–7 BBC1. *cr* Bert Schneider, Bob Rafelson. *pr* Bert Schneider, Bob Rafelson. *dr* Various, including Bob Rafelson, James Frawley, Alexander Ginger, Bruce Kessler. *wr* Various, including Bob Rafelson. *mus* Various, including Neil Diamond. *cast* Davy Jones, Peter Tork, Mickey Dolenz, Mike Nesmith.

'Hey, hey, we're the Monkees/And we like to monkey around'. So opened the theme tune of this weekly TV show about four lovable mop-top American popsters, which consciously aped the Beatles' movies, *A Hard Day's Night* and *Help!*. More than 400 applicants were screened by producers Bert Schneider and Bob Rafelson (also director of such Hollywood features as *Five Easy Pieces*) before they chose as the 'pre-fab four' Davy Jones, an English jockey and previously Ena Sharples' grandson in >*Coronation Street*, former *Circus Boy* actor Mickey Dolenz (aka Mickey Braddock), some-time folk singer Peter Tork, and Michael Nesmith, whose mother

had invented the liquid paper used in typing corrections. Each episode featured madcap antics, zany humour and bizarre happenings, plus a couple of musical numbers, to which the Monkees only contributed the vocals, since despite TV appearances most of the band could not play a note on an instrument. The writers of their songs included such luminaries as Neil Diamond ('I'm a Believer'). A notable aspect of the likeable, ingenious show was that it used such rare filming techniques as distorted focus and fast-motion. In 1966, *The Monkees* won an Emmy for Outstanding Comedy, and two years later spawned an off-the-wall movie, *Head* (directed by Rafelson).

The Munsters

USA 1964–6 70 × 25m bw CBS. MCA/Universal. *UK tx* 1965–7 BBC1. *cr* Joe Connelly, Bob Mosher. *pr* Joe Connelly, Bob Mosher. *dr* Jack Marquette, Harry Larrecq, Lawrence Dobkin, Ezra Stone, Charles Rondeau. Donald Richardson, Gene Reynolds, Joseph Pevney, Earl Bellamy, Norman Abbott. *wr* Bob Mosher, Joe Connelly, James Allardice, Dick Conway, Richard Baer, Dennis Whitcomb. *mus* Jack Marshall. *cast* **Herman Munster** Fred Gwynne **Lily Munster** Yvonne De Carlo **Grandpa Munster** Al Lewis **Edward Wolfgang (Eddie) Munster** Butch Patrick **Marilyn Munster** Beverly Owen (1964)/Pat Priest (1964–6). *Video* CIC.

Spoof horror show created by Bob Mosher and Joe Connelly, (also *Amos 'n' Andy* and >*Leave it to Beaver*). Contemporary with, and seen by some as cruder than, >*The Addams Family*, with which it has similarities. The Munsters live at number 43 Mockingbird Lane, a peaceful, elm-shaded, average suburban street in America. But the Munsters are a little different from ordinary folks. Their three-storey Victorian house has not seen a paintbrush since it was built. Shutters hang askew, weeds grow abundantly, vultures nest in the trees and there's a dungeon in the basement. In the garage stands the fabulous (if archaic) Munster Koach and drag speedster the Dragula. The Munsters hail from Transylvania and the head of the household is Herman (played by Fred Gwynne, formerly of *Car 54*), modelled on Frankenstein's monster, seven foot three with a flat head, a lantern jaw, an overhanging brow, a jagged scar on his forehead and bolts through his neck. A devoted family man, Herman works hard at the Gateman, Goodbury & Grave Funeral Home to provide for his family, wife Lily, Grandpa, son Eddie and niece Marilyn. Lily (maiden name Dracula) is aged 137, with long black hair with a white streak and a penchant for Chanel No. 13. Hauntingly beautiful, she is almost as pretty as the day she died. Grandpa Munster, somewhere between sixty-two and 479 years of age, is a practical joker who sleeps in a coffin in the cellar. He is idolised by ten-year-old Eddie, a happy youngster with Wolfboy fangs and pointed ears. Eddie thinks Grandpa's tricks are 'neat'. Innocent of the effect they have on others, the Munsters think it is other people who are odd. And none more unfortunate than blonde-haired, blue-eyed niece Marilyn who has lived with Lily and Herman all her life and does not realise that a man loves a girl for her brains.

Most of the jokes in *The Munsters* come from straightforward inversions. Niece Marilyn is in fact a ravishing Monroe lookalike and Lily's response to a handsome male is, 'He looks like Cary Grant, poor man'. Standard family advice is, 'Remember, every cloud has a dark lining'. The gags wore a little thin by the last two seasons, but there was a message of mid-sixties tolerance behind the affectionate characterisation of the gentle giant and his weird but happy family. (The creators of *The Munsters* themselves came from recent American immigrant families.)

After many fruitless weeks were spent in Los Angeles and the Mid West looking for a suitable Victorian-Gothic structure the Munster house was built in its entirety on the studio lot and aged with chemicals and powerful lights. The main stars spent hours in make-up. Aside from his flat head and bolt through the neck, Fred Gwynne, even though the series was filmed in black and white, wore green make up. Lily had a chalk-white face and fiendish fingernails. *The Munsters* ran for seventy episodes, followed by numerous repeats on both sides of the Atlantic. Memorable episodes include 'Movie Star Munster' when Herman is conned by insurance salesmen posing as Hollywood talent scouts; 'Herman the Great' in which Herman tries to earn extra cash by wrestling;

and 'Local Munster' in which Lily forces Herman to diet for his army reunion. The series also spawned two Munster films, *Munster Go Home*, 1966, and *The Munsters' Revenge*, 1981. The first starred the original cast of the series. The second, made seventeen years after the original series finished, is a best-forgotten disaster – as was the 1988–91 series *The Munsters Today*, an attempt to revamp the formula with an entirely new cast.

Nightingales

UK 1990–92 13 × 30m col Channel 4. An ALOMO Production for Channel 4. *cr* Paul Makin. *pr* Esta Charkham, Laurie Greenwood, Rosie Bunting. *dr* Tony Dow. *wr* Paul Makin. *mus* Clever Music. *cast* **Carter** Robert Lindsay **Bell** David Threlfall **Sarge** James Ellis **The Inspector** Peter Vaughan.

'There's nobody here but us chickens!' is the constant refrain (accompanied by obligatory wing-flapping gestures) of the three security guards who are the cast of *Nightingales*. A bleak, surreal, and highly cerebral black comedy, *Nightingales* takes place in only two sets, the rest room and the toilets, both intentionally 'broken-down', and uses no location shots or extras. Nor is there any action to speak of. The three men sit around a table whiling away their inactive hours with flights of fantasy, pregnant pauses, power play, pranks and squabbles, interrupted only by the occasional visitor, or indeed visitation (because of the inertia of the three main characters, creator Makin felt he had to add a catalyst in the form of another person, who has variously taken forms from Eric the Werewolf to Terence Oblong the Gorilla). A fourth nightwatchman, Mr Smith, has been dead for three years but his body has been kept on the premises so that the others can claim his salary. The night-time setting only adds to the unreal atmosphere of this TV *Waiting for Godot*.

Storylines include Bell having to attend a psychiatrist because he has raped a horse (it is revealed that he harbours a hidden fantasy to sleep with Carter, while Sarge has a secret longing to be a psychiatrist), a competition for Security Guard of the year (the prizes are an egg cup and a house brick), Carter and Bell forgetting Sarge's birthday while Eric the Werewolf remembers and turns up, and the arrival of a distressed and heavily pregnant Mary on Christmas Eve, who is allowed to stay if she signs a contract stating that she is not an allegory and proceeds to give birth to a goldfish in a plastic bag and a succession of ever larger consumer goods.

Paul Makin, creator and writer of the series, was inspired by a job he took after leaving drama school. He worked twelve-hour shifts from seven at night to seven in the morning as a part-time security guard at the National Exhibition Centre in Birmingham. 'I was struck by the strange nature of the majority of the guards and the nature of the job. You didn't actually do anything, you just had to be there.'

The series stars three of Britain's best character actors, David Threlfall has been a member of the Royal Shakespeare Company, and starred as Leslie Titmus in Euston Films' John Mortimer adaptation *Paradise Postponed*, 1985, and *Titmus Regained*, 1991. James Ellis played Bert Lynch in the legendary >*Z Cars* (1962–78) and opposite Bernard Hill in Alan Bleasdale's *Yosser's Story*. Other TV credits include working with Warren Mitchell in *So You Think You've Got Troubles*, 1991, and *In Sickness and in Health*. Robert Lindsay shot to fame in 1979 as Wolfie in the BBC comedy series >*Citizen Smith*. His other TV credits include Edmund in *King Lear* (with Sir Laurence Olivier) and the lead role of Michael Murray in Alan Bleasdale's *GBH*. His prolific stage work includes the title role of *Cyrano de Bergerac* at the Theatre Royal in London. Series director Tony Dow is a TV veteran, having directed, among others, *Only Fools and Horses*.

On the Buses

UK 1970–5 70 × 25m col ITV. London Weekend Television. *cr* Ronald Wolfe and Ronald Chesney. *pr* Stuart Allen. *dr* Stuart Allen. *wr* Ronald Wolfe and Ronald Chesney. *cast* **Stan Butler** Reg Varney **Inspector Blakey** Stephen Lewis **Mum** Cicely Courtneidge/Doris Hare **Arthur** Michael Robbins **Olive** Anna Karen **Jack** Bob Grant. *Video* Video Collection/LWT.

'I 'ate you, Butler!' says malevolent Inspector Blakey (Stephen Lewis, left) to driver Butler (Reg Varney, right) in LWT's *On the Buses*. Conductor Jack (Bob Grant, centre) looks on. For 7.8 million viewers in December 1970, the gorblimey series was just the ticket and went to the top of the ratings.

Like Chesney and Wolfe's earlier series, *The Rag Trade*, this was a workplace sitcom of cheerfully lowbrow humour. The setting was The Luxton Bus Company, ruled over by the black-hearted Inspector Blakey, tormentor of ferrety driver Stan (Reg Varney, *The Rag Trade, Beggar Thy Neighbour, Down the Gate*) and his lothario conductor, Jack. Stan lived with his mum, his plain sister Olive (former stripper Anna Karen, also *The Rag Trade*) and layabout brother-in-law, Arthur (Michael Robbins). Stories centred on Stan and Jack's labour–capital battles with the dim-witted Blakey (catchphrase: 'I 'ate you, Butler') and the attempts by the 'lads' to woo the conductresses. A bus depot in Wood Green, London, provided the series' exteriors. Three movies based on the show were released in the cinema, none of which were worth the fare to see them, *On the Buses, Mutiny on the Buses, Holiday on the Buses*.

The Phil Silvers Show

USA 1955–9 138 × 30m CBS. *UK tx* 1957–61 BBC1. *cr* Nat Hiken. *pr* Nat Hiken, Al De Caprio, Edward J Montagne. *dr* Nat Hiken, Al De Caprio. *wr* Various, including Nat Hiken, Arnold Auerbach, Terry Ryan, Barry Blitzer, Vincent Bogert, Harvey Orkin, Tony Webster, Coleman Jacoby, Arnie Rosen, Billy Friedberg, Leonard Stern, Phil Sharp, Neil Simon. *mus* John Strauss. *cast* **M/Sgt Ernie Bilko** Phil Silvers **Cpl Rocco Barbella** Harvey Lembeck **Pvt Sam Fender** Herbie Faye **Col John Hall** Paul Ford **Pvt Duane Doberman** Maurice Gosfield **Sgt Rupert Ritzik** Joe E Ross **Cpl Henshaw** Allan Melvin **Pvt Dino Paparelli** Billy Sands **Pvt Zimmerman** Mickey Freeman **Nell Hall** Hope Sansberry **Sgt Grover** Jimmy Little **Sgt Joan Hogan** Elisabeth Fraser. *Video* Fox.

Master Sergeant Ernie Bilko, based at the mythical Fort Baxter, Kansas, was the biggest – and most charming – rogue in the US Army. With little to do in the wilds of middle America Bilko was incurably occupied in get-rich-quick schemes, spending most of his time gambling (in the episode, 'The Twitch', he even managed to run a book on an officer's lectures on Beethoven), conjuring up scams and out-manoeuvring his unfortunate and all too trusting commanding officer, the hapless Colonel

Phil Silvers as wily Master Sergeant Ernie Bilko (serial number 15042699) in *The Phil Silvers Show*. Also pictured is Elisabeth Fraser as Bilko's sometime romantic interest at Fort Baxter, Sergeant Joan Hogan. Silvers later expressed concern that the series increased enlistments into the US Army.

Hall, who was reduced to calling his post 'the little Las Vegas'. The Bilko–Hall relationship was central to the genius of the show, a modern working of the dumb master–clever servant relationship found as far back in time as Ancient Greece. Highly resourceful, Bilko could talk his way out of any situation. His example was followed by most of his subordinates whom he involved as willing aides and accomplices. In times of hardship, though, the motor pool sergeant would willingly fleece his own platoon. A favourite target for the con tricks was the ill-fated cook, Rupert Ritzik. Joan Hogan, who worked in the base's office, was Bilko's mild romantic interest during the first three seasons but was later phased out. Bilko also endlessly flattered the Colonel's wife ('Hello Miss – the Colonel didn't tell me his daughter was visiting – Why! It's *Mrs* Hall . . .') with the result that she was one of his biggest defenders. Bilko's wooing technique was known as the 'Bilko blitz', an unbeatable combination of 'a man in uniform, moonlight and music'. Of course, underneath the Machiavellian exterior, Bilko had a heart of gold; in the classic spoof on Elvis Presley joining the army, 'Rock 'n' Roll Rookie', Bilko eventually refused to exploit his new recruit 'Elvin Pelvin', after hearing him sing 'Bilko is the Best' to the tune of 'Love Me Tender'. In a moral conclusion to the long-running satire on army life, the final episode, 'Weekend Colonel' saw Bilko behind bars. Colonel Hall had won the contest.

The original title of the series was *You'll Never Get Rich* which remained as the subtitle when the series became *The Phil Silvers Show* two months after its première. The *Bilko* character later turned up as a cartoon cat in Hanna-Barbera's >*Top Cat* (aka *Boss Cat*), and in 1996 an execrable movie version of Sergeant Bilko (*dr* Jonathon Lynn) was released starring Steve Martin as the eponymous conman.

Bilko series creator, producer and director, Nat Hiken, was born Philip Silversmith in Brooklyn, New York, the son of Jewish immigrants. He made his professional showbusiness début at the age of eleven, and featured in numerous films and musicals over the next decade. The Sergeant Bilko character he created overshadowed everything he did thereafter, although he did find success as the creative mover of *Car 54, Where Are You?*

(1961–2), an anarchic comedy about enormously dense New York cops, led by Joe E Ross as Gunther Toody and Fred Gwynne as Francis Muldoon. (Ross had previously been Ritzik in *Bilko*, in which Gwynne, later Herman in >*The Munsters*, had a couple of guest spots.) After several years of illness, Hiken died in 1985.

Please Sir!

UK 1968–9 40 × 25m col ITV. London Weekend TV. *cr* John Esmonde, Bob Larbey. *pr* Mark Stuart. *dr* Mark Stuart. *wr* John Esmonde, Bob Larbey. *cast* **Bernard Hedges** John Alderton **Price** Richard Davies **Doris Ewell** Joan Sanderson **Potter** Derek Guyler **Smith** Eric Chitty **Eric Duffy** Peter Cleall **Frankie Abbott** David Barry **Maureen Bullock** Liz Gebhardt **Peter Craven** Malcolm McFee **Dennis Dunstable** Peter Denyer **Sharon Eversleigh** Penny Spencer.

Actor John Alderton, in his first starring TV role since playing Dr Moon in >*Emergency Ward 10*, was sensitive teacher Bernard 'Privet' Hedges, the form master of unruly 5C at inner-city The Fenn Street School. The class – played by actors clearly much older than fifth formers – caused Bernard considerable heartache, but many of the show's best moments came in the staff room with the interchanges between the cynical Welsh teacher Price, and the straight-laced Doris Ewell. Potter was the uniformed, Hitlerian school porter. The show was inspired by the 1967 movie *To Sir with Love* which starred Sidney Poitier, Judy Geeson and Lulu.

After Alderton left *Please Sir!*, the series continued for several seasons as *The Fenn Street Gang*, concentrating on 5C's antics after leaving their alma mater. Writers Esmonde and Larbey went on to write *Get Some In*, the twee self-sufficiency sitcom *The Good Life* (BBC, 1974–8, with Richard Briers, Felicity Kendal, Paul Eddington, Penelope Keith), *Ever Decreasing Circles* and *A Fine Romance*.

An American version of *Please Sir!*, *Welcome Back Cotter*, played on ABC between 1975 and 1979. It featured John Travolta as tough Brooklyn teenager Vinnie Barbarino, and launched the actor as a major star.

Police Squad

USA 1982 6 × 30m col ABC. Paramount TV. *UK tx* 1982. *cr*
Jim Abrahams, David Zucker, Jerry Zucker. *pr* Bob Weiss. *dr*
Jerry Zucker, Reza S Badiyi, Paul Krasny, Joe Dante, George
Stafford Brown. *wr* Various, including Jim Abrahams, David
Zucker, Jerry Zucker, Tino Insana, Robert Wuhl, Nancy
Steen. *mus* Ira Newborn. *cast* **Detective Frank Drebin**
Leslie Nielsen **Ed Hocken** Alan North **Norberg** Peter Lupus
Johnny William Duell **Al** John Wardell **Ted Olson** Ed
Williams. *Video* CIC.

Spoof police show. This short-lived series came from the
creators of *Airplane!* and featured that film's star, Leslie
Nielsen (also *The New Breed* and >*The Golden Girls*) as
dead-pan, fearless, Inspector Frank Drebin of the Police
Squad. The comedy came from a deluge of sight gags (giant
policeman Al was only ever filmed from the neck down),
non sequiturs, and literalisms; when Drebin said to a fellow
officer in a dangerous situation, 'Cover me!' the officer did
– with a coat. In his fight to keep the streets safe, Drebin was
helped by forensic scientist Ted Olson (who had an
unhealthy interest in young boys), and the stoolie shoeshine
Johnny, who could give more information on a given subject
than the *Encyclopedia Americana* – for a price. Guest stars
were invariably killed off within seconds of the episode's
start. Although it fared abysmally on TV (ABC executives
allegedly considered it too complicated for the average
viewer), it provided the basis for the successful theatrical
features *The Naked Gun* (subtitled 'From the Files of Police
Squad'), *Naked Gun 2½* and *Naked Gun 33⅓*.

The episodes of *Police Squad* were: A Substantial
Gift/The Butler Did It/Ring of Fear/Revenge and
Remorse/Rendezvous at Big Gulch/Testimony of Evil (in
which Drebin assumes the guise of nightclub singer and
comedian, Tony DiWonderful, to nail a drugs ring based
at Mr V's nightspot).

Rhoda

USA 1974–8 110 × 25m col CBS. MTM. *UK tx* 1974–80
BBC2. *cr* James L Brooks, Allan Burns. *exec pr* James L
Brooks, Allan Burns. *pr* Lorenzo Music, David Davis,
Charlotte Brown. *dr* Various. *wr* Various. *mus* Billy
Goldenburg. *cast* **Rhoda Morgenstern Gerard** Valerie
Harper **Brenda Morgenstern** Julie Kavner **Ida
Morgenstern** Nancy Walker **Martin Morgenstern** Harold J
Gould **Joe Gerard** David Groh **Gary Levy** Ron Silver.

The character of Rhoda first appeared as the over-
weight, over-anxious neighbour in the >*The Mary Tyler
Moore Show* before being slimmed down, made more
obviously Jewish, and given a series of her own. She was
also relocated to New York, where she initially lived with
her parents, Ida and Martin, before moving in with her
dowdy sister Brenda (played by Julie Kavner, later Marge
in >*The Simpsons*). She also got a job as a window
dresser, and fell in love with Joe, owner of the New York
Wrecking Company. They married, but separated soon
after – largely because the scriptwriters decided that
abrasive but vulnerable Rhoda worked comically best as
a single girl. In Britain the show was first aired in BBC2's
'Yankee Treble' slot in Autumn 1974, and was so popular
it was screened weekly from February 1975. Valerie
Harper won an Outstanding Lead Comedy Actress for
Rhoda in 1976.

Rising Damp

UK 1974–8 Approx 24 × 30m col ITV. Yorkshire TV. *cr* Eric
Chapell. *pr* Vernon Lawrence. *dr* Vernon Lawrence, Ronnie
Baxter, Len Lurcuck. *wr* Eric Chapell. *cast* **Rigsby** Leonard
Rossiter **Philip** Don Warrington **Alan** Richard Beckinsale
Miss Jones Frances de la Tour. *Video* C/VIS/BMG.

Originally a stage show called *Banana Box*, Eric
Chapell's masterly series about the repulsive, jeering
landlord Rigsby and his seedy boarding house was one of
ITV's few quality comedy hits in the seventies. Almost as
obnoxious a character as the elder Steptoe or Alf Garnett,
the arms-folded, tongue-flickering Rigsby (dressed
always in a sleeveless cardigan) lusted ceaselessly after
his one female boarder, Miss Ruth Jones, and endlessly
battled with his two male boarders, effete medical
student Alan and the scion of an African chieftain, Philip.

Rigsby's snide manner was splendidly evidenced in the first episode when the fashionably hirsute Alan defended himself saying 'Jesus had long hair'. 'Yes,' replied Rigsby with perfect timing, 'but I bet he never had a hairdryer.' The series was not only compelling because of its writing and acting (especially Rossiter's virtuoso performance as Rigsby), but because it struck a chord with anybody who had ever lived in rented digs.

Of the TV cast only Richard Beckinsale (also Godber in *Porridge*) did not appear in the original play, and both Rossiter and Frances de la Tour had distinguished stage careers. An insurance clerk until he was twenty-seven, Rossiter had achieved notable success in the theatre for his renditions of Arturo Ui, and Richard III. On television he had put in a long spell in >Z *Cars* in the sixties. After *Rising Damp*, the lugubrious, Liverpudlian actor appeared in the 1980 film version of the series, and the TV situation comedy *The Fall and Rise of Reginald Perrin* (1976–80). He died during a production of Joe Orton's *Loot* in 1984.

Roseanne

USA 1988– 130+ × 25m col ABC. Carsey-Werner Production. *UK tx* 1989– C4. *cr* Matt Williams. *exec pr* Marcy Carsey, Tom Werner, Roseanne Barr, Tom Arnold. *pr* Various. *dr* Various. *wr* Various. *cast* **Roseanne Connor** Roseanne Barr **Dan Conner** John Goodman **Darlene Connor** Sara Gilbert **D J Connor** Michael Fishman **Becky Connor** Lecy Goranson/Sarah Chalke **Jackie Harris** Laurie Metcalf **Crystal Anderson** Natalie West **David** Johnny Galecki **Mark** Glenn Quinn **Leon** Martin Mull.

A blue-collar comedy about a caustic and corpulent mother, Roseanne Connor, which was set in the American Mid West town of Lanford. Making up the rest of her family were equally large husband Dan, and assorted children: boy-mad Becky, small son D J and cynical Darlene. Jackie was Roseanne's single sister, and much disliked by Dan. Though Roseanne mercilessly put down her kids (when one once complained of being bored, she responded 'Go play in the traffic'), the viewer was never left in any doubt that she loved the brats. She also worked outside the home in a variety of dead-end jobs, including on the production line at a plastics factory, and waiting on tables at Lobo's Lounge. After Dan gave up his dry-wall business for a motorbike shop, the family enjoyed a middle-class income, until the early nineties recession forced Dan out of business. Roseanne was obliged to use young son D J to con the electricity man. Aside from the problems of cash-shortage, the comedy focused on the 'usual' problems of family life, including generational conflict. Stories of this type included Dan's father Ed marrying Roseanne's friend Crystal, and Becky's elopement with Mark.

The series was based on a character created by Roseanne Barr, a Jewish waitress turned stand-up comic from Salt Lake City who came to prominence after an appearance on *The Johnny Carson Show*. Not long after the instant, sky-rocket success of *Roseanne*, Barr divorced husband Bill Pentland; in 1991 she married reformed cocaine addict Tom Arnold, whom she brought into the series as Co-Executive Producer and the character Arnie, a neighbour of the Connors. Arnold subsequently starred in *The Jackie Thomas Show*, a ratings disaster for the ABC network. Aside from the regular cast, those appearing in *Roseanne* (which grossed over $91 million a year at its peak) have included Shelley Winters as Roseanne's grandmother Mary, Estelle Parsons as Roseanne's mother Bev, Sandra Bernhard as neighbour Nancy, and Mariel Hemingway appeared as a lesbian stripper (who gave Roseanne a much publicised 'lesbian kiss'). With a famously fast turnover of writers – a scriptwriter's life on *Roseanne* averages that of a subaltern in the trenches of World War I – the show deteriorated somewhat in its latter seasons, as Roseanne remodelled her character into something distinctly glamorous, rather than proletarian, looking. A vein of sentimentality also became evident.

The Simpsons

USA 1989– 90+ × 30m Fox. *UK tx* 1990– Sky. *cr* Matt Groening. *exec pr* James L Brooks, Matt Groening, Sam Simon, Al Jean, Mike Reiss, Josh Weinstein. *pr* Various, including George Meyer, Richard Sakai, David Silverman,

Jon Vitti, Jon Swartzwelder. *dr* Various, including Rich Moore. *wr* Various, including John Swartzwelder, Adam I Lapidus. *mus* Danny Elfman (theme), Alf Clausen. *cast* (voices) **Homer Simpson** Dan Castellaneta **Marge Simpson** Julie Kavner **Bartholomew J 'Bart' Simpson** Yeardley Smith **Lisa Simpson** Nancy Cartwright **Mrs Karbappel** Marcia Wallace **Mr Burns/Principal Skinner/Ned Flanders/Smithers/Otto the Bus Driver and others** Harry Shearer **Moe/Spu/Chief Wiggum/Dr Nick Riviera** Hank Azaria. *Video* Fox.

Bart Simpson, ten years old with spiky hair, golfball eyes and catchphrases 'Aye, Carumba' and 'Don't have a cow, man' and 'I'm Bart Simpson, who the hell are you?' was America's anti-hero for the nineties. The first attempt at a prime-time animated series since >*The Flintstones* two decades before, *The Simpsons* jumped to the top of the ratings as well as garnering critical acclaim for its brilliant writing. Bart lived with his dysfunctional, blue-collar family in the seemingly idyllic town of Springfield. Springfield had all the important amenities of a modern city – a mall, a prison, a dump site, toxic waste and a nuclear power plant. Pop Simpson, a grouchy Joe-six-pack and lazy slob of a man worked as safety inspector at the plant, where his nickname was 'Bonehead'. Homer's wife and Bart's mother was Marge, the family peacemaker, a gentle, caring woman with an enormous blue beehive held together by a single bobby pin. Maggie, the youngest infant, perpetually crawled around with a dummy in her mouth. Her older sister Lisa (aged eight), an eternally optimistic second-grader and baritone saxophone prodigy, was the smartest one in the family, attempting to conduct doomed polysyllabic existential discussions with her father.

The Simpsons was a runaway success. Fox's market research showed that people saw *The Simpsons* as 'a family like us', unlike the too-good-to-be-true Ewings or Huxtables of the Reagan era. *The Simpsons* had realistic, get-by-as-best-as-you-can values. When Bart was beaten up at school pop Homer advised him lovingly, 'Never say anything unless you're sure everyone else feels exactly the same way.' One of Bart's favourite sayings was 'Make sure there are plenty of escape routes'. *Newsweek* declared *The Simpsons* 'a genuine sociological force', a sign that Americans were 'beginning to revolt against the

'I'm Bart Simpson, who the hell are you?' The family of TV's most famous underachiever seated at the table left to right: infant Maggie, Bart (an anagram of brat), polysyllabic prodigy Lisa, beehived mother Marge and 'Bonehead' father Homer. *The Simpsons* first hit the small screen in the form of animated segments framing the commercial breaks in *The Tracey Ullman Show*. The dysfunctional blue-collar family became an instant cult and earned a half-hour prime-time slot on Murdoch's Fox TV. The series was the first prime-time cartoon since *The Flintstones*, and the first animation to feature as a *Newsweek* cover story. The magazine declared *The Simpsons* to be 'a genuine sociological force'.

The establishment, however, was irritated by the show. The Bush administration campaigned for election on the slogan 'We need a nation closer to the Waltons than the Simpsons'. Bart replied: 'We're just like the Waltons – we're praying for the Depression to end, too.' The Simpsons had the last laugh in an episode which saw George and Barbara Bush buy a house opposite the yellow-skinned family. Among the havoc wreaked on the hapless Bushes was Bart's accidental trashing of the ex-President's memoirs.

tube's idealised image of family life'. The family got more fan mail than Janet Jackson, teenagers shaved 'Bart' into their hair in capital letters and the series was top viewing among males. Eager fans could buy Simpsons air fresheners, dolls, beach towels, toothbrushes, posters, hats, bed linen, sweets, biscuits and bath bubbles. Celebrities vied for the opportunity to guest voice and included Penny Marshall, Brooke Shields, Jackie Mason, Ringo Starr, Tony Bennett, Danny De Vito and Tom Jones.

The Simpsons was dreamed up by thirty-six-year-old artist Matt Groening, whose only previous published work was a left-wing comic strip called *Life in Hell*. Groening was also executive producer on the series, along with comedy deity James L Brooks (*Broadcast News*, >*The Mary Tyler Moore Show*, >*Taxi*, *The Tracey Ullman Show*) and brilliant sitcom scribe Sam Simon (>*Taxi*, >*Cheers*). It was at Brooks' behest that the series was first introduced on *The Tracey Ullman Show* as short vignettes in 1988 and then spun out into a separate series the following year (Tracey Ullman sued to the tune of $56 million for a share of the profits). One hundred and fifty animators, most of them in South Korea, toil for six months to produce each episode. Creator Matt Groening swore the series was not autobiographical – although his parents and two sisters had the same names as the Simpsons.

When, in the mid nineties, the show suffered a dip in interest, Groening penned a storyline – inspired by >*Dallas* – which set the TV nation talking. This was the summer 1995 shooting of Mr Burns, the tyrannical, 104-year-old owner of the town's nuclear power plant. The answer to the whodunnit 'Who Shot Mr Burns?' was revealed in the opening episode of the new season: it was an accident caused by the Simpson's baby, Maggie. Mr Burns, like J R, survived.

Soap

USA 1977–82 93 × 30m ABC. Whit/Thomas/Harris Productions. *UK tx* 1978–82 ITV. *cr* Susan Harris. *exec pr* Tony Thomas, Paul Junger Witt. *pr* Susan Harris. *dr* Jay Sandrich. *wr* Susan Harris. *cast* **Chester Tate** Robert

Mandan **Jessica Tate** Katherine Helmond **Corrine Tate** Diane Canova **Eunice Tate** Jennifer Salt **Billy Tate** Jimmy Baio **Benson** Robert Guillaume **The Major** Arthur Peterson **Mary Dallas Campbell** Cathryn Damon **Burt Campbell** Richard Mulligan **Jodie Campbell** Billy Crystal **Danny Campbell** Ted Wass **The Godfather** Richard Libertini **Claire** Kathryn Reynolds **Peter Campbell** Robert Ulrich **Chuck/Bob Campbell** Jay Johnson **Father Timothy Flotsky** Sal Viscuso **Dutch** Donnelly Rhodes **Detective Donahue** John Byner **Carlos 'El Puerco' Valdez** Gregory Sierra.

Outrageous prime-time satire on American daytime soaps, which provoked storms of protest while still in production after magazine reports accurately listed its themes as adultery, transvestism, impotency, frigidity, voyeurism, premarital sex and homosexuality. Religious groups organised campaigns to ban the programme and sponsors were urged to boycott the show (which a few did). The furore subsided only after ABC promised to tone down future episodes. *Soap*, however, was pure, irreverent comedy. Revelling in the series' intentionally incomprehensible storylines, each episode started with a cast snapshot and plot summary which ended 'Confused? You will be!' But *Soap* was really just a good old-fashioned tale of the families of two sisters – the upper-class Tates and the blue-collar Campbells – the members of which, like any other family, had their hang-ups. The elder sister was charming but nervy Jessica Tate, whose super-rich stockbroker husband, Chester, had a tendency towards extramarital affairs. Their children were sexy Corinne, quiet Eunice and Billy, a fourteen-year-old wisecracking brat. The Tate household was completed by Jessica's father, 'the Major', who wore uniform and believed he was still living World War II and sardonic black butler Benson, who habitually insulted his employers and refused to cook anything he didn't like himself (an act so successful that Robert Guillaume left for his own spin-off show, *Benson*, 1979, in which he worked as butler for the state governor).

Across town lived Jessica's sister, Mary Campbell, who together with second husband Burt had to deal with son Jodie, a gay ventriloquist (he insisted on his dummy being treated as an equal) and Danny, who was involved in organised crime and had a shotgun marriage to a Mafia boss's daughter. This might all have seemed unusual to the viewer, but *Soap*'s inhabitants were blasé. A typical *Soap* joke had Mary Campbell catching her gay son trying on her dress and rebuking him 'I've told you a hundred times that dress fastens at the back.'

As with the soaps the series aped, ever more far-fetched fare was to come. First Burt's son, handsome tennis pro Peter, was murdered and unlikely criminal Jessica convicted of the crime. Chester, however, turned out to be the real culprit and he was sent to prison, only to escape with Dutch, a convicted murderer. Chester then lost his memory and wandered out west to work as a cook while Dutch and Eunice fell in love and eloped, and Jessica fell in love with Detective Donahue, whom she had hired to find Chester. Meanwhile, Burt found himself kidnapped in a spacecraft and replaced on earth by an alien who inhabited his body, Corinne gave birth to a baby possessed by the devil and Jessica had another fling, with a South American revolutionary.

Creator Susan Harris has been one of television's hottest writers since the late eighties. She followed *Soap* with >*Golden Girls*, *Empty Nest* and *Nurses*, all three hits on NBC during the 1991–2 season, as well as *Good and Evil* which ran at the same time on ABC. Her husband, Paul Junger Witt, was executive producer on the series.

Steptoe and Son

UK 1964–73 40 × 30m bw/col BBC1. BBC. *cr* Ray Galton, Alan Simpson. *pr* Duncan Wood, David Croft, John Howard Davies, Douglas Argent. *dr* Various, including Douglas Argent. *wr* Ray Galton, Alan Simpson. *mus* Ron Grainger, Dennis Wilson. *cast* **Albert Steptoe** Wilfred Brambell **Harold Steptoe** Harry H Corbett. *Video* BBC.

Created by >*Hancock's Half-Hour* scriptwriters, Ray Galton and Alan Simpson, this situation comedy about a malicious rag-and-bone man and his frustrated son premièred as a one-off play, *The Offer*, in the BBC's fertile *Comedy Playhouse* slot. From the outset, the show broke most of the rules of TV comedy, ebbing with pathos (even tragedy) rather than laughs. The central characters were the tattered-mitten-wearing father

Steptoe and Son starred Harry H Corbett as socially aspiring Harold (left) and Dublin-born Wilfred Bramble (right) as his wheedling 'dirty old man' father, Albert. In 1964 Labour Party leader Harold Wilson persuaded the BBC not to screen an episode of the rag and bone comedy on General Election night – a move Wilson thought won him thirteen extra seats and victory.

Albert ('you dirty old man') and his thirty-eight-year-old son, Harold ('you great lummox'). It was Harold's dream to better himself, and to this end he read such tomes as G B Shaw's *Everybody's Political What's What* and listened to classical music on the gramophone in the cluttered sitting room. Yet every time he tried to escape the yard his petty, jealous father blackmailed him ('Harold . . . I think I'm having an 'art attack, Harold') into staying. The ties of blood were simply too strong to escape. And beneath the bickering and hate there was a love and mutual need: 'He's not a bad boy,' Albert tells the old burglar who hides out with them in 'Desperate Hours', with real pride on his face. (This classic episode featured Leonard 'Rising Damp' Rossiter as the old burglar's partner and the burglars' relationship mirrored that between Steptoe and son.) If the humour of the show was dark, it struck a chord at a time when many considered the nation trapped in decline, and it topped the ratings in 1964. In the General Election of that year, Labour leader Harold Wilson persuaded BBC Director General Hugh C Greene to postpone transmission of *Steptoe and Son* until after the polls closed, a move Wilson thought won him victory. Greene was knighted months later. The series spawned two feature films, *Steptoe and Son* (1972) and *Steptoe and Son Ride Again* (1973), and was remade in America as *Sandford and Son* (with a black cast of Redd Fox and Desmond Wilson), in Holland as *Stiefbeen En Zoom*, and in Sweden as *Albert Og Herbert*.

Taxi

USA 1978–83 113 × 30m col ABC. John Charles Walters Productions. *UK tx* 1980–5 BBC1. *cr* James L Brooks, Stan Daniels, David Davis, Ed Weinberger. *exec pr* James L Brooks, Stan Daniels, David Davis, Ed Weinberger. *pr* Glen Charles, Les Charles. *dr* Various, including James Burrows, Noam Pitlik, Danny De Vito, Harvey Miller, Richard Sakai, David Lloyd, Michael Zinberg. *wr* Various, including James L Brooks, Stan Daniels, David Davis, Ed Weinberger, Glen Charles, Les Charles, Earl Pomerantz, Barry Kemp, Holly Holmberg Brooks, Ken Estin, Sam Simon, Dari Daniels, Michael Leeson. *mus* Bob James. *cast* **Alex Reiger** Judd

Danny De Vito as slimeball dispatcher Louie DePalma who took a sadistic interest in seeing his part-time cabbies fail in *Taxi*. De Vito married occasional *Taxi* co-star Rhea Perlman, later of *Cheers*, on set during a lunch break. Ted Danson made one of his first TV appearances in the show as an egotistical hairdresser and gave a quality performance that led *Taxi* producers James Brooks, Glen Charles and Les Charles to suggest he auditioned for their new show, *Cheers*.

Hirsch **Louie DePalma** Danny De Vito **Elaine Nardo** Marilu Henner **Bobby Wheeler** Jeff Conaway **Jim Caldwell Igatowski** Christopher Lloyd **Tony Banta** Tony Danza **Latka Gravas** Andy Kaufman **Simka Dahblitz Gravas** Carol Kane **Zena Sherman** Rhea Perlman **John Burns** Randall Carver **Jeff Bennett** J Alan Thomas.

The aspirations and frustrations of the staff of New York's Sunshine Cab Company were the focal point of this comedy, which was created by ex-MTM staffers, James L Brooks, Stan Daniels, David Davis and Ed Weinberger. Having spent some years on MTM's series about single, middle-class women (>*Mary Tyler Moore Show*, *Phyllis*, >*Rhoda*), the group wanted to do a blue-collar comedy about 'guys'. The principal character of the show was Alex (Judd Hirsch, *Delvecchio*), a philosophical cabbie, and the only sensible person in the garage. Louie DePalma (Danny De Vito, husband of Rhea 'Cheers' Perlman, who also occasionally appeared in the series) was the malevolent, dwarfish dispatcher, who sat in his cage giving orders. Latka was the mechanic, and possessor of only the most fractured English. Reverend Jim (Christopher Lloyd) was a mind-warped ex-hippie, Bobby, a bit actor, Elaine, an art gallery assistant, Tony, a boxer, and John, a student, were all part-time drivers who used the garage as a way station on the road to better things (or so they hoped). In the 1980–1 season Latka married a daffy woman from his homeland by the name of Simka. Although the show finished its first two seasons in the top twenty, it slid down the ratings thereafter. ABC unceremoniously cancelled the show, despite critical acclaim for its scripts and ensemble acting (it won three consecutive Emmys for Outstanding Comedy Series). In 1981 the NBC network picked up the series for a year, but were unable to revive its ratings fortunes. Popular taste was changing, and the show's sympathy for its misfit characters just did not fit Reaganite times.

Terry and June

UK 1979–87 65 × 30m col BBC1. BBC TV. *cr* John Kane. *pr* Peter Whitmore. *dr* Various, including David Taylor, Peter Whitmore. *wr* Various, including John Kane. *cast* **Terry** Terry Scott **June** June Whitfield.

Suburban sitcom about marital ups and downs set in Purley, Surrey, with Terry Scott and June Whitfield playing Terry and June Medford. The series was a virtual TV synonym for niceness; the crises from which *Terry and June* made dramas included visits from Terry's boss, looking after a friend's dog, and Terry's misunderstanding about his wife's 'infidelity'. Throughout all these innocent misadventures tubby Terry (played to overgrown-schoolboy perfection by Scott) blustered and June smiled knowingly. Although not described as such, the bland show was a sequel to *Happy Ever After* (1974–8), in which Scott and Whitfield played the Fletchers, trying to get along together after the leaving home of their children.

June Whitfield, archetypal sitcom woman, originally came to prominence as Eth, the fiancée of Ron Glum in radio's *Take It From Here*. She first worked with Terry Scott in 1969 in *Scott On*, and among her other small-screen appearances are *Beggar Thy Neighbour*, the nurse in Hancock's classic 'The Blood Donor' sketch and more recently >*Absolutely Fabulous*. Terry Scott's other television credits include *Hugh and I*, and *Son of the Bride*.

Till Death Us Do Part

UK 1966–74 50 × 30m bw/col BBC1. BBC. *cr* Johnny Speight. *pr* Dennis Main Wilson. *dr* Various, including Douglas Argent. *wr* Johnny Speight. *mus* Dennis Wilson. *cast* **Alf Garnett** Warren Mitchell **Else** Dandy Nichols **Rita** Una Stubbs **Mike** Anthony (Tony) Booth. *Video* BBC.

The monstrous caricature of an East End working-class Tory that was Alf Garnett (Ex-Radio Luxembourg DJ, Warren Mitchell), West Ham supporter and hater of 'yer coons', first appeared in a 1965 BBC *Comedy Playhouse*. There the family was known as the Ramseys and Gretchen Franklin (later *EastEnders*) played the 'silly old moo', otherwise known as disdainful wife Else. In translation to a regular series, the cast stabilised as Mitchell, Dandy Nichols (aka Daisy Nichols) as Else,

Una Stubbs as daughter Rita, and Anthony Booth as son-in-law, Mike ('yer randy scouse git'). To Alf's eternal ire, Mike had longish hair (occasioning the epithet 'Shirley Temple') and was a Trotskyist, a reader of the *Keep Left* newspaper. (In real life, actor Tony Booth, who later married >*Coronation Street*'s Pat Phoenix, was also a left-winger.) Week after week, docker Alf treated his family to rants on whatever subject happened to catch his fancy, delivering his diatribes from his armchair below the flying ducks and the pictures of 'yer Majesty' and Winnie Churchill. Particular targets were blacks ('should go back where they came from'), women, Edward Heath (for taking Britain into the Common Market and for going to a grammar school, rather than a 'proper' school like Eton) and the permissive society. The series attracted numerous complaints – not least from moral guardian Mary Whitehouse, who once counted seventy-eight 'bladdys' in one episode and from those who failed to see that Alf was an ironic portrait, not a role model. Mitchell's performance was a tour-de-force, perfect in every word and physical gesture, but the rest of the superlative cast were as important as counterpoints and comic foils. A 1985 sequel, *In Sickness and In Health*, in which only Mitchell appeared regularly, was mediocre in comparison. Also, the fact that a Conservative government was in power made Alf's outrages difficult to pull off with plausibility, while his particular prejudices seemed dated. A more telling parody of eighties working-class Tory man was the ultra-Thatcherite creation of Harry Enfield, Loadsamoney.

An American version of *Till Death Us Do Part*, *All in the Family* (where Alf Garnett was translated into Archie Bunker) became a prime-time hit. The show was also transposed to Germany, with the Garnetts becoming the Tetzlaffs.

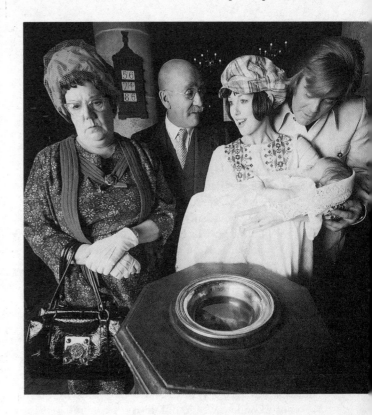

Yer original armchair critic was East End bigot Alf Garnett (Warren Mitchell, second from left) who ranted on whatever happened to pass his tunnel vision. His long-suffering family were wife Else (Dandy Nichols, left) the 'silly old moo', daughter Rita (Una Stubbs, holding baby) and leftist 'yer randy git' son-in-law Mike (Tony Booth, right).

Up Pompeii

UK 1969–72 32 × 30m col BBC1/BBC2. BBC. *cr* Talbot Rothwell. *pr* Michael Mills, David Croft, Sidney Lotterby. *dr* Various. *wr* Talbot Rothwell, Sid Colin. *mus* Alan Braden. *cast* **Lurcio** Frankie Howerd **Senna** Jeanne Mockford **Plautus** William Rushton **Ammonia** Elizabeth Larner

Nausius Kerry Gardner *Ludicrus* Max Adrian *Erotica*
Georgina Moon. *Video* BBC.

Ancient Roman costume romp, loosely derived from the
plays of Plautus (by way of *A Funny Thing Happened on
the Way to the Forum*), featuring Frankie Howerd as
Lurcio, the slave to the household of philandering
senator, Ludicrus Sextus. The double entendres in this
TV orgy of bad taste, with household slave Lurcio
playing middle-aged Cupid to everyone from
nymphomaniacal daughter Erotica to effete, lovelorn son
Nausius, were considered daring at the time. Legend even
has it that the puns caused the veteran ex-musician hall
star to 'blink a bit'. In between matchmaking, cynical
Lurcio commentated on the bawdiness around him in
asides to camera. As the seventies progressed the show
became tagged as sexist, although its seaside postcard-
like humour actually poked fun at sex, rather than
treated women as sex objects (the case was entirely
different with *The Benny Hill Show* of the same era).

In the early nineties, Howerd (and thus *Up Pompeii*)
was rediscovered by a new generation of TV watchers,
and the 'weary camel', as Howerd once described
himself, achieved a revered status in youth circles. In
response London Weekend Television commissioned a
1991 pilot (unsuccessful) for a new version of the show
entitled *Up Pompeii, Missus*. Following Howerd's death
in 1992, the British satellite station UK Gold BBC aired
the BBC series *Then Churchill Said to Me*, in which
Howerd played one of the minions in Churchill's wartime
bunker. Originally made in the early eighties the series
had been banned during the Falklands conflict, and never
previously screened.

The catchphrases of *Up Pompeii* were: 'Titter ye not,
missus' and 'Nay, nay, thrice nay'.

The Young Ones

UK 1982–4 12 × 35m col BBC2. BBC. *pr* Paul Jackson. *wr*
Ben Elton, Rik Mayall, Lise Mayer. *mus* Peter Brewis. *cast*
Rick Rik Mayall **Neil** Nigel Planer **Vyvyan** Ade Edmondson
Mike Christopher Ryan **Jerzy Balowski and family** Alexei
Sayle. *Video* BBC.

Along with C4's *The Comic Strip Presents* this was one
of the first TV appearances of ideologically sound
'alternative comedy' in Britain. The movement began in
1980 when Peter Richardson opened 'London's newest
anarchic cabaret' above the Raymond Revuebar in
London's Soho and took with him the loud-mouthed
compere from The Comedy Store as well as its most
talented acts. The nucleus of the new club were three
partnerships: the Outer Limits (Peter Richardson and
Nigel Planer), 20th Century Coyote (Rik Mayall and
Adrian Edmondson) and Dawn French and Jennifer
Saunders. The team was neither from Oxbridge nor the
northern clubs but a variety of backgrounds, sharing
little but their humour. But word spread and the first TV
production was commissioned. *The Comic Strip Presents
. . .* was screened on Channel 4 on its opening night in
1982 featuring *Five Go Mad in Dorset*, an Enid Blyton
parody. By 1987 Channel 4 had commissioned twenty-
one programmes and the Comic Strip had made two
feature films, *Supergrass* and *Eat the Rich*.

The Young Ones, though named after a Cliff Richard
song, were not all sweetness and light. Spotty Rick (a
Cliff Richard admirer) was a violent vegetarian, Vyvyan
was a headbanging punk with studs in his forehead and
spikes in his hair who owned a hamster called 'Special
Patrol Group'. This sneering, loud-mouthed duo shared
their decrepit household with Neil, a lentil freak with
lank hair down to his navel, who refused to use wooden
cocktail sticks in order to save the rain forest and Mike,
a Bogartian wide-boy with delusions of the paranoid-
conspiratorial variety. Last but not least came a pair of
speaking rats. This unattractive bunch regularly indulged
in cartoon-style violence, kicking the hell out of the
house, each other and where possible the dominant
ideology. Porkpie-hatted landlord Jerzy Balowski (who,
along with the rest of his family, was played by Alexei
Sayle) was not a happy man. All the characters derived
from routines that Mayall and the others had performed
at the Comedy Store with Rik Mayall's (aka Kevin
Turvey) rubber-limbed, swivel-eyed manic indignation
perhaps the most extreme.

The Young Ones were eternal students and the
situation producing the comedy was essentially a student
flat with comic exaggeration taken to its wildest extreme.
Arguments were regularly about who should cook, clean

and tidy or who had stolen Rick's half an apple that he left in the fridge. Left-over food stood for so long that it became animated. Loud music became guest bands in the living room. Jokes were slapstick, surreal (stepping outside the door could lead to different landscapes or eras) or based on sex – or the lack of it in this all-male, heterosexual household.

The series was, however – not surprisingly given the calibre of the performers – brilliant and highly successful. But it was also very much the product of a middle-class, university education. Rik Mayall and Adrian Edmondson met at Manchester University where they first did shows together and Nigel Planer had dropped out of African and Asian Studies at Sussex University to go on to drama school. It ran for two seasons and spawned three best-selling books and two hit records by Planer as Neil (whom the actor described as 'an unpleasant, self-pitying bastard'). It also launched high-profile careers for its stars. Mayall, Edmondson and Planer went on to star in *Filthy Rich and Catflap*, a sendup of celebrity with Mayall as Richie Rich. Mayall and Edmondson had their own series, >*Bottom*, Rik Mayall starred as the unscrupulous self-seeking Alan B'stard MP in *The New Statesman*, 1987, Alexei Sayle had his own series of sketches and Planer invented an 'actor' who gave tips to aspiring actors in first a radio and then a TV series. A less glorious moment in their upward progression was *Hardwicke House*, 1987, which was terminated after only two of its intended seven episodes.

Index

Numbers in *italics* denote main subject entry. Numbers in **bold** denote an illustration.